The Essential Mystery Lists

For Readers, Collectors, and Librarians

2007 Edition

The Essential Mystery Lists

For Readers, Collectors, and Librarians

2007 Edition

Compiled and Edited by
Roger M. Sobin

Poisoned Pen Press
6962 E. First Ave. Ste 103
Scottsdale, AZ 85251
www.poisonedpenpress.com
info@poisonedpenpress.com
Printed in the United States of America

Contents

Publisher's Note

Nearly twenty years ago, I helped my wife Barbara Peters open The Poisoned Pen, a Mystery Bookstore... and more. Since its opening we have frequently seen customers who want advice as to what to read. When Roger M. Sobin contacted me to ask if we might be interested in publishing the book you hold in your hands, I jumped at the opportunity.

For the first time in one place, Mr. Sobin has compiled a list of nominees and award winners of virtually every mystery award ever presented. Furthermore, and perhaps of even greater importance, he has included many of the "best of" lists by over fifty of the most important contributors to the genre. It is certainly possible to search bookshelves, libraries, computer web sites, and other sources in an attempt to find this information, but the task is made nearly impossible because so much of the data is incomplete, misplaced, or inaccurate. For those of us who love mysteries, it is wonderful to have before us a compilation of these many lists as the essential ones to consider.

Roger M. Sobin spent over two decades gathering the data and lists in this volume. Much of that was spent rechecking the accuracy of the material he had collected. While there have been several earlier attempts to create books containing some of these data, in most cases they have only contained the winners of various awards—not the other nominated titles. Additionally, there are several "best of" lists that appear here for the first time in book form and several others that have been unavailable for a number of years.

Of special note, Mr. Sobin extensively researched Anthony Boucher's writings as one of the major mystery reviewers of all time. Reviewing for the *San Francisco Chronicle, Ellery Queen Mystery Magazine*, and the *New York Times*, Boucher offered his annual Best Picks for the Year, as well as a list of very important works that Boucher felt should be read. From these resources Mr. Sobin created "Boucher's Best" and "Important Lists to Consider." These two lists provide insight into important writings in the field from 1942 through Boucher's death in 1968. Mystery fans, collectors, and librarians will find these important contributions to be an invaluable resource.

It is with great pleasure that we have made this volume available. I hope you find it to be a useful a tool. I know we will.

Preface

A project such as this comes with wishing for a resource, dreaming of creating one, and then the task of making all of that become a reality. I especially want to thank Marv Lachman for encouraging me in February of 2005 at the Left Coast Crime Conference in El Paso, Texas. We continue to discuss the merits and approaches to these lists. Marv's vast knowledge of the mystery field has been invaluable during the process of research. Also, Francis M. Nevins (Mike) who shared with me the resources from Anthony Boucher's days of reviewing mystery books and giving us a better understanding of this time period (1942-1968). That resulted in creating the very important Boucher Mystery Lists you will find inside. Another person who has been very helpful is Geoff Bradley in England (editor of CADS magazine) who helped to obtain much of the difficult to find titles from the Crime Writers Association in Great Britain especially the short-list or nominees from the early years.

I also want to thank several others who gave of their time, resources, knowledge, suggestions, etc., in this project: Douglas Greene, Kate Derie, Gary Warren Niebuhr, Ted Fitzgerald, Jim Huang, Susan Oleksiw, George Easter, Al Hubin, Randy Cox, Toni Plummer, Rick Blechta, Cheryl Freedman, Ted Hertel and others who checked their files for some of the hard to locate nominated titles of the past, shared lists, and offered suggestions in many areas. It takes friends to create a work such as this.

Also, I want to thank Sarah Blaskovitz, my sister-in-law, for editing the early sections of texts.

I want to thank Robert Rosenwald, the publisher and president of Poisoned Pen Press and his staff for assisting the publication of the project. The layout of the pages in itself is a monstrous task. Last minute additions, changes, and corrections just seem standard in the production of a resource such as this one.

Finally, my wife, Genie, who was patient for the many hours upon hours I spent in researching in books, journals, magazines, and especially online. The checking and double checking of sources, and the many phone calls in talking with individuals isolated me for many hours in my study. She was most understanding.

Section I: Introduction

Part 1: A Place to Begin

A couple of months ago, I was in a used bookstore wandering around in the mystery section. A woman was in the same section, and she seemed to be looking at everything without selecting anything. After a brief conversation, she noted that she liked reading mysteries and had found several authors she liked, but was looking for some new authors to read. She noticed that I had a list of books and asked what was on my list. I told her that I was in the same position some years ago. I then started looking for books that had been nominated for or won some of the mystery awards or were on the classic or best lists. I had already selected eight or nine titles on my list. I wrote down some computer web sites for her to look at, offered some ideas on collecting, and even selected several books that she took with her.

My wife and I left Chicago and the 2005 Bouchercon gathering of 1,600 or so mystery writers and fans. We pulled into St. Louis early on Monday morning and stopped for gas. As I went in to pay for the gas and get a cup of coffee, the clerk behind the counter noticed my (new) Bouchercon t-shirt and said, "I always wanted to attend that convention." I was surprised that she knew what Bouchercon was, but then again there are fans everywhere.

**This resource book
is dedicated to these individuals and others
who love to read in the mystery field.**

This resource can be used in various ways:

1. By new readers who want to explore the mystery field.

2. By book collectors to help them better understand what they have and arrange their books in some kind of order.

3. By librarians who want to increase selections in the mystery field, make specific lists for library patrons, and create special displays or opportunities (mystery month, youth mystery month, historic mysteries, hardboiled, cozies, thrillers, etc.).

4. By people who use the library system to read specific works and want suggestions.

5. By people who want to have at their fingertips specific lists of award winners and nominees, and classic or "best" lists.

Part 2: The Reader's Collection: New and Used Mystery Books

Reading in the mystery field is very enjoyable, and for many of us leads to an addiction. Several years ago I wondered, should I purchase the new mysteries—those on the bestseller list—some of the classic mysteries, or a combination? Where should I start?

Some readers go to the local library and check out books. They read several books a week, return those, and take home some more. Others purchase books and keep them or pass them along to friends.

Some readers purchase first editions and have them signed by the authors. There are two choices for signing: 1) personal "To xxxxx, hope you enjoy this story, xxxxx xxxxx," or 2) author's signature only (this appears to be more valuable at resale, if you ever need to part with the book).

What I want to share is my system for collecting a reading library of nominated, award winning, and classic or "best" mystery books. Both new and used books are a fine way to accomplish this.

Database of books. After looking at the many mystery awards and mystery lists I located using various sources including web sites, I entered the data to my computer. Then I made columns of: a) year published, b) award or best list, c) book title, and d) author. I decided to collect both the winners and the nominees of the novel category as well as various classic or best lists. Later I added true crime, nonfiction, critical, short story, juvenile and youth or young adult, and other categories.

The fun of finding books. After making my list, I discovered the great joy of searching for and finding the books. I began by looking at the books in my own library and placing those I already owned in a separate place. I looked in the local phone book for used bookstores and discount or closeout bookstores and visited them when I could. Even though some of the titles on my list are out of print—they are out there. I learned to ask personnel at the stores when a sale would be held. Most used bookstores charge one-half of the original list price and offer additional savings from time to time. The local library also has great book sales. In San Antonio, the downtown main public library sells hardbacks at $1.00. Many of the books come with plastic covers, and most of them are in good to excellent condition.

The real adventure. At Bouchercon 2003 in Las Vegas, the "Kiss Kiss, Bang Bang" panel was comprised of Dana Stabenow, Laurie King, Val McDermid, and Stephen Booth. Each panelist read four or five preselected first lines from other authors and noted how they suck the reader into the world of the novel. It was a stimulating session. I wrote down the titles, and when I arrived home, I checked my list. I had almost all of the books discussed and jumped right into reading many of them. If I did not have this collection underway and wanted to pursue some of these authors' suggestions, I would have either had to order them from a bookseller (which can get expensive) or visit the local library (which takes time). Many of the books could be out of print and ordered online.

Before leaving to take a vacation or business trip, I check the online yellow pages for mystery and/or used bookstores in the cities I will visit. Sometimes I call in advance to inquire if a store has a mystery section. I also ask if there are other bookstores nearby. Visiting a store usually takes one to two hours, sometimes longer. For example, at one store the manager pointed me toward the mystery section. After carefully going through the mystery section, I found that the next aisle held suspense books. Then, there was a thriller section. Then after covering those from A to Z, I found a newer books section that had mystery, suspense, and thrillers together. I was in that used bookstore for four hours, but came out with numerous books on my list. Some stores also have a classic or oldies-but-goodies section.

Most used bookstores file their books in alphabetical order by author. However, I have come across a few stores that do not.

I see my collection as a reader's collection. I found that when I started this collection I already had a number of books on my list. You probably do as well.

Classic or best list mystery books. There are numerous lists of classic or best list mystery books including *Haycraft-Queen Cornerstones, Sandoe's Honor Roll of Crime Fiction, Barzun and Taylor's A Catalogue of Crime*, and *Keating's Crime and Mystery: The 100 Best Books* to name a few. These are wonderful lists. Many of the books are out of print; some are in newer editions. However, you can find most of them in used bookstores.

Reading the classics today. At a Bouchercon session entitled: "Double Down: Hammett & Chandler: Who is Greater?" (panelists: Joe Gores, Stephen Mertz, and William Nolan) a panelist commented that Michael Connelly read many of the mystery classics before he started writing and that discipline made him a better author. Another person said that if some of the younger writers today would read the classics they would write better books.

Other books. Some collectors purchase anything written by a favorite author whether the book is on one of the above-mentioned lists or if the reviews are positive. That is another way of collecting. While reading some of the books on the lists that follow, I found authors that I had not read (or even heard of) and then purchased other books by them.

Storage. This can be a problem. I shelve my books this way: the first section is for the *Top 100 Mystery Novels of All Time* as selected by the Mystery Writers of America in 1995 (see, *The Crown Crime Companion: The Top 100 Mystery Novels of All Time: Selected by the Mystery Writers of America,* annotated by Otto Penzler, compiled by Mickey Friedman) by order number, 1 through 100. Next, I place all of the Edgar® winners (best novel, best first novel, best paperback). Following those, all other award winners (Agatha, Barry, Shamus, etc.). These are followed by all of the books nominated for awards. I have another place for the classic or best lists (like *Haycraft-Queen Cornerstones, Keating, Lachman,* etc.). Each section is in alphabetical order by author except the first section that I keep in their top 100 listing. To keep them straight, I place small colored dots I purchase from an office supply store on the lower right back corner (green for winners and wrote which award, orange for nominees, and red for the classic or best lists) to easily return them to the correct area.

Personality types. This reader's collection is not for everyone. One must enjoy looking and searching for books, building a database or using this resource volume, updating the list, placing the books in order, etc. Some might call us active compulsive types. Others might not want to try this approach, but I love it. I meet new acquaintances in big and small towns at bookstores that I have never previously visited. Checking and double-checking my list, is all part of the hobby. While on vacation in Omaha, Nebraska, I visited the Antiquarian Bookstore. All paperbacks were $1.50, and the owner has a very funny story about Mary Higgins Clark and Carol Higgins Clark. Stop by and visit him or call him on the phone for the story.

Updating the listings. Each year, nominees are announced. I build another database for that year, and I add them to the total listings at the end of the year. The search is on. I purchase some books when they are new, but titles end up in the used bookstores quickly. In addition, some book titles are on more than one mystery list. Some win in one or two categories, and others are just on the nominated lists. I have this list with me at all times. You never know when you will see a garage sale, a used bookstore, a library sale, or stop in a bookseller and see titles on discount table.

Part 3: Researching the Awards and Best Lists

The beginnings. This resource project/book started out as a hobby to collect books for myself. In the early 1980s, I purchased a copy of *The Edgar Winners, 33rd Annual Anthology of the Mystery Writers of America: Twenty-Four Stories Selected from the Winners of the Edgar Allan Poe Award for Excellence,* edited by Bill Pronzini. In the back section of the book was a list of the *Edgar®* winners. I copied the list of novels and started looking for some of the titles. That was before home computers, so I used a typewriter and worked on the lists the old-fashioned way. Most of the other awards did not even exist then. The *Shamus Awards* began in 1982, *Arthur Ellis Awards* in 1984, *Anthony Awards* in 1986, *Macavity Awards* in 1987, *Agatha Awards* in 1989, *Hammett Awards* in 1992, and *Barry Awards* in 1997. In those days I subscribed to *The Armchair Detective (TAD), The Mystery FANcier, Spiderweb, Mystery Magazine, The Saint Magazine, Michael Shayne Mystery Magazine,* and of course *Ellery Queen Mystery Magazine* and *Alfred Hitchcock Mystery Magazine.* I read them then and have kept them over the years. Those issues of *TAD* (I have all of the issues from 1976 to 1997) are a staple for any collector or library.

In 2002, my wife and I attended our first Bouchercon conference in Austin, Texas. It was at that conference that I decided to renew my commitment to collecting mystery related books. With the insight of the many awards and classic or best lists, I created a database on the computer as the basis for my renewed hobby.

First, I set my goals: award winners and nominees. Sitting at the banquet awards dinner at the 2002 Bouchercon, I heard several people comment that many of the books that do not win each year in the various categories were just as good and sometimes better than the books that do win. Books are personal. Not everyone likes every book or author (award winning or not). Therefore, I set my parameters high and wide. Second, I like the classic or older mysteries as well. I knew from the start that I must include those titles.

Face it—some very important authors are not on any of these lists. Maybe you will consider adding a new best list (for yourself or share with us) of important authors or titles.

At that point, I expanded my circle to all of the awards and classic or best lists I could locate. I was mainly concerned with the novels and made separate computer files for each of the lists and then a central database for all of the novels as described in Part 2.

At various points, I had to purchase more bookshelves and redirect some from other locations around the house. Today, when I want to find a certain title or place a book back, I can look on the list, check the colored dot on the lower back right side, and go directly to the location.

Several people suggested that I share my collecting methods and research because other people might like to collect books and/or make better sense of the books they already had.

I expanded my list to include other lists that I came across. Each year I still needed to add the newly nominated books to the list from all of the award groups. Most of the fan magazines listed the different awards for the year as well as organizational web sites. Also, using the web I searched for mystery awards and started locating titles of past years.

Then I decided to print out the list and see if someone was interested in publishing a resource book for others. I showed the project to Marvin Lachman and Francis M. Nevins at the 2005 Boucheron, and they both said that this project needed to be published. No one had taken this direction in the past, and it would be wonderful to have all of the suggested lists in one place.

Why these books in the project? When considering the award or nominated titles, we of course limit ourselves to just those titles. Let us say that an awards group (*Mystery Writers of America, Malice Domestic, Hammett,* etc.) present a list of five or six nominees each year in various categories (best novel, best first novel, best paperback, etc.). In 2006, there were about 290 titles in the novel category, nominated for the various awards. Were those the best novels of the year? Not necessarily. Nevertheless, they were the ones nominated by each group, and they have guidelines for selection. For instance, *Agatha* nominated titles are usually not the same type of titles nominated by *The Private Eye Writers of America*, for the *Shamus Awards,* or for the *Edgar®* *Awards.* There is a place for the hardboiled detective novels as well as the thriller, suspense, and cozy novel.

Yes, there are many great books not on the list. In some ways, these selections are like the motion picture industry awards. The *Golden Globes* or the *Academy Awards* select several film titles as finalists or nominees for their awards. Then, at a special ceremony, the winners are announced. Maybe your favorite did not win. Maybe your favorite is not even on the list of nominees to be considered. That's OK, because you will see the movie anyway, watch it on TV, and even purchase the video or DVD of the film. The same is true with the mystery awards. Out of the thousands of book titles up for consideration, only a small number of these are in the final selection or cut.

On the other hand, just as there are overlooked movies in the motion picture arena, there are overlooked books and authors in the mystery field. Jim Huang in his book, *They Died in Vain: Overlooked, Underappreciated and Forgotten Mystery Novels* brings this point home.

As the years move on, the good titles will find a way of being reprinted and available. What is confusing is what the publishers and new booksellers do to initiate book sales. High-tech marketing is in full gear. They have their leading authors and inundate us with promotions for the book, be it outstanding, great, good, or even a weak offering. They have author's contracts, printing costs, publicity, promotion, etc., and they want sales. Walk in to a Barnes and Noble, Borders, or other chain bookstores and the special displays are right there for us—we cannot miss the promotion.

Yet, an unknown author can publish a great new book and just a couple of copies are shelved somewhere in the store—not in view. Many stores will promote the books of local area or regional authors and even have them present from time to time for book signings.

I have found that readers, in the mystery field or any other field (westerns, science fiction, romance, etc.), seek their favorite authors no matter what. Sometimes they check their web pages and are even sent e-mail messages from various authors announcing their new books.

I was in a mystery bookstore, and as I was looking through the used book section, overheard one of the store personnel making calls to some of their regular customers telling them that some new books that they might enjoy had just arrived.

Part 4: The Task of Research — Challenges

Some of the challenges. When I was encouraged by Marvin Lachman and Francis M. Nevins to pursue my project for printing, I went home and began the task of reexamining my lists and considering other lists. As I examined my work up to that point, I realized there was a problem with almost every list. Errors and mistakes abounded in the original and secondary sources. In the past, I had taken the information from web sites or typed from books or magazines at face value. I had not examined the original materials for correctness. A great deal of work needed to be accomplished in the fine-tuning of this project.

On the web sites of various organizations and mystery fan sites, some of the information was wrong, incomplete, and even lacking. Some sources presented several years with both winners and nominated titles, but then changed and listed just the winners, omitting the nominees. I realized that I could simply not reproduce the errors again and needed to complete the missing information.

I used Allen J. Hubin's latest CD-ROM of *Crime Fiction IV: A Comprehensive Bibliography, 1749-2000* as one checking source, as well as several web sites such as Amazon.com, BarnesandNoble.com, Abebooks.com. Many times on those sites there would be a copy of the book cover, and in some cases, the table of contents. I received valuable help from individuals as noted in the Preface.

Computer data researchers tell me that no list is free from problems. We will always be making corrections and changes. Therefore, as this project is presented here—I offer any of you to assist in making further corrections and changes. Simply e-mail me your information and suggestions at: Rsobin@yahoo.com.

More examples. Some web sites listing the *Haycraft-Queen Cornerstones* were missing titles. I e-mailed one key site, and they responded back that they did not know how they could have missed the titles and thanked me for the correction.

Several web lists of Susan Oleksiw's *100 Classics of the Genre* (in *A Reader's Guide to the Classic British Mystery)* omitted two titles. Purchasing a copy of the book and double-checking, I found the two titles and entered them into this book.

I decided to obtain all of the books that I could to double-check the lists myself. I had several of them and ordered the rest via Amazon.com. I did this as far as I could by obtaining the *Lehman, Lachman, Oleksiw, Winks, Haycraft, Niebuhr, Bourgeau, Barzun and Taylor, Independent Mystery Booksellers Association* (three titles), *Keating, Queen's Quorum, Mystery Writers of America* (three titles) books for this research. Yet, a number of those books, had wrong information, wrong spellings, and wrong titles.

After dealing with the nonfiction lists, I decided that obtaining the complete title or subtitle might be very helpful for some people wanting to obtain books or at least have a better knowledge of what the book might be about. Here is an example: the 1997 title—*Outrage* by Vincent Bugliosi. By itself, the title does not tell us much. However, seeing the subtitle tells us a great deal—*Outrage: The Five Reasons Why O.J. Simpson Got Away With Murder*. Another example, a title that was up for four nonfiction or critical writing awards was listed as, *Who Was that Lady?* Again, seeing the subtitle helps: *Who Was that Lady? Craig Rice: The Queen of Screwball Mystery*. *Savage Art* by Robert Polito (nominated for three awards) is better seen as, *Savage Art: A Biography of Jim Thompson*.

I added the original or key source to find the short stories, including the editor—if there was one. Most lists did not do this. I used Al Hubin's CD-ROM and other sites to accomplish this task.

The challenges of dates. Dates can vary for different reasons. Here are some of the challenges.

Publication date is usually the key date listed. Yet, that date could vary. In the United States, it could have one date. In Great Britain, it could be another. A French mystery published in France might have one date, and different dates when translated and published in other countries.

Georges Simenon wrote 75 novels and 28 short stories featuring Inspector Maigret between 1931 and 1972. *Maigret and the Yellow Dog* is listed in Hubin as published by Harcourt in 1987, also under the title *A Face for a Clue* (translated by Geoffrey Sainsbury) in 1939 by Routledge. The work continued to be published in England, Canada, and the United States under this second title. In 1980, it was released as *Maigret and the Concarneau Murders* (again translated by Sainsbury) in England. Then in 1987, it was published in the United States as *Maigret and the Yellow Dog* (translated by Linder Asher). Doing some research, I found that it was originally written and published in French in 1931 as *Le Chien Jaune*. Thus, dates vary. I should list it as 1987, because that is probably the date we would find today in most bookstores. Yet, the work was a product of the early 1930s and reflects the writing style of that time, therefore, I list it as 1931/39. That raises a question, is one after the date of the writing of the book or the date it was published? If published, where and when? Therefore, dates can be misleading.

Furthermore, almost all of the awards list the year the book was nominated and not the year of publication. *California Girl* by T. Jefferson Parker was published in 2004, but nominated in 2005 for five awards *(Anthony, Edgar®, Hammett, Macavity,* and *Gumshoe* awards) and won the *Edgar® Best Novel*. It is listed in this resource as a 2005 book, but it was published in 2004. In the future, another list might be offered as to the best books of the decade and list that title with a date of 2004. The dates in the left-hand column are only guides in many cases.

Authors names and title confusion. There is also the problem of which name of an author to use or list first. There are resources that list pseudonyms and other name concerns.

James Hilton wrote 22 novels and several plays, and many of them were made into motion pictures. One book originally written in 1931 is titled *Murder at School* written under the name of Glen Trevor and published in England. Two years later in 1933, it was published in the United States as *Was it Murder?* under the name James Hilton. Thus, we have one book with two titles, two dates, and two author names. British lists of course carry it the first way as *Murder at School* by Glen Trevor, and most United States lists go the other way as *Was it Murder?* by James Hilton. It appears that Hilton only used the name Glen Trevor for that one book. I tried to list a number of the key titles in both places, also making reference to the secondary name or title, for instance:

Was it Murder? (Murder at School)   James Hilton (as Glen Trevor).

Another example is the 1969 Edgar® Best Novel winner, *A Case of Need* listed as written by Jeffery Hudson. That is a pseudonym of Michael Crichton. The early copies of that title have Jeffery Hudson as author; later copies have changed it to Crichton (writing as Jeffery Hudson). Again, that creates the problem of how you list it and where you shelve it, under Hudson or Crichton?

In this resource, I kept the titles and authors under the original listing, with the alternative titles and authors in parenthesis. I will indicate when titles have two names (or more) and most of the authors who use different names and list them in both places. As to the award/nominated dates, in most cases, I have kept the date as to the award year which will differ from the publication year.

Kenneth Millar is an excellent example. He wrote under the pen names John Macdonald, John Ross Macdonald, and of course Ross Macdonald. Earlier editions of his novels will list John Macdonald, while later editions of that same work will list Ross Macdonald. In most cases I have kept the original name that the list maker offers and in parentheses will add the key name (Ross Macdonald). Or, as: Ross Macdonald (as, John Ross Macdonald) and sometimes: Ross Macdonald (as, Kenneth Millar). There could be confusion with another writer John D. MacDonald.

Lists can vary with some titles. I have changed or added to some titles for the sake of the reader or collector today. Some list R. Austin Freeman's, *The Singing Bone* written in 1918, but later it was reissued as *The Adventures of Dr. Thorndyke* in 1947, and noted as "originally published under the title of *The Singing Bone*." I have placed both names with the listings:

1918	*Singing Bone, The (The Adventures of Dr. Thorndyke)*	R. Austin Freeman	___
1918	*Adventures of Dr. Thorndyke, The (The Singing Bone)*	R. Austin Freeman	___

Publishers. As the compiler and editor of this resource, I had to make some decisions from the start. One of those decisions was to not list the publisher of the books or titles. There were multiple problems here. With newer books the publishers are known. Older books have often been reprinted in some cases, numerous times, and it would be difficult for the collector of interest to deal with that and myself as the researcher to complete that task. Other resources have that specific information. My concern here was to offer the authors and titles of works for the collector and other interested folks. Also, the layout of this book called for columns, and there is only so much space on the page. My apologies to the publishers for without them we would not have any books. I hope they will understand.

Part 5: Concluding Thoughts

The discussion in Parts 3 and 4 might help alert the reader and collector to the various problems involved in obtaining these lists. However, it is my hope that what is contained in this volume will encourage further reading and collecting. Again, I invite you to offer suggestions, corrections, and even other lists to consider. Here are several areas for consideration and conversation:

Older books and short stories online. Numerous computer web sites offer many of the older works online.

www.freeonlinereading.com/links.htm
digital.library.upenn.edu/books/

For instance, *The Leavenworth Case* (1878) by Anna Katharine Green can be found at: www.gutenberg.org/etext/4047—I checked it against my personal copy and it is all there.

They have the works of Edgar Allan Poe with text and audio:
www.gutenberg.org/browse/authors/p#a481

Wilkie Collins works are there, such as *The Moonstone* (1868). *The Thirty-Nine Steps* (1915) by John Buchan, *The Extraordinary Adventures of Arsene Lupin: Gentleman-Burglar* (1907) by Maurice Leblanc and many more. In fact, a number of titles from the *Queen's Quorum* are available.

Libraries and librarians. Public and school libraries do offer mystery books. Some libraries have special events, speakers, and displays about the mystery field. I feel this resource might be used as a collection development tool by librarians. They would have before them all of the classic or best lists and the award lists for ordering of books, holding of already housed books, and creating different approaches to mystery events. Some individuals might want to read books from these lists and check them out from a library and not own or collect them in any permanent way.

Juvenile/youth/young adult mysteries. Librarians, parents, and interested youth might want to zero in on titles in those categories (see: Agatha, Anthony, Edgar®, Arthur Ellis, CWAA awards—all have titles listed in this book). Mystery Writers of America has a program, Kids Love a Mystery, with information and ideas available on their web site. Students can receive an Eddie Award certificate for their participation in the program. For further information go to www.mysterywriters.org/pages/news/klam.htm

Nonfiction. I list all of the awards and nominees, and classic and best lists that I could locate which offered books in the nonfiction, true crime, critical, or biography categories. After one reads numerous mystery novels, they might want to expand in the mystery field.

After reading two or three Raymond Chandler novels followed by watching several of the 1940s movies taken from the books—one might look for a biography about Chandler and learn how he developed his style, and how his writings are tied together in the history of the mystery genre. The same is true with many other favorite writers. Agatha Christie lovers do not just read Agatha's novels and plays, but at one point want to read her biography and books about her.

There are numerous nonfiction books about the mystery field that assist the mystery lover in gaining depth of knowledge. Titles like David Lehman's *The Perfect Murder* that weaves just what we have in different patterns to paint larger pictures of the genre. Also, Robin W. Winks' *Modus Operandi: An Excursion Into Detective Fiction* is poetry in prose and brings alive this love of the mystery.

One should not just stop at the mystery story, but read Marvin Lachman's book *The Heirs of Anthony Boucher: A History of Mystery Fandom* and better understand the faithful followers and the turns and bends in the field as the mystery hobby continues over the years and decades.

All of this leads to many thousands of individuals attending the various mystery book conventions around the world, if it be Bouchercon meeting annually as kind of the international gathering or the many regional or group conventions that do meet. Planning for these takes effort and committed time. Moreover, for the fan, it takes making trip plans, hotel reservations, etc., well in advance.

Remember when the list was offered. Some classic or best lists have been around a while, and some have uniqueness in their approach. We need to remember when looking at the titles in these lists—and wondering why they did not include this or that title or author—that there is a cutoff point involved. That is why I included the dates in the introduction to most of the lists that follow. Of course, nothing could be in a list after the list was completed. Therefore, if *Sandoe's* list from 1945 is reviewed, he will not list Michael Connelly writing in the 1990s. However, notice how many titles he has within five years of his list (that is 1940-1945)—36 percent! In addition, some lists placed restrictions like *They Died in Vain* and *Must-Read Thrillers* could only have one book per author; *Robin Winks Personal Favorites* had a limit to no more than three titles per author. Winks also indicated that not many titles were from the early classic period (pre-1930). On the other side, *Lachman's 100 Notable American Novels of Detection* lists twelve titles by John Dickson Carr (Carter Dickson), that is twelve percent by one author. Therefore, there are applicable controls to the outcome.

Updates and possible changes. I have included the Francis M. Nevins list of *Top Ten* mystery writers. His qualifiers are they must be American, male, and dead. In talking with him recently, he pointed out that he put that list together in 1997. But in light of all of the first-rate authors who have died since then, it might look different if he were to do it over again today. It is important to remember that a list of books or titles were created at a certain point in time. Titles after that point cannot be added nor considered, unless there is a revision or update of some kind by the author or creator of the original list.

I have the feeling that as a new list of best mystery titles is created either by a single person (such as, Lehman, Bourgeau, Sandoe, etc.) or a group community (such as, *They Died in Vain),* it can show their influence of the more current titles of their time. With all of the fanfare of publishers, booksellers, and so forth, the creators of the lists might lean a bit toward certain titles.

A new cornerstone list—1950-2000. There are a lot of lists and suggestions for the key mystery books from 1748 to 1950. *Haycraft-Queen Cornerstones, Sandoe's Honor Roll,* and other lists give us a good feel for those titles. Since 1950, there have been some best lists but more weight on awards by various groups and organizations and not really many that cover the period from 1950 to 2000. However, most of these award lists did not start until after 1982. In editing the *100 Favorite Mysteries of the Century*, Jim Huang is one source that approaches this task. Yet the influence was on the twenty years from 1980 to 2000 because fifty percent of the titles were from that time period.

One of the new best lists appearing for the first time in this resource is titles considered between 1942 to 1968 by Anthony Boucher. I have compiled his annual best lists and other important titles that he offered readers during his reviewing and mystery critic days. Please see those entries on pages 299 through 324. His suggestions give us a wonderful window to consider as important titles during those years.

I am suggesting that a special panel or group be created to consider establishing such a list. Maybe a fan magazine or several magazines could oversee this project. The panel should include people from several areas: reviewers, historians, authors, college professors, and fans. After reviewing that fifty-year time span, they could present a list. That could create a list of some 250 titles. There should probably be no limit to a number of titles by an author. The panel should include different mystery fields: detective, hardboiled, cozy, thriller, suspense, etc. In the end, I believe that we need a cornerstone or essentials list from 1950 to 2000. We are now seven years or more removed from 2000, and that gives us a better perspective on those fifty years of mystery writing.

Part 6: List of Reference Books

Listed here are resources I used for this project. I have found them very useful in my research over the past year, and I recommend all of them to you for your library or use:

Ashley, Mike, compiler, *The Mammoth Encyclopedia of Modern Crime Fiction: The Authors, Their Works and Their Most Famous Creations*, 2002, Carroll & Graf, New York.

Ball, John, editor, *The Mystery Story*, 1976, University of California, San Diego., in cooperation with Publisher's Inc., Del Mar, California.

Barzun, Jacques and Wendell Hertig Taylor, *A Catalogue of Crime: Being a Reader's Guide to the Literature of Mystery, Detection, and Related Genres*, 1989, Harper & Row, New York.

Bourgeau, Art, *The Mystery Lover's Companion*, 1986, Crown Publishers, Inc., New York.

Contento, William G., *Mystery Short Fiction: 1990-2006, An Index to Mystery Magazines, Anthologies, and Single-Author Collections*, 2007, Locus Press, Oakland, California. (web), www.philsp.com/homeville/msf/0start.htm

Gorman, Ed, Martin H. Greenberg, Larry Segriff, with Jon L. Breen, editors *The Fine Art of Murder: The Mystery Reader's Indispensable Companion*, 1993, Carroll & Graf, New York.

Grafton, Sue, editor, with Jan Burke and Barry Zeman, *Writing Mysteries: A Handbook by the Mystery Writers of America*, 2nd edition, 2002, Writer's Digest Books, Cincinnati, Ohio.

Haycraft, Howard, editor with a commentary, *The Art of the Mystery Story: A Collection of Critical Essays*, 1947, Biblo and Tannen, New York.

Haycraft, Howard, *Murder for Pleasure: The Life and Times of the Detective Story*, 1941, D. Appleton-Century Company, New York.

Huang, Jim, editor, *100 Favorite Mysteries of the Century, Selected by the Independent Mystery Booksellers Association*, 2000, The Crum Creek Press, Carmel, Indiana.

Huang, Jim, editor, *They Died in Vain: Overlooked, Underappreciated and Forgotten Mystery Novels*, 2002, The Crum Creek Press, Carmel, Indiana.

Huang, Jim and Austin Lugar, editors, *Mystery Muses: 100 Classics That Inspire Today's Mystery Writers*, 2006, The Crum Creek Press, Carmel, Indiana.

Hubin, Allen J., *Crime Fiction IV: A Comprehensive Bibliography, 1749-2000*, (CD-ROM), 2005, Locus Press, Oakland, California.

Jarvis, Mary J., *A Reader's Guide to the Suspense Novel*, 1997, G. K. Hall & Company, New York.

Keating, H.R.F., *Crime and Mystery: The 100 Best Books*, 1987, Carroll & Graf, New York.

Knight, Stephen, *Crime Fiction 1800-2000: Detection, Death, Diversity*, 2004, Palgrave MacMillian, New York.

Lachman, Marvin, *A Reader's Guide to the American Novel of Detection*, 1993, G.K. Hall & Company, New York.

Lachman, Marvin, *The Heirs of Anthony Boucher: A History of Mystery Fandom*, 2005, Poisoned Pen Press, Scottsdale, Arizona.

Lehman, David, *The Perfect Murder: A Study in Detection*, 2000, The University of Michigan Press, Ann Arbor, Michigan.

Lyles, William H., *Putting Dell on the Map: A History of the Dell Paperbacks*, 1983, Greenwood Press, Westport, Connecticut.

Mystery Writers of America. Penzler, Otto, annotated. Mickey Friedman, compiler, *The Crown Crime Companion: The Top 100 Mystery Novels of All Time: Selected by the Mystery Writers of America*, annotated by Otto Penzler, 1995, Crown Trade Paperbacks, New York.

Mystery Writers Annual: Edgar Allan Poe Awards Dinner (booklet), Mystery Writers of America, Inc., New York. (numerous years)

Nevins, Jr., Francis M., editor, *The Anthony Boucher Chronicles: Review and Commentary 1942-1947*, 2001, Ramble House, Shreveport, Louisiana.

Nevins, Jr., Francis M., editor, *The Mystery Writer's Art*, 1970, Bowling Green University Popular Press, Bowling Green, Ohio.

Niebuhr, Gary Warren, *A Reader's Guide to the Private Eye Novel*, 1993, G.K. Hall & Company, New York.

Oleksiw, Susan, *A Reader's Guide to the Classic British Mystery*, 1988, G.K. Hall & Company, New York.

Pronzini, Bill, editor, *The Edgar Winners, 33rd Annual Anthology of the Mystery Writers of America: Twenty-Four Stories Selected from the Winners of the Edgar Allan Poe Award for Excellence*, 1980, Random House, New York.

Queen, Ellery, *Queen's Quorum: A History of the Detective-Crime Short Story as Revealed by the 125 Most Important Books Published in this Field, 1845-1967*, 1969, Greenhall Books, London.

Stine, Kate, editor, *The Armchair Detective Book of Lists: A Complete Guide to the Best Mystery, Crime, and Suspense Fiction*, 1995, Otto Penzler Books, New York.

Stone, Nancy-Stephanie, *A Reader's Guide to the Spy and Thriller Novel*, 1997, G. K. Hall & Company, New York.

Vicarel, Jo Ann, *A Reader's Guide to the Police Procedural*, 1995, G. K. Hall & Company, New York.

Winks, Robin W., editor, *Colloquium on Crime: Eleven Renowned Mystery Writers Discuss Their Work*, 1986, Charles Scribner's Sons, New York.

Winks, Robin W., editor, *Detective Fiction: A Collection of Critical Essays*, 1988, A Foul Play Press Book, The Countryman Press, Woodstock, Vermont.

Winks, Robin W., *Modus Operandi: An Excursion Into Detective Fiction*, 1982, David R. Godine, Publisher, Boston.

Mystery journals consulted:

Crime and Detective Stories (CADS) magazine, Geoff Bradley, editor.

Crimespree Magazine, Jon and Ruth Jordan, editors.

Deadly Pleasures Mystery Magazine, George Easter, editor.

Mystery Scene: You Guide to the Best in Mystery, Crime and Suspense, Kate Stine, editor.

The Armchair Detective (TAD), 1976-1997.

◇ ◇ ◇ ◇ ◇ ◇ ◇ ◇

To better use this resource:

1. The column on the right is placed there as a check space for those wanting to make reference to titles collected, read or needed.

2. Titles in BOLD print have won an award. Names in BOLD print were honored in some way (grandmasters and other honored titles).

3. If there was a tie for an award, (Tie) is next to the award title.

4. *Abbreviations: ed. (editor), eds. (editors), pre. (presenters, several books have a behind the scenes editor, but marketed the book with a more famous writer as the presenter with an article to introduce the book). Also, several magazines in the short story sections like: EQMM (Ellery Queen Mystery Magazine) and AHMM (Alfred Hitchcock Mystery Magazine).*

5. Years. In the case of magazines or journals, dates are given with just the last two digits of the year because of spacing concerns. Example: *EQMM*, Jul 98. Meaning *Ellery Queen Mystery Magazine,* July 1998.

6. If the awards or classic or best lists have a web site for information, sites are listed at the end of that listing on the right side of the page. The quality of some of these sites vary as discussed above. Therefore, when possible, refer to the original sources.

7. Several times I updated the date of a reference work when that title had been updated since the original list was compiled.

8. Some titles are listed by an author that used two names. Sometimes an author used a pen name when a book was published and later published that same title under there own name or another pen name. Here is an example:

   1949   Boucher 49 Best   *Blue Harpsichord*   Keith, David (Francis Steegmuller)   ___

9. Alternate titles. Numerous times the publisher/author will change a title when a book is published in another country. Other times, a different title is utilized on future publications of the work. These brackets ( ) indicate those titles.

10. The award lists that follow are not complete lists of the organizations, but only the awards that deal with books and authors. Other awards, such as best mystery film, television, play, support individuals, web sites, etc., are not the scope of this research.

In conclusion. The primary purpose of this resource is to have in one book the award winners and nominees and classic or best lists.

I could go on checking and double-checking for further problems and resolving a few questions here and there, but then the project would never be published. Some of the awards were extremely difficult to complete. With the help of individuals from many of the award organizations, most of those voids were completed, especially with the nominee listings. Sometimes this was from notes of individuals, looking in older program articles, or just recalling memories. There is still some work to be completed and we need your help. The plan now is to update this volume in the near future with corrections, additions, new lists, etc. In addition, the latest awards with nominees and winners will be added. You are invited to offer suggestions, corrections, and ideas to: Rsobin@yahoo.com

Good luck in your reading and collecting.

Roger M. Sobin
Helotes, Texas
October 2007

A Basic Understanding of the Task:

We, in the mystery related fields—have the pleasurable task to name, to read, and talk about the books that have paved the way and make the mystery/suspense/murder/adventure/thriller/cozies, etc.—continue to live and be passed down to the present-future. If that is true, we have some continual work to do.

Section II: The Mystery Awards

Agatha Awards

Malice Domestic was established in 1989 to celebrate the traditional mystery a subgenre, typified by the writings of Agatha Christie. At its annual convention in the metropolitan Washington, DC area, the organization presents the Agatha Awards, honoring authors who write in this genre. These works do not contain explicit sex, excessive gore, or gratuitous violence. They usually feature an amateur detective, a confined setting, and characters who know one another. Police officers and private detectives may be featured, but "hard-boiled" types are not appropriate. The awards are presented annually for works by living authors, published during the previous year in the United States.

The awards are fan generated and voted on by ballot by registered convention attendees. The award is a teapot, its ceramic teabag tag emblazoned with a skull.

[Editor's note: I have dated the award years to the award presentation year to conform to the other mystery awards rather than to the Malice Domestic web site.]

Agatha Best Novel

2007

Virgin of Small Plains, The	Nancy Pickard	____
Saddlemaker's Wife, The	Earlene Fowler	____
Why Casey Had to Die	L.C. Hayden	____
All Mortal Flesh	Julia Spencer-Fleming	____
Messenger of Truth	Jacqueline Winspear	____

2006

Body in the Snowdrift, The	Katherine Hall Page	____
Owls Well that Ends Well	Donna Andrews	____
Rituals of the Season	Margaret Maron	____
Belen Hitch, The	Pari Noskin Taichert	____
Trouble in Spades	Heather Webber	____
Pardonable Lies	Jacqueline Winspear	____

2005

Birds of a Feather	Jacqueline Winspear	____
We'll Always Have Parrots	Donna Andrews	____
By a Spider's Thread	Laura Lippman	____
High Country Fall	Margaret Maron	____
Pearl Diver, The	Sujata Massey	____

2004

Letter From Home	Carolyn G. Hart	____
Crouching Buzzard, Leaping Loon	Donna Andrews	____
Mumbo Gumbo	Jerrilyn Farmer	____
Dream House	Rochelle Krich	____
Last Lessons of Summer	Margaret Maron	____
Shop Till You Drop	Elaine Viets	____

2003

You've Got Murder	Donna Andrews	___
Death of Riley	Rhys Bowen	___
Blues in the Night	Rochelle Krich	___
Body in the Bonfire, The	Katherine Hall Page	___
Golden One, The	Elizabeth Peters	___

2002

Murphy's Law	Rhys Bowen	___
Arkansas Traveler	Earlene Fowler	___
Dead Until Dark	Charlaine Harris	___
Shadows of Sin	Rochelle Krich	___
Bride's Kimono, The	Sujata Massey	___

2001

Storm Track	Margaret Maron	___
Guns and Roses	Taffy Cannon	___
Killer Wedding	Jerrilyn Farmer	___
Floating Girl, The	Sujata Massey	___
He Shall Thunder in the Sky (Thunder in the Sky)	Elizabeth Peters	___

2000

Mariner's Compass	Earlene Fowler	___
Immaculate Reception	Jerrilyn Farmer	___
Death on the River Walk	Carolyn G. Hart	___
In Big Trouble	Laura Lippman	___
Flower Master, The	Sujata Massey	___

1999

Butchers Hill	Laura Lippman	___
Liar	Jan Burke	___
Dove in the Window	Earlene Fowler	___
Blind Bloodhound Justice	Virginia Lanier	___
Home Fires	Margaret Maron	___
Ape Who Guards the Balance, The	Elizabeth Peters	___

1998

Devil in Music, The	Kate Ross	___
Hocus	Jan Burke	___
Dreaming of the Bones	Deborah Crombie	___
Goose in a Pond	Earlene Fowler	___
Seeing a Large Cat	Elizabeth Peters	___

1997

Up Jumps the Devil	Margaret Maron	___
Kansas Troubles	Earlene Fowler	___
Grass Widow, The	Teri Holbrook	___
Hearts and Bones	Margaret Lawrence	___
Strong as Death	Sharan Newman	___

1996

If I'd Killed Him When I Met Him	Sharyn McCrumb	____
Miracles in Maggody	Joan Hess	____
Wandering Arm, The	Sharan Newman	____
Twilight	Nancy Pickard	____
Escapade	Walter Satterthwait	____

1995

She Walks These Hills	Sharyn McCrumb	____
Scandal in Fair Haven	Carolyn G. Hart	____
Beekeeper's Apprentice, The	Laurie R. King	____
Angel of Death	Rochelle Krich	____
Night Train to Memphis	Elizabeth Peters	____

1994

Dead Man's Island	Carolyn G. Hart	____
Old Scores	Aaron Elkins	____
O Little Town of Maggody	Joan Hess	____
Fair Game	Rochelle Majer Krich	____
Southern Discomfort	Margaret Maron	____
To Live and Die in Dixie	Kathy Hogan Trocheck	____

1993

Bootlegger's Daughter	Margaret Maron	____
Southern Ghost	Carolyn G. Hart	____
Hangman's Beautiful Daughter, The	Sharyn McCrumb	____
Defend and Betray	Anne Perry	____
Snake, the Crocodile and the Dog, The	Elizabeth Peters	____

1992

I.O.U.	Nancy Pickard	____
Make No Bones	Aaron Elkins	____
Christie Caper, The	Carolyn G. Hart	____
Owl too Many, An	Charlotte MacLeod	____
Last Camel Died at Noon, The	Elizabeth Peters	____

1991

Bum Steer (Cross Bones)	Nancy Pickard	____
Real Murders	Charlaine Harris	____
Deadly Valentine	Carolyn G. Hart	____
Face of a Stranger, The	Anne Perry	____
Potter's Field, The	Ellis Peters	____

1990

Naked Once More	Elizabeth Peters	____
Sirens Sang of Murder, The	Sarah Caudwell	____
Little Class on Murder, A	Carolyn G. Hart	____
Corpus Christmas	Margaret Maron	____
Philly Stakes	Gillian Roberts	____

1989
Something Wicked	Carolyn G. Hart	___
Widow's Club, The	Dorothy Cannell	___
Mischief in Maggody	Joan Hess	___
Paying the Piper	Sharyn McCrumb	___
Dead Crazy	Nancy Pickard	___

Agatha Best 1st Novel

2007
Heat of the Moon, The	Sandra Parshall	___
Consigned to Death	Jane Cleland	___
Chef Who Died Sauteing, The	Honora Finklestein & Susan Smily	___
Feint of Art	Hailey Lind	___
Murder on The Rocks	Karen Macinerney	___

2006
Better Off Wed	Laura Durham	___
Jury of One	Laura Bradford	___
Witch Way to Murder	Shirley Damsgaard	___
Knit One, Kill Two	Maggie Sefton	___
Blood Relations	Lisa Tillman	___

2005
Dating Dead Men	Harley Jane Kozak	___
Till the Cows Come Home	Judy Clemens	___
Arson and Old Lace	Patricia Harwin	___
I Dreamed I Married Perry Mason	Susan Kandel	___
Clovis Incident, The	Pari Noskin Taichert	___

2004
Maisie Dobbs	Jacqueline Winspear	___
Dealing in Murder	Elaine Flinn	___
Haunted Ground	Erin Hart	___
Take the Bait	S.W. Hubbard	___
Alpine for You	Maddy Hunter	___
Murder Off Mike	Joyce Krieg	___
O' Artful Death	Sarah Stewart Taylor	___

2003
In the Bleak Midwinter	Julia Spencer-Fleming	___
Not All Tarts are Apple	Pip Granger	___
Six Strokes Under	Roberta Isleib	___
Beat Until Stiff	Claire M. Johnson	___
How to Murder a Millionaire	Nancy Martin	___
Shadows at the Fair	Lea Wait	___

2002
Bubbles Unbound — Sarah Strohmeyer — ____
Innkeeping With Murder — Tim Myers — ____
Mute Witness — Charles O'Brien — ____
Witness Above, A — Andy Straka — ____
Affinity for Murder, An — Anne White — ____

2001
Death on a Silver Tray — Rosemary Stevens — ____
Death Dances to a Reggae Beat — Kate Grilley — ____
Three Dirty Women and the Garden of Death — Julie Wray Herman — ____
Death of an Amiable Child — Irene Marcuse — ____
Murder of a Small Town Honey — Denise Swanson — ____

2000
Murder With Peacocks — Donna Andrews — ____
Circles of Confusion — April Henry — ____
Revenge of the Gypsy Queen — Kris Neri — ____
By Blood Possessed — Elena Santangelo — ____
Sing It to Her Bones — Marcia Talley — ____

1999
Doctor Digs a Grave, The — Robin Hathaway — ____
Sympathy for the Devil — Jerrilyn Farmer — ____
Tiger's Palette — Jacqueline Fiedler — ____
Dying to Get Published — Judy Fitzwater — ____
Fax Me a Bagel — Sharon Kahn — ____

1998
Salaryman's Wife, The — Sujata Massey — ____
Quieter Than Sleep — Joanne Dobson — ____
Butter Did It, The — Phyllis Richman — ____
Dead Body Language — Penny Warner — ____
Death Brims Over — Barbara Jaye Wilson — ____

1997
Murder on a Girl's Night Out — Anne George — ____
Biggie and the Poisoned Politician — Nancy Bell — ____
Death in Little Tokyo — Dale Furutani — ____
Somebody Else's Child — Terris McMahan Grimes — ____
Riding for a Fall — Lillian Roberts — ____

1996
Body in the Transept, The — Jeanne M. Dams — ____
Far and Deadly Cry, A — Teri Holbrook — ____
Horse of a Different Killer — Jody Jaffe — ____
Death in Bloodhound Red — Virginia Lanier — ____
Murder in Scorpio — Martha C. Lawrence — ____

1995

Do Unto Others	Jeff Abbott	___
One for the Money	Janet Evanovich	___
Fool's Puzzle	Earlene Fowler	___
Writers of the Purple Sage	Barbara Burnett Smith	___
Until Death	Polly Whitney	___

1994

Track of the Cat	Nevada Barr	___
Goodnight, Irene	Jan Burke	___
Share in Death, A	Deborah Crombie	___
Death Comes as Epiphany	Sharan Newman	___
Child of Silence	Abigail Padgett	___

1993

Blanche on the Lam	Barbara Neely	___
All the Great Pretenders	Deborah Adams	___
Thyme of Death	Susan Wittig Albert	___
Decked	Carol Higgins Clark	___
Seneca Falls Inheritance	Miriam Grace Monfredo	___

1992

Zero at the Bone	Mary Willis Walker	___
Carpool	Mary Cahill	___
Just Desserts	Mary Daheim	___
Bulrush Murders, The	Rebecca Rothenberg	___
Flowers for the Dead	Ann Williams	___

1991

Body in the Belfry, The	Katherine Hall Page	___
Screaming Bones	Pat Burden	___
Catering to Nobody	Diane Mott Davidson	___
Chartreuse Clue, The	William F. Love	___
Sea of Troubles	Janet L. Smith	___

1990

Grime and Punishment	Jill Churchill	___
Working Murder	Eleanor Boylan	___
Question of Guilt, A	Frances Fyfield	___
Mother Shadow, The	Melodie Johnson Howe	___
Mark Twain Murders, The	Edith Skom	___

1989

Great Deliverance, A	Elizabeth George	___
Killings at Badger's Drift, The	Caroline Graham	___
J. Alfred Prufrock Murders, The	Corinne Holt Sawyer	___
Goodbye, Nanny Grey	Susannah Stacey	___
Dead Men Don't Give Seminars	Dorothy Sucher	___

Agatha Best Non-Fiction

2007

Don't Murder Your Mystery: 24 Fiction-Writing Chris Roerden ____
 Techniques to Save Your Manuscript from
 Turning Up…D.O.A.

Mystery Muses: 100 Classics that Inspire Today's Jim Huang & Austin Lugar, eds. ____
 Mystery Writers

Beautiful Cigar Girl, The: Mary Rogers, Edgar Daniel Stashower ____
 Allan Poe, and the Invention of Murder

2006

Girl Sleuth: Nancy Drew and the Women Melanie Rehak ____
 Who Created Her

Behind the Mystery: Top Mystery Writers Stuart M. Kaminsky; ____
 Interviewed photos by Laurie Roberts

New Annotated Sherlock Holmes, The: The Novels Leslie S. Klinger, ed. ____

Heirs of Anthony Boucher, The: A History of Marvin Lachman ____
 Mystery Fandom

2005

Private Eye-Lashes: Radio's Lady Detectives Jack French ____

New Annotated Sherlock Holmes, The: Leslie S. Klinger, ed. ____
 The Complete Short Stories

2004

Amelia Peabody's Egypt: A Compendium Elizabeth Peters & ____
  Kristen Whitbread, eds.

Mystery Women: An Encyclopedia of Leading Colleen A. Barnett ____
 Women Characters in Mystery Fiction,
 Vol. 3, parts 1 & 2

Second Helping of Murder, A: More Diabolically Jo Grossman & ____
 Delicious Recipes From Contemporary Mystery Robert Weibezahl, eds.
 Writers

Atomic Renaissance: Women Mystery Jeffrey Marks ____
 Writers of the 1940s and 1950s

Dick Francis Companion, The Jean Swanson & Dean James ____

2003

They Died in Vain: Overlooked, Under- Jim Huang, ed. ____
 appreciated and Forgotten Mystery Novels

Mammoth Encyclopedia of Modern Crime Fiction, The Mike Ashley, compiler ____

Mystery Women: An Encyclopedia of Leading Colleen A. Barnett ____
 Women Characters in Mystery Fiction

Kitchen Privileges: A Memoir Mary Higgins Clark ____

Writing Mysteries: A Handbook by the Mystery Sue Grafton, ed., with ____
 Writers of America Jan Burke & Barry Zeman

2002

Seldom Disappointed: A Memoir — Tony Hillerman — ___
History of Mystery, The — Max Allan Collins — ___
Writing the Mystery: A Start-to-Finish Guide for Both Novice and Professional — G. Miki Hayden — ___
Who was that Lady? Craig Rice: The Queen of Screwball Mystery — Jeffrey Marks — ___
Food, Drink, and the Female Sleuth — The Sisters Wells (Patricia Wells Lunneborg & Roberta Wells Ryan) — ___

2001

100 Favorite Mysteries of the Century — Jim Huang, ed. — ___
Complete Christie, The: An Agatha Christie Encyclopedia — Matthew Bunson — ___
Women of Mystery: The Lives and Works of Notable Women Crime Novelists — Martha Hailey DuBose — ___
American Regional Mystery, The — Marvin Lachman — ___
They Wrote the Book: Thirteen Women Mystery Writers Tell — Helen Windrath, ed. — ___

2000

Teller of Tales: The Life of Arthur Conan Doyle — Daniel Stashower — ___
Deadly Directory 1999, The: Your Complete Guide to the International Mystery, Crime, and Detective Fiction Community — Kate Derie, ed. — ___
Taste of Murder, A: Diabolically Delicious Recipes From Contemporary Mystery Writers — Jo Grossman & Robert Weibezahl, eds. — ___
Detecting Women 3: A Reader's Guide and Checklist for Mystery Series Written by Women — Willetta L. Heising — ___
Oxford Companion to Crime and Mystery Writing, The — Rosemary Herbert, ed. — ___

1999

Mystery Reader's Walking Guide to Washington, D.C. — Alzina Stone Dale — ___
Speaking of Murder: Interviews With the Masters of Mystery and Suspense — Ed Gorman & Martin H. Greenberg, eds. — ___
Deadly Women: The Woman Mystery Reader's Indispensable Companion — Jan Grape, Dean James & Ellen Nehr, eds. — ___
Silk Stalkings II: More Women Write of Murder — Victoria Nichols & Susan Thompson — ___
Killer Books: A Reader's Guide to Exploring the Popular World of Mystery and Suspense — Jean Swanson & Dean James — ___

1998

Detecting Men: A Reader's Guide and Checklist   Willetta L. Heising   ____
for Mystery Series Written by Men

Crimes of the Scene: A Mystery Novel Guide for the   Nina King & Robin W. Winks   ____
International Traveler

Guilty Parties: A Mystery Lover's Companion   Ian Ousby   ____

1997

Detecting Women 2: A Reader's Guide and   Willetta L. Heising   ____
Checklist for Mystery Series Written by
Women

Amateur Detectives: A Writer's Guide to How   Elaine Raco Chase &   ____
Private Citizens Solve Criminal Cases   Anne Wingate

Mystery!: A Celebration: Stalking Public   Ron Miller & Karen Sharpe, eds.   ____
Television's Greatest Sleuths

Letters of Dorothy L. Sayers, The: 1899-1936: The   Barbara Reynolds, ed.   ____
Making of a Detective Novelist

By a Woman's Hand: A Guide to Mystery Fiction   Jean Swanson & Dean James, eds.   ____
by Women, 2nd ed.

1996

Mystery Readers Walking Guide: Chicago   Alzina Stone Dale   ____

John Dickson Carr: The Man Who Explained   Douglas G. Greene   ____
Miracles

Ngaio Marsh: The Woman and Her Work   B.J. Rahn, ed.   ____

Armchair Detective Book of Lists, The, 2nd ed.   Kate Stine, ed.   ____

Cadfael Companion, The: The World of Brother   Robin Whiteman   ____
Cadfael, 2nd ed.

1995

By a Woman's Hand: A Guide to Mystery   Jean Swanson & Dean James, eds.   ____
Fiction by Women

Encyclopedia Mysteriosa: A Comprehensive Guide   William L. DeAndrea   ____
to the Art of Detection in Print, Film, Radio,
and Television

Crime Fiction II: A Comprehensive Bibliography,   Allen J. Hubin   ____
1749-1990

Great Women Mystery Writers: Classic to   Kathleen Gregory Klein, ed.   ____
Contemporary

Had She but Known: A Biography of   Charlotte MacLeod   ____
Mary Roberts Rinehart

1994

Doctor, the Murder, the Mystery, The: *The True Story of the Dr. John* *Branion Murder Case*	Barbara D'Amato	____
Maker and Craftsman: The Story of *Dorothy L. Sayers*	Alzina Stone Dale	____
Poisonous Pen of Agatha Christie, The	Michael C. Gerald	____
Fine Art of Murder, The: The Mystery Reader's *Indispensable Companion*	Ed Gorman, Martin H. Greenberg, Larry Segriff & Jon L. Breen, eds.	____
Reader's Guide to the American Novel of Detection, A	Marvin Lachman	____
Doubleday Crime Club Compendium 1928-1991	Ellen Nehr	____

Agatha Best Short Story

2007

"Sleeping With the Plush"	Toni L.P. Kelner	*AHMM,* May 06	____
"Old Couple, The "	Robert Barnard	*EQMM,* Mar/Apr 06	____
"Provenance"	Robert Barnard	*EQMM,* Jul 06	____
"Yankee Swap"	Maurissa Guibord	*EQMM,* Mar/Apr 06	____
"Disturbance In The Field"	Roberta Isleib	*Seasmoke: Crime Stories by* *New England Writers;* Flora, McCarty, & Oleksiw, eds.	____

2006

"Driven to Distraction"	Marcia Talley	*Chesapeake Crimes II;* Andrews & Lima, eds.	____
"Rear View Murder"	Carla Coupe	*Chesapeake Crimes II;* Andrews & Lima, eds.	____
"Murder at Sleuthfest"	Barb Goffman	*Chesapeake Crimes II;* Andrews & Lima, eds.	____
"House Rules"	Libby Fischer Hellmann	*Murder in Vegas: New Crime* *Tales of Gambling &* *Desperation;* Connelly, ed.	____
"Mother Love"	Harriette Sackler	*Chesapeake Crimes II;* Andrews & Lima, eds.	____

2005

"Wedding Knife"	Elaine Viets	*Chesapeake Crimes;* Andrews, ed.	____
"Butler Didn't Do It, The"	Maria Y. Lima	*Chesapeake Crimes;* Andrews, ed.	____
"Two Marys, The"	Katherine Hall Page	*Mistletoe and Mayhem*	____

2004

"No Man's Land"	Elizabeth Foxwell	*Blood on Their Hands;* Block, ed.	____
"Doppleganger"	Rhys Bowen	*Blood on Their Hands;* Block, ed.	____
"Safety First"	Marcia Talley	*Blood on Their Hands;* Block, ed.	____
"Red Meat"	Elaine Viets	*Blood on Their Hands;* Block, ed.	____
"Sex and Bingo"	Elaine Viets	*High Stakes;* Randisi, ed.	____

2003

"Dog that Didn't Bark, The" (Tie)	Margaret Maron	*EQMM,* Dec 02	____
"Too Many Cooks" (Tie)	Marcia Talley	*Much Ado About Murder;* Perry, ed.	____
"Dognapped"	Robert Barnard	*EQMM,* Jun 02	____
"Devotion"	Jan Burke	18	____
"What He Needed"	Laura Lippman	*Tart Noir;* Duffy & Henderson, eds.	____

2002

"Would-Be Widower, The"	Katherine Hall Page	Malice Domestic 10; Barr, pre.	____
"Bitter Waters"	Rochelle Krich	*Criminal Kabbalah;* Raphael, ed.	____
"Virgo in Sapphires"	Margaret Maron	*EQMM,* Dec 01	____
"Peculiar Events on Riverside Drive, The"	Maan Meyers	*Mystery Street;* Randisi, ed.	____
"Juggernaut"	Nancy Springer	*EQMM,* Jun 01	____

2001

"Man in the Civil Suit, The"	Jan Burke	Malice Domestic 9; Hess, pre.	____
"Nothing to Lose"	Robert Barnard	Malice Domestic 9; Hess, pre.	____
"Seal of the Confessional, The"	Rhys Bowen	*Unholy Orders;* Stevens, ed.	____
"Amish Butter"	Jacqueline Fiedler	*Unholy Orders;* Stevens, ed.	____
"Miss Parker and the Cutter-Sanborn Tables"	Gay Toltl Kinman	*A Deadly Dozen;* Casmier, Harmetz & Lawrence, eds.	____
"Widow's Peak"	Rochelle Krich	*Unholy Orders;* Stevens, ed.	____

2000

"Out of Africa"	Nancy Pickard	*Mom, Apple Pie, & Murder;* Pickard, ed.	____
"Maubi and the Jumbies"	Kate Grilley	Murderous Intent, Fall 99	____
"Golden Rounds, The"	Susan Holtzer	Malice Domestic 8; Maron, pre.	____
"With Thanks to Agatha Christie"	Sarah J. Mason	*Mom, Apple Pie, & Murder;* Pickard, ed.	____
"With Love, Marjorie Ann"	Marcia Talley	Murderous Intent, Fall 99	____

1999

"Of Course You Know that Chocolate is a Vegetable"	Barbara D'Amato	*EQMM,* Nov 98	___
"Sleeping Dogs Lie"	Laurien Berenson	*Canine Crimes;* Marks, ed.	___
"Simple Philosophy, A"	Harlan Coben	Malice Domestic 7; McCrumb, pre.	___
"Village Vampire and the Oboe of Death, The"	Dean James	Malice Domestic 7; McCrumb, pre.	___
"Deliberate Form of Frenzy, A"	Daniel Stashower	Malice Domestic 7; McCrumb, pre.	___

1998

"Tea for Two"	M.D. Lake	*Funny Bones;* Hess, ed.	___
"Heavenly Bodies"	Simon Brett	*Funny Bones;* Hess, ed.	___
"Come to Tea"	Janet Laurence	*Murder They Wrote;* Greenberg & Foxwell, eds.	___
"Corbett Correspondence, The"	Edward Marston & Peter Lovesey	Malice Domestic 6; Perry, pre.	___
"Two Ladies of Rose Cottage, The"	Peter Robinson	Malice Domestic 6; Perry, pre.	___

1997

"Accidents Will Happen"	Carolyn Wheat	Malice Domestic 5; Whitney, pre.	___
"Bun Also Rises, The"	Jill Churchill	Malice Domestic 5; Whitney, pre.	___
"Death of Erik the Redneck, The"	Toni L.P. Kelner	Malice Domestic 5; Whitney, pre.	___
"Parrot is Forever A"	Peter Lovesey	Malice Domestic 5; Whitney, pre.	___
"Bugged"	Eve K. Sandstrom	Malice Domestic 5; Whitney, pre.	___

1996

"Dog Who Remembered too Much, The"	Elizabeth Daniels Squire	Malice Domestic 4; Hart, pre.	___
"Rule of Law"	K.K. Beck	Malice Domestic 4; Hart, pre.	___
"Cupid's Arrow"	Dorothy Cannell	*Crimes of the Heart;* Hart, ed.	___
"Contest Fit for a Queen, A"	Susan Dunlap	*Crimes of the Heart;* Hart, ed.	___
"Murder Game, The"	Jean Hager	Malice Domestic 4; Hart, pre.	___

1995

"Family Jewels, The"	Dorothy Cannell	Malice Domestic 3; Pickard, pre.	___
"Cast Your Fate to the Wind"	Deborah Adams	Malice Domestic 3; Pickard, pre.	—
"Gentleman in the Lake, The"	Robert Barnard	*EQMM,* Jun 94	___
"Soon to be a Minor Motion Picture"	Barbara D'Amato	*Partners in Crime;* Chase, ed.	___
"Dying Light, The"	Taylor McCafferty	Malice Domestic 3; Pickard, pre.	___

1994

"Kim's Game"	M.D Lake	Malice Domestic 2; Clark, pre.	____
"Romance in the Rockies, A"	K.K. Beck	Malice Domestic 2; Clark, pre.	____
"Sax and the Single Cat"	Carole Nelson Douglas	*Danger in D.C.*; Greenberg & Gorman, eds.	____
"Checkout"	Susan Dunlap	Malice Domestic 2; Clark, pre.	____
"…That Married Dear Old Dad"	Margaret Maron	Malice Domestic 2; Clark, pre.	____

1993

"Nice Gorilla"	Aaron & Charlotte Elkins	Malice Domestic 1; Peters, pre.	____
"Jersey Lily, The"	P.M. Carlson	Malice Domestic 1; Peters, pre.	____
"Country Hospitality"	Jean Hager	Sisters in Crime 5; Wallace, ed.	____
"Last to Know, The"	Joan Hess	Malice Domestic 1; Peters, pre.	____
"Happiness is a Dead Poet"	Sharyn McCrumb	Malice Domestic 1; Peters, pre.	____

1992

"Deborah's Judgment"	Margaret Maron	*A Women's Eye*; Paretsky, ed.	____
"Habit of Widowhood, The"	Robert Barnard	Winter's Crimes 23; Rejt, ed.	____
"January Sales Stowaway, The"	Dorothy Cannell	*Christmas Stalkings*; MacLeod, ed.	____
"Crime of Miss Oyster Brown, The"	Peter Lovesey	*EQMM*, May 91	____
"Long Live the Queen"	Ruth Rendell	*EQMM*, Jul 91	____

1991

"Too Much to Bare"	Joan Hess	Sisters in Crime 2; Wallace, ed.	____
"High Cost of Living, The"	Dorothy Cannell	Sisters in Crime 3; Wallace, ed.	____
"Proxime Accessit"	Reginald Hill	*The Armchair Detective*, Summer 90	____
"Family Affair, A"	Janet Neel	*EQMM*, Feb 90	____
"Wearing of Purple, The"	Anne Woodward	*AHMM*, Apr 90	____

1990

"Wee Doch and Doris, A"	Sharyn McCrumb	*Mistletoe Mysteries*; MacLeod, ed.	____
"Live It Up, Bert"	Patricia Derozier	*EQMM*, Nov 89	____
"Amanda"	Ellie Grossman	*EQMM*, Oct 89	____
"Cozy for Christmas, A"	Charlotte MacLeod	*Mistletoe Mysteries*; MacLeod, ed.	____
"Afraid All the Time"	Nancy Pickard	Sisters in Crime; Wallace, ed.	____

1989

"More Final Than Divorce"	Robert Barnard	*EQMM*, Oct 88	___
"Prodigal Grandson"	Elizabeth Byrd	*EQMM*, Aug 88	___
"Father of the Bride"	P.M. Carlson	Mr. President, Private Eye; Greenberg & Nevins Jr., eds.	___
"Double Vision"	Mary Higgins Clark	*Woman's Day*, Aug 23, 88	___
"Dutiful Son"	Ralph McInerny	*AHMM*, May 88	___

Agatha Best Children/Young Adult Ficton

2007

Pea Soup Poisonings	Nancy Means Wright	___
Behind the Curtain	Peter Abrahams	___
Room One a Mystery or Two	Andrew Clements	___
Sherlock Holmes and the Baker Street Irregulars: The Fall of the Amazing Zalindas	Tracy Mack & Michael Citrin	___

2006

Down the Rabbit Hole (Tie)	Peter Abrahams	___
Flush (Tie)	Carl Hiaasen	___
Curse of Ravenscourt, The	Sarah Masters Buckey	___
Danger at the Zoo	Kathleen Ernst	___
Coastwatcher, The	Elise Weston	___

2005

Chasing Vermeer	Blue Balliett	___
Betrayal at Cross Creek	Kathleen Ernst	___
Green Streak	Daniel J. Hale & Matthew LaBrot	___

2004

7th Knot, The	Kathleen Karr	___
Gangsters at the Grand Atlantic	Sarah Masters Buckey	___
Danger, Dynamite!	Anne Capeci	___
Ghost Light on Graveyard Shoal	Elizabeth McDavid Jones	___
Secret of the Equestrian Park, The	Gay Toltl Kinman	___

2003

Red Card	Daniel J. Hale & Matthew LaBrot	___
Whistler in the Dark	Kathleen Ernst	___
Hoot	Carl Hiaasen	___
Secret of the Red Flame, The	K.M. Kimball	___
Maltese Kitten, The	Linda Stewart	___

2002

Mystery of the Haunted Caves, The	Penny Warner	___
Viking Claw, The	Michael Dahl	___
Death on Sacred Ground	Harriet K. Feder	___
Mystery of the Octagon House, The	Gay Toltl Kinman	___
Ring Out Wild Bells	Carroll Thomas	___

Malice Domestic Award for Lifetime Achievement

The Malice Domestic Award for Lifetime Achievement is given in recognition of a significant body of distinguished work in the Malice Domestic genre. The award is bestowed by the Malice Domestic Board of Directors and presented at the Malice Domestic conference; the award is usually given annually.

2007	Carolyn Hart
2006	Robert Barnard
2005	H.R.F. Keating
2004	Marian Babson
2003	Barbara Mertz/Elizabeth Peters/Barbara Michaels
2002	Tony Hillerman
2001	Mildred Wirt Benson
2000	Dick Francis
1999	Patricia Moyes
1998	Charlotte MacLeod
1997	Emma Lathen (Mary Jane Latsis & Martha Henissar)
1996	Mary Stewart
1994	Mignon G. Eberhart
1990	Phyllis A. Whitney

www.malicedomestic.org/agatha.htm

Anthony Awards

The Anthony Awards are given in memory of Anthony Boucher, long-time author, critic, reviewer, and fan, who died in 1968. In 1970, the first World Mystery Convention, called Bouchercon was held at Santa Monica, California in his honor. The first awards were given in 1986; they are voted on by the people attending Bouchercon.

Anthony Best Novel

2007

No Good Deeds	Laura Lippman	____
Kidnapped	Jan Burke	____
Dead Hour, The	Denise Mina	____
Virgin of Small Plains, The	Nancy Pickard	____
All Mortal Flesh	Julia Spencer-Fleming	____

2006

Mercy Falls	William Kent Krueger	____
Bloodlines	Jan Burke	____
Lincoln Lawyer, The	Michael Connelly	____
Red Leaves	Thomas H. Cook	____
To the Power of Three	Laura Lippman	____

2005

Blood Hollow	William Kent Krueger	____
Killing of the Tinkers, The	Ken Bruen	____
Madman's Tale, The	John Katzenbach	____
By a Spider's Thread	Laura Lippman	____
California Girl	T. Jefferson Parker	____
Out of the Deep I Cry	Julia Spencer-Fleming	____

2004

Every Secret Thing	Laura Lippman	____
Delicate Storm, The	Giles Blunt	____
Blood is the Sky	Steve Hamilton	____
Shutter Island	Dennis Lehane	____
Close to Home (The Summer that Never Was)	Peter Robinson	____

2003

City of Bones	Michael Connelly	____
Murder in the Sentier	Cara Black	____
North of Nowhere	Steve Hamilton	____
Hell to Pay	George P. Pelecanos	____
Winter and Night	S.J. Rozan	____

2002
Mystic River	Dennis Lehane	____
Flight	Jan Burke	____
Tell No One	Harlan Coben	____
Devil Went Down to Austin, The	Rick Riordan	____
Reflecting the Sky	S.J. Rozan	____

2001
Place of Execution, A	Val McDermid	____
Deep South	Nevada Barr	____
Bottoms, The	Joe R. Lansdale	____
Listen to the Silence	Marcia Muller	____
He Shall Thunder in the Sky (Thunder in the Sky)	Elizabeth Peters	____
Legacy of the Dead	Charles Todd	____

2000
In a Dry Season	Peter Robinson	____
River of Darkness	Rennie Airth	____
Bones	Jan Burke	____
L.A. Requiem	Robert Crais	____
High Five	Janet Evanovich	____

1999
Blood Work	Michael Connelly	____
Blind Descent	Nevada Barr	____
On Beulah Height	Reginald Hill	____
Gone, Baby, Gone	Dennis Lehane	____
Framework for Death	Aileen Schumacher	____

1998
No Colder Place	S.J. Rozan	____
Devil's Food	Anthony Bruno	____
Deception Pass	Earl Emerson	____
Club Dumas, The (Dumas Club)	Arturo Perez-Reverte	____
Eye of the Cricket	James Sallis	____

1997
Poet, The	Michael Connelly	____
Firestorm	Nevada Barr	____
Lethal Genes	Linda Grant	____
Hearts and Bones	Margaret Lawrence	____
Multiple Wounds	Alan Russell	____

1996
Under the Beetle's Cellar	Mary Willis Walker	____
Last Coyote, The	Michael Connelly	____
Hard Christmas	Barbara D'Amato	____
True Crime	Andrew Klavan	____
Blue Lonesome	Bill Pronzini	____

1995

She Walks These Hills	Sharyn McCrumb	____
Concrete Blonde, The	Michael Connelly	____
Kolymsky Heights	Lionel Davidson	____
One for the Money	Janet Evanovich	____
"K" is for Killer	Sue Grafton	____
Murder on the Kibbutz	Bayta Gur	____
Pictures of Perfection	Reginald Hill	____
Cold Shoulder	Lynda La Plante	____
Thirteenth Juror, The	John Lescroart	____
Crack Down	Val McDermid	____
Black Betty	Walter Mosley	____
Not Till the Red Fog Rises	Derek Raymond	____
Just a Corpse at Twilight	Janwillem van de Wetering	____

1994

Wolf in the Shadows	Marcia Muller	____
Black Ice, The	Michael Connelly	____
Morons and Madmen	Earl Emerson	____
O Little Town of Maggody	Joan Hess	____
Sacred Clowns	Tony Hillerman	____
Old Enemies	Janet LaPierre	____
Southern Discomfort	Margaret Maron	____
To Live and Die in Dixie	Kathy Hogan Trocheck	____
Sculptress, The	Minette Walters	____
Consider the Crows	Charlene Weir	____

1993

Bootlegger's Daughter	Margaret Maron	____
Lullaby Town	Robert Crais	____
Booked to Die	John Dunning	____
Southern Ghost	Carolyn G. Hart	____
Hangman's Beautiful Daughter, The	Sharyn McCrumb	____

1992

Last Detective, The	Peter Lovesey	____
Rogue Wave	Susan Dunlap	____
Love Nor Money	Linda Grant	____
Hour of the Hunter	J.A. Jance	____
I.O.U.	Nancy Pickard	____
Single Stone, A	Marilyn Wallace	____

1991

"G" is for Gumshoe	Sue Grafton	____
Ticket to the Boneyard, A	Lawrence Block	____
Good Fight, The	Lia Matera	____
If Ever I Return, Pretty Peggy-O (If Ever I Return)	Sharyn McCrumb	____
New Orleans Mourning	Julie Smith	____

1990
Sirens Sang of Murder, The   Sarah Caudwell   ____
Pious Deception   Susan Dunlap   ____
Little Class on Murder, A   Carolyn G. Hart   ____
Corpus Christmas   Margaret Maron   ____

1989
Silence of the Lambs, The   Thomas Harris   ____
Widow's Club, The   Dorothy Cannell   ____
"E" is for Evidence   Sue Grafton   ____
Thief of Time, A   Tony Hillerman   ____
Blood Shot (Toxic Shock)   Sara Paretsky   ____
Dead Crazy   Nancy Pickard   ____
Shackles   Bill Pronzini   ____
Pepper Pike   Les Roberts   ____

1988
Skinwalkers   Tony Hillerman   ____
Trouble of Fools, A   Linda Barnes   ____
Old Bones   Aaron Elkins   ____
Trojan Gold   Elizabeth Peters   ____
Marriage is Murder   Nancy Pickard   ____

1987
"C" is for Corpse   Sue Grafton   ____
When the Sacred Ginmill Closes   Lawrence Block   ____
Tropical Heat   John Lutz   ____
No Body   Nancy Pickard   ____
Life's Work   Jonathan Valin   ____

1986
"B" is for Burglar   Sue Grafton   ____
Shortest Way to Hades, The   Sarah Caudwell   ____
Plain Old Man, The   Charlotte MacLeod   ____
Lonely Silver Rain, The   John D. MacDonald   ____
Killing Orders   Sara Paretsky   ____

Anthony Best 1st Novel

2007
Still Life   Louise Penny   ____
King of Lies, The   John Hart   ____
Holmes on the Range   Steve Hockensmith   ____
Field of Darkness, A   Cornelia Read   ____
Harrowing, The   Alexandra Sokoloff   ____

2006
Tilt-a-Whirl — Chris Grabenstein — ____
Die a Little — Megan Abbott — ____
Immoral — Brian Freeman — ____
Baby Game, The — Randall Hicks — ____
Officer Down — Theresa Schwegel — ____

2005
Dating Dead Men — Harley Jane Kozak — ____
Uncommon Grounds — Sandra Balzo — ____
Till the Cows Come Home — Judy Clemens — ____
Retribution — Juliane P. Hoffman — ____
Whiskey Sour — J.A. Konrath — ____

2004
Monkeewrench — P.J. Tracy — ____
Haunted Ground — Erin Hart — ____
Death of a Nationalist — Rebecca C. Pawel — ____
Maisie Dobbs — Jacqueline Winspear — ____
Wiley's Lament — Lono Waiwaiole — ____

2003
In the Bleak Midwinter — Julia Spencer-Fleming — ____
Devil's Redhead, The — David Corbett — ____
Eye for Murder, An — Libby Fischer Hellmann — ____
Blue Edge of Midnight, The — Jonathon King — ____
Distance, The — Eddie Muller — ____

2002
Open Season — C.J. Box — ____
Third Person Singular — K.J. Erickson — ____
Austin City Blue — Jan Grape — ____
Jasmine Trade, The — Denise Hamilton — ____
Witness Above, A — Andy Straka — ____

2001
Death of a Red Heroine — Qiu Xiaolong — ____
Black Dog — Stephen Booth — ____
Conspiracy of Paper, A — David Liss — ____
Ice Harvest, The — Scott Phillips — ____
Street Level — Bob Truluck — ____
Run — Douglas E. Winter — ____

2000
Murder With Peacocks — Donna Andrews — ____
Murder in the Marais — Cara Black — ____
Circles of Confusion — April Henry — ____
Revenge of the Gypsy Queen — Kris Neri — ____
Inner City Blues — Paula L. Woods — ____

1999

Iron Lake	William Kent Krueger	___
Sympathy for the Devil	Jerrilyn Farmer	___
Tiger's Palette	Jacqueline Fiedler	___
Cold Day in Paradise, A	Steve Hamilton	___
Eleven Days	Donald Harstad	___

1998

Killing Floor	Lee Child	___
If I Should Die	Grace Edwards	___
Except the Dying	Maureen Jennings	___
Bird Dog	Philip Reed	___
Skin Deep, Blood Red	Robert E. Skinner	___

1997

Death in Little Tokyo (Tie)	Dale Furutani	___
Somebody Else's Child (Tie)	Terris McMahan Grimes	___
Tularosa	Michael McGarrity	___
Test of Wills, A	Charles Todd	___
Brother's Blood, A	Michael C. White	___

1996

Death in Bloodhound Red	Virginia Lanier	___
Innocents, The	Richard Barre	___
Who in Hell is Wanda Fuca?	G.M. Ford	___
Hammurabi's Code	Charles Kenney	___
Murder in Scorpio	Martha C. Lawrence	___

1995

Alienist, The	Caleb Carr	___
Snow Falling on Cedars	David Guterson	___
Cuckoo	Alex Keegan	___
Drink Before the War, A	Dennis Lehane	___
Mallory's Oracle	Carol O'Connell	___
Shinju	Laura Joh Rowland	___
Every Breath You Take	Michelle Spring	___
Big Town	Doug J. Swanson	___
Death of a Blue Lantern	Christopher West	___

1994

Track of the Cat	Nevada Barr	___
Goodnight, Irene	Jan Burke	___
Grave Talent, A	Laurie R. King	___
Death Comes as Epiphany	Sharan Newman	___
Child of Silence	Abigail Padgett	___

1993
> *Blanche on the Lam* — Barbara Neely ____
> *Thyme of Death* — Susan Wittig Albert ____
> *Decked* — Carol Higgins Clark ____
> *Black Echo, The* — Michael Connelly ____
> *Winter Widow, The* — Charlene Weir ____

1992
> *Murder on the Iditarod Trail* — Sue Henry ____
> *Carpool* — Mary Cahill ____
> *Relative Stranger, A* — Margaret Lucke ____
> *Bulrush Murders, The* — Rebecca Rothenberg ____
> *Chocolate Box, The* — Leslie Watts ____
> *Murder on the Run* — Gloria White ____

1991
> *Postmortem* — Patricia Cornwell ____
> *Catering to Nobody* — Diane Mott Davidson ____
> *Kindred Crimes* — Janet Dawson ____
> *Where's Mommy Now?* — Rochelle Krich ____
> *Grave Undertaking* — James McCahery ____

1990
> *Katwalk* — Karen Kijewski ____
> *Grime and Punishment* — Jill Churchill ____
> *Mother Shadow, The* — Melodie Johnson Howe ____
> *Mark Twain Murders, The* — Edith Skom ____
> *Last Billable Hour, The* — Susan Wolfe ____

1989
> *Great Deliverance, A* — Elizabeth George ____
> *Murder Once Done* — Mary Lou Bennett ____
> *Killings at Badger's Drift, The* — Caroline Graham ____
> *Random Access Murder* — Linda Grant ____
> *Fear of the Dark* — Gar Anthony Haywood ____
> *Carolina Skeletons* — David Stout ____

1988
> *Caught Dead in Philadelphia* — Gillian Roberts ____
> *Death on the Rocks* — Michael Allegretto ____
> *House of Blue Lights, The* — Robert Bowman ____
> *Murder at the War (Knight Fall)* — Mary Monica Pulver ____
> *Infinite Number of Monkeys, An* — Les Roberts ____

1987

Too Late to Die	Bill Crider	____
Strangled Prose	Joan Hess	____
Ritual Bath, The	Faye Kellerman	____
Floater	Joseph Koenig	____
Dead Air	Mike Lupica	____

1986

When the Bough Breaks (Shrunken Heads)	Jonathan Kellerman	____
Gemini Man, The	Susan Kelly	____
Sleeping Dog	Dick Lochte	____
Doubting Thomas	Robert Reeves	____
Flood	Andrew Vachss	____

Anthony Best Paperback Original

2007

Ashes and Bones	Dana Cameron	____
47 Rules of Highly Effective Bank Robbers	Troy Cook	____
Cleanup, The	Sean Doolittle	____
Baby Shark	Robert Fate	____
Shotgun Opera	Victor Gischler	____
Snakeskin Shamisen	Naomi Hirahara	____
Dangerous Man, A	Charlie Huston	____

2006

James Deans, The	Reed Farrel Coleman	____
Kiss Her Goodbye	Allan Guthrie	____
Six Bad Things	Charlie Huston	____
Good Girl's Guide to Murder	Susan McBride	____
Killing Rain, A	P.J. Parrish	____

2005

Twisted City	Jason Starr	____
Cold Case	Robin Burcell	____
Putt to Death	Roberta Isleib	____
Blue Blood	Susan McBride	____
Halo Effect, The	M.J. Rose	____

2004

Deadly Legacy	Robin Burcell	____
Dealing in Murder	Elaine Flinn	____
Thicker Than Water	P.J. Parrish	____
Tough Luck	Jason Starr	____
Find Me Again	Sylvia Maultash Warsh	____

2003

Fatal Truth	Robin Burcell	___
Black Jack Point	Jeff Abbott	___
Six Strokes Under	Roberta Isleib	___
Paint It Black	P.J. Parrish	___
Killing Sky, A	Andy Straka	___

2002

Dead Until Dark	Charlaine Harris	___
Kiss Gone Bad, A	Jeff Abbott	___
Dim Sum Dead	Jerrilyn Farmer	___
Dead of Winter	P.J. Parrish	___
Houdini Specter, The	Daniel Stashower	___

2001

Death Dances to a Reggae Beat	Kate Grilley	___
Bad to the Bone	Katy Munger	___
Floating Lady Murder, The	Daniel Stashower	___
Killing Kin	Chassie West	___
Little Death, A	Laura Wilson	___
Kidnapping of Rosie Dawn, The	Eric Wright	___

2000

In Big Trouble	Laura Lippman	___
Every Move She Makes	Robin Burcell	___
Lucky Man	Tony Dunbar	___
Outcast, The	Jose Latour	___
Antidote for Avarice, An	Caroline Roe	___

1999

Butchers Hill	Laura Lippman	___
Zen Attitude	Sujata Massey	___
Widower's Two-Step, The	Rick Riordan	___
Remedy for Treason	Caroline Roe	___
Murder Manual	Steven Womack	___

1998

Big Red Tequila	Rick Riordan	___
Charm City	Laura Lippman	___
Salaryman's Wife, The	Sujata Massey	___
Time Release	Martin J. Smith	___
23 Shades of Black	K.j.a. Wishnia	___

1997

Somebody Else's Child	Terris McMahan Grimes	___
Fade Away	Harlan Coben	___
Grass Widow, The	Teri Holbrook	___
Walking Rain	Susan Wade	___
Chain of Fools	Steven Womack	___

1996

Deal Breaker	Harlan Coben	____
Bad Medicine	Eileen Dreyer	____
Far and Deadly Cry, A	Teri Holbrook	____
Charged With Guilt	Gloria White	____
Closet	R.D. Zimmerman	____

1991

Grave Undertaking (Tie)	James McCahery	____
Where's Mommy Now? (Tie)	Rochelle Krich	____
Not a Creature was Stirring	Jane Haddam	____
Dead in the Scrub	B.J. Oliphant	____
Sisters in Crime 2	Marilyn Wallace, ed.	____

1990

Honeymoon for Murder	Carolyn G. Hart	____
On My Honor	Malachai Black	____
Murder by Deception	D.R. Meredith	____
Rough Justice	Keith Peterson (Andrew Kalvan)	____
Collector of Photographs, A	Deborah Valentine	____

1989

Something Wicked	Carolyn G. Hart	____
High Noon at Midnight	Michael Avallone	____
Murder Unrenovated	P.M. Carlson	____
Man Who Died Laughing, The	David Handler	____
Radical Departure, A	Lia Matera	____
Paying the Piper	Sharyn McCrumb	____
Murder by Impulse	D.R. Meredith	____
Primary Target	Marilyn Wallace	____

1988

Monkey's Raincoat, The	Robert Crais	____
Cat Who Played Brahms, The	Lilian Jackson Braun	____
Death on Demand	Carolyn G. Hart	____
Bishop's Gambit, Declined	Conrad Haynes	____
Where Lawyers Fear to Tread	Lia Matera	____
Bimbos of the Death Sun	Sharyn McCrumb	____

1987

Junkyard Dog, The	Robert Campbell	____
Cat Who Saw Red, The	Lilian Jackson Braun	____
Trial by Fury	J.A. Jance	____
Back-Door Man, The	Rob Kantner	____
Trace: Too Old a Cat	Warren Murphy	____

1986

Say No to Murder	Nancy Pickard	___
Murder is Academic	P.M. Carlson	___
Poverty Bay	Earl Emerson	___
Shattered Moon	Kate Green	___
Sleightly Murder	Patrick A. Kelley	___

Anthony Best Short Story

2007

"My Father's Secret"	Simon Wood	*Crime Spree Magazine,* B-Con Special Issue 06	___
"Policy"	Megan Abbott	*Damn Near Dead: An Anthology of Geezer Noir;* Swiercyznski, ed.	___
"Lords of Misrule, The"	Dana Cameron	*Sugarplums and Scandal*	___
"Cranked"	Bill Crider	*Damn Near Dead: An Anthology of Geezer Noir;* Swiercyznski, ed.	___
"Sleeping with the Plush"	Toni L.P. Kelner	*AHMM,* May 06	___
"After the Fall"	Elaine Viets	*AHMM,* Jan/Feb 06	___

2006

"Misdirection"	Barbara Seranella	*Greatest Hits: Original Stories of Hitmen, Hired Guns, & Private Eyes*; Randisi, ed.	___
"House Rules"	Libby Fischer Hellmann	*Murder in Vegas: New Crime Tales of Gambling & Desperation*; Connelly, ed.	___
"There is No Crime on Easter Island"	Nancy Pickard	*EQMM,* Sept/Oct 05	___
"Driven to Distraction"	Marcia Talley	Chesapeake Crimes II; Andrews & Lima, eds.	___
"Killer Blonde"	Elaine Viets	*Drop-Dead Blond*	___

2005

"Wedding Knife"	Elaine Viets	Chesapeake Crimes; Andrews, ed.	___
"Voodoo"	Rhys Bowen	*AHMM,* Nov 04	___
"Widow of Slane, The"	Terence Faherty	*EQMM,* Mar/Apr 04	___
"It's Crackers to Slip a Rozzer the Dropsey in Snide"	Ted Hertel, Jr.	*Small Crimes*; Bracken, ed.	___
"Hunter Trapper"	Arthur Nersesian	*Brooklyn Noir;* McLoughlin, ed.	___

2004

"Doppelganger"	Rhys Bowen	*Blood on Their Hands;* Block, ed.	___
"Grass is Always Greener, The"	Sandra Balzo	*EQMM,* Mar 03	___
"Munchies"	Jack Bludis	*Hardbroiled;* Bracken, ed.	___
"Wanda Wilcox is Trapped"	Eddie Muller	*Plots With Guns,* Sept/Oct 03	___
"Red Meat"	Elaine Viets	*Blood on Their Hands;* Block, ed.	___

2003

"Too Many Cooks"	Marcia Talley	*Much Ado About Murder;* Perry, ed.	___
"Murder in the Land of Wawat"	Lauren Haney	*Mammoth Book of Egyptian Whodunnits;* Ashley, ed.	___
"To Live and Die in Midland, Texas"	Clark Howard	*EQMM,* Sept/Oct 02	___
"Bible Belt"	Toni Kelner	*EQMM,* Jun 02	___
"Man Called Ready, A "	Bob Truluck	*Measures of Poison;* McMillan, ed.	___

2002

"Chocolate Moose"	Bill & Judy Crider	*Death Dines at 8:30;* Bishop & DiChario, eds.	___
"My Bonnie Lies…"	Ted Hertel, Jr.	*Mammoth Book of Legal Thrillers;* Hemmingson, ed.	___
"Bitter Waters"	Rochelle Krich	*Criminal Kabbalah;* Raphael, ed.	___
"Virgo in Sapphires"	Margaret Maron	*EQMM,* Dec 01	___
"Double-Crossing Delancy"	S.J. Rozan	*Mystery Street;* Randisi, ed.	___

2001

"Problem of the Potting Shed"	Edward D. Hoch	*EQMM,* Jul 00	___
"Seal of the Confessional, The"	Rhys Bowen	*Unholy Orders;* Stevens, ed.	___
"Widow's Peak"	Rochelle Krich	*Unholy Orders;* Stevens, ed.	___
"Don't Go Upstairs"	Donald Olson	*EQMM,* Aug 00	___
"Missing in Action"	Peter Robinson	*EQMM,* Nov 00	___

2000

"Noir Lite"	Margaret Chittenden	*EQMM,* Jan 99	___
"Bit of a Treat, A"	Barry Baldwin	*AHMM,* Sept 99	___
"At the Hop"	Bill & Judy Crider	*Till Death Do Us Part;* Morgan & Greenberg, eds.	___
"Triangle"	Jeffery Deaver	*EQMM,* Mar 99	___
"Paleta Man"	Laurie R. King	*Irreconcilable Differences;* Matera, ed.	___

1999
"Of Course You Know that Chocolate is a Vegetable" — Barbara D'Amato — *EQMM,* Nov 98 — ___
"Two Bits" — Jan Burke — *EQMM,* May 98 — ___
"Simple Philosophy, A" — Harlan Coben — Malice Domestic 7; McCrumb, pre. — ___
"Small Silver Gun, A" — Rick Riordan — *MHCMM,* Summer 98 — ___
"Two Ladies of Rose Cottage, The" — Peter Robinson — Malice Domestic 6; Perry, pre. — ___

1998
"Front-Row Seat, A" (Tie) — Jan Grape — *Vengeance is Hers;* Spillane & Collins, eds. — ___
"One Bag of Coconuts" (Tie) — Edward D. Hoch — *EQMM,* Nov 97 — ___
"Ways to Kill a Cat" — Simon Brett — Malice Domestic 6; Perry, pre. — ___
"Fog of Many Colors, A" — James DeFilippi — *New Mystery,* Summer 97 — ___
"Paperboxing Art" — James Dorr — *New Mystery,* Summer 97 — ___

1997
"Accidents Will Happen" — Carolyn Wheat — Malice Domestic 5; Whitney, pre. — ___
"Dark Snow, The" — Brendan DuBois — *Playboy,* Nov 96 — ___
"Luminarias Make It Christmas-y" — Janet LaPierre — *EQMM,* Feb 96 — ___
"Bugged" — Eve K. Sandstrom — Malice Domestic 5; Whitney, pre. — ___

1996
"And Pray Nobody Sees You" — Gar Anthony Haywood — *Spooks, Spies & Private Eyes;* Woods, ed. — ___
"Rule of Law" — K.K. Beck — Malice Domestic 4; Hart, pre. — ___
"Judge's Boy, The" — Jean B. Cooper — *EQMM,* Aug 95 — ___
"How I Found A Cat, Lost True Love, and Broke the Bank at Monte Carlo" — Bill Crider — *Cat Crimes Takes a Vacation;* Greenberg & Gorman, eds.
"Dog Who Remembered too Much, The" — Elizabeth Daniels Squire — Malice Domestic 4; Hart, pre. — ___

1995
"Monster of Glarnis, The" — Sharyn McCrumb — *Royal Crimes;* Jakubowski & Greenberg, eds. — ___
"Gentleman in the Lake, The" — Robert Barnard — *EQMM,* Jun 94 — ___
"One of Those Days, One of Those Nights" — Ed Gorman — *Crime Yellow;* Jakubowski, ed. — ___
"Deep Hole, A" — Ian Rankin — *London Noir;* Jakubowski, ed. — ___

1994

"Checkout"	Susan Dunlap	Malice Domestic 2; Clark, pre.	___
"Romance in the Rockies, A"	K.K. Beck	Malice Domestic 2; Clark, pre.	___
"Kim's Game"	M.D. Lake	Malice Domestic 2; Clark, pre.	___
"Crow's Feat"	Robert Lopresti	*Constable New Crimes 2*; Jakubowski, ed.	___

1993

"Cold Turkey"	Diane Mott Davidson	Sisters in Crime 5; Wallace, ed.	___
"Candles in the Rain"	Doug Allyn	*EQMM,* Nov 92	___
"Summer of Our Discontent, The"	Edward D. Hoch	*EQMM,* Nov 92	___
"One Hit Wonder"	Gabrielle Kraft	Sisters in Crime 5; Wallace, ed.	___
"Golden Opportunity, A "	Rochelle Krich	Sisters in Crime 5; Wallace, ed.	___

1992

"Lucky Dip"	Liza Cody	*A Woman's Eye*; Paretsky, ed.	___
"Last Rites"	Linda Grant	Sisters in Crime 4; Wallace, ed.	___
"Nine Sons"	Wendy Hornsby	Sisters in Crime 4; Wallace, ed.	___
"Deborah's Judgment"	Margaret Maron	*A Woman's Eye;* Paretsky, ed.	___
"Crime of Miss Oyster Brown, The"	Peter Lovesey	*EQMM,* May 91	___
"Wolf Winter"	Maxine O'Callahan	Sisters in Crime 4; Wallace, ed.	___

1991

"Celestial Buffet, The"	Susan Dunlap	Sisters in Crime 2; Wallace, ed.	___
"Luncheon, The"	Sharyn McCrumb	Sisters in Crime 2; Wallace, ed.	___
"Remains to Be Seen"	Sharyn McCrumb	*Mummy Stories*; Greenberg, ed.	___
"Say You're Sorry"	Sarah Shankman	Sisters in Crime 3; Wallace, ed.	___
"Tale of Two Pretties, A "	Marilyn Wallace	Sisters in Crime 3; Wallace, ed.	___

1990

"Afraid All the Time"	Nancy Pickard	Sisters in Crime; Wallace, ed.	___
"No Safety"	Susan Dunlap	Sisters in Crime; Wallace, ed.	___
"Wee Doch and Doris, A"	Sharyn McCrumb	*Mistletoe Mysteries*; MacLeod, ed.	___
"Terrible Thing, A"	Shelley Singer	Sisters in Crime; Wallace, ed.	___

1988

"Breakfast Television"	Robert Barnard	*EQMM,* Jan 87	____
"Scrap"	Max Allan Collins	*Black Lizard Anthology of Crime Fiction;* Gorman, ed.	
"Soft Monkey"	Harlan Ellison	Mystery Scene Reader #1; Gorman, ed.	____
"Turn Away"	Ed Gorman	*Black Lizard Anthology of Crime Fiction*; Gorman, ed.	
"Au Pair Girl, The"	Joyce Harrington	*Matter of Crime #1*; Bruccoli & Layman, eds.	____

1987

"Parker Shotgun, The"	Sue Grafton	*Mean Streets*; Randisi, ed.	____
"Body Count"	Wayne D. Dundee	*Mean Streets*; Randisi, ed.	____
"Scalplock"	Clark Howard	*EQMM,* Jul 86	____

1986

"Lucky Penny"	Linda Barnes	*New Black Mask #3,* 85	____
"Eight Mile and Dequindre"	Loren D. Estleman	*AHMM,* May 85	____
"Vandals"	Peter Lovesey	*EQMM,* Dec 85	____
"Ride the Lightning"	John Lutz	*AHMM,* Jan 85	____
"Convolvulus Clock, The"	Ruth Rendell	*EQMM,* Aug 85	____

Anthony Best Anthology/Short Story Collection

2001

Master's Choice: Mystery Stories by Today's Top Writers and the Masters Who Inspired Them, Vol. II	Lawrence Block, ed.	____
Malice Domestic 9	Joan Hess, pre.	____
Magnolias and Mayhem	Jeffrey Marks, ed.	____
Unholy Orders	Serita Stevens, ed.	____
Tales Out of School	Carolyn Wheat	____

1996

McCone Files, The	Marcia Muller	____
Cat Crimes Takes A Vacation	Ed Gorman, ed.	____
Crimes of The Heart	Carolyn G. Hart, ed.	____
Malice Domestic 4	Carolyn G. Hart, pre.	____
Spooks, Spies and Private Eyes	Paula Woods, ed.	____

1995

Mysterious West, The	Tony Hillerman, ed.	____
Hollywood Nocturnes (Dick Contino's Blues)	James Ellroy	____
Modern Treasury of Great Detective Stories, A	Ed Gorman, ed.	____
London Noir	Maxim Jakubowski, ed.	____
Murder for Halloween	Michelle Slung & Roland Hartman, eds.	____

47

1994

Malice Domestic 2	Mary Higgins Clark, pre.	____
Some Days You Get the Bear	Lawrence Block	____
Bohannon's Country	Joseph Hansen	____
Year's Best Mystery and Suspense Stories	Edward Hoch, ed.	____
Criminal Intent	Marcia Muller, Bill Pronzini, &	____
	Ed Gorman, eds.	

1992

Woman's Eye, A	Sara Paretsky, ed.	____
Cat Crimes	Martin Greenberg &	____
	Ed Gorman, eds.	
Alfred Hitchcock's Home Sweet Homicide: Stories From Alfred Hitchcock's Mystery Magazine	Cathleen Jordan, ed.	____
Christmas Stalkings: Tales of Yuletide Murder	Charlotte MacLeod, ed.	____
50 Years of the Best From Ellery Queen's Mystery Magazine	Eleanor Sullivan, ed.	____
Sisters in Crime 4	MarilynWallace, ed.	____

Anthony Best Non-Fiction/Critical Work

2007

Mystery Muses: 100 Classics that Inspire Today's Mystery Writers	Jim Huang & Austin Lugar, eds.	____
Read 'Em Their Writes: A Handbook for Mystery and Crime Fiction Book Discussions	Gary Warren Niebuhr	____
Don't Murder Your Mystery: 24 Fiction-Writing Techniques to Save Your Manuscript From Ending Up...D.O.A.	Chris Roerden	____
Beautiful Cigar Girl, The: Mary Rogers, Edgar Allen Poe, and the Invention of Murder	Daniel Stashower	____
Science of Sherlock Holmes, The: From Baskerville Hall to the Valley of Fear, the Real Forensics Behind the Great Detectives Greatest Cases	E.J. Wagner	____

2006

Heirs of Anthony Boucher, The: A History of Mystery Fandom	Marvin Lachman	____
Writing and Selling Your Mystery Novel: How to Knock 'em Dead With Style	Hallie Ephron	____
Behind the Mystery: Top Mystery Writers Interviewed	Stuart M. Kaminsky; photos by Laurie Roberts	____
New Annotated Sherlock Holmes, The: The Novels	Leslie S. Klinger, ed.	____
Girl Sleuth: Nancy Drew and the Women Who Created Her	Melanie Rehak	____

2005

Men's Adventure Magazines — Max Allan Collins — ____

Famous American Crimes and Trials — Frankie Y. Bailey &
 Steven Chermak — ____

Blue Blood — Edward Conlon — ____

*New Annotated Sherlock Holmes, The: The
 Complete Short Stories* — Leslie S. Klinger, ed. — ____

*Ballad of the Whiskey Robber, The: A True Story of
 Bank Heists, Ice Hockey, Transylvanian Pelt
 Smuggling, Moonlighting Detectives, and Broken
 Hearts* — Julian Rubinstein — ____

2004

*Make Mine a Mystery: A Reader's Guide to
 Mystery and Detective Fiction* — Gary Warren Niebuhr — ____

*Mystery Women: An Encyclopedia of Leading
 Women Characters in Mystery Fiction, Vol. 3* — Colleen A. Barnett — ____

Story of Jane Doe, The: A Book About Rape — Jane Doe — ____

Interrogations — Jon Jordan — ____

Beautiful Shadow: A Life of Patricia Highsmith — Andrew Wilson — ____

2003

*They Died in Vain: Overlooked, Underappreciated
 and Forgotten Mystery Novels* — Jim Huang, ed. — ____

Mammoth Encyclopedia of Modern Crime Fiction, The — Mike Ashley, compiler — ____

Intent to Sell: Marketing the Genre Novel — Jeffrey Marks — ____

2002

Seldom Disappointed: A Memoir — Tony Hillerman — ____

History of Mystery, The — Max Allan Collins — ____

Dashiell Hammett: A Daughter Remembers — Jo Hammett — ____

*Writing the Mystery: A Start-to-Finish Guide for
 Both Novice and Professional* — G. Miki Hayden — ____

*Who was that Lady? Craig Rice: The Queen of
 Screwball Mystery* — Jeffrey Marks — ____

2001

100 Favorite Mysteries of the Century — Jim Huang, ed. — ____

*Complete Christie, The: An Agatha Christie
 Encyclopedia* — Matthew Bunson — ____

*Women of Mystery: The Lives and Works of
 Notable Women Crime Novelists* — Martha Hailey DuBose — ____

American Regional Mystery, The — Marvin Lachman — ____

*Hard-Boiled: Working-Class Readers and Pulp
 Magazines* — Erin A. Smith — ____

2000

Detecting Women 3: A Reader's Guide and — Willetta L. Heising — ____
Checklist for Mystery Series Written by
Women
Mystery Review Magazine, The — Barbara Davey, ed. — ____
Deadly Pleasures Magazine — George Easter, ed. — ____
Ross Macdonald — Tom Nolan — ____
Teller of Tales: The Life of Arthur Conan Doyle — Daniel Stashower — ____

1999

Deadly Pleasures Magazine — George Easter, ed. — ____
Mystery Reader's Walking Guide to Washington, D.C. — Alzina Stone Dale — ____
Dark City: The Lost World of Film Noir — Eddie Muller — ____
Silk Stalkings II: More Women Write of Murder — Victoria Nichols & — ____
Susan Thompson

Mystery and Suspense Writers: The Literature of — Robin W. Winks & — ____
Crime, Detection, and Espionage — Maureen Corrigan, eds.

1997

Detecting Women 2: A Reader's Guide and — Willetta L. Heising — ____
Checklist for Mystery Series Written by Women
Mystery!: A Celebration: Stalking Public — Ron Miller & — ____
Television's Greatest Sleuths — Karen Sharpe, eds.
Letters of Dorothy L. Sayers, The: 1899-1936: The — Barbara Reynolds, ed. — ____
Making of a Detective Novelist
By a Woman's Hand: A Guide to Mystery Fiction — Jean Swanson & — ____
by Women, 2nd ed. — Dean James, eds.

1996

Armchair Detective Book of Lists, The, 2nd ed. — Kate Stine, ed. — ____
Gentle Madness, A: Bibliophiles, Bibliomanes and — Nicholas Basbanes — ____
the Eternal Passion for Books
John Dickson Carr: The Man Who Explained — Douglas G. Greene — ____
Miracles
Savage Art: A Biography of Jim Thompson — Robert Polito — ____
Ngaio Marsh: The Woman and Her Work — B.J. Rahn, ed. — ____

1995

Detective Fiction: The Collector's Guide, 2nd ed. — John Cooper & B.A. Pike — ____
Encyclopedia Mysteriosa: A Comprehensive Guide — William L. DeAndrea — ____
to the Art of Detection in Print, Film, Radio,
and Television
Tony Hillerman Companion, The: A — Martin H. Greenberg, ed. — ____
Comprehensive Guide to His Life and Work
Fatal Art of Entertainment, The: Interviews With — Rosemary Herbert — ____
Mystery Writers

1994

*Fine Art of Murder, The: The Mystery Reader's
  Indispensable Companion*

Ed Gorman, Martin H.
  Greenberg, Larry Segriff &   ___
  Jon L. Breen, eds.

*Saint, The: A Complete History in Print, Radio,
  Film and Television of Leslie Charteris' Robin
  Hood of Modern Crime, Simon Templar,
  1928-1992*

Burl Barer   ___

Reader's Guide to the American Novel of Detection, A   Marvin Lachman   ___
Reader's Guide to the Private Eye Novel, A   Gary Warren Niebuhr   ___
Dorothy L. Sayers: Her Life and Soul   Barbara Reynolds   ___

1993

Doubleday Crime Club Compendium 1928-1991   Ellen Nehr   ___
Dorothy L. Sayers: A Careless Rage for Life   David Coomes   ___
*Alias S.S. Van Dine: The Man Who Created Philo
  Vance*

John Loughery   ___

1992

100 Great Detectives: Or, The Detective Directory   Maxim Jakubowski, ed.   ___
*Locked Room Murders and Other Impossible
  Crimes: A Comprehensive Bibliography*

Robert Adey   ___

*Out of the Woodpile: Black Characters in Crime
  and Detective Fiction*

Frankie Y. Bailey   ___

*Twentieth Century Crime and Mystery Writers,
  3rd ed.*

Lesley Henderson, ed.   ___

*Talking Mysteries: A Conversation With Tony
  Hillerman*

Tony Hillerman & Ernie Bulow   ___

*Jim Thompson: Sleep With the Devil: A Biography
  of America's Greatest Noir Writer*

Michael J. McCauley   ___

1991

Synod of Sleuths   Jon L. Breen & Martin H.
  Greenberg, eds.   ___

*Trouble is Their Business: Private Eyes in Fiction,
  Film, and Television, 1927-1988*

John Conquest   ___

John Dickson Carr: A Critical Study   S.T. Joshi   ___
Eric Ambler   Peter Lewis   ___
Deadly Doses: A Writer's Guide to Poisons   Senita Deborah Stevens   ___

Anthony Best True Crime

1996

Dead by Sunset: Perfect Husband, Perfect Killer? — Ann Rule — ____

Man Overboard: The Counterfeit Resurrection of Phil Champagne — Burl Barer — ____

Mindhunter: Inside the FBI's Elite Serial Crime Unit — John E. Douglas & Mark Olshaker — ____

Circumstantial Evidence: Death, Life, and Justice in a Southern Town — Pete Earley — ____

Born to Kill: America's Most Notorious Vietnamese Gang, and the Changing Face of Organized Crime — T.J. English — ____

1995

Criminal Shadows: Inside the Mind of the Serial Killer — David Canter — ____

Shot in the Heart: One Family's History in Murder — Mikal Gilmore — ____

Dillinger: The Untold Story — G. Russell Girardin & William J. Helmar — ____

Faber Book of Murder, The — Simon Rae, ed. — ____

Complete History of Jack the Ripper, The — Philip Sugden — ____

1994

Rose for Her Grave and Other True Cases, A (Ann Rule's Crime Files: Vol. 1) — Ann Rule — ____

Driven to Kill: The Terrifying True Account of Sex Killer Westley Allan Dodd — Gary King — ____

Misbegotten Son, The: A Serial Killer and His Victims: The True Story of Arthur J. Shawcross — Jack Olsen — ____

Until the Twelfth of Never: The Deadly Divorce of Dan and Betty Broderick — Bella Stumbo — ____

1993

Doctor, the Murder, the Mystery, The: The True Story of the Dr. John Branion Murder Case — Barbara D'Amato — ____

Trunk Murderess, The: Winnie Ruth Judd: The Truth About an American Crime Legend Revealed at Last — Jana Bommersbach — ____

Blood Echoes: The True Story of an Infamous Mass Murder and Its Aftermath — Thomas H. Cook — ____

Shadow of Death, The: The Hunt for a Serial Killer — Philip E. Ginsburg — ____

Everything She Ever Wanted: A True Story of Obsessive Love, Murder and Betrayal — Ann Rule — ____

1992
> *Homicide: A Year on the Killing Streets*   David Simon   ___
> *And the Sea Will Tell: Murder on a Desert Island and Justice*   Vincent Bugliosi   ___
> *Sins of the Father: The Landmark Franklin Case: A Daughter, a Memory, and a Murder*   Eileen Franklin & W.M. Wright   ___
> *Witnesses From the Grave: The Stories Bones Tell*   Christopher Joyce & Eric Stover   ___
> *Plausible Denial: Was the CIA Involved in the Assassination of JFK?*   Mark Lane   ___
> *Cruel Doubt*   Joe McGinniss   ___

Anthony Best Historical Mystery

2004
> *For the Love of Mike*   Rhys Bowen   ___
> *Let Loose the Dogs*   Maureen Jennings   ___
> *Bridge of Sighs, The*   Olen Steinhauer   ___
> *Find Me Again*   Sylvia Maultash Warsh   ___
> *Maisie Dobbs*   Jacqueline Winspear   ___

Anthony Best Young Adult Mystery

2004
> *Harry Potter and the Order of the Phoenix*   J.K. Rowling   ___
> *Artemis Fowl - The Eternity Code*   Eoin Colfer   ___
> *Feast of Fools*   Bridget Crowley   ___
> *Seventh Knot*   Kathleen Karr   ___
> *No Escape*   Norah McClintock   ___

2002
> *Mystery of the Haunted Caves, The*   Penny Warner   ___
> *Viking Claw, The*   Michael Dahl   ___
> *Death on Sacred Ground*   Harriet K. Feder   ___
> *Matthew's Web*   Jeri Fink & Donna Paltrowitz   ___
> *Ghost Sitter*   Peni R. Griffin   ___

Anthony Best Novel/Series/Writer of the 20th Century

The 2000 Bouchercon in Denver, saw the "Millennium Awards" and were voted on by fans for the best series, mystery writer, and novel of the 20th century. The final results were

Best Mystery Novel of the Century:

1938	*Rebecca*	**du Maurier, Daphne**	___
1939	*Big Sleep, The*	Chandler, Raymond	___
1926	*Murder of Roger Ackroyd, The*	Christie, Agatha	___
1930	*Maltese Falcon, The*	Hammett, Dashiell	___
1935	*Gaudy Night*	Sayers, Dorothy L.	___

Best Series of the Century:

Agatha Christie's	**Hercule Poirot**
Ed McBain's	87th Precinct
Marcia Muller's	Sharon McCone
Dorothy L. Sayers's	Lord Peter Wimsey
Rex Stout's	Nero Wolfe

Best Writer of the Century:

Christie, Agatha
Chandler, Raymond
Hammett, Dashiell
Sayers, Dorothy L.
Stout, Rex

Anthony Lifetime Achievement

2007	James Sallis
2006	Robert B. Parker
2005	Marcia Muller
2005	Bill Pronzini
2004	Bernard Cornwell
2001	Edward D. Hoch
2000	Jane Langton
1999	Len and June Moffatt
1997	Donald Westlake
1994	Tony Hillerman
1993	Hammond Innes
1993	Ralph McInerny
1992	Charlotte MacLeod
1991	William Campbell Gault
1990	Michael Gilbert
1989	Dorothy Salisbury Davis
1986	Barbara Mertz (aka Elizabeth Peters and Barbara Michaels)

(the award was called Grand Master in 1986)

bouchercon.info/
www.hycyber.com/MYST/anthonys.html

Audie Mystery Awards

The Audies® are annual awards honoring excellence in audio publishing. There are 32 categories and since 1997 they have offered one for a "Mystery Award" and in 2007 one for "Thriller/Suspense." The Audies® are sponsored by the Audio Publishers Association (APA). Along with the title and author, the narrator/s are listed here.

Audie Mystery Award

2007
Echo Park	Cariou, Len, narrator	Michael Connelly	____
Field of Darkness, A	Huber, Hillary, narrator	Cornelia Redd	____
Dark Tort	Marvel, Elizabeth, narrator	Diane Mott Davidson	____
Dead Center	Gardner, Grover, narrator	David Rosenfelt	____
Definitely Dead	Parker, Johanna, narrator	Charlaine Harris	____
Crimes of Jordan Wise, The	Ferrone, Richard, narrator	Bill Pronzini	____

2006
Serpent on the Crown	Rosenblat, Barbara, narrator	Elizabeth Peters	____
Away with the Fairies	Daniel, Stephanie, narrator	Kerry Greenwood	____
Hidden River	Goyle, Gerard, narrator	Adrian McKinty	____
Hot Kid	Arliss, Howard, narrator	Elmore Leonard	____
One Dangerous Lady	Rosenblat, Barbara, narrator	Jane Stanton Hitchcock	____

2005
Twisted: Selected Unabridged Stories of Jeffery Deaver	Gaines, Boyd, Michele Pawk & Frederick Weller	Jeffery Deaver	____
Brimstone	Brick, Scott, narrator	Douglas Preston & Lincoln Child	____
Double Homicide	Rubinstein, John, narrator	Faye & Jonathan Kellerman	____
Hark!	McLarty, Ron, narrator	Ed McBain	____
Man in My Basement, The	Hudson, Ernie, narrator	Walter Mosley	____

2004
Lost Light	Cariou, Len, narrator	Michael Connelly	____
Bangkok 8	Wong, B.D., narrator	John Burdett	____
Fear Itself	Cheadle, Don, narrator	Walter Mosley	____
Last Detective, The	Daniels, James, narrator	Robert Crais	____

2003
Jolie Blon's Bounce	Patton, Will, narrator	James Lee Burke	____
Diviner's Son, The	Veitch, Michael, narrator	Gary Crew	____
"Q" is for Quarry	Kaye, Judy, narrator	Sue Grafton	____
Rumpole's Return	Hardy, Robert, narrator	John Mortimer	____
Tishomingo Blues	Rudd, Paul, narrator	Elmore Leonard	____

2002

Tell No One	Weber, Steven, narrator	Harlan Coben	___
Blue Nowhere, The	Dufris, William, narrator	Jeffery Deaver	___
Vendetta Defense, The	Rosenblat, Barbara, narrator	Lisa Scottoline	___

2001

Naked Detective, The	McLarty, Ron, narrator	Laurence Shames	___
Hugger Mugger	Mantegna, Joe, narrator	Robert B.Parker	___
Moment of Truth	Rosenblat, Barbara, narrator	Lisa Scottoline	___

2000

Breaker, The	Powell, Robert, narrator	Minette Walters	___
"O" is for Outlaw	Kaye, Judy, narrator	Sue Grafton	___
Prayers for Rain	Brown, Thomas J.S., narrator	Dennis Lehane	___

1999

Third Man, The	Jarvis, Martin, narrator	Graham Greene	___
Black Coffee	Thomas, Alexandra, narrator	Agatha Christie; Charles Osborne, adapted by	___
Job, The	Slattery, John, narrator	Douglas Kennedy	___

1998

Vintage Crime Stories	Malahide, Patrick, narrator	authors	___
Cimarron Rose	Patton, Will, narrator	James Lee Burke	___
Red Harvest	Dufris, William, narrator	Dashiell Hammett	___

1997

Mysterious Affair at Styles, The	Suchet, David, narrator	Agatha Christie	___
Cadillac Jukebox	Patton, Will, narrator	James Lee Burke	___
"M" is for Malice	Kaye, Judy, narrator	Sue Grafton	___

Audie Thriller/Suspense

2007

Dead Yard, The	Doyle, Gerard, narrator	Adrian McKinty	___
Night of the Jaguar	Davis, Jonathan, narrator	Michael Gruber	___
Surrender	Bower, Humphrey, narrator	Sonya Hartnett	___
Foreign Correspondent, The	Molina, Alfred, narrator	Alan Furst	___
Wall, The	Gardner, Grover, narrator	Jeff Long	___

Barry Awards

In 1997, *Deadly Pleasures Magazine* began their awards called "The Barry." This annual award is named for Barry Gardner, a fan reviewer, to keep his memory alive. A committee selects the nominees and the subscribers/readers of *Deadly Pleasures* vote for the winners. Beginning in 2007, the Barry Awards were co-sponsored by *Mystery News*.

Barry Best Novel

2007
Night Gardener, The	George P. Pelecanos	____
White Shadow	Ace Atkins	____
Oh Danny Boy	Rhys Bowen	____
Last Assassin, The	Barry Eisler	____
Prisoner of Guantanamo, The	Dan Fesperman	____
City of Shadows	Ariana Franklin	____

2006
Red Leaves	Thomas H. Cook	____
Bloodlines	Jan Burke	____
Mercy Falls	William Kent Krueger	____
Sudden Death	David Rosenfelt	____
Mr. Lucky	James Swain	____
Power of the Dog, The	Don Winslow	____

2005
Enemy, The	Lee Child	____
Alone at Night	K.J. Erickson	____
Darkly Dreaming Dexter	Jeff Lindsay	____
Remembering Sarah	Chris Mooney	____
Little Scarlet	Walter Mosley	____
Hard Revolution	George P. Pelecanos	____

2004
Every Secret Thing	Laura Lippman	____
Guards, The	Ken Bruen	____
Small Boat of Great Sorrows, The	Dan Fesperman	____
Keeping Watch	Laurie R. King	____
Shutter Island	Dennis Lehane	____
Fountain Filled With Blood, A	Julia Spencer-Fleming	____

2003
City of Bones	Michael Connelly	____
Without Fail	Lee Child	____
Hearse Case Scenario, The	Tim Cockey	____
North of Nowhere	Steve Hamilton	____
Hell to Pay	George P. Pelecanos	____
Winter and Night	S.J. Rozan	____

2002

Mystic River	Dennis Lehane	___
Tell No One	Harlan Coben	___
Darkness More Than Night	Michael Connelly	___
Purgatory Ridge	William Kent Krueger	___
Silent Joe	T. Jefferson Parker	___
Right as Rain	George P. Pelecanos	___
Bad News	Donald E. Westlake	___

2001

Deep South	Nevada Barr	___
Running Blind (The Visitor)	Lee Child	___
Places in the Dark	Thomas H. Cook	___
Cross Dressing	Bill Fitzhugh	___
Winter of the Wolf Moon	Steve Hamilton	___
Unwanted Company	Barbara Seranella	___

2000

In a Dry Season	Peter Robinson	___
Angels Flight	Michael Connelly	___
L.A. Requiem	Robert Crais	___
High Five	Janet Evanovich	___
Hart's War	John Katzenbach	___
Prayers for Rain	Dennis Lehane	___

1999

On Beulah Height (Tie)	Reginald Hill	___
Gone, Baby, Gone (Tie)	Dennis Lehane	___
Evan Help Us	Rhys Bowen	___
Blood Work	Michael Connelly	___
Coffin Dancer, The	Jeffery Deaver	___
Judas Child	Carol O'Connell	___
Hanging Garden, The	Ian Rankin	___
All the Dead Lie Down	Mary Willis Walker	___

1998

Trunk Music	Michael Connelly	___
Cimarron Rose	James Lee Burke	___
Hocus	Jan Burke	___
Dreaming of the Bones	Deborah Crombie	___
Wasteland of Strangers, A	Bill Pronzini	___
No Colder Place	S.J. Rozan	___
Death and Life of Bobby Z, The	Don Winslow	___

1997
Bloodhounds	Peter Lovesey
Chatham School Affair, The	Thomas H. Cook
Wood Beyond, The	Reginald Hill
Speak No Evil	Rochelle Krich
Hearts and Bones	Margaret Lawrence
Dance of the Dead	Thomas Perry

Barry Best 1st Novel Published in the U.S.

2007
Still Life	Louise Penny
Faithful Spy, The	Alex Berenson
Sharp Objects	Gillian Flynn
Berlin Conspiracy, The	Tom Gabbay
King of Lies, The	John Hart
Field of Darkness, A	Cornelia Read

2006
Cold Granite	Stuart MacBride
Die a Little	Megan Abbott
Immoral	Brian Freeman
Baby Game, The	Randall Hicks
Dark Harbor	David Hosp

2005
Shadow of the Wind, The	Carlos Ruiz Zafon
Relative Danger	Charles Benoit
Walking Money	James O. Born
Coroner's Lunch, The	Colin Cotterill
Skinny-Dipping	Claire Matturro
Some Danger Involved	Will Thomas

2004
Monkeewrench	P.J. Tracy
Mission Flats	William Landay
Bridge of Sighs, The	Olen Steinhauer
Barbed-Wire Kiss, The	Wallace Stroby
Maisie Dobbs	Jacqueline Winspear
Clea's Moon	Edward Wright

2003
In the Bleak Midwinter	Julia Spencer-Fleming
Devil's Redhead, The	David Corbett
Not All Tarts are Apple	Pip Granger
Blue Edge of Midnight, The	Jonathan King
Distance, The	Eddie Muller
Buck Fever	Ben Rehder

2002

Open Season — C.J. Box ___
Third Person Singular — K.J. Erickson ___
Chasing the Devil's Tail — David Fulmer ___
Perhaps She'll Die — M.K. Preston ___
Blindsighted — Karin Slaughter ___
Bubbles Unbound — Sarah Strohmeyer ___

2001

Conspiracy of Paper, A — David Liss ___
In Her Defense — Stephen Horn ___
Ice Harvest, The — Scott Phillips ___
Street Level — Bob Truluck ___
Death of a Red Heroine — Qiu Xiaolong ___

2000

Murder With Peacocks — Donna Andrews ___
Immortal Game, The — Mark Coggins ___
Lie in the Dark — Dan Fesperman ___
White Sky, Black Ice — Stan Jones ___
Every Trace — Greg Main ___

1999

Iron Lake — William Kent Krueger ___
Contrary Blues, The — John Billheimer ___
Cold Day in Paradise, A — Steve Hamilton ___
Doctor Digs a Grave, The — Robin Hathaway ___
Tidewater Blood — William Hoffman ___
Likeness in Stone, A — J. Wallis Martin ___
Billy Dead — Lisa Reardon ___
Criminal Appeal, A — D.R. Schanker ___

1998

Killing Floor — Lee Child ___
Free Reign — Rosemary Aubert ___
Except the Dying — Maureen Jennings ___
Los Alamos — Joseph Kanon ___
Flower Net — Lisa See ___
No Human Involved — Barbara Seranella ___

1997

Test of Wills, A — Charles Todd ___
Killing in Quail County, A — Jameson Cole ___
Fatal Gift — H. Michael Frase ___
Lie Down With Dogs — Jan Gleiter ___
What the Deaf Mute Heard — G.D. Gearino ___
Brother's Blood, A — Michael C. White ___

Barry Best British Novel Published in the U.K.

2007
Priest	Ken Bruen	____
Dying Light	Stuart McBride	____
Sovereign	C.J. Sansom	____
Case of the Missing Books, The	Ian Sansom	____
Mr. Clarinet	Nick Stone	____
Red Sky Lament	Edward Wright	____

2006
Field of Blood, The	Denise Mina	____
Blood-Dimmed Tide	Rennie Airth	____
Lifeless	Mark Billingham	____
Silence of the Grave	Arnaldur Indridason	____
Good Day to Die, A	Simon Kernick	____
Lost	Michael Robotham	____

2005
Flesh and Blood	John Harvey	____
Burning Girl, The	Mark Billingham	____
Dramatist, The	Ken Bruen	____
Tokyo (The Devil of Nanking)	Mo Hayder	____
Crime Trade, The	Simon Kernick	____
First Drop	Zoe Sharp	____

2004
Distant Echo, The	Val McDermid	____
Lazybones	Mark Billingham	____
Full Dark House	Christopher Fowler	____
Murder Exchange, The	Simon Kernick	____
House Sitter, The	Peter Lovesey	____
American Boy, The (An Unpardonable Crime)	Andrew Taylor	____

2003
White Road, The	John Connolly	____
Scaredy Cat	Mark Billingham	____
Master of Rain, The	Tom Bradby	____
Business of Dying, The	Simon Kernick	____
Diamond Dust	Peter Lovesey	____
Yeare's Midnight, The	Ed O'Connor	____

2002
Dancing With the Virgins .... Stephen Booth .... ___
Blood Junction .... Caroline Carver .... ___
   (as, Caroline Seed)
Killing Kind, The .... John Connolly .... ___
Dialogues of the Dead .... Reginald Hill .... ___
Death in Holy Orders .... P.D. James .... ___
Killing the Shadows .... Val McDermid .... ___
Falls, The .... Ian Rankin .... ___

2001
Black Dog .... Stephen Booth .... ___
Dark Hollow .... John Connolly .... ___
Beach Road, The .... Sarah Diamond .... ___
Certainty of Doing Evil, The .... Colin Falconer .... ___
Reaper, The .... Peter Lovesey .... ___

2000
Place of Execution, A .... Val McDermid .... ___
River of Darkness .... Rennie Airth .... ___
Every Dead Thing .... John Connolly .... ___
Rough Justice .... Colin Falconer .... ___
Chalon Heads, The .... Barry Maitland .... ___

Barry Best Paperback Original Novel

2007
Cleanup, The .... Sean Doolittle .... ___
Bust .... Ken Bruen & Jason Starr .... ___
Last Quarry, The .... Max Allan Collins .... ___
Live Wire .... Jay MacLarty .... ___
Deadman's Poker .... James Swain .... ___
Crooked .... Brian M. Wiprud .... ___

2006
James Deans, The .... Reed Farrel Coleman .... ___
Night's Child .... Maureen Jennings .... ___
Six Bad Things .... Charlie Huston .... ___
Now You See Me .... Rochelle Krich .... ___
Dead Don't Get Out Much, The .... Mary Jane Maffini .... ___
Inside Out .... John Ramsey Miller .... ___

2005
Tagged for Murder .... Elaine Flinn .... ___
Librarian, The .... Larry Beinhart .... ___
Into the Web .... Thomas H. Cook .... ___
Last Seen in Aberdeen .... M.G. Kincaid .... ___
Confession, The .... Domenic Stansberry .... ___
Twisted City .... Jason Starr .... ___

2004

Tough Luck — Jason Starr — ____
Dealing in Murder — Elaine Flinn — ____
Wisdom of the Bones — Christopher Hyde — ____
Courier, The — Jay MacLarty — ____
Shadow of Venus, The — Judith Van Gieson — ____
Murder Between the Covers — Elaine Viets — ____

2003

Cold Silence — Danielle Girard — ____
Black Jack Point — Jeff Abbott — ____
Fatal Truth — Robin Burcell — ____
Bone Orchard, The — D. Daniel Judson — ____
Prison Blues — Anna Salter — ____
Pipsqueak — Brian M. Wiprud — ____

2002

Killing Gifts — Deborah Woodworth — ____
Rode Hard, Put Away Dead — Sinclair Browning — ____
Death is a Cabaret — Deborah Morgan — ____
Fourth Wall, The — Beth Saulnier — ____
Straw Men — Martin J. Smith — ____

2001

Kidnapping of Rosie Dawn, The — Eric Wright — ____
Dive Deep and Deadly — Glynn Marsh Alam — ____
Death Dances to a Reggae Beat — Kate Grilley — ____
Little Mexico — Cathie John — ____
Distemper — Beth Saulnier — ____

2000

Every Move She Makes (Tie) — Robin Burcell — ____
Antidote for Avarice, An (Tie) — Caroline Roe — ____
Last Song Dogs, The — Sinclair Browning — ____
Them Bones — Carolyn Haines — ____
Hunted, The — Jerry Kennealy — ____

1998

Back Spin — Harlan Coben — ____
Salaryman's Wife, The — Sujata Massey — ____
Big Red Tequila — Rick Riordan — ____
Dead Body Language — Penny Warner — ____

1997

Walking Rain — Susan Wade — ____
Fade Away — Harlan Coben — ____
Grass Widow, The — Teri Holbrook — ____

Barry Best Thriller

2007

Messinger, The	Daniel Silva	___
Killer Instinct	Joe Finder	___
Foreign Correspondent, The	Alan Furst	___
Relentless	Simon Kernick	___
Cold Kill	Stephen Leather	___
Kill Me	Stephen White	___

2006

Company Man	Joseph Finder	___
Consent to Kill	Vince Flynn	___
Inside Ring, The	Michael Lawson	___
Seven Deadly Wonders	Matthew Reilly	___
Map of Bones	James Rollins	___
Private Wars	Greg Rucka	___

2005

Rain Storm	Barry Eisler	___
Paranoia	Joseph Finder	___
Whirlwind	Joseph Garber	___
Bagman	Jay MacLarty	___
Scarecrow	Matthew Reilly	___
Death in Vienna, A	Daniel Silva	___

Barry Best Non-Fiction

1997

Detecting Women 2: A Reader's Guide and Checklist for Mystery Series Written by Women	Willetta L. Heising	___

Barry Best Mystery Short Story

2007

"Right Call, The"	Brendan DuBois	*EQMM,* Sept/Oct 06	___
"Cain was Innocent"	Simon Brett	*Thou Shalt Not Kill,* Perry, ed.	___
"Shaping the Ends"	Judith Cutler	*EQMM,* May, 06	___
"Man of Taste, A"	Kate Ellis	*EQMM,* Mar/Apr, 06	___
"Flower Girl, The"	Halter Paul	*The Night of the Wolf*	___
"Case for Inspector Ghote, A"	June Thomson	*The Verdict of Us All,* Lovesey, ed.	___

2006

"There is No Crime on Easter Island"	Nancy Pickard	*EQMM*, Sept/Oct 05	___
"Big Road, The"	Steve Hockensmith	*AHMM*, May 05	___
"Needle Match"	Peter Lovesey	*Murder is My Racquet*; Penzler, ed.	___
"Love and Death in Africa"	Joan Richter	*EQMM*, Jan 05	___
"Method in Her Madness, The"	Tom Savage	*AHMM*, Jun 05	___

2005

"War in Wonderland, The"	Edward D. Hoch	*Green for Danger*; Edwards, ed.	___
"Cold Comfort"	Catherine Aird	*Chapter & Hearse: & Other Mysteries*	___
"Facing Up"	Melodie Johnson Howe	*EQMM*, Jul 04	___
"Rumpole and the Christmas Break"	John Mortimer	*Strand Mag*, #14, 04	___
"Murder, the Missing Heir and the Boiled Egg"	Amy Myers	*Criminal Appetites*; Marks, ed.	___
"Ledgers"	Neil Schofield	*EQMM*, Jul 04	___

2004

"Rogues' Gallery"	Robert Barnard	*EQMM*, Mar 03	___
"Blind Pig, The"	Doug Allyn	*EQMM*, May 03	___
"Always Another War"	Brendan BuBois	*AHMM*, Jul/Aug 03	___
"Mask of Peter, The"	Clark Howard	*EQMM*, Apr 03	___
"Rogue's Run"	Donald Olson	*EQMM*, Apr 03	___

www.deadlypleasures.com/Barry.htm

Al Blanchard Short Story Award

The New England Crime Bake Conference offers the Al Blanchard Award (for short story) and began in 2005. This award is in memory of author Al Blanchard who was the co-chair of the first three conferences and president of NEMWA. Blanchard passed away in 2004.

The short story must be a crime story by a New England author or with a New England setting. In addition, the story must be previously unpublished and no longer than 5,000 words. The story may be a mystery, thriller, suspense, caper, or horror (no torture/killing of children or animals).

Al Blanchard Short Story Award

2007

"Misery 101"	Pat Remick		___
"Soldiers"	Mike Wiecek		___
"Fish to Fry"	Suzanne Rorhus		___
"Susie Cue"	Stephen Liskow		___
"Caring for Jose"	Steven Torres		___

2006

"Roundhouse Medeiros and the Jade Dragon"	Jim Shannon	*Seasmoke: Crime Stories by New England Writers*; Flora, McCarty, & Oleksiw, eds.	___
"Cow Track Caper, The"	Julie Hennrikus	Honorable Mention	___
"Dirty Laundry"	Todd Robinson	Out of the Gutter, mag #1	___
"Island Shots"	Suzanne Rorhus	Honorable Mention	___
"Winter Rental"	Barbara Ross	*Seasmoke: Crime Stories by New England Writers*; Flora, McCarty, & Oleksiw, eds.	___

2005

"Forever Reunion, The"	Brendan DuBois	*Windchill: Crime Stories by New England Writers*; Alexander, Flora & Oleksiw, eds.	___

www.mwane.org/crimebake/default.htm

Crime Writers Association of Australia

The Crime Writers Association of Australia (CWAA) began in the mid-1990s to promote and encourage Australian crime writing through the establishment of the Ned Kelly Awards beginning in 1996. The annual "Neddies," named for a notorious Australian outlaw of the 19th century, have become an eagerly anticipated fixture on the Australian literary scene.

CWAA Best Novel

2007

Chain of Evidence	Garry Disher	____
Undertow	Sydney Bauer	____
Cleaner, The	Paul Cleave	____
Unknown Terrorist, The	Richard Flanagan	____
Spider Trap	Barry Maitland	____
Night Ferry, The	Michael Robotham	____

2006

Crook as Rookwood (Tie)	Chris Nyst	____
Broken Shore, The (Tie)	Peter Temple	____
Rendezvous at Kamakura Inn	Marshall Browne	____
Saving Billie	Peter Corris	____
Rubdown	Leigh Redhead	____
Five Oranges	Graham Reilly	____

2005

Lost	Michael Robotham	____
Happiness Punch, The	Kirsty Brooks	____
Hand in the Bush, A	Jane Clifton	____
Private Dicks and Fiesty Chicks	Cathy Cole	____
Dangerous Deception	Sandy Curtis	____
Heavenly Pleasures	Kerry Greenwood	____
Queen of the Flowers	Kerry Greenwood	____
Static	Randall Longmire	____
No Trace	Barry Maitland	____
Spiking the Girl	Gabrielle Lord	____
Covet	Tara Moss	____
Murder by Manuscript	Steve J. Spears	____
Domino Game, The	Greg Wilson	____

2004

Degrees of Connection	Jon Cleary	___
Wrong Door, The	Bunty Avieson	___
Vodka Dialogue, The	Kirsty Brooks	___
Master's Mates	Peter Corris	___
Until Death	Sandy Curtis	___
Who Killed Camilla?	Emma Darcy	___
Castlemaine Murders, The	Kerry Greenwood	___
Earthly Delights	Kerry Greenwood	___

2003

White Dog	Peter Temple	___
Affair, The	Bunty Avieson	___
Open for Inspection	Carmel Bird	___
Eye of the Abyss, The	Marshall Browne	___
Salt and Blood	Peter Corris	___
Deadly Tide	Sandy Curtis	___
Who Killed Bianca?	Emma Darcy	___
Kitty Hawk Down	Garry Disher	___
Murder in Montparnasse	Kerry Greenwood	___
Analyst, The	Fred Guilhaus	___
Breakfastinfur	Michael Herrmann	___
Baby Did a Bad Bad Thing	Gabrielle Lord	___
Babel	Barry Maitland	___
Something Fishy	Shane Maloney	___
Chance, The	Andy Shea	___
Empty Bed, The	Paul Thomas	___
Evidence	Emma Tom	___

2002

Death Delights	Gabrielle Lord	___
Inspector Anders and the Ship of Fools	Marshall Browne	___
Crime of Silence	Patricia Carlon	___
Yesterday's Shadow	Jon Cleary	___
Skin Deep	Cathy Cole	___
Lugarno	Peter Corris	___
Death Club	Claire McNab	___
Death of the Author	Andrew Masterson	___
Simple Death, A	Carolyn Morwood	___
Disciples, The	Andy Shea	___
In the Evil Day	Peter Temple	___

2001

Second Coming, The (Tie)	Andrew Masterson	___
Dead Point (Tie)	Peter Temple	___

2000

Shooting Star	Peter Temple	___
Dilemma	Jon Cleary	___
Other Side of Sorrow	Peter Corris	___
Dragon Man	Garry Disher	___
Death Before Wicket	Kerry Greenwood	___
Our Man	Nicholas Hasluck	___
Inquisitor	Catherine Jinks	___
Chalon Heads, The	Barry Maitland	___
Silvermeadow	Barry Maitland	___
Set Up	Claire McNab	___
Uncertain Death, An	Carolyn Morwood	___
Black Tide	Peter Temple	___
Final Cut	Paul Thomas	___
Exxxpresso	Dave Warner	___
Murder in the Frame	Dave Warner	___

1999

Amaze Your Friends	Peter Doyle	___
Cheaters	J.R. Carroll	___
Black Prince, the	Peter Corris	___
Dogs are Barking, The	John Dale	___
Sharp End, The	Gabrielle Lord	___

1997

Brush-Off	Shane Maloney	___
Clan, The	J.R. Carroll	___
Endpeace	Jon Cleary	___
Bad Debts	Peter Temple	___
Get Rich Quick	Peter Doyle	___

1996

Malcontenta, The (Tie)	Barry Maitland	___
Inside Dope (Tie)	Paul Thomas	___
Scream Black Murder	Philip McLaren	___
Wildfire	Susan Geason	___

CWAA Best 1st Novel

2007
Diamond Dove	Adrian Hyland	___
Betrayal of Bindi Mackenzie, The	Jaclyn Moriaty	___
Behind the Night Bazaar	Angela Savage	___
Better Dead Than Never	Laurent Boulanger	___

2006
Out of Silence: A Story of Love, Betrayal, Politics and Murder	Wendy James	___
Head Shot	Jarad Henry	___
Dead Set	Kel Robertson	___

2005
Private Man, A	Malcolm Knox	___
Malicious Intent	Kathryn Fox	___
Groundsman, The	William Youatt-Pine	___

2004
Walker, The (Tie)	Jane Goodall	___
Junkie Pilgrim (Tie)	Wayne Grogan	___
Misconceptions	Terry McGee	___
Far Horizon	Tony Park	___
Rogue Element	David A. Rollins	___

2003
Blood Redemption	Alex Palmer	___
Lady Luck	Kirsty Brooks	___
Half Past Dead	Jane Clifton	___
Games, The	Peter de Vries	___
Final Account, The	Greg Wilson	___

2002
Apartment 255 (Tie)	Bunty Avieson	___
Who Killed Angelique? (Tie)	Emma Darcy	___
On Probation: Detective Ludowski's Casebook	Margaret Bevege	___
Black Ice	Sandy Curtis	___
Artist is a Thief, The	Stephen Gray	___

2001
Last Drinks	Andrew McGahn	___
April Fools	Yvonne Fein	___
Fedora Walk	Merrilee Moss	___

2000
Wooden Leg of Inspector Anders, The	Marshall Browne	___
Unholy Writ	Carmel Bird	___
Dry Dock	Cathy Cole	___
Trojan Dog, The	Dorothy Johnston	___

Angels in the Architecture	Mary Rose MacColl	____
Fetish	Tara Moss	____
Cop This	Chris Nyst	____
Cat Catcher	Caroline Shaw	____

1999

Last Days, The	Andrew Masterson	____

1997

Get Rich Quick (Tie)	Peter Doyle	____
Bad Debts (Tie)	Peter Temple	____
Final Dismissal, The	Anne Hawking	____
Kokoda Club, The	Geoff Stewart	____
Scarlet Rider, The	Lucy Sussex	____

1996

Dark Angel	John Dale	____
Cross, The	Mandy Sayer	____

CWAA Best True Crime

2007

Killing for Pleasure: The Definitive Story of the Snowtown Serial Murders (Tie)	Debi Marshall	____
Written on the Skin: An Australian Forensic Casebook (Tie)	Liz Porter	____
Justice for the Dead: Forensic Pathology in the Hot Zone	Malcolm Dodd & Beverly Knight	____
Things a Killer Would Know: The True Story of Leonard Fraser; Is He Australia's Worst Serial Killer?	Paula Doneman	____
Silent Death: The Killing of Julie Ramage	Karen Kissane	____
Intractable: Hell has a Name: Katingal - Life Inside Australia's First Super Max Prison	Bernie Matthews	____
Dodger, The: Inside the World of Roger Rogerson	Duncan McNab	____
Australian Outlaw: The True Story of Postcard Bandit Brenden Abbott	Derek Pedley	____
Overboard: The Stories Cruise Ships Don't Want Told	Gywn Topham	____

2006

Packing Death	Lachlan McCulloch	____
You'll Never Take Me Alive: The Life and Death of Bushranger Ben Hall	Nick Bleszynski	____
In Your Face: The Life and Times of Billy 'The Texan' Longley	Rochelle Jackson	____
Norfolk, Island of Secrets: The Mystery of Janelle Patton's Death	Tim Latham	____
And Then the Darkness: The Disappearance of Peter Falconio and the Trials of Joanne Lees	Sue Williams	____

2005

Mr. Big: The True Story of Lennie McPherson and His Life of Crime (Tie)	Tony Reeves	____
Jo Cinque's Consolation: A True Story of Death, Grief and the Law (Tie)	Helen Garner	____
Gatton Murders, The: A True Story of Lust, Vengeance and Vile Retribution	Stephanie Bennett	____
Wild Life: A Story of Family, Infidelity and a Fatal Shooting	John Dale	____
Almost Perfect: The True Story of the Brutal, Unsolved Crawford Family Murders	Greg Fogarty	____
Coroner, The: Investigating Sudden Death	Derrick Hand & Janet Fife-Yeomans	____
Bagman, The: Final Confessions of Jack Herbert	Jack Herbert with Tom Gilling	____
All Things Bright and Beautiful: Murder in the City of Light	Susan Mitchell	____
Phillip Island Murder, The: The True Account of a Brutal Killing	Vikki Petraitis & Paul Daley	____
Leadbelly: Inside Australia's Underworld Wars	John Silvester & Andrew Rule	____
Underbelly 8: More True Crime Stories	John Silvester & Andrew Rule	____
Bound by Blood	John Suter Winton	____

2003

Blood Stain: The True Story of Katherine Knight, the Mother and Abattoir Worker Who Became Australia's Worst Female Killer	Peter Lalor	____
What Happened to Freeda Hayes?	Robin Bowles	____
Just Another Little Murder: A Brother's Pursuit of Justice	Phil Cleary	____
Beyond Bad: The Life and Crime of Katherine Knight, Australia's Hannibal	Sandra Lee	____
Blood Brothers: The Criminal Underworld of Asia	Bertil Lintner	____
Mickelberg Stitch, The	Avon Lovell	____
Reasons of State: To Kill a Polish Priest	Kevin Ruane	____
Tough: 101 Australian Gangsters, A Crime Companion	John Silvester & Andrew Rule	____
Underbelly 6: More True Crime Stories	John Silvester & Andrew Rule	____
Brotherhoods, The: Inside the Outlaw Motorcycle Gangs	Arthu Veno	____

2002

Razor: A True Story of Slashers, Gangsters, Prostitutes, and Sly Grog (Tie)	Larry Writer	____
Hanged Man, The: The Life and Death of Ronald Ryan (Tie)	Mike Richards	____
Poison Principle, The	Stephanie Bennett	____
Taken in Contempt: When Parents Abduct Their Own Children	Robin Bowles	____

73

Touched by the Devil: Inside the Mind of a Psychopath	John Clarke & Andy Shea	___
10 Months in Laos: A Vast Web of Intrigue, Missing Millions, and Murder	Paul Conroy	___
Death at Bondi: Cops, Cocaine, Corruption and the Killing of Roni Levi	Darren Goodsir	___
On Murder 2: True Crime Writing in Australia	Kerry Greenwood, ed.	___
More…Cops Crooks and Catastrophes	Shirley Hardy-Rix	___
True Story of Jimmy Governor, The	Laurie Moore & Stephan Williams	___
Young Blood: The Story of the Family Murders	Bob O'Brien	___
Underbelly 5: More True Crime Stories	John Silvester & Andrew Rule	___
Writing on Gravestones: A Compelling Collection of True-Crime Writing	Gary Tippett & Ian Munro	___
Moran v. Moran: A Family, a Suicide and the Court Case that Gripped a Nation	Murray Waldren	___

2001

Broken Lives: Serial Killer Eric Edgar Cooke's Secret Crimes, the Women Who Survived Them, and the Man Still Paying the Price	Estelle Blackburn	___

2000

Huckstepp: A Dangerous Life (Tie)	John Dale	___
Underbelly 3: Some More True Crime Stories (Tie)	John Silvester & Andrew Rule	___
Justice Denied: An Investigation into the Death of Jaidyn Leskie	Robin Bowles	___
Heart and Soul: Personal Recollections of Life in the Police Force	Barry Dickins	___
Shark Net: Memories and Murder	Robert Drewe	___
Arrested Development: The Aaron Cohen Story	Paul Little	___

CWAA Best Non-Fiction

1997

How to Write Crime	Marele Day, ed.	___

CWAA Best Teenage/Young Adult Fiction

2002

Blue Murder	Ken Catran	___
Blood on the Microphone	Ian Bone	___
Dead Red	Ruth Starke	___
Star Struck	Ruth Starke	___

CWAA Readers' Favourite

2002
Apartment 255   Bunty Avieson   ____

2001
Bleeding Hearts   Lindy Cameron   ____

CWAA Lifetime Achievement Award

2007	**Sandra Harvey** and **Lindsay Simpson**
2006	**John Silvester** and **Andrew Rule**
2005	**Stuart Coupe**
2003	**Kerry Greenwood**
2002	**Patrick Gallagher**, managing director of Allen & Unwin
2001	**Stephen Knight**, professor
1999	**Peter Corris**
1997	**Alan Yates** (aka Carter Brown)
1996	**Jon Cleary**

www.crimedownunder.com/nedkellyawards.html

Crime Writers Association (UK)

The Crime Writers' Association was founded in 1953 by John Creasey with the aim of supporting professional writers and promoting the genre. Over the years, a number of different awards and honours have been offered in support of crime writing. There have been different sponsors and some of the awards have changed names.

[Editor's note: This has been one of the most difficult groups to assemble and below (with the assistance of several individuals, books, and journals) is the result of several years of research. There is room for improvement because of a lack of record keeping in the earlier days, conflicts in some of the posted titles, and some lost materials. Rather than presenting a history of the CWA awards in this resource, I will concentrate mainly on the titles researched with a brief introduction to some of the awards.]

CWA Duncan Lawrie Dagger

Initially titled the Crossed Red Herring Award, it was first presented in 1955 to Winston Graham for *The Little Walls*. The award was renamed the Gold Dagger in 1960. The Silver Dagger goes to the runner-up and came into being in 1969. Some of the sponsor's have been The Macallan, distillers of Single Highland Malt Whisky; the membership of the Crime Writers Association (CWA); The BCA (Book Club Associates); and The Duncan Lawrie Private Bank. The judges for these awards are mainly reviewers for British publications, the reason being that their work will have required them to have read most of the 150 or more titles that are submitted each year. Winners receive ornamental daggers and a financial gift.

2007
Broken Shore, The	Peter Temple	____
Fields of Grief	Giles Blunt	____
Pegasus Descending	James Lee Burke	____
Sharp Objects	Gillian Flynn	____
Brother Grimm	Craig Russell	____
Sovereign	C.J. Sansom	____

2006
Raven Black	Ann Cleeves	____
Chemistry of Death, The	Simon Beckett	____
Red Leaves	Thomas H. Cook	____
Safer Than Houses	Frances Fyfield	____
Wolves of Memory	Bill James	____
Thousand Lies, A	Laura Wilson	____

2005

CWA Gold Dagger
Silence of the Grave   Arnaldur Indridason   ___

CWA Silver Dagger
Deadly Web   Barbara Nadel   ___

CWA Dagger Short-List
Calling Out for You   Karin Fossum   ___
In Matto's Realm   Friedrich Glauser   ___
Skinny Dip   Carl Hiaasen   ___
Seeking Whom He May Devour   Fred Vargas   ___

2004

CWA/BCA Gold Dagger
Blacklist   Sara Paretsky   ___

CWA/BCA Silver Dagger
Flesh and Blood   John Harvey   ___

CWA/BCA Dagger Short-List
Tokyo (The Devil of Nanking)   Mo Hayder   ___
Torment of Others, The   Val McDermid   ___
Midnight Cab   James W. Nichol   ___
Lover, The   Laura Wilson   ___

2003

CWA Gold Dagger
Fox Evil   Minette Walters   ___

CWA Silver Dagger
Half Broken Things   Morag Joss   ___

CWA Dagger Short-List
Winter Queen, The   Boris Akunin   ___
Company, The   Robert Littell   ___
Almost Blue   Carlo Lucarelli   ___
Blind Man of Seville, The   Robert Wilson   ___

2002

MACALLAN Gold Dagger
Athenian Murders, The   Jose Carlos Samoza   ___

MACALLAN Silver Dagger
Final Country, The   James Crumley   ___

MACALLAN Dagger Short-List
Scaredy Cat	Mark Billingham	___
Jolie Blon's Bounce	James Lee Burke	___
City of Bones	Michael Connelly	___
Acid Row	Minette Walters	___

2001

MACALLAN Gold Dagger
Sidetracked	Henning Mankell	___

MACALLAN Silver Dagger
Forty Words for Sorrow	Giles Blunt	___

MACALLIAN Dagger Short-List
Dancing With the Virgins	Stephen Booth	___
Baby Love	Denise Danks	___
Right as Rain	George P. Pelecanos	___
Ice Harvest, The	Scott Phillips	___

2000

MACALLAN Gold Dagger
Motherless Brooklyn	Jonathan Lethem	___

MACALLAN Silver Dagger
Friends in High Places	Donna Leon	___

MACALLAN Dagger Short-List
Purple Cane Road	James Lee Burke	___
Havana Bay	Martin Cruz Smith	___
Skull Mantra, The	Eliot Pattison	___
Lost	Lucy Wadham	___

1999

MACALLAN Gold Dagger
Small Death in Lisbon, A	Robert Wilson	___

MACALLAN Silver Dagger
Vienna Blood	Adrian Mathews	___

MACALLAN Dagger Short-List
Angels Flight	Michael Connelly	___
Phreak	Denise Danks	___
Staring at the Light	Frances Fyfield	___
Place of Execution, A	Val McDermid	___
Dead Souls	Ian Rankin	___

1998

MACALLAN Gold Dagger
Sunset Limited	James Lee Burke	___

MACALLAN Silver Dagger
Manchester Slingback   Nicholas Blincoe   ____

MACALLAN Dagger Short-List
Fire Hawk   Geoffrey Archer   ____
Long Finish, A   Michael Dibdin   ____
On Beulah Height   Reginald Hill   ____
King Suckerman   George P. Pelecanos   ____

1997

MACALLAN Gold Dagger
Black and Blue   Ian Rankin   ____

MACALLAN Silver Dagger
Three to Get Deadly   Janet Evanovich   ____

MACALLAN Dagger Short-List
Church of Dead Girls, The   Stephen Dobyns   ____
Transgressions   Sarah Dunant   ____
Ruluctant Investigator, The   Frank Lean   ____
Black Hornet   James Sallis   ____

1996

MACALLAN Gold Dagger
Popcorn   Ben Elton   ____

MACALLAN Silver Dagger
Bloodhounds   Peter Lovesey   ____

MACALLAN Dagger Short-List
Cadillac Jukebox   James Lee Burke   ____
Death Is Now My Neighbor   Colin Dexter   ____
Bookman's Wake, The   John Dunning   ____
Private Enquiry, A   Jessica Mann   ____

1995

MACALLAN Gold Dagger
Mermaids Singing, The   Val McDermid   ____

MACALLAN Silver Dagger
Summons, The   Peter Lovesey   ____

MACALLAN Dagger Short-List
Dark Spectre   Michael Dibdin   ____
Death in the Garden   Elizabeth Ironside   ____
Piece of Justice, A   Jill Paton Walsh   ____
Dark Room, The   Minette Walters   ____

1994

CWA Gold Dagger
Scold's Bridle, The   Minette Walters   ____

CWA Silver Dagger
Miss Smilla's Feeling for Snow (Smilla's Sense of Snow)   Peter Hoeg   ____

CWA Dagger Short-List
Clear Conscience, A	Frances Fyfield	____
"K" is for Killer	Sue Grafton	____
Crack Down	Val McDermid	____
Black Betty	Walter Mosley	____
Tunnel Vision	Sara Paretsky	____

1993

CWA Gold Dagger
Cruel and Unusual   Patricia Cornwell   ____

CWA Silver Dagger
Fatlands   Sarah Dunant   ____

CWA Dagger Short-List
Dead Meat (Grushko)	Philip Kerr	____
White Butterfly	Walter Mosley	____
Death Among the Dons	Janet Neel	____
Hand of Strange Children, The	Robert Richardson	____

1992

CWA Gold Dagger
Way Through the Woods, The   Colin Dexter   ____

CWA Silver Dagger
Bucket Nut   Liza Cody   ____

CWA Dagger Short-List
Cabal	Michael Dibdin	____
"I" is for Innocent	Sue Grafton	____
Recalled to Life	Reginald Hill	____
Red Death, A	Walter Mosley	____

1991

CWA Gold Dagger
King Solomon's Carpet   Barbara Vine   ____

CWA Silver Dagger
Deep Sleep   Frances Fyfield   ____

CWA Dagger Short-List
Fifth Rapunzel, The   B.M. Gill   ____
Birth Marks   Sarah Dunant   ____
Play Dead   Peter Dickinson   ____
Dirty Tricks   Michael Dibdin   ____
Death of a Partner   Janet Neel   ____

1990

CWA Gold Dagger
Bones and Silence   Reginald Hill   ____

CWA Silver Dagger
Late Candidate, The   Mike Phillips   ____

CWA Dagger Short-List
Listening in the Dusk   Celia Fremlin   ____
Trial by Fire (Not that Kind of Place)   Frances Fyfield   ____
Rough Treatment   John Harvey   ____
Going Wrong   Ruth Rendell   ____

1989

CWA Gold Dagger
Wench is Dead, The   Colin Dexter   ____

CWA Silver Dagger
Shadow Run, The   Desmond Lowden   ____

CWA Dagger Short-List
Touch of the Past   Jon L. Breen   ____
Silent Thunder   Loren D. Estleman   ____
Very Particular Murder, A   S.T. Haymon   ____
Way We Die Now, The   Charles Willeford   ____

1988

CWA Gold Dagger
Ratking   Michael Dibdin   ____

CWA Silver Dagger
Toxic Shock (Blood Shot)   Sara Paretsky   ____

CWA Dagger Short-List
At Death's Door   Robert Barnard   ____
Greek Gifts   T.J. Binyon   ____
Sheep's Clothing   Celia Dale   ____
Underworld   Reginald Hill   ____

1987

CWA Gold Dagger
Fatal Inversion, A   Barbara Vine   ___

CWA Silver Dagger
Presumed Innocent   Scott Turow   ___

CWA Dagger Short-List
Death of a God   S.T. Haymon   ___
Child's Play   Reginald Hill   ___
Colour of Blood (Color of Blood)   Brian Moore   ___
Dead Reckoning (Deadly Reunion)   Ivan Ruff   ___

1986

CWA Gold Dagger
Live Flesh   Ruth Rendell   ___

CWA Silver Dagger
Taste of Death, A   P.D. James   ___

CWA Dagger Short-List
Under Contract   Liza Cody   ___
Secret of Annexe Three, The   Colin Dexter   ___
Intensive Care   Peter Dunant   ___
Dark-Adapted Eye, A   Barbara Vine   ___

1985

CWA Gold Dagger
Monkey Puzzle   Paula Gosling   ___

CWA Silver Dagger
Last Seen Alive   Dorothy Simpson   ___

CWA Dagger Short-List
Weekend for Murder (Murder on a Mystery Tour)   Marian Babson   ___
Disposal of the Living, The (Fete Fatale)   Robert Barnard   ___
Performance   Douglas Clark   ___
Head Case   Liza Cody   ___
You'd Better Believe It   Bill James   ___
Elberg Collection, The   Anthony Oliver   ___
Field of Blood   Gerald Seymour   ___
*Criminal Comedy of the Contented Couple, The (A   Julian Symons   ___
    Criminal Comedy)*
Our Fathers' Lies   Andrew Taylor   ___

1984
CWA Gold Dagger
Twelfth Juror, The   B.M. Gill   ___

CWA Silver Dagger
  Tree of Hands, The   Ruth Rendell   ____

CWA Dagger Short-List
  Not Dead, Only Resting   Simon Brett   ____
  Rats' Alley   William Garner   ____
  Stately Homicide   S.T. Haymon   ____
  Die Again, Macready   Jack Livingston   ____
  Penny Black   Susan Moody   ____
  May Day in Magadan   Anthony Olcott   ____
  Sound Evidence   June Thomson   ____
  Big Money   Peter Turnbull   ____
  Advertise for Treasure   David Williams   ____
  Smooth Face of Evil, The   Margaret Yorke   ____

1983

CWA Gold Dagger
  Accidental Crimes   John Hutton   ____

CWA Silver Dagger
  Papers of Tony Veitch, The   William McIlvanney   ____

CWA Dagger Short-List
  Berlin Game   Len Deighton   ____
  Riddle of the Third Mile, The   Colin Dexter   ____
  Danger, The   Dick Francis   ____
  Black Seraphim, The   Michael Gilbert   ____
  Deadheads   Reginald Hill   ____
  Twelfth Night of Ramadan, The   Kendal J. Peel   ____
  Speaker of Mandarin, The   Ruth Rendell   ____

1982

CWA Gold Dagger
  False Inspector Dew, The   Peter Lovesey   ____

CWA Silver Dagger
  Ritual Murder   S.T. Haymon   ____

CWA Dagger Short-List
  By Frequent Anguish   S.F.X. Dean   ____
  Banker   Dick Francis   ____
  Skull Beneath the Skin, The   P.D. James   ____
  Conduct of Major Maxim, The   Gavin Lyall   ____
  Old Vengeful, The   Anthony Price   ____
  Shot in the Arm, A (Death at the BBC)   John Sherwood   ____
  To Make a Killing (Portrait of Lilith)   June Thomson   ____

1981

CWA Gold Dagger
Gorky Park   Martin Cruz Smith   ____

CWA Silver Dagger
Dead of Jericho, The   Colin Dexter   ____

CWA Dagger Short-List
Big Bear, Little Bear   David Brierley   ____
Off Duty   Andrew Coburn   ____
Twice Shy   Dick Francis   ____
Funeral of Gondolas, A   Timothy Holme   ____
Fiddle City   Dan Kavanagh   ____
Amateur, The   Robert Littell   ____
Murder Has a Pretty Face   Jennie Melville   ____

1980

CWA Gold Dagger
Murder of the Maharajah, The   H.R.F. Keating   ____

CWA Sliver Dagger
Monk's Hood   Ellis Peters   ____

CWA Dagger Short-List
Bruce, The   Michael de Larrabeiti   ____
Reflex   Dick Francis   ____
Garden of Weapons, The   John Gardner   ____
Innocent Blood   P.D. James   ____
Sweet Adelaide   Julian Symons   ____
Dissident, The   Peter Van Greenaway   ____
Murder for Treasure   David Williams   ____

1979

CWA Gold Dagger
Whip Hand   Dick Francis   ____

CWA Silver Dagger
Service of All the Dead   Colin Dexter   ____

CWA Dagger Short-List
Nostradamus Traitor, The   John Gardner   ____
Take Murder...   John Wainwright   ____

1978

CWA Gold Dagger
Chelsea Murders, The (Murder Games)   Lionel Davidson   ____

CWA Silver Dagger
Waxworks   Peter Lovesey   ____

CWA Dagger Short-List

X Marks the Spot	Michael Butterworth	____
Trial Run	Dick Francis	____
Dancing Dodo, The	John Gardner	____
Last Sentence, The	Jonathan Goodman	____
Blackheath Poisonings, The	Julian Symons	____
Coppergold (Copper Gold)	Pauline Glen Winslow	____

1977

CWA Gold Dagger

Honourable Schoolboy, The	John le Carre	____

CWA Silver Dagger

Laidlaw	William McIlvanney	____

CWA Dagger Short-List

Send No More Roses (Siege of the Villa Lipp)	Eric Ambler	____
Enemy, The	Desmond Bagley	____
Glimpses of the Moon	Edmund Crispin	____
Death of an Expert Witness	P.D. James	____
Judgement in Stone, A	Ruth Rendell	____
Day of the Peppercorn Kill, The	John Wainwright	____

1976

CWA Gold Dagger

Demon in My View, A	Ruth Rendell	____

CWA Silver Dagger

Rogue Eagle	James McClure	____

1975

CWA Gold Dagger

Seven-Per-Cent Solution, The	Nicholas Meyer	____

CWA Silver Dagger

Black Tower, The	P.D. James	____

CWA Dagger Short-List

Man Who Loved Zoos, The (Stricken)	Malcolm Bosse	____
Lively Dead, The	Peter Dickinson	____
Curtain	Agatha Christie	____
High Stakes	Dick Francis	____
Troublemaker	Joseph Hansen	____

1974

CWA Gold Dagger

Other Paths to Glory	Anthony Price	____

CWA Silver Dagger
Grosvenor Square Goodbye, The (Good-Bye and   Francis Clifford   ____
Amen)

CWA Dagger Short-List
Doctor Frigo   Eric Ambler   ____
Poison Oracle, The   Peter Dickinson   ____
Knock Down   Dick Francis   ____
Ripley's Game   Patricia Highsmith   ____
Tinker, Tailor, Soldier, Spy   John le Carre   ____

1973

CWA Gold Dagger
Defection of A.J. Lewinter, The   Robert Littell   ____

CWA Silver Dagger
Coffin for Pandora, A   Gwendoline Butler   ____

CWA Dagger Short-List
Riverside Villas Murder   Kingsley Amis   ____
Tightrope Men, The   Desmond Bagley   ____
Finger of Saturn, The   Victor Canning   ____
Amigo, Amigo   Francis Clifford   ____
Slay-Ride   Dick Francis   ____
Mad Hatter's Holiday   Peter Lovesey   ____
Jasius Pursuit, The   Douglas Orgill   ____

1972

CWA Gold Dagger
Levanter, The   Eric Ambler   ____

CWA Silver Dagger
Rainbird Pattern, The (Family Plot)   Victor Canning   ____

CWA Dagger Short-List
Odessa File, The   Frederick Forsyth   ____
Smokescreen   Dick Francis   ____
Long Silence, A (Aupres de ma blonde)   Nicolas Freeling   ____
Friends of Eddie Coyle, The   George V. Higgins   ____
Unsuitable Job for a Woman, An   P.D. James   ____
Ask the Right Question   Michael Z. Lewin   ____
Blame the Dead   Gavin Lyall   ____
Caterpillar Cop, The   James McClure   ____
Players and the Game, The   Julian Symons   ____

1971

CWA Gold Dagger
Steam Pig, The   James McClure   ____

CWA Silver Dagger
Shroud for a Nightingale   P.D. James   ____

CWA Dagger Short-List
Blind Side, The   Francis Clifford   ____
Sleep and His Brother   Peter Dickinson   ____
Bonecrack   Dick Francis   ____
Warsaw Document, The   Adam Hall   ____
Ripley Under Ground   Patricia Highsmith   ____
Dossier 51   Gilles Perrault   ____
Laughing Policeman, The   Maj Sjowall & Per Wahloo   ____
Alamut Ambush, The   Anthony Price   ____

1970

CWA Gold Dagger
Young Man, I Think You're Dying   Joan Fleming   ____

CWA Silver Dagger
Labyrinth Makers, The   Anthony Price   ____

CWA Dagger Short-List
Intercom Conspiracy, The (Quiet Conspiracy)   Eric Ambler
Seals, The (The Sinful Stones)   Peter Dickinson
Rat Race   Dick Francis   ____
Inspector Ghote Breaks an Egg   H.R.F. Keating   ____
Homicidal Colonel, The   Robert Player   ____
Man Who Lost His Wife, The   Julian Symons   ____

1969

CWA Gold Dagger
Pride of Heroes, A (The Old English Peep Show)   Peter Dickinson   ____

CWA Silver Dagger
Another Way of Dying   Francis Clifford   ____

CWA Dagger Short-List
Odds on Death, The   Charles Drummond   ____
Enquiry   Dick Francis   ____
Possession   Celia Fremlin   ____
Write on Both Sides of the Paper   Mary Kelly   ____
Sunday the Rabbi Stayed Home   Harry Kemelman   ____
Hunter in the Shadows, The (Complicity)   Jennie Melville   ____
Flaxborough Crab, The (Just What the Doctor Ordered)   Colin Watson   ____

1968

CWA Gold Dagger
Skin Deep (The Glass-Sided Ants' Nest)   Peter Dickinson   ____

CWA Runner-Up
Private Wound, The   Nicholas Blake   ____

CWA Dagger Short-List
Cargo of Eagles, A   Margery Allingham   ____
Burden of Proof, The (Villain)   James Barlow   ____
I Love, I Kill (Good Old Charlie)   John Bingham   ____
Miranda Must Die   Henry Calvin   ____
Forfeit   Dick Francis   ____
Dust and the Heat, The (Overdrive)   Michael Gilbert   ____
Sweet Sister Seduced   S.B. Hough   ____
Appleby at Allington (Death by Water)   Michael Innes   ____
Inspector Ghote Hunts the Peacock   H.R.F. Keating   ____
Last One Left, The   John D. MacDonald   ____
Three Minus Two (The Quiet Killer)   Donald Mackenzie   ____
Lie Down, I Want to Talk to You   William P. McGivern   ____
Bird-Cage, The   Kenneth O'Hara   ____
Dance of Death, The   Jeremy Potter   ____
Man Whose Dreams Came True   Julian Symons   ____
Place for the Wicked, A   Elleston Trevor   ____
One is One   Miles Tripp   ____

1967

CWA Gold Dagger
Murder Against the Grain   Emma Lathen   ____

CWA Runner-Up
Lonelyheart 4122   Colin Watson   ____

CWA Dagger Short-List
All Men are Lonely Now   Francis Clifford   ____
Those Who Walk Away   Patricia Highsmith   ____
Run Man Run   Chester Himes   ____
Face of Danger, The   Miriam Sharman   ____
Last Best Friend, The   George Sims   ____
Man Who Killed Himself, The   Julian Symons   ____

1966

CWA Gold Dagger
Long Way to Shiloh, A (The Menorah Men)   Lionel Davidson   ____

CWA Silver Dagger
Double Agent, The   John Bingham   ____

CWA Dagger Short-List

Naked Runner, The	Francis Clifford	____
Billion Dollar Brain	Len Deighton	____
Tall, Balding, Thirty-Five (The Limbo Affair)	Anthony Firth	____
Flying Finish	Dick Francis	____
King of the Rainy Country, The	Nicolas Freeling	____
Crack in the Teacup, The	Michael Gilbert	____
Provenance of Death, A (Picture of Death)	Kenneth Giles	____
Power Play	The Gordons	____
Dead Corse	Mary Kelly	____
Seeds of Violence	Miriam Sharman	____
Doorbell Rang, The	Rex Stout	____
Murder in Canton	Robert van Gulik	____

1965

CWA Gold Dagger

Far Side of the Dollar, The	Ross Macdonald	____

CWA Runner-Up

For Kicks	Dick Francis	____
Accounting for Murder	Emma Lathen	____

CWA Dagger Short-List

Fragment of Fear, A	John Bingham	____
Ring of Roses, A (A Wreath of Roses)	John Blackburn	____
Odds Against	Dick Francis	____
Loner, The	Otto Friedrich	____
Jealous One, The	Celia Fremlin	____
Hard Sell, The	William Haggard	____
Holm Oaks, The	P.M. Hubbard	____
Friday the Rabbi Slept Late	Harry Kemelman	____
May You Die in Ireland	Michael Kenyon	____
Airs Above the Ground	Mary Stewart	____
Belting Inheritance, The	Julian Symons	____
End of a Party	Hillary Waugh	____

1964

CWA Gold Dagger

Perfect Murder, The	H.R.F. Keating	____

CWA Runner-Up

Most Dangerous Game, The	Gavin Lyall	____
Chill, The	Ross Macdonald	____

CWA Dagger Short-List

Kind of Anger, A	Eric Ambler	____
Simple Case of Ill-Will, A	Evelyn Berckman	____
Sad Variety, The	Nicholas Blake	____
Funeral in Berlin	Len Deighton	____
Nerve	Dick Francis	____
Double-Barrel	Nicolas Freeling	____
Liquidator, The	John Gardner	____
March to the Gallows	Mary Kelly	____
Monkey on a Chain	Edwin Lanhan	____
Drowner, The	John D. MacDonald	____
Fiend, The	Margaret Millar	____
Two Men in Twenty	Maurice Procter	____
End of Solomon Grundy, The	Julian Symons	____
Crime of Colin Wise, The	Michael Underwood	____
Dead Calm	Charles Williams	____

1963

CWA Gold Dagger

Spy Who Came in From the Cold, The	John le Carre	____
Gun Before Butter (Question of Loyalty)	Nicolas Freeling	____
High Wire, The	William Haggard	____

1962

When I Grow Rich	Joan Fleming	____
Light of Day, The	Eric Ambler	____
Hopjoy was Here	Colin Watson	____

1961

Spoilt Kill, The	Mary Kelly	____
Call for the Dead (The Deadly Affair)	John le Carre	____
One Away	Allan Prior	____

1960

Night of Wenceslas	Lionel Davidson	____
My Brother Michael	Mary Stewart	____
Progress of a Crime, The	Julian Symons	____

1959

Crossed Red Herring

Passage of Arms	Eric Ambler	____
Strike for a Kingdom	Menna Gallie	____
Way Back, A (The Way Back)	James Mitchell	____

1958

Someone From the Past	Margot Bennett	____
Hide My Eyes (Tether's End; Ten Were Missing)	Margery Allingham	____
Or Be He Dead	James Byrom	____
Undiplomatic Exit	John Sherwood	____

1957

Colour of Murder, The (The Color of Murder)	Julian Symons	____
Off With His Head (Death of a Fool)	Ngaio Marsh	____
Your Money or Your Life	George Milner	____
Long Echo, The	Douglas Rutherford	____

1956

Second Man, The	Edward Grierson	____
Time Right Deadly	Sarah Gainham	____
Gideon's Week	J.J. Marric (John Creasey)	____
Man of Two Tribes	Arthur W. Upfield	____

1955

Little Walls, The (Bridge to Vengeance)	Winston Graham	____
Man Who Didn't Fly, The	Margot Bennett	____
Blind Date (Chance Meeting)	Leigh Howard	____
Scales of Justice	Ngaio Marsh	____

CWA Special Silver Dagger Award

1980

Ferrars, Elizabeth	in recognition of 50 outstanding books

CWA Special Award

1975

Gladys Mitchell	in honour of 50 outstanding books

CWA Special Merit Award

1966

Crime and Detection,	Symons, Julian	____
An Illustrated History From 1840		

CWA Police Review Awards

From 1985 to 1987 the publication, *The Police Review,* sponsored an award for the best police procedural crime novel.

1987

Snowman	Roger Busby	___
Pretty Place for a Murder, A	Roy Hart	___
Halo Parade	Bill James	___
Element of Doubt	Dorothy Simpson	___
Serious Crimes (Silver Spoon Murders)	D.W. Smith	___

1986

Crossfire Killings, The	Bill Knox	___
Hunting of Mr. Gloves, The	Phillip Daniels	___
No Flowers, By Request	June Thomson	___

1985

Murder After the Holiday	Andrew Arncliffe	___
Hunter, The	Roger Busby	___
All Through the Night	John Wainwright	___

CWA Ian Fleming Steel Dagger for Best Thriller

This award was introduced in 2002 and is sponsored by Ian Fleming Publications Ltd. to celebrate the best of contemporary thriller writing in the vein of James Bond. The judges (agents, authors, booksellers, and reviewers) choose the winner who receives a financial gift and a steel dagger.

2007

Sharp Objects	Gillian Flynn	___
Faithful Spy, The	Alex Berenson	___
Woods, The	Harlan Coben	___
City of Lies	Roger Jon Ellory	___
Intruders, The	Michael Marshall	___
Night Ferry, The	Michael Robotham	___
Triptych	Karin Slaughter	___

2006

Mr. Clarinet	Nick Stone	___
Lincoln Lawyer, The	Michael Connelly	___
Sweet Gum	Jo-Ann Goodwin	___
Pig Island	Mo Hayder	___
English Assassin, The	Daniel Silva	___
Mercy Seat, The	Martyn Waites	___
Contact Zero	David Wolstencroft	___

2005

Brandenburg	Henry Porter	___
Blind Eye, A	G.M. Ford	___
Good Day to Die, A	Simon Kernick	___
Apothecary's House, The	Adrian Mathews	___
Labyrinth	Kate Mosse	___
Double Cross Blind	Joel Ross	___
Death in Vienna, A	Daniel Silva	___

2004

Garden of Beasts	Jeffery Deaver	___
Warlord's Son, The	Dan Fesperman	___
Paranoia	Joseph Finder	___
Tokyo (The Devil of Nanking)	Mo Hayder	___
Hard Landing	Stephen Leather	___
Dead I May Well Be	Adrian McKinty	___
Confessor, The	Daniel Silva	___

2003

Small Boat of Great Sorrows, The	Dan Fesperman	___
Persuader	Lee Child	___
Candlemoth	Roger Jon Ellory	___
Nightspinners, The	Lucretia Grindle	___
Company, The	Robert Littell	___
Empire State	Henry Porter	___
Traitor's Kiss	Gerald Seymour	___

2002

Sirius Crossing, The	John Creed	___
Master of Rain, The	Tom Bradby	___
Without Fail	Lee Child	___
Hostage	Robert Crais	___
Lime's Photograph	Leif Davidsen	___
French Executioner, The	C.C. Humphreys	___
Tango One	Stephen Leather	___

CWA Duncan Lawrie International Dagger

The Duncan Lawrie International Dagger is awarded by the Crime Writers Association for crime novels translated into English from their original language. Books eligible for the new dagger include thrillers, suspense novels, and spy fiction. They must be written in a language other than English and have been translated into English for UK publication. The author and the book's translator of the winning title receive a financial award. This award began in 2006.

2007

Wash This Blood Clean From My Hand	Fred Vargas	____
Shame	Karin Alvtegan	____
Exception, The	Christian Jungersen	____
Attack, The	Yasmina Khadra	____
Savage Altar, The	Åsa Larsson	____
Redbreast, The	Jo Nesbø	____

2006

Three Evangelists, The	Fred Vargas	____
Excursion to Tindari	Andrea Camilleri	____
Autumn of the Phantoms	Yasmina Khadra	____
Dead Horsemeat	Dominique Manotti	____
Borkmann's Point	Hakan Nesser	____
Blood on the Saddle	Rafael Reig	____

CWA New Blood Fiction Dagger

This award for best crime novel by a debuting author was named after John Creasey, one of the Association's founders. Publisher Chivers Press was the sponsor from the award's introduction in 1973 until 2002. Since 2003, it has been sponsored by BBC Audiobooks. The award was called the CWA Creasey Award and is now referred to as the CWA New Blood Dagger; the prize consists of an ornamental dagger and a financial gift.

CWA New Blood Dagger

2007

Sharp Objects	Gillian Flynn	____
Objects of Desire	C.J. Emerson	____
Wrong Kind of Blood, The	Declan Hughes	____
Borderlands	Brian McGilloway	____
Last Days of Newgate	Andrew Pepper	____
Dead of Summer	Camilla Way	____

2006

Still Life	Louise Penny	____
Immoral	Brian Freeman	____
Ice Trap	Kitty Sewell	____

CWA Creasey

2005
Running Hot   Dreda Say Mitchell   ___
Great Stink, The   Clare Clark   ___
Grip   David McKeowen   ___
Bloody Harvests   Richard Kunzmann   ___

2004
Amagansett   Mark Mills   ___
Jasmine Trade, The   Denise Hamilton   ___
Three Body Problem, The Catherine Shaw   ___
Devil's Playground   Stav Sherez   ___

2003
Mission Flats   William Landay   ___
Backlash   Rod Duncan   ___
Dissolution   C.J. Sansom   ___

2002
Cutting Room, The   Louise Welsh   ___
25th Hour, The   David Benioff   ___
Emperor of Ocean Park, The Stephen L. Carter   ___
Dark Fields, The   Alan Glynn   ___
Water Clock, The   Jim Kelly   ___

2001
Earthquake Bird, The   Susanna Jones   ___
Paradise Salvage   John Fusco   ___
Ice Harvest, The   Scott Phillips   ___
Blindsighted   Karin Slaughter   ___
Good Bad Woman   Elizabeth Woodcraft   ___

2000
God is a Bullet   Boston Teran   ___
Stone Baby   Joolz Denby   ___
Lost Girls   Andrew Pyper   ___

1999
Lie in the Dark   Dan Fesperman   ___
Provocation   Charlotte Grimshaw   ___
Quinn   Seumas Smyth   ___

1998
Garnethill   Denise Mina   ___
Locust Farm, The   Jeremy Dronfield   ___
Down on Ponce   Fred Willard   ___

1997
> ***Body Politic***   Paul Johnston   ___
> *Riot Act, The*   Jon Stock   ___
> *Test of Wills, A*   Charles Todd   ___

1996

No award given, but there was an award by an independent group of critics, *Quite Ugly One Morning*, by Christopher Brookmyre. See later in this section, "1st Blood Award," page 117.

1995
> ***One for the Money (Tie)***   Janet Evanovich   ___
> ***Grave Talent, A (Tie)***   Laurie R. King   ___
> *Greenaway, The*   Jane Adams   ___
> *Dark Backward, The*   Gregory Hall   ___

1994
> ***Big Town***   Doug J. Swanson   ___
> *Marx Sisters, The*   Barry Maitland   ___
> *Looking for Trouble*   Cath Staincliffe   ___

1993

no award was made, but there was a short-list:
> *Night's Black Angel*   David Armstrong   ___
> *Skinner's Rules*   Quintin Jardine   ___
> *Devil's Juggler, The*   Murray Smith   ___

1992
> ***Ice House, The***   Minette Walters   ___
> *File Under: Deceased*   Sarah Lacey   ___
> *Unseen Witness*   Lew Matthews   ___

1991
> ***Devil in a Blue Dress***   Walter Mosley   ___
> *Deadly Errand*   Christine Green   ___
> *One Oblique One*   Keith Wright   ___

1990
> ***Postmortem***   Patricia Cornwell   ___
> *Becket Factor, The*   Michael David Anthony   ___

1989
> ***Real Shot in the Arm, A***   Annette Roome   ___
> *Midsummer Killing, A (A Midsummer Night's Killing)*   Trevor Barnes   ___
> *Nobody's Fool*   Marten Claridge   ___
> *Murder at the Nineteenth*   J.M. Gregson   ___
> *Personal Possession, A (Fetish)*   Jeanne Hart   ___
> *March Violets*   Philip Kerr   ___
> *Count the Days*   Lin Summerfield   ___
> *Frost at Christmas*   R.D. Wingfield   ___

1988
Death's Bright Angel   Janet Neel   ___
Death in Tokyo   Stanley Guy   ___
Cold Light of Dawn, The   Graham Ison   ___
Fine Art of Murder, The   Anthony Quogan   ___
Hawk, The   Peter Ransley   ___

1987
Dark Apostle, The   Denis Kilcommons   ___
Traveler, The   John Katzenbach   ___
Ritual Bath, The   Faye Kellerman   ___
Death in Time, A   Francis Lyall   ___
Forests of the Night   Margaret Moore   ___
Jumping the Cracks   Rebecca O'Rourke   ___
Infinite Number of Monkeys, An   Les Roberts   ___
Gallows View   Peter Robinson   ___
Masculine Ending, A   Joan Smith   ___
Goodbye, Nanny Grey   Susannah Stacey   ___

1986
Tinplate   Neville Steed   ___
Student Body (An Educated Murder)   J.R. Hulland   ___
Death in Leningrad   John Lear   ___
Sleeping Dog   Dick Lochte   ___
Slow Turn   Mike Marqusee   ___
Murder for Lunch   Haughton Murphy   ___
Dangerous Age, A   Martin Sylvester   ___
Unorthodox Murder of Rabbi Wahl, The   Joseph Telushkin   ___
   (Unorthodox Murder of Rabbi Moss)

1985
Latimer Mercy, The   Robert Richardson   ___
Disorderly Elements   Bob Cook   ___
Patterns in the Dust (Death on Widow's Walk)   Lesley Grant-Adamson   ___
Trouble at Aquitaine, The   Nancy Livingston   ___
Death at Charity's Point   William G. Tapply   ___
Organized Crimes   Nicholas von Hoffman   ___

1984
Very Private Enterprise, A   Elizabeth Ironside   ___
Rembrandt Panel, The (The Rembrandt File)   Oliver Banks   ___
Vicar's Roses (Listen for the Click)   Jon L. Breen   ___
Outbid   David Hume   ___
Healthy Body, A   Gillian Linscott   ___
Back Room in Somers Town, A   John Malcolm   ___
Dead in the Water   Ted Wood   ___

1983

Ariadne Clue, The (Tie)	Carol Clemeau	___
Night the Gods Smiled, The (Tie)	Eric Wright	___
Name of the Rose, The	Umberto Eco	___
Tender Prey	Patricia Roberts	___

1982

Caroline Minuscule	Andrew Taylor	___
Swan Song	T.J. Binyon	___
Spytrap	William Crips	___
Corridors of Death	Ruth Dudley Edwards	___
Devil's Prison, The	Michael O'Donnell	___
Murder at the Red October	Anthony Olcott	___
Indemnity Only	Sara Paretsky	___
Butcher's Boy, The	Thomas Perry	___
Post Mortem	Peter Whalley	___
Converging Parallels (The Red Citroen)	Timothy Williams	___

1981

Ludi Victor, The	James Leigh	___
Thus Was Adonis Murdered	Sarah Caudwell	___
Sale of Lot 236, The	Michael Delahaye	___
Tondo for Short	Peter Inchbald	___
Death of an Englishman	Magdalen Nabb	___
Man on Fire	A.J. Quinnell	___
Deep and Crisp and Even	Peter Turnbull	___
Lime Pit, The	Jonathan Valin	___
Odd's End	Tim Wynne-Jones	___

1980

Dupe	Liza Cody	___
Trick of Diamonds, A	Alex Auswaks	___
In the Midst of Death	Helen Luce	___
In the Secret State	Robert McCrum	___

1979

Saturday of Glory	David Serafin	___
Cold War	David Brierley	___
Troika	David Gurr	___
Peripheral Spy, The	Bernard Peterson	___

1978

Running Duck, A (Fair Game)	Paula Gosling	___
Inside Job, An	Stella Allan	___
Head of the Force	James Barnett	___
Aristotle, Detective	Margaret Doody	___
Housespy	Maureen Duffy	___
Death and the Maiden (Death in the Morning)	Sheila Radley	___

1977
Judas Pair, The	Jonathan Gash	____
Fire in the Barley (not eligible)	Frank Parrish	____

1976
Death of a Thin Skinned Animal	Patrick Alexander	____

1975
Acid Drop	Sara George	____
Last Bus to Woodstock, The	Colin Dexter	____
Six Days of the Condor (Three Days of the Condor)	James Grady	____
Robespierre Serial, The	Nicholas Luard	____
Target Practice	Nicholas Meyer	____
Harry's Game	Gerald Seymour	____

1974
Big Fix, The	Roger L. Simon	____
See the Woman	Dallas Barnes	____
Scorpion	Christopher Hill	____

1973
Don't Point that Thing at Me (Mortdecai's Endgame)	Kryil Bonfiglioli	____
Perfumes of Arabia	Evelyn Dewar	____
Hotels With Empty Rooms	Harriet Gilbert	____
Unbecoming Habits	Tim Heald	____
Sorry, Wrong Number	Margaret Simpson	____

CWA Ellis Peters Historical Crime Award

Started in 1999 in memory of Ellis Peters, author of the medieval Brother Cadfael series, this award is sponsored by the Estate of Ellis Peters and her publishers—Headline and Little Brown. A financial gift and an ornamental dagger are presented for a novel with a crime theme and a historical background from any period up to the 1960s. The judging panel is made up of the most recent winner as well as reviewers and historians.

2007
Mistress of the Art of Death	Ariana Franklin	____
Snake Stone, The	Jason Goodwin	____
One From the Other, The	Philip Kerr	____
Murder at Deviation Junction	Andrew Martin	____
Savage Garden, The	Mark Mills	____
Tenderness of Wolves, The	Stef Penney	____

2006
Red Sky Lament	Edward Wright	____
Pale Blue Eye, The	Louis Bayard	____
Nefertiti: The Book of the Dead	Nick Drake	____
Janissary Tree, The	Jason Goodwin	____
Sovereign	C.J. Sansom	____
Sultan's Seal, The	Jenny White	____

2005
Dark Fire	C.J. Sansom	____
God of Chaos, The	Tom Bradby	____
Palace Tiger, The	Barbara Cleverly	____
After the Armistice Ball	Catriona McPherson	____
Portrait, The	Iain Pears	____
Mortal Mischief	Frank Tallis	____

2004
Damascened Blade, The	Barbara Cleverly	____
Shape of Sand, The	Marjorie Eccles	____
Hell at the Breech	Tom Franklin	____
Thief-Taker, The	Janet Gleeson	____
Dante Club, The	Matthew Pearl	____
Judgment of Caesar, The	Steven Saylor	____
Lover, The	Laura Wilson	____

2003
American Boy, The (An Unpardonable Crime)	Andrew Taylor	____
White Russian, The	Tom Bradby	____
Advocate, The	Marcello Fois	____
London Dust	Lee Jackson	____
Blood on the Wood	Gillian Linscott	____
Dissolution	C.J. Sansom	____
Bridge of Sighs, The	Olen Steinhauer	____

2002
Fingersmith	Sarah Waters	____
Jupiter Myth, The	Lindsey Davis	____
Pale Companion, The	Philip Gooden	____
Dead Man Riding	Gillian Linscott	____
Athenian Murders, The	Jose Carlos Samoza	____
Desperate Remedy, The	Martin Stephen	____

2001
Office of the Dead, The		Andrew Taylor	____
Cold Touch of Ice, A	Runner-up	Michael Pearce	____
Ode to a Banker		Lindsey Davis	____
Distinction of Blood, A		Hannah March	____
Last Seen in Massilia		Steven Saylor	____
Mortal Sins		Penn Williamson	____

2000
Absent Friends	Gillian Linscott	____
River of Darkness	Rennie Airth	____
Guilty Knowledge	Clare Curzon	____
Murdered House, The	Pierre Magnan	____
Devil's Highway, The	Hannah March	____

Death of an Effendi	Michael Pearce	___
Little Death, A	Laura Wilson	___

1999

Two for the Lions	Lindsey Davis	___
Falconer and the Great Beast	Ian Morson	___
Wings of Fire	Charles Todd	___

CWA Debut Dagger

This is the CWA's annual new writing competition, which is open to anyone in the world who writes in the English language but whose work has not been published before. Most previous winners, as well as some nominees, have subsequently had their manuscripts published. The entrants submit an opening chapter and synopsis. The winning entry is selected by agents and publishers, and its author receives a financial gift. It began life in 1998 as The CWA New Writers Competition and is now sponsored by leading publisher Orion.

2007

Sweetness at the Bottom of the Pie, The	Alan Bradley	Canada	___
Malestki's Motive	Martin Brackstone	UK	___
With a View to Death	Nesta Brzozowski	UK	___
Cry Baby	Fay Cunningham	UK	___
Rome was Never Like This	Gordon W. Dale	USA	___
Solitaire	Martie de Villiers	UK	___
Shadow of the Dead, The	C.J. Harper	USA	___
Pariah	David Jackson	UK	___
Witch of Babylon, The	D.J. McIntosh	Canada	___
White Lion	Gerard O'Donovan	UK	___
Natural Causes	James Oswald	UK	___
Towers of London	Peter James Peacock	UK	___

2006

Imp: Being the Lost Notebooks of Rufus Wilmot Griswold In the Matter of the Death of Edgar Allan Poe		Otis Twelve (D.V. Wesslemann)	USA	___
Moonshadow	Runner-up	Diane Janes	UK	___
House on Fever Street, The		Celina Alcock	UK	___
Belfast Boy, The		Paul Curd	UK	___
Special Delivery		Sarah Kotler	USA	___
Fiddle Game		Richard A. Thompson	USA	___
One of Us		Iain Rowan	UK	___
Ikumo		Elizabeth Saccente	UK	___
Carrion Death, A		Michael Sears Stanley Trollip	South Africa/ USA	___
Random Act of Generosity, A		Megan Toogood	UK	___

2005

Woman Before Me, The	Ruth Dugdall	UK	___
Mystery of the Third Lucretia, The Runner-up	Susan Runholt	USA	___
Truth Lake, The	Shakuntala Banaji	UK	___
Gilded Lives	Karen Beck	USA	___
Pure Mad	Gary J. Byrnes	Ireland	___
Die With Me	Elena Forbes	UK	___
Namarrkun	Nick Forbes	Australia	___
Taking the Village	Regina Harvey	USA	___
Animal Instinct	Gabriella Herkert	USA	___
Splinter	Rebecca Snape	UK	___
Dead Man Dancing	Otis Twelve	USA	___
	(D.V. Wesselmann)		
Dogs of a Low Degree	George Winter	UK	___
You Think You Know Someone	Simon Woodham	UK	___

2004

Doll Makers, The	Ellen Grubb	UK	___
Still Life Runner-up	Louise Penny	Canada	___
George Trenque and the Old School Tie	Paula Bouwer	Ireland	___
Gardener, The	Kenneth Carlisle	UK	___
Sleeping Dogs	Fay Cunningham	UK	___
Obscure Grave, An	Jim Doherty	USA	___
Cheap Day Return	Tom Flynn	Australia	___
Dead Meat	Jude Larkin	Australia	___
Red Man's Revenge	Andrew Murphy	N. Ireland	___
Margarita Nights	Phyllis Smallman	Canada	___
Fallen Women	Germaine Stafford	Italy	___
Sometimes a Prozac Notion	Otis Twelve	USA	___
	(D.V. Wesselmann)		
Murder in Crowded Hours	Eugene Wang	Hawaii	___
Deadly Contact	Geoffrey West	UK	___

2003

Cuckoo, The	Kirsty Evans	UK	___
Speak Now Runner-up	Margaret Dumas	USA	___
Woman From Smyrna, The	Duncan Brewer	UK	___
Third Room, The	Sandra Charan	UK	___
Speak No Evil	Avriel Genesen	Israel	___
Days of Future Past	Betty Jacque	USA	___
Dead Cat Bounce	Jude Larkin	Australia	___
Long Train, The	Peter Norris	UK	___
Lunchbox Hero	Bryon Quertermous	USA	___
Driftlines	Chris Rose	Italy	___
Mouths of Men, The	Melissa Kate Rowberry	UK	___
Soul of the Desert	Maria E. Schneider	USA	___
Amazing GM Dog, The	Michael Shenton	UK	___

On the Albino Farm		Otis Twelve (D.V. Wesselmann)	UK ___

2002

Sugarmilk Falls		Ilona Van Mil	Canada ___
Heaven's Door	Runner-up	Carol Baier	USA ___
Murders and Acquisitions		Leigh Boyer	New Zealand ___
Unhealthy Heritage, An		Wayne Caldwell	Australia ___
Stealing Babies		Gill Chilton	UK ___
Unlucky With Women		J. Huw Evans	UK ___
Fortress in the Sea, The		Kirsty Evans	UK ___
Dying Angels		Alan Frost	UK ___
Talking Back to the Night		Almuth Heuner	Germany ___
Strength of Silk, The		Heidi Holzer	USA ___
Good Times and Hate Crimes		Joshua Kuritzky	USA ___
Backrun		Sue Lord	UK ___
Past Sins		Karen Lucas	UK ___
Fact or Fiction		Jane McCoy	UK ___
Celtic Connection, The		Marsali McDonald	UK ___
Beware the Anger		Lilias Odell	UK ___
Fattening Frogs for Snakes		Patricia Rainsford	Ireland ___
King's Desire, The		Shirley Rhodes	UK ___
Rough House		Marion Roberts	UK ___
Craze, The		Paul Southern	UK ___

2001

Clea's Moon		Edward Wright	USA ___
Blighted Cliffs, The	Runner-up	Edwin Thomas	UK ___
Blithe Psychopaths (Two-way Split)		Allan Buchan (Allan Guthrie)	Scotland ___

2000

Flowery Death, A		Simon Levack	___

1999

Blood Junction		Caroline Carver	___
Third Eye		Bernadette Brown	___
Question of Despair		Maureen Carter	___
Last Kashmiri Rose, The		Barbara Cleverly	___
Damned If You Do		M.P. Gillick	___
Babushka		Ann Monks	___
Eating People		Madaline Holland	___
Fatal Lie, A		Brian Hollywood	___
Colour Wheel, The		Sue Richards	___
Smoke's First Folly		Eric Sanborn	___

1998

Stone Baby	Joolz Denby	____
Top Hard	Stephen Booth	____
Blood Ties	Mrs F. Cunningham	____
Street Called Straight, The	Frederick Highland	____
Animals After Dark, The	Jeremy Holford	____
Mystery of Koenigberg, The	Michael G. Jacob	____
Estrella Damn	Matthew Loukes	____
Acid Gene, The	Roderick Maude	____
Bones in the Womb, The (Reckoning, The)	Patricia Tyrrell	____
Sleeping Cupid, The	M.J. Ward	____

CWA Last Laugh Daggers

First presented in 1988, and formerly known as The Punch Award, this award is for most humorous crime novel.

1996

Two for the Dough	Janet Evanovich	____
Of Wee Sweetie Mice and Men	Colin Bateman	____
Stormy Weather	Carl Hiaasen	____

1995

Sunburn	Laurence Shames	____
Ten Lords A-Leaping	Ruth Dudley Edwards	____
One for the Money	Janet Evanovich	____
Maxwell's Flame	M.J. Trow	____

1994

Villian of the Earth, The	Simon Shaw	____
Written in Blood	Caroline Graham	____
After All These Years	Susan Isaacs	____

1993

Mamur Zapt and the Spoils of Egypt	Michael Pearce	____
Poseidon's Gold	Lindsey Davis	____
Blood Sympathy	Reginald Hill	____

1992

Native Tongue	Carl Hiaasen	____
Clubbed to Death	Ruth Dudley Edwards	____
Mamur Zapt and the Girl in the Nile, The	Michael Pearce	____

1991

Angels in Arms	Mike Ripley	____
Corporate Bodies	Simon Brett	____
Mamur Zapt and the Men Behind, The	Michael Pearce	____

1990
Killer Cinderella — Simon Shaw — ____
Bertie and the Seven Bodies — Peter Lovesey — ____
Lestrade and the Guardian Angel — M.J. Trow — ____

1989
Angel Touch — Mike Ripley — ____
Monsieur Pamplemousse Aloft — Michael Bond — ____
Sirens Sang of Murder, The — Sarah Caudwell — ____
Rigby File, The (stories) — Tim Heald (ed.) — ____
Vane Pursuits — Charlotte MacLeod — ____

CWA Punch Prize

1988
Death in a Distant Land — Nancy Livingston — ____
Just Another Angel — Mike Ripley — ____

CWA Gold Dagger for Non-Fiction

In 1978, the CWA instituted the Gold Dagger for Non-Fiction Award, and for the years 1978-1979 also awarded The CWA Silver Dagger for Non-Fiction to the runner-up. Between 1995 and 2002, this award was sponsored by The Macallan and renamed The Macallan Gold Dagger for Non-Fiction. The award is currently sponsored by the membership of the CWA. The winner receives a financial gift as well as an ornamental dagger. This is a biennial award and will be presented in 2008.

2006
Dagenham Murder, The: The Brutal Killing of PC George Clark, 1846 — Linda Rhodes, Lee Sheldon & Kathryn Abnett — ____
Death in Belmont, A — Sebastian Junger — ____
Story of Chicago May, The — Nuala O'Faolain — ____
Death of Innocents, The: An Eyewitness Account of Wrongful Executions — Sister Helen Prejean — ____
Under and Alone: The True Story of the Undercover Agent Who Infiltrated America's Most Violent Outlaw Motercycle Gang — William Queen — ____
And Then the Darkness: The Disappearance of Peter Falconio and the Trials of Joanne Lees — Sue Williams — ____

2005
On the Run: A Life Lost in the Witness Protection Program — Gregg Hill & Gina Hill — ____
Wreckers, The: A Story of Killing Seas, False Lights and Plundered Ships — Bella Bathurst — ____
Last Duel, The: A True Story of Crime, Scandal, and Trial by Combat in Medieval France — Eric Jager — ____
Trial, The: A History, From Socrates to O.J. Simpson — Sadakat Kadri — ____
Serpent in Eden, A: The Greatest Murder Mystery of All Time — James Owen — ____

2004

Cosa Nostra: A History of the Sicilian Mafia (Tie)	John Dickie	____
Italian Boy, The: Murder and Grave Robbery in 1830s London (Tie)	Sarah Wise	____
Swamp of Death, The: A True Tale of Victorian Lies and Murder	Rebecca Gowers	____
Trials of Hank Janson, The: The True Story Behind the Censorship and Banning of Hank Janson's Books in the UK	Steve Holland	____
Slave: The True Story of a Girl's Lost Childhood and Her Fight for Survival	Mende Nazer & Damien Lewis	____

2003

Pointing From the Grave: A True Story of Murder and DNA	Samantha Weinberg	____
Wicked Beyond Belief: The Hunt for the Yorkshire Ripper	Michael Bilton	____
Devil in the White City, The: Murder, Magic, and Madness at the Fair that Changed America	Erik Larson	____
Imprint of the Raj: How Fingerprinting was Born in Colonial India	Chandak Sengoopta	____
Underworld at War: Spivs, Deserters, Racketeers and Civilians in the Second World War	Donald Thomas	____
Gang War: The Inside Story of the Manchester Gangs	Peter Walsh	____

2002

Dead Man's Wages	Lilian Pizzichini	____
Anthony Blunt, His Lives	Miranda Carter	____
Town Without Pity: The Fight to Clear Stephen Downing of the Bakewell Murder	Don Hale	____

2001

Infiltrators, The: Guns, Drugs, Deception, and Murder Duty Calls (Undercover With Scotland Yard)	Philip Etienne, Maynard Martin & Tony Thompson	____
Maggots, Murder and Men: Memories and Reflections of a Forensic Entomologist	Dr. Zacaria Erzinclioglu	____
Patriot Traitors: Roger Casement, John Amery, and the Real Meaning of Treason	Adrian Weale	____

2000

Mr. Blue: Memoirs of a Renegade	Edward Bunker ___
Cocky: The Rise and Fall of Curtis Warren,	Tony Barnes, Richard Elisa ___
Britain's Biggest Drug Baron	& Peter Walsh
Wainewright the Poisoner	Andrew Motion ___
Bloggs 19: The Story of the Essex Range Rover	Tony Thompson ___
Triple Murders	
Life and Death of Lord Erroll, The: The Truth	Errol Trzebinski ___
Behind the Happy Valley Murder	

1999

Case of Stephen Lawrence, The	Brian Cathcart ___
Dragon Syndicates, The: The Global Phenomenon	Martin Booth ___
of the Triads	
Sceptical Witness, The: Concerning the Scientific	Stuart S. Kind ___
Investigation of Crime Against a Human	
Background	

1998

Cries Unheard: Why Children Kill: The Story of	Gitta Sereny ___
Mary Bell	
Informer, The: The Real Life Story of One Man's	Sean O'Callaghan ___
War Against Terrorism	
Victorian Underworld, The	Donald Thomas ___

1997

Jigsaw Man, The: The Remarkable Career of	Paul Britton ___
Britain's Foremost Criminal Psychologist	
Unnatural Murder: Poison at the Court of James I	Anne Somerset ___
– The Overbury Murder	
Wild Justice: The Lynn Siddons Murder	Harry Pugh ___

1996

Gunpowder Plot, The: Terror and Faith in 1605	Antonia Fraser ___
Power to Harm, The: Mind, Medicine, and	John Cornwell ___
Murder on Trial	
Mindhunter: Inside the FBI's Elite Serial Crime Unit	John E. Douglas & Mark Olshaker ___

1995

Dead Not Buried	Martin Beales ___
Sellout: Aldrich Ames and the Corruption of the CIA	James Adams ___
Landmarks in 20th Century Murder	Robin Odell ___
Supergrasses and Informers: An Informal History of	James Morton ___
Undercover Police Work	

1994

Criminal Shadows: Inside the Mind of the Serial Killer — David Canter ——

Capone: The Man and the Era — Laurence Bergreen ——

Gangland: How the FBI Broke the Mob — Howard Blum ——

Crime: An Encyclopedia — Oliver Cyriax ——

Father's Story, A: One Man's Anguish at Confronting the Evil in His Son — Lionel Dahmer ——

Shot in the Heart: One Family's History in Murder — Mikal Gilmore ——

Death Benefit: A Lawyer Uncovers a Twenty-Year Pattern of Seduction, Arson and Murder — David Heilbroner ——

Gangland 2: The Underworld in Britain and Ireland — James Morton ——

Stranger Beside Me, The: Ted Bundy, The Shocking Inside Story — Ann Rule ——

Complete History of Jack the Ripper, The — Philip Sugden ——

Oscar Slater: Mystery Solved, The — Thomas Toughill ——

Blood Relations: Jeremy Bamber and the White House Farm Murders — Roger Wilkes ——

Remembering Satan: A Case of Recovered Memory and the Shattering of an American Family — Lawrence Wright ——

1993

Murder in the Heart: A True Life Psychological Thriller — Alexandra Artley ——

1992

Reckoning, The: The Murder of Christopher Marlow — Charles Nicholl ——

1991

Giordano Bruno and the Embassy Affair — John Bossy ——

Porthole Murder Case, The: The Death of Gay Gibson — Denis Herbstein ——

Women Who Kill: A Vivid History of America's Female Murderers from Colonial Times to the Present — Ann Jones ——

Lundy: The Destruction of Scotland Yard's Finest Detective — Martin Short ——

1990

Passing of Starr Faithfull, The — Jonathan Goodman ——

1989

Gathering of Saints, A: A True Story of Money, Murder and Deceit — Robert Lindsey ——

Thief in the Night, A: The Death of Pope John Paul I — John Cornwell ——

Bermondsey Horror, The: The Murder that Shocked Victorian England — Albert Borowitz ——

Who Framed Colin Wallace? — Paul Foot ——

Gumshoe: Reflections in a Private Eye — Josiah Thompson ——

Blooding, The: The True Story of the Narborough Village Murders — Joseph Wambaugh ——

1988

Secret Lives of Trebitsch Lincoln, The	Bernard Wasserstein	___
Thurtell-Hunt Muder Case, The: Dark Mirror to Regency England	Albert Borowitz	___
Mystery Reader's Walking Guide: London	Alzina Stone Dale & Barbara Sloan Hendershott	___
Bodysnatchers: A History of the Resurrectionists, 1742-1832	Martin Fido	___
Negotiator, The: Memoirs of the World's Most Successful Kidnap Expert	James March	___
Stalker	John Stalker	___
Murder at the Priory: The Mysterious Poisoning of Charles Bravo	Barnard Taylor & Kate Clarke	___
Criminal Justice: The True Story of Edith Thompson	Rene Weis	___

1987

Perfect Murder: A Century of Unsolved Homicides	Bernard Taylor & Stephen Knight	___

1986

Evil Angels: The Case of Lindy Chamberlain	John Bryson	___
At Mother's Request: A True Story of Money, Murder and Betrayal	Jonathan Coleman	___
Memories of Murder: The Great Cases of a Finger-Print Expert	Tony Fletcher	___
Murder at the Farm: Who Killed Carl Bridgewater?	Paul Foot	___
Surgeons at the Bailey: English Forensic Medicine to 1878	Thomas Forbes	___
A Cast of Killers: Murder of William Desmond Taylor	Sydney Kirkpatrick	___
Operation Seal Day	Pat Malloy	___

1985

Killing for Company: The Case of Dennis Nilsen	Brian Masters	___

1984

In God's Name: An Investigation into the Murder of Pope John Paul I	David Yallop	___

1983

Double Dealer	Peter Watson	___

1982

Earth to Earth: A True Story of the Lives and Violent Deaths of a Devon Farming Family	John Cornwell	___

1981

Prisoner Without a Name, Cell Without a Number	Jacobo Timerman	___

1980

Conspiracy: Who Killed President Kennedy?	Anthony Summers	___

1979

Rachman: The Slum Landlord Whose Name Became a Byword for Evil (G)	Shirley Green	___
Fraud: The Amazing Career of Dr. Savundra (S)	Jon Connell & Douglas Sutherland	___
Murderer's Who's Who, The: Outstanding Internation Cases from the Literature of Murder in the Last 150 Years	J.H.H. Gaute & Robin Odell	___
Menten Affair, The: For 30 Years the Dutch Millionaire Art Collector Hid the Terrible Secret of His Nazi Crimes	Hans Knoop	___
Life and Crimes of Charles Sobraj, The	Richard Neville & Julie Clarke	___
Murder of Rudolf Hess, The	Hugh Thomas	___

1978

Mystery of the Princes, The: An Investigation into a Supposed Murder (G)	Audrey Williamson	___
Capture of the Black Panther, The: Casebook of a Killer (S)	Harry Hawkes	___
Cops and Robbers: An Investigation Into Armed Bank Robbery	John Ball, Lewis Chester & Roy Parrott	___
Legend: The Secret World of Lee Harvey Oswald	E.J. Epstein	___
Forty Years of Murder: An Autobiography	Keith Simpson (professor)	___
Crime and the Penal Policy: Reflections on Fifty Years' Experience	Barbara Wootton	___

CWA Dagger in the Library

Formerly called the Golden Handcuffs, this prize is awarded to the (living) author who has given the most pleasure to readers. It is nominated by UK libraries and judged by a panel of librarians. New sponsorship from the Random House Group has enabled this award to be reinstated after a break of some years. The prize consists of an ornamental dagger and a financial gift.

2007	**Stuart MacBride**
2006	**Jim Kelly**
2005	**Jake Arnott**
2004	**Alexander McCall Smith**
2003	**Stephen Booth**
2002	**Peter Robinson**
1997–2001	in abeyance
1996	**Marian Babson**
1995	**Lindsey Davis**
1994	**Robert Barnard**
1993	**Margaret Yorke**
1992	**Catherine Aird**

CWA Cartier Diamond Dagger Lifetime Achievement Award

As the name suggests, this coveted award is sponsored by Cartier. The CWA committee selects writers nominated by the membership. Nominees have to meet two essential criteria: first, their careers must be marked by sustained excellence, and second, they must have made a significant contribution to crime fiction published in the English language, whether originally or in translation. The award is made purely on merit without reference to age, gender, or nationality.

2007	John Harvey
2006	Elmore Leonard
2005	Ian Rankin
2004	Lawrence Block
2003	Robert Barnard
2002	Sara Paretsky
2001	Lionel Davidson
2000	Peter Lovesey
1999	Margaret Yorke
1998	Ed McBain
1997	Colin Dexter
1996	H.R.F. Keating
1995	Reginald Hill
1994	Michael Gilbert
1993	Ellis Peters
1992	Leslie Charteris
1991	Ruth Rendell
1990	Julian Symons
1989	Dick Francis
1988	John le Carré
1987	P.D. James
1986	Eric Ambler

CWA Mystery Thriller Book Club People's Choice

Voted on by members of the Thriller Book Club.

2004

Good Morning, Midnight	Reginald Hill	___
Just One Look	Harlan Coben	___
Narrows, The	Michael Connelly	___
Torment of Others, The	Val McDermid	___
Third Degree	James Patterson	___
Indelible	Karin Slaughter	___

CWA Best Foreign Novel

1969

Father Hunter, The	Rex Stout	___

1968
Lady in the Car With Glasses and a Gun, The   Sebastien Japrisot   ____

1966
In the Heat of the Night   John Ball   ____

1964
Two Faces of January, The   Patricia Highsmith   ____

CWA Best British Novel

1967
Dirty Story   Eric Ambler   ____

1965
Midnight Plus One   Gavin Lyall   ____

CWA Short Story Award

This award was introduced in 1993 and was called The Short Story Dagger Award, later it was sponsored by The Macallan between 1995 and 2002. It is now sponsored by the membership of the CWA.

2007

"Needle Match"	Peter Lovesey	*Murder is My Racquet,* Penzler, ed.	____
"Epitaph"	J.A. Konrath	*Thriller: Stories to Keep You Up All Night*; Patterson, ed.	____
"Empathy"	James Siegel	*Thriller: Stories to Keep You Up All Night*; Patterson, ed.	____
"Retrospective"	Kevin Wignall	*Greatest Hits: Original Stories of Hitmen, Hired Guns, and Private Eyes*; Randisi, ed.	____

2006

"Sins of Scarlet"	Robert Barnard	*I.D. Crimes of Identity: The Crime Writers Association Anthology*, Edwards, ed.	____
"Loaded"	Ken Bruen	*London Noir: Capital Crime Fiction*, Unsworth, ed.	____
"Part-Time Job, The"	P.D. James	*The Detection Collection*	____
"Les's Story"	Stuart Pawson	*I.D. Crimes of Identity: The Crime Writers Association Anthology*, Edwards, ed.	____
"Love"	Martyn Waites	*London Noir: Capital Crime Fiction*, Unsworth, ed.	____

2005

"No Flies on Frank"	Danuta Reah	*Sherlock Mag*, issue 64	___
"Miss Froom, Vampire"	John Connolly	*Nocturnes*; Connolly	___
"Test Drive"	Martin Edwards	*Crime on the Move*; Edwards, ed.	___
"Top Deck"	Kate Ellis	*Crime on the Move*; Edwards, ed.	___
"Wrong Hands, The"	Peter Robinson	*Not Safe After Dark & Other Short Works*; Robinson	___

2004

"Weekender, The"	Jeffery Deaver	*Twisted*; Deaver	___
"Dancing Towards the Blade"	Mark Billingham	*Men From Boys*; Harvey, ed.	___
"Persons Reported"	Mat Coward	*Green for Danger*; Edwards, ed.	___
"Consolation Blonde, The"	Val McDermid	*Mysterious Pleasures*; Edwards, ed.	___
"Douggie Doughnuts"	Don Winslow	*Men From Boys*; Harvey, ed.	___

2003

"Closer to the Flame"	Jerry Sykes	*Crime in the City*; Edwards, ed.	___
"Dollface"	Marion Arnott	*Sleepwalkers*; Arnott	___
"Doctor's Orders"	Judith Cutler	*Best British Mysteries*; Jakubowski, Allison & Busby, eds.	___
"Les Inconnus"	Kate Ellis	*Crime in the City*; Edwards, ed.	___
"Ester Gordon Framlingham"	Anthony Mann	*Crimewave 7: The Last Sunset*; Cox, ed.	___

2002

"Martha Grace"	Stella Duffy	*Tart Noir*; Duffy & Henderson, eds.	___
"Marbles"	Marion Arnott	*Crimewave 6: Breaking Point*; Cox, ed.	___
"Plater, The"	Ann Cleeves	*Murder Squad*; Edwards, ed.	___
"Kick in the Lunchbucket, A"	Sean Doolittle	*Crimewave 5: Dark Before Dawn*; Cox, ed.	___

2001

"Prussian Snowdrops"	Marion Arnott	*Crimewave 4: Mood Indigo*; Cox, ed.	___
"Leaving Seven Sisters"	Simon Avery	*Crimewave 4: Mood Indigo*; Cox, ed.	___
"Trebuchet Murder, The"	Susanna Gregory	*Murder Through the Ages*; Jakubowski, ed.	___
"Dark Mirror"	Lauren Henderson	*Murder Through the Ages*; Jakubowski, ed.	___
"Miles to Go Before I Weep"	Brian Hodge	*Crimewave 4: Mood Indigo*; Cox, ed.	___

2000

"Helena and the Babies"	Denise Mina	*Fresh Blood 3*; Ripley & Jakubowski, eds.
"Bad Boyz Klub"	Doug Allyn	*Diagnosis Dead;* Kellerman, ed.
"For All the Saints"	Gillian Linscott	*Chronicles of Crime*; Jakubowski, ed.
"Blue Devils"	James Sallis	*AHMM,* Aug 96

1999

"Taking Care of Frank"	Anthony Mann	*Crimewave 2: Deepest Red;* Coward & Cox, eds.
"Damned Spot"	Julian Rathbone	*Past Poisons*; Jakuboswki, ed.
"Symptoms of Loss"	Jerry Sykes	*Crimewave 1 - EQMM,* Apr 00

1998

"Roots"	Jerry Sykes	*Mean Time;* Sykes, ed.
"Master Eld, His Wayzgoose"	Chaz Brenchley	*Shakespearean Detectives*; Ashley, ed.
"Hanged Man, The"	Ian Rankin	*BBC Radio,* for broadcast
"Unknown Pleasures"	Ian Rankin	*Mean Time*; Sykes, ed.

1997

"On the Psychiatrist's Couch"	Reginald Hill	*Whydunit*; Edwards, ed.
"Bampot Central"	Christopher Brookmyre	*Fresh Blood 2;* Ripley & Jakubowski, eds.
"Stranglehold"	Phil Lovesey	*Fresh Blood 2*; Ripley & Jakubowski, eds.

1996

"Herbert in Motion"	Ian Rankin	*Perfectly Criminal*; Edwards, ed.
"Day I Gave Up Smoking, The"	Chaz Benchley	*Blood Waters*; Benchley
"Surprise of His Life, The"	Elizabeth George	*Women on the Case*; Paretsky, ed.
"Disposing of Mrs. Cronk"	Peter Lovesey	*Perfectly Criminal*; Edwards, ed.

1995

"Funny Story"	Larry Beinhart	*No Alibi*; Jakubowski, ed.
"News, As It Happens"	Denise Danks	*No Alibi*; Jakubowski, ed.
"Where the Snow Lay Dinted"	Reginald Hill	*Northern Blood II*; Edwards, ed.
"Quite Please–We're Rolling"	Peter Lovesey	*No Alibi*; Jakubowski, ed.
"Guilty Party, The"	Susan Moody	*No Alibi*; Jakubowski, ed.
"Odd Coincidence, An"	James Pattinson	*Anglian Blood*; Church & Edwards, eds.
"Blood Lines"	Ruth Rendell	*Blood Lines*; Rendell
"Flat Share"	Judith Saxton	*Anglian Blood*; Church & Edwards, eds.
"Dead-Head"	Penny Sumner	*Reader, I Murdered Him, Too*; Windrath, ed.

1994

"Deep Hole, A"	Ian Rankin	London Noir; Jakubowski, ed.	___
"Last of Kin"	Jo Bannister	Crime Yellow; Jakubowski, ed.	___
"One of Those Days, One of Those Nights"	Ed Gorman	Crime Yellow; Jakubowski, ed.	___
"And She Laughed"	Liz Holliday	London Noir; Jakubowski, ed.	___

1993

"Some Sunny Day"	Julian Rathbone	Constable New Crimes 2; Jakubowski, ed.	___
"History Repeats Itself and Doesn't Even Say Pardon"	Mat Coward	Constable New Crimes 2; Jakubowski, ed.	___
"Mood Cuckoo, The"	Jonathan Gash	2nd Culprit; Cody & Lewin, eds.	___
"Vacance en Campagne, A"	Tim Heald	*EQMM,* Jun 93	___
"Death of a Dead Man"	Gillian Linscott	Midwinter Mysteries 3; Hale, ed.	___
"Sweetheart of the Rodeo"	Mark Timlin	Constable New Crimes 2; Jakubowski, ed.	___

CWA Rumpole Award

The *Rumpole Award* was given for the best crime novel portraying the British legal procedure.

1992

Hatred and Contempt	Peter Rawlinson	___

1990

Trial by Fire (Not that Kind of Place)	Frances Fyfield	___

CWA '92 Award

The best crime novel set in Continental Europe (in honour of the European Economic Community).

1992

Black August	Timothy Williams	___
Peckover Joins the Choir	Michael Kenyon	___
Hard News	James Long	___

1991

Gaudi Collective	Barbara Wilson	___
Dante Game, The	Jane Langton	___
Sister Beneath the Sheet	Gillian Linscott	___
Dangerous Games	Julian Rathbone	___

1990

Vendetta	Michael Dibdin	___
Raphael Affair, The	Iain Pears	___
End of Lieutenant Boruvka, The	Josef Skvorecky	___

CWA Rusty Dagger—Best Crime Novel of the 1930s

1934	*Nine Tailors, The*	Dorothy L. Sayers	____
1939	*Mask of Dimitrios, The (A Coffin for Dimitrios)*	Eric Ambler	____
1938	*Brighton Rock*	Graham Greene	____
1939	*Rogue Male (Man Hunt)*	Geoffrey Household	____
1932	*Malice Aforethought*	Francis Iles	____

CWA Dagger of Daggers (2005)

On the Golden Jubilee year, 2005, the membership of the CWA voted the "best of the best" novel from all of the previous Crossed Red Herring and Gold Dagger winners of the past. The results were:

1963	*Spy Who Came in From the Cold, The*	John le Carre	____
1990	*Bones and Silence*	Reginald Hill	____
1982	*False Inspector Dew, The*	Peter Lovesey	____
1995	*Mermaids Singing, The*	Val McDermid	____
1974	*Other Paths to Glory*	Anthony Price	____
1981	*Gorky Park*	Martin Cruz Smith	____
1987	*Fatal Inversion, A*	Barbara Vine	____

www.thecwa.co.uk/

CWA—The Crime Writer's Crimewriter

In 1998, to commemorate the 500th issue of the *Red Herring* magazine of CWA, the members conducted a poll with the following results.

The Crimewriter's Crimewriter
> **Raymond Chandler**
> Agatha Christie
> Dorothy L. Sayers

The Crimewriters' Crime Novel

1934	*Nine Tailors, The*	Dorothy L. Sayers	____
1939	*Big Sleep, The*	Raymond Chandler	____
1868	*Moonstone, The*	Wilkie Collins	____

The Crimewriters' Crime Series
> **Raymond Chandler's Philip Marlowe series**
> Dorothy L. Sayers's Lord Peter Wimsey series
> Sir Arthur Conan Doyle's Sherlock Holmes series

First Blood Award for Best 1st Crime Novel (Outside the CWA)

CWA did not name a winner for the Creasey Award in 1996, but an independent group of critics did name a book for that year and issued the First Blood Award for Best 1st Crime Novel.

1996

Quite Ugly One Morning	Christopher Brookmyre	____
Rilke on Black	Ken Bruen	____
Ruby	Gerry Byrne	____
Monkey House, The	John Fullerton	____
Goodnight, My Angel	Margaret Murphy	____
Hen's Teeth	Manda Scott	____

Derringer Awards

The Derringer Awards were created in 1997 by the Short Mystery Fiction Society (SMFS) to honor excellence in the creative artform of short mystery and crime fiction stories. The name "Derringer," after the palm-sized handgun, was chosen as a metaphor for a short Mystery or Crime story—small, but deadly.

Any mystery or crime story published in a professional print or electronic magazine or book length anthology is eligible for a Derringer. The author does not have to be a member of SMFS to be considered. Winners in each category are chosen by an SMFS member vote. In September 2007, the membership voted to change the award groupings to the following:

> Best Story 1,000 words or less
> Best Story 1,001 to 4,000 words
> Best Story 4,001 to 8,000 words
> Best Story 8,001 to 17,500 words

Many of these stories can be found online and others in books and magazines of short stories. Some of the sources listed have ceased publication or online availability. Try computer search engines to locate some of these works.

Derringer Best Flash Story

(up to 500 words)

2007

"Vigilante"	Barry Ergang	Mysterical-E, Summer 06	____
"Matched Set"	Jan Christensen	*Long Story Short*, Winter 06	____
"Snowflake Therapy"	Michelle Mach	*Thereby Hangs a Tale*, Jun 06	____
"Flight School"	Jill Maser	*Flashshots*, Aug 28, 06	____
"Home Entertainment"	Sandra Seamans	*A Cruel World*, Jul/Aug 06	____

2006

"Secondhand Shoe"	Patricia Harrington	*A Flasher's Dozen*, Winter 05	____
"Hell Hath No Fury"	B.J Bourg	Mysterical-E, Mar 05	____
"Word Power"	Michelle Mach	*Flashshot*, Mar 05	____
"No Atheists in Foxholes"	Stephen D. Rogers	*Kwichee*, May 05	____
"Last Journey, The"	Mary Schenten	*Flashshot*, Jul 05	____

2005

"Big Guys, The"	J.A. Konrath	*Small Bites;* Peck & Gouveia, eds.	____
"Sand Scam"	Nick Andreychuk	*Crimestalker Casebook*, Fall 04	____
"Theda"	Beverly Brackett	*Flash Fantastic*, Nov 04	____
"Housesitter"	J.K. Cummins	*Futures*, Summer 04	____
"Widow's Peak"	S.A. Daynard	*Riptide: Crime Stories by New England Writers;* Alexander, Flora & Oleksiw, eds.	____

2004

"All My Yesterdays"	Michael Bracken	*Suddenly V*; Pelham, ed.	___
"Patience"	Nick Andreychuk	*Futures,* Fall 03	___
"Motive for Murder"	Guy Belleranti	*Futures,* Spring 03	___
"How to Become a Rodeo Queen"	Michelle Mach	*Mslexia,* Oct 03	___
"At Thirty Paces"	Graydon Miller	*The Havana Brotherhood*	___

2001

"Polls Don't Lie" (Tie)	Earl McGill	*Blue Murder Mag*	___
"New Lawyer, The" (Tie)	Mike Wiecek	*Crimestalker Casebook,* Spring 00	___
"Accident"	Guy Belleranti	*About.com Mysteries,* May 9, 00	___
"Sunken Dreams"	Tim Myers	*Futures,* Dec 00	___
"Lucky Man"	Ali Seay	*About.com Mysteries*	___

1999

"Pretty Kitty"	Joyce Holland	*Murderous Intent,* Winter 98	___
"Exchange of Information"	Kimberly Brown	*TheCase.com* (Flash 49), Feb 6, 98	___
"Key to Success"	Richard Ciciarelli	*TheCase.com* (Twist 98), Nov 4, 98	___
"Christmas Guest, The"	Dorothy Francis	*TheCase.com* (Twist 103), Dec 16, 98	___
"Checkmate!"	Dale B. Hall	*TheCase.com* (Flash 65), Oct 2, 98	___
"Rough Times"	Paul Harrison	*TheCase.com* (Flash 51), Mar 6, 98	___
"Mother's Helper"	John Hermann	*Murderous Intent,* Spring 98	___
"Pocket Picked"	Jesse Knight	*TheCase.com* (Twist 69), Mar 18, 98	___
"Used Car, The"	Sheryl Snell-Massie	*TheCase.com* (Flash 55), May 1, 98	___
"Daddy's Pet"	Fay Thompson	*TheCase.com* (Twist), Jan 14, 98	___
"Other Woman, The"	Kate Thornton	*TheCase.com* (Twist 96), Oct 21, 98	___
"Anything for the Chief"	Linda K. Wright (as, Geri Myerson)	*TheCase.com* (Twist 95), Oct 14, 98	___

1998

"Curiosity Kills"	Michael Mallory	*Murderous Intent,* Fall 97	___

Derringer Best Short-Short Story

(501 - 2,000 words)

2007

"Four for Dinner" (Tie)	John M. Floyd	*Seven by Seven*; Burton, ed.	____
"Elena Speaks of the City, Under Siege" (Tie)	Steven Torres	*Crimespree Mag* Sept/Oct 06	____
"Even Steven"	Gail Farrelly	*Mouth Full of Bullets*, Winter 06	____
"Interview"	Justin Gustainis	*Cape Fear Crime Festival*, Oct 06	____
"Worst Door, The "	Frank Zafiro	*Dispatch*, Jan 06	____

2006

"Zipped"	Stephen D. Rogers	*Windchill: Crime Stories by New England Writers*; Alexander, Flora & Oleksiw, eds.	____
"Hangman's Tree"	Deanne Boast	*Crime and Suspense*, Dec 05	____
"Day the Bad Men Came, The"	Andy Henion	*Thieves Jargon*, Jan 14, 05	____
"Roses at His Feet"	Todd Robinson	*ThugLit*, Issue #4, Dec 05	____
"Twilight of the Fireflies"	John Weagly	*Big Muddy, A Journal of the Mississippi River Valley*, Dec 05	____

2005

"Test, The"	Mike Wiecek	*Woman's World*, Nov 20, 04	____
"Up in Smoke"	Jan Christensen	*Futures*, Jan/Mar 04	____
"Experience Required"	Michael Giorgio	*Lunatic Chameleon*, Mar 04	____
"Sweet Smell of Success"	Beverle Graves Myers	*Who Died in Here?*, Dennis, ed.	____
"Big Store, The"	Stephen D. Rogers	*Hardluck Stories*, Spring 04	____

2004

"Nailbiter"	Robert Lopresti	*AHMM*, Sept 03	____
"Coyotes Find"	Gay Toltl Kinman	*Detective Mystery Stories*, Feb 03	____
"Waiter, There's a Clue in My Soup"	Camille LaGuire	*Futures*, Spring 03	____
"Children Seen and Heard"	K.G. McAbee	*EWG Presents: Without a Clue*, Jul 03	____
"Packy Run"	Stephen D. Rogers	*Hardluck Stories*, Spring 03	____
"Silky's Getaway"	Earl Staggs	*Futures*, Summer 03	____

2003

"Cut Above, A"	Del Tinsley	*Hardluck Stories,* Fall 02	___
"Sending Out an S.O.S."	Nick Andreychuk	*Futures,* Apr/Jun 02	___
"Jumping the Fence"	Stephen D. Rogers	*Hardluck Stories,* Fall 02	___
"What a Day"	Seymour Shubin	*Futures,* Jan 02	___
"Shark Infested Pudding"	John Weagly	*Judas Ezine,* Nov 02	___

2002

"In the Heat of the Moment"	Nick Andreychuk	*Futures,* Feb 01	___
"Greenhouse Pest"	Tim Myers	*Futures,* Nov 01	___
"Matter of Interest, A"	Stephen D. Rogers	*Hand Held Crime,* Sept 01	___
"Lucrezia and the Thief"	Henry Slesar	*EQMM,* Apr 01	___

2000

"When in Rome" (Tie)	Dorothy Francis	*Murderous Intent,* Dec/Jan 00	___
"Just a Man on the Sidewalk" (Tie)	Carol Kilgore	*TheCase.com* Mar 99	___
"Blind Justice"	Lynda Douglas	*Novel Advice,* Aug 15, 99	___
"Absent-Minded"	L.C. Mohr	*Futures,* Jun/Jul 99	___
"Armored Car, The"	Tim Myers	*MysteryNet Twist,* Aug 4, 99 (Woman's World, Feb 17, 97)	___

1998

"Guavaberry Christmas"	Kate Grilley	*Murderous Intent,* v3 #4, Fall 97	___

Derringer Best Mid-Length Short Story

(2,001 - 6,000 words)

2007

"Cranked"	Bill Crider	*Damn Near Dead: An Anthology of Geezer Noir;* Swierczynski, ed.	___
"Eden's Bodyguard"	David Bareford	*ThugLit,* Sept 06	___
"Shadow People"	Rex Burns	*AHMM,* Jun 06	___
"Uncle Blinky's Corner of the World"	Robert S. Levinson	*EQMM,* Mar/Apr 06	___
"Shanks on the Prowl"	Robert Lopresti	*AHMM,* May 06	___

2006

"One Step Closer"	Iain Rowan	*Hardluck Stories,* Spring 05	____
"Best Wishes"	J.R. Chabot	*Futures* (FMAM), Sept/Oct 05	____
"Spare, The"	Woody Hanstein	*Windchill: Crime Stories by New England Writers;* Alexander, Flora & Oleksiw, eds.	____
"Johnny Cash is Dead"	Jordan Harper	*ThugLit,* Issue #2, Oct 05	____
"Death in Ueno, A"	Mike Wiecek	*AHMM,* Mar 05	____

2005

"Viscery"	Sandra Balzo	*EQMM,* Dec 04	____
"Phillie's Last Dance"	Ray Banks	*Shots Mag,* Mar 04	____
"Brethren of the Sea"	Joan Druett	*AHMM,* Nov 04	____
"Freddie Swings In"	David Terrenoire	*Fedora III;* Bracken, ed.	____
"Hilly Palmer's Last Case"	Duane Swierczynski	*Plots With Guns,* Sept/Oct 04	____

2004

"Notions of the Real World"	Dorothy Rellas	*Futures,* Summer 03	____
"Mother Scorned, A"	Michele R. Bardsley	Writer's Digest/ mobipocket.com /A Mother Scorned & Other Stories	____
"Big Winner"	Terry Black	*AHMM,* Nov 03	____
"Sara Morningsky"	Lee Driver	*A Mystery in Mind,* Mar 03	____
"Wanda Wilcox is Trapped"	Eddie Muller	*Plots With Guns,* Sept/Oct 03	____

Derringer Best Longer Short Story

(6,001 - 15,000 words)

2007

"Strictly Business"	Julie Hyzy	*These Guns for Hire;* Konrath, ed.	____
"Signature in Blood"	Annette Dashofy	Mysterical-E, Winter 2006	____
"Daphne MacAndrews and the Smack-Head Junkies"	Stuart MacBride	*Damn Near Dead: An Anthology of Geezer Noir;* Swierczynski, ed.	____
"See Also Murder"	Larry Sweazy	*Amazon Shorts,* Dec 11, 06	____
"Valley of Angustias, The"	Steven Torres	*AHMM,* Oct 06	____

2006

"Safest Place on Earth, The"	Mark Best	*Thrilling Detective,* Spring 05	____
"Monday, Sweet Monday"	John F. Dobbyn	*AHMM,* Jun 05	____
"Fish"	Stephen Johnston	*Web Mystery Mag.,* Fall 05	____
"Cherries of Lucullus, The"	Steven Saylor	*EQMM,* May 05	____
"Good Shepherd"	Frank Zafiro	*Ascent Aspirations,* Nov 05	____

2005

"Secondhand Heart"	Doug Allyn	*AHMM,* Jan/Feb 04	___
"Sunday in Ordinary Time, A"	Terence Faherty	*EQMM,* Aug 04	___
"Girl in Apartment 2A, The"	G. Miki Hayden	*Dime* 2004; Lakey, ed.	___
"Franklin Fiasco, The"	Beverle Graves Myers	*AHMM,* Sept 04	___
"God's Dice"	David White	Thrilling Detective web site, Spring 04	___

2004

"Mask of Peter, The"	Clark Howard	*EQMM,* Apr 03	___
"Bombshell"	Loren D. Estleman	*EQMM,* Aug 03	___
"Windsor Ballet, The"	Deborah Morgan	*Flesh and Blood: Guilty as Sin*; Collins & Gelb, eds.	___
"Henry and the Idiots"	Robert J. Randisi	*High Stakes*; Randisi, ed.	___
"Amazing Grace"	Harriet Rzetelny	*AHMM,* Feb 03	___

2003

"Murder Ballads, The"	Doug Allyn	*EQMM,* Mar 02	___
"Medicine Water"	David Edgerley Gates	*AHMM,* Sept 02	___
"To Live and Die in Midland, Texas"	Clark Howard	*EQMM,* Sept/Oct 02	___
"Painter of the Seven-Eyed Beast"	Catherine Mambretti	*AHMM,* Nov 02	___
"Henry's Power"	Bob Stevens	*Hand Held Crime,* Mar 02	___

2002

"Early Morning Rain"	Jean McCord	*Futures,* Oct 01	___
"Harry's Lament"	Bentley Dadmun	*EQMM,* Jun 01	___
"Lesser-Included Offense"	Jeffery Deaver	*EQMM,* May 01	___
"Mondo Whammy, The"	David Handler	*EQMM,* Sept/Oct 01	___
"Avenging Miriam"	Peter Sellers	*EQMM,* Dec 01	___

Derringer Best Novella

2001

Lilacs and Lace	Lynda Douglas	*Futures,* Jun 00	___
Death Row Pet Show, The	Doug Allyn	*EQMM,* Apr 00	___
Attitude Thing	William J. Carroll. Jr.	*AHMM,* May 00	___
Blood Paths	Clark Howard	*EQMM,* Jun 00	___
Sedgemoor Strangler, The	Peter Lovesey	*Criminal Records*; Penzler, ed.	___

2000

Saint Bobby	Doug Allyn	*EQMM,* Apr 99	___
Death in the Dales	C.M. Chan	*AHMM,* Jan 99	___
Annie's Dream	Bentley Dadmun	*AHMM,* Dec 99	___

1998

Image of Conspiracy"	Margo Power	*Image of Conspiracy: A Mystery Adventure*	___

Derringer Best Short Story

2003

"Closure"	David White	Thrilling Detective web site, Fall 02	___
"Top of the World"	Bill Crider	*Flesh and Blood: Dark Desires*; Collins & Gelb, eds.	___
"Just Looking"	Bill Pronzini	*Flesh and Blood: Dark Desires*; Collins & Gelb, eds.	___
"Mexican Gatsby"	Raymond Steiber	*EQMM,* Mar 02	___
"More Than a Scam"	Dave Zeltserman	Mysterical-E	___

2002

"All the Fine Actors"	Earl Staggs	*EWG Presents: Without a Clue,* Apr 01	___
"Cuts Like a Knife"	Michael Bracken	*Fedora: Private Eyes & Tough Guys;* Bracken, ed.	___
"Smoky Didn't Send Me"	Charles Cutter	*AHMM,* Dec 01	___
"Tunnel of Malice"	Margaret DiCanio	*Futures,* Oct 01	___
"Last Letter, The"	Mike Wiecek	*AHMM,* Jan 02	___

2001

"Erie's Last Day"	Steve Hockensmith	*AHMM,* May 00	___
"Disappearance of Miss Sarah Oswald, The"	Jennifer Ashley	*Over My Dead Body #7,* Spring 00	___
"Amish Butter"	Jacqueline Fiedler	*Unholy Orders*; Stevens, ed.	___
"Dark Tower, The"	Gwen Moffat	Malice Domestic 9; Hess, pre.	___
"Tom Wasp and Anybody's Child"	Amy Myers	*Scenes of Crime*; Edwards, ed.	___

2000

"Way to a Man's Heart, The"	Elizabeth Dearl	TheCase.Com Twist, Feb 10, 99	___
"One More Kill"	Matt Hughes	*Blue Murder Mag,* Dec 99	___
"Let Sleeping Dogs Lie"	Chris Huntington	*Blue Murder Mag #9*	___
"Bread of Affliction, The"	Michael A. Kahn	*EQMM,* Sept/Oct 99	___
"Taking Care of Frank"	Anthony Mann	*Crimewave 2: Deepest Red*; Coward & Cox, eds.	___

1999

"Capital Justice"	Kris Neri	*Blue Murder Mag #1*	___
"Murder of Ernest Trapnell, The"	Erik Arneson	*Mary Higgins Clark Mystery Mag,* Fall 98	___
"Gator Bayou"	Joyce Holland	*Fogfire Mag,* Spring 98	___
"Deadly Diamonds, The"	Robert Iles	*Blue Murder Mag #5,* 98	___
"To the Farm"	Dina Leacock (as, Dianne Arrelle)	*Blue Murder Mag #2*	___
"Loss of Income, A"	Seymour Shubin	*Murderous Intent,* Spring 98	___

"Just Like in the Movies"	Kate Thornton	*Blue Murder Mag*	___
"Drop Dead Zone"	M.E. Troy	*Mystery Buff Mag*, Apr 98	___
"Two Tickets to Paradise"	Barbara White-Rayczek	*Death Knell III*	___

1998

"Adventurers, The" (Tie)	Barbara White-Rayczek	*Murderous Intent,* Winter 97	___
"L.A. Justice" (Tie)	Kris Neri	*Murder by 13*; English, Seidman & Woods, eds.	___

Derringer Best 1st Short Story

2000

"Death in Full Bloom"	Ray Wonderly	*Futures,* Aug 99	___

1998

"Back Stairs"	Eileen Brosnan	*Murderous Intent,* Fall 97	___

Derringer Best Puzzle Story

2001

"Cabin Killer, The"	Henry Slesar	*EQMM,* Jul 00	___
"Happy Acres Homicide"	Richard Ciciarelli	Solve-It #227, MysteryNet.com	___
"Killing the Old Survivors"	Gary Sensening	Solve-It #215, MysteryNet.com	___

Golden Derringer for Lifetime Achievement

2001	**John Lutz**
2000	**Henry Slesar**
1999	**Edward D. Hoch**

www.shortmystery.net/derringers.html

Edgar Allan Poe Sesquicentennial Homage Award

The Short Mystery Fiction Society along with *Murderous Intent Mystery Magazine* sponsored a Poe Tribute Short Story Contest on the 150th anniversary of the passing of Edgar Allan Poe. The contest was open to members of SMFS and the readers of *MIMM*. This award was not connected in any way to the Mystery Writers of America or the Edgar® Awards. The results are as follows:

1999

"Montressor Hit, The"	Mark Troy	*Murderous Intent Mystery Mag*; Fall 99	___
"Cave Cask"	Glynn Marsh Alam		___
"Second Hand Smoke"	E.J. McGill		___
"Poetic Justice"	James L. Oddie		___
"Midnight Dreary"	D.C. Thomas		___

Text of the winning selection: www.tamu.edu/marshome/staff_pages/Montress.pdf

Dilys Award

The Dilys Award was named for pioneering mystery bookseller Dilys Winn, the founder of the first specialty bookseller of mystery books in the United States. It is awarded each year by the Independent Mystery Booksellers Association (IMBA) to the book members most enjoyed selling over the past year. The award began in 1992 and is usually presented at the Left Coast Crime Conference.

Dilys Award

2007
Still Life	Louise Penny	____
Billy Boyle	James R. Benn	____
Holmes on the Range	Steve Hockensmith	____
Mournful Teddy, The	John J. Lamb	____
Virgin of Small Plains, The	Nancy Pickard	____
Thirteenth Tale, The	Diane Setterfield	____

2006
Thirty-Three Teeth	Colin Cotterill	____
In a Teapot	Terence Faherty	____
Half Broken Things	Morag Joss	____
Cold Dish, The	Craig Johnson	____
Power of the Dog, The	Don Winslow	____
Tenor Wore Tap Shoes, The	Mark Schweizer	____

2005
Darkly Dreaming Dexter	Jeff Lindsay	____
Enemy, The	Lee Child	____
Something Rotten	Jasper Fforde	____
Intelligencer, The	Leslie Silbert	____
Birds of a Feather	Jacqueline Winspear	____
Shadow of the Wind, The	Carlos Ruiz Zafon	____

2004
Lost in a Good Book	Jasper Fforde	____
Crouching Buzzard, Leaping Loon	Donna Andrews	____
Sixth Larnentation, The	William Brodrick	____
Monkeewrench	P.J. Tracy	____
Maisie Dobbs	Jacqueline Winspear	____

2003
In the Bleak Midwinter	Julia Spencer-Fleming	____
You've Got Murder	Donna Andrews	____
Without Fail	Lee Child	____
Eyre Affair, The	Jasper Fforde	____
Hell to Pay	George P. Pelecanos	____

2002
Mystic River — Dennis Lehane — ___
Cold Blue Blood, The — David Handler — ___
Dead Until Dark — Charlaine Harris — ___
Purgatory Ridge — William Kent Krueger — ___
Reaper, The — Peter Lovesey — ___

2001
Place of Execution, A — Val McDermid — ___
Sibyl in Her Grave, The — Sarah Caudwell — ___
Demolition Angel — Robert Crais — ___
Hot Six — Janet Evanovich — ___
Hearse You Came in On, The — Tim Cockey — ___

2000
L.A. Requiem — Robert Crais — ___
River of Darkness — Rennie Airth — ___
Murder With Peacocks — Donna Andrews — ___
Boundary Waters — William Kent Krueger — ___
California Fire and Life — Don Winslow — ___

1999
Gone, Baby, Gone — Dennis Lehane — ___
Blind Descent — Nevada Barr — ___
Ghosts of Morning, The — Richard Barre — ___
Sunset Limited — James Lee Burke — ___
Iron Lake — William Kent Krueger — ___
Wings of Fire — Charles Todd — ___

1998
Three to Get Deadly — Janet Evanovich — ___
Killing Floor — Lee Child — ___
Back Spin — Harlan Coben — ___
Sacred — Dennis Lehane — ___
Deja Dead — Kathy Reichs — ___
Devil in Music, The — Kate Ross — ___

1997
Poet, The — Michael Connelly — ___
Fade Away — Harlan Coben — ___
Hearts and Bones — Margaret Lawrence — ___
Darkness, Take My Hand — Dennis Lehane — ___
Tularosa — Michael McGarrity — ___
Moody Gets the Blues — Steve Oliver — ___
Dance for the Dead — Thomas Perry — ___
Test of Wills, A — Charles Todd — ___

1996

Last Coyote, The	Michael Connelly	____
Voodoo River	Robert Crais	____
Who in Hell is Wanda Fuca?	G.M. Ford	____
If I'd Killed Him When I Met Him	Sharyn McCrumb	____
Codicil, The	Tom Topor	____

1995

One for the Money	Janet Evanovich	____
Do Unto Others	Jeff Abbott	____
Aunt Dimity and the Duke	Nancy Atherton	____
Superior Death, A	Nevada Barr	____
Concrete Blonde, The	Michael Connelly	____
Mallory's Oracle	Carol O'Connell	____
Walking Rain	Susan Wade	____

1994

Smilla's Sense of Snow (Miss Smilla's Feeling for Snow)	Peter Hoeg	____
Death Comes as Epiphany	Sharan Newman	____
Wolf in the Shadows	Marcia Muller	____
By Evil Means	Sandra West Prowell	____
Catilina's Riddle	Steven Saylor	____
Sculptress, The	Minette Walters	____
Way Down on the High Lonely	Don Winslow	____

1993

Booked to Die	John Dunning	____
Black Echo, The	Michael Connelly	____
Bootlegger's Daughter	Margaret Maron	____
Ice House, The	Minette Walters	____

1992

Native Tongue	Carl Hiaasen	____
Suitable Vengeance, A	Elizabeth George	____
Book Case	Stephen Greenleaf	____
Hour of the Hunter	J.A. Jance	____
We Wish You a Merry Murder	Valerie Wolzien	____

www.mysterybooksellers.com/dilys.html

Edgar® Mystery Awards
Mystery Writers of America

The Mystery Writers of America (MWA) was founded in 1945. It is the premier organization for mystery writers, professionals related to the crime writing field, aspiring crime writers, and those who are devoted to the genre in America. Each spring they present the coveted Edgar® Allan Poe Awards in New York City in numerous categories. The "Edgar®," given in name of Edgar Allan Poe, was first presented in 1946.

As an organization, MWA promotes crime writing in numerous ways. They provide scholarships for writers, sponsor Kids Love a Mystery, sponsor symposia and conferences, conduct activities to further the appreciation and high regard for crime writing, and present the Edgar® Awards.

They have a wonderful web site with a comprehensive list of their awards and various activities: mysterywriters.org/index.htm.

Edgar® Best Novel

2007

Janissary Tree, The	Jason Goodwin	____
Pale Blue Eye, The	Louis Bayard	____
Gentleman and Players	Joanne Harris	____
Dead Hour, The	Denise Mina	____
Virgin of Small Plains, The	Nancy Pickard	____
Liberation Movements, The	Olen Steinhauer	____

2006

Citizen Vince	Jess Walter	____
Lincoln Lawyer, The	Michael Connelly	____
Red Leaves	Thomas H. Cook	____
Vanish	Tess Gerritsen	____
Drama City	George P. Pelecanos	____

2005

California Girl	T. Jefferson Parker	____
Evan's Gate	Rhys Bowen	____
By a Spider's Thread	Laura Lippman	____
Remembering Sarah	Chris Mooney	____
Out of the Deep I Cry	Julia Spencer-Fleming	____

2004

Resurrection Men	Ian Rankin	____
Guards, The	Ken Bruen	____
Lost Light (withdrawn, he served as president)	Michael Connelly	____
Out	Natsuo Kirino	____
Maisie Dobbs	Jacqueline Winspear	____

2003
Winter and Night	S.J. Rozan	___
Savannah Blues	Mary Kay Andrews	___
Jolie Blon's Bounce	James Lee Burke	___
City of Bones	Michael Connelly	___
No Good Deed	Manda Scott	___

2002
Silent Joe	T. Jefferson Parker	___
Judgment, The	D.W. Buffa	___
Tell No One	Harlan Coben	___
Money, Money, Money	Ed McBain	___
Reflecting the Sky	S.J. Rozan	___

2001
Bottoms, The	Joe R. Lansdale	___
Dangerous Road, A	Kris Nelscott	___
Place of Execution, A	Val McDermid	___
Red Light	T. Jefferson Parker	___
Whole Truth, The	Nancy Pickard	___

2000
Bones	Jan Burke	___
River of Darkness	Rennie Airth	___
L.A. Requiem	Robert Crais	___
Strawberry Sunday	Stephen Greenleaf	___
In a Dry Season	Peter Robinson	___

1999
Mr. White's Confession	Robert Clark	___
Blood Work	Michael Connelly	___
Beyond Recall	Robert Goddard	___
Likeness in Stone, A	J. Wallis Martin	___
Last Days of Il Duce, The	Domenic Stansberry	___

1998
Cimarron Rose	James Lee Burke	___
Dreaming of the Bones	Deborah Crombie	___
Wasteland of Strangers, A	Bill Pronzini	___
Black and Blue	Ian Rankin	___
Purification Ceremony, The	Mark T. Sullivan	___

1997
Chatham School Affair, The	Thomas H. Cook	___
With Child	Laurie R. King	___
Hearts and Bones	Margaret Lawrence	___
Pentecost Alley	Anne Perry	___
Mean Streak	Carolyn Wheat	___

1996
  Come to Grief   Dick Francis   ___
  Bookman's Wake, The   John Dunning   ___
  Shadow Man, The   John Katzenbach   ___
  Summons, The   Peter Lovesey   ___
  Roaring Boy, The   Edward Marston   ___

1995
  Red Scream, The   Mary Willis Walker   ___
  Lights Out   Peter Abrahams   ___
  Long Line of Dead Men, A   Lawrence Block   ___
  Miami, It's Murder   Edna Buchanan   ___
  Wednesday's Child   Peter Robinson   ___

1994
  Sculptress, The   Minette Walters   ___
  Free Fall   Robert Crais   ___
  Smilla's Sense of Snow (Miss Smilla's Feeling for Snow)   Peter Hoeg   ___
  Wolf in the Shadows   Marcia Muller   ___
  Journeyman Tailor, The   Gerald Seymour   ___

1993
  Bootlegger's Daughter   Margaret Maron   ___
  Backhand   Liza Cody   ___
  32 Cadillacs   Joe Gores   ___
  Pomona Queen   Kem Nunn   ___
  White Butterfly   Walter Mosley   ___

1992
  Dance at the Slaughterhouse, A   Lawrence Block   ___
  Don't Say a Word   Andrew Klavan   ___
  Prior Convictions   Lia Matera   ___
  I.O.U.   Nancy Pickard   ___
  Palindrome   Stuart Woods   ___

1991
  New Orleans Mourning   Julie Smith   ___
  Fade the Heat   Jay Brandon   ___
  Whiskey River   Loren D. Estleman   ___
  Bones and Silence   Reginald Hill   ___
  Deadfall in Berlin   R.D. Zimmerman   ___

1990
  Black Cherry Blues   James Lee Burke   ___
  Goldilocks   Andrew Coburn   ___
  Question of Guilt, A   Frances Fyfield   ___
  Death of a Joyce Scholar   Bartholomew Gill   ___
  Booster, The   Eugene Izzi   ___

1989
> ***Cold Red Sunrise, A***   Stuart M. Kaminsky   ___
> *Joey's Case*   K.C. Constantine   ___
> *Sacrificial Ground*   Thomas H. Cook   ___
> *Thief of Time, A*   Tony Hillerman   ___
> *In the Lake of the Moon*   David L. Lindsey   ___

1988
> ***Old Bones***   Aaron Elkins   ___
> *Trouble of Fools, A*   Linda Barnes   ___
> *Nursery Crimes*   B.M. Gill   ___
> *Rough Cider*   Peter Lovesey   ___
> *Corpse in Oozak's Pond, The*   Charlotte MacLeod   ___

1987
> ***Dark-Adapted Eye, A***   Barbara Vine   ___
> *Blind Run, The (Charlie Muffin and Russian Rose)*   Brian Freemantle   ___
> *Come Morning*   Joe Gores   ___
> *Taste of Death, A*   P.D. James   ___
> *Straight Man, The*   Roger L. Simon   ___

1986
> ***Suspect, The***   L.R. Wright   ___
> *City of Glass: The New York Trilogy, Part 1*   Paul Auster   ___
> *Shock to the System, A*   Simon Brett   ___
> *Tree of Hands, The*   Ruth Rendell   ___
> *Unkindness of Ravens, An*   Ruth Rendell   ___

1985
> ***Briarpatch***   Ross Thomas   ___
> *Black Seraphim, The*   Michael Gilbert   ___
> *Twelfth Juror, The*   B.M. Gill   ___
> *Emily Dickinson is Dead*   Jane Langton   ___
> *Chessplayer*   William Pearson   ___

1984
> ***LaBrava***   Elmore Leonard   ___
> *Name of the Rose, The*   Umberto Eco   ___
> *Little Drummer Girl, The*   John le Carre   ___
> *Texas Station (Blood Games)*   Christopher Leach   ___
> *Papers of Tony Veitch, The*   William McIlvanney   ___

1983
> ***Billingsgate Shoal***   Rick Boyer   ___
> *Eight Million Ways to Die*   Lawrence Block   ___
> *Split Images*   Elmore Leonard   ___
> *Captain, The*   Seymour Shubin   ___
> *Kahawa*   Donald E. Westlake   ___

1982
Peregrine	William Bayer	____
Other Side of Silence, The	Ted Allbeury	____
Death in a Cold Climate	Robert Barnard	____
Dupe	Liza Cody	____
Amateur, The	Robert Littell	____
Bogmail	Patrick McGinley	____

1981
Whip Hand	Dick Francis	____
Death of a Literary Widow (Posthumous Papers)	Robert Barnard	____
Death Drop	B.M. Gill	____
Spy's Wife, The	Reginald Hill	____
Man on Fire	A.J. Quinnell	____

1980
Rheingold Route, The	Arthur Maling	____
Death of a Mystery Writer (Unruly Son)	Robert Barnard	____
Coat of Varnish, A	C.P. Snow	____
Fire in the Barley	Frank Parrish	____
Make Death Love Me	Ruth Rendell	____

1979
Eye of the Needle (Storm Island)	Ken Follett	____
Snake, The	John Godey	____
Listening Woman	Tony Hillerman	____
Sleeping Life, A	Ruth Rendell	____
Shallow Grave, The	Jack S. Scott	____

1978
Catch Me: Kill Me	William H. Hallahan	____
Laidlaw	William McIlvanney	____
Nightwing	Martin Cruz Smith	____

1977
Promised Land	Robert B. Parker	____
Cavanaugh Quest, The	Thomas Gifford	____
Madness of the Heart, A	Richard Neely	____
Glory Boys, The	Gerald Seymour	____
Main, The	Trevanian	____

1976
Hopscotch	Brian Garfield	____
Gargoyle Conspiracy, The	Marvin H. Albert	____
Operation Alcestis	Maggie Rennert	____
Harry's Game	Gerald Seymour	____
Money Harvest, The	Ross Thomas	____

1975

Peter's Pence — Jon Cleary ____
Man Who Loved Zoos, The (Stricken) — Malcolm Bosse ____
Goodbye and Amen (The Grosvenor Square Goodbye) — Francis Clifford ____
Silver Bears, The — Paul E. Erdman ____
Lester Affair, The (The File on Lester) — Andrew Garve ____

1974

Dance Hall of the Dead — Tony Hillerman ____
Rainbird Pattern, The (Family Plot) — Victor Canning ____
Amigo, Amigo — Francis Clifford ____
Unsuitable Job for a Woman, An — P.D. James ____
Dear Laura — Jean Stubbs ____

1973

Lingala Code, The — Warren Kiefer ____
Five Pieces of Jade — John Ball ____
Tied Up in Tinsel — Ngaio Marsh ____
Shooting Gallery, The — Hugh C. Rae ____
Canto for a Gypsy — Martin Cruz Smith ____

1972

Day of the Jackal, The — Frederick Forsyth ____
Fly on the Wall, The — Tony Hillerman ____
Shroud for a Nightingale — P.D. James ____
Sir, You Bastard (Rogue Cop) — G.F. Newman ____
Who Killed Enoch Powell? — Arthur Wise ____

1971

Laughing Policeman, The — Maj Sjowall & Per Wahloo ____
Hound and the Fox and the Harper, The — Shaun Herron ____
Beyond This Point are Monsters — Margaret Millar ____
Many Deadly Returns (Who Saw Her Die?) — Patricia Moyes ____
Autumn of a Hunter (The Murder Hunt) — Pat Stadley ____
Hot Rock, The — Donald E. Westlake ____

1970

Forfeit — Dick Francis ____
Where the Dark Streets Go — Dorothy Salisbury Davis ____
Old English Peep Show, The (A Pride of Heroes) — Peter Dickinson ____
Miro — Shaun Herron ____
Blind Man With a Pistol (Hot Day, Hot Night) — Chester Himes ____
When in Greece — Emma Lathen ____

1969

Case of Need, A	Jeffery Hudson (Michael Crichton)	___
Picture Miss Seeton	Heron Carvic	___
God Speed the Night	Dorothy S. Davis & Jerome Ross	___
Glass-Sided Ants' Nest, The (Skin Deep)	Peter Dickinson	___
Valentine Estate, The	Stanley Ellin	___
Blood Sport	Dick Francis	___

1968

God Save the Mark	Donald E. Westlake	___
Gift Shop, The	Charlotte Armstrong	___
Lemon in the Basket	Charlotte Armstrong	___
Parade of Cockeyed Creatures, A: Or Did Someone Murder Our Wandering Boy?	George Baxt	___
Flying Finish	Dick Francis	___
Rosemary's Baby	Ira Levin	___

1967

King of the Rainy Country, The	Nicolas Freeling	___
Odds Against	Dick Francis	___
Killer Dolphin (Death at the Dolphin)	Ngaio Marsh	___
Busy Body, The	Donald E. Westlake	___

1966

Quiller Memorandum, The (The Berlin Memorandum)	Adam Hall	___
Pale Betrayer, The	Dorothy Salisbury Davis	___
Funeral in Berlin	Len Deighton	___
Perfect Murder, The	H.R.F. Keating	___
Far Side of the Dollar, The	Ross Macdonald	___
Airs Above the Ground	Mary Stewart	___

1965

Spy Who Came in From the Cold, The	John le Carre	___
Night of the Generals, The	Hans Hellmut Kirst	___
Fiend, The	Margaret Millar	___
This Rough Magic	Mary Stewart	___

1964

Light of Day, The	Eric Ambler	___
Make-Believe Man, The	Elizabeth Fenwick	___
Grieve for the Past	Stanton Forbes	___
Expendable Man, The	Dorothy B. Hughes	___
Player on the Other Side, The	Ellery Queen (by, Theodore Sturgeon)	___

1963

Death and the Joyful Woman	Ellis Peters	___
Zebra-Striped Hearse, The	Ross Macdonald	___
Seance (Séance on a Wet Afternoon)	Mark McShane	___
Evil Wish, The	Jean Potts	___
Knave of Hearts	Dell Shannon	___
Ballad of the Running Man, The	Shelley Smith	___

1962

Gideon's Fire	J.J. Marric (John Creasey)	___
Nightmare	Anne Blaisdell	___
Green Stone, The	Suzanne Blanc	___
Night of Wenceslas	Lionel Davidson	___
Wycherly Woman, The	Ross Macdonald	___

1961

Progress of a Crime, The	Julian Symons	___
Traces of Brillhart, The	Herbert Brean	___
Devil's Own, The (Witches; and, The Little Wax Doll, by Norah Lofts)	Peter Curtis (Norah Lofts)	___
Watcher in the Shadows	Geoffrey Household	___

1960

Hours Before Dawn, The	Celia Fremlin	___
List of Adrian Messenger, The	Philip MacDonald	___

1959

Eighth Circle, The	Stanley Ellin	___
Madhouse in Washington Square, The	David Alexander	___
Woman in the Woods, The (Miss Fenny)	Lee Blackstock (Charity Blackstock)	___
Gentleman Called, A	Dorothy Salisbury Davis	___

1958

Room to Swing	Ed Lacy	___
Longest Second, The	Bill Ballinger	___
Night of the Good Children, The (One Night of Terror)	Marjorie Carleton	___
Bushman Who Came Back, The (Bony Buys a Woman)	Arthur W. Upfield	___

1957

Dram of Poison, A	Charlotte Armstrong	___
Man Who Didn't Fly, The	Margot Bennett	___

1956

Beast in View	Margaret Millar	___
Case of the Talking Bug, The (Playback)	The Gordons	___
Talented Mr. Ripley, The	Patricia Highsmith	___

1955
Long Goodbye, The (The Long Good-bye) Raymond Chandler ____

1954
Beat Not the Bones Charlotte Jay ____

Edgar® Best 1st Novel by an American Author

2007
Faithful Spy, The Alex Berenson ____
Sharp Objects Gillian Flynn ____
King of Lies, The John Hart ____
Holmes on the Range Steve Hockensmith ____
Field of Darkness, A Cornelia Read ____

2006
Officer Down Theresa Schwegel ____
Die a Little Megan Abbott ____
Immoral Brian Freeman ____
Run the Risk Scott Frost ____
Hide Your Eyes Alison Gaylin ____

2005
Country of Origin Don Lee ____
Little Girl Lost Richard Aleas ____
Relative Danger Charles Benoit ____
Cloud Atlas Liam Callanan ____
Tonight I Said Goodbye Michael Koryta ____
Bahamarama Bob Morris ____

2004
Death of a Nationalist Rebecca C. Pawel ____
12 Bliss Street Martha Conway ____
Offer of Proof Robert Heilbrun ____
Night of the Dance, The James Hime ____
Bridge of Sighs, The Olen Steinhauer ____

2003
Blue Edge of Midnight, The Jonathon King ____
Southern Latitudes Stephen J. Clark ____
High Wire Kam Majd ____
Buck Fever Ben Rehder ____
Open and Shut David Rosenfelt ____

2002
Line of Vision David Ellis ____
Open Season C.J. Box ____
Red Hook Gabriel Cohen ____
Gun Monkeys Victor Gischler ____
Jasmine Trade, The Denise Hamilton ____

2001
>   *Conspiracy of Paper, A*   David Liss   ___
>   *Ice Harvest, The*   Scott Phillips   ___
>   *Crow in Stolen Colors*   Marcia Simpson   ___
>   *Raveling*   Peter Moore Smith   ___
>   *Death of a Red Heroine*   Qiu Xiaolong   ___

2000
>   *Skull Mantra, The*   Eliot Pattison   ___
>   *Big Trouble*   Dave Barry   ___
>   *Certifiably Insane*   Arthur W. Bahr   ___
>   *God is a Bullet*   Boston Teran   ___
>   *Inner City Blues*   Paula L. Woods   ___

1999
>   *Cold Day in Paradise, A*   Steve Hamilton   ___
>   *Reckless Homicide*   Ira Genberg   ___
>   *Numbered Account*   Christopher Reich   ___
>   *Nice*   Jen Sacks   ___
>   *Criminal Appeal, A*   D.R. Schanker   ___

1998
>   *Los Alamos*   Joseph Kanon   ___
>   *Crime in the Neighborhood, A*   Suzanne Berne   ___
>   *Bird Dog*   Philip Reed   ___
>   *Flower Net*   Lisa See   ___
>   *23 Shades of Black*   K.j.a. Wishnia   ___

1997
>   *Simple Justice*   John Morgan Wilson ___
>   *Bonita Faye*   Margaret Moseley   ___
>   *Queen's Man, The*   Sharon Kay Penman   ___
>   *Test of Wills, A*   Charles Todd   ___
>   *Brother's Blood, A*   Michael C. White   ___

1996
>   *Penance*   David Housewright   ___
>   *Tight Shot*   Kevin Allman   ___
>   *Murder in Scorpio*   Martha C. Lawrence ___
>   *Harry Chronicles, The*   Allan Pedrazas   ___
>   *Fixed in His Folly*   David J. Walker   ___

1995
>   *Caveman's Valentine, The (Caveman)*   George Dawes Green   ___
>   *One for the Money*   Janet Evanovich   ___
>   *Mallory's Oracle*   Carol O'Connell   ___
>   *Suspicion of Innocence*   Barbara Parker   ___
>   *Big Town*   Doug J. Swanson   ___

1994
Grave Talent, A — Laurie R. King — ___
List of 7, The — Mark Frost — ___
Criminal Seduction — Darian North — ___
Ballad of Rocky Ruiz, The: Death of a Martyr — Manuel Ramos — ___
Zaddik — David Rosenbaum — ___

1993
Black Echo, The — Michael Connelly — ___
Trail of Murder — Christine Andreae — ___
Trick of the Eye — Jane Stanton Hitchcock — ___
Ladystinger — Craig Smith — ___

1992
Slow Motion Riot — Peter Blauner — ___
Deadstick — Terence Faherty — ___
Deadline — Marcy Heidish — ___
Zero at the Bone — Mary Willis Walker — ___
Cool Breeze on the Underground, A — Don Winslow — ___

1991
Postmortem — Patricia Cornwell — ___
Come Nightfall — Gary Amo — ___
Passion Play — W. Edward Blain — ___
Nobody Lives Forever — Edna Buchanan — ___
Devil in a Blue Dress — Walter Mosley — ___

1990
Last Billable Hour, The — Susan Wolfe — ___
Hide and Seek — Barry Berg — ___
Story of Annie D., The — Susan Taylor Chehak — ___
Mother Shadow, The — Melodie Johnson Howe — ___
Blood Under the Bridge — Bruce Zimmerman — ___

1989
Carolina Skeletons — David Stout — ___
Murder Once Done — Mary Lou Bennett — ___
Murder of Frau Schutz, The — J. Madison Davis — ___
Great Deliverance, A — Elizabeth George — ___
Julian Solo — Shelley Reuben — ___

1988
Death Among Strangers — Deidre S. Laiken — ___
Detective — Parnell Hall — ___
Heat Lightning — John Lantigua — ___
Lover Man — Dallas Murphy — ___
Spoiler, The — Domenic Stansberry — ___

1987
No One Rides for Free   Larry Beinhart   ____
Lost   Gary Devon   ____
Riceburner   Richard Hyer   ____
Floater   Joseph Koenig   ____
Dead Air   Mike Lupica   ____

1986
When the Bough Breaks (Shrunken Heads)   Jonathan Kellerman   ____
Glory Hole Murders, The   Tony Fennelly   ____
Sleeping Dog   Dick Lochte   ____
Adventure of the Ectoplasmic Man, The   Daniel Stashower   ____

1985
Strike Three You're Dead   R.D. Rosen   ____
Creative Kind of Killer, A   Jack Early (as, Sandra Scoppetone) ____
Foul Shot   Doug Hornig   ____
Someone Else's Grave   Alison Smith   ____
Sweet, Savage Death   Orania Papazoglou   ____
                                                         (Jane Haddam)

1984
Bay Psalm Book Murder, The   Will Harriss   ____
Gold Solution, The   Herbert Resnicow   ____
Red Diamond, Private Eye   Mark Schorr   ____
Caroline Minuscule   Andrew Taylor   ____
Dead Man's Thoughts   Carolyn Wheat   ____

1983
Butcher's Boy, The   Thomas Perry   ____
By Frequent Anguish   S.F.X. Dean   ____
Unholy Communion   Richard Hughes   ____
In the Heat of the Summer (The Mean Season)   John Katzenbach   ____
Two If by Sea   Ernest Savage   ____

1982
Chiefs   Stuart Woods   ____
Giant Killer   Vernon Tom Hyman   ____
Not a Through Street   Ernest Larsen   ____
Black Glove, The   Geoffrey Miller   ____
Murder at the Red October   Anthony Olcott   ____

1981
Watcher, The   Kay Nolte Smith   ____
Winds of the Old Days   Betsy Aswald   ____
Rembrandt Panel, The (The Rembrandt File)   Oliver Banks   ____
Double Negative   David Carkeet   ____
Other Ann Fletcher, The   Susanne Jaffe   ____

1980
> ***Lasko Tangent, The*** Richard North Patterson ___
> *Night Trains* Peter Heath Fine ___
> *Follow the Leader* John Logue ___

1979
> ***Killed in the Ratings*** William L. DeAndrea ___
> *Scourge, The* Thomas L. Dunne ___
> *Falling Angel* William Hjortsberg ___
> *Blood Secrets* Craig Jones ___
> *Memory of Eva Ryker, The* Donald A. Stanwood ___

1978
> ***French Finish, A*** Robert Ross ___
> *Dewey Decimated* Charles A. Goodrum ___
> *Fan, The* Bob Randall ___

1977
> ***Thomas Berryman Number, The*** James Patterson ___
> *Your Day in the Barrel* Alan Furst ___
> *Straight* Steve Knickmeyer ___
> *Big Payoff, The* Janice Law ___
> *Final Proof* Marie R. Reno ___

1976
> ***Alvarez Journal, The*** Rex Burns ___
> *Waltz Across Texas* Max Crawford ___
> *Harmattan* Thomas Klop ___
> *Paperback Thriller* Lynn Meyer ___
> *Devalino Caper, The* A.J. Russell ___

1975
> ***Fletch*** Gregory McDonald ___
> *Kreutzman Formula, The* Dominic Koski & Virgil Scott ___
> *Saturday Games* Brown Meggs ___
> *Target Practice* Nicholas Meyer ___
> *Jones Men, The* Vern E. Smith ___

1974
> ***Billion Dollar Sure Thing, The*** Paul E. Erdman ___
> ***(The Billion Dollar Killing)***
> *Kicked to Death by a Camel* Clarence Jackson ___
> *Someone's Death* Charles Larson ___
> *Many Happy Returns* Justin Scott ___
> *Man on a String* Michael Wolfe ___

1973
Squaw Point — R.H. Shimer — ___
Person Shouldn't Die Like That, A — Arthur D. Goldstein — ___
Dead of Winter, The — William H. Hallahan — ___
Box 100 — Frank Leonard — ___
Heart of the Dog, The — Thomas A. Roberts — ___

1972
Finding Maubee (The Calypso Murders) — A.H.Z. Carr — ___
To Spite Her Face — Hildegarde Dolson — ___
Ask the Right Question — Michael Z. Lewin — ___
Stalker, The — Bill Pronzini — ___
Gypsy in Amber — Martin Cruz Smith — ___

1971
Anderson Tapes, The — Lawrence Sanders — ___
Incident at 125th Street — J.E. Brown — ___
Taking Gary Feldman (The Abduction) — Stanley Cohen — ___
Blessing Way, The — Tony Hillerman — ___
Naked Face, The — Sidney Sheldon — ___

1970
Time for Predators, A — Joe Gores — ___
You'll Like My Mother (The House with the Watching Eye) — Naomi Hintze — ___
Quicksand — Myrick Land — ___

1969
Silver Street (The Silver Street Killer) (Tie) — E. Richard Johnson — ___
Bait, The (Tie) — Dorothy Uhnak — ___
Dinosaur, The — Lawrence Kamarck — ___

1968
Act of Fear — Michael Collins (Dennis Lynds) — ___
Hell Gate — James Dawson — ___
Mortissimo — P.E.H. Dunston — ___
Tigers are Hungry, The — Charles Early — ___
Killing Season, The — John Redgate — ___

1967
Cold War Swap, The (Spy in the Vodka) — Ross Thomas — ___
Fancy's Knell — Babs Deal — ___
Kind of Treason, A — Robert S. Elegant — ___
Pedestal, The — George Lanning — ___

1966
In the Heat of the Night — John Ball — ___
Expendable Spy, The — Jack D. Hunter — ___
French Doll, The — Vincent McConnor — ___
Before the Ball was Over (A Season for Death) — Alexandra Roudybush — ___

1965
Friday the Rabbi Slept Late — Harry Kemelman ___
In the Last Analysis — Amanda Cross ___
Grave-Maker's House, The — Rubin Weber ___

1964
Florentine Finish — Cornelius Hirschberg ___
Fifth Woman, The — M. Fagyas ___
Prowler, The — Frances Rickett ___
Neon Haystack, The — James Michael Ullman ___

1963
Fugitive, The — Robert L. Fish ___
Counterweight — Daniel Broun ___
Chase, The (Pursuit; Dirty Mary, Crazy Larry) — Richard Unekis ___

1962
Green Stone, The — Suzanne Blanc ___
Felony Tank — Malcolm Braly ___
Close His Eyes — Olivia Dwight ___
Cipher, The — Alex Gordon (Gordon Cotler) ___
Night of the Kill — Breni James ___
Shock Treatment — Winfred Van Atta ___

1961
Man in the Cage, The — John Holbrook Vance (Jack Vance) ___

Marriage Cage, The — William Johnston ___
Killing at Big Tree, The — David McCarthy ___
Case Pending — Dell Shannon ___
Mercenaries, The (The Smashers) — Donald E. Westlake ___

1960
Grey Flannel Shroud, The — Henry Slesar ___
Dream of Falling, A (Dream of Death) — Mary O. Rank ___

1959
Bright Road to Fear, The — Richard Martin Stern ___
Man Who Disappeared, The — Edgar J. Bohle ___
Death of a Spinster — Frances Duncombe ___
Now, Will You Try for Murder? — Harry Olesker ___

1958
Knock and Wait a While — William Rawle Weeks ___
Bay of the Damned (A Hell of a Murder) — Warren Carrier ___
Root of Evil — James Cross ___

1957
Rebecca's Pride — Donald McNutt Douglass ___

1956
   Perfectionist, The (Kill the Beloved)   Lane Kauffmann   ____
   In His Blood   Harold R. Daniels   ____
   Much Ado About Murder   Fred Levon   ____

1955
   Go, Lovely Rose   Jean Potts   ____

1954
   Kiss Before Dying, A   Ira Levin   ____

1953
   Don't Cry for Me   William Campbell Gault   ____
   Inward Eye, The (Lady Marked for Murder)   Peggy Bacon   ____

1952
   Strangle Hold (Death of Miss X)   Mary McMullen   ____
   Carry My Coffin Slowly   Lee Herrington   ____
   Christmas Card Murders, The   David William Meredith   ____
   Cure It With Honey (I'll Get Mine)   Thurston Scott   ____
   Eleventh Hour, The   Robert B. Sinclair   ____

1951
   Nightmare in Manhattan   Thomas Walsh   ____
   Strangers on a Train   Patricia Highsmith   ____
   Happy Holiday!   Thaddeus O'Finn   ____
   House Without a Door, The   Thomas Sterling   ____

1950
   What a Body!   Alan Green   ____
   End is Known, The   Geoffrey Holiday Hall   ____
   Walk the Dark Streets   William Krasner   ____
   Shadow and the Blot, The   N.D. & G.G. Lobell   ____
   Dark Light, The   Bart Spicer   ____
   Innocent, The   Evelyn Piper   ____

1949
   Room Upstairs, The   Mildred Davis   ____
   Wilders Walk Away   Herbert Brean   ____
   Shoot the Works   Richard Ellington   ____

1948
   Fabulous Clipjoint, The   Fredric Brown   ____

1947
   Horizontal Man, The   Helen Eustis   ____

1946
   Watchful at Night   Julius Fast   ____

Edgar® Best Paperback Original

2007

Snakeskin Shamisen	Naomi Hirahara	____
Goodbye Kiss, The	Massimo Carlotto	____
Open Curtain, The	Brian Evenson	____
Deep Blue Alibi, The	Paul Levine	____
City of Tiny Lights	Patrick Neate	____

2006

Girl in the Glass	Jeffrey Ford	____
Homicide My Own	Anne Argula	____
James Deans, The	Reed Farrel Coleman	____
Kiss Her Goodbye	Allan Guthrie	____
Six Bad Things	Charlie Huston	____

2005

Confession, The	Domenic Stansberry	____
Librarian, The	Larry Beinhart	____
Into the Web	Thomas H. Cook	____
Dead Men Rise Up Never	Ron Faust	____
Twelve-Step Fandango	Chris Haslam	____

2004

Find Me Again	Sylvia Maultash Warsh	____
Cut and Run	Jeff Abbott	____
Last Witness, The	Joel Goldman	____
Wisdom of the Bones	Christopher Hyde	____
Southland	Nina Revoyr	____

2003

Out of Sight	T.J. MacGregor	____
Black Jack Point	Jeff Abbott	____
Night Watcher, The	John Lutz	____
Trauma	Graham Masterton	____
Prison Blues	Anna Salter	____

2002

Adios Muchachos	Daniel Chavarria	____
Hell's Kitchen	Jeffery Deaver (as, William Jefferies)	____
Mother Tongue, The	Teri Holbrook	____
Dead of Winter	P.J. Parrish	____
Straw Men	Martin J. Smith	____

2001

Black Maria, The	Mark Graham	____
Murder on St. Mark's Place	Victoria Thompson	____
Killing Kin	Chassie West	____
Kidnapping of Rosie Dawn, The	Eric Wright	____
Pursuit and Persuasion	Sally S. Wright	____

2000

Fulton County Blues	Ruth Birmingham	___
Lucky Man	Tony Dunbar	___
Resurrectionist, The	Mark Graham	___
Outcast, The	Jose Latour	___
In Big Trouble	Laura Lippman	___

1999

Widower's Two-Step, The	Rick Riordan	___
Atlanta Graves	Ruth Birmingham	___
Butchers Hill	Laura Lippman	___
Zen Attitude	Sujata Massey	___
Murder Manual	Steven Womack	___

1998

Charm City	Laura Lippman	___
Prioress' Tale, The	Margaret Frazer	___
Tarnished Icons	Stuart M. Kaminsky	___
Home Again, Home Again	Susan Cooper Rogers	___
Sunset and Santiago	Gloria White	___

1997

Fade Away	Harlan Coben	___
Silent Words	Joan M. Drury	___
Grass Widow, The	Teri Holbrook	___
Walking Rain	Susan Wade	___
Tribe	R.D. Zimmerman	___

1996

Tarnished Blue	William Heffernan	___
Deal Breaker	Harlan Coben	___
High Desert Malice	Kirk Mitchell	___
Charged With Guilt	Gloria White	___
Hard Frost	R.D. Wingfield	___

1995

Final Appeal	Lisa Scottoline	___
Broken-Hearted Detective, The	Milton Bass	___
Viper Quarry	Dean Feldmeyer	___
Power of Attorney	Walter Sorrells	___
Sunrise	Chassie West	___

1994

Dead Folks' Blues	Steven Womack	___
Servant's Tale, The	Margaret Frazer	___
Tony's Justice	Eugene Izzi	___
Beyond Saru	Thomas A. Roberts	___
Everywhere that Mary Went	Lisa Scottoline	___

1993
Cold Day for Murder, A — Dana Stabenow — ___
Good Friday Murder, The — Lee Harris — ___
Principal Defense — Gini Hartzmark — ___
Shallow Graves — William Jefferies — ___
Night Cruise — Billie Sue Mosiman — ___

1992
Dark Maze — Thomas Adcock — ___
Murder in the Dog Days — P.M. Carlson — ___
Cracking Up — Ed Naha — ___
Midtown North — Christopher Newman — ___
Fine Distinctions — Deborah Valentine — ___

1991
Man Who Would be F. Scott Fitzgerald — David Handler — ___
Comeback — L.L Enger — ___
Not a Creature was Stirring — Jane Haddam — ___
Dead in the Scrub — B.J. Oliphant — ___
SPQR — John Maddox Roberts — ___

1990
Rain, The — Keith Peterson (Andrew Kalvan) — ___
Manhattan is My Beat — Jeffery Deaver — ___
King of the Hustlers — Eugene Izzi — ___
Hot Wire — Randy Russell — ___
Collector of Photographs, A — Deborah Valentine — ___

1989
Telling of Lies, The — Timothy Findley — ___
Judgement by Fire — Fredrick D. Huebner — ___
Radical Departure, A — Lia Matera — ___
Trapdoor — Keith Peterson (Andrew Kalvan) — ___
Preacher — Ted Thackrey. Jr. — ___

1988
Bimbos of the Death Sun — Sharyn McCrumb — ___
Monkey's Raincoat, The — Robert Crais — ___
Deadly Intrusion — Walter Dillon — ___
Long Way to Die, The — James N. Frey — ___
Bullshot — Gabrielle Kraft — ___

1987
Junkyard Dog, The — Robert Campbell — ___
Cat Who Saw Red, The — Lilian Jackson Braun — ___
Hazzard — R.D. Brown — ___
Ronin — Nick Christian — ___
Shattered Moon — Kate Green — ___

1986
Pigs Get Fat .... Warren Murphy .... _____
Poverty Bay .... Earl Emerson .... _____
Broken Idols .... Sean Flannery .... _____
Blue Heron .... Philip Ross .... _____
Black Gravity .... Conall Ryan .... _____

1985
Grandmaster .... Warren Murphy & Molly Cochran .... _____
Keys to Billy Tillio, The .... Eric Blau .... _____
Seventh Sacrament, The .... Roland Cutler .... _____
Words Can Kill .... Kenn Davis .... _____
Black Knight in Red Square .... Stuart M. Kaminsky .... _____

1984
Mrs. White .... Margaret Tracy .... _____
False Prophets .... Sean Flannery .... _____
Hunter .... Eric Sauter .... _____
Kill Factor, The .... Richard Harper .... _____
Trace .... Warren Murphy .... _____

1983
Triangle .... Teri White .... _____
Vital Signs .... Ralph Burrows, M.D. .... _____
Clandestine .... James Ellroy .... _____
Missing and the Dead, The .... Jack Lynch .... _____

1982
Old Dick, The .... L.A. Morse .... _____
Deadline .... John Dunning .... _____
Unforgiven, The .... Patricia J. MacDonald .... _____
Pin .... Andrew Neiderman .... _____
Dead Heat .... Ray Obstfeld .... _____

1981
Public Murders .... Bill Granger .... _____
Blood Innocents .... Thomas H. Cook .... _____
Looking for Ginger North .... John Dunning .... _____
Tough Luck L.A. .... Murray Sinclair .... _____

1980
Hog Murders, The .... William L. DeAndrea .... _____
Kremlin Conspiracy, The .... Sean Flannery .... _____
Vortex .... David Heller .... _____
Queen is Dead, The .... Glen Keger .... _____
Infernal Device, The .... Michael Kurland .... _____

1979
Deceit and Deadly Lies — Frank Bandy — ___
Stud Game — David Anthony — ___
Switch, The — Elmore Leonard — ___
Heartstone — Philip Margolin — ___
Charnel House — Graham Masterton — ___

1978
Quark Maneuver, The — Mike Jahn — ___
Time to Murder and Create — Lawrence Block — ___
Terrorizers, The — Donald Hamilton — ___
They've Killed Anna — Marc Olden — ___

1977
Confess, Fletch — Gregory McDonald — ___
Captive City, The — Daniel Da Cruz — ___
Dark Side, The — Kenn Davis & John Stanley — ___
Retaliators, The — Donald Hamilton — ___
Freeze Frame — R.R. Irvine — ___

1976
Autopsy — John R. Feegel — ___
Set-Up, The — Milt Machlin & Robin Moore — ___
Charlie's Back in Town — Jacqueline Park — ___
Midas Coffin, The — Simon Quinn — ___
Assassinator, The — David Vowell — ___

1975
Corpse that Walked, The — Roy Winsor — ___
Who Killed Mr. Garland's Mistress? — Richard Forrest — ___
Jump Cut — R.R. Irvine — ___
Gravy Train Hit, The — Curtis Stevens — ___
Flats Fixed-Among Other Things — Don Tracy — ___

1974
Death of an Informer — Will Perry — ___
Mediterranean Caper, The (Mayday!) — Clive Cussler — ___
Deadlocked! — Leo P. Kelley — ___
Starling Street — Dinah Palmtag — ___
Big Fix, The — Roger L. Simon — ___

1973
Invader, The — Richard Wormser — ___
Not Dead Yet — Daniel Banko — ___
Smith Conspiracy, The — Richard Neely — ___
Power Kill — Charles Runyon — ___

1972
For Murder I Charge More	Frank McAuliffe	____
White Wolverine Contract, The	Philip Atlee	____
Space for Hire	William F. Nolan	____
Nor Spell Nor Charm	Alicen White	____
And the Deep Blue Sea	Charles Williams	____

1971
Flashpoint (Operation Flashpoint)	Dan J. Marlowe	____
Drowning, The	Jack Ehrlich	____
O.D. at Sweet Claude's	Matt Gattzden	____
After Things Fell Apart	Ron Goulart	____
Grave Descend	John Lange	____
Mafioso	Peter McCurtin	____

1970
Dragon's Eye, The	Scott C.S. Stone	____
Assault on Ming	Alan Caillou	____
Governess, The (Guardian of Love)	Elsie Cromwell	____
Plague of Spies, A	Michael Kurland	____
Sour Lemon Score, The	Richard Stark (Donald E. Westlake)	____

Edgar® Best Short Story

2007
"Home Front, The"	Charles Ardai	*Death Do Us Part*; Coben, ed.	____
"Rain"	Thomas H. Cook	*Manhattan Noir*; Block, ed.	____
"Cranked"	Bill Crider	*Damn Near Dead: An Anthology of Geezer Noir*; Swierczynski, ed.	____
"White Trash Noir"	Michael Malone	*Murder at the Foul Line*; Penzler, ed.	____
"Building"	S.J. Rozan	*Manhattan Noir*; Block, ed.	____

2006
"Catch, The"	James W. Hall	*Greatest Hits*; Randisi, ed.	____
"Born Bad"	Jeffery Deaver	*Dangerous Women*; Penzler, ed.	____
"Her Lord and Master"	Andrew Klavan	*Dangerous Women*; Penzler, ed.	____
"Misdirection"	Barbara Seranella	*Greatest Hits*; Randisi, ed.	____
"Welcome to Monroe"	Daniel Wallace	A Kudzu Christmas; Gilbert & Waller, eds.	____

2005

"Something About a Scar"	Laurie Lynn Drummond	*Anything You Say Can and Will Be Used Against You*	___
"Widow of Slane, The"	Terence Faherty	*EQMM,* Mar/Apr 04	___
"Book Signing, The"	Pete Hamill	*Brooklyn Noir;* McLoughlin, ed.	___
"Adventure of the Missing Detective"	Gary Lovisi	*Sherlock Holmes: The Hidden Years;* Kurland, ed.	___
"Imitate the Sun"	Luke Sholer	*EQMM,* Nov 04	___

2004

"Maids, The"	G. Miki Hayden	*Blood on Their Hands;* Block, ed.	___
"Bet on Red"	Jeff Abbott	*High Stakes;* Randisi, ed.	___
"Black Heart and Cabin Girl"	Shelley Costa	*Blood on Their Hands;* Block, ed.	___
"Aces and Eights"	David Edgerley Gates	*AHMM,* Dec 03	___
"Cowboy Grace"	Kristine Kathryn Rusch	*The Silver Gryphon;* Turner & Halpern, eds.	___

2003

"Mexican Gatsby"	Raymond Steiber	*EQMM,* Mar 02	___
"Murder Ballads, The"	Doug Allyn	*EQMM,* Mar 02	___
"To Live and Die in Midland, Texas"	Clark Howard	*EQMM,* Sept/Oct 02	___
"Rumpole and the Primrose Path"	John Mortimer	*The Strand,* #8	___
"Angel of Wrath"	Joyce Carol Oates	*EQMM,* Jun 02	___

2002

"Double-Crossing Delancy"	S.J. Rozan	*Mystery Street;* Randisi, ed.	___
"Abbey Ghosts, The"	Jan Burke	*AHMM,* Jan 01	___
"Horrible Senseless Murder of Two Elderly Women, The"	Michael Collins (Dennis Lynds)	*Fedora: Private Eyes & Tough Guys;* Bracken, ed	___
"If the Glove Fits"	Michael Z. Lewin	*EQMM,* Sept/Oct 01	___
"Virgo in Sapphires"	Margaret Maron	*EQMM,* Dec 01	___

2001

"Missing in Action"	Peter Robinson	*EQMM,* Nov 00	___
"Delta Double-Deal"	Noreen Ayres	*The Night Awakens-MWA Anthology;* Clark, ed.	___
"Twelve Little Buggers"	Mat Coward	*EQMM,* Jan 00	___
"Candle for Christmas, A"	Reginald Hill	*EQMM,* Jan 00	___
"Spinning"	Kristine Kathryn Rusch	*EQMM,* Jul 00	___

2000

"Heroes"	Anne Perry	*Murder and Obsession*; Penzler, ed.	___
"Triangle"	Jeffery Deaver	*EQMM*, Mar 99	___
"Crack"	James W. Hall	*Murder and Obsession*; Penzler, ed.	___
"Snow"	Stuart M. Kaminsky	*First Cases*, Vol 3; Randisi, ed.	___
"Paleta Man"	Laurie R. King	*Irreconcilable Differences*; Matera, ed.	___

1999

"Poachers"	Tom Franklin	*Texas Review*, Fall/Winter 98	___
"Looking for David"	Lawrence Block	*EQMM*, Feb 98	___
"Halfway Woman, The"	Clark Howard	*EQMM*, Feb 98	___
"For Jeff"	Perry Michael Smith	*EQMM*, Feb 98	___
"Sacrifice"	L.L. Thrasher	*Murderous Intent*, Summer/Fall 98	___

1998

"Keller on the Spot"	Lawrence Block	*Playboy*, Nov 97	___
"Ways to Kill a Cat"	Simon Brett	Malice Domestic 6; Perry, pre.	___
"Kneeling Soldier, The"	Jeffery Deaver	*EQMM*, Mar 97	___
"Find Miriam"	Stuart M. Kaminsky	*New Mystery*, Summer 97	___
"Man Who Beat the System, The"	Stuart M. Kaminsky	*Funny Bones*; Hess, ed.	___

1997

"Red Clay"	Michael Malone	*Murder for Love*; Penzler, ed.	___
"My Murder"	David Corn	*Unusual Suspects*; Grady, ed.	___
"Dark Snow, The"	Brendan DuBois	*Playboy*, Nov 96	___
"Kiss the Sky"	James Grady	*Unusual Suspects*; Grady, ed.	___
"Hoops"	S.J. Rozan	*EQMM*, Jan 96	___

1996

"Judge's Boy, The"	Jean B. Cooper	*EQMM*, Aug 95	___
"Rule of Law"	K.K. Beck	Malice Domestic 4; Hart, pre.	___
"Death in a Small Town"	Larry Beinhart	*New Mystery*, Spring 95	___
"When Your Breath Freezes"	Kathleen Dougherty	*EQMM*, Sept 95	___
"Plain and Honest Death, A"	Bill Pomidor	*EQMM*, Sept 95	___

1995

"Dancing Bear, The"	Doug Allyn	*AHMM*, Mar 94	___
"Gentleman in the Lake, The"	Robert Barnard	*EQMM*, Jun 94	___
"Necessary Brother, The"	Brendan DuBois	*EQMM*, May 94	___
"Tennis Court, The"	Brenda Melton Burnham	*AHMM*, Jul 94	___
"Eye for a Tooth, An "	Justin Scott	*Justice in Manhattan*; Clark & Chastain, eds.	___

1994

"Keller's Therapy"	Lawrence Block	*Playboy*, May 93	___
"Ghost Show, The"	Doug Allyn	*EQMM*, Dec 93	___
"Mefisto in Onyx"	Harlan Ellison	*Omni*, Oct 93	___
"McIntyre's Donald"	Joseph Hansen	*Bohannon's Country*	___
"Enduring as Dust"	Bruce Holland Rogers	*Danger in D.C.;* Greenberg & Gorman, eds.	___

1993

"Mary, Mary, Shut the Door"	Benjamin M. Schutz	*Deadly Allies*; Randisi & Wallace, eds.	___
"Candles in the Rain"	Doug Allyn	*EQMM*, Nov 92	___
"Howler"	Jo Bannister	*EQMM*, Oct 92	___
"Louise"	Max Allan Collins	*Deadly Allies*; Randisi & Wallace, eds.	___
"One Hit Wonder"	Gabrielle Kraft	Sisters in Crime 5; Wallace, ed.	___

1992

"Nine Sons"	Wendy Hornsby	Sisters in Crime 4; Wallace, ed.	___
"Sleeper"	Doug Allyn	*EQMM*, May 91	___
"Blow for Freedom, A"	Lawrence Block	*Playboy*, Oct 91	___
"Spasmo"	Liza Cody	A Classic English Crime; *Heald, ed.*	___
"Dreaming in Black and White"	Susan Schwartz	Psycho-Paths; Block, ed.	___

1991

"Elvis Lives"	Lynne Barrett	*EQMM*, Sept 90	___
"Answers to Soldiers"	Lawrence Block	*Playboy*, Jun 90	___
"Prisoners"	Ed Gorman	*New Crimes*; Jakubowski, ed.	___
"Poison that Leaves No Trace, A"	Sue Grafton	Sisters in Crime 2; Wallace, ed.	___
"Challenge the Widow-Maker"	Clark Howard	*EQMM*, Aug 90	___

1990

"Too Many Crooks"	Donald E. Westlake	*Playboy*, Aug 89	___
"Ted Bundy's Father"	Ruth Graviros	*EQMM*, Nov 89	___
"Girl and the Gator, The"	Robert Halsted	*AHMM*, Dec 89	___
"Afraid All the Time"	Nancy Pickard	Sisters in Crime; Wallace, ed.	___
"For Loyal Service"	Stephen Wasylyk	*AHMM*, Aug 89	___

1989

"Flicks"	Bill Crenshaw	*AHMM*, Aug 88	___
"Deja Vu"	Doug Allyn	*AHMM*, Jun 88	___
"Bridey's Caller"	Judith O'Neill	*AHMM*, May 88	___
"Incident in a Neighborhood Tavern"	Bill Pronzini	*An Eye For Justice*; Randisi, ed.	___
"Alley, The"	Stephen Wasylyk	*AHMM*, Nov 88	___

1988
"Soft Monkey"	Harlan Ellison	*Mystery Scene Reader* #1; Gorman, ed.	___
"Breakfast Television"	Robert Barnard	*EQMM,* Jan 87	___
"Stroke of Genius"	George Baxt	*EQMM,* Jun 87	___
"Mr. Felix"	Paula Gosling	*EQMM,* Jul 87	___
"Au Pair Girl, The"	Joyce Harrington	*Matter of Crime* #1; Bruccoli & Layman, eds.	___

1987
"Rain in Pinton County"	Robert Sampson	*New Black Mask,* May 86	___
"Christmas Cop"	Thomas Adcock	*EQMM,* Nov 86	___
"Puddle Diver, The"	Doug Allyn	*AHMM,* Oct 86	___
"Driven"	Brendan DuBois	*EQMM,* Nov 86	___
"Body Count"	Wayne D. Dundee	*Mean Streets*; Randisi, ed.	___

1986
"Ride the Lightning"	John Lutz	*AHMM,* Jan 85	___
"What's in a Name?"	Robert Barnard	*EQMM,* Jun 85	___
"Trouble in Paradise"	Arthur Lyons	New Black Mask, Jan 85	___
"Yellow One-Eyed Cat"	Robert Twohy	*EQMM,* May 85	___
"There Goes Ravelaar"	Janwillem van de Wetering	*EQMM,* Jan 85	___

1985
"By the Dawn's Early Light"	Lawrence Block	*Playboy,* Aug 84	___
"Reluctant Detective, The"	Michael Z. Lewin	*The Eyes Have It*; Randisi, ed.	___
"Breakfast at Ojai"	Robert Twohy	*EQMM,* Sept 84	___
"After I'm Gone"	Donald E. Westlake	*EQMM,* Jun 84	___
"Season Pass"	Chet Williamson	*AHMM,* Oct 84	___

1984
"New Girlfriend, The"	Ruth Rendell	*EQMM,* Aug 83	___
"Big Boy, Little Boy"	Simon Brett	*EQMM,* Jul 83	___
"Graffiti"	Stanley Ellin	*EQMM,* Mar 83	___
"Anderson Boy, The"	Joseph Hansen	*EQMM,* Sept 83	___
"Puerto Rican Blues"	Clark Howard	*EQMM,* Apr 83	___

1983
"There are No Snakes in Ireland"	Frederick Forsyth	*No Comebacks*	___
"Decent Price for a Painting, A"	James Holding	*EQMM,* Aug 82	___
"All the Heroes are Dead"	Clark Howard	*EQMM,* Dec 82	___
"Tall Tommy and the Millionaire"	R.R. Rafferty	*AHMM,* Sept 82	___

1982

"Absence of Emily, The"	Jack Ritchie	*EQMM*, Jan 81	___
"Seeds of Murder"	Nan Hamilton	*AHMM*, Dec 81	___
"Token of Appreciation, A"	Donald Olson	*AHMM*, Jun 81	___
"Miracle Day, The"	Ernest Savage	*EQMM*, Feb 81	___
"Mousie"	Robert Twohy	*EQMM*, Nov 81	___

1981

"Horn Man"	Clark Howard	*EQMM*, Jul 80	___
"Choirboy, The"	William Bankier	*AHMM*, Dec 80	___
"Most Dangerous Man Alive, The"	Edward D. Hoch	*EQMM*, May 80	___
"Until You are Dead"	John Lutz	*EQMM*, Jan 80	___

1980

"Armed and Dangerous"	Geoffrey Norman	*Esquire*, Mar 79	___
"Used in Evidence"	Frederick Forsyth	*Playboy*, Dec 79	___
"Scrimshaw"	Brian Garfield	*EQMM*, Dec 79	___
"Boiler, The"	Julian Symons	*EQMM*, Nov 79	___
"Imperial Ice House, The"	Paul Theroux	*Atlantic Monthly*, Apr 79	___

1979

"Cloud Beneath The Eaves, The"	Barbara Owens	*EQMM*, Jan 78	___
"Going Backward"	David Ely	*EQMM*, Nov 78	___
"Strangers in the Fog"	Bill Pronzini	*EQMM*, Jun 78	___
"Closed Door, The"	Thomas Walsh	*EQMM*, May 78	___
"This is Death"	Donald E. Westlake	*EQMM*, Nov 78	___

1978

"Chance After Chance"	Thomas Walsh	*EQMM*, Nov 77	___
"Last Rendezvous, The"	Jean Backus	*EQMM*, Sept 77	___
"Problem of Li T'ang, The"	Geoffrey Bush	Atlantic Monthly, Aug 77	___
"Jode's Last Hunt"	Brian Garfield	*EQMM*, Jan 77	___
"Johore Murders, The"	Paul Theroux	Atlantic Monthly, Mar 77	___

1977

"Like a Terrible Scream"	Etta Revesz	*EQMM*, May 76	___
"Lavender Lady"	Barbara Callahan	*EQMM*, Apr 76	___
"Crazy Old Lady"	Avram Davidson	*EQMM*, Mar 76	___
"People Don't Do Such Things"	Ruth Rendell	The Fallen Curtain	___
"Nobody Tells Me Anything"	Jack Ritchie	*EQMM*, Oct 76	___

1976

"Jail, The"	Jesse Hill Ford	*Playboy*, Mar 75	____
"Old Friends"	Dorothy Salisbury Davis	*EQMM*, Sept 75	____
"Night Crawlers"	Joyce Harrington	*EQMM*, Jan 75	____
"Fall of the Coin, The"	Ruth Rendell	*EQMM*, Jun 75	____
"Many-Flavored Crime, The"	Jack Ritchie	*Mystery Digest Mag*, Dec 75	____

1975

"Fallen Curtain, The"	Ruth Rendell	*EQMM*, Aug 74	____
"Light in the Cottage, The"	David Ely	*Playboy*, Oct 74	____
"Night Out With the Boys, A"	Elsin Ann Gardner	*EQMM*, Feb 74	____
"Cabin in the Hollow"	Joyce Harrington	*EQMM*, Oct 74	____
"Screams and Echoes"	Donald Olson	*EQMM*, Aug 74	____
"Game, The"	Thomasina Weber	*Killers of the Mind*; Freeman, ed.	____

1974

"Whimper of Whipped Dogs, The"	Harlan Ellison	*Bad Moon Rising*; Disch, ed.	____
"Fifty Years After"	Anthony Gilbert	*EQMM*, Mar 73	____
"O'Bannon Blarney File, The"	Joe Gores	*Men & Malice*; Dickensheet, ed.	____
"Do With Me What You Will"	Joyce Carol Oates	*Playboy*, Jun 73	____
"Ghosts at Iron River, The"	Chelsea Quinn Yarbro	*Men & Malice*; Dickensheet, ed.	____

1973

"Purple Shroud, The"	Joyce Harrington	*EQMM*, Sept 72	____
"Celestine"	George Bradshaw	*Ladies' Home Journal*, Oct 72	____
"Island of Bright Birds"	John Christopher	*EQMM*, Feb 72	____
"Frightened Lady"	C.B. Gilford	*AHMM*, Jul 72	____
"Hijack"	Robert L. Fish	*Playboy*, Aug 72	____

1972

"Moonlight Gardener"	Robert L. Fish	*Argosy*, Dec 71	____
"Sardinian Incident"	Evan Hunter	*Playboy*, Oct 71	____
"Spivvleton Mystery, The"	Katherine Anne Porter	*Ladies' Home Journal*, Aug 71	____
"My Daughter is Dead"	Pauline C. Smith	*AHMM*, Nov 71	____

1971

"In the Forests of Riga the Beasts are Very Wild Indeed"	Maragret Finn Brown	*McCall's*, Jul 70	____
"Door to a Different World"	Anthony Gilbert	*EQMM*, Mar 70	____
"Miss Paisley on a Diet"	John Pierce	*EQMM*, Feb 70	____

1970

"Goodbye, Pops"	Joe Gores	*EQMM,* Dec 69	___
"Poison in the Cup"	Christianna Brand	*EQMM,* Feb 69	___
"Double Entry"	Robert L. Fish	*EQMM,* Jan 69	___
"Death's Door"	Robert McNear	*Playboy,* Mar 69	___
"Promise of Oranges"	Duveen Polk	*Good Housekeeping,* Feb 69	___

1969

"Man Who Fooled the World, The"	Warner Law	*Sat. Evening Post,* Aug 24, 68	___
"Success of a Mission"	William Arden (Dennis Lynds)	*Argosy,* Apr 68	___
"Last Bottle in the World, The"	Stanley Ellin	*EQMM,* Feb 68	___
"Crooked Bone"	Gerald Kersh	*Sat. Evening Post,* Aug 10, 68	___
"Moment of Power"	P.D. James	*EQMM,* Jul 68	___

1968

"Oblong Room, The"	Edward D. Hoch	*The Saint,* Jul 67	___
"Twist for Twist"	Christianna Brand	*EQMM,* May 67	___
"Dare I Weep? Dare I Mourn?"	John le Carre	*Sat. Evening Post,* Jan 28, 67	___
"Salad Maker, The"	Robert McNear	*EQMM,* Jun 67	___

1967

"Chosen One, The"	Rhys Davies	*The New Yorker,* Jun 4, 66	___
"Splintered Monday, The"	Charlotte Armstrong	*EQMM,* Mar 66	___
"Master of the Hounds"	Algis Budrys	*Sat. Evening Post,* Aug 27, 66	___
"Hochmann Miniatures, The"	Robert L. Fish	*Argosy,* Mar 66	___

1966

"Possibility of Evil, The"	Shirley Jackson	*Sat. Evening Post,* Dec 18, 65	___
"Case for Miss Peacock, The"	Charlotte Armstrong	*EQMM,* Feb 65	___
"Foxer"	Brian Cleeve	*Sat. Evening Post,* Dec 18, 65	___
"Who Walks Behind"	Holly Roth	*EQMM,* Sept 65	___

1965

"H as in Homicide"	Lawrence Treat	*EQMM,* Mar 64	___
"Purple is Everything, The"	Dorothy Salisbury Davis	*EQMM,* Jun 64	___
"Solilokquy in Tongues, A"	William Wiser	*Cosmopolitan,* May 64	___

1964

"Man Gehorcht"	Leslie Ann Brownrigg	*Story Mag,* Jan/Feb 63	___
"Ballad of Jesse Neighbors, The"	William Humphrey	*Esquire,* Sept 63	___
"Crime of Ezechiele Coen, The"	Stanley Ellin	*EQMM,* Nov 63	___

1963
"Sailing Club, The"   David Ely   *Cosmopolitan,* Oct 62   ____
"Terrapin, The"   Patricia Highsmith   *EQMM,* Oct 62   ____
"Order, An"   Carl Erik Soya   Story Mag, Oct 62   ____

1962
"Affair at Lahore Cantonment" Avram Davidson   *EQMM,* Jun 61   ____
"Ellery Queen's 1962   Ellery Queen   *Queen,* Volume: 61   ____
   Anthology"
"Children of Alda Nuova, The" Robert Wallston   *EQMM,* Aug 61   ____

1961
"Tiger"   John Durham   *Cosmopolitan,* Feb 60   ____
"Real Live Murder, A"   Donald Honig   *AHMM,* Oct 60   ____
"Louisa, Please"   Shirley Jackson   *Ladies' Home Journal,* Feb 60 ____
"Summer Evil"   Nora Kaplan   *AHMM,* Oct 60   ____
"View From the Terrace, A"   Mike Marmer   *Cosmopolitan,* Dec 60   ____

1960
"Landlady, The"   Roald Dahl   *The New Yorker,* Nov 59   ____
"Day of the Bullet, The"   Stanley Ellin   *EQMM,* Oct 59   ____

1959
"Over There, Darkness"   William O'Farrell   *Sleuth,* Oct 58   ____

1958
"Secret of the Bottle, The"   Gerald Kersh   *Sat. Evening Post,* Dec 7, 57 ____
"And Already Lost"   Charlotte Armstrong   *EQMM,* Jun 57   ____

1957
"Blessington Method, The"   Stanley Ellin   *EQMM,* Jun 56   ____
"Gentlest of the Brothers, The" David Alexander   *EQMM,* Feb 56   ____
"Last Spin, The"   Evan Hunter   *Manhunt,* Sept 56   ____

1956
"Dream No More"   Philip MacDonald   *EQMM,* Nov 55   ____
"Invitation to an Accident"   Wade Miller   *EQMM,* Jul 55   ____

1955
"House Party, The"   Stanley Ellin   *EQMM,* May 54   ____

1954
"Someone Like You"   Roald Dahl   *Someone Like You*   ____

1953
"Something to Hide"   Philip MacDonald   *Something to Hide (Fingers of* ____
                                                    Fear)

1952

"Fancies and Goodnights"	John Collier	*Fancies and Goodnights*	____
"Handbook for Poisoners"	Raymond T. Bond	*Handbook for Poisoners*	____
"Memoirs of Solar Pons, The"	August Derleth	*Memoirs of Solar Pons*	____
"Full Cargo"	Wilbur D. Steele	*Full Cargo*	____
"Twenty Great Tales of Murder"		*McCloy*, Helen & Brett Halliday, eds.	____

1951

"Diagnosis: Homicide"	Lawrence G. Blochman	*Diagnosis: Homicide*	____

Some of the above are on-line; example: www.classicshorts.com/stories/lastspin.html

Edgar® Best Fact Crime

2007

Manhunt: The 12-Day Chase for Lincoln's Killer	James L. Swanson	____
Strange Piece of Paradise: A Return to the American West to Investigate My Attempted Murder – and Solve the Riddle of Myself	Terri Jentz	____
Death in Belmont, A	Sebastian Junger	
Finding Amy: A True Story of Murder in Maine	Joseph K. Loughlin (Capt.) & Kate Clark Flora	____
Ripperology: A Study of the World's First Serial Killer	Robin Odell	____
Beautiful Cigar Girl, The: Mary Rogers, Edgar Allan Poe and the Invention of Murder	Daniel Stashower	____

2006

Rescue Artist, The : A True Story of Art, Thieves, and the Hunt for a Missing Masterpiece	Edward Dolnick	____
Elements of Murder, The: The History of Poison	John Emsley	
Written in Blood: A True Story of Murder and a Deadly 16-Year-Old Secret that Tore a Family Apart	Diane Fanning	____
True Story: Murder, Memoir, Mea Culpa	Michael Finkel	____
Desire Street: A True Story of Death and Deliverance in New Orleans	Jed Horne	____

2005

Conviction: Solving the Moxley Murder: A Reporter and a Detective's Twenty-Year Search for Justice	Leonard Levitt	____
Ready for the People: My Most Chilling Cases as Prosecutor	Marissa N. Batt	____
Forensics for Dummies	D.P. Lyle, M.D.	____
Are You There Alone?: The Unspeakable Crime of Andrea Yates	Suzanne O'Malley	____
Ballad of the Whiskey Robber, The: A True Story of Bank Heists, Ice Hockey, Transylvanian Pelt Smuggling, Moonlighting Detectives, and Broken Hearts	Julian Rubinstein	____

Green River, Running Red: The Real Story of the Green River Killer - America's Deadliest Serial Murderer	Ann Rule	___

2004

Devil in the White City, The: Murder, Magic, and Madness at the Fair that Changed America	Erik Larson	___
Black Dahlia Avenger - The True Story	Steve Hodel	___
Judgment Ridge: The True Story Behind the Dartmouth Murders	Dick Lehr & Mitchell Zuckoff	___
And the Dead Shall Rise: The Murder of Mary Phagan and the Lynching of Leo Frank	Steve Oney	___
Rothstein: The Life, Times, and Murder of the Criminal Genius Who Fixed the 1919 World Series	David Pietrusza	___

2003

Fire Lover: A True Story	Joseph Wambaugh	___
Blood and Ink: International Guide to Fact-Based Crime Literature	Albert Borowitz	___
Takedown: The Fall of the Last Mafia Empire	Rick Cowan & Douglas Century	___
Death at the Priory: Sex, Love and Murder in Victorian England	James Ruddick	___
Count and the Confession, The: A True Murder Mystery	John Taylor	___

2002

Son of a Grifter: The Twisted Tale of Sante and Kenny Kimes, the Most Notorious Con Artists in America	Kent Walker w/ Mark Schone	___
Dark Dreams: Sexual Violence, Homicide and the Criminal Mind	Roy Hazelwood & Stephen G. Michaud	___
Leavenworth Train: A Fugitive's Search for Justice in the Vanishing West	Joe Jackson	___
Wrong Man, The: The Final Verdict in the Dr. Sam Sheppard Murder Case	James Neff	___
Base Instincts: What Makes Killers Kill?	Jonathan H. Pincus, M.D.	___

2001

Black Mass: The Irish Mob, the FBI, and a Devil's Deal	Dick Lehr & Gerard O'Neill	___
Seekers, The: Finding Felons and Guiding Men: A Bounty Hunter's Story	Joshua Armstron & Anthony Bruno	___
Portraits of Guilt: The Woman Who Profiles the Faces of America's Deadliest Criminals	Jeanne Boylan	___
Author Unknown: On the Trail of Anonymous	Don Foster	___
Moonlight: Abraham Lincoln and the Almanac Trial	John Evangelist Walsh	___

2000

Blind Eye: The Terrifying Story of a Doctor Who   James B. Stewart   ____
Got Away With Murder

Ghosts of Hopewell, The: Setting the Record   Jim Fisher   ____
Straight in the Lindbergh Case

Mean Justice: A Town's Terror, A Prosecutor's   Edward Humes   ____
Power, A Betrayal of Innocence

And Never Let Her Go: Thomas Capano: The   Ann Rule   ____
Deadly Seducer

Disco Bloodbath: A Fabulous but True Tale of   James St. James   ____
Murder in Clubland

1999

To the Last Breath: Three Women Fight For the   Carlton Stowers   ____
Truth Behind a Child's Tragic Murder

Death Sentence: The True Story of Velma Barfield's   Jerry Bledsoe   ____
Life, Crimes and Execution

Tough Jews: Fathers, Sons, and Gangster Dreams   Rich Cohen   ____

Greentown: Murder and Mystery in Greenwich,   Timothy Dumas   ____
America's Wealthiest Community

One of Ours: Timothy McVeigh and the Oklahoma   Richard A. Serrano   ____
City Bombing

1998

Death of Innocents, The: A True Story of   Richard Firstman & Jamie Talan   ____
Murder, Medicine, and High-Stake Science

Our Guys: The Glen Ridge Rape and the Secret Life   Bernard Lefkowitz   ____
of the Perfect Suburb

Napoleon of Crime, The: The Life and Times of   Ben Macintyre   ____
Adam Worth, Master Thief

Bitter Harvest: A Woman's Fury, a Mother's Sacrifice   Ann Rule   ____

May God Have Mercy: A True Story of Crime and   John C. Tucker   ____
Punishment

1997

Power to Hurt: Inside a Judge's Chambers: Darcy O'Brien   ____
Sexual Assault, Corruption, and the Ultimate
Reversal of Justice for Women

Outrage: The Five Reasons Why O.J. Simpson Got   Vincent Bugliosi   ____
Away With Murder

Fall Guys: False Confessions and the Politics of Murder   Jim Fisher   ____

No Matter How Loud I Shout: A Year in the Life   Edward Humes   ____
of Juvenile Court

Trespasses: Portrait of a Serial Rapist   Howard Swindle   ____

1996

Circumstantial Evidence: Death, Life, and — Pete Earley — ____
Justice in a Southern Town
Mindhunter: Inside the FBI's Elite Serial Crime Unit — John E. Douglas & Mark Olshaker — ____
Born to Kill: America's Most Notorious Vietnamese — T.J. English — ____
Gang, and the Changing Face of Organized Crime
Unfinished Murder: The Capture of a Serial Rapist — James Neff — ____
By Two and Two: The Shocking True Story of Twin — Jim Schutze — ____
Sisters Torn Apart by Lies, Injustice, and Murder

1995

To Protect and Serve: The LAPD's Century of — Joe Domanick — ____
War in the City of Dreams
Before He Wakes: A True Story of Money, — Jerry Bledsoe — ____
Marriage, Sex and Murder
Breakdown: Sex, Suicide, and the Harvard — McNamara Eileen — ____
Psychiatrist
Mississippi Mud: Southern Justice and the Dixie Mafia — Edward Humes — ____
In the Best of Families: The Anatomy of a True Tragedy — Dennis McDougal — ____

1994

Until the Twelfth of Never: The Deadly Divorce — Bella Stumbo — ____
of Dan and Betty Broderick
Lindbergh: The Crime — Noel Behn — ____
Final Justice: The True Story of the Richest Man — Steven Naifeh & — ____
Ever Tried for Murder — Gregory White Smith
Misbegotten Son, The: A Serial Killer and His — Jack Olsen — ____
Victims: The True Story of Arthur J. Shawcross
Gone in the Night: The Dowaliby Family's — David Protess & Rob Warden — ____
Encounter With Murder and the Law

1993

Swift Justice: Murder and Vengeance in a — Harry Farrell — ____
California Town
Trunk Murderess, The: Winnie Ruth Judd: The — Jana Bommersbach — ____
Truth About an American Crime Legend
Revealed at Last
Blood Echoes: The True Story of an Infamous Mass — Thomas H. Cook — ____
Murder and Its Aftermath
Everything She Ever Wanted: A True Story of — Ann Rule — ____
Obsessive Love, Murder and Betrayal
"My Husband's Trying to Kill Me!": A True Story — Jim Schutze — ____
of Money, Marriage and Murderous Intent

1992

Homicide: A Year on the Killing Streets — David Simon ___
Witnesses From the Grave: The Stories Bones Tell — Christopher Joyce & Eric Stover ___
Boss of Bosses: The Fall of the Godfather: The FBI and Paul Castellano — Andris Kurins & Joseph F. O'Brien ___
Den of Thieves: The Untold Story of Men Who Plundered Wall Street and the Chase that Brought Them Down — James B. Stewart ___
Death of Elvis: What Really Happened — Charles C. Thompson II & James P. Cole ___

1991

In a Child's Name: The Legacy of a Mother's Murder — Peter Maas ___
Goombata: The Improbable Rise and Fall of John Gotti and His Gang — John Cummings & Ernest Volkman ___
Beyond Reason: The True Story of a Shocking Double Murder, a Brilliant and Beautiful Virginia Socialite, and a Deadly Psychotic Obsession — Ken Englade ___
Death in White Bear Lake, A: The True Chronicle of an All-American Town — Barry Siegel ___

1990

Doc: The Rape of the Town of Lovell — Jack Olsen ___
Death Shift, The: The True Story of Nurse Genene Jones and the Texas Baby Murders — Peter Elkind ___
Murder in Little Egypt — Darcy O'Brien ___
Blooding, The: The True Story of the Narborough Village Murders — Joseph Wambaugh ___
Wasted: The Preppie Murder — Linda Wolfe ___

1989

In Broad Daylight: A Murder in Skidmore, Missouri — Harry N. MacLean ___
Family of Spies: Inside the John Walker Spy Ring — Pete Earley ___
Cocaine Wars, The: Murder, Money, Corruption and the World's Most Valuable Commodity — Paul Eddy, Sara Walden w/Hugo Sabogal ___
Monkey on a Stick: Murder, Madness, and the Hare Krishnas — John Hubner & Lindsey Gruson ___
Gathering of Saints, A: A True Story of Money, Murder and Deceit — Robert Lindsey ___

1988

CBS Murders: A True Story of Greed and   Richard Hammer   ____
Violence in New York's Diamond District

Man Who Robbed the Pierre, The: The Story of Bobby   Ira Berkow   ____
Comfort and the Biggest Hotel Robbery Ever

Dreams of Ada: A True Story of Murder,   Robert Mayer   ____
Obsession, and a Small Town

Engaged to Murder: The Inside Story of the Main   Loretta Schwartz-Noble   ____
Line Murders

Talked to Death: The Murder of Alan Berg and the   Stephen Singular   ____
Rise of the Neo-Nazis

1987

Careless Whispers: The True Story of a Triple   Carlton Stowers   ____
Murder and the Determined Lawman Who
Wouldn't Give Up

Incident at Big Sky: Sheriff Johnny France and the   Johnny France &   ____
Mountain Men   Malcolm McConnell

Unveiling Claudia: A True Story of Serial Murder   Daniel Keyes   ____

Wiseguy: Life in a Mafia Family   Nicholas Pileggi   ____

Poison Tree, The: A True Story of Family Violence   Alan Prendergast   ____
and Revenge

1986

Savage Grace: The Story of a Doomed Family   Natalie Robins &   ____
    Stephen M.L. Aronson

Nutcracker: Money, Madness, Murder: A Family   Shana Alexander   ____
Album

Somebody's Husband, Somebody's Son: The Story of   Gordon Burn   ____
the Yorkshire Ripper

At Mother's Request: A True Story of Money,   Jonathan Coleman   ____
Murder and Betrayal

Airman and the Carpenter, The: The Lindbergh   Ludovic Kennedy   ____
Kidnapping and the Framing of Richard Hauptmann

Murder of a Shopping Bag Lady, The   Brian Kates   ____

1985

Double Play: The San Francisco City Hall Killings   Mike Weiss   ____

Evidence of Love: A True Story of Passion and   Jim Atkinson & John Bloom   ____
Death in the Suburbs

Murder at the Met: Based on the Exclusive   David Black   ____
Accounts of Detectives Mike Struk and Jerry
Giorgio of How They Solved the Phantom of the
Opera Case

Earth to Earth: A True Story of the Lives and   John Cornwell   ____
Violent Deaths of a Devon Farming Family

Molineux Affair, The: The True Story of the High Society   Jane Pejsa   ____
Murder that Rocked Turn-of-the-Century New York

1984

Very Much a Lady: The Untold Story of Jean — Shana Alexander — ____
Harris and Dr. Herman Tarnower
Judgement Day — B.C. Hall & Bob Lancaster — ____
Deadly Force: The Wrongful Death of James — Lawrence O'Donnell, Jr. — ____
Bouden Jr.: A True Story of How a Badge can
Become a License to Kill
Son — Jack Olsen — ____
Von Bulow Affair, The — William Wright — ____

1983

Vatican Connection, The: The Explosive Expose — Richard Hammer — ____
of a Billion- Dollar Counterfeit Stock Deal
Between the Mafia and the Church
Somebody is Lying: The Story of Doctor X. — Myron Farber — ____
Indecent Exposure: A True Story of Hollywood and — David McClintock — ____
Wall Street
Deadly Intentions: An Extraordinary Crime, The — William Randolph Stevens — ____
Prosecutor's Own Account
Big Bucks: The True, Outrageous Story of the — Ernest Tidyman — ____
Plymouth Mail Robbery... and How They Got
Away With It

1982

Sting Man, The: The Inside Story of Abscam — Robert W. Greene — ____
By Reason of Doubt: The Belshaw Case — Ellen Godfrey — ____
Minds of Billy Milligan, The — Daniel Keyes — ____
Day They Stole the Mona Lisa, The — Seymore V. Reit — ____
Papa's Game — Gregory Wallance — ____

1981

True Deliverance, A: The Joan Little Case — Fred Harwell — ____
Assassination on Embassy Row — John Dinges & — ____
Saul Landeau
Trial of Policeman Thomas Shea, The — Thomas Hawser — ____

1980

Falcon and the Snowman, The: A True Story of — Robert Lindsey — ____
Friendship and Espionage
Anyone's Daughter: The Times and Trials of — Shana Alexander — ____
Patricia Hearst
Blood Will Tell: The Murder Trials of T. Cullen Davis — Gary Cartwright — ____
Sentenced to Die: The People, the Crimes, and the — Stephen H. Gettinger — ____
Controversy
Zebra: The True Account of the 179 Days of Terror — Clark Howard — ____
in San Francisco

1979

Till Death Do Us Part: A True Murder Mystery   Vincent Bugliosi & Ken Hurwitz   ___

Why Have They Taken Our Children?:   Jack W. Baugh &   ___
  Chowchilla, July 15, 1976   Jefferson Morgan

Criminal Violence Criminal Justice   Charles E. Silberman   ___

Perjury: The Hiss-Chambers Case   Alan Weinstein   ___

1978

By Persons Unknown: The Strange Death of   George Jonas & Barbara Amiel   ___
Christine Demeter

Justice Crucified: The Story of Sacco and Vanzetti   Roberta S. Feuerlicht   ___

Closing Time: The True Story of the "Goodbar" Murder   Lacey Fosburgh   ___

Six Against the Rock   Clark Howard   ___

Voice of Guns, The: The Definitive and Dramatic Story   Vin McLellan & Paul Avery   ___
  of the Twenty-Two-Month Career of the Symbionese
  Liberation Army - One of the Most Bizarre Chapters
  in the History of the American Left

1977

Blood and Money   Thomas Thompson   ___

Murder in Coweta County   Margaret Anne Barnes   ___

Michigan Murders, The   Edward Keyes   ___

1976

Time to Die, A: The Attica Prison Revolt   Tom Wicker   ___

House on Garibaldi Street, The: The First Full   Isser Harel   ___
  Account of the Capture of Adolf Eichmann

Invitation to a Lynching   Gene Miller   ___

1975

Helter Skelter: The True Story of the Manson   Vincent Bugliosi & Curt Gentry   ___
Murders

Memphis Murders, The   Gerald Meyer   ___

Dummy   Ernest Tidyman   ___

1974

Legacy of Death: The Remarkable Saga of the   Barbara Levy   ___
Sanson Family, Who Served as Executioners of
France for Seven Generations

Medical Detectives, The   Paulette Cooper   ___

Burden of Proof: The Case of Juan Corona   Ed Cray   ___

Implosion Conspiracy, The   Louis Nizer   ___

Profession of Violence, The: The Rise and Fall of the   John Pearson   ___
  Kray Twins

1973

Hoax: The Inside Story of the Howard Hughes -   Lewis Chester, Stephen Fay   ____
   Clifford Irving Affair   & Magnus Linkletter
Santa Claus Bank Robbery, The   A.C. Greene   ____
They Got to Find Me Guilty Yet   T.P. Slattery   ____
Shipwreck: The Strange Fate of the Morro Castle   Gordon Witts &   ____
     Max Morgan Witts

1972

Beyond a Reasonable Doubt   Sandor Frankel   ____
Girl on the Volkswagen Floor, The: A True Tale of   William A. Clark   ____
   Murder
Disappearance of Dr. Parkman, The   Robert Sullivan   ____

1971

Great Fall, A: A Murder and Its Consequences   Mildred Savage   ____
Ninth Juror, The: A True Account of a Murder   Giraud Chester   ____
   Trial as Seen From Jury Box and Jury Room
Crime in America: Observations on Its Nature,   Ramsey Clark   ____
   Causes, Prevention, and Control

1970

Case that Will Not Die, The: Commonwealth   Herbert B. Ehrmann   ____
   Vs. Sacco and Vanzetti
Scottsboro: A Tragedy of the American South   Dan T. Carter   ____
Victims, The: The Wylie-Hoffert Murder Case and   Bernard Lefkowitz &   ____
   It's Strange Aftermath   Kenneth G.Gross
Whitmore: The Sensational Story of the   Fred C. Shapiro   ____
   Wylie-Hoffert Rape Murders

1969

Poe the Detective: The Curious Circumstances   John Evangelist Walsh   ____
   Behind 'The Mystery of Marie Roget'
Mulberry Tree, The   John Frasca   ____
Three Sisters in Black   Norman Zierold   ____

1968

Private Disgrace, A: Lizzie Borden in Daylight   Vicotria Lincoln   ____
Frame-Up: The Incredible Case of Tom Mooney   Curt Gentry   ____
   and Warren Billings
Black Market Medicine   Margaret Kreig   ____
Justice in the Back Room: The Explosive Story of   Selwyn Raab   ____
   Forced Confessions

1967

Boston Strangler, The   Gerold Frank   ____
Last Two to Hang, The   Elwyn Jones   ____
Crime and Detection, An Illustrated History From 1840   Julian Symons   ____

1966

In Cold Blood: A True Account of a Multiple   Truman Capote   _____
Murder and Its Consequences
Power of Life and Death, The   Lawrence G. Blochman &   _____
      Michael V. DiSalle
Murderers Sane and Mad: Case Histories in the   Miriam Allen deFord   _____
Motivation and Rationale of Murder
Little Girl is Dead, A   Harry Golden   _____
Century of the Detective, The   Jurgen Thorwald   _____

1965

Gideon's Trumpet   Anthony Lewis   _____
Molly Maguires, The   Wayne G. Broehl, Jr.   _____
Minister and the Choir Singer, The: The   William Kunstler   _____
Hall-Mills Murder Case
Lament for the Molly Maguires   Arthur H. Lewis   _____
Honored Society, The: A Searching Look at the Mafia   Norman Lewis   _____

1964

Deed, The   Gerold Frank   _____
Flight 967: A Startling Solution of One of the Most   Brad Williams   _____
Mysterious Crashes in the History of U.S.
Commercial Aviation
Hired Killers, The   Peter Wyden   _____

1963

Tragedy in Dedham: The Story of the   Francis Russell   _____
Sacco-Vanzettti Case

1962

Death and the Supreme Court   E. Barrett Prettyman, Jr.   _____
Sheppard Murder Case, The   Paul Holmes   _____
Lizzie Borden: The Untold Story   Edward D. Radin   _____
Kidnap: The Shocking Story of the Lindbergh Case   George Waller   _____

1961

Overbury Affair, The   Miriam Allen deFord   _____
Heaven Knows Who   Christianna Brand   _____
Mostly Murder   Sir Sydney Smith   _____

1960

Fire at Sea: The Story of the Morro Castle   Thomas Gallager   _____
Great Train Robberies of the West (1870-1933)   Eugene B. Block   _____

1959

They Died in the Chair: The Dramatic True   Wenzell Brown   ___
    Stories of Six Women Who Committed the
    Deadliest Sin
Royal Vultures, The   Sam Kollman   ___
        (as told to Hillel Black)
Murder and the Trial, The   Edgar Lustgarten   ___
Deadly Reasons, The   Edward D. Radin   ___
Incurable Wound, and Further Narratives of   Berton Roueche   ___
    Medical Detection, The

1958

D.A.'s Man, The   Harold R. Danforth &   ___
        James D. Horan
Memoirs of a Bow Street Runner   Henry Goddard & Patrick   ___
        Pringle (Intro.)
Girl in the Belfry, The   Joseph Henry Jackson &   ___
        Lenore Glen Offord

1957

Night Fell on Georgia   Charles & Louise Samuels   ___
Ruby McCollum: Woman in the Suwannee Jail   William Bradford Huie   ___
Historical Whodunits   Hugh Ross Williamson   ___

1956

Dead and Gone: Classic Crimes of North Carolina   Manly Wade Wellman   ___
Truth About Belle Guinness, The   Lillian de la Torre   ___
Assassins, The   Robert J. Donovan   ___

1955

Girl With the Scarlet Brand, The   Charles Boswell &   ___
        Lewis Thompson

1954

Why Did They Kill?   John Bartlow Martin   ___

1953

Court of Last Resort, The   Erle Stanley Gardner   ___

1952

True Tales From the Annals of Crime and Rascality   St. Clair McKelway   ___
Lady: Killers   W.T. Brannon   ___

1951

Twelve Against Crime: True Stories of the Men   Edward D. Radin   ___
    Who Solve America's Most Notorious Crimes

1950

Bad Company: The Story of California's Legendary   Joseph Henry Jackson   ___
    and Actual Stage-Robbers, Bandits, Highwaymen
    and Outlaws From the Fifties to the Eighties

1948

Twelve Against the Law: Twelve Outstanding Edward D. Radin ___
Cases in the Recent Annals of American Crime

Edgar® Best Critical/Biographical Work

2007

Science of Sherlock Holmes, The: From E.J. Wagner ___
Baskerville Hall to the Valley of Fear, the Real
Forensics Behind the Great Detective's
Greatest Cases
Unless the Threat of Death is Behind Them: John T. Irwin ___
Hard-Boiled Fiction and Film Noir

2006

Girl Sleuth: Nancy Drew and the Women Who Melanie Rehak ___
Created Her
Writing and Selling Your Mystery Novel: How to Hallie Ephron ___
Knock 'em Dead With Style
Behind the Mystery: Top Mystery Writers Stuart M. Kaminsky; photos ___
Interviewed by Laurie Roberts
New Annotated Sherlock Holmes, The: The Novels Leslie S. Klinger, ed.
Discovering the Maltese Falcon and Sam Spade: Richard Layman, ed. ___
The Evolution of Dashiell Hammett's
Masterpiece, Including John Huston's Movie
With Humphrey Bogart

2005

New Annotated Sherlock Holmes, The: The Leslie S. Klinger, ed. ___
Complete Short Stories
Latin American Mystery Writers: An A-to-Z Guide Darrell B. Lockhart ___
Booze and the Private Eye: Alcohol in the Rita Elizabeth Rippetoe ___
Hard-Boiled Novel
Life of Graham Greene, The: Volume III: 1956-1991 Norman Sherry ___

2004

Beautiful Shadow: A Life of Patricia Highsmith Andrew Wilson ___
Mystery Women: An Encyclopedia of Leading Colleen A. Barnett ___
Women Characters in Mystery Fiction, Vol. 3
Alfred Hitchcock: A Life in Darkness and Light Patrick McGillian ___
American Police Novel, The: A History Leroy Lad Panek ___
Amelia Peabody's Egypt: A Compendium Elizabeth Peters & ___
  Kristen Whitbread

2003

Mammoth Encyclopedia of Modern Crime   Mike Ashley, compiler   ____
    Fiction, The
Classic Era of Crime Fiction   Peter Haining   ____
Crime Films   Thomas Leitch   ____
Art of Noir, The: The Posters and Graphics From   Eddie Muller   ____
    the Classic Era of Film Noir

2002

Edgar Allan Poe: A to Z   Dawn B. Sova   ____
History of Mystery, The   Max Allan Collins   ____
Dashiell Hammett: A Daughter Remembers   Jo Hammett   ____
My Name's Friday: The Unauthorized but True   Michael J. Hayde   ____
    Story of Dragnet and the Films of Jack Webb
Selected Letters of Dashiell Hammett: 1921-1960   Richard Layman &   ____
                                        Julie M. Rivett, eds.
Who was that Lady? Craig Rice: The Queen of   Jeffrey Marks   ____
    Screwball Mystery

2001

Conundrums for the Long Week-End   Ethan Lewis & Robert Kuhn ____
                                        McGregor
Doctor and the Detective, The: A Biography of Sir Martin Booth   ____
    Arthur Conan Doyle
Women of Mystery: The Lives and Works of   Martha Hailey DuBose   ____
    Notable Women Crime Novelists   (some essays by Margaret
                                        Caldwell Thomas)
Red-Hot Typewriter, The: The Life and Times of   Hugh Merrill   ____
    John D. MacDonald

2000

Teller of Tales: The Life of Arthur Conan Doyle   Daniel Stashower   ____
Oxford Companion to Crime and Mystery Writing, The Rosemary Herbert, ed.   ____
Suitable Job for a Woman, A: Inside the World of   Val McDermid   ____
    Women Private Eyes
Web of Iniquity, The: Early Detective Fiction by   Catherine Ross Nickerson   ____
    American Women
Ross Macdonald   Tom Nolan   ____

1999

Mystery and Suspense Writers: The Literature of   Robin W. Winks &   ____
    Crime, Detection, and Espionage   Maureen Corrigan, eds.
Seven Deadly Sins in the Work of Dorothy L. Sayers, The Janice Brown   ____
Cordially Yours, Brother Cadfael   K. Anne Kaler, ed.   ____
Dark City: The Lost World of Film Noir   Eddie Muller   ____
Midnight Dreary: The Mysterious Death of Edgar   John Evangelist Walsh   ____
    Allan Poe

1998

"G" is for Grafton: The World of Kinsey Millhone	Natalie Hevener Kaufman & Carol McGinnis Kay	___
Reader and the Detective Story, The	George M. Dove	___
Crime Fiction and Film in the Sunshine State: *Florida Noir*	Steve Glassman & Maurice O'Sullivan	___
Deadly Women: The Woman Mystery Readers' *Indispensable Companion*	Jan Grape, Dean James & Ellen Nehr, eds.	___
AZ Murder Goes…Classic	Susan Malling & Barbara Peters	___

1997

Secret Marriage of Sherlock Holmes and Other *Eccentric Readings, The*	Michael Atkinson	___
Detecting Women 2: A Reader's Guide and *Checklist for Mystery Series Written by Women*	Willetta L. Heising	___
Blues Detective, The: A Study of African-American *Detective Fiction*	Stephen F. Soitos	___
Agatha Christie: A to Z	Dawn B. Sova	___
Elusion Aforethought: The Life and Writing of *Anthony Berkeley Cox*	Malcolm J. Turnbull	___

1996

Savage Art: A Biography of Jim Thompson	Robert Polito	___
John Dickson Carr: The Man Who Explained Miracles	Douglas G. Greene	___
Life of Graham Greene, The: Volume II: 1939-1955	Norman Sherry	___
Cadfael Companion, The: The World of Brother *Cadfael, 2nd ed.*	Robin Whiteman	___

1995

Encyclopedia Mysteriosa: A Comprehensive *Guide to the Art of Detection in Print, Film,* *Radio, and Television*	William L. DeAndrea	___
Tony Hillerman Companion, The: A *Comprehensive Guide to His Life and Work*	Martin H. Greenberg, ed.	___
Great Women Mystery Writers: Classic to Contemporary	Kathleen Gregory Klein, ed.	___
Dick Tracey and American Culture	Garyn G. Roberts	___
By a Woman's Hand: A Guide to Mystery Fiction *by Women*	Jean Swanson & Dean James, eds.	___

1994

Saint, The: A Complete History in Print, Radio, Film *and Television of Leslie Charteris' Robin Hood of* *Modern Crime, Simon Templar, 1928-1992*	Burl Barer	___
Fine Art of Murder, The: The Mystery Reader's *Indispensable Companion*	Ed Gorman, Martin H. Greenberg, Larry Segriff & Jon L. Breen, eds.	___
Reader's Guide to the American Novel of Detection, A	Marvin Lachman	___
Man Who Wasn't Maigret, The	Patrick Marnham	___
Dorothy L. Sayers: Her Life and Soul	Barbara Reynolds	___

1993

Alias S.S. Van Dine: The Man Who Created   John Loughery   ___
Philo Vance
Dorothy L. Sayers: A Careless Rage for Life   David Coomes   ___
Edgar Allan Poe: His Life and Legacy   Jeffrey Meyers   ___
Doubleday Crime Club Compendium 1928-1991   Ellen Nehr   ___

1992

Edgar A. Poe: Mournful and Never-Ending   Kenneth Silverman   ___
Remembrance
Out of the Woodpile: Black Characters in Crime   Frankie Y. Bailey   ___
and Detective Fiction
Agatha Christie: Murder in Four Acts   Peter Haining   ___
Talking Mysteries: A Conversation With Tony   Tony Hillerman & Ernie Bulow   ___
Hillerman
Jim Thompson: Sleep With the Devil: A Biography   Michael J. McCauley   ___
of America's Greatest Noir Writer

1991

Trouble is Their Business: Private Eyes in   John Conquest   ___
Fiction, Film, and Television, 1927-1988
John Dickson Carr: A Critical Study   S.T. Joshi   ___
Remarkable Case of Dorothy L. Sayers, The   Catherine Kenney   ___
Eric Ambler   Peter Lewis   ___
Hillary Waugh's Guide to Mysteries and Mystery   Hillary Waugh   ___
Writing

1990

Life of Graham Greene, The: Volume I: Norman Sherry   ___
1904-1939
Film Noir: Reflections in a Dark Mirror   Bruce Crowther   ___
Perfect Murder, The: A Study in Detection   David Lehman   ___
Murder on the Air: Television's Great Mystery Series   Ric Meyers   ___
Mysterium and Mystery: The Clerical Crime Novel   William David Spencer   ___

1989

Cornell Woolrich: First You Dream, Then You Die   Francis M. Nevins, Jr.   ___
Dime Detectives, The: A Comprehensive History of   Ron Goulart   ___
the Detective Fiction Pulps
Silk Stalkings: When Women Write of Murder   Victoria Nichols &   ___
    Susan Thompson
Sisters in Crime: Feminism and the Crime Novel   Maureen T. Reddy   ___

1988

Introduction to the Detective Story   Leroy Lad Panek   ___
Crime and Mystery, The 100 Best Books   H.R.F. Keating   ___
Campion's Career: A Study of the Novels of   B.A. Pike   ___
Margery Allingham
Corridors of Deceit: The World of John le Carre   Peter Wolfe   ___

1987
Here Lies: An Autobiography   Eric Ambler   ____
Secret of the Stratemeyer Syndicate, The: Nancy   Carol Billman   ____
  Drew, The Hardy Boys and the Million Dollar
  Fiction Factory
Mystery Lover's Companion, The   Art Bourgeau   ____
13 Mistresses of Murder   Elaine Budd   ____
1001 Midnights: The Aficionado's Guide to   Marcia Muller & Bill Pronzini   ____
  Mystery and Detective Fiction

1986
John le Carre   Peter Lewis   ____
Private Eyes: 101 Knights: A Survey of American   Robert A. Baker &   ____
  Detective Fiction, 1922-1984   Michael T. Nietzel
Lord Peter Wimsey Companion, The   Stephan P. Clarke   ____
American Private Eye, The: The Image in Fiction   David Geherin   ____
Agatha Christie: A Biography   Janet Morgan   ____

1985
Novel Verdicts: A Guide to Courtroom Fiction   Jon L. Breen   ____
James Bond Bedside Companion, The: All About   Raymond Benson   ____
  the World According to 007
Ross Macdonald   Matthew J. Bruccoli   ____
One Lonely Knight: Mickey Spillane's Mike Hammer   Max Allan Collins &   ____
                                                                  James L. Traylor
Inward Journey: Ross Macdonald   Ralph B. Sipper, ed.   ____

1984
Dark Side of Genius, The: The Life of Alfred   Donald Spoto   ____
  Hitchcock
Mystery of Georges Simenon, The   Fenton Bresler   ____
Dashiell Hammett: A Life   Diane Johnson   ____
Poetics of Murder, The: Detective Fiction and   Glenn W. Most &   ____
  Literary Theory   William W. Stowe, eds.

1983
Cain; The Biography of James M. Cain   Roy Hoopes   ____
Police Procedural, The   George M. Dove   ____
Gun in Cheek: A Study of "Alternative" Crime Fiction   Bill Pronzini   ____
Modus Operandi: An Excursion into Detective Fiction   Robin W. Winks   ____

1982
What About Murder? A Guide to Books About   Jon L. Breen   ____
  Mystery and Detective Fiction
Whodunit, The: An Informal History of Detective   Stefano Benvenuti &   ____
  Fiction   Gianni Rizzoni
Selected Letters of Raymond Chandler   Frank MacShane, ed.   ____
TV Detectives   Richard Meyers   ____
Annotated Tales of Edgar Allan Poe, The   Stephen Peithman, ed.   ____

1981

Twentieth Century Crime and Mystery Writers,   John M. Reilly, ed.   ____
    1st edition

Talent to Deceive, A: An Appreciation of Agatha   Robert Barnard   ____
    Christie

Watteau's Shepherds: The Detective Novel in   Leroy Lad Panek   ____
    Britain 1914-1940

1980

Dorothy L. Sayers, A Literary Biography   Ralph E. Hone   ____

Secret of Grown-Ups, The: An Autobiography   Vera Caspary   ____

As Her Whimsey Took Her: Critical Essays on the   Margaret Hannay, ed.   ____
    Work of Dorothy L. Sayers

Sherlock Holmes, The Man and His World   H.R.F. Keating   ____

1979

Mystery of Agatha Christie, The: An Intimate   Gwen Robins   ____
    Biography of the First Lady of Crime

Erle Stanley Gardner: The Case of the Real Perry   Dorothy B. Hughes   ____
    Mason

Tell-Tale Heart, The: The Life and Work of Edgar   Julian Symons   ____
    Allan Poe

Detective in Hollywood, The: The Movie Careers of   John Tuska   ____
    the Great Fictional Private Eyes and Their Creators

1978

Rex Stout: A Biography   John McAleer   ____

Agatha Christie: An Autobiography   Agatha Christie   ____

Encyclopedia Sherlockiana, The: A Universal   Jack Tracy   ____
    Dictionary of Sherlock Holmes and His
    Biographer John H. Watson, M.D.

1977

Encyclopedia of Mystery and Detection   Chris Steinbrunner & Otto   ____
       Penzler, eds. in chief, Marvin
       Lachman & Charles Shibuk,
       senior eds.

Mystery Story, The: Introduction to   John Ball, ed.   ____
    Detective-Mystery Fiction

Dangerous Edge, The   Gavin Lambert   ____

Life of Raymond Chandler, The   Frank MacShane   ____

Agatha Christie Mystery, The   Derrick Murdoch   ____

Edgar® Best Young Adult

2007

Buried	Robin Merrow MacCready	____
Road of the Dead, The	Kevin Brooks	____
Christopher Killer, The	Alane Ferguson	____
Crunch Time	Mariah Fredericks	____
Night My Sister Went Missing, The	Carol Plum-Ucci	____

2006

Last Shot	John Feinstein	____
Down the Rabbit Hole	Peter Abrahams	____
Quid Pro Quo	Vicki Grant	____
Young Bond, Book One: Silverfin, A James Bond Adventure	Charlie Higson	____
Spy Goddess, Book One: Live and Let Shop	Michael P. Spradlin	____

2005

In Darkness, Death	Dorothy & Thomas Hoobler	____
Story Time	Edward Bloor	____
Jude	Kate Morgenroth	____
Book of Dead Days, The	Marcus Sedgwick	____
Missing Abby	Lee Weatherly	____

2004

Acceleration	Graham McNamee	____
Last Treasure, The	Janet Anderson	____
Feast of Fools	Bridget Crowley	____
Death and the Arrow	Chris Priestly	____
Uncovering Sadie's Secrets	Libby Sternberg	____

2003

Wessex Papers, The: Vols. 1-3	Daniel Parker	____
Safe House	Jenny Carroll	____
Cheating Lessons	Nan Willard Cappo	____
Hit and Run	Mark Delaney	____
Night the Penningtons Vanished, The	Marianna Heusler	____

2002

Boy in the Burning House, The	Tim Wynne-Jones	____
Dark Secrets Don't Tell	Elizabeth Chandler	____
Death on Sacred Ground	Harriet K. Feder	____
Shades of Simon Gray	Joyce McDonald	____
Witch Hill	Marcus Sedgwick	____

2001

Counterfeit Son	Elaine Marie Alphin	____
Silent to the Bone	E.L. Konigsburg	____
Body of Christopher Creed, The	Carol Plum-Ucci	____
Locked Inside	Nancy Werlin	____

2000
Never Trust a Dead Man   Vivian Vande Velde   ____
Speak   Laurie Halse Anderson   ____
That Kind of Money   Vicki Cameron   ____
Ghost in the Tokaido Inn, The Dorothy & Thomas Hoobler   ____
Monster   Walter Dean Myers   ____

1999
Killer's Cousin, The   Nancy Werlin   ____
Finn   Katharine Jay Bacon   ____
Maze, The   Will Hobbs   ____
Paperquake   Kathryn Reiss   ____
For Mike   Shelley Sykes   ____

1998
Ghost Canoe   Will Hobbs
Tangerine   Edward Bloor   ____
Yesterday's Child   Sonia Levitin   ____
Thin Ice   Marsha Qualey   ____
Deal With a Ghost   Marilyn Sanger   ____

1997
Twisted Summer   Willo Davis Roberts   ____
Who Killed Mr. Chippendale?   Mel Glenn
Mr. Was   Pete Hautman   ____
Flyers   Daniel Hayes   ____
Hawk Moon   Rob MacGregor   ____

1996
Prophecy Rock   Rob MacGregor   ____
Spying on Miss Muller   Eve Bunting   ____
In the Middle of the Night   Robert Cormier   ____
Angel's Gate   Gary Crew   ____
Spirit Seeker   Joan Lowery Nixon   ____

1995
Toughing It   Nancy Springer   ____
Poison   Alane Ferguson   ____
Shadowmaker   Joan Lowery Nixon   ____
Midnight Club, The   Christopher Pike   ____
Pale Phoenix   Kathryn Reiss   ____

1994
Name of the Game was Murder, The Joan Lowery Nixon   ____
Strange Objects   Gary Crew   ____
Help Wanted   Richie Tankersley Cusick   ____
Class Trip   Bebe Faas Rice   ____
Silent Witness   Patricia H. Rushford   ____

1993

Little Bit Dead, A	Chap Reaver	___
Breaking the Fall	Michael Cadnum	___
Highest Form of Killing, The	Malcolm Rose	___
One Who Came Back, The	Joann Mazzio	___
Weekend was Murder, The	Joan Lowery Nixon	___

1992

Weirdo, The	Theodore Taylor	___
Calling Home	Michael Cadnum	___
We All Fall Down	Robert Cormier	___
Scarface	Peter Nelson	___
Chrismas Killers, The	Patricia Windsor	___

1991

Mote	Chap Reaver	___
Zachary	Ernest Pintoff	___
Guilt Trip	Stephen Schwandt	___
Secret Keeper, The	Gloria Whelan	___

1990

Show Me the Evidence	Alane Ferguson	___
Man Who was Poe, The		___
Fell Back	M.E. Kerr	___
Remember Me	Christopher Pike	___
Sniper	Theodore Taylor	___

1989

Incident at Loring Groves	Sonia Levitin	___
Falcon Sting, The	Barbara Brenner	___
Second Fiddle	Ronald Kidd	___
Shadow in the North	Philip Pullman	___
Accident, The	Todd Strasser	___

Edgar® Best Juvenile

2007

Room One: A Mystery or Two	Andrew Clements	___
Gilda Joyce: The Ladies of the Lake	Jennifer Allison	___
Stolen Sapphire: A Samantha Mystery, The	Sarah Masters Buckey	___
Bloodwater Mysteries: Snatched, The	Pete Hautman & Mary Logue	___
Case of the Missing Marquess, The	Nancy Springer	___

2006

Boys of San Joaquin, The	D. James Smith	___
Shakespeare's Secret	Elise Broach	___
Case of the Nana-Napper, The: A Wright & Wrong Mystery	Laura J. Burns & Melinda Metz	___
Missing Manatee, The	Cynthia DeFelice	___
Flush	Carl Hiassen	___

2005
Chasing Vermeer — Blue Balliett — ___
Abduction! — Peg Kehret — ___
Assassin — Patricia Finney — ___
Looking for Bobowicz — Daniel Pinkwate — ___
Unseen, The — Zilpha Keatley Snyder — ___

2004
Bernie Magruder and the Bats in the Belfry — Phyllis Reynolds Naylor — ___
Malted Falcon, The — Bruce Hale — ___
Lily's Ghosts — Laura Ruby — ___
Dust — Arthur Slade — ___
Sammy Keyes and the Art of Deception — Wendelin Van Draanen — ___

2003
Harriet Spies Again — Helen Ericson — ___
O'Dwyer and Grady: Starring in Acting Innocent — Eileen Heyes — ___
Case of the Greedy Granny, The: Jake Gander, Storyville Detective — George McClements — ___
Riding the Flume — Patricia Curtis Pfitsch — ___
Sammy Keyes and the Search for Snake Eye — Wendelin Van Draanen — ___

2002
Dangling — Lillian Eige — ___
Ghost Soldier — Elaine Marie Alphin — ___
Ghost Sitter — Peni R. Griffin — ___
Following Fake Man — Barbara Ware Holmes — ___
Bug Muldoon — Paul Shipton — ___

2001
Dovey Coe — Frances O'Roark Dowell — ___
Trouble at Fort La Pointe — Kathleen Ernst — ___
Walking to the Bus Rider Blues — Harriette Gillem Robinet — ___
Sammy Keyes and the Curse of Mustache Mary — Wendelin Van Draanen — ___
Ghosts in the Gallery — Barbara Brooks Wallace — ___

2000
Night Flyers, The — Elizabeth McDavid Jones — ___
Howie Bowles, Secret Agent — Kate Banks — ___
Shadow Horse — Alison Hart — ___
Dolphin Luck — Hilary McKay — ___
Green Thumb — Rob Thomas — ___

1999
Sammy Keyes and the Hotel Thief — Wendelin Van Draanen — ___
Alice Rose and Sam — Kathryn Lasky — ___
Wreckers, The — Iain Lawrence — ___
Kidnappers, The — Willo Davis Roberts — ___
Holes — Louis Sachar — ___

1998

Sparrows in the Scullery   Barbara Brooks Wallace   ___
Wolf Stalker   Alane Ferguson &   ___
    Gloria Skurzynski

Turn the Cup Around   Barbara Mariconda   ___
Christie and Company Down East   Katherine Hall Page   ___
Secrets at Hidden Valley   Willo Davis Roberts   ___

1997

Clearing, The   Dorothy Reynolds Miller   ___
Last Piper, The   Helen Cavanagh   ___
Case of the Wiggling Wig, The   E.W. Hildick   ___
Gaps in Stone Walls   John Neufield   ___
Cousins in the Castle   Barbara Brooks Wallace   ___

1996

Looking for Jamie Bridger   Nancy Springer   ___
13th Floor, The   Sid Fleischman   ___
Running Out of Time   Margaret Peterson Haddix   ___
Marvelous Marvin and the Pioneer Ghost   Bonnie Pryor   ___
Bones in the Cliff, The   James Stevenson   ___

1995

Absolutely True Story, The…How I Visited   Willo Davis Roberts   ___
    Yellowstone Park With the Terrible Rubes
Harvey's Mystifying Racoon Mix Up   Clifford Eth   ___
Hester Bidgood Investigatrix of Evill Deedes   E.W. Hildick   ___
Trouble Will Find You   Joan M. Lexau   ___
Caught   Willo Davis Roberts   ___

1994

Twin in the Tavern, The   Barbara Brooks Wallace   ___
Tangled Web   Eloise Jarvis McGraw
Face in the Bessledorf Funeral Parlor, The   Phyllis Reynolds Naylor   ___
Spider Kane and the Mystery at Jumbo Nightcrawler's   Mary Pope Osborne   ___
Sam the Cat, Detective   Linda Stewart   ___

1993

Coffin on a Case!   Eve Bunting   ___
Susannah and the Purple Mongoose   Patricia Elmore   ___
Treasure Bird, The   Peni R. Griffin   ___
Fish and Bones   Ray Prather   ___
Widow's Broom, The   Chris Van Allsburg   ___

1992
Wanted...Mud Blossom — Betsy Byars — ____
Mystery on October Road — Alison Cragin Herzig & Jane Lawrence Mali — ____

Double Trouble Squared — Kathryn Lasky — ____
Witch Weed — Phyllis Reynolds Naylor — ____
Finding Buck McHenry — Alfred Slote — ____

1991
Stonewords — Pam Conrad — ____
Midnight Horse, The — Sid Fleischman — ____
Tormentors, The — Lynn Hall — ____
To Grandmother's House We Go — Willo Davis Roberts — ____
Cave Ghost — Barbara Steiner — ____

1989
Megan's Island — Willo Davis Roberts — ____
Something Upstairs — Avi — ____
Lamp From the Warlock's Tomb, The — John Bellairs — ____
Is There Anybody There? — Eve Bunting — ____
Following the Mystery Man — Mary Downing Hahn — ____

1988
Lucy Forever and Miss Rosetree, Shrinks — Susan Shreve — ____
Bury the Dead — Peter Carter — ____
Twisted Windows, The — Lois Duncan — ____
House on the Hill, The — Eileen Dunlop — ____
Through the Hidden Door — Rosemary Wells — ____

1987
Other Side of Dark, The — Joan Lowery Nixon — ____
Skeleton Man, The — Jay Bennett — ____
Secret Life of Dilly McBean, The — Dorothy Haas — ____
Bodies in the Bessledorf Hotel, The — Phyllis Reynolds Naylor — ____
Floating Illusions — Chelsea Quinn Yarbro — ____

1986
Sandman's Eyes, The — Patricia Windsor — ____
Locked in Time — Lois Duncan — ____
On the Edge — Gillian Cross — ____
Screaming High — David Line — ____
Playing Murder — Sandra Scoppettone — ____

1985
Night Cry — Phyllis Reynolds Naylor — ____
Third Eye, The — Lois Duncan — ____
Chameleon the Spy and the Case of the Vanishing Jewels — Diane Redfield Massie — ____
Ghosts of Now, The — Joan Lowery Nixon — ____
Island on Bird Street, The — Uri Orlev — ____

1984

Callender Papers, The	Cynthia Voigt	___
Shadrach's Crossing	Avi	___
Maze Stone, The	Eileen Dunlop	___
Griffin Legacy, The	Jan O'Donnell Klaveness	___
Dollhouse Murders, The	Betty Ren Wright	___

1983

Murder of Hound Dog Bates, The	Robbie Branscum	___
Kept in the Dark	Nina Bawden	___
Case of the Cop Catchers, The	Terrance Dicks	___
Clone Catcher	Alfred Slote	___
Cadbury's Coffin	Glendon & Kathryn Swarthout	___

1982

Taking Terri Mueller	Norma Fox Mazer	___
Hoops	Walter Dean Myers	___
Village of the Vampire Cat	Lensey Namioka	___
Detective Mole and the Halloween Mystery	Robert Quackenbush	___
Detour to Danger	Eva-Lis Wuorio	___

1981

Séance, The	Joan Lowery Nixon	___
Doggone Mystery, The	Mary Blount Christian	___
We Dare Not Go A-Hunting	Charlotte MacLeod	___
More Minden Curses	Willo Davis Roberts	___
When No One was Looking	Rosemary Wells	___

1980

Kidnapping of Christina Lattimore, The	Joan Lowery Nixon	___
Mystery Cottage in Left Field	Remus F. Caroselli	___
Whispered Horse, The	Lynn Hall	___
Chameleon was a Spy	Diane Redfield Massie	___
Mystery of the Eagle's Claw	Frances Wosmek	___

1979

Alone in Wolf Hollow	Dana Brookins	___
Emily Upham's Revenge	Avi	___
Bassumtyte Treasure, The	Jean Louise Curry	___
Case of the Secret Scribbler, The	E.W. Hildick	___
Halloween Pumpkin Smasher, The	Judith St. George	___

1978

Really Weird Summer, A	Eloise Jarvis McGraw	___
Miss Nelson is Missing!	Harry Allard & James Marshall	___
Night Spell	Robert Newman	___
Poor Tom's Ghost	Jean Louise Curry	___

1977
> ***Are You in the House Alone?***   Richard Peck   ___
> *Wiley and the Hairy Man*   Molly Garrett Bang   ___
> *Chalk Cross, The*   Berthe Amoss   ___
> *Mr. Moon's Last Case*   Brian Patten   ___
> *Master Puppeteer, The*   Katherine Peterson   ___

1976
> ***Z for Zachariah***   Robert C. O'Brien   ___
> *No More Magic*   Avi   ___
> *Tattooed Potato and Other Clues, The*   Ellen Raskin   ___
> *Great Steamboat Mystery*   Richard Scarry   ___

1975
> ***Dangling Witness, The***   Jay Bennett   ___
> *Here Lies the Body*   Scott Corbett   ___
> *Mysterious Red Tape Gang, The*   Joan Lowery Nixon   ___
> *Girl in the Grove, The*   David Severn   ___
> *Fire in the Stone*   Colin Thiele   ___

1974
> ***Long Black Coat, The***   Jay Bennett   ___
> *Dreamland Lake*   Richard Peck   ___
> *Secret of the Seven Crows, The*   Wylly Folk St. John   ___
> *Mystery of the Scowling Boy*   Phyllis A. Whitney   ___

1973
> ***Deathwatch***   Robb White   ___
> *Uncle Robert's Secret*   Wylly Folk St. John   ___
> *Catch a Killer*   George A. Woods   ___
> *Elizabeth's Tower*   A.C. Stewart   ___

1972
> ***Nightfall***   Joan Aiken   ___
> *Mystery in Wales*   Mabel Esther Allan   ___
> *Goody Hall*   Natalie Babbitt   ___
> *Ghost of Ballyhooly, The*   Betty Cavanna   ___

1971
> ***Intruder, The***   John Rowe Townsend   ___
> *Mystery Man, The*   Scott Corbett   ___
> *Secret of the Missing Footprint, The*   Phyllis A. Whitney   ___

1970
> ***Danger at Black Dyke***   Winfred Finlay   ___
> *Spice Island Mystery*   Betty Cavanna   ___
> *They Never Came Home*   Lois Duncan   ___
> *Mystery of the Witch Who Wouldn't*   Kin Platt   ___

1969
> *House of Dies Drear, The*   Virginia Hamilton   ____
> *Forgery!*   Phyllis Bentley   ____
> *Mystery of the Fat Cat*   Frank Bonham   ____
> *Smugglers' Road*   Hal G. Evarts   ____

1968
> *Signpost to Terror*   Gretchen Sprague   ____
> *Secret of the Missing Boat, The*   Paul Berna   ____
> *Witches' Bridge, The*   Barbee Oliver Carleton   ____

1967
> *Sinbad and Me*   Kin Platt   ____
> *Mystery of the Red Tide*   Frank Bonham   ____
> *Ransom*   Lois Duncan   ____
> *Danger Beats the Drum*   Arnold Madison   ____

1966
> *Mystery of 22 East, The*   Leon Ware   ____
> *Secret of the Simple Code, The*   Nancy Faulkner   ____
> *Secret of the Haunted Crags*   Lawrence J. Hunt   ____
> *Apache Gold Mystery, The*   Eileen Thompson   ____

1965
> *Mystery at Crane's Landing*   Marcella Thum   ____
> *Spell is Cast, A*   Eleanor Cameron   ____
> *Treasure River*   Hal G. Evarts   ____
> *Private Eyes*   Leo Kingman   ____

1964
> *Mystery of the Hidden Hand*   Phyllis A. Whitney   ____
> *Honor Bound*   Frank Bonham   ____
> *Mystery of the Velvet Box*   Margaret Scherf   ____

1963
> *Cutlass Island*   Scott Corbett   ____
> *Mystery of Ghost Valley, The*   Harriett Carr   ____
> *House on Charlton Street, The*   Dola de John   ____
> *Diamond in the Window, The*   Jane Langton   ____

1962
> *Phantom of Walkaway Hill. The*   Edward Fenton   ____
> *Secret of the Tiger's Eye, The*   Phyllis A. Whitney   ____

1961
> *Mystery of the Haunted Pool, The*   Phyllis A. Whitney   ____

Edgar® Grand Master Award

The Grand Master Award, given yearly by the MWA, represents the pinnacle of achievement in the mystery field. This prestigious and highly coveted award was established to recognize not only important contributions to the mystery field but also a significant output of consistently high quality.

2007	Stephen King
2006	Stuart M. Kaminsky
2005	Marcia Muller
2004	Joseph Wambaugh
2003	Ira Levin
2002	Robert B. Parker
2001	Edward D. Hoch
2000	Mary Higgins Clark
1999	P.D. James
1998	Barbara Mertz (Elizabeth Peters and Barbara Michaels)
1997	Ruth Rendell
1996	Dick Francis
1995	Mickey Spillane
1994	Lawrence Block
1993	Donald E. Westlake
1992	Elmore Leonard
1991	Tony Hillerman
1990	Helen McCloy
1989	Hillary Waugh
1988	Phyllis A. Whitney
1987	Michael Gilbert
1986	Ed McBain
1985	Dorothy Salisbury Davis
1984	John le Carre
1983	Margaret Millar
1982	Julian Symons
1981	Stanley Ellin
1980	W.R. Burnett
1979	Aaron Marc Stein
1978	Daphne du Maurier
1978	Dorothy B. Hughes
1978	Ngaio Marsh
1976	Graham Greene
1975	Eric Ambler
1974	Ross Macdonald
1973	Alfred Hitchcock
1973	Judson Philips
1972	John D. MacDonald

1971	Mignon G. Eberhart
1970	James M. Cain
1969	John Creasey
1967	Baynard Kendrick
1966	Georges Simenon
1964	George Harmon Coxe
1963	John Dickson Carr
1962	Erle Stanley Gardner
1961	Ellery Queen (Frederic Dannay and Manfred B. Lee)
1959	Rex Stout
1958	Vincent Starrett
1955	Agatha Christie

Mary Higgins Clark Award
The Simon & Schuster—Mary Higgins Clark Award

Each year this award, sponsored by Simon & Schuster, is presented to an author in suspense fiction writing in the tradition of Mary Higgins Clark. The award began in 2001. The winner is selected by a special Mystery Writers of America committee and follows guidelines set forth by Mary Higgins Clark:

❖ The protagonist is a very nice young woman, 27-38 or so, whose life is suddenly invaded. She is not looking for trouble—she is doing exactly what she should be doing and something cuts across her bow (as in ship).

❖ She solves her problem by her own courage and intelligence.

❖ She has an interesting job.

❖ She's self-made—independent—has primarily good family relationships.

❖ No on-scene violence.

❖ No four-letter words or explicit sex scenes.

❖ Think Rhett Butler, "You'll not shut me out of your bedroom tonight, my dear."

Mary Higgins Clark Award

2007
Bloodline   Fiona Mountain   ____

2006
Dark Angel   Karen Harper   ____
Breaking Faith   Jo Bannister   ____
Shadow Valley   Gwen Hunter   ____

2005
Grave Endings   Rochelle Krich   ____
Perfect Sax   Jerrilyn Farmer   ____
Drowning Tree, The   Carol Goodman   ____
Scent of a Killer   Christiane Heggan   ____
Murder in a Mill Town   P.B. Ryan   ____

2004
Song of the Bones   M.K. Preston   ____
Ricochet   Nancy Baker Jacobs   ____
Bloodhound to Die For, A   Virginia Lanier   ____
Samurai's Daughter   Sujata Massey   ____
Body in the Lighthouse, The   Katherine Hall Page   ____

2003

Absolute Certainty	Rose Connors	___
Stone Forest, The	Karen Harper	___
Truth Hurts, The	Nancy Pickard	___
Bad Witness, The	Laura Van Wormer	___

2002

Summer of Storms	Judith Kelman	___
Murphy's Law	Rhys Bowen	___
Perhaps She'll Die	M.K. Preston	___
Murder of a Sweet Old Lady	Denise Swanson	___

2001

Authorized Personnel Only	Barbara D'Amato	___
Demolition Angel	Robert Crais	___
Debt Collector, The	Lynn Hightower	___
False Witness	Lelia Kelly	___
Plain Truth	Jodi Picoult	___

Robert L. Fish Memorial Award

This award is administered by the Mystery Writers of America and is sponsored by the Robert L. Fish estate. The award is to recognize and encourage promising new writers. Each year the Edgar® Short Story Committee selects the best first mystery short story by an American author whose fiction has not been previously published. The award began in 1984.

Robert L. Fish Memorial Award

2007
"Evening Gold" — William Dylan Powell *EQMM*, Nov 06 ___

2006
"Home" — Eddie Newton — *EQMM*, May 05 ___

2005
"Can't Catch Me" — Thomas Morrissey — *Brooklyn Noir*; McLoughlin, ed. ___

2004
"Grass is Always Greener, The" — Sandra Balzo — *EQMM*, Mar 03 ___

2003
"War Can Be Murder" — Mike Doogan — *Mysterious North*; Stabenow, ed. ___

2002
"My Bonnie Lies…" — Ted Hertel, Jr. — *Mammoth Book of Legal Thrillers*; Hemmingson, ed. ___

2001
"Witch and the Relic Thief, The" — M.J. Jones — *AHMM*, Oct 00 ___

2000
"Cro-Magnon, P.I." — Mike Reiss — *AHMM*, Jul/Aug 99 ___

1999
"Clarity" — Bryn Bonner — *EQMM*, May 98 ___

1998
"If Thine Eye Offend Thee" — Rosalind Roland — *Murder by 13*; English, Seidman & Woods, eds. ___

1997
"Prosecutor of DuPrey, The" — David Vaughn — *EQMM*, Jan 96 ___

1996
"Word for Breaking August Sky, The" — James Sarafin — *AHMM*, Jul 95 ___

1995
"Me and Mr. Harry" — Batya Swift Yasgur — *EQMM*, Dec 94 ___

1994
"Wicked Twist"   D.A. McGuire   *AHMM*, Oct 93   ___

1993
"Will is a Way, A"   Steven Saylor   *EQMM*, Mar 92   ___

1991
"Willie's Story"   Jerry F. Skarky   *AHMM*, Jun 90   ___

1990
"Hawks"   Connie Colt   *AHMM*, Jun 89   ___

1989
"Different Drummers"   Linda O. Johnston   *EQMM*, Jul 88   ___

1988
"Roger, Mr. Whilkie!"   Eric M. Heideman   *AHMM*, Jul 87   ___

1987
"Father to the Man"   Mary Kittredge   *AHMM*, Nov 86   ___

1986
"Final Rites"   Doug Allyn   *AHMM*, Dec 85   ___

1985
"Poor Dumb Mouths"   Bill Crenshaw   *AHMM*, May 84   ___

1984
"Locked Doors"   Lilly Carlson   *EQMM*, Oct 83   ___

Database for all of the Edgar® Awards: mysterywriters.org/edgarsDB/edgarDB.php

Arthur Ellis Awards
Crime Writers of Canada

The Arthur Ellis Awards, named after the *nom de travail* of Canada's official hangman, are presented for works in the crime genre published for the first time in the previous year by authors living in Canada, regardless of their nationality, or by Canadian writers living outside of Canada. The award, the "Arthur," is hand-carved by Canadian artisan Barry Lambeck and based on a design and prototype by artist Peter Blais. "Arthur" is a wooden articulated jumping-jack figure with a noose around its neck that "dances" when a string is pulled. The Arthur Ellis Awards were established in 1983 and begin in 1984 by the Crime Writers of Canada.

Arthur Ellis Best Novel

2007

Honour Among Men	Barbara Fradkin	___
Lone Wolf	Linwood Barclay	___
Every Secret Thing	Emma Cole	___
Break No Bones	Kathy Reichs	___
Piece of My Heart	Peter Robinson	___

2006

April Fool	William Deverell	___
Cemetery of the Nameless	Rick Blechta	___
Black Fly Season	Giles Blunt	___
Cold Dark Matter	Alex Brett	___
Strange Affair	Peter Robinson	___

2005

Fifth Son	Barbara Fradkin	___
Last Good Day, The	Gail Bowen	___
Magyar Venus, The	Lyn Hamilton	___
Playing With Fire	Peter Robinson	___
Sweep Lotus	Mark Zuehlke	___

2004

Delicate Storm, The	Giles Blunt	___
Lament for a Lounge Lizard	Mary Jane Maffini	___
Glenwood Treasure, The	Kim Moritsugu	___
Hua Shan Hospital Murders, The	David Rotenberg	___
Summer that Never Was, The (Close to Home)	Peter Robinson	___

2003

Blood of Others	Rick Mofina	___
Blackflies are Murder	Lou Allin	___
Once Upon a Time	Barbara Fradkin	___
Hot Pursuit	Nora Kelly	___
Grave Secrets	Kathy Reichs	___

2002

In the Midnight Hour	Michelle Spring	——
Laughing Falcon, The	William Deverell	——
Ice Lake	John Farrow	——
Cold Fear	Rick Mofina	——
Aftermath	Peter Robinson	——

2001

Cold is the Grave	Peter Robinson	——
Forty Words for Sorrow	Giles Blunt	——
One-Eyed Jacks	Brad Smith	——
Kidnap	L.R. Wright	——
Kidnapping of Rosie Dawn, The	Eric Wright	——

2000

Feast of Stephen, The	Rosemary Aubert	——
Dead of Winter, The	Lisa Appignanesi	——
Slander	William Deverell	——
City of Ice	John Farrow	——
In a Dry Season	Peter Robinson	——

1999

Old Wounds	Nora Kelly	——
Verdict in Blood	Gail Bowen	——
Cold Comfort	Scott Mackay	——
Remedy for Treason	Caroline Roe	——
Next Week Will Be Better	Jean Ruryk	——
Standing in the Shadows	Michelle Spring	——

1998

Trial of Passion	William Deverell	——
Free Reign	Rosemary Aubert	——
Death at Sandringham House	C.C. Benison	——
Ghirlandaio's Daughter	John Spencer Hill	——
Dead Right (Blood at the Root)	Peter Robinson	——
Illegal Alien	Robert J. Sawyer	——

1997

Innocent Graves	Peter Robinson	——
Alias Grace	Margaret Atwood	——
Light From Dead Stars	Martin S. Cohen	——
Nice Girls Finish Last	Sparkle Hayter	——
Fatal Flaw	Frank Smith	——

1996
  Mother Love   L.R. Wright   ____
  Street Legal   William Deverell   ____
  Striking Out   Alison Gordon   ____
  Heartbreaker   Laurence Gough   ____
  No Cure for Love   Peter Robinson   ____

1995
  Colder Kind of Death, A   Gail Bowen   ____
  Lights Out   Peter Abrahams   ____
  Good Life, The   John Brady   ____
  Solitary Dancer   John Lawrence Reynolds   ____
  Touch of Panic, A   L.R. Wright   ____

1994
  Gypsy Sins   John Lawrence Reynolds   ____
  All Souls   John Brady   ____
  There was an Old Woman   Howard Engel   ____
  Virtual Light   William Gibson   ____
  Water Damage   Gregory Ward   ____
  Prized Possessions   L.R. Wright   ____

1993
  Lizardskin   Carsten Stroud   ____
  Wandering Soul Murders, The   Gail Bowen   ____
  Fall Down Easy   Laurence Gough   ____
  Wednesday's Child   Peter Robinson   ____
  Pursued by Shadows   Medora Sale   ____

1992
  Past Reason Hated   Peter Robinson   ____
  Accidental Deaths   Laurence Gough   ____
  Fall From Grace   L.R. Wright   ____

1991
  Chill Rain in January, A   L.R. Wright   ____
  Kaddish in Dublin   John Brady   ____
  Serious Crimes   Laurence Gough   ____
  Lies of Silence   Brian Moore   ____
  And Leave Her Lay Dying   John Lawrence Reynolds   ____
  Caedmon's Song   Peter Robinson   ____

1990
  Hot Shots   Laurence Gough   ____
  Straight No Chaser   Jack Batten   ____
  Unholy Ground   John Brady   ____
  Mindfield   William Deverell   ____
  Hanging Valley, The   Peter Robinson   ____

1989
Jack   Chris Scott   ___
Platinum Blues   William Deverell   ___
Death on a No. 8 Hook (Silent Knives)   Laurence Gough   ___
Dedicated Man, A   Peter Robinson   ___

1988
Swann (Mary Swann)   Carol Shields   ___
Madelaine   Joseph Louis   ___
Mortal Sins   Anna Porter   ___
Body Surrounded by Water, A   Eric Wright   ___

1987
Buried on Sunday   Edward O. Phillips   ___
Telling of Lies, The   Timothy Findley   ___
To an Easy Grave   Alexander Law   ___
Murder on the Run**   Medora Sale   ___
Fool's Gold   Ted Wood   ___
Single Death, A   Eric Wright   ___

** A prize was awarded to Medora Sale for Best First Novel, which subsequently became an annual event.

1986
Death in the Old Country   Eric Wright   ___
Inner Ring, The   Maurice Gagnon   ___
Red Fox, The   Anthony Hyde   ___
Murder With Muskets   John Reeves   ___
Suspect, The   L.R. Wright   ___

1985
Murder Sees the Light   Howard Engel   ___
Dance of Shiva, The   William Deverell   ___
Precious   Douglas Glover   ___
Murder Before Matins   John Reeves   ___
Smoke Detector   Eric Wright   ___

1984
Night the Gods Smiled, The   Eric Wright   ___
Mecca   William Deverell   ___
Dead in the Water   Ted Wood   ___

Arthur Ellis Best 1st Novel

(Medora Sale was nominated for Best Novel, was recognized, and the next year a new category was established here; Best 1st Novel)

2007

Sign of the Cross	Anne Emery	____
Elvis Interviews, The	Glen Bonham	____
Reparations	Stephen Kimber	____
Dead Money	Grant McCrea	____
Deadly Lessons	David Russell	____

2006

Still Life	Louise Penny	____
Joining of Dingo Radish, The	Rob Harasymchuk	____
All Shook Up	Mike Harrison	____
Blue Mercy	Illona Haus	____
Sugarmilk Falls	Ilona Van Mil	____

2005

Dark Places	Jon Evans	____
Death in the Age of Steam	Mel Bradshaw	____
Raw Deal	Rick Gadziola	____
Mad Money	Linda L. Richards	____
Border Guards, The	Mark Sinnett	____

2004

Just Murder	Jan Rehner	____
Amuse Bouche	Anthony Bidulka	____
Confession in Moscow	Michael Johansen	____
Mazovia Legacy	Michael E. Rose	____
Sleeping Boy, The	Barbara J. Stewart	____

2003

Midnight Cab	James W. Nichol	____
Unlikely Victims, The	Alvin Abram	____
Undertow	Thomas Rendell Curran	____
Work of Idle Hands	Jonathon Platz	____
Come Clean	Kevin J. Porter	____

2002

Boy Must Die, The	Jon Redfern	____
Thief-Taker, The: Memoirs of a Bow Street Runner	T.F. Banks	____
Devil in Me, The	J. David Carpenter	____
Missing: Presumed Dead	James Hawkins	____
Every Wickedness	Cathy Vasas-Brown	____

2001
Hands Like Clouds — Mark Zuehlke — ____
Dying by Degrees — Eileen Coughlin — ____
If Angels Fall — Rick Mofina — ____
To Die in Spring — Sylvia Maultash Warsh — ____
Diamond Dogs — Alan Watt — ____

2000
Lost Girls — Andrew Pyper — ____
Crimes of War — Peter Hogg — ____
Pluto Rising — Karen Irving — ____
Speak Ill of the Dead — Mary Jane Maffini — ____
Guilty Addictions — Garrett Wilson — ____

1999
Sudden Blow — Liz Brady — ____
Lethal Practice — Peter Clement — ____
Hoot to Kill — Karen Dudley — ____
Down in the Dumps — H. Mel Malton — ____
Electrical Field, The — Kerri Sakamoto — ____

1998
Deja Dead — Kathy Reichs — ____
Shanghai Alley — Jim Christy — ____
Xibalba Murders, The — Lyn Hamilton — ____
Except the Dying — Maureen Jennings — ____
Blood Libel — Allan Levine — ____
Undercut — John Worsley Simpson — ____

1997
Death at Buckingham Palace — C.C. Benison — ____
Plane Death — Anne M. Dooley — ____
Throwaway Angels — Nancy Richler — ____
Gas Head Willy — Richard J. Thomas — ____

1996
Last Castrato (Tie) — John Spencer Hill — ____
Moonlit Days and Nights (Tie) — D.H. Toole — ____
Deadly by Nature — Meredith Andrew — ____
No Blood Relative — Terry Carroll — ____
Debut for a Spy — Harry Currie — ____

1995
What's a Girl Gotta Do? — Sparkle Hayter — ____
Healthy, Wealthy and Dead — Suzanne North — ____
Every Breath You Take — Michelle Spring — ____

1994
Memory Trace — Gavin Scott ___
Bloody Man, The — Bevan Amberhill ___
Dead and Living — Jane Bow ___
Deadlock — Stuart Langford ___
Alaska Highway Two-Step — Caroline Woodward ___

1993
Passion Play — Sean Stewart ___
Sense of Honour, A — Roy French ___
Murder of Crows, A — Margaret Haffner ___
Very Palpable Hit, A — Douglas Marshall ___
Found: A Body — Betsy Struthers ___

1992
Flesh Wound — Paul Grescoe ___
Jacamar Nest, The — David Parry & Patrick Withrow ___
Chocolate Box, The — Leslie Watts ___

1991
Sniper's Moon — Carsten Stroud ___
Fatal Choices — James Burke ___
Last Rights — David Laing Dawson ___

1990
Man Who Murdered God, The — John Lawrence Reynolds ___
Death on 30 Beat — Maynard Collins ___
Rempal Inquest, The — Keith McKinnon ___

1989
Stone of the Heart, A — John Brady ___
Ladies Night — Elisabeth Bowers ___
Stalking Horse, The (The Third Circle) — Brendan Howley ___
Murder in a Cold Climate — Scott Young ___

1988
Goldfish Bowl, The — Laurence Gough ___
Merlin's Web — Susan Mayse ___
Gallows View — Peter Robinson ___

1987
Murder on the Run — Medora Sale ___

Arthur Ellis Best Non-Fiction (True Crime)

2007

High: Confessions of a Pot Smuggler	Brian O'Dea ____
Desperate Ones, The: Forgotten Canadian Outlaws	Edward Butts ____
Brotherhoods, The: The True Story of Two Cops Who Murdered for the Mafia	Guy Lawson & William Oldham ____
To the Grave: Inside a Spectacular RCMP Sting	Mike McIntyre ____
Who Named the Knife?: A True Story of Murder and Memory	Linda Spalding ____

2006

Under the Bridge: The True Story of the Murder of Reena Virk	Rebecca Godfrey ____
Betrayed: The Assassination of Digna Ochoa	Linda Diebel ____
Starlight Tour: The Last, Lonely Night of Neil Stonechild	Susanne Reber & Robert Renaud ____
Hell's Witness	Daniel Sanger ____

2005

Irish Game: A True Story of Crime and Art	Matthew Hart ____
Mobsters, Gangsters and Men of Honour: Cracking the Mafia Code	Pierre de Champlain ____
Night Justice: The True Story of the Black Donnellys	Peter Edwards ____
Instruments of Murder	Max Haines ____
Crime School: Money Laundering: True Crime Meets the World of Business and Finance	Chris Mathers ____

2004

Road to Hell, The: How the Biker Gangs are Conquering Canada	Julian Sher & William Marsden ____
Story of Jane Doe, The: A Book About Rape	Jane Doe ____
Nowhere to Run: The Killing of Constable Dennis Strongquill	Mike McIntyre ____
Where There's Life, There's Lawsuits: Not Altogether Serious Ruminations on Law and Life	Jeffrey Miller ____

2003

Covert Entry: Spies, Lies and Crimes Inside Canada's Secret Service	Andrew Mitrovica ____
Dark Paths, Cold Trails: A Mountie's Quest to Link Serial Killers to Their Victims	Doug Clark ____
Unnatural Causes	Max Haines ____
Nasty Business: One Biker Gang's War Against the Hells Angels	Peter Paradis ____
Letters From Prison: Felons Write About the Struggle for Life and Sanity Behind Bars	Shawn Thompson ____

2002

Saboteurs: Wiebo Ludwig's War Against Big Oil (Tie)	Andrew Nikiforuk	___
Last Amigo, The: Karlheinz Schreiber and the Anatomy of Scandal (Tie)	Stevie Cameron & Harvey Cashore	___
One Dead Indian: The Premier, the Police, and the Ipperwash Crisis	Peter Edwards	___
No Kill No Thrill: The Shocking True Story of Charles Ng: One of America's Most Ruthless Serial Killers	Darcy Henton & Greg Owens	___
Free Rider: How a Bay Street Whiz Kid Stole and Spent $20 Million	John Lawrence Reynolds	___
Quicksand: One Woman's Escape From the Husband Who Stalked Her — A True Story	Ellen Singer	___

2001

Spinster and the Prophet, The: Florence Deeks, H.G. Wells, and the Mystery of the Purloined Past	A.B. McKillip	___
No Tears to the Gallows: The Strange Case of Frank McCullough	Mark Johnson	___
Who Killed Ty Conn?	Linden MacIntyre & Theresa Burke	___
Mad Notions: A True Tale of Murder and Mayhem	John Lawrence Reynolds	___

2000

Cowboys and Indians: The Shooting of J.J. Harper	Gordon Sinclair, Jr.	___
Hell's Angels at War: The Alarming Story Behind the Headlines	Yves Lavigne	___
Big Red Fox, The: The Incredible Story of Norman "Red" Ryan, Canada's Most Notorious Criminal	Peter McSherry	___
Money for Nothing: The Ten Best Ways to Make Money Illegally in North America	Jeremy Mercer	___
Mother's Story, A: My Battle to Free David Milgaard	Joyce Millgaard & Peter Edwards	___

1999

No Claim to Mercy: Elizabeth Bain and Robert Baltovich, A Suburban Mystery	Derek Finkle	___
Blue Trust: The Author, the Lawyer, His Wife and Her Money	Stevie Cameron	___
Getting Away With Murder: The Canadian Criminal Justice System	David M. Paciocco	___
Hand in the Water, A: The Many Lies of Albert Walker	Bill Schiller	___
Friend of the Family, A: The True Story of David Snow	Alison Shaw	___
Stolen Life, A: The Journey of a Cree Woman	Rudy Wiebe and Yvonne Johnson	___

1998

When She was Bad: Violent Women and the Myth of Innocence	Patricia Pearson	____
Cheats, Charlatans, and Chicanery: More Outrageous Tales of Skullduggery	Andreas Schroeder	____
Churchill and Secret Service	David Stafford	____

1997

Cassock and the Crown, The: Canada's Most Controversial Murder Trial	Jean Monet	____
Graham Greene Thrillers and the 1930s	Brian Diemert	____
Lord High Executioner: An Unashamed Look at Hangmen, Headsmen, and Their Kind	Howard Engel	____
Great Pulp Heroes, The	Don Hutchison	____
Convict Lover, The: A True Story	Merilyn Simonds	____

1996

Secret Lives of Sgt. John Wilson, The : A True Story of Love and Murder	Lois Simmie	____
Mind over Murder: DNA and Other Forensic Adventures	Jack Batten	____
Judas Kiss, The: The Undercover Life of Patrick Kelly	Michael Harris	____

1995

Prodigal Husband, The: The Tragedy of Helmuth and Hanna Buxbaum	Michael Harris	____
Arsenic Milkshake, The: And Other Mysteries Solved by Forensic Science	Sylvia Barrett	____
Comrade Criminal: Russia's New Mafiya	Stephen Handelman	____
Without Conscience: The Disturbing World of the Psychopaths Among Us	Robert D. Hare	____
Killing Time: The Senseless Murder of Joseph Fritch	Wade Hemsworth	____
Murder at McDonald's: The Killers Next Door	Phonse Jessome	____

1994

With Malice Aforethought: Six Spectacular Canadian Trials	David R. Williams	____
Descent into Madness: The Diary of a Killer	Vernon Frolick	____
Canada's Enemies: Spies and Spying in the Peaceable Kingdom	Graeme S. Mount	____
Contempt of Court: The Betrayal of Justice in Canada	Carsten Stroud	____

1993

Redrum the Innocent: The Murder of Christine   Kirk Makin   ____
Jessop and the Controversial Conviction of Her
Next-Door Neighbour, Guy Paul Morin

Unholy Alliances: Terrorists, Extremists, Front   Warren Kinsella   ____
   Companies and the Libyan Connection in Canada

Terror's End: Allan Legere on Trial: The Complete   Rick Maclean, Andre Veniot &   ____
   Story of New Brunswick's Serial Killer   Shaun Waters

Stopwatch Gang, The: The True Story of Three   Greg Weston   ____
   Affable Canadians Who Stormed American's
   Banks and Drove the FBI Crazy

1992

Arms and the Man: Dr. Gerald Bull, Iraq and   William Lowther   ____
the Supergun

Crime and Punishment in Canada: A History   Owen D. Carrigan   ____

Fatal Cruise: The Trial of Robert Frisbee   William Deverell   ____

Undercover: Cases of the RCMP's Most Secret   James Dubros & Robin Rowland   ____
   Operative

Crime Wave: Con Men, Rogues and Scoundrels   Dean Jobb   ____
   From Nova Scotia's Past

1991

Ginger: The Life and Death of Albert Goodwin   Susan Mayse   ____

Blood Brothers: How Canada's Most Powerful   Peter Edwards   ____
   Mafia Family Runs Its Business

Spy Wars: Espionage and Canada From Gouzenko   J.L. Granatstein & David Stafford   ____
   to "Glasnost"

Sole Survivor: Children Who Murder Their Families   Elliott Leyton   ____

From Police Headquarters: True Tales From the   Jocko Thomas   ____
   Big City Crime Beat

1990

Conspiracy of Silence: The Riveting Real-Life   Lisa Priest   ____
Account of the Pas Murder and Cover-Up that
Rocked the Nation

Merchants of Misery: Inside Canada's Illegal Drug Scene   Victor Malarak   ____

1989

Conspiracy of Brothers: A True Story of Murder,   Mick Lowe   ____
Bikers and the Law

Gross Misconduct: The Life of Spinner Spencer   Martin O'Malley   ____

Silent Game, The: The Real World of Imaginary Spies   David Stafford   ____

1988

Stung: The Incredible Obsession of Brian Molony — Gary Ross ___

King of the Mob: Rocco Perri and the Women Who Ran His Rackets — James Dubro & Robin Rowland ___

Greenspan: The Case for the Defence — Edward L. Greenspan & George Jonas ___

Close Pursuit: A Week in the Life of an NYPD Homicide Cop — Carsten Stroud ___

1987

Hunting Humans: The Rise of the Modern Multiple Murderer — Elliott Leyton ___

Case of Valentine Shortis, The: A True Story of Crime and Politics in Canada — Martin L. Friedland ___

Justice Denied: The Law Versus Donald Marshall — Michael Harris ___

1986

Canadian Tragedy, A: Joan and Colin Thatcher a Story of Love and Hate — Maggie Siggins ___

1985

Trials of Israel Lipsky, The — Martin L. Friedland ___

Vengeance: The True Story of an Israel Counter-Terrorist Team — George Jonas ___

Armchair Guide to Murder and Detection, The — David Peat ___

Who Killed Janet Smith?: The 1924 Vancouver Killing that Remains Canada's Most Intriguing Unsolved Murder — Edward Starkins ___

Arthur Ellis Best Genre Criticism/Reference

1992

Spy Fiction, Spy Films and Real Intelligence — Wesley K. Wark, ed. ___

Rough Justice: Essays on Crime in Literature — Martin L. Friedland ___

1991

Sherlock Holmes Among the Pirates: Copyright and Conan Doyle in America, 1890-1930 — Donald A. Redmond ___

Lawmen in Scarlet: An Annotated Guide to Royal Canadian Mounted Police in Print and Performance — Bernard Drew ___

Agatha Christie's Poirot: The Life and Times of Hercule Poirot — Anne Hart ___

Arthur Ellis Best Juvenile Award

2007
Hamish X and the Cheese Pirates	Sean Cullen	___
Mystery of the Graffiti Ghoul, The	Marty Chan	___
Devil, The Banshee and Me, The	L.M. Falcone	___
Tell	Norah McClintock	___
All In	Monique Polak	___

2006
Quid Pro Quo	Vicki Grant	___
Remember, Remember	Sheldon Goldfarb	___
Wild Ride	Jacqueline Guest	___
Not a Trace	Norah McClintock	___
Red Sea	Diane Tullson	___

2005
Beckoners, The	Carrie Mac	___
Thread of Deceit	Susan Cliffe	___
Hippie House, The	Katherine Holubitsky	___
Kat's Fall	Shelley Hrdlitschka	___
Sea Chase	Curtis Parkinson	___

2004
Acceleration	Graham McNamee	___
Theories of Relativity	Barbara Haworth-Attard	___
Truth	Tanya Lloyd Kyi	___
Deep End Gang, The	Peggy Dymond Leavey	___
No Escape	Norah McClintock	___

2003
Break and Enter	Norah McClintock	___
What's a Serious Detective Like Me Doing in Such a Silly Movie?	Linda Bailey	___
Maze, The	Monica Hughes	___
Out of the Ashes	Valerie Sherrard	___
Camp X	Eric Walters	___

2002
Scared to Death	Norah McClintock	___
Seeing Stars	Gary Barwin	___
Body, Crime, Suspect	Norah McClintock	___
Bone Beds of the Badlands	Shane Peacock	___

2001
Boy in the Burning House, The	Tim Wynne-Jones	___
Liberty Circle, The	Phil Campagna	___
Grave, The	James Heneghan	___
Stormwarning	Monica Hughes	___
Secret Under My Skin, The	Janet McNaughton	___

2000
How Can a Brilliant Detective Shine in the Dark? — Linda Bailey
That Kind of Money — Vicki Cameron
Ghost of Captain Briggs, The — Mary Labatt
Grave Secrets — Sylvia McNicholl
Mystery of Ireland's Eye, The — Shane Peacock

1999
Sins of the Father — Norah McClintock
Surfers of Snow — Kim Askew
Trial by Fire — Sheila Dalton
Secret of Devils Lake, The — Robert Sutherland
Intrepid Polly McDoodle, The — Mary Woodbury

1998
Body in the Basement, The — Norah McClintock
What's a Daring Detective Like Me Doing in the Doghouse? — Linda Bailey
Maxim Gunn: The Demon Plan — Nicholas Boving
Terror in Florida — Roy MacGregor
Vanishing Act — Cora Taylor

1997
How Can a Frozen Detective Stay Hot on the Trail? — Linda Bailey
Who Took Henry and Mr. Z? — Dave Glaze
Case of the Blue Raccoon, The — James Heneghan
Ear Witness — Mary Ann Scott

1996
Mistaken Identity — Norah McClintock
Time to Choose — Martha Attema
Mystery at Lake Placid — Roy MacGregor
Night They Stole the Stanley Cup, The — Roy MacGregor
Jacob Two-Two's First Spy Case — Mordecai Richler

1995
Torn Away — James Heneghan
Trouble on Wheels — Ann Aveling
Who's Got Gertie and How Can We Get Her Back? — Linda Bailey

1994
Abalone Summer — John Dowd
How Can I Be a Detective if I Have to Babysit? — Linda Bailey
Suspicion Summer — Jeni Mayer

Arthur Ellis Best Crime Work in the French Language

2007
no French awards for 2007

2006
Motel Riviera   Gérard Galarneau   ____
La Trace de l'escargot   Benoit Bouthillette   ____
La Rive noire   Jacques Côté   ____

2005
Les douze pierres   Ann Lamontagne   ____
La Souris et le rat   Jean-Pierre Charland   ____
Le Transmetteur   Jacques Diamant   ____
Virgo intacta   Louise Levesque   ____
La Femme de Berlin   Pauline Vincent   ____

2004
On finit toujours par payer   Jean Lemieux   ____
Indesirables   Chrystine Brouillet   ____
La Salaire de la honte   Maxime Houde   ____
Les effets sont secondaires   Andre Marois   ____
Au nom de Compostelle   Maryse Rouy   ____

2003
Le rouge ideal   Jacques Côté   ____
La Mort dans l'ame   Maxime Houde   ____
Sac de noeuds   Robert Malacci   ____
La Derniere Enquete de Julie Juillet   Sylvain Meunier   ____
Les Sept Jours du talion   Patrick Senecal   ____

2002
Fleur invitait au troisième   Anne-Michèle Lévesque   ____
L'Attentat   Michel Auger   ____
La Trajectoire du pion   Michel Jobin   ____
Trente-huit morts dont neuf femmes   André Marois   ____
L'Espion du 307   Louise-Michelle Sauriol   ____

2001
Le roman policier en Amerique francaise   Norbert Spehner   ____
Soins lntensifs   Chrystine Brouillet   ____
Nebulosite croissante en fin de journee   Jacques Côté   ____
Pitie pour les pigeons   Jean-Pierre Davidts   ____
La voix sur la montagne   Maxime Houde   ____

2000

Louna	Lionel Noel	____
Les fiancees de l'enfer	Chystine Brouillet	____
Blockhaus	Arthur Ghost	____
Therapie mortelle	Gilles Ouimet &	____
	Anne-Marie Pons	
Le Temps s'enfuit	Stanley Pean	____

Arthur Ellis Best Short Story Award

2007

"Fuzzy Wuzzy"	Dennis Richard Murphy	*EQMM,* Aug 06	____
"Lady in Violet Satin"	Vicki Cameron	*Storyteller,* Fall 06	
"Curious Case of the Book Baron, The"	Karl El-Koura	*Storyteller,* Spring 06	____
"Voices from the Deep"	Barbara Fradkin	*Dead in the Water,* Greenwood & Malan, eds.	____
"Canadian Diamonds"	Jennifer Geens	*Storyteller,* Summer 06	____

2006

"Lightning Rider"	Rick Mofina	*Murder in Vegas: New Crime Tales of Gambling & Desperation;* Connelly, ed.	____
"Plenty of Time"	Melanie Fogel	*When Boomers Go Bad;* Boswell, Pike, Wiken, eds.	____
"Red Pagoda, The"	Day's Lee	*When Boomers Go Bad;* Boswell, Pike, Wiken, eds.	____
"Headless Horseman and the Horseless Carriage, The"	James Powell	*EQMM,* Sept/Oct 05	____
"Knitting Circle, The"	Coleen Steele	*Storyteller,* Winter 05	____

2005

"Crocodile Tears"	Leslie Watts	*Revenge: A Noir Anthology;* Schooley & Sellers, eds.	____
"Robbie Burns Revival, The"	Cecilia Kennedy	*Robbie Burns Revival*	____
" Sounds of Silence"	Dennis Richard Murphy	*EQMM,* Dec 04	____
"Death of a Dry-Stone Wall"	Dennis Richard Murphy	*Storyteller,* Summer 04	____
"Sunnyside"	Coleen Steele	*Storyteller,* Summer 04	____

2004

"Dead Wood"	Gregory Ward	*Hard Boiled Love*; Schooley & Sellers, eds.	___
"Christmas Bauble, A"	Therese Greenwood	*Kingston Whig-Standard*, Dec 24, 03	___
"Dead in the Water"	Dennis Murphy	*Storyteller*, Summer 03	___
"When Laura Smiles"	Liz Palmer	*Bone Dance*; Pike & Boswell, eds.	___
"Gimmick, The "	Vern Smith	*Hard Boiled Love*; Schooley & Sellers, eds.	___

2003

"Bottom Walker"	James Powell	*EQMM*, May 02	___
"Timber Town Justice"	Barbara Fradkin	*Storyteller*, Summer 02	___
"Last Name, The"	Cecilia Kennedy	*Storyteller*, Summer 02	___
"Christmas Tree Farm, The"	Scott Mackay	*EQMM*, Jan 02	___
"Maisie's Safe House"	Wes Smiderle	*Storyteller*, Winter 02	___
"Taking Care of Howard"	Linda Wiken	*Over My Dead Body*, Special Issue 02	___

2002

"Sign of the Times"	Mary Jane Maffini	*Fit to Die*; Boswell & Pike, eds.	___
"Coup de Grace"	Barbara Fradkin	*Iced: The New Noir Anthology of Cold, Hard Fiction*; Schooley & Sellers, eds.	
"Double Trouble"	Barbara Fradkin	*Fit to Die*; Boswell & Pike, eds.	___
"Blind Alley"	Mary Jane Maffini	*EQMM*, Nov 01	___
"Avenging Miriam"	Peter Sellers	*EQMM*, Dec 01	___

2001

"Murder in Utopia"	Peter Robinson	*Crime Through Time III*; Newman, ed.	___
"Weeping Time, The"	Maureen Jennings	*Crime Through Time III*, Newman, ed.	___
"Collusionists, The"	Scott Mackay	*EQMM*, Sept/Oct 00	___
"Murder on the Polar Bear Express"	Peter Sellers	*EQMM*, Jan 01	___
"Catabolism"	Edo van Belkom	*Felonious Felines*; Gorman/s, eds.	___

2000

"One More Kill"	Matt Hughes	*Blue Murder Mag*, Dec 99	____
"Fair Lady"	Therese Greenwood	*Menopause is Murder*; Cameron & Maffini, eds.	____
"Kicking the Habit"	Mary Jane Maffini	*Menopause is Murder*; Cameron & Maffini, eds.	____
"Jerrold's Meat"	James Powell	*EQMM*, Apr 99	____
"Murdoch's Wife"	Peter Sellers	*Whistling Past the Graveyard / EQMM* May 93	____

1999

"Last Inning"	Scott Mackay	*EQMM*, Feb 98	____
"Do You Take This Man?"	Barry Baldwin	*EQMM*, Dec 98	____
"Hunter of the Guileless, The"	J.S. Lyster	*Storyteller*, Fall 98	____
"Strangers on a Sleigh"	James Powell	*EQMM*, Jan 98	____
"Getting Ahead"	Wayne Yetman	*Storyteller*, Spring 98	____

1998

"Widow's Weeds"	Sue Pike	*Cottage Country Killers*; Cameron & Wiken, eds.	____
"Rigged to Blow"	John Ballem	*Secret Tales of the Artic Trails*; Skene-Melvin, ed.	____
"Two Ladies of Rose Cottage, The"	Peter Robinson	Malice Domestic 6; Perry, pre.	____
"Hand You're Dealt, The"	Robert J. Sawyer	Free Space/Fictionwise.com.	____
"Rug, The"	Edo van Belkom	*Robert Bloch's - Psychos*; Bloch, ed.	____

1997

"Dead Run"	Richard K. Bercuson	*Storyteller*, Winter 96/97	____
"Too Broke for Bullets"	Jane Dias	*Storyteller*	____
"Dogs in Winter"	Eden Robinson	*Traplines: Stories*	____
"Murder in the Abbey"	Brad Spurgeon	*Murderous Intent*; Spring 96	____
"Piano Player Has No Fingers, The"	Edo van Belkom	*The Piano Players has No Fingers*; Edwards, Wayne & John Marshall, eds.	____

1996

"Cotton Armour"	Mary Jane Maffini	*Ladies Killing Circle*; Cameron & Audrey, eds.	____
"This Town Ain't Big Enough"	Tanya Huff	*Vampire Detectives*; Greenberg, ed.	____
"Rasputin Faberge, The"	James Powell	*EQMM*, Oct 95	____
"Breakout From Mistletoe Five"	James Powell	*EQMM*, mid-Dec 95	____
"Carrion"	Peter Robinson	*No Alibi*; Jakubowski, ed.	____

1995

"Midnight Boat to Palermo"	Rosemary Aubert	*Cold Blood V;* Sellers & North, eds.	___
"Big Lonely, The"	William Bankier	*Cold Blood V;* Sellers & North, eds.	___
"Death of a Dragon"	Eliza Moorhouse	*Cold Blood V;* Sellers & North, eds.	___
"Midnight at Manger's Bird and Beast"	James Powell	*EQMM,* Dec 94	___
"Lawn Sale"	Peter Robinson	*Cold Blood V;* Sellers & North, ed.	___
"Summer Rain"	Peter Robinson	*EQMM,* Dec 94	___

1994

"Just Like Old Times"	Robert J. Sawyer	*On Spec,* Summer 93	___
"East End Safe"	Jas. R. Petrin	*AHMM,* Jun 93	___
"Fixer-Upper, The"	James Powell	*EQMM,* May 93	___
"Casebook of Dr. Billingsgate, The"	Eric Wright	*New Mystery;* Charyn, ed.	___
"Duke, The"	Eric Wright	*2nd Culprit;* Cody & Lewin, eds.	___

1993

"Mantrap"	Nancy Kilpatrick	*Murder, Mayhem and the Macabre*	___
"Wade in the Balance"	William Bankier	*Criminal Shorts;* Wright & Engel, eds.	___
"Custom Killing"	Howard Engel	*Criminal Shorts;* Wright & Engel, eds.	___
"Fracture Patterns"	Gail Helgason	*Grain*	___
"Murder at Louisburg"	Ted Wood	*Cold Blood IV;* Sellers, ed.	___

1992

"Two in the Bush"	Eric Wright	*Christmas Stalkings;* MacLeod, ed.	___
"Wild Stock"	Gail Helgason	*Great Canadian Murder & Mystery Stories;* Bailey & Unruh, eds.	___
"Santa's Way"	James Powell	*EQMM,* mid-Dec 91	___
"Winter Hiatus"	James Powell	*EQMM,* Oct 91	___
"This One's Trouble"	Peter Sellers	*AHMM,* Jul 91	___

1991

"Innocence"	Peter Robinson	*Cold Blood III;* Sellers, ed.	___
"Out of Bounds"	John North	*Cold Blood III;* Sellers, ed.	___
"Man on the Roof"	Jas. R. Petrin	*Cold Blood III;* Sellers, ed.	___
"Blind Date"	Sara Plews	*Cold Blood III;* Sellers, ed.	___
"Tamerlane Crutch, The"	James Powell	*Cold Blood III;* Sellers, ed.	___

1990

"**Humbug**"	Josef Skvorecky	*The End of Lieutenant Boruvka*	___
"One Day at a Time"	William Bankier	*Cold Blood II*; Sellers, ed.	___
"Safe as Houses"	Elaine Mitchell Matlow	*Cold Blood II*; Sellers, ed.	___
"Burning Bridges"	James Powell	*EQMM*, Feb 89	___
"Kaput"	Eric Wright	*Mistletoe Mysteries*; MacLeod, ed.	___

1989

"**Killer in the House**"	Jas. R. Petrin	*AHMM*, Mid-Dec 88	___
"One Day at a Time"	William Bankier	*EQMM*, Oct 88	___
"Still Life With Orioles"	James Powell	*EQMM*, Dec 88	___

1988

"**Looking for an Honest Man**"	Eric Wright	*Cold Blood: Murder in Canada*; Sellers, ed.	___
"Murder by Half"	Tony Aspler	*Cold Blood: Murder in Canada*; Sellers, ed.	___
"Magic Nights"	Jas. R. Petrin	*AHMM*, Mar 87	___
"Prairie Heat"	Jas. R. Petrin	*AHMM*, Nov 87	___
"Pit Bull"	Ted Wood	*Cold Blood: Murder in Canada*; Sellers, ed.	___

Arthur Ellis Unhanged Arthur for the Best Unpublished 1st Crime Novel

2007

Margarita Nights	Phyllis Smallman	___
Murder in a Cold Climate	Jennifer Hemstock	___
Ego Tenderloin	Meika Erinn McClurg	___
Last Date	Rosemary McCracken	___
Condemned	Kevin Thornton	___

Derrick Murdoch Award

The Derrick Murdoch Award is given for outstanding contribution to the genre of crime writing in Canada. The Award is named in honor of Canada's premier crime fiction reviewer, who was the driving force behind the creation of the Crime Writers of Canada.

Derrick Murdoch Award for Outstanding Contribution	
2007	No award
2006	Mary Jane Maffini
2005	Max Haines
2004	Cheryl Freedman
2003	Margaret Cannon
2002	Caro Soles
2002	James Dubro
2001	L.R. Wright
2000	Eddie Barber
2000	Rick Blechta
2000	John North
2000	David Skene-Melvin
1999	Ted Wood
1998	Howard Engel
1998	Eric Wright
1995	Jim and Margaret McBride
1992	William Bankier
1992	James Powell
1992	Sellers Peter
1990	Eric Wilson
1988	J.D. Singh
1988	Jim Reicke
1987	The CBC Drama Department
1986	Margaret Millar
1985	Tony Aspler
1984	Derrick Murdoch

www.crimewriterscanada.com/
www.thrillingdetective.com/trivia/triv65.html
crimewriterscanada.com/cwc/pages/awards.html

Gumshoe Mystery Awards

The Gumshoe Awards are given by Mystery Ink to recognize the best achievements in crime fiction. These awards were presented for the first time in 2002.

Gumshoe Best Novel

2007

All Mortal Flesh	Julia Spencer-Fleming	____
White Shadow	Ace Atkins	____
City of Shadows	Ariana Franklin	____
Night Gardener, The	George P. Pelecanos	____
Hollywood Station	Joseph Wambaugh	____

2006

To the Power of Three	Laura Lippman	____
As Dog is My Witness	Jeffrey Cohen	____
James Deans, The	Reed Farrel Coleman	____
Savage Garden	Denise Hamilton	____
Wheelman, The	Duane Swierczynski	____

2005

Hard, Hard City	Jim Fusilli	____
Last Lullaby	Denise Hamilton	____
By a Spider's Thread	Laura Lippman	____
California Girl	T. Jefferson Parker	____
Absent Friends	S.J. Rozan	____

2004

Blood is the Sky	Steve Hamilton	____
Eye of the Abyss, The	Marshall Browne	____
Persuader	Lee Child	____
Hard Rain	Barry Eisler	____
Tribeca Blues	Jim Fusilli	____

2003

Hell to Pay	George P. Pelecanos	____
Dark End of the Street	Ace Atkins	____
Nine	Jan Burke	____
City of Bones	Michael Connelly	____
Stone Monkey, The	Jeffery Deaver	____

2002

Pursuit	Thomas Perry	____
Cons, Scams & Grifts	Joe Gores	____
Silent Joe	T. Jefferson Parker	____
Right as Rain	George P. Pelecanos	____
Death Benefits	Thomas Perry	____

Gumshoe Best 1st Novel

2007

King of Lies, The	John Hart	___
Out of Cabrini	Dave Case	___
Corpse in the Koyro, A	James Church	___
Shadow Catchers, The	Thomas Lakeman	___
Field of Darkness, A	Cornelia Read	___

2006

Baby Game, The	Randall Hicks	___
Color of Law, The	Mark Gimenez	___
Tilt-a-Whirl	Chris Grabenstein	___
Sacred Cows	Karen E. Olson	___
Beneath a Panamanian Moon	David Terrenoire	___

2005

Misdemeanor Man	Dylan Schaffer	___
Rift Zone	Raelynn Hillhouse	___
Caught Stealing	Charlie Huston	___
Whiskey Sour	J.A. Konrath	___
Dating Dead Men	Harley Jane Kozak	___

2004

Monkeewrench	P.J. Tracy	___
Hex	Maggie Estep	___
Dealing in Murder	Elaine Flinn	___
Curious Incident of the Dog in the Night-Time, The	Mark Haddon	___
Cutting Room, The	Louise Welsh	___

2003

Distance, The	Eddie Muller	___
Rain Fall	Barry Eisler	___
Blue Edge of Midnight, The	Jonathon King	___
Open and Shut	David Rosenfelt	___
In the Bleak Midwinter	Julia Spencer-Fleming	___

2002

Open Season	C.J. Box	___
Hollowpoint	Rob Reuland	___
Blindsighted	Karin Slaughter	___

Gumshoe Best Thriller

2007

Prayers for the Assassin	Robert Ferrigno	___
Hard Way, The	Lee Child	___
Last Assassin, The	Barry Eisler	___
Marked Man	William Lashner	___
Venus Fix, The	M.J. Rose	___

2006

Company Man	Joseph Finder	____
Lincoln Lawyer, The	Michael Connelly	____
Only Suspect, The	Jonnie Jacobs	____
Falls the Shadow	William Lashner	____
Creepers	David Morrell	____

2005

Rain Storm	Barry Eisler	____
Wake-Up, The	Robert Ferrigno	____
Dark Voyage	Alan Furst	____
Life Expectancy	Dean Koontz	____
Death in Vienna, A	Daniel Silva	____

Gumshoe Best European Crime

2007

When the Devil Holds the Candle	Karin Fossum	____
Dramatist, The	Ken Bruen	____
Walk in the Dark, A	Gianrico Carofiglio	____
By a Slow River	Philippe Claudel	____
Minotaur, The	Barbara Vine	____

2006

Vanished Hands, The	Robert Wilson	____
Big Over Easy, The	Jasper Fforde	____
Kiss Her Goodbye	Allan Guthrie	____
Jar City	Arnaldur Indridason	____
Have Mercy on Us All	Fred Vargas	____

2005

Return of the Dancing Master, The	Henning Mankell	____
Murder on the Leviathan	Boris Akunin	____
Doctored Evidence	Donna Leon	____
Question of Blood, A	Ian Rankin	____
Shadow of the Wind, The	Carlos Ruiz Zafon	____

Gumshoe Lifetime Achievement

2007	**Robert B. Parker**
2006	**Ed McBain**
2005	**Lawrence Block**
2004	**Ruth Rendell**
2003	**Dick Francis**
2002	**Ross Thomas**

www.mysteryinkonline.com/gumshoe.html

Dashiell Hammett Award

The Dashiell Hammett Award is presented by the North American Branch of the International Association of Crime Writers, for a work of literary excellence (fiction or non-fiction) in the field of crime writing by a US or Canadian author. The nominees do not have to be hardboiled or detective novels.

"Crime writing" is defined as any published work of adult fiction or narrative nonfiction that encompasses such areas as "crime," "suspense," "thriller," "mystery," or "espionage" as those terms are normally understood in the writing and publishing fields. A collection of short stories by a single author would qualify.

The winning title is selected by a reading committee of IACW/NA, based on recommendations from other members and the publishing community, and the winner is chosen by three distinguished outside judges. The award is a bronze trophy, designed by West Coast sculptor, Peter Boiger, whose falcon-headed "Thin Man" symbolizes Dashiell Hammett's literary spirit. The Dashiell Hammett Awards began in 1992.

Hammett Best Novel

2007

Prisoner of Guantanamo, The	Dan Fesperman	____
Ghost Dancer	John Case	____
Dark Companion	Jim Nisbet	____
Crimes of Jordan Wise, The	Bill Pronzini	____
Four Kinds of Rain	Robert Ward	____

2006

Alibi: A Novel	Joseph Kanon	____
Islandbridge	John Brady	____
Door to Bitterness, The	Martin Limon	____
No Country for Old Men	Cormac McCarthy	____
Power of the Dog, The	Don Winslow	____

2005

Prince of Thieves	Chuck Hogan	____
Madman's Tale, The	John Katzenbach	____
Havana Room, The	Colin Harrison	____
California Girl	T. Jefferson Parker	____
Playing With Fire	Peter Robinson	____

2004

Seduction of Water, The	Carol Goodman	____
Delicate Storm, The	Giles Blunt	____
Tropic of Night	Michael Gruber	____
Shutter Island	Dennis Lehane	____
Every Secret Thing	Laura Lippman	____

2003
 Honor's Kingdom   Owen Parry   ____
 Jolie Blon's Bounce   James Lee Burke   ____
 Eighth Day, The   John Case   ____
 Flykiller   J. Robert Janes   ____
 Bad Boy Brawly Brown   Walter Mosley   ____

2002
 Kingdom of Shadows   Alan Furst   ____
 Mystic River   Dennis Lehane   ____
 Silent Joe   T. Jefferson Parker   ____
 Right as Rain   George P. Pelecanos   ____
 Hollowpoint   Rob Reuland   ____

2001
 Blind Assassin, The   Margaret Atwood   ____
 Hot Springs   Stephen Hunter   ____
 Bottoms, The   Joe R. Lansdale   ____
 Ice Harvest, The   Scott Phillips   ____
 One-Eyed Jacks   Brad Smith   ____

2000
 Havana Bay   Martin Cruz Smith   ____
 Heartwood   James Lee Burke   ____
 L.A. Requiem   Robert Crais   ____
 In a Dry Season   Peter Robinson   ____
 Personal Injuries   Scott Turow   ____

1999
 Tidewater Blood   William Hoffman   ____
 Praying to a Laughing God   Kevin McColley   ____
 Man Who Stole the Mona Lisa, The   Robert Noah   ____
 Last Days of Il Duce, The   Domenic Stansberry   ____
 Tomato Red   Daniel Woodrell   ____

1998
 Trial of Passion   William Deverell   ____
 Cimarron Rose   James Lee Burke   ____
 Trunk Music   Michael Connelly   ____
 Wasteland of Strangers, A   Bill Pronzini   ____
 Acts of Murder   L.R. Wright   ____

1997
 Rose   Martin Cruz Smith   ____
 Poet, The   Michael Connelly   ____
 Buzz Cut   James W. Hall   ____
 Innocent Graves   Peter Robinson   ____
 Damaged Goods   Stephen Solomita   ____

1996

Under the Beetle's Cellar	Mary Willis Walker	____
Smithereens	Susan Taylor Chehak	____
Last Coyote, The	Michael Connelly	____
Breakheart Hill	Thomas H. Cook	____
True Crime	Andrew Klavan	____

1995

Dixie City Jam	James Lee Burke	____
Dogs of God	Pinckney Benedict	____
Shot in the Heart: One Family's History in Murder	Mikal Gilmore	____
Third and Indiana	Steve Lopez	____
Shinju	Laura Joh Rowland	____

1994

Mexican Tree Duck, The	James Crumley	____
Black Ice, The	Michael Connelly	____
By Evil Means	Sandra West Prowell	____
Occasional Hell, An	Randall Silvis	____
Catilina's Riddle	Steven Saylor	____

1993

Turtle Moon	Alice Hoffman	____
Trick of the Eye	Jane Stanton Hitchcock	____
White Butterfly	Walter Mosley	____
Humans	Donald E. Westlake	____
Ones You Do, The (Special Mention)	Daniel Woodrell	____

1992

Maximum Bob	Elmore Leonard	____
Elsinore	Jerome Charyn	____
Murther and Walking Spirits	Robertson Davies	____
Harlot's Ghost	Norman Mailer	____
Women of Whitechapel and Jack the Ripper, The	Paul West	____

www.crimewritersna.org/

217

Herodotus Historical Awards

The Historical Mystery Appreciation Society was under the direction of Sue Feder until she passed away in 2005. The awards were presented between 1999 and 2002 and were to honor excellence in historical mysteries. The award called, The Herodotus, is in honor the Greek "Father of History" who never let history stand in the way of a good story. Herodotus was born in Turkey in the fifth century BCE and best known as the author of the first important narrative history produced in the ancient world, The History of the Greco-Persian Wars.

[Editor's note: Mystery Readers International have instituted a new award to honor the memory of Sue Feder and her love of historical mysteries. In 2006 they announced the Macavity Sue Feder Historical Mystery Award. Look to the Macavity awards for the listings.]

Herodotus Best Historical Mystery Award

2002
Brothers of Cain	Miriam Grace Monfredo	____
Last Kashmiri Rose, The	Beverly Cleverly	____
Good German, The	Joseph Kanon	____
Call Each River Jordan	Owen Parry	____
Island of Tears	Troy Soos	____

Herodotus Best US Historical Mystery

2001
Dangerous Road, A	Kris Nelscott	____

2000
Rubicon	Steven Saylor	____

1999
Cursed in the Blood	Sharan Newman	____

Herodotus Best 1st US Historical Mystery Award

2002
Murphy's Law	Rhys Bowen	____
Carter Beats the Devil	Glen David Gold	____
Mute Witness	Charles O'Brien	____
Right Hand of Sleep, The	John Wray	____
Birth of Blue Satan, The: Introducing Blue Satan and Mrs. Kean	Patricia Wynn	____

2001
Bottoms, The	Joe R. Lansdale	____

2000
Faded Coat of Blue	Owen Parry	____

1999
Last Kabbalist of Lisbon, The	Richard Zimler	____

Herodotus Best International Historical Mystery

2001
Company, The: The Story of a Murderer   Arabella Edge   ____

2000
Absent Friends   Gillian Linscott   ____

1999
Ex-Libris   Ross King   ____

Herodotus 1st International Historical

2001
Bone House   Betsy Tobin   ____

2000
Guilty Knowledge   Clare Curzon   ____

1999
no award given

Herodotus Best Short Story Historical Mystery

2002

"Kisses of Death"	Max Allan Collins	*Kisses of Death*	____
"Invisible Spy, The"	Brendan DuBois	*The Blue & the Gray Underground*; Gorman, ed.	____
"Hobson's Choice"	John Lutz	*The Blue & the Gray Underground*; Gorman, ed.	____
"Beyond the Lost Man Mountains"	Anne Weston	*AHMM*, Jul/Aug 01	____
"Perfect Crime, A"	Derek Wilson	*Mammoth Book of More Historical Whodunits*; Ashley, ed.	____

2001

"Man Who Never Was, The"	Charles Todd	Malice Domestic 9; Hess, pre.	____

2000

"Neither Pity, Love Nor Fear"	Margaret Frazer	*Royal Whodunits*; Ashley, ed.	____

1999

"Fatherhood"	Thomas H. Cook	*Murder for Revenge*; Penzler, ed.	____

Herodotus Historical Lifetime Achievement Award

2002	**Max Allan Collins**
2001	**Lindsey Davis**
2000	**Paul Doherty** (aka Anna Apostolou, Michael Clynes, P.C. Doherty, Ann Dukthas, C.L. Grace, and Paul Harding)
1999	**Ann Perry**

mywebpages.comcast.net/monkshould/EmptyForNow.htm

Chester Himes Award

The Chester Himes Black Mystery Award is given annually to a published African American mystery writer by the Friends of Chester Himes (FOCH) as a way of keeping Mr. Himes' memory alive while honoring the accomplishments of contemporary black writers. Chester Himes, the first nationally published black mystery writer, wrote numerous works including *Cotton Comes to Harlem* and *Blind Man With a Pistol (Hot Day, Hot Night)*. Himes lived the last 30 years of his life in Europe and died in Spain in 1984.

FOCH was established by Jan Faulkner under the auspices of the Oakland Museum of California's Education Department's Education and History Guild. In 1994, Ms. Faulkner saw a need to educate the public about the extensive contributions African Americans have made in the literary world and specifically the mystery genre. She also wanted to create a vehicle for authors to be accessible to readers and fans.

FOCH sponsors a Mystery Writer's Conference each year, a student writing contest for Oakland High School students, and presents an annual award to a published African American mystery writer.

Note: No longer active.

Chester Himes Award

2003	Gary Phillips
2002	Renay Jackson
2001	Alice Holman
2000	Eleanor Taylor Bland
1999	Robert Greer
1998	Walter Mosley
1997	Terris Grimes
1996	Gar Anthony Haywood

www.friendsofchesterhimes.org/winners.html

International Thriller Writers

The International Thriller Writers present awards for works in the thriller genre. These awards began in 2006 at their conference: ThrillerFest.

International Thriller Best Novel

2007

Killer Instinct	Joseph Finder	____
False Impression	Jeffrey Archer	____
Cold Kill	Stephen Leather	____
Messenger, The	Daniel Silva	____
Beautiful Lies	Lisa Unger	____

2006

Patriots Club, The	Christopher Reich	____
Panic	Jeff Abbott	____
Consent to Kill	Vince Flynn	____
Velocity	Dean Koontz	____
Citizen Vince	Jess Walter	____

International Thriller Best 1st Novel

2007

Mr. Clarinet	Nick Stone	____
Shadow of Death	Patricia Gussin	____
Switchback	Matthew Klein	____
Thousand Suns, A	Alex Scarrow	____
18 Seconds	George D. Shuman	____

2006

Improbable	Adam Fawer	____
Color of Law, The	Mark Gimenez	____
Cold Granite	Stuart MacBride	____
Painkiller	Will Staeger	____
Beneath a Panamanian Moon	David Terrenoire	____

International Thriller Best Paperback Original

2007

Unquiet Grave, An	P.J. Parrish	____
Skeleton Coast	Clive Cussler with Jack DuBrul	____
Deep Blue Alibi, The	Paul Levine	____
Headstone City	Tom Piccirilli	____
Mortal Faults	Michael Prescott	____

2006

Pride Runs Deep	R. Cameron Cooke	___
Sleeper Cell	Jeffrey Anderson	___
Upside Down	John Ramsey Miller	___
Dying Hour, The	Rick Mofina	___
Exit Strategy	Mike Wiecek	___

International ThrillerMaster Award

2007	**James Patterson**
2006	**Clive Cussler**

www.thrillerwriters.org/

222

Lambda Mystery Awards

The awards are sponsored by the Lambda Literary Foundation and are given annually to recognize excellence in gay and lesbian writing published in the United States in 25 categories. The winners are announced at Book Expo America. Novels, novellas, short story collections, and anthologies are eligible for the awards. Here, of course, we are looking at the awards for mystery writing.

[Editor's note: I have dated the award years to the award presentation year to conform to the other mystery awards rather than to the Lambda Literary Foundation web site.]

Lambda Lesbian Mystery Awards

2007

Art of Detection, The	Laurie R. King	___
Sleep of Reason	Rose Beecham	___
Night Vision	Ellen Hart	___
Idaho Code	Joan Opyr	___
Weekend Visitor, The	Jessica Thomas	___

2006

Desert Blood: The Juarez Murders	Alicia Gaspar de Alba	___
Women of Mystery	Katherine V. Forrest, ed.	___
Iron Girl, The	Ellen Hart	___
Darkness Descending	Penny Mickelbury	___
Justice Served	Radclyffe	___

2005

Hancock Park	Katherine V. Forrest	___
Wombat Strategy, The	Claire McNab	___
Intimate Ghost, An	Ellen Hart	___
Commitment to Die	Jennifer Jordan	___
Death by Discount	Mary Vermillion	___

2004

Damn Straight	Elizabeth Sims	___
Cry Havoc	Baxter Clare	___
Epitaph for an Angel	Lauren Maddison	___
Owl of the Desert	Ida Swearingen	___
Woman Who Found Grace, The	Bett Reece Johnson	___

2003

Good Bad Woman	Elizabeth Woodcraft	___
Immaculate Midnight	Ellen Hart	___
Weeping Buddha, The	Heather Dune Macadam	___
Death by Prophecy	Lauren Maddison	___
Accidental Murder	Claire McNab	___

2002
Merchant of Venus, The	Ellen Hart	___
Witchfire	Lauren Maddison	___
Kiss the Girls and Make Them Spy	Mabel Maney	___
Back to Salem	Alex Marcoux	___
Moving Targets	Pat Welch	___

2001
Mommy Deadest	Jean Marcy	___
Booked for Murder	Val McDermid	___
Death Understood	Claire McNab	___
When Evil Changes Face	Therese Szymanski	___
Case of the Orphaned Bassoonists, The	Barbara Wilson	___

2000
Hunting the Witch	Ellen Hart	___
Sleeping Bones	Katherine V. Forrest	___
Murder Undercover	Claire McNab	___
Lost Daughters	J.M. Redmann	___
She Came in Drag	Mary Wings	___

1999
Shaman's Moon (Tie)	Sarah Dreher	___
Blue Place, The (Tie)	Nicola Griffith	___
Wicked Games	Ellen Hart	___
Mother May I	Randye Lordon	___
Past Due	Claire McNab	___

1998
Father, Forgive Me	Randye Lordon	___
Apparition Alley	Katherine V. Forrest	___
Evil Dead Center	Carole laFavor	___
Old Black Magic	Jaye Maiman	___
No Daughter of the South	Cynthia Webb	___

1997
Robber's Wine	Ellen Hart	___
Liberty Square	Katherine V. Forrest	___
Baby, It's Cold	Jaye Maiman	___
Final Take	Jackie Manthorne	___
Inner Circle	Claire McNab	___

1996
Intersection of Law and Desire	J.M. Redmann	___
Faint Praise	Ellen Hart	___
Someone to Watch	Jaye Maiman	___
Night Songs	Penny Mickelbury	___
Hangdog Hustle	Elizabeth Pincus	___

1995
 Small Sacrifice   Ellen Hart   ____
 Sister's Keeper   Randye Lordon   ____
 Case of the Good-For-Nothing Girlfriend   Mabel Maney   ____
 Body Guard   Claire McNab   ____
 My Sweet Untraceable You   Sandra Scoppettone   ____

1994
 Divine Victim   Mary Wings   ____
 Long Goodbyes   Nikki Baker   ____
 Case of the Not-So-Nice Nurse   Mabel Maney   ____
 I'll Be Leaving You Always   Sandra Scoppettone   ____
 Trouble in Transylvania   Barbara Wilson   ____

1993
 Crazy for Loving (Tie)   Jaye Maiman   ____
 Two-Bit Tango, The (Tie)   Elizabeth Pincus   ____
 Lavender House Murder   Nikki Baker   ____
 Stage Fright   Ellen Hart   ____
 Deaths of Jocasta   J.M. Redmann   ____

1992
 Murder by Tradition   Katherine V. Forrest   ____
 Cop Out   Claire McNab   ____
 Final Session   Mary Morell   ____
 Everything You Have is Mine   Sandra Scoppettone   ____
 Providence File, The   Amanda Kyle Williams   ____

1991
 Ninth Life (Tie)   Lauren Wright Douglas   ____
 Gaudi Afternoon (Tie)   Barbara Wilson   ____
 Captive in Time, A   Sarah Dreher   ____
 Slick   Camarin Grae   ____
 Death Down Under   Claire McNab   ____

1990
 Beverly Malibu, The   Katherine V. Forrest   ____
 Contactees Die Young, The   Antoinette Azolakov   ____
 Hallowed Murder   Ellen Hart   ____
 Fatal Reunion   Claire McNab   ____
 Dog Collar Murders   Barbara Wilson   ____

1989
 Skiptrace   Antoinette Azolakov   ____
 Crystal Curtain, The   Sandy Bayer   ____
 Mundane's World   Judy Grahn   ____
 Heavy Gilt   Dolores Klaich   ____
 Lessons In Murder   Claire McNab   ____

Lambda Gay Mystery Awards

2007

Lucky Elephant Restaurant, The	Garry Ryan	____
Mardi Gras Mambo	Greg Herren	____
Hell You Say, The	Josh Lanyon	____
Back Passage, The	James Lear	____
Provincetown Follies, Bangkok Blues	Randall Peffer	____

2006

One of These Things is Not Like the Other	D. Travers Scott	____
Actor's Guide to Greed, The	Rick Copp	____
White Tiger	Michael Allen Dymmoch	____
Paper Mirror, The	Dorien Grey	____
Cajun Snuff	W. Randy Haynes	____

2005

Flight of Aquavit	Anthony Bidulka	____
Role Players, The	Dorien Grey	____
Jackson Square Jazz	Greg Herren	____
Moth and Flame	John Morgan Wilson	____
Someone You Know	Gary Zebrun	____

2004

Blind Eye	John Morgan Wilson	____
Bourbon Street Blues	Greg Herren	____
It Takes Two	Elliott Mackle	____
Wearing Black to the White Party	David Stukas	____
Dead Egotistical Morons	Mark Richard Zubro	____

2003

Snow Garden, The	Christopher Rice	____
Hot Spot	Michael Craft	____
Hired Man, The	Dorien Grey	____
Lodger, The	Drew Gummerson	____
Murder in the Rue Dauphine	Greg Herren	____

2002

Rag and Bone	Michael Nava	____
Boy Toy	Michael Craft	____
Making a Killing	Warren Dunford	____
Butcher's Son, The	Dorien Grey	____
Sex and Murder.Com	Mark Richard Zubro	____

2001

Limits of Justice, The	John Morgan Wilson	____
Name Games	Michael Craft	____
Love's Last Chance	Krandall Kraus	____
Nothing Gold Can Stay	Casey Nelson	____
Density of Souls, A	Christopher Rice	____

2000
Justice at Risk — John Morgan Wilson ____
Gumshoe, the Witch, and the Virtual Corpse, The — Keith Hartman ____
Death of a Constant Lover, The — Lev Raphael ____
Innuendo — R.D. Zimmerman ____
Drop Dead — Mark Richard Zubro ____

1999
Outburst — R.D. Zimmerman ____
Uprising — Randy Boyd ____
Federal Fag — Fred Hunter ____
Dead as a Doornail — Grant Michaels ____
Strachey's Folly — Richard Stevenson ____

1998
Magician's Tale, The — David Hunt ____
Gossip — Christopher Bram ____
Burning Plain, The — Michael Nava ____
Revision of Justice — John Morgan Wilson ____
Hostage — R.D. Zimmerman ____

1997
Death of Friends, The — Michael Nava ____
Time to Check Out — Grant Michaels ____
Murder on the Appian Way — Steven Saylor ____
Simple Justice — John Morgan Wilson ____
Tribe — R.D. Zimmerman ____

1996
Closet — R.D. Zimmerman ____
Queer Kind of Umbrella — George Baxt ____
Venus Throw — Steven Saylor ____
Shock to the System — Richard Stevenson ____
Another Dead Teenager — Mark Richard Zubro ____

1995
Midnight in the Garden of Good and Evil — John Berendt ____
Queer Kind of Love — George Baxt ____
Alienist, The — Caleb Carr ____
Mad Man — Samuel Delaney ____
Mask for a Diva — Grant Michaels ____

1994
Catilina's Riddle — Steven Saylor ____
Mae West Murder Case — George Baxt ____
Torsos — John Cooke ____
Bohannon's Country — Joseph Hansen ____
Dead on Your Feet — Grant Michaels ____

1993

Hidden Law, The	Michael Nava	——
Final Atonement	Steve Johnson	——
Love You to Death	Grant Michaels	——
Third Man Out	Richard Stevenson	——
One for the Master, Two for the Fool	Larry Townsend	——

1992

Country of Old Men, A	Joseph Hansen	——
Best Performance by a Patsy	Stan Cutler	——
Face on the Cutting Room Floor, The	Stan Cutler	——
Master's Counterpoints	Larry Townsend	——
Sorry Now?	Mark Richard Zubro	——

1991

Howtown	Michael Nava	——
Boy Who was Buried This Morning	Joseph Hansen	——
Black Marble Pool	Stan Leventhal	——
Body to Dye For	Grant Michaels	——
Why Isn't Becky Twitchell Dead?	Mark Richard Zubro	——

1990

Simple Suburban Murder, A	Mark Richard Zubro	——
Faultlines: Stories of Suspense	Stan Leventhal	——
Somewhere in the Night	Jeffrey N. McMahan	——
Finale	Michael Nava, ed.	——
Caravaggio Shawl	Samuel M. Steward	——

1989

Goldenboy	Michael Nava	——
Who's Next	George Baxt	——
Unicorn Mountain	Michael Bishop	——
Obedience	Joseph Hansen	——
Death Takes the Stage	Donald Ward	——

www.lambdaliterary.org

Left Coast Crime Conference

Left Coast Crime is an annual mystery conference sponsored by mystery fans, for mystery fans. It is held during the first quarter of the calendar year usually in Western North America, as defined by the Mountain Time Zone and all time zones westward to Hawaii. The first event was held in 1991. The Lefty, an award for the best humorous mystery, is to be awarded at each Left Coast Crime. Furthermore, up to three other awards may be awarded at the discretion of individual Left Coast Crime conventions each year.

Lefty Award

2007

Go to Helena Handbasket	Donna Moore	____
No Nest for the Wicket	Donna Andrews	____
Monkey Man	Steve Brewer	____
47 Rules of Highly Effective Bank Robbers	Troy Cook	____
Murder Unleashed	Elaine Viets	____

2006

Cast Adrift	Peter Guttridge	____
Cue the Easter Bunny	Liz Evans	____
Big Over Easy, The	Jasper Fforde	____
Highway 61 Resurfaced	Bill Fitzhugh	____
Fags and Lager	Charlie Williams	____

2005

We'll Always Have Parrots (Tie)	Donna Andrews	____
Blue Blood (Tie)	Susan McBride	____
Carnage on the Committee	Ruth Dudley Edwards	____
Holy Guacamole	Nancy Fairbanks	____
Perfect Sax	Jerrilyn Farmer	____

2004

Mumbo Gumbo	Jerrilyn Farmer	____
Crouching Buzzard, Leaping Loon	Donna Andrews	____
Shop Till You Drop	Elaine Viets	____

2003

Hearse Case Scenario, The (Tie)	Tim Cockey	____
Pipsqueak (Tie)	Brian M. Wiprud	____
Hard Eight	Janet Evanovich	____
This Pen for Hire	Laura Levine	____
Rival Queens, The	Fidelis Morgan	____
Buck Fever	Ben Rehder	____

2002
Dim Sum Dead (Tie)	Jerrilyn Farmer	____
Fender Benders (Tie)	Bill Fitzhugh	____
Revenge of the Wrought-iron Flamingos	Donna Andrews	____
Murder Can Upset Your Mother	Selma Eichler	____
Long Time No See	Susan Isaacs	____

2001
No award presented

2000
Murder With Peacocks	Donna Andrews	____
Big Trouble	Dave Barry	____
High Five	Janet Evanovich	____
Immaculate Reception	Jerrilyn Farmer	____
Murder Shoots the Bull	Anne George	____

1999
Four to Score	Janet Evanovich	____

1998
Three to Get Deadly	Janet Evanovich	____
Dead Men Don't Dance	Margaret Chittenden	____
Scam	Parnell Hall	____
I Still Miss My Man But My Aim Is Getting Better	Sarah Shankman	____
Death and Life of Bobby Z, The	Don Winslow	____

1997
No award presented

1996
Fat Innkeeper, The	Alan Russell	____
God Bless John Wayne	Kinky Friedman	____
Who in Hell is Wanda Fuca?	G.M. Ford	____
Movie	Parnell Hall	____
Miracles in Maggody	Joan Hess	____
If I'd Killed Him When I Met Him	Sharyn McCrumb	____

www.leftcoastcrime.org/

Special Left Coast Crime Awards

The Bylaws for Left Coast Crime state: "Furthermore, up to three other awards may be awarded at the discretion of individual Left Coast Crime conventions in categories to be chosen by the current organizing committee. Subsequent committees may but are not required to continue any of these awards." Several different awards have been selected and presented.

Calavera Award

Mysteries set in the geographical area covered by Left Coast Crime were announced at the conference held in El Paso, Texas in 2005.

2005

Grave Endings	Rochelle Krich	___
Snap Shot	Meg Chittenden	___
Shadow Play	David Cole	___
What Others Know	L.C. Hayden	___
Family Claims	Twist Phelan	___

Otter Award

Mysteries set in the geographical area covered by Left Coast Crime were announced at the conference held in Monterey, California in 2004.

2004

More Than You Know	Margaret Chittenden	___
Dragonfly Bones	David Cole	___
Murder Pans Out	Emily Toll	___

Bruce Alexander Historical Award

The Bruce Alexander History Mystery Award is for the best historical crime novel (set anywhere in the time period to fifty years before the conference) published in the previous year. This award honors the memory of historical crime novelist Bruce Alexander (aka Bruce Cook). The award is presented at the Left Coast Crime Conference.

Bruce Alexander History

2006
Spectres in the Smoke	Tony Broadbent	___
Night's Child	Maureen Jennings	___
Pardonable Lies	Jacqueline Winspear	___

2005
Witch in the Well, The	Sharan Newman	___
Five for Silver	Mary Reed & Eric Mayer	___
Tyrant of the Mind	Priscilla Royal	___
Murder on Marble Row	Victoria Thompson	___
Birds of a Feather	Jacqueline Winspear	___

2004
For the Love of Mike	Rhys Bowen	___
Silver Lies	Ann Parker	___
Four for a Boy	Mary Reed & Eric Mayer	___

Los Angeles Times Book Prize for a Mystery/Thriller Novel

The Los Angeles Times Festival of Books awards several prizes to honor achievement in literature by recognizing writers who have demonstrated outstanding craftsmanship and vision. One of the categories is "Mystery/Thriller." A writer need not be an American citizen and need not have written originally in English, but the winning book must have been published in English in the United States during the eligible year. The prize for Mystery/Thriller was first awarded in 2001.

L.A. Times Mystery/Thriller

2007
Echo Park	Michael Connelly	___
City of Tiny Lights	Patrick Neate	___
Night Gardener, The	George P. Pelecanos	___
Zero, The	Jess Walter	___
Winter of Frankie Machine, The	Don Winslow	___

2006
Legends: A Novel of Dissimulation	Robert Littell	___
Lincoln Lawyer, The	Michael Connelly	___
Right Madness, The	James Crumley	___
Ash and Bone	John Harvey	___
Strange Affair	Peter Robinson	___

2005
Tijuana Straits	Kem Nunn	___
Dark Voyage	Alan Furst	___
Return of the Dancing Master, The	Henning Mankell	___
Old Boys	Charles McCarry	___
Question of Blood, A	Ian Rankin	___

2004
Soul Circus	George P. Pelecanos	___
Company You Keep, The	Neil Gordon	___
House Sitter, The	Peter Lovesey	___
Dogs of Riga, The	Henning Mankell	___
Death of a Nationalist	Rebecca C. Pawel	___

2003
Hell to Pay	George P. Pelecanos	___
Emperor of Ocean Park, The	Stephen L. Carter	___
Living Dead Girl	Tod Goldberg	___
One Step Behind	Henning Mankell	___
Reversible Errors	Scott Turow	___

2002

Silent Joe	T. Jefferson Parker	___
Open Season	C.J. Box	___
Little America	Henry Bromell	___
Wooden Leg of Inspector Anders, The	Marshall Browne	___
Chasing the Devil's Tail	David Fulmer	___

2001

Place of Execution, A	Val McDermid	___
Purple Cane Road	James Lee Burke	___
Blood Rain	Michael Dibdin	___
Shame the Devil	George P. Pelecanos	___
Cold is the Grave	Peter Robinson	___

www.latimes.com/extras/bookprizes/

Lovey Awards
(Love is Murder Conference)

At the Love is Murder Conference, a number of mystery awards are offered and have been called the Readers' Choice Awards through 2006. Some of the guidelines and categories have changed over the years. The awards here are for works in the mystery field. Beginning in 2007, the awards were changed to the Lovey Awards. These are fan-based and voted on by conference attendees, and the winner of the award must register to attend.

[Editor's note: Some titles were nominated for two different award categories; also, some were nominated in two different years. Some of the earlier years' information has been lost and several members have tried to reconstruct the results.]

Lovey Best 1st Novel

2007

Chef Who Died Sauteing, The	Honora Finkelstein & Susan Smily	____
Murder Passes the Buck	Deb Baker	____
Dark Backward, The	Julia Buckley	____
Safe Place for Dying, A	Jack Fredrickson	____
Destroying Angels	Gail Lukasik	____
Two Wrongs	Morgan Mandel	____
Another Lost Angel	Steven B. Mandel	____
Blade Itself, The	Marcus Sakey	____
Shepherd's Pie	J.D. Webb	____

Readers Choice 1st Novel

2006

Cast of Shadows	Kevin Guilfoile	____
May Day	Jess Lourey	____
Destroying Angels	Gail Lukasik	____
Two Wrongs	Morgan Mandel	____
Lost in the Ivy	Randy Richardson	____
Operation: Stiletto	T.A. Ridgell	____
Dangerous Affairs	Kelle Z. Riley	____
Vengeance is Mine	Helen Sanders	____
Deadly Choices	Jennie Spallone	____

2005
Whiskey Sour	J.A. Konrath	___
Uncommon Grounds	Sandra Balzo	___
Rosary Bride, The: A Cloistered Death	Luisa Buehler	___
Penal Fires	Bill Fietzer	___
Circle of Sodom, The	Pat Mullan	___
Second Advent	Tony Perona	___
For the Defendant	E.G. Schrader	___
Murmurings, The	David Walks-As-Bear	___
Fall of White City, The	N.S. Wikarski	___

2003
Eye for Murder, An	Libby Fischer Hellmann	___

2002
When the Dead Speak	S.D. Tooley	___

2000
Deadly Little Christmas, A	Mary V. Welk	___

Lovey Best Traditional/Amateur Sleuth

2007
Deadly Interest	Julie Hyzy	___
Scout Master, The: A Prepared Death	Luisa Buehler	___
Bones to Pick	Carolyn Haines	___
Grave Surprise	Charlaine Harris	___
Minor Case of Murder	Jeff Markowitz	___
Horse Power	Linda Mickey	___
Love You Madly	Linda Palmer	___
Intrigue in Italics	Gayle Wigglesworth	___

Readers Choice Traditional/Amateur Sleuth

2006
Shot to Die For, A	Libby Fischer Hellmann	___
Murder a la Carte	Prudy Taylor Board	___
Something to Build Upon	Tim Broderick	___
Station Master, The: A Scheduled Death	Luisa Buehler	___
Deadly Blessing	Julie Hyzy	___
Who Is Killing Doah's Deer?	Jeff Markowitz	___
Scarecrow Murders, The	Mary V. Welk	___
Bound for Eternity	Sarah Wisseman	___

2005

Artistic License	Julie Hyzy	____
Uncommon Grounds	Sandra Balzo	____
Murder a la Carte	Prudy Taylor Board	____
Lion Tamer, The: A Caged Death	Luisa Buehler	____
Office Party, The	Chari Davenport	____
Skullduggery	Silvia Foti	____
Scent of Murder, The	Jeffrey Marks	____
Wedding's Window	Alex Matthews	____
Fatal Vision	Monette Michaels	____
Defective Goods	Linda Mickey	____
Scarecrow Murders, The	Mary V. Welk	____

2002

Something Wicked in the Air	Mary V. Welk	____

2000

Hard Evidence	Barbara D'Amato	____

Lovey Best PI/Police Procedural

2007

Final Judgment, A	Michael A. Black	____
Dramatist, The	Ken Bruen	____
Out of Cabrini	Dave Case	____
Married in Metropolis	Lonnie Cruse	____
Blown Away	Shane Gericke	____
Murder Most Holy	Mike Manno	____

Readers Choice PI/Police Procedural

2006

Bloody Mary	J.A. Konrath	____
Turn Left at September	Dennis Collins	____
Tarnished Eye, The	Judith Guest	____
Mercy Falls	William Kent Krueger	____
Murder Most Holy	Mike Manno	____
Dooley's Back	Sam Reaves (aka Allen Salter)	____
All the Dead Fathers	David J. Walker	____

2005

Death of a Thousand Cuts	Barbara D'Amato	____
Windy City Knights	Michael A. Black	____
One Last Breath	Stephen Booth	____
Troubleshooter, The	Austin S. Camacho	____
Whiskey Sour	J.A. Konrath	____

2003
Purgatory Ridge   William Kent Krueger   ____

2002
Boundary Waters   William Kent Krueger   ____

2000
Left Hand of God   Hugh Holton   ____

Lovey Best Paranormal/Sci Fi/Horror

2007
Definitely Dead   Charlaine Harris   ____
Sins of Orville Sand, The   Phil Locascio   ____
Telling, The   Jane Shoup   ____

Readers Choice Paranormal/Sci Fi/Horror

2006
Heartstone   D.C. Brod   ____
Academy, The   Scarlett Dean   ____
Eye of Newt   Denise Dietz   ____
Saving Jake   Ophelia Julien   ____
"Unwanted Pregnancy, An" (S.S.)   J. Michael Major   ____
Secret Portrait, The   Lillian Stewart Carl   ____

2005
Unseen, The   Lee Driver   ____
Oblivion   Jay Bonansinga   ____
Hell Hath No Fury Anthology; Wood, ed.   Scarlett Dean   ____
Undertow of Small Town Dreams, The   John Weagly   ____

Lovey Best Suspense

2007
Virgin of Small Plains, The   Nancy Pickard   ____
Dark Backward, The   Julia Buckley   ____
Rome Affair, The   Laura Caldwell   ____
Dangerous Affairs   Kelle Z. Riley   ____
Dead Sea Codex, The   Sarah Wisseman   ____

Readers Choice Suspense

2006

Heist, The	Michael A. Black	___
Look Closely	Laura Caldwell	___
Documentia	Darren Callahan	___
White Tiger	Michael Allen Dymmoch	___
Vengeance	Brian Pinkerton	___
Best Defense, The	Todd A. Stone	___
Absolute Instinct	Robert W. Walker	___

Lovey Best Thriller

2007

Sweetie's Diamonds	Raymond Benson	___
Last Quarry, The	Max Allan Collins	___
Another Lost Angel	Steven B. Mandel	___
PSI: Blue	Robert W. Walker	___

Readers Choice Thriller

2006

Creepers	David Morrell	___
Cracks in the Rainbow	Mark Bouton	___
Payback Assignment, The	Austin S. Camacho	___
Killing Rain	Barry Eisler	___
In the Company of Liars	David Ellis	___
Tom Clancy's Splinter Cell: Operation Barracuda	David Michaels (aka Raymond Benson)	___
L.P., The	David Walks-As-Bear	___

Lovey Best Suspense Thriller

2005

Fall, The	Michael Allen Dymmoch	___
Tom Clancy's Splinter Cell	David Michaels (aka Raymond Benson)	___
Oblivion	Jay Bonansinga	___
Deader by the Lake	Doug M. Cummings	___
Rain Storm	Barry Eisler	___
Dirty Fire	Earl Merkel	___
Circle of Sodom, The	Pat Mullan	___
Abducted	Brian Pinkerton	___
Sandstorm	James Rollins	___
Catch a Falling Lawyer	Robert W. Smith	___
Best Defense, The	Todd A. Stone	___
Grave Instinct	Robert W. Walker	___
Murmurings, The	David Walks-As-Bear	___

2003
Unnatural Instinct   Robert W. Walker   ____

2002
Oblivion   Jay Bonansinga   ____

2000
Windows to the Soul   J.M. Barlog   ____

Lovey Best Historical

2007
Dark Assassin   Anne Perry   ____
Shadow of the Bomb   Robert Goldsborough   ____
Penumbra   Carolyn Haines   ____

Readers Choice Historical

2006
Three Strikes You're Dead   Robert Goldsborough   ____
And Only to Deceive   Tasha Alexander   ____
All Roads Lead to Murder: A Case from the   Albert A. Bell, Jr.   ____
    Notebooks of Pliny the Younger
Shrouded in Thought   N.S. Wikarski   ____

2005
Shifting Tide, The   Anne Perry   ____
Good Soldier, A   Jeffrey Marks   ____
Missing From Haymarker Square   Harriette Gillem Robinet   ____
Fall of White City, The   N.S. Wikarski   ____

Lovey Best Crime Related Nonfiction

2005
They Died in Vain: Overlooked, Underappreciated   Jim Huang, ed.   ____
    and Forgotten Mystery Novels
Island of Lost Maps, The: A True Story of   Miles Harvey   ____
    Cartographic Crime
Return Again to the Scene of the Crime: A Guide to   Richard Lindberg   ____
    Even More Infamous Places in Chicago
Alchemy of Bones: Chicago's Luetgert Murder Case   Robert Loerzel   ____
    of 1897
Atomic Renaissance: Women Mystery Writers of the   Jeffrey Marks   ____
    1940s and 1950s

Lovey Best Short Story

2007

"Family Affair, A"	Mary V. Welk	*Deadly Ink 2006 Short Story Collection*; Buchanan, ed.	____
"Another Rock 'N' Roll Hit"	Raymond Benson	*These Guns for Hire*; Konrath, ed.	____
"Black Rose, The"	Michael A. Black	*These Guns for Hire*; Konrath, ed.	____
"Black Stuff"	Ken Bruen	*Dublin Noir;* Bruen, ed.	____
"Way I See It, The"	Dave Case	*Crimespree Mag*, Nov/Dec 06	____
"Tacky"	Charlaine Harris	*My Big Fat Supernatural Wedding*, Elrod, ed.	____
"Detour"	Libby Fischer Hellmann	*These Guns for Hire*; Konrath, ed.	____
"Strictly Business"	Julie Hyzy	*These Guns for Hire*; Konrath, ed.	____
"Book of Truth, The"	Nancy Pickard	*EQMM*, Sept 06	____

www.loveismurder.net/PeopleCh.htm

Macavity Awards

The Macavity Award is named for the "mystery cat" of T.S. Eliot's *Old Possum's Book of Practical Cats*. Each year the members of Mystery Readers International nominate and vote for their favorite mysteries in five categories. The awards began in 1987.

Macavity Best Mystery Novel

2007
Virgin of Small Plains, The	Nancy Pickard	____
Christine Falls	Benjamin Black	____
Janissary Tree, The	Jason Goodwin	____
Dead Hour, The	Denise Mina	____
Piece of My Heart	Peter Robinson	____
All Mortal Flesh	Julia Spencer-Fleming	____

2006
Lincoln Lawyer, The	Michael Connelly	____
One Shot	Lee Child	____
James Deans, The	Reed Farrel Coleman	____
Vanish	Tess Gerritsen	____
Solomon vs. Lord	Paul Levine	____
Strange Affair	Peter Robinson	____
Power of the Dog, The	Don Winslow	____

2005
Killing of the Tinkers, The	Ken Bruen	____
Cold Case	Robin Burcell	____
Darkly Dreaming Dexter	Jeff Lindsay	____
High Country Fall	Margaret Maron	____
California Girl	T. Jefferson Parker	____
Playing With Fire	Peter Robinson	____

2004
House Sitter, The	Peter Lovesey	____
Delicate Storm, The	Giles Blunt	____
For the Love of Mike	Rhys Bowen	____
Gurads, The	Ken Bruen	____
Done for a Dime	David Corbett	____

2003
Winter and Night	S.J. Rozan	____
Savannah Blues	Mary Kay Andrews	____
Jolie Blon's Bounce	James Lee Burke	____
Nine	Jan Burke	____
City of Bones	Michael Connelly	____

2002
>*Folly*   Laurie R. King   ____
>*Tell No One*   Harlan Coben   ____
>*Deadhouse, The*   Linda Fairstein   ____
>*Mystic River*   Dennis Lehane   ____
>*Silent Joe*   T. Jefferson Parker   ____

2001
>*Place of Execution, A*   Val McDermid   ____
>*Guns and Roses*   Taffy Cannon   ____
>*Bottoms, The*   Joe R. Lansdale   ____
>*Half Moon Street*   Anne Perry   ____
>*Whole Truth, The*   Nancy Pickard   ____

2000
>*Flower Master, The*   Sujata Massey   ____
>*River of Darkness*   Rennie Airth   ____
>*L.A. Requiem*   Robert Crais   ____
>*In a Dry Season*   Peter Robinson   ____

1999
>*Blood Work*   Michael Connelly   ____
>*Blind Descent*   Nevada Barr   ____
>*Butchers Hill*   Laura Lippman   ____
>*Home Fires*   Margaret Maron   ____
>*Blue*   Abigail Padgett   ____

1998
>*Dreaming of the Bones*   Deborah Crombie   ____
>*Hocus*   Jan Burke   ____
>*Trunk Music*   Michael Connelly   ____
>*Club Dumas, The (Dumas Club)*   Arturo Perez-Reverte   ____
>*Ax, The (Axe, The)*   Donald E. Westlake   ____

1997
>*Bloodhounds*   Peter Lovesey   ____
>*Chatham School Affair, The*   Thomas H. Cook   ____
>*Two for the Dough*   Janet Evanovich   ____
>*Grass Widow, The*   Teri Holbrook   ____
>*Hearts and Bones*   Margaret Lawrence   ____
>*Multiple Wounds*   Alan Russell   ____

1996
>*Under the Beetle's Cellar*   Mary Willis Walker   ____
>*Hard Christmas*   Barbara D'Amato   ____
>*Last Coyote, The*   Michael Connelly   ____
>*Bookman's Wake, The*   John Dunning   ____
>*Wild and Lonely Place, A*   Marcia Muller   ____

1995

She Walks These Hills	Sharyn McCrumb	____
Concrete Blonde, The	Michael Connelly	____
Playing for the Ashes	Elizabeth George	____
Scandal in Fair Haven	Carolyn G. Hart	____
Red Scream, The	Mary Willis Walker	____

1994

Sculptress, The	Minette Walters	____
Missing Joseph	Elizabeth George	____
Dead Man's Island	Carolyn G. Hart	____
Old Enemies	Janet LaPierre	____
To Live and Die in Dixie	Kathy Hogan Trocheck	____

1993

Bootlegger's Daughter	Margaret Maron	____
Booked to Die	John Dunning	____
Hangman's Beautiful Daughter, The	Sharyn McCrumb	____
White Butterfly	Walter Mosley	____

1992

I.O.U.	Nancy Pickard	____
Christie Caper, The	Carolyn G. Hart	____
Red Death, A	Walter Mosley	____

1991

If Ever I Return, Pretty Peggy-O (If Ever I Return)	Sharyn McCrumb	____
Well-Schooled in Murder	Elizabeth George	____
Deadly Valentine	Carolyn G. Hart	____
Burn Marks	Sara Paretsky	____
Face of a Stranger, The	Anne Perry	____

1990

Little Class on Murder, A	Carolyn G. Hart	____
Black Cherry Blues	James Lee Burke	____
Bone	George C. Chesbro	____
Death of a Joyce Scholar	Bartholomew Gill	____

1989

Thief of Time, A	Tony Hillerman	____
Murder Unrenovated	P.M. Carlson	____
Great Deliverance, A	Elizabeth George	____
"E" is for Evidence	Sue Grafton	____
Silence of the Lambs, The	Thomas Harris	____
Blood Shot (Toxic Shock)	Sara Paretsky	____

1988
Marriage is Murder	Nancy Pickard	___
Primary Target	Max Allan Collins	___
Project Named Desire, A	John William Corrington & Joyce H.	___
Venetian Mask	Mickey Friedman	___
Right Jack, The	Margaret Maron	___
Bitter Medicine	Sara Paretsky	___
Fatal Inversion, A	Barbara Vine	___
Tenth Interview, The	John Wainwright	___

1987
Taste for Death, A	P.D. James	___
When the Sacred Ginmill Closes	Lawrence Block	___
Million Dollar Wound, The	Max Allan Collins	___
Come Morning	Joe Gores	___
Beyond Blame	Stephen Greenleaf	___
Skinwalkers	Tony Hillerman	___
Perfect Spy, A	John le Carre	___
Deadfall	Bill Pronzini	___
Lady Killer	MasakoTogawa	___
Night Games	Collin Wilcox	___

Macavity Best 1st Mystery Novel

2007
Mr. Clarinet	Nick Stone	___
Consigned to Death	Jane K. Cleland	___
47 Rules of Highly Effective Bank Robbers	Troy Cook	___
King of Lies, The	John Hart	___
Field of Darkness, A	Cornelia Read	___

2006
Immoral	Brian Freeman	___
All Shook Up	Mike Harrison	___
Baby Game, The	Randall Hicks	___

2005
Dating Dead Men	Harley Jane Kozak	___
Uncommon Grounds	Sandra Balzo	___
Summer of the Big Bachi	Naomi Hirahara	___
Whiskey Sour	J.A. Konrath	___
Misdemeanor Man	Dylan Schaffer	___

2004
Maisie Dobbs	Jacqueline Winspear	___
Night of the Dance, The	James Hime	___
Death of a Nationalist	Rebecca C. Pawel	___
Bridge of Sighs, The	Olen Steinhauer	___

2003

In the Bleak Midwinter	Julia Spencer-Fleming	____
Blue Edge of Midnight, The	Jonathon King	____
Distance, The	Eddie Muller	____
Valley to Die For, A	Radine Trees Nehring	____

2002

Open Season	C.J. Box	____
Jasmine Trade, The	Denise Hamilton	____
Perhaps She'll Die	M.K. Preston	____
Blindsighted	Karin Slaughter	____

2001

Conspiracy of Paper, A	David Liss	____
Death Dances to a Reggae Beat	Kate Grilley	____
Three Dirty Women and the Garden of Death	Julie Wray Herman	____
Crow in Stolen Colors	Marcia Simpson	____

2000

Inner City Blues	Paula L. Woods	____
Murder With Peacocks	Donna Andrews	____
Murder in the Marais	Cara Black	____
Revenge of the Gypsy Queen	Kris Neri	____

1999

Sympathy for the Devil	Jerrilyn Farmer	____
Tiger's Palette	Jacqueline Fiedler	____
Doctor Digs a Grave, The	Robin Hathaway	____

1998

Dead Body Language	Penny Warner	____
Killing Floor	Lee Child	____
Off the Face of the Earth	Aljean Harmetz	____
Charm City	Laura Lippman	____
Salaryman's Wife, The	Sujata Massey	____

1997

Death in Little Tokyo	Dale Furutani	____
Final Jeopardy	Linda Fairstein	____
Murder on a Girl's Night Out	Anne George	____
Brother's Blood, A	Michael C. White	____

1996

Strange Files of Fremont Jones, The	Dianne Day	____
Body in the Transept, The	Jeanne M. Dams	____
Far and Deadly Cry, A	Teri Holbrook	____
Horse of a Different Killer	Jody Jaffe	____
Death in Bloodhound Red	Virginia Lanier	____

1995
Do Unto Others   Jeff Abbott   ___
One for the Money   Janet Evanovich   ___
Murder in the Place of Anubis   Lynda Robinson   ___
North of Montana   April Smith   ___

1994
Death Comes as Epiphany   Sharan Newman   ___
Track of the Cat   Nevada Barr   ___
Share in Death, A   Deborah Crombie   ___
Grave Talent, A   Laurie R. King   ___
Child of Silence   Abigail Padgett   ___

1993
Blanche on the Lam   Barbara Neely   ___
Aunt Dimity's Death   Nancy Atherton   ___
Every Crooked Nanny   Kathy Hogan Trocheck   ___

1992
Murder on the Iditarod Trail (Tie)   Sue Henry   ___
Zero at the Bone (Tie)   Mary Willis Walker   ___
Bulrush Murders, The   Rebecca Rothenberg   ___
Roman Blood   Steven Saylor   ___
Flowers for the Dead   Ann Williams   ___

1991
Postmortem   Patricia Cornwell   ___
Catering to Nobody   Diane Mott Davidson   ___
Kindred Crimes   Janet Dawson   ___
Chartresue Clue, The   William F. Love   ___

1990
Grime and Punishment   Jill Churchill   ___
Cherrio Killings, The   Doug Allyn   ___
Mark Twain Murders, The   Edith Skom   ___
Collector of Photographs, A   Deborah Valentine   ___
Last Billable Hour, The   Susan Wolfe   ___

1989
Killings at Badger's Drift, The   Caroline Graham   ___
Murder Once Done   Mary Lou Bennett   ___

1988

Monkey's Raincoat, The	Robert Crais	___
Death on the Rocks	Michael Allegretto	___
Death on Demand	Carolyn G. Hart	___
Fetish (A Personal Possession)	Jeanne Hart	___
Unquiet Grave, The	Janet LaPierre	___
Where Lawyers Fear to Tread	Lia Matera	___
Lover Man	Dallas Murphy	___
Neon Flamingo	Matt & Bonnie Taylor	___
Unorthodox Murder of Rabbi Wahl, The (Unorthodox Murder of Rabbi Moss)	Joseph Telushkin	___
Presumed Innocent	Scott Turow	___

1987

Ritual Bath, The (Tie)	Faye Kellerman	___
Case of Loyalties, A (Tie)	Marilyn Wallace	___
Too Late to Die	Bill Crider	___
Floater	Joseph Koenig	___
Dead Air	Mike Lupica	___
From a High Place	Edward Mathis	___
Kiss Me Once	Thomas Maxwell	___

Macavity Best Non-Fiction

2007

Mystery Muses: 100 Classics That Inspire Today's Mystery Writers	Jim Huang & Austin Lugar, eds.	___
Don't Murder Your Mystery: 24 Fiction-Writing Techniques to Save Your Manuscript From Ending Up...D.O.A.	Chris Roerden	___
Beautiful Cigar Girl, The: Mary Rogers, Edgar Allan Poe, and the Invention of Murder	Daniel Stashower	___

2006

Girl Sleuth: Nancy Drew and the Women Who Created Her	Melanie Rehak	___
Tracks to Murder: A Witty and Informative Look at Classic American Murder Cases	Jonathan Goodman	___
Behind the Mystery: Top Mystery Writers Interviewed	Stuart M. Kaminsky; photos by Laurie Roberts	___
New Annotated Sherlock Holmes, The: The Novels	Leslie S. Klinger, ed.	___
Spook: Science Tackles the Afterlife	Mary Roach	___

2005
Forensics for Dummies   D.P. Lyle, M.D.   ____
Famous American Crimes and Trials, Vol. 1   Frankie Y. Bailey &   ____
                                                         Steven Chermak
Just the Facts: True Tales of Cops and Criminals   Jim Doherty   ____
New Annotated Sherlock Holmes, The: The   Leslie S. Klinger, ed.   ____
   Complete Short Stories
Latin American Mystery Writers: An A-to-Z Guide   Darrell B. Lockhart   ____

2004
Make Mine a Mystery: A Reader's Guide to   Gary Warren Niebuhr   ____
   Mystery and Detective Fiction
Mystery Women: An Encyclopedia of Leading   Colleen A. Barnett   ____
   Women Characters in Mystery Fiction, Vol. 3
Second Helping of Murder, A: More Diabolically   Jo Grossman &   ____
   Delicious Recipes From Contemporary Mystery   Robert Weibezahl, eds.
   Writers
Beautiful Shadow: A Life of Patricia Highsmith   Andrew Wilson   ____

2003
They Died in Vain: Overlooked, Underappreciated   Jim Huang, ed.   ____
   and Forgotten Mystery Novels
Mammoth Encyclopedia of Modern Crime Fiction, The   Mike Ashley, compiler   ____
Intent to Sell: Marketing the Genre Novel   Jeffrey Marks   ____
Art of Noir, The: The Posters and Graphics From   Eddie Muller   ____
   the Classic Era of Film Noir

2002
Writing the Mystery: A Start-to-Finish Guide for   G. Miki Hayden   ____
   Both Novice and Professional
History of Mystery, The   Max Allan Collins   ____
Seldom Disappointed: A Memoir   Tony Hillerman   ____
My Name's Friday: The Unauthorized but True   Michael J. Hayde   ____
   Story of Dragnet and the Films of Jack Webb
Who was that Lady? Craig Rice: The Queen of   Jeffrey Marks   ____
   Screwball Mystery

2001
American Regional Mystery, The   Marvin Lachman   ____
Doctor and the Detective, The: A Biography of Sir   Martin Booth   ____
   Arthur Conan Doyle
Women of Mystery: The Lives and Works of   Martha Hailey DuBose   ____
   Notable Women Crime Novelists
100 Favorite Mysteries of the Century   Jim Huang, ed.   ____

2000

Ross Macdonald   Tom Nolan   ____

Taste of Murder, A: Diabolically Delicious Recipes   Jo Grossman &   ____
From Contemporary Mystery Writers   Robert Weibezahl, eds.

Teller of Tales: The Life of Arthur Conan Doyle   Daniel Stashower   ____

1999

Killer Books: A Reader's Guide to Exploring the   Jean Swanson & Dean James   ____
Popular World of Mystery and Suspense

Mystery Reader's Walking Guide to Washington, D.C.   Alzina Stone Dale   ____

Speaking of Murder: Interviews With the Masters of   Ed Gorman &   ____
Mystery and Suspense   Martin H. Greenberg, eds.

Dark City: The Lost World of Film Noir   Eddie Muller   ____

Silk Stalkings II: More Women Write of Murder   Victoria Nichols &   ____
                                                                          Susan Thompson

1998

Deadly Women: The Woman Mystery Reader's   Jan Grape, Dean James &   ____
Indispensable Companion   Ellen Nehr, eds.

"G" is for Grafton: The World of Kinsey Millhone   Natalie Hevener Kaufman   ____
                                                                          & Carol McGinnis Kay

Napoleon of Crime, The: The Life and Times of   Ben Macintyre   ____
Adam Worth, Master Thief

Guilty Parties: A Mystery Lover's Companion   Ian Ousby   ____

1997

Detecting Women 2: A Reader's Guide and   Willetta L. Heising   ____
Checklist for Mystery Series Written by Women

Mystery!: A Celebration: Stalking Public   Ron Miller & Karen Sharpe, eds.   ____
Television's Greatest Sleuths

St. James Guide to Crime and Mystery, 4th ed.   Jay Pederson, ed.   ____

1996

Detecting Women: A Reader's Guide and   Willetta L. Heising   ____
Checklist for Mystery Series Written by Women

John Dickson Carr: The Man Who Explained Miracles   Douglas G. Greene   ____

Armchair Detective Book of Lists, The, 2nd ed.   Kate Stine, ed.   ____

Spooks, Spies and Private Eyes   Paula Woods   ____

1995

By a Woman's Hand: A Guide to Mystery   Jean Swanson & Dean James, eds.   ____
Fiction by Women

Crime Fiction II: A Comprehensive Bibliography,   Allen J. Hubin   ____
1749-1990

1994
Fine Art of Murder, The: The Mystery Reader's   Ed Gorman, Martin H.   ____
    Indispensable Companion   Greenberg, Larry Segriff
    & Jon L. Breen, eds.

Dorothy L. Sayers: A Centenary Celebration   Alzina Stone Dale   ____
Poisonous Pen of Agatha Christie, The   Michael C. Gerald   ____
Reader's Guide to the American Novel of Detection, A   Marvin Lachman   ____

1993
Doubleday Crime Club Compendium 1928-1991   Ellen Nehr   ____
Alias S.S. Van Dine   John Loughery   ____

1992
Talking Mysteries: A Conversation With Tony   Tony Hillerman & Ernie Bulow   ____
    Hillerman
Margery Allingham: A Biography   Julia Thorogood   ____

1991
Agatha Christie: The Woman and Her Mysteries   Gillian Gill   ____

1990
Bedside Companion to Crime   H.R.F. Keating   ____
Perfect Murder, The   David Lehman   ____
Murder on the Air   Ric Meyers   ____

1989
Silk Stalkings: When Women Write of Murder   Victoria Nichols &   ____
    Susan Thompson
Mystery Reader's Walking Guide: England   Alzina Stone Dale &   ____
    Barbara Sloan Hendershott
Mystery Lovers' Book of Quotations: The Wit and   Jane E. Horning, compiled and   ____
    Wisdom of the World's Great Crime Writers   arranged by

1988
Son of Gun in Cheek   Bill Pronzini   ____

1987
1001 Midnights: The Aficionado's Guide to   Marcia Muller & Bill Pronzini   ____
    Mystery and Detective Fiction

Macavity Best Short Story

2007
"Till Death Do Us Part"   Tim Maleeny   *Death Do Us Part: New Stories*   ____
    about Love, Lust, and Murder
    (MWA); Coben, ed.
"Provenance"   Robert Barnard   *EQMM*, Jul 06   ____
"Disturbance in the Field"   Roberta Isleib   *Seasmoke: Crime Stories by*   ____
    New England Writers; Flora,
    McCarty, & Oleksiw, eds.

2006

"There is No Crime on Easter Island"	Nancy Pickard	*EQMM*, Sept/Oct 05	___
"Everybody's Girl"	Robert Barnard	*EQMM*, May 05	___
"It Can Happen"	David Corbett	*San Francisco Noir*; Maravelis, ed.	___
"Big Road, The"	Steve Hockensmith	*AHMM*, May 05	___

2005

"Widow of Slane, The"	Terence Faherty	*EQMM*, Mar/Apr 04	___
"Viscery"	Sandra Balzo	*EQMM*, Dec 04	___
"Lady's Not for Dying, The"	Alana White	*Futures*, Winter 04	___

2004

"Grass is Always Greener, The"	Sandy Balzo	*EQMM*, Mar 03	___
"Rogues' Gallery"	Robert Barnard	*EQMM*, Mar 03	___
"Texas Two-Step"	Diana Deverell	*AHMM*, Feb 03	___
"No Man's Land"	Beth Foxwell	*Blood on Their Hands*; Block, ed.	___
"War Crimes"	G. Miki Hayden	*A Hot & Sultry Night for Crime*; Deaver, ed.	___
"Child Support"	Ronnie Klaskin	*A Hot & Sultry Night for Crime*; Deaver, ed.	___
"Red Meat"	Elaine Viets	*Blood on Their Hands*; Block, ed.	___

2003

"Voice Mail"	Janet Dawson	*Scam & Eggs*	___
"Boot Scoot"	Diana Deverell	*AHMM*, Oct 02	___
"Empire's Reach, An"	Brendan DuBois	*AHMM*, Nov 02	___
"Bible Belt"	Toni L.P. Kelner	*EQMM*, Jun 02	___
"Too Many Cooks"	Marcia Talley	*Much Ado About Murder*; Perry, ed.	___
"Adventure of the Rara Avis, The"	Carolyn Wheat	*Murder, My Dear Watson*; Greenbery, Lellenberg & Stashower, eds.	___

2002

"Abbey Ghosts, The"	Jan Burke	*AHMM*, Jan 01	___
"My Bonnie Lies…"	Ted Hertel, Jr.	*Mammoth Book of Legal Thrillers*; Hemmingson, ed.	___
"Bitter Waters"	Rochelle Krich	*Criminal Kabbalah*; Raphael, ed.	___
"Would-Be Widower, The"	Katherine Hall Page	Malice Domestic 10; Barr, pre.	___

2001
"Candle for Christmas, A"	Reginald Hill	*EQMM,* Jan 00	____
"Man in the Civil Suit, The"	Jan Burke	Malice Domestic 9; Hess, pre.	____
"Chosen, The"	Joyce Christmas	*Unholy Orders*; Stevens, ed.	____

2000
"Maubi and the Jumbies"	Kate Grilley	*Murderous Intent,* Fall 99	____
"Paleta Man"	Laurie R. King	*Irreconcilable Differences*; Matera, ed.	____
"Heroes"	Anne Perry	*Murder and Obsession*; Penzler, ed.	____
"Show Me the Bones"	Carolyn Wheat	*Diagnosis Dead*; Kellerman, ed.	____

1999
"Of Course You Know that Chocolate is a Vegetable"	Barbara D'Amato	*EQMM,* Nov 98	____
"Sleeping Dogs Lie"	Laurien Berenson	*Canine Crimes*; Marks, ed.	____
"Simple Philosophy, A"	Harlan Coben	Malice Domestic 7; McCrumb, pre.	____
"Village Vampire and the Oboe of Death, The"	Dean James	Malice Domestic 7; McCrumb, pre.	____

1998
"Two Ladies of Rose Cottage, The"	Peter Robinson	Malice Domestic 6; Perry, pre.	____
"Real Bullets This Time"	William Bankier	*EQMM,* Jul 97	____
"Find Miriam"	Stuart M. Kaminsky	*New Mystery,* Summer 97	____
"Corbett Correspondence, The"	Edward Marston & Peter Lovesey	Malice Domestic 6; Perry, pre.	____
"Etiquette Lesson"	Polly Whitney	*Murderous Intent,* Fall 97	____

1997
"Cruel and Unusual"	Carolyn Wheat	*Guilty as Charged*; Turlow, ed.	____
"Takeout"	Joyce Christmas	Malice Domestic 5; Whitney, pre.	____
"Bun Also Rises, The"	Jill Churchill	Malice Domestic 5; Whitney, pre.	____
"Red Clay"	Michael Malone	*Murder for Love*; Penzler, ed.	____
"Music Lesson, The"	Rosemarie Santini	*New Mystery,* v4 #2, No.9, 96	____

1996
"Evans Tries an O-Level"	Colin Dexter	*Morse's Greatest Mystery*	____
"Rule of Law"	K.K. Beck	Malice Domestic 4; Hart, pre.	____
"Cupid's Arrow"	Dorothy Cannell	*Crimes of the Heart*; Hart, ed.	____

1995
"Cast Your Fate to the Wind" (Tie)	Deborah Adams	Malice Domestic 3; Pickard, pre.	____
"Unharmed" (Tie)	Jan Burke	*EQMM,* Mid-Dec 94	____

1994
"Checkout"	Susan Dunlap	Malice Domestic 2; Clark, pre.	____
"Kim's Game"	M.D. Lake	Malice Domestic 2; Clark, pre.	____

1993
"Henrie O's Holiday"	Carolyn G. Hart	Malice Domestic 1; Peters, pre.	____
"Last to Know, The"	Joan Hess	Malice Domestic 1; Peters, pre.	____
"Hand of Carlos, The"	Charles McCarry	*The Armchair Detective*, Fall 92	____

1992
"Deborah's Judgment"	Margaret Maron	*A Woman's Eye*; Paretsky, ed.	____
"Dance of the Dead"	Joe Gores	*The Armchair Detective*, Spring 91	____
"Life, for Short"	Carolyn Wheat	Sisters in Crime 4, Wallace, ed.	____

1991
"Too Much to Bare"	Joan Hess	Sisters in Crime 2; Wallace, ed.	____

1990
"Afraid All the Time"	Nancy Pickard	Sisters in Crime; Wallace, ed.	____
"Fire Burning Bright"	Brendan DuBois	*AHMM*, Winter 89	____
"One Eye Open"	Jeremiah Healy	*EQMM*, Jul 89	____
"Too Many Crooks"	Donald E. Westlake	*Playboy*, Aug 89	____

1989
"Déjà Vu"	Doug Allyn	*AHMM*, Jun 88	____
"Fatherly Love"	Carl Martin	*EQMM*, Jul 88	____

1988
"Woman in the Wardrobe, The"	Robert Barnard	*EQMM*, Dec 87	____

1987
"Parker Shotgun, The"	Sue Grafton	*Mean Streets*; Randisi, ed	____

Macavity Sue Feder Historical Mystery Award

This award is in honor of the late Sue Feder, reviewer, scholar and dedicated mystery fan. The award is nominated and voted on by members of Mystery Readers International and presented at Bouchercon each year in the fall. Sue Feder founded the Historical Mystery Appreciation Society with its quarterly journal, *Murder: Past Tense,* dedicated to Ellis Peters. HMAS bestowed the Herodotus Awards for many years, and the Sue Feder Historical Mystery Award continues this tradition in her memory. To see the earlier awards, look at the Herodotus Historical Awards. Sue passed away in 2005 and was the wife of Larry Miller and sister of Nanette Williams, who have both given their permission and support for this award.

Macavity Sue Feder Historical

2007
Oh Danny Boy	Rhys Bowen	___
Lightning Rule, The	Brett Ellen Block	___
Bee's Kiss, The	Barbara Cleverly	___
Dark Assassin	Anne Perry	___
Messenger of Truth	Jacqueline Winspear	___

2006
Pardonable Lies	Jacqueline Winspear	___
In Like Flynn	Rhys Bowen	___
Spectres in the Smoke	Tony Broadbent	___
War of the World Murders, The	Max Allan Collins	___
Night's Child	Maureen Jennings	___

www.mysteryreaders.org/macavity.html

Quill Award

The Quills (Literacy Foundation) is a national book awards program in which the people, not the critics, decide who is the best of the best. Quill Award's staff identifies thousands of English-language titles, released in the U.S between August 1 and July 31 yielding five top titles in each of nineteen categories, one being "Mystery/Suspense/Thriller." The titles are ones that received starred reviews or appeared on national bestseller lists during the year. An invited group of booksellers and librarians serve as a nominating board voting for their favorites, yielding five top titles in each of nineteen categories. Between August 15 and September 15, America's readers have the final say by casting their votes at www.quillsvote.com, or at voting kiosks in select Borders® Books & Music Stores. The Quill Awards began in 2005.

Quill Mystery/Suspense/Thriller Award

2007

What the Dead Know	Laura Lippman	____
Overlook, The	Michael Connelly	____
Body of Lies	David Ignatius	____
Welcome Grave, A	Michael Koryta	____
Collaborator of Bethlehem, The	Matt BeynonRees	____

2006

Twelve Sharp	Janet Evanovich	____
Lincoln Lawyer, The	Michael Connelly	____
Promise Me	Harlan Coben	____
New Annotated Sherlock Holmes, (nonfiction) The: The Novels	Leslie S. Klinger, ed.	____
Tomb of the Golden Bird	Elizabeth Peters	____

2005

Eleven on Top	Janet Evanovich	____
Closers, The	Michael Connelly	____
With No One as Witness	Elizabeth George	____
Historian, The	Elizabeth Kostova	____
In the Company of Cheerful Ladies	Alexander McCall Smith	____

www.quillsliteracy.org/index.html

St. Martin's Press Competition

There are now four contests sponsored by St. Martin's Press in conjunction with four different mystery organizations. These are contests for unpublished manuscripts with the winner obtaining a book publishing offer with a $10,000 advance.

St. Martin's Minotaur/PWA 1st Private Eye Novel Competition

In 1986, the Private Eye Writers of America teamed up with St. Martin's Minotaur to sponsor the St. Martin's Minotaur/PWA First Private Eye Novel Competition. This is a competition for unpublished manuscripts.

2007
Father's Day   Keith Gilman   ____

2006
Last Striptease, The   Michael Wiley   ____

2005
no winner

2004
First Kill   Michael Kronenwetter   ____

2003
Tonight I Said Goodbye   Michael Koryta   ____

2002
Sterling Inheritance, The   Michael Siverling   ____

2001
no winner

2000
Catching Water in a Net   J.L. Abramo   ____

1999
Street Level   Bob Truluck   ____

1998
Losers' Club, The   Lise S. Baker   ____

1997
Cold Day in Paradise, A   Steve Hamilton   ____

1996
no winner

1995
Diamond Head   Charles Knief   ____

1994
Harry Chronicles, The   Allan Pedrazas   ____

1993
Heaven Stone, The   David Daniel   ____

1992
Hour of the Manatee   A.C. Ayres   ____

1991
Sudden Death at the Norfolk Café, A   Winona Sullivan   ____

1990
Loud Adios, The   Ken Kuhlken   ____

1989
Kindred Crimes   Janet Dawson   ____

1988
Katwalk   Karen Kijewski   ____

1987
Fear of the Dark   Gar Anthony Haywood   ____

1986
Infinite Number of Monkeys, An   Les Roberts   ____

St. Martin's Minotaur/MWA 1st Crime Novel Competition

Mystery Writers of America (Edgar® Awards) and St. Martin's Minotaur will offer a first crime novel competition beginning in 2008 and announce the winner at the annual Edgar® Awards banquet. The competition is open to any writer who has never been the author of a published novel.

St. Martin's Minotaur/Malice Domestic 1st Traditional Mystery Novel

Malice Domestic (Agatha Awards) and St. Martin's Minotaur offer a first traditional mystery novel competition and announce the winner at the Malice Domestic Awards banquet. The competition is open to any professional or non-professional writer, regardless of nationality, who has never been the author of a published traditional mystery, and is not under contract with a publisher for publication of a traditional mystery.

2007
Posed for Murder   Meredith S.Cole   ____

2006
Stranger Lies There, A   Stephen Santogrossi   ____

2005
Murder in Exile   Vincent H. O'Neil   ____

2004
Eight of Swords   David Skibbins   ____

2003
Southern Fried   Cathy Pickens   ____

2002
  Murder Off Mike   Joyce Krieg   ____

2001
  In the Bleak Midwinter   Julia Spencer-Fleming   ____

2000
  Gripping Beast, The   Margot Wadley   ____

1999
  Jackpot Justice   Marilyn Wooley   ____

1998
  Murder With Peacocks   Donna Andrews   ____

1997
  Doctor Digs a Grave, The   Robin Hathaway   ____

1996
  Simon Said   Sarah R. Shaber   ____

1995
  Lie Down With Dogs   Jan Gleiter   ____

1994
  Death in Still Waters   Barbara Lee   ____

1993
  Something to Kill For   Susan Holtzer   ____

1992
  Man Who Understood Cats, The   Michael Allen Dymmoch   ____

1991
  Winter Widow, The   Charlene Weir   ____

1990
  Piano Man, The   Noreen Gilpatrick   ____

Shamus Awards

The Private Eye Writers of America (PWA) is an organization devoted to private-eye detective fiction, and offers the Shamus Awards. Membership is open to fans, writers, and publishing professionals. The Shamus Awards have been offered since 1982.

Shamus Best P.I. Novel

2007
Dramatist, The	Ken Bruen	____
Darkest Place, The	Daniel Judson	____
Do-Re-Mi, The	Ken Kuhlken	____
Vanishing Point	Marcia Muller	____
Days of Rage	KrisNelscott	____

2006
Lincoln Lawyer, The	Michael Connelly	____
Oblivion	Peter Abrahams	____
Forgotten Man, The	Robert Crais	____
In a Teapot	Terence Faherty	____
Man With the Iron-On Badge, The	Lee Goldberg	____
Cinnamon Kiss	Walter Mosley	____

2005
While I Disappear	Edward Wright	____
Fade to Clear	Leonard Chang	____
Wake-Up, The	Robert Ferrigno	____
After the Rain	Chuck Logan	____
Choke Point	James C. Mitchell	____

2004
Guards, The	Ken Bruen	____
Scavenger Hunt	Robert Ferrigno	____
Blood is the Sky	Steve Hamilton	____
Visible Darkness, A	Jonathon King	____
Fatal Flaw	William Lashner	____

2003
Blackwater Sound	James W. Hall	____
North of Nowhere	Steve Hamilton	____
Last Place, The	Laura Lippman	____
Hell to Pay	George P. Pelecanos	____
Winter and Night	S.J. Rozan	____

2002
Reflecting the Sky	S.J. Rozan	___
Angel in Black	Max Allan Collins	___
Ashes of Aries	Martha C. Lawrence	___
Devil Went Down to Austin, The	Rick Riordan	___
Cold Water Burning	John Straley	___

2001
Havana Heat	Carolina Garcia-Aguilera	___
Smile on the Face of the Tiger, A	Loren D. Estleman	___
Deader the Better, The	G.M. Ford	___
Ellipsis	Stephen Greenleaf	___
Listen to the Silence	Marcia Muller	___

2000
California Fire and Life	Don Winslow	___
L.A. Requiem	Robert Crais	___
Monster	Jonathan Kellerman	___
Prayers for Rain	Dennis Lehane	___
Stone Quarry	S.J. Rozan	___

1999
Boobytrap	Bill Pronzini	___
No Badge, No Gun	Harold Adams	___
Flying Blind	Max Allan Collins	___
Only Good Lawyer, The	Jeremiah Healy	___
Gone, Baby, Gone	Dennis Lehane	___

1998
Come Back Dead	Terence Faherty	___
Indigo Slam	Robert Crais	___
Deception Pass	Earl Emerson	___
Sacred	Dennis Lehane	___
Down for the Count	Maxine O'Callaghan	___
No Colder Place	S.J. Rozan	___

1997
Sunset Express	Robert Crais	___
Damned in Paradise	Max Allan Collins	___
Flesh Wounds	Stephen Greenleaf	___
Invasion of Privacy	Jeremiah Healy	___
Sentinels	Bill Pronzini	___
When Wallflowers Die	Sandra West Prowell	___

1996

Concourse	S.J. Rozan	___
Vanishing Smile, The	Earl Emerson	___
Come to Grief	Dick Francis	___
Movie	Parnell Hall	___
Neon Smile, The	Dick Lochte	___

1995

"K" is for Killer	Sue Grafton	___
Long Line of Dead Men, A	Lawrence Block	___
Carnal Hours	Max Allan Collins	___
Killing of Monday Brown, The	Sandra West Prowell	___
Lake Effect, The	Les Roberts	___

1994

Devil Knows You're Dead, The	Lawrence Block	___
Foursome	Jeremiah Healy	___
Wolf in the Shadows	Marcia Muller	___
Moth	James Sallis	___
Lies that Bind, The	Judith Van Gieson	___

1993

Man Who was Taller Than God, The	Harold Adams	___
Cassandra in Red	Michael Collins (Dennis Lynds)	___
Lullaby Town	Robert Crais	___
Shallow Graves	Jeremiah Healy	___
Special Delivery	Jerry Kennealy	___

1992

Stolen Away: A Novel of the Lindbergh Kidnapping	Max Allan Collins	___
Dance at the Slaughterhouse, A	Lawrence Block	___
Where Echoes Live	Marcia Muller	___
Fistful of Empty, A	Benjamin Schutz	___
Second Chance	Jonathan Valin	___

1991

"G" is for Gumshoe	Sue Grafton	___
Ticket to the Boneyard, A	Lawrence Block	___
Poor Butterfly	Stuart M. Kaminsky	___
Polo's Wild Card	Jerry Kennealy	___
Dead Irish	John Lescroart	___
Desert Look, The	Bernard Schopen	___

1990

Extenuating Circumstances	Jonathan Valin	____
Out on the Cutting Edge	Lawrence Block	____
Skintight Shroud, The	Wayne D. Dundee	____
Shape of Dread, The	Marcia Muller	____
Killing Man, The	Mickey Spillane	____

1989

Kiss	John Lutz	____
Neon Mirage	Max Allan Collins	____
Deviant Behavior	Earl Emerson	____
Swan Dive	Jeremiah Healy	____
Blood Shot (Toxic Shock)	Sara Paretsky	____

1988

Tax in Blood, A	Benjamin Schutz	____
Trouble of Fools, A	Linda Barnes	____
Lady Yesterday	Loren D. Estleman	____
Autumn Dead, The	Ed Gorman	____
Ride the Lightning	John Lutz	____

1987

Staked Goat, The (The Tethered Goat)	Jeremiah Healy	____
When the Sacred Ginmill Closes	Lawrence Block	____
In La-La Land We Trust	Robert Campbell	____
Million Dollar Wound, The	Max Allan Collins	____
"C" is for Corpse	Sue Grafton	____

1986

"B" is for Burglar	Sue Grafton	____
Naked Liar, The	Harold Adams	____
Hardball	Doug Hornig	____
Catskill Eagle, A	Robert B. Parker	____
Bones	Bill Pronzini	____

1985

Sugartown	Loren D. Estleman	____
True Crime	Max Allan Collins	____
Die Again, Macready	Jack Livingston	____
Nightlines	John Lutz	____
Full Contact	Robert J. Randisi	____

1984

True Detective	Max Allan Collins	____
Dancing Bear	James Crumley	____
Dark Fantastic, The	Stanley Ellin	____
Glass Highway, The	Loren D. Estleman	____
Widening Gyre, The	Robert B. Parker	____

1983
Eight Million Ways to Die	Lawrence Block	____
"A" is for Alibi	Sue Grafton	____
Gravedigger	Joseph Hansen	____
Piece of the Silence, A	Jack Livingston	____
Ceremony	Robert B. Parker	____

1982
Hoodwink	Bill Pronzini	____
Stab in the Dark, A	Lawrence Block	____
30 for a Harry	Richard Hoyt	____
Hard Trade	Arthur Lyons	____
Early Autumn	Robert B. Parker	____

Shamus Best Paperback Original P.I. Novel

2007
Unquiet Grave, An	P.J. Parrish	____
Hallowed Ground	Lori G. Armstrong	____
Prop, The	Pete Hautman	____
Uncomfortable Dead, The: What's Missing is Missing	Paco Ignacio Taibo II & Subcomandante Marcos	____
Crooked	Brian M. Wiprud	____

2006
James Deans, The	Reed Farrel Coleman	____
Falling Down	David Cole	____
Deadlocked	Joel Goldman	____
Cordite Wine	Richard Helms	____
Killing Rain, A	P.J. Parrish	____

2005
Fade to Blonde	Max Phillips	____
Call the Devil by His Oldest Name	Sallie Bissell	____
Shadow of the Dahlia	Jack Bludis	____
London Blitz Murders, The	Max Allan Collins	____
Island of Bones	P.J. Parrish	____

2004
Cold Quarry	Andy Straka	____
Dragonfly Bones	David Cole	____
Wet Debt	Richard Helms	____
Thicker Than Water	P.J. Parrish	____

2003
Poisoned Rose, The	D. Daniel Judson	____
Cash Out	Paul Boray	____
Lusitania Murders, The	Max Allan Collins	____
Juicy Watusi	Richard Helms	____
Paint It Black	P.J. Parrish	____

2002
Archangel Protocol — Lyda Morehouse ___
Keepers — Janet LaPierre ___
Ancient Enemy — Robert Westbrook ___

2001
Death in the Steel City — Thomas Lipinski ___
Blazing Tree, The — Mary Jo Adamson ___
Sporting Club, The — Sinclair Browning ___
Hindenburg Murders, The — Max Allan Collins ___
Bad to the Bone — Katy Munger ___
Dirty Money — Steven Womack ___

2000
In Big Trouble — Laura Lippman ___
Deadbeat — Leo Atkins ___
Fulton County Blues — Ruth Birmingham ___
Last Song Dogs, The — Sinclair Browning ___
Steel City Confessions — Thomas Lipinski ___

1999
Murder Manual — Steven Womack ___
Too Easy — Phillip Depoy ___
Butchers Hill — Laura Lippman ___
Widower's Two-Step, The — Rick Riordan ___
Death in a City of Mystics — Janice Steinberg ___

1998
Charm City — Laura Lippman ___
Back Spin — Harlan Coben ___
Whisper of Rage, A — Tim Hemlin ___
Father, Forgive Me — Randye Lordon ___
Sunset and Santiago — Gloria White ___

1997
Fade Away — Harlan Coben ___
Natural Death, A — Ruthe Furie ___
Chain of Fools — Steven Womack ___

1996
Native Angels — William Jaspersohn ___
Zero Tolerance — J.D. Knight ___
Interview With Mattie — Shelley Singer ___
Charged With Guilt — Gloria White ___
Way Past Dead — Steven Womack ___

1995

Served Cold	Ed Goldberg	____
Double Plot	Leo Axler	____
Lament for a Dead Cowboy	Catherine Dain	____
Dead Ahead	Bridget McKenna	____
Deadly Devotion	Patricia Wallace	____

1994

Brothers and Sinners	Rodman Philbrick	____
Half-Hearted Detective, The	Milton Bass	____
Minyon for the Dead, A	Richard Fliegel	____
Shadow Games	Ed Gorman	____
Torch Town Boogie	Steven Womack	____

1993

Last Tango of Delores Delgado, The	Marele Day	____
Lay It on the Line	Catherine Dain	____
Dirty Money	Mark Davis	____
Brutal Ballet, The	Wayne D. Dundee	____

1992

Cool Blue Tomb	Paul Kemprecos	____
Black Light	Daniel Hearn	____
House of Cards	Kay Hooper	____
Thousand Yard Stare, The	Rob Kantner	____

1991

Rafferty: Fatal Sisters (Fatal Sisters)	W. Glenn Duncan	____
Bimbo Heaven	Marvin H. Albert	____
Queen's Mare, The	John Birkett	____
Made in Detroit	Rob Kantner	____
Blue Room, The	Monroe Thompson	____

1990

Hell's Only Half Full	Rob Kantner	____
Muscle and Blood	Gaylord Dold	____
Behind the Fact	Richard Hilary	____
Tough Enough	W.R. Philbrick	____
Collector of Photographs, A	Deborah Valentine	____

1989

Dirty Work	Rob Kantner	____
Last Private Eye, The	John Birkett	____
Bonepile	Gaylord Dold	____
Rebound	David Everson	____
Crystal Blue Persuasion, The	W.R. Philbrick	____

1988

Wild Night .... L.J. Washburn ___
Monkey's Raincoat, The .... Robert Crais ___
Snake Eyes .... Gaylord Dold ___
Recount .... David Everson ___
Madelaine .... Joseph Louis ___

1987

Back Door Man, The .... Rob Kantner ___
Melting Point .... Kenn Davis ___
Nervous Laughter .... Earl Emerson ___
Dark Fields .... T.J. MacGregor ___
Trace: Too Old a Cat .... Warren Murphy ___

1986

Poverty Bay .... Earl Emerson ___
Rainy City, The .... Earl Emerson ___
Kill, The .... Douglas Heyes ___
Trace: Pigs Get Fat .... Warren Murphy ___
Blue Heron .... Philip Ross ___

1985

Ceiling of Hell .... Warren Murphy ___
Squeeze Play .... Paul Benjamin ___
San Quentin .... Jack Lynch ___
Trace and 47 Miles of Rope .... Warren Murphy ___
Man Who Risked His Partner, The .... Reed Stephens ___

1984

Dead in Centerfield .... Paul Engleman ___
Finders Weepers .... Max Byrd ___
Death and the Single Girl .... Elliot Lewis ___
Trace .... Warren Murphy ___
Steinway Collection, The .... Robert J. Randisi ___

1983

Cana Diversion, The .... William Campbell Gault ___
Nevsky's Return .... Dimitri Gat ___
Pieces of Death .... Jack Lynch ___
Smoked Out (Digger Smoked Out) .... Warren Murphy ___

1982

California Thriller .... Max Byrd ___
Carpenter, Detective .... Hamilton T. Caine ___
Brown's Requiem .... James Ellroy ___
Old Dick, The .... L.A. Morse ___
Murder in the Wind .... George Ogan ___

Shamus Best 1st P.I. Novel

2007
Wrong Kind of Blood, The	Declan Hughes	___
Lost Angel	Mike Doogan	___
Safe Place for Dying, A	Jack Fredrickson	___
Holmes on the Range	Steve Hockensmith	___
18 Seconds	George D. Shuman	___

2006
Forcing Amaryllis	Louise Ure	___
Blood Ties	Lori G. Armstrong	___
Still River	Harry Hunsicker	___
Devil's Right Hand, The	J.D. Rhoades	___

2005
Dead, The	Ingrid Black	___
Little Girl Lost	Richard Aleas	___
Last Goodbye, The	Reed Arvin	___
Aspen Pulp	Patrick Hasburgh	___
Some Danger Involved	Will Thomas	___

2004
Black Maps	Peter Spiegelman	___
Spiked	Mark Arsenault	___
Lovers Crossing	James C. Mitchell	___

2003
Distance, The	Eddie Muller	___
Private Heat	Robert Bailey	___
Westerfield's Chain	Jack Clark	___
Bone Orchard, The	D. Daniel Judson	___
Open and Shut	David Rosenfelt	___

2002
Chasing the Devil's Tail	David Fulmer	___
Rat City	Curt Colbert	___
Epitaph	James Siegel	___
Witness Above, A	Andy Straka	___
Pilikia is My Business	Mark Troy	___

2001
Street Level	Bob Truluck	___
Brigham's Day	John Gates	___
Heir Hunter, The	Chris Larsgaard	___
Resurrection Angel	William Mize	___
Lost Girls	Andrew Pyper	___

2000
Every Dead Thing   John Connolly   ____
East of A   Russell Atwood   ____
Immortal Game, The   Mark Coggins   ____
Maximum Insecurity   P.J. Grady   ____
Answer Man, The   Roy Johansen   ____

1999
Cold Day in Paradise, A   Steve Hamilton   ____
Like a Hole in the Head   Jen Banbury   ____
Zen and the Art of Murder   Elizabeth Cosin   ____
Dead Low Tide   Jamie Katz   ____

1998
Big Red Tequila   Rick Riordan   ____
Baltimore Blues   Laura Lippman   ____
Legwork   Katy Munger   ____

1997
This Dog for Hire   Carol Lea Benjamin   ____
Keeper   Greg Rucka   ____
Low End of Nowhere, The   Michael Stone   ____
This Far, No Further   John Wessel   ____

1996
Innocents, The   Richard Barre   ____
Who in Hell is Wanda Fuca?   G.M. Ford   ____
If Looks Could Kill   Ruthe Furie   ____
Penance   David Housewright   ____
Harry Chronicles, The   Allan Pedrazas   ____

1995
Drink Before the War, A   Dennis Lehane   ____
Heaven Stone, The   David Daniel   ____
One for the Money   Janet Evanovich   ____
Fall-Down Artist, The   Thomas Lipinski   ____
When Death Comes Stealing   Valerie Wilson Wesley   ____

1994
Satan's Lambs   Lynn Hightower   ____
Brotherly Love   Randye Lordon   ____
By Evil Means   Sandra West Prowell   ____

1993
Woman Who Married a Bear, The   John Straley   ____
Return Trip Ticket   David C. Hall   ____
Switching the Odds   Phyllis Knight   ____
Long-Legged Fly, The   James Sallis   ____

1992

Suffer Little Children	Thomas Davis	____
January Corpse, The	Neil Albert	____
Dead on the Island	Bill Crider	____
Best Performance by a Patsy	Stan Cutler	____
Cool Breeze on the Underground, A	Don Winslow	____

1991

Devil in a Blue Dress	Walter Mosley	____
Kindred Crimes	Janet Dawson	____
Body Scissors	Jerome Doolittle	____
Stone Veil, The	Ronald Tierney	____

1990

Katwalk	Karen Kijewski	____
Medicine Dog	Geoff Peterson	____
Cold Night	Al Sarrantonio	____
Rock Critic Murders	Jesse Sublett	____

1989

Fear of the Dark	Gar Anthony Haywood	____
Lost Daughter	Michael Cormany	____
Burning Season	Wayne D. Dundee	____
Wall of Glass	Walter Satterthwait	____
Slow Dance in Autumn	Philip Lee Williams	____

1988

Death on the Rocks	Michael Allegretto	____
House of Blue Lights, The	Robert Bowman	____
Shawnee Alley Fire	John Douglas	____
Detective	Parnell Hall	____
Infinite Number of Monkeys, An	Les Roberts	____

1987

Jersey Tomatoes	J.W. Rider	____
No One Rides for Free	Larry Beinhart	____
Tourist Season	Carl Hiaasen	____

1986

Hardcover	Wayne Warga	____
New, Improved Murder	Ed Gorman	____
Sleeping Dog	Dick Lochte	____
Embrace the Wolf	Benjamin Schutz	____
Flood	Andrew Vachss	____

1985

Creative Kind of Killer, A	Jack Early (as, Sandra Scoppetone)	____
Blunt Darts	Jeremiah Healy	____
Nebraska Quotient, The	William J. Reynolds	____

Shamus Best P.I. Short Story

2007

"Heart Has Reasons, The"	O'Neil De Noux	*AHMM*, Sept 06	___
"Sudden Stop	Mitch Alderman	*AHMM*, Nov 06	___
"Square One"	Loren D.Estleman	*AHMM*, Nov 06	___
"Devil's Brew"	Bill Pronzini	*EQMM*, Dec 06	___
"Smoke Got In My Eyes"	Bruce Rubenstein	Twin Cities Noir; Schaper & Horwitz, eds.	___

2006

"Death in Ueno, A"	Mike Wiecek	*AHMM*, Mar 05	___
"Oh, What a Tangled Lanyard We Weave	Parnell Hall	Murder Most Crafty; Bruce, ed.	___
"Two Birds With One Stone"	Jeremiah Healy	*AHMM*, Jan/Feb 05	___
"Big Road, The"	Steve Hockensmith	*AHMM*, May 05	___
"Breaks, The"	Timothy Williams	*EQMM*, Sept/Oct 05	___

2005

"Hasidic Noir"	Pearl Abraham	Brooklyn Noir; McLoughlin, ed.	___
"Burnt Wood"	Mitch Alderman	*AHMM*, Jul 04	___
"Trumpeter Swan"	John F. Dobbyn	*AHMM*, Jan/Feb 04	___
"Dog on Fire"	Gregory S. Fallis	*AHMM*, May 04	___
"Tricks"	Steve Hockensmith	*AHMM*, Aug 04	___

2004

"Lady on Ice"	Loren D. Estleman	A Hot & Sultry Night for Crime; Deaver, ed.	___
"Valhalla"	Doug Allyn	*EQMM*, Jan 03	___
"Rock in the Orange Grove, The"	Mitch Alderman	*AHMM*, Jun 03	___
"Munchies"	Jack Bludis	Hardbroiled; Bracken, ed.	___
"Slayer Statute"	Janet Dawson	*EQMM*, Sept/Oct 03	___

2003

"Second Coming, The"	Terence Faherty	*EQMM*, Nov 02	___
"Setting Up the Kill"	J. Michael Blue	HandHeldCrime, Summer 02	___
"Aftermath"	Jeremiah Healy	Most Wanted; Randisi, ed.	___
"Second Story Sunlight"	John Lutz	Most Wanted; Randisi, ed.	___
"Jewels of Atlantis, The"	James Powell	*EQMM*, Nov 02	___

2002

"Rough Justice"	Ceri Jordan	*AHMM*, Jul 01	___
"Cobalt Blues, The"	Clark Howard	*EQMM*, Sept 01	___
"Jungle, The"	John Lantigua	And the Dying is Easy; Pittman & Riffle, eds.	___
"Golden Retriever"	Barbara Paul	*EQMM*, Dec 01	___
"Last Kiss"	Tom Sweeney	Mystery Street; Randisi, ed.	___

2001

"Road's End, The"	Brendan DuBois	*EQMM*, Apr 00	___
"What's in a Name?"	Jeremiah Healy	The Shamus Game; Randisi, ed.	___
"Sleeping Detective, The"	Gary Phillips	The Shamus Game; Randisi, ed.	___
"Big Bite, The"	Bill Pronzini	The Shamus Game; Randisi, ed.	___
"Good Daughter, The"	Mike Wiecek	*AHMM*, Dec 00	___

2000

"Akitada's First Case"	I.J. Parker	*AHMM*, Jul/Aug 99	___
"Unchained Melody"	Doug Allyn	*EQMM*, Jan 99	___
"Hodegetria"	Jeremiah Healy	Death Cruise; Block, ed.	___
"Reluctant Op, The"	Barbara Paul	*EQMM*, Sept/Oct, 99	___
"Cro-Magnon, P.I."	Mike Reiss	*AHMM*, Jul/Aug 99	___

1999

"Another Day, Another Dollar"	Warren Murphy	Murder on the Run	___
"Sidewinder"	David Edgerley Gates	*AHMM*, Jul/Aug 89	___
"No, Thank You, John"	Michelle Knowlden	*AHMM*, Mar 98	___
"All About Heroes"	Dan A. Sproul	*AHMM*, Dec 98	___
"More Light"	James Sallis	New Mystery, Summer 98	___

1998

"Love Me For My Yellow Hair Alone"	Carolyn Wheat	Marilyn: Shades of Blonde; Douglas, ed.	___
"Copperhead Run"	Doug Allyn	*EQMM*, Jun 97	___
"Lord of Obstacles"	Gregory S. Fallis	*AHMM*, Jan 97	___
"Front-Row Seat, A"	Jan Grape	Vengeance is Hers; Spillane & Collins, eds.	___
"Nightcrawlers"	John Lutz	*EQMM*, Apr 97	___

1997

"Dead Drunk"	Lia Matera	Guilty as Charged; Turow, ed.	___
"Eye of the Beholder"	Ed Gorman	The Autumn Dead & A Cry of Shadows	___
"Turning the Witness"	Jeremiah Healy	Guilty as Charged; Turow, ed.	___
"One About the Green Detective, The"	John Lethan	Unusual Suspects; Grady, ed.	___
"Girl Who Talked to Horses, The"	Robert J. Randisi	Homicide Hosts Presents; Olmsted, ed.	___

1996

"And Pray Nobody Sees You"	Gar Anthony Haywood	*Spooks, Spies & Private Eyes*; Woods, ed.	____
"Trial by Fire"	David Dean	*EQMM*, Feb 95	____
"Plain and Honest Death, A"	Bill Pomidor	*EQMM*, Sept 95	____
"Home is the Place Where"	Bill Pronzini	*EQMM*, Nov 95	____
"Enigma"	D.H. Reddall	*AHMM*, Dec 95	____

1995

"Necessary Brother, The"	Brendan DuBois	*EQMM*, May 94	____
"Matter of Character, A"	Michael Collins (Dennis Lynds)	*Partners in Crime*; Chase, ed.	____
"Slipstream"	Loren D. Estleman	*Deadly Allies II*; Randisi & Dunlap, eds.	____
"Split Decision"	Clark Howard	*EQMM*, Dec 94	____
"Romantics, The"	John Lutz	*Deadly Allies II*; Randisi & Dunlap, eds.	____

1994

"Merciful Angel of Death, The"	Lawrence Block	*New Mystery*; Charyn, ed.	____
"Sultans of Soul, The"	Doug Allyn	*EQMM*, Mar 93	____
"Nobody Wins"	Charles Ardai	*AHMM*, Mid-Dec 93	____
"Bagged Man, The"	Jeremiah Healy	*EQMM*, Feb 93	____
"Watt's Lion, The"	Walter Mosley	*New Mystery*; Charyn, ed.	____

1993

"Mary, Mary, Shut the Door"	Benjamin M. Schutz	*Deadly Allies*; Randisi & Wallace, eds.	____
"Messenger, The"	Jacklyn Butler	*AHMM*, Oct 92	____
"Safe House"	Loren D. Estleman	*Deadly Allies*; Randisi & Wallace, eds.	____
"Little Missionary Work, A"	Sue Grafton	*Deadly Allies*; Randisi & Wallace, eds.	____
"Rest Stop"	Jeremiah Healy	*AHMM*, May 92	____

1992

"Dust Devil"	Nancy Pickard	*The Armchair Detective*, Winter 91	____
"Dying in the Post-War World"	Max Allan Collins	*Dying in the Post-War World*	____
"Man Who Loved Noir, The"	Loren D. Estleman	*AHMM*, Feb 91	____
"Full Circle"	Sue Grafton	*A Woman's Eye*; Paretsky, ed.	____

1991

"Final Resting Place"	Marcia Muller	*Justice for Hire;* Randisi, ed.	___
"Naughty, Naughty"	Wayne D. Dundee	*Justice for Hire;* Randisi, ed.	___
"Cigarette Stop"	Loren D. Estleman	*Justice for Hire;* Randisi, ed.	___
"Poison that Leaves No Trace, A"	Sue Grafton	Sisters in Crime 2; Wallace, ed.	___
"Battered Spouse"	Jeremiah Healy	*The Armchair Detective,* Fall 90	___
"Bypass to Murder"	Dick Stodghill	*Justice for Hire;* Randisi, ed.	___

1990

"Killing Man, The"	Mickey Spillane	*Playboy,* Dec 89	___
"Deadly Fantasies"	Marcia Muller	*AHMM,* Apr 89	___
"Here Comes Santa Claus"	Bill Pronzini	*Mistletoe Mysteries;* MacLeod, ed.	___
"Sure Thing, The"	Dan A. Sproul	*AHMM,* Jan 89	___
"Sloat's Last Case"	Robert Twohy	*EQMM,* May 89	___

1989

"Crooked Way, The"	Loren D. Estleman	*New Black Mask 88/A Matter of Crime;* Bruccoli & Layman, eds.	___
"Man Who Knew Dick Bong, The"	Robert Crais	*Raymond Chandler's Philip Marlowe;* Preiss, ed.	___
"Reason Why, The"	Ed Gorman	*Criminal Elements;* Pronzini & Greenberg, eds.	___
"In the Line of Duty"	Jeremiah Healy	*Raymond Chandler's Philip Marlowe;* Preiss, ed.	___
"Incident in a Neighborhood Tavern"	Bill Pronzini	*An Eye For Justice;* Randisi, ed.	___

1988

"Turn Away"	Ed Gorman	*Black Lizard Anthology of Crime Fiction;* Gorman, ed.	___
"Bodyguards Shoot Second"	Loren D. Estleman	*A Matter of Crime;* Bruccoli & Layman, eds.	___
"Kerman Kill, The"	William Campbell Gault	*Murder in Los Angeles;* Adams Round Table	___
"Merely Players"	Joseph Hansen	*AHMM,* Feb 87	___
"My Brother's Life"	Rob Kantner	*AHMM,* Mar 87	___

1987

"Fly Away Home"	Rob Kantner	*Mean Streets;* Randisi, ed.	___
"Quint and the Braceros"	Paul Bishop	*Hardboiled #5,* Summer 86	___
"Body Count"	Wayne D. Dundee	*Mean Streets;* Randisi, ed.	___
"I'm in the Book"	Loren D. Estleman	*Mean Streets;* Randisi, ed.	___
"Between the Sheets"	Sue Grafton	*Redbook*	___

1986

"Eight Mile and Dequindre"	Loren D. Estleman	*AHMM*, May 85	___
"Lucky Penny"	Linda Barnes	*New Black Mask #3*, 85	___
"Shooting Match"	Wayne D. Dundee	*Hardboiled #3*, Winter 85/86	___
"Perfect Pitch"	Rob Kantner	*AHMM*, Jul 85	___
"Snaphaunce The"	Robert J. Randisi	*Hardboiled #2*, Fall 85	___

1985

"By the Dawn's Early Light"	Lawrence Block	*Playboy*, Aug 84	___
"Easy Money"	John Boland	*EQMM*, Apr 84	___
"Iris"	Stephen Greenleaf	*The Eyes Have It*; Randisi, ed.	___
"Rat Line, The"	Rob Kantner	*The Eyes Have It*; Randisi, ed.	___
"Big Winners, The"	Ernest Savage	*EQMM*, Sept 84	___

1984

"Cat's-Paw"	Bill Pronzini	Waves Press	___
"Oldest Killer, The"	Michael Collins (Dennis Lynds)	*Thieftakers Journal*, Nov 83	___
"Greektown"	Loren D. Estleman	*AHMM*, Aug 83	___
"Long Slow Drive, The"	T. Robin Kanter	*AHMM*, Feb 83	___
"Only One Way to Land"	John Lutz	*AHMM*, Oct 83	___

1983

"What You Don't Know Can't Hurt You"	John Lutz	*AHMM*, Nov 82	___
"Meet Athalia Goode"	Raleigh Bond	*EQMM*, Jan 27, 82	___
"Dead Soldier"	Loren D. Estleman	*AHMM*, Mid-Sept 82	___
"My Little Girl"	Kenneth Gavrell	*AHMM*, May 82	___
"Cardula and the Locked Room"	Jack Ritchie	*AHMM*, Mar 31, 82	___

The Hammer

In recognition of a memorable private eye character/series. This honor began in 2007.

2007   **Shell Scott**, created by Richard S. Prather

The Eye (Shamus Lifetime Achievement Award)

2007	Stuart M. Kaminsky
2006	Max Allan Collins
2005	Sara Paretsky
2004	Donald Westlake
2002	Lawrence Block
2000	Edward D. Hoch
1999	Maxine O'Callaghan
1997	Stephen Marlowe
1995	John Lutz
1995	Robert B. Parker
1994	Stephen J. Cannell
1993	Marcia Muller
1992	Joseph Hansen
1991	Roy Huggins
1988	Dennis Lynds
1988	Wade Miller (Robert Wade & Bob Miller)
1987	Bill Pronzini
1986	Richard S. Prather
1985	Howard Browne
1984	William Campbell Gault
1983	Mickey Spillane
1982	Ross Macdonald

www.thrillingdetective.com/trivia/triv72.html
hometown.aol.com/rrandisi/myhomepage/writing.html

Spotted Owl Awards

The Friends of Mystery, a non-profit literary/educational organization headquartered in Portland, Oregon, presents the Spotted Owl Award for the best mystery by a Pacific Northwest author. This award began in 1996. In 2007, they began an award for the best first mystery.

Spotted Owl Best Mystery Award

2007
Days of Rage   Kris Nelscott   ____

2006
Last Victim, The   Kevin O'Brien   ____

2005
Stone Cribs   Kris Nelscott   ____

2004
Second Watch   Lowen Clausen   ____

2003
Black River   G.M. Ford   ____

2002
Desperate Measures   Kate Wilhelm   ____

2001
Crow in Stolen Colors   Marcia Simpson   ____

2000
First Avenue   Lowen Clausen   ____

1999
Charlie's Bones   L.L. Thrasher   ____

1998
Katie's Will   Tom Mitcheltree   ____

1997
Music of What Happens, The   John Straley   ____

1996
Vanishing Smile, The   Earl Emerson   ____

Spotted Owl Best 1st Mystery Award

2007
Lost Angel   Mike Doogan   ____

www.friendsofmystery.org/award.htm

Theakston's Old Peculier
Crime Novel of the Year Award

Theakstons Old Peculier Crime Writing Festival began in 2005. This award has voters casting their selection at Waterstone's bookstores throughout the UK, as well as online at the bookstore web site and festival's web sites.

Theakston's Crime Festival

2007

Two Way Split	Allan Guthrie	____
Dead Place, The	Stephen Booth	____
All Fun and Games Until Somebody Loses an Eye	Christopher Brookmyre	____
Blood and Honey	Hurley Graham	____
Death Ship of Dartmouth, The	Michael Jecks	____
Cold Granite	Stuart MacBride	____

2006

Torment of Others, The	Val McDermid	____
Strange Blood	Lindsay Ashford	____
One Last Breath	Stephen Booth	____
Coffin Trail, The	Martin Edwards	____
Various Haunts of Men, The	Susan Hill	____
Fleshmarket Close	Ian Rankin	____

2005

Lazybones	Mark Billingham	____
Murder Exchange, The	Simon Kernick	____
Distant Echo, The	Val McDermid	____
Question of Blood, A	Ian Rankin	____
American Boy, The (An Unpardonable Crime)	Andrew Taylor	____
Disordered Minds	Minette Walters	____

www.harrogate-festival.org.uk/crime/index.html

Nero Wolfe Awards

This award is presented at the Black Orchid Banquet each December by The Wolfe Pack, devotees of the works of Rex Stout, for the book that best represents the spirit of the Nero Wolfe novels. The awards began in 1979 and are presented in early December each year.

Nero Wolfe Award

2007

Kidnapped	Jan Burke	___
Stolen Season, A	Steve Hamilton	___
All Mortal Flesh	Julia Spencer-Fleming	___

2006

Vanish	Tess Gerritsen	___

2005

Enemy, The	Lee Child	___
Drowning Tree, The	Carol Goodman	___
Spectacle of Corruption, A	David Liss	___

2004

Fear Itself	Walter Mosley	___
Vanished Man, The	Jeffery Deaver	___
Burning Garbo	Robert Eversz	___
Where the Truth Lies	Rupert Holmes	___
Fat Ollie's Book	Ed McBain	___

2003

Winter and Night	S.J. Rozan	___
Gone for Good	Harlan Coben	___
Weeping Buddha, The	Heather Dune Macadam	___
Open and Shut	David Rosenfelt	___
In the Bleak Midwinter	Julia Spencer-Fleming	___

2002

Deadhouse, The	Linda Fairstein	___
Flight	Jan Burke	___
Tell No One	Harlan Coben	___
Beulah Hill	William Heffernan	___
Uncommon Clay	Margaret Maron	___

2001

Sugar House, The	Laura Lippman	___

2000

Coyote Revenge	Fred Harris	___

1999

Bone Collector, The	Jeffery Deaver	___

1998
Sacred   Dennis Lehane   ____

1997
Poet, The   Michael Connelly   ____

1996
Monstrous Regiment of Women, A   Laurie R. King   ____

1995
She Walks These Hills   Sharyn McCrumb   ____

1994
Old Scores   Aaron Elkins   ____

1993
Booked to Die   John Dunning   ____

1992
Scandal in Belgravia, A   Robert Barnard   ____

1991
Coyote Waits   Tony Hillerman   ____

1987
Corpse in Oozak's Pond, The   Charlotte MacLeod   ____

1986
Murder in E Minor   Robert Goldsborough   ____

1985
Sleeping Dog   Dick Lochte   ____

1984
Emily Dickinson is Dead   Jane Langton   ____

1983
Anodyne Necklace, The   Martha Grimes   ____

1982
Past, Present and Murder   Hugh Pentecost   ____

1981
Death in a Tenured Position (A Death in the Faculty)   Amanda Cross   ____

1980
Burn This   Helen McCloy   ____

1979
Burglar Who Liked to Quote Kipling   Lawrence Block   ____

Wolfe Pack's Black Orchid Award

Beginning in 2007, The Wolfe Pack, working with *Alfred Hitchcock Mystery Magazine,* offers an award for an original unpublished work of fiction that conforms to the tradition of the Nero Wolfe series, and contains no overt sex or violence, emphasizes the deductive skills of the sleuth, and does not include characters from the original series. This novella award must be between 15,000 and 20,000 words in length. The award is presented at the annual Black Orchid Banquet in early December.

Archie Goodwin Award for Lifetime Achievement

The Wolfe Pack instituted an award in 2005 to celebrate the many mystery authors the members worldwide enjoy and voted on. The honor is to be awarded biannually and is called the "Archie."

2005	Rex Stout
2005	Sir Arthur Conan Doyle
2005	Dame Agatha Christie

Section III: Classic or Best Lists

Authors' Choices (Miscellaneous Sources)

This list of books are the suggestions of various mystery writers in books, at conferences, and on web sites. Many of the titles are on other lists in this resource but some are not. Each author felt that these books should be read. The several sources for these list are: *Writing Mysteries*, edited by Sue Grafton; *The Armchair Detective Book of Lists* (*TAD:BL*), edited by Kate Stine; and www.Detective-Fiction.com (web site).

Isaac Asimov — TAD:BL; www.Detective-Fiction.com

1948	*Wilders Walk Away*	Herbert Brean	____
1936	*Case for Three Detectives*	Leo Bruce	____
1911	*Innocence of Father Brown, The*	G.K. Chesterton	____
1939	*And Then There Were None (Ten Little Niggers)*	Agatha Christie	____
1926.	*Murder of Roger Ackroyd, The*	Agatha Christie	____
1938	*Judas Window, The (The Crossbow Murder)*	Carter Dickson	____
1946	*Horizontal Man, The*	Helen Eustis	____
1946	*Pick Your Victim*	Patricia McGerr	____
1933	*Murder Must Advertise*	Dorothy L. Sayers	____
1951	*Daughter of Time, The*	Josephine Tey	____

Robert Barnard — TAD:BL; www.Detective-Fiction.com

1948	*More Work for the Undertaker*	Margery Allingham	____
1816	*Emma*	Jane Austen	____
1955	*Tour de Force*	Christianna Brand	____
1942	*Five Little Pigs (Murder in Retrospect)*	Agatha Christie	____
1853	*Bleak House*	Charles Dickens	____
1902	*Hound of the Baskervilles, The*	Arthur Conan Doyle	____
1962	*How Like an Angel*	Margaret Millar	____
1964	*Dover One*	Joyce Porter	____
1977	*Judgement in Stone, A*	Ruth Rendell	____
1930	*Strong Poison*	Dorothy L. Sayers	____

Robert Barnard — TAD:BL

(Top 10 in the last 20 years.)

1979	*Rose in Darkness, The*	Christianna Brand	____
1985	*Dead Romantic*	Simon Brett	____
1987	*Killings at Badger's Drift, The*	Caroline Graham	____
1983	*Deadheads*	Reginald Hill	____
1980	*Neapolitan Streak, The*	Timothy Holme	____
1986	*Spider Webs*	Margaret Millar	____
1982	*Talent for Destruction, A*	Sheila Radley	____
1977	*Judgement in Stone, A*	Ruth Rendell	____
1986	*Life's Work*	Jonathan Valin	____
1978	*Blond Baboon, The*	Janwillem van de Wetering	____

Jacques Barzun — TAD:BL

1913	*Trent's Last Case (The Woman in Black)*	E.C. Bentley	___
1960	*Furious Old Women*	Leo Bruce	___
1943	*Lady in the Lake, The*	Raymond Chandler	___
1961	*Pale Horse, The*	Agatha Christie	___
1902	*Hound of the Baskervilles, The*	Arthur Conan Doyle	___
1980	*Killing of Katie Steelstock, The (Death of a Favourite Girl)*	Michael Gilbert	___
1938	*Funeral in Eden, A (Burial Service)*	Paul McGuire	___
1966	*Salt is Leaving*	J.B. Priestley	___
1930	*Strong Poison*	Dorothy L. Sayers	___
1962	*Gambit*	Rex Stout	___

George Baxt — TAD:BL; www.Detective-Fiction.com

(Favorite mysteries with a theatrical theme.)

1989	*Death and the Chaste Apprentice*	Robert Barnard	___
1984	*Dead Heat*	Linda Barnes	___
1983	*Murder in the Title*	Simon Brett	___
1988	*Death Mask*	Jane Dentinger	___
1986	*Murder in the Wings*	Ed Gorman	___
1982	*Skull Beneath the Skin, The*	P.D. James	___
1941	*G-String Murders, The (Strip-Tease Murders; Lady of Burlesque)*	Gypsy Rose Lee (ghost written by Georgiana Ann Randolph Craig, aka, Craig Rice)	___
1960	*Show Red for Danger*	Frances & Richard Lockridge	___
1948	*Dark Wheel, The (Sweet and Deadly)*	Philip MacDonald with A. Boyd Correll	___
1942	*Repeat Performance*	William O'Farrell	___

Lawrence Block (16 favorite [deceased] writers) — TAD:BL

Anthony Boucher
Fredric Brown
James M. Cain
Raymond Chandler
Stanley Ellin
Erle Stanley Gardner
Dashiell Hammett
Chester Himes
John D. MacDonald
Ross Macdonald
Ellery Queen
Jack Ritchie
Rex Stout
Jim Thompson
Charles Willeford
Cornell Woolrich

Jan Burke — Writing Mysteries

1992	*Black Echo, The*	Michael Connelly	___
1979	*Whip Hand*	Dick Francis	___
1982	*"A" is for Alibi*	Sue Grafton	___
1985	*Sleeping Dog*	Dick Lochte	___
1975	*Crocodile on the Sandbank*	Elizabeth Peters	___
1949	*Brat Farrar (Come and Kill Me)*	Josephine Tey	___
1984	*Briarpatch*	Ross Thomas	___
1973	*Onion Field, The*	Joseph Wambaugh	___

Dorothy Salisbury Davis — TAD:BL

1939	*Coffin for Dimitrios, A (The Mask of Dimitrios)*	Eric Ambler	___
1948	*Devil Take the Blue-Tail Fly*	John Franklin Bardin	___
1983	*Dark Fantastic, The*	Stanley Ellin	___
1938.	*Brighton Rock*	Graham Greene	___
1979	*Skinflick*	Joseph Hansen	___
1962	*We Have Always Lived in the Castle*	Shirley Jackson	___
1955	*Beast in View*	Margaret Millar	___
1984	*Deadlock*	Sara Paretsky	___
1935	*Gaudy Night*	Dorothy L. Sayers	___
1938/42	*Man Who Watched the Trains Go By, The*	Georges Simenon	___

Aaron Elkins — TAD:BL

1979	*Death of a Mystery Writer (Unruly Son)*	Robert Barnard	___
1936	*ABC Murders, The (The Alphabet Murders)*	Agatha Christie	___
1868	*Moonstone, The*	Wilkie Collins	___
1946	*Moving Toyshop, The*	Edmund Crispin	___
1902	*Hound of the Baskervilles, The*	Arthur Conan Doyle	___
1969	*Forfeit*	Dick Francis	___
1973	*Dance Hall of the Dead*	Tony Hillerman	___
1960	*Case of Sonia Wayward, The (The New Sonia Wayward)*	Michael Innes	___
1972	*Tied Up in Tinsel*	Ngaio Marsh	___
1975	*Crocodile on the Sandbank*	Elizabeth Peters	___

James Ellory — TAD:BL; www.Detective-Fiction.com

1973	*No Beast So Fierce*	Edward Bunker	___
1936/43	*Double Indemnity*	James M. Cain	___
1940	*Farewell, My Lovely*	Raymond Chandler	___
1977	*True Confessions*	John Gregory Dunne	___
1929	*Red Harvest*	Dashiell Hammett	___
1981	*Red Dragon (Manhunter)*	Thomas Harris	___
1973	*Digger's Game, The*	George V. Higgins	___
1956	*Compulsion*	Meyer Levin	___
1964	*Chill, The*	Ross Macdonald	___
1975	*Choirboys, The*	Joseph Wambaugh	___

Loren D. Estleman — Writing Mysteries

(He offers a list in his article *Perspectives on Point of View* [chapter 16] with several categories.)

First Person

1918	*My Antonia*	Willa Cather	___
1939	*Big Sleep, The*	Raymond Chandler	___
1926	*Murder of Roger Ackroyd, The*	Agatha Christie	___
1978	*Last Good Kiss, The*	James Crumley	___
1946	*All the King's Men*	Robert Penn Warren	___

Omniscient

1987	*Suspects*	William J. Caunitz	___
1859	*Tale of Two Cities, A*	Charles Dickens	___
1861	*Silas Marner*	George Eliot	___
1938	*Night and the City (Dishonor)*	Gerald Kersh	___
1969	*Godfather, The*	Mario Puzo	___

Third-Person Objective

1931	*Glass Key, The*	Dashiell Hammett	___
1937	*To Have and Have Not*	Ernest Hemingway	___
1972	*Friends of Eddie Coyle, The*	George V. Higgins	___
1943	*Fountainhead, The*	Ayn Rand	___
1962	*Hunter, The (Point Blank)*	Richard Stark (Donald E. Westlake)	___

Third-Person Subjective

1909	*Martin Eden*	Jack London	___
1937	*No Pockets in a Shroud*	Horace McCoy	___
1952	*Wise Blood*	Flannery O'Connor	___
1976	*Demon in My View, A*	Ruth Rendell	___
1951	*Daughter of Time, The*	Josephine Tey	___

Shotgun (Semiomniscient)

1988	*Silence of the Lambs, The*	Thomas Harris	___
1980	*City Primeval*	Elmore Leonard	___
1934	*Appointment in Samarra*	John O'Hara	___
1886	*Strange Case of Dr. Jekyll and Mr. Hyde*	Robert Louis Stevenson	___
1973	*Law and Order*	Dorothy Uhnak	___

Linda Fairstein — Writing Mysteries

1987	*Presumed Innocent*	Scott Turow	___
1990	*Postmortem*	Patricia Cornwell	___
1963	*Spy Who Came in From the Cold, The*	John le Carre	___
1999	*L.A. Requiem*	Robert Crais	___
1958	*Anatomy of a Murder*	Robert Traver	___

John Gardner — TAD:BL

(Titles are novels of espionage.)

1983	*Berlin Game*	Len Deighton	___
1964	*Funeral in Berlin*	Len Deighton	___
1987	*Agents of Innocence*	David Ignatius	___
1980	*Smiley's People*	John le Carre	___
1963	*Spy Who Came in From the Cold, The*	John le Carre	___
1974	*Tinker, Tailor, Soldier, Spy*	John le Carre	___
1979	*Better Angels, The*	Charles McCarry	___
1977	*Secret Lovers, The*	Charles McCarry	___
1975	*Tears of Autumn, The*	Charles McCarry	___
1973	*Beria Papers, The*	Alan Williams	___

Michael Gilbert — TAD:BL; www.Detective-Fiction.com

1938	*Fashion in Shrouds, The*	Margery Allingham	___
1943	*Lady in the Lake, The*	Raymond Chandler	___
1926	*Murder of Roger Ackroyd, The*	Agatha Christie	___
1868	*Moonstone, The*	Wilkie Collins	___
1902	*Hound of the Baskervilles, The*	Arthur Conan Doyle	___
1946	*Big Clock, The (No Way Out)*	Kenneth Fearing	___
1931	*Glass Key, The*	Dashiell Hammett	___
1953	*Kiss Before Dying, A*	Ira Levin	___
1930	*Strong Poison*	Dorothy L. Sayers	___
1948	*Franchise Affair, The*	Josephine Tey	___

Sue Grafton — TAD:BL; www.Detective-Fiction.com

1936/43	*Double Indemnity*	James M. Cain	___
1942	*High Window, The*	Raymond Chandler	___
1920	*Mysterious Affair at Styles, The*	Agatha Christie	___
1983	*Berlin Game*	Len Deighton	___
1964	*Nerve*	Dick Francis	___
1979	*Death Drop*	B.M. Gill	___
1950	*Beyond a Reasonable Doubt*	C.W. Grafton	___
1982	*Cat Chaser*	Elmore Leonard	___
1950	*Drowning Pool, The*	Ross Macdonald (as John Ross Macdonald)	___
1987	*Talking to Strange Men*	Ruth Rendell	___

Jeremiah Healy — Writing Mysteries

1995	*Maiden's Grave, A*	Jeffery Deaver	___
1994	*One for the Money*	Janet Evanovich	___
1993	*Nobody's Fool*	Richard Russo	___

Reginald Hill — TAD:BL; www.Detective-Fiction.com

1913	*Trent's Last Case (The Woman in Black)*	E.C. Bentley	___
1868	*Moonstone, The*	Wilkie Collins	___
1724	*Roxana (The Fortunate Mistress, The Life and Adventures of Roxana)*	Daniel Defoe	___
1853	*Bleak House*	Charles Dickens	___
1983	*Name of the Rose, The*	Umberto Eco	___
1983	*Back of the North Wind, The*	Nicolas Freeling	___
1931	*Glass Key, The*	Dashiell Hammett	___
1954	*Maigret in Montmartre (Inspector Maigret and the Strangled Stripper)*	Georges Simenon	___
1952	*Killer Inside Me, The*	Jim Thompson	___
1867	*Last Chronicle of Barset, The*	Anthony Trollope	___

Tony Hillerman — TAD:BL; www.Detective-Fiction.com

1939	*Coffin for Dimitrios, A* (*The Mask of Dimitrios*)	Eric Ambler	____
1979	*Limits of Pain, The*	K. Arne Blom	____
1975	*Alvarez Journal, The*	Rex Burns	____
1949	*Little Sister, The (Marlow)*	Raymond Chandler	____
1950	*Third Man, The (The Third Man and the Fallen Idol)*	Graham Greene	____
1939	*Rogue Male (Man Hunt)*	Geoffrey Household	____
1974	*Tinker, Tailor, Soldier, Spy*	John le Carre	____
1977	*Unknown Man #89*	Elmore Leonard	____
1962	*Will of the Tribe, The*	Arthur W. Upfield	____
1985	*New Hope for the Dead*	Charles Willeford	____

Tony Hillerman — Writing Mysteries

2000	*Forty Words for Sorrow*	Giles Blunt	____
2001	*Best American Mystery Stories of the Century, The*	Otto Penzler & Tony Hillerman, eds.	____

Edward D. Hoch — Writing Mysteries

(Emphasis on the short story with a number of reference suggestions.)

1991	*Locked Room Murders and Other Impossible Crimes: A Comprehensive Bibliography*	Robert Adey	____
1981	*What About Murder? A Guide to Books About Mystery and Detective Fiction*	Jon L. Breen	____
1993	*What About Murder? (1981-1991): A Guide to Books About Mystery and Detective Fiction*	Jon L. Breen	____
1911	*Innocence of Father Brown, The*	G.K. Chesterton	____
1991	*Index to Crime and Mystery Anthologies*	William G. Contento & Martin H. Greenberg	____
1982	*Monthly Murders: A Checklist and Chronological Listing of Fiction in the Digest-Size Mystery Magazines in the United States and England*	Michael L. Cook, compiler	____
1988	*Mystery, Detective, and Espionage Fiction: A Checklist of Fiction in U.S. Pulp Magazines, 1915-1974 (2 volumes)*	Michael L. Cook & Stephen T. Miller	____
1983	*Mystery, Detective, and Espionage Magazines*	Michael L. Cook	____
2000	*American Regional Mystery, The*	Marvin Lachman	____
1984	*Mystery Hall of Fame: An Anthology of Classic Mystery and Suspense Stories Selected by the Mystery Writers of America*	Bill Pronzini, Martin H. Greenberg & Charles G. Waugh, eds.	____
1941	*101 Years' Entertainment: The Great Detective Stories, 1841-1941*	Ellery Queen, ed.	____

H.R.F. Keating — TAD:BL; www.Detective-Fiction.com

1968	*Private Wound, The*	Nicholas Blake	____
1868	*Moonstone, The*	Wilkie Collins	____
1974	*Poison Oracle, The*	Peter Dickinson	____
1892	*Adventures of Sherlock Holmes, The*	Arthur Conan Doyle	____
1972	*Mirror, Mirror on the Wall*	Stanley Ellin	____
1986	*Taste for Death, A*	P.D. James	____
1984	*Artful Egg, The*	James McClure	____
1970	*Beyond This Point are Monsters*	Margaret Millar	____
1918	*Uncle Abner, Master of Mysteries*	Melville Davisson Post	____
1949/57	*My Friend Maigret (Methods of Maigret)*	Georges Simenon	____

Laurie R. King — Writing Mysteries

1982	*Last Houseparty, The*	Peter Dickinson	____
1981	*Summer in the Twenties, A*	Peter Dickinson	____
1994	*Pictures of Perfection*	Reginald Hill	____

Elmore Leonard — TAD:BL

| 1972 | *Friends of Eddie Coyle, The* | George V. Higgins | ____ |

Dick Lochte — Writing Mysteries

| 2000 | *Cold Steel Rain* | Kenneth Abel | ____ |

Peter Lovesey — TAD:BL; www.Detective-Fiction.com

1946	*Deadly Percheron, The*	John Franklin Bardin	____
1934	*Postman Always Rings Twice, The*	James M. Cain	____
1953	*Long Goodbye, The (The Long Good-bye)*	Raymond Chandler	____
1892	*Adventures of Sherlock Holmes, The*	Arthur Conan Doyle	____
1902	*Hound of the Baskervilles, The*	Arthur Conan Doyle	____
1975	*Stronghold*	Stanley Ellin	____
1950	*Strangers on a Train*	Patricia Highsmith	____
1974	*Tinker, Tailor, Soldier, Spy*	John le Carre	____
1931	*Malice Aforethought*	Francis Iles	____
1974	*Fletch*	Gregory McDonald	____
1949/57	*My Friend Maigret (Methods of Maigret)*	Georges Simenon	____

John Lutz — Writing Mysteries

1982	*"A" is for Alibi*	Sue Grafton	____
1982	*Indemnity Only*	Sara Paretsky	____
1999	*California Fire and Life*	Don Winslow	____

Charlotte MacLeod — TAD:BL; www.Detective-Fiction.com

1948	*More Work for the Undertaker*	Margery Allingham	___
1984	*Corpse in a Gilded Cage*	Robert Barnard	___
1903	*Riddle of the Sands, The*	Erskine Childers	___
1961	*Pale Horse, The*	Agatha Christie	___
1942	*Tragedy at Law*	Cyril Hare	___
1949	*Case of the Journeying Boy, The*	Michael Innes	___
	(The Journeying Boy)		
1956	*Death of a Fool (Off With His Head)*	Ngaio Marsh	___
1975	*Crocodile on the Sandbank*	Elizabeth Peters	___
1986	*Miss Melville Regrets*	Evelyn Smith	___
1884	*Pudd'nhead Wilson*	Mark Twain	___
	(The Tragedy of Pudd'nhead Wilson)		

Michael Malone — TAD:BL

1977	*Who is Teddy Villanova?*	Thomas Berger	___
1940	*Farewell, My Lovely*	Raymond Chandler	___
1853	*Bleak House*	Charles Dickens	___
1866	*Crime and Punishment*	Fyodor Dostoevsky	___
1948	*Intruder in the Dust*	William Faulkner	___
1964	*Deep Blue Good-by, The*	John D. MacDonald	___
1934	*Nine Tailors, The*	Dorothy L. Sayers	___
1935	*League of Frightened Men, The*	Rex Stout	___
1978	*Chinaman's Chance*	Ross Thomas	___

Marcia Muller — TAD:BL

1943	*Lady in the Lake, The*	Raymond Chandler	___
1953	*Long Goodbye, The (The Long Good-bye)*	Raymond Chandler	___
1930	*Maltese Falcon, The*	Dashiell Hammett	___
1970	*Ripley Under Ground*	Patricia Highsmith	___
1978	*Listening Woman*	Tony Hillerman	___
1947	*In a Lonely Place*	Dorothy B. Hughes	___
1946	*Ride the Pink Horse*	Dorothy B. Hughes	___
1966	*Darker Than Amber*	John D. MacDonald	___
1966	*Black Money*	Ross Macdonald	___
1961	*Wycherly Woman, The*	Ross Macdonald	___

Sara Paretsky — TAD:BL; www.Detective-Fiction.com

1948	*More Work for the Undertaker*	Margery Allingham	___
1939	*Smiler With the Knife, The*	Nicholas Blake	___
1986	*Under Contract*	Liza Cody	___
1974	*Poison Oracle, The*	Peter Dickinson	___
1902	*Hound of the Baskervilles, The*	Arthur Conan Doyle	___
1878	*Leavenworth Case, The*	Anna Katharine Green	___
1930	*Maltese Falcon, The*	Dashiell Hammett	___
1965	*Johnny Under Ground*	Patricia Moyes	___
1961	*Spoilt Kill, The*	Mary Kelly	___
1985	*Assault, The*	Harry Mulisch	___

Robert B. Parker — TAD:BL

1939	*Big Sleep, The*	Raymond Chandler	___
1940	*Farewell, My Lovely*	Raymond Chandler	___
1942	*High Window, The*	Raymond Chandler	___
1943	*Lady in the Lake, The*	Raymond Chandler	___
1949	*Little Sister, The (Marlow)*	Raymond Chandler	___
1953	*Long Goodbye, The (The Long Good-bye)*	Raymond Chandler	___
1930	*Maltese Falcon, The*	Dashiell Hammett	___
1973	*Digger's Game, The*	George V. Higgins	___

Elizabeth Peters — TAD:BL

1937	*Burning Court, The*	John Dickson Carr	___
1961	*Pale Horse, The*	Agatha Christie	___
1902	*Hound of the Baskervilles, The*	Arthur Conan Doyle	___
1983	*Dark Place, The*	Aaron Elkins	___
1942	*Phantom Lady*	William Irish (Cornell Woolrich)	___
1950	*Through a Glass, Darkly*	Helen McCloy	___
1979	*Family Vault, The*	Charlotte MacLeod	___
1942	*Calamity Town*	Ellery Queen	___
1930	*Strong Poison*	Dorothy L. Sayers	___
1951	*Daughter of Time, The*	Josephine Tey	___

Ann Rule — Writing Mysteries

1988	*Bitter Blood: A True Story of Southern Family Pride, Madness, and Multiple Murder (non-fiction)*	Jerry Bledsoe	___
1999	*Garden of Evil*	Edna Buchanan	___
1965	*In Cold Blood: A True Account of a Multiple Murder and Its Consequences (non-fiction)*	Truman Capote	___
1995	*Shot in the Heart: One Family's History in Murder (non-fiction)*	Mikal Gilmore	___
1957	*Executioners, The (Cape Fear)*	John D. MacDonald	___
1985	*Two of a Kind: The Hilllside Stranglers (non-fiction)*	Darcy O'Brien	___
1992	*Along Came a Spider*	James Patterson	___
1972	*Murder Being Once Done*	Ruth Rendell	___
1976	*Blood and Money (non-fiction)*	Thomas Thompson	___

Peter Straub — TAD:BL

1913	*Trent's Last Case (The Woman in Black)*	E.C. Bentley	___
1986	*When the Sacred Ginmill Closes*	Lawrence Block	___
1943	*Lady in the Lake, The*	Raymond Chandler	___
1953	*Long Goodbye, The (The Long Good-bye)*	Raymond Chandler	___
1967	*James Joyce Murder, The*	Amanda Cross	___
1981	*Red Dragon (Manhunter)*	Thomas Harris	___
1968	*Pale Gray for Guilt*	John D. MacDonald	___
1975	*Mortal Stakes*	Robert B. Parker	___
1986	*Live Flesh*	Ruth Rendell	___
1973	*First Deadly Sin, The*	Lawrence Sanders	___

Julian Symons — TAD:BL; www.Detective-Fiction.com

1974	*Doctor Frigo*	Eric Ambler	___
1953	*Long Goodbye, The (The Long Good-bye)*	Raymond Chandler	___
1926	*Murder of Roger Ackroyd, The*	Agatha Christie	___
1860	*Woman in White, The*	Wilkie Collins	___
1894	*Memoirs of Sherlock Holmes, The*	Arthur Conan Doyle	___
1931	*Glass Key, The*	Dashiell Hammett	___
1974	*Cogan's Trade*	George V. Higgins	___
1964	*Two Faces of January, The*	Patricia Highsmith	___
1963	*Spy Who Came in From the Cold, The*	John le Carre	___
1845	*Tales of Mystery and Imagination*	Edgar Allan Poe	___

Donald E. Westlake — TAD:BL

1962	*Light of Day, The*	Eric Ambler	___
1971	*Sleep and His Brother*	Peter Dickinson	___
1958	*Eighth Circle, The*	Stanley Ellin	___
1974	*Interface*	Joe Gores	___
1930	*Maltese Falcon, The*	Dashiell Hammett	___
1956	*Kill the Boss Good-by*	Peter Rabe	___
1945	*Red Right Hand, The*	Joel Townsley Rogers	___

Carolyn Wheat — Writing Mysteries

1994	*Concrete Blonde, The*	Michael Connelly	___

Phyllis A. Whitney — TAD:BL

1909	*Secret Garden, The*	Frances Hodgson Burnett	___
1938	*Rebecca*	Daphne du Maurier	___
1988	*Thief of Time, A*	Tony Hillerman	___
1894	*Prisoner of Zenda, The*	Anthony Hope	___
1983	*Act of Darkness*	Francis King	___
1975	*Night of the Juggler*	William P. McGivern	___
1905.	*Scarlet Pimpernel, The*	Baroness Orczy	___
1934	*Nine Tailors, The*	Dorothy L. Sayers	___
1958	*Nine Coaches Waiting*	Mary Stewart	___
1949	*Brat Farrar (Come and Kill Me)*	Josephine Tey	___

Angela Zeman - Writing Mysteries

1998	*Good Cop, Bad Cop*	Barbara D'Amato	___

from: chapter 28, The Armchair Dectective Book of Lists, edited by Kate Stine, 1995
www.detective-fiction.com/author-recommended.htm
www.detective-fiction.com/author-recommended2.htm
from: Writing Mysteries (MWA), Grafton, ed. 2002

Barzun and Taylor's
Classic Crime Novels 1900-1975

Jacques Barzun and Wendell Hertig Taylor in their *A Catalogue of Crime* (Rev. & Enl. Edition, 1989) include descriptions of works the authors consider "Classics of Crime" between 1900-1976; 90 titles in all.

Barzun and Taylor's Classic Crime Novels

1900	*Circular Study, The*	Anna Katharine Green	___
1902	*Hound of the Baskervilles, The*	Arthur Conan Doyle	___
1913	*Trent's Last Case (The Woman in Black)*	E.C. Bentley	___
1915	*In Accordance With the Evidence*	Oliver Onions	___
1922	*Red House Mystery, The*	A.A. Milne	___
1926	*Murder of Roger Ackroyd, The*	Agatha Christie	___
1927	*Murder at Crome House, The*	G.D.H. & Margaret Cole	___
1929	*Purple Sickle Murders, The (The Box Office Murders)*	Freeman Wills Crofts	___
1929	*Murder in the Moor*	Thomas Kindon	___
1930	*Secret of High Eldersham, The (The Mystery of High Eldersham)*	Miles Burton	___
1930	*Strong Poison*	Dorothy L. Sayers	___
1931	*Found Drowned*	Eden Phillpotts	___
1931	*Who is the Next?*	Henry K. Webster	___
1932	*Death Under Sail*	C.P. Snow	___
1932	*Division Bell Mystery, The*	Ellen Wilkinson	___
1933	*Mummy Case Mystery, The (The Mummy Case)*	Dermot Morrah	___
1935	*Jury, The*	Gerald Bullett	___
1935	*Was It Murder? (Murder at School)*	James Hilton (as, Glen Trevor)	___
1937	*Dancers in Mourning (Who Killed Chloe?)*	Margery Allingham	___
1938	*Blunt Instrument, A*	Georgette Heyer	___
1938	*Funeral in Eden, A (Burial Service)*	Paul McGuire	___
1938	*Too Many Cooks*	Rex Stout	___
1938	*Bone is Pointed, The*	Arthur W. Upfield	___
1939	*African Poison Murders, The*	Elspeth Huxley	___
1941	*Measure for Murder*	Clifford Witting	___
1942	*Daffodil Affair, The*	Michael Innes	___
1943	*Lady in the Lake, The*	Raymond Chandler	___
1944	*Case of the Crooked Candle, The*	Erle Stanley Gardner	___
1944	*Alarum and Excursion*	Virginia Perdue	___
1945	*Birthday Murder, The*	Lange Lewis	___
1946	*Horizontal Man, The*	Helen Eustis	___
1946	*Big Clock, The (No Way Out)*	Kenneth Fearing	___
1946	*Pick Your Victim*	Patricia McGerr	___

1946	*Shadowy Third, The (Suspects All)*	Marco Page (Harry Kurnitz)	___
1947	*Minute for Murder*	Nicholas Blake	___
1948	*Blood on the Bosom Divine*	Thomas Kyd	___
1949	*Dark River, The*	Philip Clark	___
1949	*Buried for Pleasure*	Edmund Crispin	___
1949	*When the Wind Blows (The Wind Blows Death)*	Cyril Hare	___
1949	*Engaged to Murder*	M.V. Heberden	___
1949	*Strip Death Naked*	Norman Longmate	___
1949	*Wreath for Rivera, A (Swing, Brother, Swing)*	Ngaio Marsh	___
1950	*Death and Letters*	Elizabeth Daly	___
1950	*No Tears for Hilda*	Andrew Garve	___
1950	*Beyond a Reasonable Doubt*	C.W. Grafton	___
1950	*Congo Venus, The*	Matthew Head	___
1950	*Smallbone Deceased*	Michael Gilbert	___
1950	*Drowning Pool, The*	Ross Macdonald	___
		(as, John Ross Macdonald)	
1951	*Banner for Pegasus, A (Not in the Script)*	John & Emery Bonett	___
1952	*Deep End, The*	Fredric Brown	___
1952	*Body in the Beck, The*	Joanna Cannan	___
1952	*Key to Nicholas Street, The*	Stanley Ellin	___
1952	*One-Man Show (A Private View;*	Michael Innes	___
	Murder is an Art)		
1953	*Dead Low Tide*	John D. MacDonald	___
1953	*Singing Sands, The*	Josephine Tey	___
1954	*Narrowing Circle, The*	Julian Symons	___
1954	*Such Friends are Dangerous*	Walter Tyrer	___
1955	*Exit Charlie*	Alex H. Atkinson	___
1955	*Stone Cold Dead in the Market*	Christopher Landon	___
1955	*Hammersmith Maggot, The (Small Venom)*	William Mole	___
1956	*Second Man, The*	Edward Grierson	___
1956	*Pub Crawler, The*	Maurice Procter	___
1958	*Suffer a Witch*	Nigel Fitzgerald	___
1958	*Too Much of Water*	Bruce Hamilton	___
1958	*Murder of a Wife*	Henry Kuttner	___
1959	*Bronze Perseus, The (The Tender Killer)*	S.B. Hough	___
1960	*Furious Old Women*	Leo Bruce	___
1960	*Swan Song (The Chinese Goose)*	Helen Robertson	___
1961	*Death Finds a Foothold*	Glyn Carr	___
1961	*Dead Past, The*	Jean Scholey	___
1962	*Dead Cert*	Dick Francis	___
1962	*Cover Her Face*	P.D. James	___
1962	*Killed by Scandal*	Simon Nash	___
1963	*Sad Song Singing, A*	Thomas B. Dewey	___
1964	*In the Last Analysis*	Amanda Cross	___
1964	*Missing Man, The*	Hillary Waugh	___

1965	*Johnny Under Ground*	Patricia Moyes	____
1966	*Crayfish Dinner, The (The Elusive Epicure)*	Carlton Keith	____
1966	*Murder Makes the Wheels Go 'Round*	Emma Lathen	____
1966	*Salt is Leaving*	J.B. Priestley	____
1968	*Gideon's River*	J.J. Marric (John Creasey)	____
1969	*Swift to Its Close*	Simon Troy	____
1969	*Just What the Doctor Ordered (The Flaxborough Crab)*	Colin Watson	____
1970	*High Tide*	P.M. Hubbard	____
1970	*On the Shady Side*	Frank Swinnerton	____
1970	*Finding Maubee (The Calypso Murders)*	A.H.Z. Carr	____
1971	*Fly on the Wall, The*	Tony Hillerman	____
1973	*Man Who Liked to Look at Himself, The*	K.C. Constantine	____
1973	*Night Hunters, The*	John Miles	____
1976	*Never Pick Up Hitch Hikers!*	Ellis Peters	____

www.topmystery.com/books4.htm

home.comcast.net/~dwtaylor1/barzuntaylor.html

Anthony Boucher Best/Important Selections
1942-1968

Anthony Boucher (August 21, 1911 - April 29, 1968) was a reviewer, critic, editor, and author (novels and short stories) of mystery, fantasy, horror, and science fiction. Here, we will look to his work in the mystery genre. Between 1942 and 1947, he served as reviewer and critic of mystery fiction for the *San Francisco Chronicle*. Later he served in the same role for *Ellery Queen's Mystery Magazine,* but his major critical contribution appeared in the *New York Times* beginning in 1951 to the year of his death in 1968. He wrote more than 850 weekly review columns under the heading "Criminals at Large" for the *New York Times*. A key element in this work was listing what he felt was the "top" or "best" mystery writing at the end of each year.

Boucher won three Edgar® Awards from the Mystery Writers of America for this outstanding body of criticism and was recognized as the nation's foremost authority on crime fiction during his time. The annual mystery convention, called Bouchercon, was named in his honor.

We have access to Anthony Boucher's newspaper columns beginning in 1942.* In that year he did not list the "best" for the year but offered what he considered as some of the best mysteries ever written. Then, beginning in December 1943, he would offer a list of the best titles, usually novels, for the year.

During the year, he would mention books that he felt were important or the best of all time, some being newly available in reprint. Sometimes he referred to titles as an important work or works that should be on bookshelves. I have added those key titles that I felt he wanted listed as "important" and have placed them after the "Best of the Year" titles.

In the *San Francisco Chronicle* and *New York Times* columns, he would talk about changing trends, newer trends, and important reprints for mystery fans. He would sometimes offer one title in the "Best" list for a year in a particular genre. Then, in an accompanying article, he would offer more very important titles in that same genre. In his December 1956 article he talked about the rise of the police novel. He listed Ed McBain in the Best of '56 but added other important contributions to this new school in the article. These titles are also listed below with other important novels.

Sometimes Boucher made reference to an older title that he felt was a key book that needed to be read again. Other times a selection was an important reprint that had been out of publication or being published in paperback for the first time.

He felt that the "best" lists were untrustworthy because they were subjective or personal; nonetheless these were selections that he especially enjoyed and admired.

*See, *The Anthony Boucher Chronicles: Review and Commentary, 1942-1947*, edited by Francis
   M. Nevins.

Some titles have two dates in the left column. These are generally works written in a foreign language and later translated and published in English. The first date would be the original language publication and the second date, the later English publication date.

For several years Boucher noted that there were so many wonderful books that only space limited his selections. He often mentions "with regrets" numerous authors, wishing that he had more room. I did not list names of important authors; there had to be a title with the name.

He would discuss the advances or changes in literacy, in psychological depth, in observation of manners and character, a flood of major British imports, America spawned a new school of quasi-detective pornography…and much more.

In many ways, the "important" lists are as significant as the "best" lists during these years (1942-1968). Reprint or reissue titles are offered from earlier times, additional titles of specific genre works are offered where he only wanted one of that type in the "best" list for that year, as were other works that just were over and above the quota for the year. Therefore, I suggest we treat the "important" list with great significance.

Some years the list is longer because Boucher did not just list fifteen or so titles, but he went by genre and listed titles to different mystery trends.

There is a concern about obtaining some of these titles from the 1940s, 1950s, and 1960s. Some book search web sites like Abebooks.com, Barnesandnoble.com, Amazon.com, and Bookfinder.com have search engines and can locate most of these titles. Ordering, with a small postage fee, is one way to obtain them. Also, some used bookstores that carry older books are another great source. In addition, various libraries might have copies or can use the interlibrary loan procedures.

There are two lists that follow:

    1. Boucher's List of Best Titles—Novels
    2. Boucher's List of Important Titles—Novels

There were no Best lists written during 1947 as Boucher had concluded his work with the *San Francisco Chronicle* and would begin his work with *Ellery Queen Mystery Magazine* in 1948 and the *New York Times* a few years later.

In the end, Anthony Boucher's Best/Important Lists between 1942 and 1968 give us a most important window of titles in the mystery field. I only list here his naming of novels; I do not list his suggestions for nonfiction, collections by an author, anthologies, etc.

Boucher's List of Best Titles - Novels

Boucher 42 Best

1930	*It Walks by Night*	John Dickson Carr	____
1936	*ABC Murders, The (The Alphabet Murders)*	Agatha Christie	____
1934	*Willful and Premeditated (The 12:30 From Croydon)*	Freeman Wills Crofts	____
1935	*Red Window Murders, The*	Carter Dickson	____
1935	*Case of the Counterfeit Eye, The*	Erle Stanley Gardner	____
1938	*Death in a White Tie*	Ngaio Marsh	____
1922	*Red House Mystery, The*	A.A. Milne	____
1933	*Siamese Twin Mystery, The*	Ellery Queen	____
1930	*Strong Poison*	Dorothy L. Sayers	____
1932/40	*Liberty Bar (Maigret on the Riviera) (in: Maigret Travels South)*	Georges Simenon	____
1932/40	*Saint-Fiacre Affair, The (Maigret Goes Home; included in, Maigret Keeps a Rendezvous)*	Georges Simenon	____
1941	*Three Famous Murder Novels* (3 below)	Bennett Cert, ed.	____
1932	*Before the Fact*	Francis Iiles	____
1913	*Trent's Last Case (Woman in Black, The)*	E.C. Bentley	____
1924	*House of the Arrow, The*	A.E.W. Mason	____
1942	*Three Famous Spy Novels* (3 below)	Bennett Cert, ed.	____
1920	*Great Impersonation, The*	E. Phillips Oppenheim	____
1940	*Journey Into Fear*	Eric Ambler	____
1939	*Confidential Agent, The*	Graham Greene	____
1942	*Crime Club Encore* (4 below)	Howard Haycraft, ed.	____
1940	*Verdict of Twelve*	Raymond Postgate	____
1940	*Keep Murder Quiet*	Selwyn Jepson	____
1938	*Warrant for X (The Nursemaid Who Disappeared)*	Philip MacDonald	____
1937	*Case of the Late Pig, The (also in, Mr. Campion: Criminologist)*	Margery Allingham	____
1942	*Three Star Mystery Novels* (3 below) (Harper)	Anonymous	____
1927	*Old Dark House, The (Benighted)*	J.B. Priestley	____
1931	*Was it Murder? (Murder at School)*	James Hilton (as, Glen Trevor)	____
1936	*Wheel Spins, The (The Lady Vanishes)*	Ethel Lina White	____

Boucher 43 Best

1942	*Death of a Busybody*	George Bellairs	____
1943	*Lady in the Lake, The*	Raymond Chandler	____
1943	*Painted for the Kill*	Lucy Cores	____
1943	*Mouse in the Mountain, The (Rendezvous with Fear; Dead Little Rich Girl)*	Norbert Davis	____
1943	*She Died a Lady*	Carter Dickson	____
1943	*Unidentified Woman*	Mignon G. Eberhart	____

1943	*Ministry of Fear, The*	Graham Greene	____
1943	*Stranger and Afraid, A*	Michael Hardt	____
1943	*Smell of Money, The*	Matthew Head	____
1943	*Death in the Doll's House*	Hannah Lees &	____
		Lawrence Bachmann	
1943	*Colour Scheme*	Ngaio Marsh	____
1943	*Green Circle, The (The Green Orb)*	Chris Massie	____
1943	*Do Not Disturb*	Helen McCloy	____
1943	*Wall of Eyes*	Margaret Millar	____
1943	*Thursday Turkey Murders, The*	Craig Rice	____
1943	*Year of August, The*	Mark Saxton	____
1943	*They Deal in Death*	Robert Terrall	____
1943	*Murder Down Under (Mr. Jelly's Business)*	Arthur W. Upfield	____
1943	*Stalk the Hunter*	Mitchell Wilson	____
1943	*Black Angel, The*	Cornell Woolrich	____

Boucher 44 Best

1944	*Case of the Giant Killer*	H.C. Branson	____
1943	*Last Secret, The*	Dana Chambers	____
1944	*Jack-in-the-Box*	J.J. Connington	____
1944	*Corpse de Ballet*	Lucy Cores	____
1944	*He Wouldn't Kill Patience*	Carter Dickson	____
1944	*Case of the Crooked Candle, The*	Erle Stanley Gardner	____
1944	*To What Dread End (The Doctor Was a Lady)*	M.V. Heberden	____
1944	*Needle's Eye, The*	Edward Lee	____
1944	*Sinners Never Die*	A.E. Martin	____
1944	*Dark Tunnel, The (I Die Slowly)*	Kenneth Millar (Ross Macdonald)	____
1944	*Home Sweet Homicide*	Craig Rice	____
1944	*Crying at the Lock*	Adeline Rumsey	____
1944	*Moon was Red, The*	Dana Sage	____
1944	*Bride's Castle*	P.W. Wilson	____

Boucher 45 Best

1945	*Murder by Proxy*	Bettina & Audrey Boyers	____
1944	*Obsequies at Oxford*	Edmund Crispin	____
	(The Case of the Gilded Fly)		
1945	*Steps in the Dark*	Marten Cumberland	____
1945	*Murder on a Tangent*	Doris Miles Disney	____
1945	*Watchful at Night*	Julius Fast	____
1945	*Rumor Hath It*	Christopher Hale	____
1945	*Devil in the Bush, The*	Matthew Head	____
1945	*Dread Journey*	Dorothy B. Hughes	____
1945	*Appleby's End*	Michael Innes	____
1945	*Out of Control*	Baynard Kendrick	____
1945	*Shape of Danger (Live Dangerously)*	Axel Kielland	____

1944	*Outsiders, The (The Common People)*	A.E. Martin	___
1945	*Iron Gates, The (Taste of Fears)*	Margaret Millar	___
1945	*State Department Cat*	Mary Plum	___
1945	*Murderer is a Fox, The*	Ellery Queen	___
1945	*Red Right Hand, The*	Joel Townsley Rogers	___
1945	*Man Who Asked Why, The (The Clue of the Frightening Coin)*	Jessica Ryan	___
1945	*Dead Lie Still, The (Dead Ahead)*	William L. Stuart	___
1945	*"V" as in Victim*	Lawrence Treat	___

Boucher 46 Best

1946	*Life Sentence, The*	H.C. Bailey	___
1946	*Deadly Percheron, The*	John Franklin Bardin	___
1945	*Time to Change Hats*	Margot Bennett	___
1946	*White Mazurka, The*	Bettina Boyers	___
1946	*Crooked Wreath, The (Suddenly at His Residence)*	Christianna Brand	___
1946	*He Who Whispers*	John Dickson Carr	___
1946	*Hollow, The (Murder After Hours)*	Agatha Christie	___
1946	*My Late Wives*	Carter Dickson	___
1946	*Who Rides a Tiger (Sow the Wind)*	Doris Miles Disney	___
1946	*Curate's Crime, The*	Sibyl Erickson (Alexandra Dick)	___
1946	*Horizontal Man, The*	Helen Eustis	___
1946	*Tiger by the Tail*	Lawrence Goldman	___
1946	*Dark Passage*	David Goodis	___
1946	*Innocent Mrs. Duff, The*	Elisabeth Sanxay Holding	___
1946	*What Happened at Hazelwood?*	Michael Innes	___
1946	*Black Seven, The*	Carol Kendall	___
1946	*Pavilion, The (The Deadly Pavilion)*	Hilda Lawrence	___
1946	*Pick Your Victim*	Patricia McGerr	___
1946	*Municipal Murder, The*	Leslie W. Morris, II	___
1946	*Brass Ring, The (Murder in Brass)*	Lewis Padgett	___
1945	*Ingenious Mr. Stone, The*	Robert Player	___
1946	*Puzzle for Fiends (Love is a Deadly Weapon)*	Patrick Quentin	___
1946	*You Leave Me Cold!*	Samuel Rogers	___
1946	*Glass Room, The*	Edwin Rolfe & Lester Fuller	___
1945	*Green December Fills the Graveyard (Murder at Shots Hall)*	Maureen Sarsfield	___
1938/42	*Man Who Watched the Trains Go By, The*	Georges Simenon	___
1946	*Where There's Smoke*	Stewart Sterling	___
1946	*Assassins, The*	Hildegarde Tolman Teilhet	___
1946	*"H" as in Hunted*	Lawrence Treat	___
1946	*Chinese Doll, The*	Wilson Tucker	___

Boucher 48 Best

1948	*In Cold Blood*	George Bagby (Aaron Marc Stein)	___
1947	*Minute for Murder*	Nicholas Blake	___
1948	*Wilders Walk Away*	Herbert Brean	___
1948	*Snare for Witches*	Elinor Chamberlain	___
1948	*There is a Tide (Taken at the Flood)*	Agatha Christie	___
1948	*Wisteria Cottage (The Night Before Dying)*	Robert M. Coates	___
1948	*Love Lies Bleeding*	Edmund Crispin	___
1948	*Death Haunts the Dark Lane*	A.B. Cunningham	___
1948	*Voice Out of Darkness*	Ursula Curtiss	___
1948	*Book of the Lion, The*	Elizabeth Daly	___
1948	*Room Upstairs, The*	Mildred Davis	___
1948	*Skeleton in the Clock, The*	Carter Dickson	___
1948	*That Which is Crooked*	Doris Miles Disney	___
1948	*Mouse With Pink Eyes, The (His Dead Wife)*	Elizabeth Eastman	___
1948	*But the Patient Died*	James G. Edwards	___
1948	*Dreadful Summit (The Big Night)*	Stanley Ellin	___
1948	*It's a Crime*	Richard Ellington	___
1948	*Many a Monster*	Robert Finnegan	___
1948	*Wolf Tone*	Lawrence Goldman	___
1948	*Root of Evil*	Eaton K. Goldthwaite	___
1948	*Lock and the Key, The (Too Tough to Die; Run, Thief, Run)*	Frank Gruber	___
1948	*Steel Mirror, The*	Donald Hamilton	___
1948	*Kiss Your Elbow (Terror in Times Square)*	Alan Handley	___
1948	*Symphony in Two Time*	Alexander Irving	___
1948	*Armchair in Hell*	Henry Kane	___
1948	*Owl in the Sun, An*	Leslie Kark	___
1948	*I am the Cat*	Rosemary Kutak	___
1948	*Murder One*	Eleazar Lipsky	___
1948	*Murder is Served*	Frances & Richard Lockridge	___
1948	*Savage Breast*	Manning Long	___
1948	*Screen for Murder, A (Death Before Dinner)*	E.C.R. Lorac	___
1948	*Map of Mistrust*	Allan MacKinnon	___
1948	*Baited Blonde, The*	Robinson MacLean	___
1948	*But Death Runs Faster (The Whispering Corpse)*	William P. McGivern	___
1948	*Fatel Step*	Wade Miller	___
1948	*Ugly Woman, The*	William O'Farrell	___
1948	*Ten Days' Wonder*	Ellery Queen	___
1948	*False Bounty (I, the Executioner)*	Stephen Ransone	___
1948	*Trial of Alvin Boaker, The*	John Reywall	___
1948	*Fourth Postman, The*	Craig Rice	___
1948	*Murder Makes Me Nervous*	Margaret Scherf	___
1948	*Blowtop, The*	Alvin Schwartz	___
1948	*Woman in the Sea, The*	Shelley Smith	___

1948	*Night Cry*	William L. Stuart	___
1948	*Killer is Loose Among Us, A*	Robert Terrall	___
1948	*Where's Mr. Chumley?*	Seldon Truss	___
1948	*Sin of Angels*	Anna Mary Wells	___
1948	*Rendezvous in Black*	Cornell Woolrich	___

Boucher 49 Best

1949	*Below Suspicion*	John Dickson Carr	___
1949	*Case of the Dubious Bridegroom, The*	Erle Stanley Gardner	___
1949	*What a Body!*	Alan Green	___
1949	*Cabinda Affair, The*	Matthew Head	___
1949	*Case of the Journeying Boy, The (The Journeying Boy)*	Michael Innes	___
1949	*Blue Harpsichord*	David Keith (Francis Steegmuller)	___
1949	*Moving Target, The (Harper)*	John MacDonald (Ross Macdonald)	___
1949	*Innocent, The*	Evelyn Piper	___
1949	*Cat of Many Tails*	Ellery Queen	___
1948	*Franchise Affair, The*	Josephine Tey	___

Boucher 50 Best

1949	*Two If by Sea (Came the Dawn)*	Roger Bax (Andrew Garve)	___
1950	*Knife Behind You, The*	James Benet	___
1949	*Screaming Mimi, The*	Fredric Brown	___
1950	*So Young a Body*	Frank Bunce	___
1949	*One of Those Things (Mistress Murder)*	Peter Cheyney	___
1950	*Sudden Vengeance (Frequent Hearses)*	Edmund Crispin	___
1950	*Hunter is the Hunted, The (Blood Runs Cold)*	A.B. Cunningham	___
1950	*Clay Hand, The*	Dorothy Salisbury Davis	___
1950	*Case of the Negligent Nymph, The*	Erle Stanley Gardner	___
1949	*Death Knocks Three Times*	Anthony Gilbert	___
1949	*Wind Blows Death, The (When the Wind Blows)*	Cyril Hare	___
1950	*Fright*	George Hopley (Cornell Woolrich)	___
1950	*Slay Ride*	Frank Kane	___
1949	*Dishonest Murderer, The*	Frances & Richard Lockridge	___
1950	*Tentacles, The*	Dana Lyon	___
1949	*Death of a White Witch*	Inez Oellrichs	___
1950	*Double Identities (The Two Graphs)*	John Rhode	___
1950	*House Without a Door, The*	Thomas Sterling	___
1950	*Rim of Terror, The*	Hildegarde Tolman Teilhet	___
1949	*Brat Farrar (Come and Kill Me)*	Josephine Tey	___
1950	*Windows of Broome, The*	Arthur W. Upfield	___

Boucher 51 Best

1951	*Devil in Velvet, The*	John Dickson Carr	____
1951	*They Came to Baghdad*	Agatha Christie	____
1951	*Gentle Murderer, A*	Dorothy Salisbury Davis	____
1951	*English Murder, An (The Christmas Murder)*	Cyril Hare	____
1951	*Rough Shoot, A*	Geoffrey Household	____
1951	*Time to Kill, A*	Geoffrey Household	____
1951	*Paper Thunderbolt, The (Operation Pax)*	Michael Innes	____
1950	*Mr. Byculla*	Eric Linklater	____
1951	*Way Some People Die, The*	John Ross Macdonald (Ross Macdonald)	____
1951	*Shield for Murder*	William P. McGivern	____
1951	*Night at the Vulcan (Opening Night)*	Ngaio Marsh	____
1951	*Murder on the Left Bank*	Elliot Paul	____
1951	*Origin of Evil, The*	Ellery Queen	____
1951	*Mr. Blessington's Imperialist Plot (Mr. Blessington's Plot)*	John Sherwood	____
1951	*Black Sheep, Run*	Bart Spicer	____
1951	*Golden Door, The*	Bart Spicer	____
1951	*31st of February, The*	Julian Symons	____
1951	*Big Shot*	Lawrence Treat	____

Boucher 52 Best

1938/52	*Epitaph for a Spy*	Eric Ambler	____
1952	*Barbary Hoard (The Singing Cave)*	John Appleby	____
1952	*Inward Eye, The (Lady Marked for Murder)*	Peggy Bacon	____
1952	*Catch a Tiger*	Owen Cameron	____
1952	*Mrs. McGinty's Dead (Blood Will Tell)*	Agatha Christie	____
1952	*Key to Nicholas Street, The*	Stanley Ellin	____
1952	*Deadlock*	Ruth Fenisong	____
1952	*Bloody Bokhara, The (The Bloodstained Bokhara)*	William Campbell Gault	____
1951	*Death Has Deep Roots*	Michael Gilbert	____
1952	*They Died Laughing*	Alan Green	____
1952	*Ivory Grin, The (Marked for Murder)*	John Ross Macdonald (Ross Macdonald)	____
1952	*Vanish in an Instant*	Margaret Millar	____
1952	*Black Widow (Fatal Woman)*	Patrick Quentin	____
1952	*Long Green, The (Shadow of Fear)*	Bart Spicer	____
1951	*Daughter of Time, The*	Josephine Tey	____

Boucher 53 Best

1953	*Their Nearest and Dearest (The Frightened Widow)*	Bernice Carey	____
1953	*Post Mortem*	Guy Cullingford	____
1953	*Case of the Hesitant Hostess, The*	Erle Stanley Gardner	____

1953	*Canvas Coffin, The*	William Campbell Gault	____
1953	*Fear to Tread*	Michael Gilbert	____
1952	*Reputation for a Song*	Edward Grierson	____
1952	*Beat Not the Bones*	Charlotte Jay	____
1953	*Kiss Before Dying, A*	Ira Levin	____
1953	*Speak Justly of the Dead (Murder in Mill-Race)*	E.C.R. Lorac	____
1953	*Meet Me at the Morgue (Experience With Evil)*	John Ross Macdonald (Ross Macdonald)	____
1952	*Singing Sands, The*	Josephine Tey	____

Boucher 54 Best

1954	*Whisper in the Gloom, The (Catch and Kill* [abridged]*)*	Nicholas Blake	____
1954	*Time of the Fire, The*	Marc Brandel	____
1954	*Third Bullet and Other Stories, The*	John Dickson Carr	____
1953	*Long Goodbye, The (The Long Good-bye)*	Raymond Chandler	____
1953	*Pocket Full of Rye, A*	Agatha Christie	____
1954	*Dead Man's Shoes (Appleby Talking)*	Michael Innes	____
1953	*Fugitive Eye, The*	Charlotte Jay	____
1954	*Find a Victim*	John Ross Macdonald (Ross Macdonald)	____
1954	*Murder in Pastiche: Or, Nine Detectives All at Sea*	Marion Mainwaring	____
1954	*Rogue Cop*	William P. McGivern	____
1954	*Lucinda*	Howard Rigsby	____
1936/54	*Shilling for Candles, A*	Josephine Tey	____

Boucher 55 Best

1955	*Tour de Force*	Christianna Brand	____
1955	*Tall Dark Man, The*	Anne Chamberlain	____
1955	*Mean Streets, The*	Thomas B. Dewey	____
1955	*Room for Murder*	Doris Miles Disney	____
1954	*Rare Adventure, The*	Bernard Fergusson	____
1955	*F.O.B. Murder*	Bert & Dolores Hitchens	____
1955	*Yellow Turban, The*	Charlotte Jay	____
1955	*Best that Ever Did It, The (Visa to Death)*	Ed Lacy	____
1955	*Scales of Justice*	Ngaio Marsh	____
1955	*All Through the Night (A Cry in the Night)*	Whit Masterson	____
1955	*Beast in View*	Margaret Millar	____
1954	*Somewhere in This City (Hell is a City; Murder, Somewhere in This City)*	Maurice Procter	____
1955	*Evil of the Day, The (Murder in Venice)*	Thomas Sterling	____

Boucher 56 Best

1956	*Dram of Poison, A*	Charlotte Armstrong	____
1955	*Man Who Didn't Fly, The*	Margot Bennett	____
1956	*Tangled Web, A (Death and Daisy Bland)*	Nicholas Blake	____
1956	*Lenient Beast, The*	Fredric Brown	____
1956	*Capitol Offense, A (The Undoubted Deed)*	Jocelyn Davey	____
1956	*Second Man, The*	Edward Grierson	____
1956	*Compulsion*	Meyer Levin	____
1956	*Cop Hater*	Ed McBain	____
1956	*Mugger, The*	Ed McBain	____
1956	*Barbarous Coast, The*	John Ross Macdonald (Ross Macdonald)	____
1956	*Harm Intended*	Richard Parker	____
1956	*Inspector Queen's Own Case*	Ellery Queen	____
1956	*Murder in Haiti (Out for a Killing)*	John Vandercook	____

Boucher 57 Best

1957	*Naked Sun, The* (note: S.F. novel)	Isaac Asimov	____
1957	*Tiger Among Us, The (13 West Street; Fear No Evil)*	Leigh Brackett	____
1957	*Taste of Ashes, The*	Howard Browne (John Evans)	____
1957	*Night of the Good Children, The (One Night of Terror)*	Marjorie Carleton	____
1957	*Fire, Burn!*	John Dickson Carr	____
1957	*Death of an Old Sinner*	Dorothy Salisbury Davis	____
1957	*Scapegoat, The*	Daphne du Maurier	____
1956	*Be Shot for Sixpence*	Michael Gilbert	____
1957	*Room to Swing*	Ed Lacy	____
1957	*Stopover: Tokyo (Last of Mr. Moto; Right You are, Mr.Moto)*	John P. Marquand	____
1957	*Gideon's Night*	J.J. Marric (John Creasey)	____
1957	*Con Man, The*	Ed McBain	____
1957	*Odds Against Tomorrow*	William P. McGivern	____
1957	*Air that Kills, An (The Soft Talkers)*	Margaret Millar	____
1955	*Watson's Choice*	Gladys Mitchell	____
1957	*Bunny Lake is Missing*	Evelyn Piper	____
1956	*Lord Have Mercy, The (The Shrew Is Dead)*	Shelley Smith	____
1957	*What Rough Beast*	John Trench	____
1957	*Bushman Who Came Back, The (Bony Buys a Woman)*	Arthur W. Upfield	____
1956	*Chinese Maze Murders, The*	Robert van Gulik	____
1957	*Knock and Wait a While*	William Rawle Weeks	____

Boucher 58 Best

1958	*All Men are Murderers (The Shadow of Murder)*	Lee Blackstock (Charity Blackstock)	____
1956	*Dewey Death*	Charity Blackstock	____
1957	*Woman in the Woods, The (Miss Fenny)*	Lee Blackstock (Charity Blackstock)	____
1958	*Devil's Agent, The (Agent of the Devil)*	Hans Habe	____
1958	*Untimely Death (He Should Have Died Hereafter)*	Cyril Hare	____
1955	*Blind Date (Chance Meeting)*	Leigh Howard	____
1958	*Doomsters, The*	Ross Macdonald (John Ross Macdonald)	____
1957	*Final Exposure*	Paul H. Mansfield	____
1958	*Stir of Echoes, A*	Richard Matheson	____
1958	*Killer's Choice*	Ed McBain	____
1958	*Killer's Payoff*	Ed McBain	____
1958	*Lady Killer*	Ed McBain	____
1958	*Now, Will You Try for Murder?*	Harry Olesker	____
1957	*Midnight Plumber, The*	Maurice Procter	____
1958	*Finishing Stroke, The*	Ellery Queen	____
1958	*April Robin Murders, The*	Craig Rice & Ed McBain	____
1958	*Stopped Clock, The (Never Leave My Bed)*	Joel Townsley Rogers	____
1957	*Heat Wave*	Caesar Smith (also, Elleston Trevor)	____
1957	*Colour of Murder, The (The Color of Murder)*	Julian Symons	____

Boucher 59 Best

1959	*Duo (The Girl with a Secret; Incident at a Corner)*	Charlotte Armstrong	____
1957	*Devil by the Sea*	Nina Bawden	____
1959	*End of Violence, The*	Ben Benson	____
1959	*Seven Steps East*	Ben Benson	____
1959	*Lament for Four Brides*	Evelyn Berckman	____
1958	*Foggy, Foggy Dew, The*	Charity Blackstock	____
1959	*Psycho*	Robert Bloch	____
1959	*No Grave for a Lady*	John & Emery Bonett	____
1959	*Scandal at High Chimneys*	John Dickson Carr	____
1959	*Blood and Judgment*	Michael Gilbert	____
1958	*Hours Before Dawn, The*	Celia Fremlin	____
1959	*Killer's Wedge*	Ed McBain	____
1959	*King's Ransom*	Ed McBain	____
1959	*'Til Death*	Ed McBain	____
1959	*Listening Walls, The*	Margaret Millar	____
1959	*Twisted Ones, The*	Vin Packer	____
1959	*Dream of Falling, A (Dream of Death)*	Mary O. Rank	____
1959	*Journey to the Hangman (Bony and the Mouse)*	Arthur W. Upfield	____

| 1931/59 | *Sands of Windee, The* | Arthur W. Upfield | ___ |
| 1958 | *Chinese Bell Murders, The* | Robert van Gulik | ___ |

Boucher 60 Best

1959	*Passage of Arms*	Eric Ambler	___
1960	*Traces of Brillhart, The*	Herbert Brean	___
1959	*Cat Among the Pigeons*	Agatha Christie	___
1960	*Devil's Own, The (Witches;*	Peter Curtis (Norah Lofts)	___
	The Little Wax Doll, by Norah Lofts)		
1960	*Lust for Innocence*	Dianne Doubtfire	___
1960	*Traps (A Dangerous Game)*	Friedrich Dürrenmatt	___
1959	*Uncle Paul*	Celia Fremlin	___
1959	*Strike for a Kingdom*	Menna Gallie	___
1960	*Watcher in the Shadows*	Geoffrey Household	___
1960	*End of the Night, The*	John D. MacDonald	___
1960	*Only Girl in the Game, The*	John D. MacDonald	___
1960	*Ferguson Affair, The*	Ross Macdonald	___
1960	*Gideon's Risk*	J.J. Marric (John Creasey)	___
1959	*False Scent*	Ngaio Marsh	___
1960	*Send Another Hearse*	Harold Q. Masur	___
1960	*Give the Boys a Great Big Hand*	Ed McBain	___
1960	*Heckler, The*	Ed McBain	___
1960	*See Them Die*	Ed McBain	___
1959	*Dead Men Don't Ski*	Patricia Moyes	___
1960	*Green-Eyed Monster, The*	Patrick Quentin	___
1960	*Versus Inspector Maigret* (2 below)	Georges Simenon	___
1959	*Maigret and the Reluctant Witnesses*	Georges Simenon	___
	(Maigret and the Reluctant Witness)		
1958/58	*Maigret has Scruples*	Georges Simenon	___
1960	*My Brother Michael*	Mary Stewart	___
1960	*Progress of a Crime, The*	Julian Symons	___

Boucher 61 Best

1960	*Counsel for the Defense*	Jeffrey Ashford	___
1961	*Moonbeams, The (Faith has No Country)*	R. Vernon Beste	___
1961	*Felony Tank*	Malcolm Braly	___
1961	*Witch of the Low Tide, The*	John Dickson Carr	___
1960	*Night of Wenceslas*	Lionel Davidson	___
1961	*Wait for the Wedding (Seven Lean Years)*	Celia Fremlin	___
1961	*Case of the Spurious Spinster, The*	Erle Stanley Gardner	___
1961	*House of Soldiers, The*	Andrew Garve	___
1961	*Cipher, The*	Alex Gordon (Gordon Cotler)	___
1961	*Night of the Kill*	Breni James	___
1961	*Message From Sirius*	Cecil Jenkins	___
1961	*Old House of Fear*	Russell Kirk	___

1961	*Court of Crows*	Robert A. Knowlton	____
1961	*Wrong Side of the Sky, The*	Gavin Lyall	____
1961	*Wycherly Woman, The*	Ross Macdonald	____
1961	*Gideon's Fire*	J.J. Marric (John Creasey)	____
1961	*Some of Your Blood*	Theodore Sturgeon	____
1961	*Red Pavilion, The*	Robert van Gulik	____
1961	*Gift of Rome (66 B.C.), The*	John & Esther Wagner	____
1961	*Eye of the Needle, The*	Thomas Walsh	____
1961	*That Night It Rained*	Hillary Waugh	____
1961	*Killing Time (The Operator)*	Donald E. Westlake	____
1961	*Smartest Grave, The (1903 historical event)*	R.J. White	____

Boucher 62 Best

1961	*D.I., The (Investigations are Proceeding)*	Jeffrey Ashford	____
1961	*House Possessed, A (The Exorcism)*	Charity Blackstock	____
1961	*Scarlet Boy, The*	Arthur Calder-Marshall	____
1962	*Demoniacs, The*	John Dickson Carr	____
1961	*Pale Horse, The*	Agatha Christie	____
1962	*Fugitive, The*	Robert L. Fish	____
1962	*When I Grow Rich*	Joan Fleming	____
1962	*Murder by Proxy*	Brett Halliday	____
1959	*Bronze Perseus, The (The Tender Killer)*	S.B. Hough	____
1962	*We Have Always Lived in the Castle*	Shirley Jackson	____
1961	*Spoilt Kill, The*	Mary Kelly	____
1962	*Zebra–Striped Hearse, The*	Ross Macdonald	____
1962	*Cormorant's Isle*	Allan MacKinnon	____
1961	*Séance (Séance on a Wet Afternoon)*	Mark McShane	____
1962	*How Like an Angel*	Margaret Millar	____
1962	*Plain Man, The (The Killing of Francie Lake)*	Julian Symons	____
1961	*Chinese Nail Murders, The*	Robert van Gulik	____
1962	*361*	Donald E. Westlake	____
1962	*Perfect Pigeon*	Richard Wormser	____

1962	*Five Spy Novels* (5 below)	Howard Haycraft, ed.	____
1920	*Great Impersonation, The*	E. Phillips Oppenheim	____
1916	*Greenmantle*	John Buchan	____
1938	*Epitaph for a Spy*	Eric Ambler	____
1942	*No Surrender*	Martha Albrand	____
1958	*No Entry*	Manning Coles	____

Boucher 63 Best

1962	*Light of Day, The*	Eric Ambler	____
1963	*Little Less Than Kind, A*	Charlotte Armstrong	____
1963	*It's Different Abroad*	Henry Calvin	____

1962	*Mirror Crack'd, The (The Mirror Crack'd From Side to Side)*	Agatha Christie	____
1961/63	*Black Sister*	Dagmar Edqvist	____
1962	*Alligator: A Harvard Lampoon Parody*	I*n Fl*m*ng (Michael K. Frith & Christopher B. Cerf)	____
1962	*Love in Amsterdam (Death in Amsterdam)*	Nicolas Freeling	____
1963	*Trouble Makers, The*	Celia Fremlin	____
1962	*Massingham Affair, The*	Edward Grierson	____
1963	*Florentine Finish*	Cornelius Hirschberg	____
1963	*Grudge, The*	Bert & Dolores Hitchens	____
1963	*Expendable Man, The*	Dorothy B. Hughes	____
1962/63	*10:30 From Marseilles, The (The Sleeping Car Murders)*	Sebastien Japrisot	____
1962	*Dead of Summer, The (Due to a Death)*	Mary Kelly	____
1963	*Assassination Bureau, Ltd., The*	Jack London; completed by Robert L. Fish	____
1963	*Most Dangerous Game, The*	Gavin Lyall	____
1963	*Gideon's Ride*	J.J. Marric (John Creasey)	____
1963	*Murder a la Mode*	Patricia Moyes	____
1963	*Player on the Other Side, The*	Ellery Queen (by, Theodore Sturgeon)	____
1963	*Last Tresilians, The*	J.I.M. Steward (Michael Innes)	____
1963	*Neon Haystack, The*	James Michael Ullman	____

Boucher 64 Best

1964	*Kind of Anger, A*	Eric Ambler	____
1927/64	*Max Carrados Mysteries*	Ernest Bramah	____
1963	*Clocks, The*	Agatha Christie	____
1964	*Misty Curtain, The*	Lucy Cores	____
1963	*Question of Loyalty (Gun Before Butter)*	Nicolas Freeling	____
1964	*Frame-Up*	Andrew Garve	____
1963	*Incident at the Merry Hippo, The (The Merry Hippo)*	Elspeth Huxley	____
1964	*Friday the Rabbi Slept Late*	Harry Kemelman	____
1963	*Night of the Generals, The*	Hans Hellmut Kirst	____
1964	*Transcendental Murder, The (The Minuteman Murder)*	Jane Langton	____
1963	*Spy Who Came in From the Cold, The*	John le Carre	____
1964	*Greenmask!*	Elizabeth Linington	____
1964	*Chill, The*	Ross Macdonald	____
1964	*Gideon's Vote*	J.J. Marric (John Creasey)	____
1963	*Burning is a Substitute for Loving*	Jennie Melville	____
1964	*Fiend, The*	Margaret Millar	____
1963/64	*Road to Hell, The*	Hubert Monteilhet	____
1964	*Falling Star*	Patricia Moyes	____

1962	*Five Times Maigret (Omnibus;* 5 below)	Georges Simenon ___
1953/54	*Maigret's Mistake (also in:*	Georges Simenon ___
	Maigret Right and Wrong)	
1954/57	*Maigret Goes to School*	Georges Simenon ___
1958/59	*Maigret has Scruples (also in:*	Georges Simenon ___
	Versus Inspector Maigret)	
1959	*Maigret and the Reluctant Witnesses*	Georges Simenon ___
	(Maigret and the Reluctant Witness;	
	also in: *Versus Inspector Maigret)*	
1951/54	*Maigret in Montmartre (Inspector*	Georges Simenon ___
	Maigret and the Strangled Stripper)	
1955/64	*Accomplices, The* (with: *The Blue Room)*	Georges Simenon ___
1964	*Blue Room, The* (with: *The Accomplices)*	Geroges Simenon ___
1964	*This Rough Magic*	Mary Stewart ___
1964	*Right to Die, A*	Rex Stout ___
1877/63	*Simon Wheeler, Detective (unfinished novel,*	Mark Twain ___
	edited by Franklin R. Rogers,	
	New York Public Library)	

Boucher 65 Best

1964	*Look Three Ways at Murder*	John Creasey ___
1964	*Funeral in Berlin*	Len Deighton ___
1965	*For Kicks*	Dick Francis ___
1965	*Jealous One, The*	Celia Fremlin ___
1964	*Double-Barrel*	Nicolas Freeling ___
1965	*Quiller Memorandum, The*	Adam Hall ___
	(The Berlin Memorandum)	
1965	*Last Known Address, The*	Joseph Harrington ___
1964	*Day the Call Came, The*	Thomas Hinde ___
1965	*Legend of the Seventh Virgin, The*	Victoria Holt ___
1965	*Cunning as a Fox*	Kyle Hunt (as, Michael
		Halliday, John Creasey)
1965	*Expendable Spy, The*	Jack D. Hunter ___
1965	*Strode Venturer, The*	Hammond Innes ___
1964	*Perfect Murder, The*	H.R.F. Keating ___
1965	*Midnight Plus One*	Gavin Lyall ___
1965	*Gideon's Badge*	J.J. Marric (John Creasey) ___
1965	*Far Side of the Dollar, The*	Ross Macdonald ___
1965	*Modesty Blaise*	Peter O'Donnell ___
1965	*Before the Ball was Over (A Season for Death)*	Alexandra Roudybush ___
1964	*Firework for Oliver, A*	John Sanders ___
1965	*Petrovka 38*	Julian Semyonov ___
1965	*Airs Above the Ground*	Mary Stewart ___
1965	*Fugitive Pigeon, The*	Donald E. Westlake ___
195/65	*Bony and the Black Virgin (The Torn Branch)*	Arthur W. Upfield ___

1964	*Maigret Cinq* (5 below)	Georges Simenon	___
1950/58	*Maigret and the Old Lady*	Georges Simenon	___
1949/58	*Maigret's First Case*	Georges Simenon	___
1954/55	*Maigret and the Young Girl (Maigret and the Dead Girl; Inspector Maigret and the Dead Girl)*	Georges Simenon	___
1957	*Maigret's Little Joke (None of Maigret's Business)*	Georges Simenon	___
1951/60	*Maigret Takes a Room (Maigret Rents a Room)*	Georges Simenon	___

Boucher 66 Best

1965	*Hands of Innocence, The*	Jeffrey Ashford	___
1966	*Queer Kind of Death, A*	George Baxt	___
1965	*In a Glass Darkly (Murder Reflected)*	Janet Caird	___
1965	*In Cold Blood: A True Account of a Multiple Murder and Its Consequences*	Truman Capote	___
1965	*At Bertram's Hotel*	Agatha Christie	___
1966	*Gascoyne*	Stanley Crawford	___
1966	*House on Greenapple Road*	Harold R. Daniels	___
1965	*Highland Masquerade (Return to Glenshael)*	Mary Elgin	___
1966	*Windowmaker, The*	M. Fagyas	___
1965	*Odds Against*	Dick Francis	___
1966	*King of the Rainy Country, The*	Nicolas Freeling	___
1966	*Crack in the Teacup, The*	Michael Gilbert	___
1966	*Blind Spot*	Joseph Harrington	___
1963/66	*Death of a Fat God*	H.R.F. Keating	___
1966	*Saturday the Rabbi Went Hungry*	Harry Kemelman	___
1966	*Pedestal, The*	George Lanning	___
1966	*Death Shall Overcome*	Emma Lathen	___
1966	*Black Money*	Ross Macdonald	___
1966	*Killer Dolphin (Death at the Dolphin)*	Ngaio Marsh	___
1966	*Crimson Madness of Little Doom, The*	Mark McShane	___
1966	*Night is a Time for Listening, The*	Elliot West	___
1966	*Spy in the Ointment, The*	Donald E. Westlake	___
1966	*Sunday; and; The Little Man From Archangel* (2 below)	Georges Simenon	___
1958/60	*Sunday*	Georges Simenon	___
1956/57	*Little Man From Archangel*	Georges Simenon	___

Boucher 67 Best

1967	*Most Contagious Game, A*	Catherine Aird	___
1967	*Lemon in the Basket*	Charlotte Armstrong	___
1967	*Parade of Cockeyed Creatures; or Did Someone Murder Our Wandering Boy?, A*	George Baxt	___

1967	*Hochmann Miniatures, The*	Robert L. Fish	___
1966	*Flying Finish*	Dick Francis	___
1967	*Walking Stick, The*	Winston Graham	___
1967	*Tower, The*	P.M. Hubbard	___
1967	*Sly as a Serpent*	Kyle Hunt (as, Michael Halliday, John Creasey)	___
1967	*Murder Against the Grain*	Emma Lathen	___
1967	*Something Wrong*	Elizabeth Linington	___
1967	*Last One Left, The*	John D. MacDonald	___
1967	*Murder Fantastical*	Patricia Moyes	___
1967	*God Save the Mark*	Donald E. Westlake	___

Boucher's List of Important Titles — Novels

Boucher 43 Important

1943	*Up Jumped the Devil (Murder All Over)*	Cleve F. Adams	___
1943	*Night Over the Wood*	Hugh Addis	___
1941	*Traitor's Purse (The Sabotage Murder Mystery)*	Margery Allingham	___
1937	*Background to Danger (Uncommon Danger)*	Eric Ambler	___
1941	*Advance Agent*	John August	___
1939	*Smiler With the Knife, The*	Nicholas Blake	___
1942	*Full Crash Dive (The Submarine Signaled…Murder!; Murder Goes to Sea; Hang and Rattle)*	Allan R. Bosworth	___
1937	*Poirot Loses a Client (Dumb Witness)*	Agatha Christie	___
1938	*Death in Five Boxes*	Carter Dickson	___
1939	*Bigger They Come, The (Lam to the Slaughter)*	A.A. Fair (Erle Stanley Gardner)	___
1929	*Dain Curse, The*	Dashiell Hammett	___
1931	*Glass Key, The*	Dashiell Hammett	___
1930	*Maltese Falcon, The*	Dashiell Hammett	___
1929	*Red Harvest*	Dashiell Hammett	___
1934	*Thin Man, The*	Dashiell Hammett	___
1941	*Taste for Honey, A (A Taste for Murder)*	H.F. Heard	___
1942	*Fallen Sparrow, The*	Dorothy B. Hughes	___
1940	*Secret Vanguard, The*	Michael Innes	___
1943	*Weight of the Evidence, The*	Michael Innes	___
1943	*Blind Man's Bluff*	Baynard Kendrick	___
1932	*Valcour Meets Murder*	Rufus King	___
1938	*Dead Don't Care, The*	Jonathan Latimer	___
1913	*Lodger, The*	Marie Belloc Lowndes	___
1921/30	*Master of the Day of Judgment, The*	Leo Perutz	___
1942	*Calamity Town*	Ellery Queen	___
1932	*Egyptian Cross Mystery, The*	Ellery Queen	___
1943	*There was an Old Woman (The Quick and the Dead)*	Ellery Queen	___

1934	*Nine Tailors, The*	Dorothy L. Sayers	___
1943	*"X" Marks the Dot*	Muriel Stafford	___
1937	*Red Box, The (Case of the Red Box; in, The Nero Wolfe Omnibus)*	Rex Stout	___
1941	*Terror, The* (3 below)	Dorothy B. Hughes	___
1940	*So Blue Marble, The*	Dorothy B. Hughes	___
1940	*Cross-Eyed Bear, The (The Crossed-Eyed Bear Murders)*	Dorothy B. Hughes	___
1941	*Bamboo Blonde, The*	Dorothy B. Hughes	___

Boucher 44 Important

1944	*Avalanche*	Kay Boyle	___
1943	*See What I Mean*	Lewis Browne	___
1935	*Three Coffins, The (The Hollow Man)*	John Dickson Carr	___
1944	*Great Bustard and Other People, The: Containing: How to Tell Your Friends from the Apes and How to Become Extinct* (2 books)	Will Cuppy	___
1926	*Payment Deferred*	C.S. Forester	___
1934	*Murder of My Aunt, The*	Richard Hull	___
1942	*Phantom Lady*	William Irish (Cornell Woolrich)	___
1938	*Death From a Top Hat*	Clayton Rawson	___
1932	*Vicar's Experiments, The (Clerical Error)*	Anthony Rolls	___
1931	*Five Red Herrings, The (Suspicious Characters)*	Dorothy L Sayers	___
1944	*Jethro Hammer*	Michael Venning (Rice, Craig)	___
1892	*Big Bow Mystery, The*	Israel Zangwill	___

Boucher 45 Important

1942	*No Surrender*	Martha Albrand	___
1939	*Coffin for Dimitrios, A (The Mask of Dimitrios)*	Eric Ambler	___
1939	*Murder in Stained Glass*	Margaret Armstrong	___
1939	*Big Sleep, The*	Raymond Chandler	___
1939	*Rogue Male (Man Hunt)*	Geoffrey Household	___
1941	*Above Suspicion*	Helen MacInnes	___
1939	*Escape*	Ethel Vance	___

Boucher 46 Important

1929	*Poisoned Chocolates Case, The*	Anthony Berkeley	___
1926	*Murder of Roger Ackroyd, The*	Agatha Christie	___
1910	*At the Villa Rose*	A.E.W. Mason	___
1928	*Prisoner in the Opal, The*	A.E.W. Mason	___
1946	*Deadly Weapon*	Wade Miller	___

Boucher 48 Important

| 1938 | *Brighton Rock* | Graham Greene | ___ |

Boucher 49 Important

1949	*Drop Dead*	George Bagby (Aaron Marc Stein)	___
1949	*Deed is Drawn, The*	Willetta Barber & R.F. Schabelitz	___
1948	*Death on the Last Train*	George Bellairs	___
1949	*Private Killing, A*	James Benet	___
1949	*Murder is Contagious*	Marion Bramhall	___
1949	*Leaden Bubble, The*	H.C. Branson	___
1949	*Shadow of a Hero*	Allan Chase	___
1948	*Buried for Pleasure*	Edmund Crispin	___
1949	*Man Who Covered Mirrors, The*	Marten Cumberland	___
1949	*Policeman's Nightmare*	Marten Cumberland	___
1949	*Judas Cat, The*	Dorothy Salisbury Davis	___
1949	*Before I Wake*	Hal Debrett (Brett Halliday)	___
1949	*Family Skeleton*	Doris Miles Disney	___
1949	*Plunder of the Sun*	David Dodge	___
1949	*Give Up the Ghost*	Margaret Erskine	___
1949	*Date with Death (Shot in the Dark)*	Leslie Ford	___
1949	*Chord in Crimson*	Gale Gallagher	___
1948	*Blue Ice, The*	Hammond Innes	___
1947	*Killer Mine, The (Run by Night)*	Hammond Innes	___
1949	*Diplomatic Incident, A*	Judith Kelly	___
1949	*Madame Baltimore (Baltimore Madame)*	Helen Knowland	___
1949	*Walk the Dark Streets*	William Krasner	___
1949	*Duet of Death (Duet in Death; 2 novelettes; Death has Four Hands; The Bleeding House; The House)*	Hilda Lawrence	___
1949	*Shadow and the Blot, The*	N.D. & G.G. Lobell	___
1949	*Spin Your Web, Lady!*	Frances & Richard Lockridge	___
1949	*Matter of Taste, A*	Richard Lockridge	___
1949	*Some Like 'Em Shot*	Fred Malina	___
1949	*Cannibal Heart, The*	Margaret Millar	___
1949	*Viewless Winds, The*	Murray C. Morgan	___
1949	*Cat Wears a Mask*	D.B. Olsen	___
1949	*Body, The*	William Sansom	___
1949	*Gilbert's Last Toothache (For the Love of Murder)*	Margaret Scherf	___
1949	*Three Fears, The*	Jonathan Stagge	___
1949	*Dead Sure*	Stewart Sterling	___
1949	*Nothing More than Murder*	Jim Thompson	___
1949	*Murder at Drake's Anchorage*	E. Lee Waddell	___

Boucher 50 Important

1950	*Bullet for My Love, A*	Octavus Roy Cohen	___
1949	*Fatal Finale*	Paul H. Dobbins	___
1864	*Uncle Silas*	J. Sheridan Le Fanu	___

1950	*Causeway to the Past*	William O'Farrell	____
1950	*Something About Midnight*	D.B. Olsen	____
1949	*So Many Doors*	E.R. Punshon	____
1950	*And When She was Bad She was Murdered*	Richard Starnes	____

Boucher 51 Important
| 1951 | *Cure It with Honey (I'll Get Mine)* | Thurston Scott | ____ |

Boucher 52 Important
1951	*Dark Omnibus, The* (3 below)	Peter Cheyney	____
1951	*Stars are Dark, The*	Peter Cheyney	____
1951	*Dark Street*	Peter Cheyney	____
1951	*Sinister Errand*	Peter Cheyney	____

Boucher 53 Important
1953	*Trent's Case Book*	E.C. Bentley	____
1940	*Toast of Tomorrow, A (Pray Silence)*	Manning Coles	____
1870	*Mystery of Edwin Drood, The (Starrett, ed.)*	Charles Dickens	____
1938	*Listening House, The*	Mabel Seeley	____
1929	*Man in the Queue, The (Killer in the Crowd)*	Josephine Tey (Gordon Daviot)	____

Boucher 54 Important
1930	*Plain Murder*	C.S. Forester	____
1954	*Act of Violence*	Basil Heatter	____
1953	*Silent Women, The*	Margaret Page Hood	____
1952	*Thieves' Hole (Group Flashing Two)*	David Howarth	____
1954	*Go, Lovely Rose*	Jean Potts	____
1938	*Dead and Not Buried*	H.F.M. Prescott	____
1954	*Storm Fear*	Clinton Seeley	____
1954	*Flaw in the Crystal, The*	Godfrey Smith	____
1953	*Diamonds for Danger (Diamonds for Moscow)*	David Walker	____
1954	*To Find a Killer (Before I Die!)*	Lionel White	____
1954	*Three by Tey* (3 below)	Josephine Tey	____
1946	*Miss Pym Disposes*	Josephine Tey	____
1948	*Franchise Affair, The*	Josephine Tey	____
1949	*Brat Farrar (Come and Kill Me)*	Josephine Tey	____

Boucher 55 Important
1955	*Life and Death of a Tough Guy (Teen-Age Mobster)*	Benjamin Appel	____
1938	*Crooked Hinge, The*	John Dickson Carr	____
1948	*Witness for the Prosecution*	Agatha Christie	____
1955	*In His Blood*	Harold R. Daniels	____
1954	*Perfectionist, The (Kill the Beloved)*	Lane Kauffmann	____
1933	*Information Received*	E.R. Punshon	____
1955	*Man Who Paid His Way, The*	Walter Sheldon	____

1929	*How Like a God*	Rex Stout	___
1950	*Murdering Mr. Velfrage (Maid to Murder)*	Roy Vickers	___
1952	*Don Among the Dead Men*	C.E. Vulliamy	___
1955	*Circumstances Beyond Control (Network of Fear)*	Alvin Yudkoff	___
1948	*Full House (Nero Wolfe Omnibus; 3 below)*	Rex Stout	___
1935	*League of Frightened Men, The*	Rex Stout	___
1948	*And Be a Villain (More Deaths Than One)*	Rex Stout	___
1951	*Curtains for Three*	Rex Stout	___

Boucher 56 Important

1956	*Ninth Hour, The*	Ben Benson	___
1956	*Matter of Fact, A (Collar for the Killer; Dead Sure)*	Herbert Brean	___
1956	*Morgue for Venus*	Jonathan Craig	___
1956	*Beauty Queen Killer, The (A Beauty for Inspector West; So Young, So Cold, So Fair)*	John Creasey	___
1955	*Gelignite Gang, The (Inspector West Makes Haste)*	John Creasey	___
1956	*Unappointed Rounds (The Post Office Case)*	Doris Miles Disney	___
1956	*One-Way Ticket*	Bert & Dolores Hitchens	___
1956	*Prowl Cop*	Gregory Jones	___
1956	*Murder of Eleanor Pope, The*	Henry Kuttner	___
1956	*Dragnet: Case No. 561 (Case No. 561: Dragnet)*	David Knight (Richard S. Prather)	___
1956	*Gideon's Week*	J.J. Marric (John Creasey)	___
1956	*Seven File, The (Chicago-7)*	William P. McGivern	___
1956	*Ripper, The (I Will Speak Daggers; The Ripper Murders)*	Maurice Procter	___
1956	*Dead Right (The Hotel Murders)*	Stewart Sterling	___
1956	*Dark Window, The*	Thomas Walsh	___

Boucher 59 Important

1959	*Dame, The*	Carter Brown	___
1959	*Terror Comes Creeping*	Carter Brown	___
1959	*Late Lamented, The*	Fredric Brown	___
1956	*Fear is the Same*	Carter Dickson	___
1934	*Plague Court Murders, The*	Carter Dickson	___
1957	*Trouble at Saxby's, The (Find Inspector West)*	John Creasey	___
1959	*Did She Fall or Was She Pushed?*	Doris Miles Disney	___
1959	*Pass the Gravy*	A.A. Fair (Erle Stanley Gardner)	___
1959	*Mark Kilby Solves a Murder (R.I.S.C.; The Timid Tycoon)*	Robert Caine Frazer (John Creasey)	___
1959	*Case of the Singing Skirt, The*	Erle Stanley Gardner	___
1959	*Come Die With Me*	William Campbell Gault	___
1959	*Prelude to Murder (Third Crime Lucky)*	Anthony Gilbert	___
1935	*Keep It Quiet*	Richard Hull	___

1959	*Hare Sitting Up*	Michael Innes	____
1959	*List of Adrian Messenger, The*	Philip MacDonald	____
1959	*Galton Case, The*	Ross Macdonald (John Ross Macdonald)	____
1959	*Gideon's Staff*	J.J. Marric (John Creasey)	____
1959	*Walking Shadow*	Lenore Glen Offord	____
1959	*Double in Trouble*	Richard S. Prather & Stephen Marlowe	____
1958	*Man in Ambush*	Maurice Procter	____
1959	*Girl With No Place to Hide*	Nick Quarry (Marvin H. Albert)	____
1959	*Shadow of Guilt*	Patrick Quentin	____
1959	*Exit, Running*	Bart Spicer	____
1959	*Plot It Yourself (Murder in Style)*	Rex Stout	____

Boucher 60 Important

1959	*Way Back, The (A Way Back)*	James Mitchell	____
1960	*Midsummer's Nightmare*	Elizabeth Shenkin	____
1960	*Man in the Cage, The*	John Holbrook Vance (Jack Vance)	____
1960	*Mercenaries, The (The Smashers)*	Donald E. Westlake	____

Boucher 62 Important

1962	*Counterweight*	Daniel Broun	____
1961	*Wake in Fright*	Kenneth Cook	____
1962	*Quarry, The*	Friedrich Dürrenmatt	____
1962	*Little Treachery, A*	Phyllis Paul	____
1961	*Twig is Bent, A*	Estelle Thompson	____

Boucher 63 Important

1963	*Charlie Sent Me!*	Carter Brown	____
1915	*Thirty-Nine Steps, The*	John Buchan	____
1928	*Ashenden; or, The British Agent*	W. Somerset Maugham	____
1963	*Wife or Death*	Ellery Queen	____
1963	*Mother Hunt, The*	Rex Stout	____
1931/33	*Maigret and the Hundred Gibbets (The Crime of Inspector Maigret)*	Georges Simenon	____
1931/34	*Maigret Meets a Milord (The Crime at Lock 14)*	Georges Simenon	____
1931/33	*Maigret Stonewalled (The Death of Monsieur Gallet)*	Georges Simenon	____
1937	*Octagon House*	Phoebe Atwood Taylor	____
1962	*Hopjoy Was Here*	Colin Watson	____
1963	*Three For Midnight* (3 novels; below)	Philip MacDonald	____
1924	*Rasp, The*	Philip MacDonald	____
1931	*Murder Gone Mad*	Philip MacDonald	____
1930	*Rynox Murder, The (The Rynox Murder Mystery; The Rynox Mystery; Rynox)*	Philip MacDonald	____

Boucher 64 Important

1964	*Night Light*	Marie Bardos	___
1964	*Murder at Midnight (The Winds of Midnight)*	John Blackburn	___
1953	*Knife for the Juggler, A (The Vengeance Man)*	Manning Coles	___
1964	*In the Last Analysis*	Amanda Cross	___
1964	*Whirligig of Time, The*	Dola de Jong	___
1964	*Is There a Traitor in the House?*	Patricia McGerr	___
1964	*Bank Job*	Thomas B. Reagan	___
1964	*Long White Night, The*	Katherine Scherman	___
1964	*Real Serendipitous Kill, The*	Hampton Stone (Aaron Marc Stein)	___
1964	*Mantis and the Moth, The (A Crowded Loneliness)*	Max Weatherly	___
1964	*Grave-Maker's House, The*	Rubin Weber	___

Boucher 65 Important

1965	*Mind Readers, The* (note: S.F. novel)	Margery Allingham	___
1965	*Winds of April, The*	I.D. Baharav	___
1965	*In the Heat of the Night*	John Ball	___
1965	*Wreath of Roses, A (Ring of Roses)*	John Blackburn	___
1965	*Coffin in Malta*	Gwendoline Butler	___
1965	*Chinese Visitor, The*	James Eastwood	___
1965	*Man From the Mist, A (Visibility Nil)*	Mary Elgin	___
1965	*Understrike*	John Gardner	___
1965	*Voice, The (Knock, Knock, Who's There?)*	Anthony Gilbert	___
1965	*Waiting for a Tiger*	Ben Healey	___
1965	*Month of the Pearl , The*	Philip Jones	___
1965	*French Doll, The*	Vincent McConnor	___
1965	*Hound's Tooth, The*	Robert McDowell	___
1965	*Thicker than Water*	Madeleine Polland	___
1965	*From Doon With Death*	Ruth Rendell	___
1965	*Grave Danger*	Kelley Roos	___
1965	*Game of X, The*	Robert Sheckley	___
1960/65	*It Can't Always Be Caviar (The Monte Cristo Cover-Up)*	Johannes Mario Simmel	___

Boucher 66 Important

1966	*Magic Grandfather, The (Mask of Evil)*	Doris Miles Disney	___
1966	*Midnight Hag*	Joan Fleming	___
1966	*Betrayers, The*	Donald Hamilton	___
1929	*Murder by the Clock*	Rufus King	___
1966	*Rogue Running*	Maurice Procter	___
1966	*Burned Man, The*	Bart Spicer	___
1966	*Venus Trap, The (House of Cards)*	James Michael Ullman	___
1966	*Shepherd File, The*	Conrad Voss Bark	___

Boucher 67 Important

1907	*Red Thumb Mark, The*	R. Austin Freeman	____
1967	*Very Quiet Place, A*	Andrew Garve	____
1966/67	*Lady in the Car with Glasses and a Gun, The*	Sebastien Japrisot	____
1967	*Where Eagles Dare*	Alistair MacLean	____
1967	*Dead Woman of the Year*	Hugh Pentecost	____
1967	*Black is the Colour of My True-Love's Heart*	Ellis Peters	____
1967	*Exercise Hoodwink*	Maurice Procter	____
1967	*Who Saw Maggie Brown?*	Kelley Roos	____
1967	*Death of a Moral Person*	Alexandra Roudybush	____
1932/40	*Maigret Goes Home (The Saint-Fiacre Affair; in, Maigret Keeps a Rendezvous)*	Georges Simenon	____
1967	*Delta Factor, The*	Mickey Spillane	____
1967	*Rare Coin Score, The*	Richard Stark (Donald E. Westlake)	____

[Editor's note: Anthony Boucher died of lung cancer on April 30, 1968. The titles below were taken from his reviews January 7, 1968 through April 21, 1968 and are suggestions of what he felt were important books for the year up until that point. We can only guess that some of these would have made his Best list for the year if he had lived.]

Boucher 68 Important

1967	*Crystal Crow, The (The Ribs of Death)*	Joan Aiken	____
1967	*Swing Low, Sweet Harriet*	George Baxt	____
1968	*Topsy and Evil*	George Baxt	____
1967	*Case in Nullity, A (A Hidden Malice)*	Evelyn Berckman	____
1968	*Private Wound, The*	Nicholas Blake	____
1967	*Until Temptation Do Us Part*	Carter Brown	____
1968	*Cool Man, The*	W.R. Burnett	____
1968	*Murder Among Children*	Tucker Coe (Donald E. Westlake)	____
1968	*Money for the Taking*	Doris Miles Disney	____
1964	*Welcome, Proud Lady*	June Drummond	____
1968	*Lucifer Cell, The*	William Fennerton	____
1968	*Disturbance on Berry Hill*	Elizabeth Fenwick	____
1968	*Malice Domestic*	Rae Foley	____
1967	*Blood Sport*	Dick Francis	____
1968	*Case of the Careless Cupid, The*	Erle Stanley Gardner	____
1967	*Too Many Magicians* (note: S.F. novel)	Randall Garrett	____
1967	*Overdrive (The Dust and the Heat)*	Michael Gilbert	____
1964	*No Way to Treat a Lady*	William Goldman (Harry Longbaugh)	____
1967	*Mermaid on the Rocks*	Brett Halliday (by Robert Terrall)	____
1968	*Menacers, The*	Donald Hamilton	____
1968	*House Above Hollywood*	Velda Johnston	____

1966	*Unholy Trio (Devil to Pay; Better Wed than Dead)*	Henry Kane	___
1968	*Caught in the Act*	John Lee	
1966	*One Fearful Yellow Eye*	John D. MacDonald	___
1968	*Pale Gray for Guilt*	John D MacDonald	___
1968	*Instant Enemy, The*	Ross Macdonald	___
1968	*Ill Met By a Fish Shop on George Street*	Mark McShane	___
1968	*Big Dig, The*	Slater McGurk	___
1967	*Trash Stealer, The*	Jean Potts	___
1968	*House of Brass, The*	Ellery Queen (by, Avram Davidson)	___
1955/67	*Maigret and the Headless Corpse*	Georges Simenon	___
1967	*Last Best Friend, The*	George Sims	___
1967	*I was Following This Girl*	Desmond Skirrow	___
1967	*My Grand Enemy*	Jean Stubbs	___
1967	*Orange Wednesday*	Leslie Thomas	___
1958	*Coffin, Scarcely Used*	Colin Watson	___

In the May issue of *Good Housekeeping* magazine (GH), Ellery Queen (Frederic Dannay), a supreme authority on the detective short story, offered his "Golden Ten" books of stories. Anthony Boucher presented the list in his San Francisco newspaper column on May 28, 1944. Boucher pointed out that up until the 1920s the short story was the best detective writing. After that, the novel dominated. Boucher stated that he would rather offer *The Singing Bone* by Freeman (1912) and that the list could be stretched to eleven and include *Prince Zaleski* by M.P. Shiel (1895). He then offered a "Silver 13" list to cover the quarter century since that list closed.

Boucher GH 44

1919	*Call Mr. Fortune*	H.C. Bailey	___
1914	*Max Carrados*	Ernest Bramah	___
1911	*Innocence of Father Brown, The*	G.K. Chesterton	___
1892	*Adventures of Sherlock Holmes, The*	Arthur Conan Doyle	___
1909	*John Thorndyke's Cases (Dr. Thorndyke's Cases)*	R. Austin Freeman	___
1910	*Achievements of Luther Trant, The*	William MacHarg & Edwin Balmer	___
1894	*Martin Hewitt, Investigator*	Arthur Morrison	___
1909	*Old Man in the Corner, The (The Man in the Corner)*	Baroness Orczy	___
1845	*Tales*	Edgar Allan Poe	___
1918	*Uncle Abner, Master of Mysteries*	Melville Davisson Post	___

Boucher GH add 44

1912	*Singing Bone, The (The Adventures of Dr. Thorndyke)*	R. Austin Freeman	___
1895	*Prince Zaleski*	M P. Shiel	___

Boucher Silver List 44

1937	*Mr. Campion: Criminologist (including: "Case of the Late Pig, The")*	Margery Allingham	____
1938	*Trent Intervenes*	E.C. Bentley	____
1944	*Five Murderers*	Raymond Chandler	____
1932	*Thirteen Problems, The (The Tuesday Club Murders)*	Agatha Christie	____
1940	*Department of Queer Complaints, The*	Carter Dickson	____
1944	*Adventures of Sam Spade and Other Stories, The (They Can Only Hang You Once)*	Dashiell Hammett	____
1943	*I Wouldn't Be in Your Shoes*	William Irish (Cornell Woolrich)	____
1931	*Solange Stories, The*	F. Tennyson Jesse	____
1940	*New Adventures of Ellery Queen, The*	Ellery Queen	____
1933	*Hangman's Holiday*	Dorothy L. Sayers	____
1932	*13 Culprits, The (Les 13 Coupables)*	Georges Simenon	____
1929	*Clues of the Caribbees (Clues of the Caribees)*	T.S. Stribling	____
1925	*Mind of Mr. J.G. Reeder, The (The Murder Book of J.G. Reeder)*	Edgar Wallace	____

In their June issue, *Good Housekeeping* magazine (GH) offered "The Ten Most Important Detective Novels." Boucher posted it in his June 25, 1944 column. The list was offered for historical importance of the mystery-detective novels, with an emphasis on "firsts" rather than "bests." Boucher offered two dissents: R. Austin Freeman's *Mr. Pottermack's Oversight* (1930) rather than *Before the Fact* by Frances Iles. Also, he called for Dorothy L. Sayers' *The Nine Tailors* (1934) over *The Benson Murder Case* by S.S. Van Dine.

Boucher GH Detective 44

1913	*Trent's Last Case (The Woman in Black)*	E.C. Bentley	____
1926	*Murder of Roger Ackroyd, The*	Agatha Christie	____
1868	*Moonstone, The*	Wilkie Collins	____
1920	*Cask, The*	Freeman Wills Crofts	____
1887	*Study in Scarlet, A*	Arthur Conan Doyle	____
1866	*Widow Lerouge, The (Lerouge Case)*	Emile Gaboriau	___
1878	*Leavenworth Case, The*	Anna Katharine Green	____
1930	*Maltese Falcon, The*	Dashiell Hammett	____
1932	*Before the Fact*	Francis Iles	____
1926	*Benson Murder Case, The*	S.S. Van Dine	____

Boucher GH Detective add 44

1930	*Mr. Pottermack's Oversight*	R. Austin Freeman	____
1934	*Nine Tailors, The*	Dorothy L. Sayers	____

Bouchercon Panel
The Essentials of Mystery:
Creating a Mystery List From 1950 - 2000

At the 2006 Bouchercon conference in Madison, WI, a panel ("The Essentials of Mystery: Creating a Mystery List from 1950-2000") undertook the task to discuss the "Important" or "Best" novels between 1950 and 2000. Serving on the panel were Susan Oleksiw (M), Jim Huang, Al Hubin, Marv Lachman, and Roger M. Sobin. The lists below were a part of the handout to those present and represent some of the thinking for that forum.

Marv Lachman Important ("Best") Books 1950 – 1969		
1950	*Smallbone Deceased*	Michael Gilbert	___
1950	*Drowning Pool, The*	Ross Macdonald	___
1951	*Far Cry, The*	Fredric Brown	___
1951	*Daughter of Time, The*	Josephine Tey	___
1952	*Death Has Deep Roots*	Michael Gilbert	___
1952	*Something to Hide (Fingers of Fear)*	Philip MacDonald	___
1952	*Vanish In an Instant*	Margaret Millar	___
1952	*Last Seen Wearing*	Hillary Waugh	___
1953	*Someone Like You*	Roald Dahl	___
1953	*Kiss Before Dying, A*	Ira Levin	___
1955	*Enormous Shadow, The*	Robert Harling	___
1955	*Beast n View*	Margaret Millar	___
1955	*Dying Fall, A*	Henry Wade	___
1956	*Dram of Poison, A*	Charlotte Armstrong	___
1956	*Lenient Beast, The*	Fredric Brown	___
1956	*Mystery Stories (Quiet Horror)*	Stanley Ellin	___
1957	*Convertible Hearse, The*	William Campbell Gault	___
1957	*Room to Swing*	Ed Lacy	___
1957	*Odds Against Tomorrow*	William P. McGivern	___
1957	*Bunny Lake is Missing*	Evelyn Piper	___
1957	*Midnight Plumber, The*	Maurice Procter	___
1959	*No Next of Kin*	Doris Miles Disney	___
1959	*Dead Men Don't Ski*	Patricia Moyes	___
1960	*Heckler, The*	Ed McBain	___
1960	*Stranger in My Grave, A*	Margaret Millar	___
1961	*Gideon's Fire*	J.J. Marric (John Creasey)	___
1962	*Burden of Proof, The*	Jeffrey Ashford	___
1962	*Name of the Game is Death, The (Operation Overkill)*	Dan J. Marlowe	___
1963	*It's Different Abroad*	Henry Calvin	___
1963	*Fifth Passenger, The*	Edward Young	___
1964	*Nerve*	Dick Francis	___

1964	*Friday the Rabbi Slept Late*	Harry Kemelman	____
1964	*Chill, The*	Ross Macdonald	____
1964	*From Doon with Death*	Ruth Rendell	____
1965	*For Kicks*	Dick Francis	____
1965	*Odds Against*	Dick Francis	____
1965	*Fidelio Score, The*	Gerald Sinstadt	____
1966	*Religious Body, The*	Catherine Aird	____
1966	*Incredible Schlock Homes, The*	Robert L. Fish	____
1967	*Blood Sport*	Dick Francis	____
1967	*Murder Against The Grain*	Emma Lathen	____
1969	*Ascent of D-13, The*	Andrew Garve	____
1969	*Game Without Rules*	Michael Gilbert	____

Marv Lachman Important ("Best") Books 1970-1979

1970	*Late Phoenix, A*	Catherine Aird	____
1970	*Wobble to Death*	Peter Lovesey	____
1971	*Fly on the Wall, The*	Tony Hillerman	____
1971	*Ask the Right Question*	Michael Z. Lewin	____
1972	*Smokescreen*	Dick Francis	____
1972	*Unsuitable Job for a Woman, An*	P.D. James	____
1973	*Dance Hall of the Dead*	Tony Hillerman	____
1973	*Undercurrent*	Bill Pronzini	____
1974	*Death of an Old Goat*	Robert Barnard	____
1974	*Lester Affair, The (The File on Lester)*	Andrew Garve	____
1974	*God Save the Child*	Robert B. Parker	____
1975	*Curtain*	Agatha Christie	____
1975	*Tell Them What's-Her-NameCalled*	Mildred Davis	____
1975	*High Stakes*	Dick Francis	____
1976	*Sleeping Murder*	Agatha Christie	____
1977	*Enemy, The*	Desmond Bagley	____
1977	*Fan, The*	Bob Randall	____
1978	*Counterstroke*	Andrew Garve	____
1978	*Sting of the Honeybee*	Frank Parrish	____
1978	*Death in the Morning (Death and the Maiden)*	Sheila Radley	____

Jim Huang — Enduring Favorites from the 1980s and 1990s

1981	*Thus Was Adonis Murdered*	Sarah Caudwell	____
1984	*Briarpatch*	Ross Thomas	____
1987	*Monkey's Raincoat, The*	Robert Crais	____
1988	*Silence of the Lambs, The*	Thomas Harris	____
1989	*Black Cherry Blues*	James Lee Burke	____
1989	*Skin Tight*	Carl Hiaasen	____
1991	*Scandal in Belgravia, A*	Robert Barnard	____
1992	*Aunt Dimity's Death*	Nancy Atherton	____
1992	*Booked to Die*	John Dunning	____

1992	*Ice House, The*	Minette Walters	____
1994	*Yellow Room Conspiracy, The*	Peter Dickinson	____
1994	*Beekeeper's Apprentice, The*	Laurie R. King	____
1995	*Breakheart Hill*	Thomas H. Cook	____
1995	*Vanishing Act*	Thomas Perry	____
1995	*Concourse*	S.J. Rozan	____
1996	*Bloodhounds*	Peter Lovesey	____
1997	*Devil in Music, The*	Kate Ross	____
1998	*One False Move*	Harlan Coben	____
1998	*Iron Lake*	William Kent Krueger	____
1998	*Ax, The (Axe, The)*	Donald E. Westlake	____

Bouchercon Panel Editor's Picks—Favorite Mysteries

At the 2005 Bouchercon Conference in Chicago, six mystery magazine editors talked about their favorite mysteries on a panel: We Read Before We Write, Mystery Magazine Editors Talk About Their Favorite Mysteries. They each offered titles of: Recent Favorites, Classic Novels, and Little-known Author/Title selections. There are 49 titles dating from 1905 to 2005.

George Easter	editor, *Deadly Pleasures Mystery Magazine*	(deadlypleasures.com)
Jon Jordan	editor, *Crimespree Magazine*	(crimespreemag. Com)
Kate Stine	editor, *Mystery Scene*	(mysteryscenemag.com)
Lynn Kaczmarek	editor, *Mystery News*	(blackravenpress.com)
Janet Rudolph	editor, *Mystery Readers Journal*	(mysteryreaders.org)
Andrew Gulli	editor, *The Strand Magazine*	(strandmag.com)

2005	*Down the Rabbit Hole (YA novel)*	Peter Abrahams	____
2004	*Case Histories*	Kate Atkinson	____
1913	*Trent's Last Case (The Woman in Black)*	E.C. Bentley	____
2005	*Lifeless*	Mark Billingham	____
2005	*Heist, The*	Michael A. Black	____
1938	*Beast Must Die, The*	Nicholas Blake	____
2003	*Monsieur Pamplemousse Hits the Headlines*	Michael Bond	____
2002	*Blitz*	Ken Bruen	____
2005	*Bloodlines*	Jan Burke	____
2003	*Voice of the Violin*	Andrea Camilleri	____
1992	*Dark Chant in a Crimson Key*	George C. Chesbro	____
2005	*Asti Spumante Code*	Toby Clements	____
2004	*Road to Purgatory*	Max Allan Collins	____
2005	*Lincoln Lawyer, The*	Michael Connelly	____
1979	*Tales of the Unexpected*	Roald Dahl	____
2003	*Hard Rain*	Barry Eisler	____
1979	*Specialty of the House and Other Stories*	Stanley Ellin	____
2005	*Blood Knot*	John Galligan	____
2003	*December Heat*	Luis Alfred Garcia-Roza	____
2005	*With No One as Witness*	Elizabeth George	____
2005	*Tilt-a-Whirl*	Chris Grabenstein	____
1970	*Blessing Way, The*	Tony Hillerman	____
2001	*Seldom Disappointed: A Memoir (nonfiction)*	Tony Hillerman	____
2004	*Skeleton Man, The*	Tony Hillerman	____
2004	*Program, The*	Gregg Hurwitz	____
1972	*Unsuitable Job for a Woman, An*	P.D. James	____
2005	*Good Day to Die, A*	Simon Kernick	____
2005	*Last Refuge, The*	Chris Knopf	____
2004	*Whiskey Sour*	J.A. Konrath	____

2005	*Motive, The*	John Lescroart	___
2004	*Dearly Devoted Dexter*	Jeff Lindsay	___
2002	*Diamond Dust*	Peter Lovesey	___
1999	*Firemaker, The*	Peter May	___
2004	*Hardboiled and High Heeled:*	Linda Mizejewski	___
	The Detective in Popular Culture (nonfiction)		
2003	*Rumpole and the Primrose Path*	John Mortimer	___
2005	*Cinnamon Kiss*	Walter Mosley	___
1980	*Pew Group, The*	Anthony Oliver	___
1905	*Scarlet Pimpernel, The*	Baroness Orczy	___
2005	*Serpent on the Crown, The*	Elizabeth Peters	___
2000	*Ice Harvest, The*	Scott Phillips	___
1989	*Down in the Valley*	David M. Pierce	___
1935	*Gaudy Night*	Dorothy L. Sayers	___
2004	*First Drop*	Zoe Sharp	___
2005	*Busted Flush*	Brad Smith	___
2005	*Murder of a Smart Cookie*	Denise Swanson	___
2003	*O' Artful Death*	Sarah Stewart Taylor	___
2005	*Dead Run*	P.J. Tracy	___
2005	*Pardonable Lies*	Jacqueline Winspear	___
1985	*Suspect, The*	L.R. Wright	___

Favorite Mysteries — 2004

At the 2004 Bouchercon conference in Toronto, five mystery magazine editors and one newspaper columnist talked about their favorite mysteries on the panel All-Nighters: Books You Can't Put Down. They each offered titles of Recent Favorites, Classic Novels, Little-known Author/Title, and Reserve List selections. There are 101 titles dating from 1935 to 2004.

George Easter	editor, *Deadly Pleasures Mystery Magazine* (deadlypleasures.com)
Jim Huang	editor, *The Drood Review* (droodreview.com)
Kate Stine	editor, *Mystery Scene* (mysteryscenemag.com)
Lynn Kaczmarek	editor, *Mystery News* (blackravenpress.com)
Oline H. Cogdill	Mystery Columnist (The South Florida Sun-Sentinel)
Chris Aldrich	editor, *Mystery News* (blackravenpress.com)

2004	*Echo Bay*	Richard Barre	___
1992	*Agatha Raisin and the Quiche of Death*	M.C. Beaton	___
1998	*Contrary Blues, The*	John Billheimer	___
2001	*Forty Words for Sorrow*	Giles Blunt	___
2001	*Guards, The*	Ken Bruen	___
1981	*Thus was Adonis Murdered*	Sarah Caudwell	___
2004	*Enemy, The*	Lee Child	___
2001	*Last Kashmiri Rose, The*	Barbara Cleverly	___
1999	*Final Detail, The*	Harlan Coben	___
1992	*Black Echo, The*	Michael Connelly	___

1994	*Concrete Blonde, The*	Michael Connelly	___
1995	*Last Coyote, The*	Michael Connelly	___
1996	*Poet, The*	Michael Connelly	___
2000	*Dark Hollow*	John Connolly	___
1999	*L.A. Requiem*	Robert Crais	___
1997	*Dreaming of the Bones*	Deborah Crombie	___
2002	*White Male Infant*	Barbara D'Amato	___
2000	*Ode to a Banker*	Lindsey Davis	___
2003	*Devil's Hearth, The*	Philip DePoy	___
1993	*Dying of the Light, The*	Michael Dibdin	___
1983	*Hindsight*	Peter Dickinson	___
2001	*Grandmother Spider*	James Doss	___
1999	*Night Visitor, The*	James Doss	___
2004	*Witch's Tongue, The*	James Doss	___
2003	*Hard Rain*	Barry Eisler	___
2004	*Alone at Night*	K.J. Erickson	___
2004	*Perfect Sax*	Jerrilyn Farmer	___
2003	*Tribeca Blues*	Jim Fusilli	___
2004	*Drowning Tree, The*	Carol Goodman	___
2002	*Lake of Dead Languages, The*	Carol Goodman	___
2003	*Widow of Jerusalem, The*	Alan Gordon	___
1982	*"A" is for Alibi*	Sue Grafton	___
2003	*Curious Incident of the Dog in the Night-Time, The*	Mark Haddon	___
2003	*Blood is the Sky*	Steve Hamilton	___
2003	*Haunted Ground*	Erin Hart	___
2004	*Lake of Sorrows*	Erin Hart	___
2001	*Dialogues of the Dead*	Reginald Hill	___
2000	*In Her Defense*	Stephen Horn	___
2002	*Poisoned Rose, The*	D. Daniel Judson	___
2004	*Hundredth Man, The*	Jack Kerley	___
2002	*Business of Dying, The*	Simon Kernick	___
2002	*Blue Edge of Midnight, The*	Jonathon King	___
2001	*Folly*	Laurie R. King	___
2003	*Keeping Watch*	Laurie R. King	___
1995	*True Crime*	Andrew Klavan	___
1994	*Drink Before the War, A*	Dennis Lehane	___
1998	*Gone, Baby, Gone*	Dennis Lehane	___
2002	*This Pen for Hire*	Laura Levine	___
2000	*Perfect Daughter, The*	Gillian Linscott	___
2003	*Every Secret Thing*	Laura Lippman	___
2002	*Diamond Dust*	Peter Lovesey	___
1986	*Rough Cider*	Peter Lovesey	___
1989	*Time's Witness*	Michael Malone	___
1983	*Uncivil Seasons*	Michael Malone	___
1997	*Likeness in Stone, A*	J. Wallis Martin	___

2001	*Girl in the Face of the Clock, The*	Charles Mathes	___
1995	*Mermaids Singing, The*	Val McDermid	___
1999	*Place of Execution, A*	Val McDermid	___
2003	*Six Easy Pieces*	Walter Mosley	___
1977	*Edwin of the Iron Shoes*	Marcia Muller	___
2002	*Darkness Falls*	Margaret Murphy	___
1994	*Mallory's Oracle*	Carol OConnell	___
1982	*Indemnity Only*	Sara Paretsky	___
1973	*Godwulf Manuscript, The*	Robert B. Parker	___
2003	*Thicker Than Water*	P.J. Parrish	___
2003	*Limestone Cowboy*	Stuart Pawson	___
1998	*Sweet Forever, The*	George P. Pelecanos	___
2001	*Falls, The*	Ian Rankin	___
2001	*Aftermath*	Peter Robinson	___
2003	*Close to Home (The Summer that Never Was)*	Peter Robinson	___
1999	*In a Dry Season*	Peter Robinson	___
2004	*Absent Friends*	S.J. Rozan	___
2002	*Winter and Night*	S.J. Rozan	___
1935	*Gaudy Night*	Dorothy L. Sayers	___
2004	*First Drop*	Zoe Sharp	___
2002	*Kisscut*	Karin Slaughter	___
2003	*No.1 Ladies' Detective Agency, The*	Alexander McCall Smith	___
2003	*Black Maps*	Peter Spiegelman	___
2004	*Twisted City*	Jason Starr	___
2003	*Bridge of Sighs, The*	Olen Steinhauer	___
1976	*Dangerous Davies: The Last Detective*	Leslie Thomas	___
1984	*Briarpatch*	Ross Thomas	___
1970	*Fools in Town Are on Our Side, The*	Ross Thomas	___
2003	*Monkeewrench*	P.J. Tracy	___
1979	*Shibumi*	Trevanian	___
1992	*Ice House, The*	Minette Walters	___

www.blackravenpress.com/bouchercon2004panel.htm
www.deadlypleasures.com/ALLNIGHTERS.htm

Art Bourgeau Classic Mystery Books

In his *Mystery Lover's Companion,* Art Bourgeau used a rating scheme of one to five daggers to indicate the quality of the work he listed and briefly described. *The Mystery Lover's Companion* reviewed and rated some 2,500 books. His highest rating, five daggers, was used to indicate "A True Classic" which are listed here. The time span for this list is 1860 to 1985 with 226 titles listed.

Art Bourgeau Classic Mystery Books

1860	*Woman in White, The*	Wilkie Collins	____
1868	*Moonstone, The*	Wilkie Collins	____
1878	*Leavenworth Case, The*	Anna Katharine Green	____
1886	*Mystery of a Hansom Cab, The*	Fergus Hume	____
1894	*Pudd'nhead Wilson (The Tragedy of Pudd'nhead Wilson)*	Mark Twain	____
1905	*Scarlet Pimpernel, The*	Baroness Orczy	____
1908	*Man Who was Thursday, The*	G.K. Chesterton	____
1911	*Innocence of Father Brown, The*	G.K. Chesterton	____
1913	*Trent's Last Case (The Woman in Black)*	E.C. Bentley	____
1913	*Lodger, The*	Marie Belloc Lowndes	____
1914	*Wisdom of Father Brown, The*	G.K. Chesterton	____
1915	*Thirty-Nine Steps, The*	John Buchan	____
1919	*Haunted Bookshop, The*	Christopher Morley	____
1920	*Mysterious Affair at Styles, The*	Agatha Christie	____
1920	*Great Impersonation, The*	E. Phillips Oppenheim	____
1922	*Red House Mystery, The*	A.A. Milne	____
1925	*John Macnab*	John Buchan	____
1925	*Mousetrap, The (Three Blind Mice)*	Agatha Christie	____
1926	*Chinese Parrot, The*	Earl Derr Biggers	____
1926	*Murder of Roger Ackroyd, The*	Agatha Christie	____
1926	*Payment Deferred*	C.S. Forester	____
1927	*Canary Murder Case, The*	S.S. Van Dine	____
1927	*Complete Sherlock Holmes, The*	Arthur Conan Doyle	____
1927	*Meet Mr. Mulliner*	P.G. Wodehouse	____
1928	*Footsteps at the Lock, The*	Ronald A. Knox	____
1928	*Greene Murder Case, The*	S.S. Van Dine	____
1929	*Poisoned Chocolates Case, The*	Anthony Berkeley	____
1929	*Red Harvest*	Dashiell Hammett	____
1929	*Roman Hat Mystery, The*	Ellery Queen	____
1930	*Mr. Pottermack's Oversight*	R. Austin Freeman	____
1930	*Maltese Falcon, The*	Dashiell Hammett	____
1930	*Arundel*	Kenneth Roberts	____
1930	*Strong Poison*	Dorothy L. Sayers	____
1930	*Green Ice (The Green Ice Murders)*	Raoul Whitfield	____
1931	*Death Walks in Eastrepps*	Francis Beeding	____

1931	*Living Shadow, The*	Maxwell Grant (Walter B. Gibson)	____
1931	*Shadow Laughs, The*	Maxwell Grant (Walter B. Gibson)	____
1931	*Malice Aforethought*	Francis Iles	____
1931	*Five Red Herrings, The (Suspicious Characters)*	Dorothy L. Sayers	____
1932	*Keeper of the Keys*	Earl Derr Biggers	____
1932	*Death Under Sail*	C.P. Snow	____
1932	*Darkness at Pemberly*	T.H. White	____
1933	*Was it Murder? (Murder at School)*	James Hilton (as, Glen Trevor)	____
1933	*Oxford Tragedy, An*	J.C. Masterman	____
1933	*Rabble in Arms*	Kenneth Roberts	____
1933	*Paradine Case, The*	Robert Hichens	____
1934	*Postman Always Rings Twice, The*	James M. Cain	____
1934	*Murder on the Orient Express (Murder in the Calais Coach)*	Agatha Christie	____
1934	*Chinese Orange Mystery, The*	Ellery Queen	____
1934	*Nine Tailors, The*	Dorothy L. Sayers	____
1934	*Fer-de-Lance (Meet Nero Wolfe)*	Rex Stout	____
1934	*Mystery of Cape Cod Tavern, The*	Phoebe Atwood Taylor	____
1934	*Thank You, Jeeves*	P.G. Wodehouse	____
1935	*Three Coffins, The (The Hollow Man)*	John Dickson Carr	____
1935	*Enter a Murderer*	Ngaio Marsh	____
1935	*League of Frightened Men, The*	Rex Stout	____
1935	*Wax*	Ethel Lina White	____
1936	*Thou Shell of Death (Shell of Death)*	Nicholas Blake	____
1936	*ABC Murders, The (The Alphabet Murders)*	Agatha Christie	____
1936	*This Gun for Hire (A Gun for Sale)*	Graham Greene	____
1936	*Northwest Passage*	Kenneth Roberts	____
1936	*Lady Vanishes, The (The Wheel Spins)*	Ethel Lina White	____
1937	*Bullet in the Ballet, A*	Caryl Brahms & S.J. Simon	____
1937	*Hamlet, Revenge!*	Michael Innes	____
1938	*Beast Must Die, The*	Nicholas Blake	____
1938	*Rebecca*	Daphne du Maurier	____
1938	*Ship of the Line*	C.S. Forester	____
1938	*Stoneware Monkey, The*	R. Austin Freeman	____
1938	*Lament for a Maker*	Michael Innes	____
1938	*Death From a Top Hat*	Clayton Rawson	____
1938	*Code of the Woosters, The*	P.G. Wodehouse	____
1939	*Coffin for Dimitrios, A (The Mask of Dimitrios)*	Eric Ambler	____
1939	*No Orchids for Miss Blandish (Villain and the Virgin)*	James Hadley Chase	____
1939	*And Then There Were None (Ten Little Niggers)*	Agatha Christie	____
1939	*Rogue Male (Man Hunt)*	Geoffrey Household	____
1939	*Mysterious Mickey Finn, The; or, Murder at the Café du Dome*	Elliot Paul	____
1939	*Footprints on the Ceiling, The*	Clayton Rawson	____

1940	*Oliver Wiswell*	Kenneth Roberts	____
1940	*Bride Wore Black, The (Beware the Lady)*	Cornell Woolrich	____
1941	*Mildred Pierce*	James M. Cain	____
1941	*Pinch of Poison, A*	Frances & Richard Lockridge	____
1941	*Black Curtain, The*	Cornell Woolrich	____
1942	*Laura*	Vera Caspary	____
1942	*Cue for Murder*	Helen McCloy	____
1942	*Calamity Town*	Ellery Queen	____
1943	*Lady in the Lake, The*	Raymond Chandler	____
1943	*Ministry of Fear, The*	Graham Greene	____
1943	*Black Angel, The*	Cornell Woolrich	____
1944	*Green for Danger*	Christianna Brand	____
1944	*Black Orchids (The Case of the Black Orchids)*	Rex Stout	____
1945	*Holy Disorders*	Edmund Crispin	____
1945	*Rising of the Moon, The*	Gladys Mitchell	____
1945	*Red Right Hand, The*	Joel Townsley Rogers	____
1946	*Too Many Cousins*	Douglas G. Browne	____
1946	*Moving Toyshop, The*	Edmund Crispin	____
1946	*Big Clock, The (No Way Out)*	Kenneth Fearing	____
1946	*Double Take, The*	Roy Huggins	____
1946	*Ride the Pink Horse*	Dorothy B. Hughes	____
1946	*Pavilion, The (The Deadly Pavilion)*	Hilda Lawrence	____
1947	*Final Curtain*	Ngaio Marsh	____
1948	*Devil Take the Blue-Tail Fly*	John Franklin Bardin	____
1948	*Wilders Walk Away*	Herbert Brean	____
1948	*Skeleton in the Clock, The*	Carter Dickson	____
1948	*Sudden Fear*	Edna Sherry	____
1948	*I, the Jury*	Mickey Spillane	____
1948	*Rendezvous in Black*	Cornell Woolrich	____
1949	*Little Sister, The (Marlow)*	Raymond Chandler	____
1949	*Buried for Pleasure*	Edmund Crispin	____
1949	*Cat of Many Tails*	Ellery Queen	____
1950	*Third Man, The (The Third Man and the Fallen Idol)*	Graham Greene	____
1950	*Strangers on a Train*	Patricia Highsmith	____
1950	*In a Lonely Place*	Dorothy B. Hughes	____
1950	*My Gun is Quick*	Mickey Spillane	____
1950	*To Love and Be Wise*	Josephine Tey	____
1951	*Daughter of Time, The*	Josephine Tey	____
1952	*Tiger in the Smoke, The*	Margery Allingham	____
1952	*Ivory Grin, The (Marked for Murder)*	Ross Macdonald (as, John Ross Macdonald)	____
1952	*Killer Inside Me, The*	Jim Thompson	____
1953	*Madball*	Fredric Brown	____
1953	*Long Goodbye, The (The Long Good-bye)*	Raymond Chandler	____

1953	*High and the Mighty, The*	Ernest K. Gann	____
1953	*Night of the Hunter, The*	Davis Grubb	____
1953	*Kiss Before Dying, A*	Ira Levin	____
1954	*Black Mountain, The*	Rex Stout	____
1954	*Hell of a Woman, A*	Jim Thompson	____
1955	*Talented Mr. Ripley, The*	Patricia Highsmith	____
1955	*Beast in View*	Margaret Millar	____
1956	*Landscape With Dead Dons*	Robert Robinson	____
1958	*Our Man in Havana*	Graham Greene	____
1958	*Anatomy of a Murder*	Robert Traver	____
1959	*Psycho*	Robert Bloch	____
1959	*List of Adrian Messenger, The*	Philip MacDonald	____
1960	*Watcher in the Shadows*	Geoffrey Household	____
1962	*Sherlock Holmes of Baker Street*	W.S. Baring-Gould	____
1962	*Rose of Tibet, The*	Lionel Davidson	____
1962	*Ipcress File, The*	Len Deighton	____
1962	*Seven Days in May*	Fletcher Knebel & Charles W. Bailey	____
1962	*Zebra-Striped Hearse, The*	Ross Macdonald	____
1962	*How Like an Angel*	Margaret Millar	____
1962	*Will of the Tribe, The*	Arthur W. Upfield	____
1963	*Spy Who Came in From the Cold, The*	John le Carre	____
1963	*Ice Station Zebra*	Alistair MacLean	____
1963	*Emperor's Pearl, The*	Robert van Gulik	____
1964	*Funeral in Berlin*	Len Deighton	____
1964	*Liquidator, The*	John Gardner	____
1964	*Night of the Generals, The*	Hans Helmut Kirst	____
1964	*Minuteman Murder, The (The Transcendental Murder)*	Jane Langton	____
1964	*This Rough Magic*	Mary Stewart	____
1964	*Pop. 1280*	Jim Thompson	____
1964	*Winter of Madness*	David Walker	____
1965	*In the Heat of the Night*	John Ball	____
1965	*Who is Lewis Pinder? (Man Out of Nowhere)*	L.P. Davies	____
1965	*Quiller Memorandum, The (The Berlin Memorandum)*	Adam Hall	____
1965	*Doorbell Rang, The*	Rex Stout	____
1966	*Double Image, The*	Helen MacInnes	____
1967	*Annotated Sherlock Holmes, The*	W.S. Baring-Gould	____
1967	*Green Grow the Tresses-O*	Stanley Hyland	____
1967	*Seersucker Whipsaw, The*	Ross Thomas	____
1967	*Necklace and Calabash*	Robert van Gulik	____
1968	*Laughing Policeman, The*	Maj Sjowall & Per Wahloo	____
1969	*Flashman*	George MacDonald Fraser	____
1969	*Puppet on a Chain*	Alistair MacLean	____

1969	Godfather, The	Mario Puzo	___
1969	Fire Engine that Disappeared, The	Maj Sjowall & Per Wahloo	___
1970	Time and Again	Jack Finney	___
1971	Day of the Jackal, The	Frederick Forsyth	___
1971	Copper Beeches	Arthur H. Lewis	___
1971	Underground Man, The	Ross Macdonald	___
1971	Bear Island	Alistair MacLean	___
1972	Blood on a Harvest Moon	David Anthony	___
1972	Rainbird Pattern, The (Family Plot)	Victor Canning	___
1972	Odessa File, The	Frederick Forsyth	___
1972	Friends of Eddie Coyle, The	George V. Higgins	___
1973	Defection of A.J. Lewinter, The	Robert Littell	___
1973	First Deadly Sin, The	Lawrence Sanders	___
1973	Death of the Detective, The	Mark Smith	___
1973	Plot Against Roger Ryder, The	Julian Symons	___
1973	If You Can't Be Good	Ross Thomas	___
1974	Jaws	Peter Benchley	___
1974	Dogs of War, The	Frederick Forsyth	___
1974	Tinker, Tailor, Soldier, Spy	John le Carre	___
1974	Dreadful Lemon Sky, The	John D. MacDonald	___
1974	Other Paths to Glory	Anthony Price	___
1974	Onion Field, The	Joseph Wambaugh	___
1975	Eagle Has Landed, The	Jack Higgins	___
1975	Big Enough Wreath, A	William Gardner	___
1975	Stealing Lillian (The Kidnap Kid)	Tony Kenrick	___
1975	Eye of the Tiger, The	Wilbur Smith	___
1976	Cavanaugh Quest, The	Thomas Gifford	___
1976	Boys From Brazil, The	Ira Levin	___
1976	Someone is Killing the Great Chefs of Europe	Nan & Ivan Lyons	___
1976	Best Martin Hewitt Detective Stories	Arthur Morrison	___
1976	Cry Wolf	Wilbur Smith	___
1977	Flashman's Lady	George MacDonald Fraser	___
1977	Charlie M (Charlie Muffin)	Brian Freemantle	___
1977	Punch and Judy Murders, The	George Hart	___
1977	Judgement in Stone, A	Ruth Rendell	___
1978	Flyaway	Desmond Bagley	___
1978	Last Good Kiss, The	James Crumley	___
1978	Eye of the Needle (Storm Island)	Ken Follett	___
1978	Death Freak, The	Clifford Irving & Herbert Burkholz	___
1978	Random Factor, The	Linda LaRosa & Barry Tanenbaum	___
1979	Mobius Strip, The	William Gardner	___
1980	Fifth Horseman, The	Larry Collins & Dominique LaPierre	___

1980	*Congo*	Michael Crichton	____
1980	*Mantis*	Peter Fox	____
1980	*Mr. American*	George MacDonald Fraser	____
1981	*Woman Called Scylla, A*	David Gurr	____
1981	*Red Dragon (Manhunter)*	Thomas Harris	____
1981	*Paragon Walk*	Anne Perry	____
1982	*Queen's Messenger, The*	W.R. Duncan (Robert L. Duncan)	____
1982	*Twice Shy*	Dick Francis	____
1982	*Heights of Rimring, The*	Duff Hart-Davis	____
1983	*Fatal Vision*	Joe McGinniss	____
1983	*Adventure of the Unseen Traveler, The*	D.O. Smith	____
1984	*Dolly and the Bird of Paradise (Tropical Issue)*	Dorothy Dunnett (Dorothy Halliday)	____
1984	*King's Commissar, The*	Duncan Kyle	____
1984	*Tragedy at Tiverton, The*	Raymond Paul	____
1984	*Briarpatch*	Ross Thomas	____
1985	*Black Mask Boys, The* (from: *Black Mask* stories)	William, F. Nolan, ed.	____

Nonfiction Titles

1971	*Game of the Foxes, The: The Untold Story of German Espionage in the United States and Great Britian During World War II*	Ladislas Farago	____
1976	*Man Called Intrepid, A: The Secret War*	William Stevenson	____
1977	*Cliffhanger*	Alan G. Barbour	____
1978	*Films of Sherlock Holmes, The*	Chris Steinbrunner & Norman Michaels	____
1982	*Gun in Cheek: A Study of "Alternative" Crime Fiction*	Bill Pronzini	____
1947/84	*Illustrious Clients Case-Book (reprint, 1984)*	J.N. Williamson & H.B. Williams	____

www.topmystery.com/books2.htm
home.comcast.net/~dwtaylor1/bourgeau.html

William F. Deeck's —
My One Hundred Best Mystery Books

In January 1989, William F. Deeck began a list of his twenty favorite mystery books. He later expanded it to "My One Hundred Best Mystery Books." These lists were published in *CADS* magazine, issues #10 and #48. As Deeck has passed away, we do have this last list supplied by Charles Shibuk. One footnote is offered: "In Bill's list of Twenty Favourites in *CADS* #10 he chose Cyril's Hare's *When the Wind Blows*. This is the only one of the twenty not to be included in this later list of 100 titles;" it is included here with an * mark. There are 101 novels dating from 1918 to 1991, and 13 nonfiction titles.

Deeck Best Mystery List

1969	*Complete Steel, The* (*The Stately Home Murder*)	Catherine Aird	____
1948	*More Work for the Undertaker*	Margery Allingham	____
1954	*Caves of Steel, The*	Isaac Asimov	____
1936	*Clue for Mr. Fortune (or, any Reggie Fortune short-story collection)*	H.C. Bailey	____
1974	*Death of an Old Goat*	Robert Barnard	____
1929	*Poisoned Chocolates Case, The*	Anthony Berkeley	____
1947	*Minute for Murder*	Nicholas Blake	____
1972	*Don't Point that Thing at Me* (*Mortdecai's Endgame*)	Kryil Bonfiglioli	____
1944	*Green for Danger*	Christianna Brand	____
1949	*Leaden Bubble, The*	H.C. Branson	____
1936	*Case for Three Detectives*	Leo Bruce	____
1984	*Thin Woman, The*	Dorothy Cannell	____
1988	*Murder Unrenovated*	P.M. Carlson	____
1934	*Blind Barber, The*	John Dickson Carr	____
1937	*Burning Court, The*	John Dickson Carr	____
1968	*Picture Miss Seeton*	Heron Carvic	____
1984	*Shortest Way to Hades, The*	Sarah Caudwell	____
1939	*First Saint Omnibus, The* (13 short stories)	Leslie Charteris	____
1935	*Father Brown Omnibus, The* (stories)	G.K. Chesterton	____
1930	*Murder at the Vicarage, The*	Agatha Christie	____
1939	*Ten Little Niggers (And Then There Were None)*	Agatha Christie	____
1926	*Death at Swaythling Court*	J.J. Connington	____
1972	*Rocksburg Railroad Murders, The*	K.C. Constantine	____
1929	*Merrivale Mystery, The*	James Corbett	____
1948	*Love Lies Bleeding*	Edmund Crispin	____
1954	*Conjurer's Coffin*	Guy Cullingford	____
1950	*Death and Letters*	Elizabeth Daly	____
1991	*Hard Tack*	Barbara D'Amato	____
1950	*Clay Hand, The*	Dorothy Salisbury Davis	____

1950	*Night at the Mocking Widow*	Carter Dickson	___
1953	*Death at Crane's Court*	Eilis Dillon	___
1927	*Complete Sherlock Holmes, The*	Arthur Conan Doyle	___
1972	*Death at the Bar, A*	Charles Drummond	___
1987	*Old Bones*	Aaron Elkins	___
1969	*Death Cracks a Bottle*	Kenneth Giles	___
1972	*Person Shouldn't Die Like That, A*	Arthur D. Goldstein	___
1988	*Hoodwink*	Paula Gosling	___
1990	*Murder at Madingley Grange*	Caroline Graham	___
1949	*What a Body!*	Alan Green	___
1991	*Precious Blood*	Jane Haddam	___
1934	*Thin Man, The*	Dashiell Hammett	___
1949	*When the Wind Blows* (The Wind Blows Death)*	Cyril Hare	___
1946	*With a Bare Bodkin*	Cyril Hare	___
1969	*Last Doorbell, The*	Joseph Harrington	___
1965	*Last Known Address, The*	Joseph Harrington	___
1987	*Death on Demand*	Carolyn G. Hart	___
1941	*Envious Casca*	Georgette Heyer	___
1955	*F.O.B. Murder*	Bert & Dolores Hitchens	___
1959	*Saint Maker, The*	Leonard Holton	___
1957	*She Died Because…*	Kenneth Hopkins	___
1934	*Murder of My Aunt, The*	Richard Hull	___
1943	*Weight of the Evidence, The*	Michael Innes	___
1942	*Widening Stain, The*	W. Bolingbroke Johnson	___
1980	*Murder of the Majarajah, The*	H.R.F. Keating	___
1967	*Nine Mile Walk, The*	Harry Kemelman	___
1929	*Woman is Dead, A (Somewhere in This House; A Murderer in This House)*	Rufus King	
1934	*Still Dead*	Ronald A. Knox	___
1961	*Banking on Death*	Emma Lathen	___
1929	*Medbury Fort Murder, The*	George Limnelius	___
1973	*Mad Hatter's Holiday*	Peter Lovesey	___
1938	*Nursemaid Who Disappeared, The (Warrant for X)*	Philip MacDonald	___
1980	*Withdrawing Room, The*	Charlotte MacLeod	___
1981	*One Coffee With*	Margaret Maron	___
1955	*Gideon's Day (Gideon of Scotland Yard)*	J.J. Marric (John Creasey)	___
1941	*Death and the Dancing Footman*	Ngaio Marsh	___
1975	*Yellowthread Street*	William Marshall	___
1954	*Bridal Bed Murders, The (The Chinese Bed Murders)*	A.E. Martin	___
1965	*Of All the Bloody Cheek*	Frank McAuliffe	___
1950	*Through a Glass, Darkly*	Helen McCloy	___
1946	*Pick Your Victim*	Patricia McGerr	___
1985	*Beer and Skittles*	B.J. Morison	___

1987	*Voyage of the Chianti, The*	B.J. Morison	____
1972	*Fall Guy, The*	Ritchie Perry	____
1981	*Curse of the Pharaohs, The*	Elizabeth Peters	____
1975	*Let's Talk of Graves, of Worms, and Epitaphs*	Robert Player	____
1964	*Dover One*	Joyce Porter	____
1972	*Meddler and Her Murder, A*	Joyce Porter	____
1918	*Uncle Abner, Master of Mysteries*	Melville Davisson Post	____
1985	*Bones*	Bill Pronzini	____
1949	*Cat of Many Tails*	Ellery Queen	____
1948	*Ten Days Wonder*	Ellery Queen	____
1939	*Footprints on the Ceiling, The*	Clayton Rawson	____
1941	*No Love Lost (Come Out Killing)*	Robert Reeves	____
1952	*Kindest Use a Knife, The*	Louisa Revell	____
1941	*Trial by Fury*	Craig Rice	____
1945	*Green December Fills the Graveyard (Murder at Shots Hall)*	Maureen Sarsfield	____
1934	*Nine Tailors, The*	Dorothy L. Sayers	____
1971	*Chilean Club, The (The Yellow Room)*	George Shipway	____
1974	*Black Aura*	John Sladek	____
1979	*Reggis Arms Caper, The*	Ross H. Spencer	____
1941	*Good Night, Sheriff*	Harrison R. Steeves	____
1934	*Fer-de-Lance (Meet Nero Wolfe)*	Rex Stout	____
1938	*Too Many Cooks*	Rex Stout	____
1970	*Fools in Town Are on Our Side, The*	Ross Thomas	____
1937	*Beginning With a Bash*	Alice Tilton (Phoebe Atwood Taylor)	____
1928	*Greene Murder Case, The*	S.S. Van Dine	____
1947	*Department of Dead Ends, The*	Roy Vickers	____
1925	*Mind of Mr. J.G. Reeder, The (The Murder Book of J.G. Reeder)*	Edgar Wallace	____
1967	*Of Mice and Murder*	Beryl Whitaker	____
1942	*Tinsley's Bones*	Percival Wilde	____
1978	*Treasure Up in Smoke*	David Williams	____

Reference Works

Some of these reference works have been reprinted several times, and in some cases, have the same title and have been updated. In some cases I simply went to the newest edition available.

1991	*Locked Room Murders and Other Impossible Crimes: A Comprehensive Bibliography*	Robert Adey	____
1981	*What About Murder? A Guide to Books About Mystery and Detective Fiction*	Jon L. Breen	____
1993	*What About Murder? (1981-1991): A Guide to Books About Mystery and Detective Fiction*	Jon L. Breen	____

1941	*Murder for Pleasure: The Life and Times of the Detective Story*	Howard Haycraft	___
2005	*Crime Fiction IV, A Comprehensive Bibliography 1749–2000 (also on CD-ROM)*	Allen J. Hubin	___
1988	*Silk Stalkings: When Women Write of Murder*	Victoria Nichols & Susan Thompson	___
1999	*Silk Stalkings II: More Women Write of Murder*	Victoria Nichols & Susan Thompson	___
1982	*Gun in Cheek: A Study of "Alternative" Crime Fiction*	Bill Pronzini	___
1987	*Son of Gun in Cheek*	Bill Pronzini	___
1989	*Catalogue of Crime A: Being a Reader's Guide to the Literature of Mystery, Detection, and Related Genres (revised and enlarged)*	Jacques Barzun & Wendell Hertig Taylor	___
1980	*Twentieth Century Crime and Mystery Writers, 1st edition*	John M. Reilly, ed.	___
1985	*Twentieth Century Crime and Mystery Writers, 2nd edition*	John M. Reilly, ed.	___
1991	*Twentieth Century Crime and Mystery Writers, 3rd edition*	Lesley Henderson, ed.	___

Dell Great Mystery Library

In January 1957, Dell publishers created a series of mystery classics of either never reprinted before, or long unavailable in soft covers up until that time for the public. Along with publishing new mysteries, they wanted to reprint the best mysteries of all time, thus, *The Dell Great Mystery Library*. The titles were selected by three judges and some titles were recommended by mystery editor Lee Wright. There are 29 number titles (a large number on the cover in a circle) in the series and 27 more titles without a number. Four of the unnumbered titles were also in the first grouping, * indicates these titles. There are 56 books in all; they date from 1902 to 1962.

Dell Great Mystery Library

1940	**Dell Great Mystery Library 1**		
	Bride Wore Black, The (Beware the Lady)	Cornell Woolrich	___
1941	**Dell Great Mystery Library 2**		
	Trial by Fury	Craig Rice	___
1943	**Dell Great Mystery Library 3**		
	Laura	Vera Caspary	___
1936	**Dell Great Mystery Library 4**		
	Puzzle for Fools, A	Patrick Quentin	___
1938	**Dell Great Mystery Library 5**		
	Warrant for X (The Nursemaid Who Disappeared)	Philip MacDonald	___
1935	**Dell Great Mystery Library 6**		
	Headed for a Hearse (The Westland Case)	Jonathan Latimer	___
1908	**Dell Great Mystery Library 7**		
	Circular Staircase, The	Mary Roberts Rinehart	___
1939	**Dell Great Mystery Library 8**		
	Coffin for Dimitrios, A (The Mask of Dimitrios)	Eric Ambler	___
1945	**Dell Great Mystery Library 9**		
	Red Right Hand, The	Joel Townsley Rogers	___
1942	**Dell Great Mystery Library 10**		
	Phantom Lady	William Irish (Cornell Woolrich)	___
1932	**Dell Great Mystery Library 11**		
	Before the Fact	Francis Iles	___
1939	**Dell Great Mystery Library 12**		
	Sad Cypress	Agatha Christie	___
1934	**Dell Great Mystery Library 13**		
	Fer-de-Lance (Meet Nero Wolfe)	Rex Stout	___
1946	**Dell Great Mystery Library 14**		
	Ride the Pink Horse	Dorothy B. Hughes	___
1938	**Dell Great Mystery Library 15**		
	Beast Must Die, The	Nicholas Blake	___
1927	**Dell Great Mystery Library 16**		
	Bellamy Trial, The	Frances Noyes Hart	___

1934	**Dell Great Mystery Library 17**		
	Death of a Ghost	Margery Allingham	___
1937	**Dell Great Mystery Library 18**		
	Background to Danger (Uncommon Danger)	Eric Ambler	___
1933	**Dell Great Mystery Library 19**		
	Mystery of the Dead Police	Philip MacDonald	___
1929	**Dell Great Mystery Library 20**		
	Man in the Queue, The (Killer in the Crowd)	Josephine Tey (Gordon Daviot)	___
1952.	**Dell Great Mystery Library 21**		
	Hole in the Ground, A	Andrew Garve	___
1951	**Dell Great Mystery Library 22**		
	Gentle Murderer, A	Dorothy Salisbury Davis	___
1947	**Dell Great Mystery Library 23**		
	One More Unfortunate (A Case to Answer)	Edgar Lustgarten	___
1902	**Dell Great Mystery Library 24**		
	Hound of the Baskervilles, The	Arthur Conan Doyle	___
1922	**Dell Great Mystery Library 25**		
	Red House Mystery, The	A.A. Milne	___
1945	**Dell Great Mystery Library 26**		
	Iron Gates, The (Taste of Fears)	Margaret Millar	___
1940	**Dell Great Mystery Library 27**		
	Journey into Fear	Eric Ambler	___
1945	**Dell Great Mystery Library 28**		
	Bedelia	Vera Caspary	___
1935	**Dell Great Mystery Library 29**		
	Three Coffins, The (The Hollow Man)	John Dickson Carr	___
1939	**Dell Great Mystery Library***		
	Coffin for Dimitrios, A (The Mask of Dimitrios)	Eric Ambler	___
1940	**Dell Great Mystery Library***		
	Journey into Fear	Eric Ambler	___
1937	**Dell Great Mystery Library**		
	Trial and Error	Anthony Berkeley	___
1945	**Dell Great Mystery Library***		
	Bedelia	Vera Caspary	___
1960	**Dell Great Mystery Library**		
	Evvie	Vera Caspary	___
1943	**Dell Great Mystery Library***		
	Laura	Vera Caspary	___
1963	**Dell Great Mystery Library**		
	Nick Carter, Detective	Nicholas Carter (Robert Clurman, Introduction)	___
1960	**Dell Great Mystery Library**		
	Kiss Kiss (stories)	Roald Dahl	___
1961	**Dell Great Mystery Library**		
	Someone Like You (stories)	Roald Dahl	___

1963	**Dell Great Mystery Library**		
	Black Sheep, White Lamb	Dorothy Salisbury Davis	____
1959	**Dell Great Mystery Library**		
	No Next of Kin	Doris Miles Disney	____
1961	**Dell Great Mystery Library**		
	Promise of Murder, The (Melora)	Mignon G. Eberhart	____
1958	**Dell Great Mystery Library**		
	Eighth Circle, The	Stanley Ellin	____
1958	**Dell Great Mystery Library**		
	Hours Before Dawn, The	Celia Fremlin	____
1956	**Dell Great Mystery Library**		
	Second Man, The	Edward Grierson	____
1946	**Dell Great Mystery Library**		
	Pavilion, The (The Deadly Pavilion)	Hilda Lawrence	____
1913	**Dell Great Mystery Library**		
	Lodger, The	Marie Belloc Lowndes	____
1963	**Dell Great Mystery Library**		
	Before I Die	Helen McCloy	____
1964	**Dell Great Mystery Library**		
	Fiend, The	Margaret Millar	____
1959	**Dell Great Mystery Library**		
	Listening Walls, The	Margaret Millar	____
1962	**Dell Great Mystery Library**		
	How Like an Angel	Margaret Millar	____
1949	**Dell Great Mystery Library**		
	Affairs of the Heart	Malcolm Muggeridge	____
1950	**Dell Great Mystery Library**		
	Motive, The (Death of a Nymph)	Evelyn Piper	____
1960	**Dell Great Mystery Library**		
	Case Pending	Dell Shannon	____
1957	**Dell Great Mystery Library**		
	Colour of Murder, The (Color of Murder)	Julian Symons	____
1959	**Dell Great Mystery Library**		
	Sleep Long, My Love (Jigsaw)	Hillary Waugh	____
1956	**Dell Great Mystery Library**		
	Nightmare	Cornell Woolrich	____

Sue Feder's Favorite Fifty

Sue Feder created her "best" list of 50 mystery novels and listed them on her web site. She included a wide variety of writing styles, appealing characters, and interesting storylines. Some were historical mysteries and others were barely mysteries at all. She admittedly did not include many of her favorites. The 50 titles cover from 1930 to 1998. Sue Feder passed away in 2005.

Feder's Favorite Fifty			
1976	*Murder at the ABA (Authorized Murder)*	Isaac Asimov	___
1970	*Deadly Meeting*	Robert Bernard	___
1984	*Out of the Blackout*	Robert Barnard	___
1979	*Celestial Chess*	Thomas Bontly	___
1950	*Hardly a Man is Now Alive (Murder Now and Then)*	Herbert Brean	___
1948	*Wilders Walk Away*	Herbert Brean	___
1969	*Whispering Wall, The*	Patricia Carlon	___
1991	*Bad Blood*	P.M Carlson	___
1989	*Bone*	George C. Chesbro	___
1939	*And Then There Were None (Ten Little Niggers)*	Agatha Christie	___
1984	*Other David, The*	Carolyn Coker	___
1995	*Breakheart Hill*	Thomas H. Cook	___
1991	*Blood Marks*	Bill Crider	___
1983	*Dark Place, The*	Aaron Elkins	___
1987	*Old Bones*	Aaron Elkins	___
1983	*Dark Fantastic, The*	Stanley Ellin	___
1963	*Seconds*	David Ely	___
1970	*Time and Again*	Jack Finney	___
1971	*Day of the Jackal, The*	Frederick Forsyth	___
1992	*Shadow Queen*	Tony Gibbs	___
1973	*Taking of Pelham One Two Three, The*	John Godey	___
1987	*Best Cellar, The*	Charles A. Goodrum	___
1986	*Replay*	Ken Grimwood	___
1974	*Search for Joseph Tully, The*	William H. Hallahan	___
1992	*Good Friday Murder, The*	Lee Harris	___
1986	*Unknown Soldier, The*	Michael Hastings	___
1930	*Secret of the Old Clock, The (Nancy Drew, #1)*	Carolyn Keene	___
1998	*Last Days of Summer*	Steve Kluger	___
1989	*Death in Verona*	Roy Harley Lewis	___
1984	*Too Sane a Murder*	Lee Martin	___
1979	*Back Bay*	William Martin	___
1960	*Stranger in My Grave, A*	Margaret Millar	___
1978	*Mirror, The*	Marlys Millhiser	___
1986	*Beyond the Grave*	Marcia Muller & Bill Pronzini	___

1988	*Eight, The*	Katherine Neville	___
1993	*Death Comes as Epiphany*	Sharan Newman	___
1979	*Cosgrove Report, The*	G.J.A. O'Toole	___
1982	*Poor Richard's Game*	G.J.A. O'Toole	___
1951	*Fallen into the Pit*	Ellis Peters	___
1968	*Grass-Widow's Tale, The*	Ellis Peters	___
1977	*Morbid Taste for Bones, A*	Ellis Peters	___
1976	*Never Pick Up Hitch-Hikers!*	Ellis Peters	___
1989	*Potter's Field, The*	Ellis Peters	___
1969	*Godfather, The*	Mario Puzo	___
1973	*First Deadly Sin, The*	Lawrence Sanders	___
1951	*Daughter of Time, The*	Josephine Tey	___
1975	*Choirboys, The*	Joseph Wambaugh	___
1996	*Brother's Blood, A*	Michael C. White	___
1958	*Secret of the Samurai Sword*	Phyllis A. Whitney	___
1978	*Murder in the Hellfire Club*	Donald Zochert	___

mywebpages.comcast.net/monkshould/

Douglas G. Greene's Twenty-Five Greatest Volumes of Detective Short Stories
(or so Doug Greene proclaims)

Douglas G. Greene is an expert on the short story format. In the July 1988 issue of *CADS #9* magazine, he offers a list of the "Twenty-Five Greatest Volumes of Detective Short Stories" for conversation. In his note to the article he writes, "You'll notice that I do not include Poe's *Tales* (1845) as it is *sui generis*." These stories date from 1892 to 1983.

Greene's 25 Greatest SS			
1892	Adventures of Sherlock Holmes, The	Arthur Conan Doyle	___
1907	Thinking Machine, The	Jacques Futrelle	___
1909	Old Man in the Corner, The (The Man in the Corner)	Baroness Orczy	___
1911	Innocence of Father Brown, The	G.K. Chesterton	___
1912	Singing Bone, The (The Adventures of Dr. Thorndyke)	R. Austin Freeman	___
1918	Uncle Abner, Master of Mysteries	Melville Davisson Post	___
1924	Giglamps	Will Scott	___
1928	Lord Peter Views the Body	Dorothy L. Sayers	___
1934	Adventures of Ellery Queen, The	Ellery Queen	___
1937	Mr. Campion, Criminologist	Margery Allingham	___
1940	Department of Queer Complaints, The	Carter Dickson	___
1945	Continental Op, The (stories)	Dashiell Hammett	___
1974	Continental Op, The (later collected edition)	Dashiell Hammett	___
1946	Dr. Sam: Johnson, Detector	Lillian de la Torre	___
1947	Labours of Hercules, The	Agatha Christie	___
1951	Simple Art of Murder, The	Raymond Chandler	___
1952	Little Tales of Smethers, The	Lord Dunsany	___
1953	Beware of the Trains	Edmund Crispin	___
1955	Name is Archer, The	John Ross Macdonald (Kenneth Millar; Ross Macdonald)	___
1967	Nine Mile Walk, The	Harry Kemelman	___
1968	Asimov's Mysteries	Isaac Asimov	___
1971	Spy and the Thief, The	Edward D. Hoch	___
1979	Murder and Magic	Randall Garrett	___
1979	Pascoe's Ghost	Reginald Hill	___
1983	Casefile: The Best of the 'Nameless Detective' Stories	Bill Pronzini	___

Douglas G. Greene's Additions to Queen's Quorum, Post-Queen's Quorum, and Extended Queen's Quorum

Douglas G. Greene offers his suggestions for 54 additional writings to expand the Queen's Quorum of 125 titles, dates from 1827 to 1967. This was offered in the August 1990 issue of *CADS* #14. In November 1990, he offered 50 more titles in a Post-Queen's Quorum, with dates between 1968 to 1989. Finally, in the August 1993 issue #21, he offered an expansion on this list with 10 more titles dating between 1990–1992. In March, 2007, he expanded the list by nine titles and removed one title; an asterisk marks the additional titles, the removed title has a strikethrough line.

Greene's Additions to Queen's Quorum		
1827	*Richmond: or, Scenes in the Life of a Bow Street Runner*	Anonymous	——
1829*	*Tales and Sketches of a Country Schoolmaster*	William Leggett	——
1860	*John Horsleydown; or, Confessions of a Thief*	Thomas Littleton Holt	——
1861	*Curiosities of Crime in Edinburgh*	James M'Levy	——
1865	*Chronological History of the Boston Watch and Police, A*	Edward H. Savage	——
1873	*Murphy's Master and Other Stories*	James Payn	——
1874	*Johnny Ludlow*	Mrs. Henry Wood	——
1879	*Criminal Reminiscences and Detective Sketches*	Allan Pinkerton	——
1880	*In the Force*	Bracebridge Hemyng	——
1882	*Historic China and Other Sketches*	Herbert A. Giles	——
1888*	*Plain Tales from the Hills*	Rudyard Kipling	——
1894	*Jewel Mysteries I Have Known*	Max Pemberton	——
1898	*Hagar of the Pawn-Shop*	Fergus Hume	——
1899*	*Ghosts: Being the Experiences of Flaxman Low (The Experiences of Flaxman Low)*	K. & H. Prichard (E. & H. Heron)	——
1900	*Prince of Swindlers, A*	Guy Boothby	——
1900	*Diplomatic Woman, A*	Huan Mee	——
1902	*Master Spy, The*	Robert John Buckley	——
1903	*Secrets of the Foreign Office*	William Le Queux	——
1905	*Memoirs of Constantine Dix, The*	Barry Pain	——
1906	*Burglar's Club, The*	Henry A. Hering	——
1908	*John Silence, Physician Extraordinary*	Algernon Blackwood	——
1912	*Amazing Mr. Bunn, The*	Bertram Atkey	——
1917	*Adventures of Jimmy Dale, The*	Frank L. Packard	——
1920	*Ambrose Lavendale, Diplomat*	E. Phillips Oppenheim	——
1924	*Giglamps*	Will Scott	——
1926	*Madame Storey*	Hulbert Footner	——

1928	~~Runagates Club, The~~	~~John Buchan~~	____
	(removed from list by Greene)		
1928	*Incredible Adventures of Rowland Hern, The*	Nicholas Olde	____
1928	*Baffle Book, The*	Lassiter Wren & Randle McKay	____
1929	*McLean of Scotland Yard*	George Goodchild	____
1929	*Thieves' Nights*	Harry Stephen Keeler	____
1930	*Mysterious Mr. Quin, The*	Agatha Christie	____
1932	*Thirteen Problems, The*	Agatha Christie	____
1936	*Seven Seas Murders, The*	Van Wych Mason	____
1941	*Mr. Caution, Mr. Callaghan*	Peter Cheyney	____
1942	*Three Plots for Asey Mayo*	Phoebe Atwood Taylor	____
1944*	*Les nouvelles enquêtes de Maigret*	Georges Simenon	____
1945	*"In Re Sherlock Holmes"*	August Derleth	____
1946	*Seven Slayers*	Paul Cain	____
1946	*Flash Casey, Detective*	George Harmon Coxe	____
1946	*Mrs. Pym of Scotland Yard*	Nigel Morland	____
1946*	*Confidences dans Ma Nuit*	Thomas Narcejac	____
1947	*Make Mine MacLain*	Baynard Kendrick	____
1947/48	*Murderers Make Mistakes*	Freeman Wills Crofts	____
1948	*Michael Shayne's Triple Mystery*	Brett Halliday	____
1949	*Report For a Corpse*	Henry Kane	____
1949	*Triple Threat*	Kelley Roos	____
1949	*Trouble in Triplicate*	Rex Stout	____
1950	*Six Deadly Dames*	Frederick Nebel	____
1953	*Mostly Murder*	Fredric Brown	____
1954	*Death Under the Table*	Peter Godfrey	____
1955	*Name is Archer, The*	John Ross Macdonald	____
		(Kenneth Millar; Ross Macdonald)	
1957	*Have Gat — Will Travel*	Richard S. Prather	____
1959	*Best Detective Stories of Cyril Hare*	Cyril Hare	____
1960*	*Nothing to Declare*	Manning Coles	____
1960	*For Your Eyes Only*	Ian Fleming	____
1961	*Murder! Murder!*	Julian Symons	____
1962	*Name is Jordan, The*	Harold Q. Masur	____
1964	*Strange Cases of Magistrate Pao, The*	Leon Comber ("translated and	____
		retold" from ancient sources)	
1966	*Brass Knuckles: The Oliver Quade,*	Frank Gruber	____
	Human Encyclopedia		
1967	*Judge Dee at Work*	Robert van Gulik	____

Post-Queen's Quorum

1968	*Asimov's Mysteries*	Isaac Asimov	_____
1968	*What Dread Hand*	Christianna Brand	_____
1968	*Exploits of the Chevalier Dupin, The*	Michael Harrison	_____
1970	*Case of the Crimson Kiss, The*	Erle Stanley Gardner	_____
1970	*Legacy of Danger*	Patricia McGerr	_____
1970	*"P" as in Police*	Lawrence Treat	_____
1971	*Spy and the Thief, The*	Edward D. Hoch	_____
1972	*Pieces of Modesty*	Peter O'Donnell	_____
1973	*Mournful Demeanour of Lieutenant Boruvka, The*	Josef Skvorecky	_____
1974	*Tales of the Black Widowers*	Isaac Asimov	_____
1974.	*View From Daniel Pike, The*	Edward Boyd & Bill Knox	_____
1974	*Raffles Revisited*	Barry Perowne	_____
1975	*Enquiries of Doctor Eszterhazy, The*	Avram Davidson	_____
1978	*Norgil the Magician*	Maxwell Grant	_____
1978	*Rumpole of the Bailey*	John Mortimer	_____
1979	*Fatal Flourishes*	S.S. Rafferty	_____
1979.	*Great Merlini, The*	Clayton Rawson	_____
1979	*Means of Evil*	Ruth Rendell	_____
1979	*Murder and Magic*	Randall Garrett	_____
1979	*Pascoe's Ghost*	Reginald Hill	_____
1980	*Designs on Life*	E.X. Ferrars	_____
1981	*Checkpoint Charlie*	Brian Garfield	_____
1982	*Hair of the Sleuthhound*	Jon L. Breen	_____
1982	*Good Old Stuff, The*	John D. MacDonald	_____
1983	*Dan Turner, Hollywood Detective*	Robert Leslie Bellem	_____
1983	*Sometimes They Bite*	Lawrence Block	_____
1983	*Exeunt Murderers*	Anthony Boucher	_____
1983	*Casefile: The Best of the "Nameless Detective" Stories*	Bill Pronzini	_____
1984	*Night Nemesis, The*	Frederick C. Davis	_____
1984	*Tales For a Stormy Night*	Dorothy Salisbury Davis	_____
1984	*Brandstetter and Others*	Joseph Hansen	_____
1984	*Best Short Stories, The*	"Sapper" (H.C. McNeile)	_____
1985	*Box of Tricks, A (Tickled to Death)*	Simon Brett	_____
1985	*House on Plymouth Street, The*	Ursula Curtiss	_____
1985	*Butchers*	Peter Lovesey	_____
1985	*Murder Round the Clock*	Hugh Pentecost	_____
1985	*Inspector Saito's Small Satori*	Janwillem van de Wetering	_____
1986	*Army of the Shadows, The*	Eric Ambler	_____
1986	*Tales of the Wolf*	Lawrence Sanders	_____
1986	*Jemima Shore's First Case*	Antonia Fraser	_____
1987	*Adventures of Henry Turnbuckle, The*	Jack Ritchie	_____
1987	*Murder By the Tale*	Dell Shannon	_____
1988	*Adventures of Max Latin, The*	Norbert Davis	_____

1988	*General Murders*	Loren D. Estleman	___
1988	*Better Mousetraps*	John Lutz	___
1988	*Rare Benedictine, A*	Ellis Peters	___
1989	*Death of a Salesperson*	Robert Barnard	___
1989	*Adventures of Race Williams, The*	Carroll John Daly	___
1989	*Four on the Floor*	Ralph McInerny	___
1989	*Collected Short Fiction of Ngaio Marsh, The*	Ngaio Marsh	___

Additions to Queen's Quorum

1990	*Murder Coming, A*	James Powell	___
1990	*Factory, The*	Brian Freemantle	___
1990	*Other Kinds of Treason*	Ted Allbeury	___
1991	*Secret Pilgrim, The*	John le Carre	___
1991	*Deceptions*	Marcia Muller	___
1991	*Kinsey and Me*	Sue Grafton	___
1991	*Dying in the Post War World*	Max Allan Collins	___
1992	*Crime, Punishment and Resurrection*	Michael Collins (Dennis Lynds)	___
1992	*Good Hanging and Other Stories, A*	Ian Rankin	___
1992	*Death in Store*	Jennifer Rowe	___
1992*	*Flowers for the Dead*	June Thomson	___
1992*	*Prisoners and Other Stories*	Ed Gorman	___

Douglas G. Greene—Locked-Room and Impossible—Crime Novels of All Time

As published in *The Armchair Detective Book of Lists*, edited by Kate Stine, 1995, there are 20 titles selected as "locked-room" and "impossible-crime" novels and they date from 1891 though 1977. Greene has added a new selection, *Bloodhounds* by Peter Lovesey making the list now 21.

Greene - Locked Room

1938	*Judas Window, The (The Crossbow Murder)*	John Dickson Carr	___
1935	*Three Coffins, The (The Hollow Man)*	John Dickson Carr	___
1944	*He Wouldn't Kill Patience*	John Dickson Carr (as, Carter Dickson)	___
1944	*Till Death Do Us Part*	John Dickson Carr	___
1937	*Peacock Feathers Murders, The (The Ten Teacups)*	John Dickson Carr (as, Carter Dickson)	___
1946	*He Who Whispers*	John Dickson Carr	___
1938	*Crooked Hinge, The*	John Dickson Carr	___
1934	*White Priory Murders, The*	John Dickson Carr (as, Carter Dickson)	___
1943	*She Died a Lady*	John Dickson Carr (as, Carter Dickson)	___
1965	*House at Satan's Elbow, The*	John Dickson Carr	___

1967	*Too Many Magicians*	Randall Garrett	___
1940	*Nine Times Nine*	H.H. Holmes (Anthony Boucher)	___
1996	*Bloodhounds*	Peter Lovesey	___
1982	*Scattershot*	Bill Pronzini	___
1934	*Chinese Orange Mystery, The*	Ellery Queen	___
1938	*Death From a Top Hat*	Clayton Rawson	___
1977	*Invisible Green*	John Sladek	___
1944	*Rim of the Pit*	Hake Talbot	___
1942	*Hangman's Handyman, The*	Hake Talbot	___
1934	*Talking Sparrow Murders, The*	Darwin L. Teilhet	___
1891	*Big Bow Mystery, The*	Israel Zangwill	___

Haycraft-Queen Cornerstones

The Haycraft-Queen Definitive Library of Detective-Crime-Mystery Fiction: Two Centuries of Cornerstones, 1748-1948 (1952)

In 1941, Howard Haycraft compiled a list of detective stories for a book entitled *Murder for Pleasure: The Life and Times of the Detective Story*. The chapter is entitled, "A Detective Story Bookshelf." The list was prepared for "unpretentious detective story fans who may care to assemble for their own pleasure 'cornerstone' libraries of the best and most influential writing in the medium....The list which follows...is primarily a 'readers' list." The list contains books written between 1845 and 1938.

In 1951, Haycraft updated his selections (it had been ten years) with book titles published before 1948.

Adding to this list was Ellery Queen (Frederic Dannay, half of the famous writing team), selecting a broader and more historical approach to books in the mystery field (these titles are noted with an asterisk mark). This became known as The Definitive Library of Detective- Crime-Mystery Fiction: Two Centuries of Cornerstones, 1748-1948. The first edition of this list appeared in 1951 in EQMM. It was then revised to its final form in 1956 with books published through 1952 in the Mystery Writers Handbook, edited by Herbert Brean.

The list is to be viewed in the original chronological order by date of publication.

[Editor's note: In Haycraft's original list, he listed *The Arabian Nights Murder* by Carr and *The Plague Court Murders* by Carter Dickson (same author), but on page 493 of Haycraft's *The Art of the Mystery Story* (1946), he wrote: "After careful, and possibly maturer, re-reading I beg to change my vote" to *The Crooked Hinge* (Carr) and *The Judas Window* (Dickson). I have listed all four titles below with ## for the 1941 titles and @@ for the 1946 titles.]

Thus it took some fifteen years to create this list of cornerstones; it numbers 187 titles.

The list offers many Sherlock Holmes (Doyle) titles; one might want to select *The Complete Sherlock Holmes* for a one-volume edition of the Holmes stories.

Following the list is a special list of anthologies that Haycraft felt important to the mystery field.

Haycraft-Queen Cornerstones

1748*	*Zadig; or, The Book of Fate*	Voltaire	___
1794*	*Things as They Are; or, The Adventures of* *Caleb Williams (Caleb Williams;* *The Adventures of Caleb Williams)*	William Godwin	___
1828-9*	*Memoires de Vidocq (Memoirs of Vidocq:* *Master of Crime)*	Francois Eugéne Vidocq	___
1845	*Tales*	Edgar Allan Poe	___
1852-53	*Bleak House*	Charles Dickens	___
1856*	*Recollections of a Detective Police-Officer*	"Waters" (William Russell)	___
1860*	*Woman in White, The*	Wilkie Collins	___
1862*	*Les Misérables*	Victor Hugo	___
1866*	*Crime and Punishment*	Fyodor Dostoevsky (Feodor Dostoevski)	___
1866	*Widow Lerouge, The (Lerouge Case;* *L'Affaire Lerouge)*	Émile Gaboriau	___
1866*	*Dead Letter, The*	Seeley Regester (Metta V. Victor)	___
1867*	*File No. 113 (Dossier No. 113;* *The Blackmailers; Le Dossier N 113)*	Émile Gaboriau	___
1868*	*Mystery of Orcival, The (Crime at Orcival; Le* *Crime D'Orcival)*	Émile Gaboriau	___
1868	*Moonstone, The*	Wilkie Collins	___
1869	*Monsieur Lecoq (Lecoq the Detective)*	Émile Gaboriau	___
1870	*Mystery of Edwin Drood, The*	Charles Dickens	___
1872/85*	*Old Sleuth, The Detective; or,* *The Bay Ridge Mystery*	Old Sleuth (Harlan Page Halsey)	___
1874*	*Expressman and the Detective, The*	Allan Pinkerton	___
1878	*Leavenworth Case, The*	Anna Katharine Green	___
1882*	*New Arabian Nights*	Robert Louis Stevenson	___
1886*	*Strange Case of Dr. Jekyll and Mr. Hyde*	Robert Louis Stevenson	___
1887	*Study in Scarlet, A*	Arthur Conan Doyle	___
1887*	*Mystery of a Hansom Cab, The*	Fergus W. Hume	___
1890	*Sign of the Four, The*	Arthur Conan Doyle	___
1892	*Adventures of Sherlock Holmes, The*	Arthur Conan Doyle	___
1892	*Big Bow Mystery, The*	Israel Zangwill	___
1894	*Memoirs of Sherlock Holmes, The*	Arthur Conan Doyle	___
1894	*Martin Hewitt, Investigator*	Arthur Morrison	___
1894*	*Tragedy of Pudd'nhead Wilson, The* *(Pudd'nhead Wilson)*	Mark Twain	___
1895*	*Prince Zaleski*	M.P. Shiel	___
1897*	*Dracula*	Bram Stoker	___
1899*	*Amateur Cracksman, The (Raffles,* *the Amateur Crasksman; Raffles)*	E.W. Hornung	___
1902	*Hound of the Baskervilles, The*	Arthur Conan Doyle	___
1903*	*Riddle of the Sands, The*	Erskine Childers	___

1905	*Return of Sherlock Holmes, The*	Arthur Conan Doyle	____
1905*	*Scarlet Pimpernel, The*	Baroness Orczy	____
1906	*Tracks in the Snow*	Godfrey R. Benson (Lord Charnwood)	____
1906	*Triumphs of Eugéne Valmont, The*	Robert Barr	____
1907	*Thinking Machine, The*	Jacques Futrelle	____
1907*	*Ásene Lupin, Gentleman-Cambrioleur (The Exploits of Ársene Lupin; The Seven of Hearts)*	Maurice Leblanc	____
1907	*Mystery of the Yellow Room, The (Murder in the Bedroom; Le Mystére de la Chambre Jaune)*	Gaston Leroux	____
1907	*Red Thumb Mark, The*	R. Austin Freeman	____
1907*	*Secret Agent, The*	Joseph Conrad	____
1908	*Circular Staircase, The*	Mary Roberts Rinehart	____
1908*	*Gentle Grafter, The*	O. Henry	____
1908*	*Man Who was Thursday, The*	G.K. Chesterton	____
1909	*Old Man in the Corner, The (The Man in the Corner)*	Baroness Orczy	____
1909*	*John Thorndyke's Cases (Dr. Thorndyke's Cases)*	R. Austin Freeman	____
1909*	*Perfume of the Lady in Black, The*	Gaston Leroux	____
1909*	*Through the Wall*	Cleveland Moffett	____
1909	*Clue, The*	Carolyn Wells	____
1910	*813*	Maurice Leblanc	____
1910	*At the Villa Rose*	A.E.W. Mason	____
1910*	*Achievements of Luther Trant, The*	William MacHarg & Edwin Balmer	____
1911*	*Eye of Osiris, The (The Vanishing Man)*	R. Austin Freeman	____
1911	*Innocence of Father Brown, The*	G.K. Chesterton	____
1912	*Singing Bone, The (The Adventures of Dr. Thorndyke)*	R. Austin Freeman	____
1912.	*Silent Bullet, The (The Black Hand)*	Arthur B. Reeve	____
1913	*Lodger, The*	Mrs. Marie Belloc Lowndes	____
1913*	*Mystery of Dr. Fu-Manchu, The (The Insidious Dr. Fu-Manchu)*	Sax Rohmer	____
1913	*Trent's Last Case (The Woman in Black)*	E.C. Bentley	____
1914	*Max Carrados*	Ernest Bramah	____
1914*	*Lone Wolf, The*	Louis Joseph Vance	____
1915*	*Thirty-Nine Steps, The*	John Buchan	____
1915	*Valley of Fear, The*	Arthur Conan Doyle	____
1916*	*Limehouse Nights*	Thomas Burke	____
1917	*His Last Bow*	Arthur Conan Doyle	____
1918	*Uncle Abner, Master of Mysteries*	Melville Davisson Post	____
1919	*Middle Temple Murder, The*	J.S. Fletcher	____
1920*	*Mysterious Affair at Styles, The*	Agatha Christie	____
1920	*Cask, The*	Freeman Wills Crofts	____

1920	*Call Mr. Fortune*	H.C. Bailey	____
1920*	*Bulldog Drummond (Bull-Dog Drummond)*	"Sapper" (H.C. McNeile)	____
1920*	*Tutt and Mr. Tutt*	Arthur Train	____
1920*	*Great Impersonation, The*	E. Phillips Oppenheim	____
1921	*Grey Room, The*	Eden Phillpotts	____
1922	*Eight Strokes of the Clock, The* (*Les Huits Coups de l'Horloge*)	Maurice Leblanc	____
1922	*Red House Mystery, The*	A.A. Milne	____
1923	*Brooklyn Murders, The*	G.D.H. Cole	____
1923*	*Whose Body?*	Dorothy L. Sayers	____
1924	*House of the Arrow, The*	A.E.W. Mason	____
1924	*Inspector French's Greatest Case*	Freeman Wills Crofts	____
1924	*Rasp, The*	Philip MacDonald	____
1925	*Mind of Mr. J.G. Reeder, The* (*The Murder Book of J.G. Reeder*)	Edgar Wallace	____
1925	*Paddington Mystery, The*	John Rhode	____
1925	*House Without a Key, The*	Earl Derr Biggers	____
1925*	*American Tragedy, An*	Theodore Dreiser	____
1925*	*Informer, The*	Liam O'Flaherty	____
1925	*Viaduct Murder, The*	Ronald A. Knox	____
1926	*Benson Murder Case, The*	S.S. Van Dine	____
1926*	*Payment Deferred*	C.S. Forester	____
1926	*Murder of Roger Ackroyd, The*	Agatha Christie	____
1927	*Case-Book of Sherlock Holmes, The*	Arthur Conan Doyle	____
1927	*"Canary" Murder Case, The*	S.S. Van Dine	____
1927	*Bellamy Trial, The*	Frances Noyes Hart	____
1928*	*Murders in Praed Street, The*	John Rhode	____
1928*	*Ashenden; or, The British Agent*	W. Somerset Maugham	____
1928*	*Meet the Tiger! (Meet—The Tiger!; The Saint Meets the Tiger; Crooked Gold)*	Leslie Charteris	____
1929	*Poisoned Chocolates Case, The*	Anthony Berkeley	____
1929	*Roman Hat Mystery, The*	Ellery Queen	____
1929*	*Murder by the Clock*	Rufus King	____
1929*	*Little Caesar*	W.R. Burnett	____
1929*	*Clues of the Caribbees (Clues of the Caribees)*	T.S. Stribling	____
1929*	*Detective Duff Unravels It*	Harvey J. O'Higgins	____
1929	*Patient in Room 18, The*	Mignon G. Eberhart	____
1930	*Book of Murder, The*	Frederick Irving Anderson	____
1930	*Maltese Falcon, The*	Dashiell Hammett	____
1930	*Hammersmith Murders, The*	David Frome	____
1930	*Documents in the Case, The*	Dorothy L. Sayers & Robert Eustace	____
1931*	*Glass Key, The*	Dashiell Hammett	____
1931*	*Penguin Pool Murder, The*	Stuart Palmer	____
1931*	*Death Walks in Eastrepps*	Francis Beeding	____

1931*	Murder at School (Was It Murder?)	Glen Trevor (James Hilton)	___
1931*	Guys and Dolls	Damon Runyon	___
1931	Cape Cod Mystery, The	Phoebe Atwood Taylor	___
1932	Red Castle, The (The Red Castle Mystery)	H.C. Bailey	___
1932	Before the Fact	Francis Iles	___
1932	Tragedy of X, The	Barnaby Ross (Ellery Queen)	___
1932*	Tragedy of Y, The	Barnaby Ross (Ellery Queen)	___
1932	Fatal Five Minutes, The	R.A.J. Walling	___
1932	Re-Enter Sir John	Clemence Dane & Helen Simpson	___
1933	Case of the Sulky Girl, The	Erle Stanley Gardner	___
1933*	Case of the Velvet Claws, The	Erle Stanley Gardner	___
1934	Nine Tailors, The	Dorothy L. Sayers	___
1934	Death of a Ghost	Margery Allingham	___
1934*	Postman Always Rings Twice, The	James M. Cain	___
1934	Fer-de-Lance (Meet Nero Wolfe)	Rex Stout	___
1934	Murder of My Aunt, The	Richard Hull	___
1934##	Plague Court Murders, The	Carter Dickson	___
1935*	No Hero (Mr. Moto Takes a Hand; Your Turn, Mr Moto)	John P. Marquand	___
1935*	League of Frightened Men, The	Rex Stout	___
1936##	Arabian Nights Murder, The	John Dickson Carr	___
1937	Trial and Error	Anthony Berkeley	___
1938*	Warrant for X (The Nursemaid Who Disappeared)	Philip MacDonald	___
1938@@	Crooked Hinge, The	John Dickson Carr	___
1938@@	Judas Window, The (The Crossbow Murder)	Carter Dickson	___
1938	Beast Must Die, The	Nicholas Blake	___
1938	Lament for a Maker	Michael Innes	___
1938*	Death From a Top Hat	Clayton Rawson	___
1938*	Brighton Rock	Graham Greene	___
1938*	Rebecca	Daphne du Maurier	___
1938	Listening House, The	Mabel Seeley	___
1939	Overture to Death	Ngaio Marsh	___
1939	Coffin for Dimitrios, A (The Mask of Dimitrios)	Eric Ambler	___
1939	Big Sleep, The	Raymond Chandler	___
1939	Patience of Maigret, The (2 books: A Battle of Nerves; A Face for a Clue)	Georges Simenon	___
1939*	Mysterious Mickey Finn, The; or, Murder at the Café du Dome	Elliot Paul	___
1940	Verdict of Twelve	Raymond Postgate	___
1940	Norths Meet Murder, The (Mr. & Mrs. North Meet Murder; A Taste for Murder)	Frances & Richard Lockridge	___
1940	So Blue Marble, The	Dorothy B. Hughes	___
1940*	Bride Wore Black, The (Beware the Lady)	Cornell Woolrich	___
1940	Farewell, My Lovely	Raymond Chandler	___

1940	*Drink to Yesterday*	Manning Coles	____
1941	*Toast to Tomorrow, A (Pray Silence)*	Manning Coles	____
1941*	*Taste for Honey, A (A Taste for Murder)*	H.F. Heard	____
1941	*Trial by Fury*	Craig Rice	____
1942*	*Calamity Town*	Ellery Queen	____
1942*	*Rocket to the Morgue*	H.H. Holmes (Anthony Boucher)	____
1942	*Phantom Lady*	William Irish (Cornell Woolrich)	____
1942*	*Just and the Unjust, The*	James Gould Cozzens	____
1943*	*Laura*	Vera Caspary	____
1944*	*Adventures of Sam Spade and Other Stories, The (They Can Only Hang You Once)*	Dashiell Hammett	____
1944	*Home Sweet Homicide*	Craig Rice	____
1944	*Blood Upon the Snow*	Hilda Lawrence	____
1945*	*Curse of the Bronze Lamp, The (Lord of the Sorcerers)*	Carter Dickson	____
1946	*Horizontal Man, The*	Helen Eustis	____
1946*	*Unsuspected, The*	Charlotte Armstrong	____
1946*	*Dr. Sam: Johnson, Detector*	Lillian de la Torre	____
1946	*Moving Toyshop, The*	Edmund Crispin	____
1947	*In a Lonely Place*	Dorothy B. Hughes	____
1947	*One More Unfortunate (A Case to Answer)*	Edgar Lustgarten	____
1947*	*Department of Dead Ends, The*	Roy Vickers	____
1948	*Franchise Affair, The*	Josephine Tey	____
1948*	*Intruder in the Dust*	William Faulkner	____
1948	*Wisteria Cottage (The Night Before Dying)*	Robert M. Coates	____
1948	*Dreadful Summit (The Big Night)*	Stanley Ellin	____
1948	*Love Lies Bleeding*	Edmund Crispin	____
1949	*Moving Target, The (Harper)*	Ross Macdonald (as, John Macdonald)	____
1950	*People Against O'Hara, The*	Eleazar Lipsky	____
1950	*Motive, The (Death of a Nymph)*	Evelyn Piper	____
1950	*Nightmare in Manhattan*	Thomas Walsh	____
1950	*Through a Glass, Darkly*	Helen McCloy	____
1950	*Blues for the Prince*	Bart Spicer	____
1950	*Mischief*	Charlotte Armstrong	____
1950	*Simple Art of Murder, The* (1 essay and stories)	Raymond Chandler	____
1951	*Gentle Murderer, A*	Dorothy Salisbury Davis	____
1952	*Little Tales of Smethers, The*	Lord Dunsany	____

A Selected List of Detective Story Anthologies, by Howard Haycraft

1931	*Sleuths: Twenty-Three Great Detectives of Fiction and their Best Stories*	Kenneth MacGowan	___
1938	*Challenge to the Reader: An Anthology*	Ellery Queen	___
1929	*Omnibus of Crime, The*	Dorothy L. Sayers, ed.	___
1932	*Second Omnibus of Crime, The: The World's Great Crime Stories*	Dorothy L. Sayers, ed.	___
1935	*Third Omnibus of Crime 1935, The*	Dorothy L. Sayers, ed.	___
1936	*Tales of Detection*	Dorothy L. Sayers, ed.	___
1928	*Fourteen Great Detective Stories*	Starrett Vincent, ed.	___
1929	*World's Best 100 Detective Stories, The*	Eugene Thwing, ed.	___
1941	*Pocket Book of Great Detectives, The*	Lee Wright, ed.	___
1927	*Great Detective Stories, The*	Wright Willard Huntington, ed.	___
1926	*Crime and Detection*	E.M. Wrong	___

Haycraft Juvenile

1938	*Boys' Book of Great Detective Stories, The*	Howard Haycraft, ed.	___
1940	*Boys' Second Book of Great Detective Stories, The*	Howard Haycraft, ed.	___

Haycraft Specialties

1936	*Six Against Scotland Yard (Six Against the Yard)*	Detection Club of London	___
1931	*Floating Admiral, The*	Detection Club of London	___
1933	*Ask a Policeman*	Detection Club of London	___
1940	*Line-Up*	John Rhode, ed. (for the Detection Club)	___

www.topmystery.com/books15.htm
www.classiccrimefiction.com/haycraftqueen.htm
home.comcast.net/~dwtaylor1/haycraftqueen.html
www.detective-fiction.com/haycraftqueen-cornerstones.htm

Independent Mystery Booksellers Association (IMBA) 100 Favorite Mysteries of the Century

Selected by the Independent Mystery Booksellers Association (IMBA), Edited by Jim Huang

Members of the Independent Mystery Booksellers Association's have looked back at a century of mysteries and murder and compiled a list of the *100 Favorite Mysteries of the Century*. This was accomplished by an online discussion group that spent nearly two months considering and debating hundreds of titles recommended by mystery booksellers throughout the country. Each title has a short essay about the work. IMBA's book, *100 Favorite Mysteries of the Century*, was published in December 2000 by The Crum Creek Press/Drood Review Books. The titles date from 1902 to 1998.

IMBA 100 Mysteries			
1952	*Tiger in the Smoke, The*	Margery Allingham	____
1939	*Coffin for Dimitrios, A (The Mask of Dimitrios)*	Eric Ambler	____
1956	*Dram of Poison, A*	Charlotte Armstrong	____
1992	*Aunt Dimity's Death*	Nancy Atherton	____
1965	*In the Heat of the Night*	John Ball	____
1982	*Death by Sheer Torture (Sheer Torture)*	Robert Barnard	____
1993	*Track of the Cat*	Nevada Barr	____
1938	*Beast Must Die, The*	Nicholas Blake	____
1986	*When the Sacred Ginmill Closes*	Lawrence Block	____
1944	*Green for Danger*	Christianna Brand	____
1947	*Fabulous Clipjoint, The*	Fredric Brown	____
1915	*Thirty-Nine Steps, The*	John Buchan	____
1989	*Black Cherry Blues*	James Lee Burke	____
1934	*Postman Always Rings Twice, The*	James M. Cain	____
1984	*Thin Woman, The*	Dorothy Cannell	____
1935	*Three Coffins, The (The Hollow Man)*	John Dickson Carr	____
1981	*Thus was Adonis Murdered*	Sarah Caudwell	____
1939	*Big Sleep, The*	Raymond Chandler	____
1926	*Murder of Roger Ackroyd, The*	Agatha Christie	____
1994	*Concrete Blonde, The*	Michael Connelly	____
1982	*Man Who Liked Slow Tomatoes, The*	K.C. Constantine	____
1987	*Monkey's Raincoat, The*	Robert Crais	____
1946	*Moving Toyshop, The*	Edmund Crispin	____
1997	*Dreaming of the Bones*	Deborah Crombie	____
1978	*Last Good Kiss, The*	James Crumley	____
1994	*Yellow Room Conspiracy, The*	Peter Dickinson	____
1902	*Hound of the Baskervilles, The*	Arthur Conan Doyle	____
1938	*Rebecca*	Daphne du Maurier	____
1992	*Booked to Die*	John Dunning	____

1987	*Old Bones*	Aaron Elkins	___
1994	*One for the Money*	Janet Evanovich	___
1970	*Time and Again*	Jack Finney	___
1995	*Who in Hell is Wanda Fuca?*	G.M. Ford	___
1979	*Whip Hand*	Dick Francis	___
1958	*Hours Before Dawn, The*	Celia Fremlin	___
1988	*Great Deliverance, A*	Elizabeth George	___
1950	*Smallbone Deceased*	Michael Gilbert	___
1982	*"A" is for Alibi*	Sue Grafton	___
1987	*Killings at Badger's Drift, The*	Caroline Graham	___
1981	*Man With a Load of Mischief, The*	Martha Grimes	___
1930	*Maltese Falcon, The*	Dashiell Hammett	___
1951	*English Murder, An (The Christmas Murder)*	Cyril Hare	___
1988	*Silence of the Lambs, The*	Thomas Harris	___
1986	*Tourist Season*	Carl Hiaasen	___
1955	*Talented Mr. Ripley, The*	Patricia Highsmith	___
1998	*On Beulah Height*	Reginald Hill	___
1988	*Thief of Time, A*	Tony Hillerman	___
1965	*Cotton Comes to Harlem*	Chester Himes	___
1937	*Hamlet, Revenge!*	Michael Innes	___
1972	*Unsuitable Job for a Woman, An*	P.D. James	___
1986	*Ritual Bath, The*	Faye Kellerman	___
1985	*When the Bough Breaks (Shrunken Heads)*	Jonathan Kellerman	___
1994	*Beekeeper's Apprentice, The*	Laurie R. King	___
1975	*Dark Nantucket Noon*	Jane Langton	___
1963	*Spy Who Came in From the Cold, The*	John le Carre	___
1960	*To Kill a Mockingbird*	Harper Lee	___
1996	*Darkness, Take My Hand*	Dennis Lehane	___
1990	*Get Shorty*	Elmore Leonard	___
1985	*Sleeping Dog*	Dick Lochte	___
1986	*Rough Cider*	Peter Lovesey	___
1964	*Deep Blue Good-by, The*	John D. MacDonald	___
1959	*List of Adrian Messenger, The*	Philip MacDonald	___
1964	*Chill, The*	Ross Macdonald	___
1992	*Bootlegger's Daughter*	Margaret Maron	___
1940	*Death of a Peer (Surfeit of Lampreys)*	Ngaio Marsh	___
1972	*Sadie When She Died*	Ed McBain	___
1977	*Sunday Hangman, The*	James McClure	___
1990	*If Ever I Return, Pretty Peggy-O (If Ever I Return)*	Sharyn McCrumb	___
1960	*Stranger in My Grave, A*	Margaret Millar	___
1990	*Devil in a Blue Dress*	Walter Mosley	___
1977	*Edwin of the Iron Shoes*	Marcia Muller	___
1988	*Death's Bright Angel*	Janet Neel	___
1994	*Mallory's Oracle*	Carol O'Connell	___
1993	*Child of Silence*	Abigail Padgett	___

1984	*Deadlock*	Sara Paretsky	_____
1980	*Looking for Rachel Wallace*	Robert B. Parker	_____
1996	*Club Dumas, The (Dumas Club)*	Arturo Perez-Reverte	_____
1995	*Vanishing Act*	Thomas Perry	_____
1975	*Crocodile on the Sandbank*	Elizabeth Peters	_____
1979	*One Corpse too Many*	Ellis Peters	_____
1995	*Blue Lonesome*	Bill Pronzini	_____
1949	*Cat of Many Tails*	Ellery Queen	_____
1971	*No More Dying Then*	Ruth Rendell	_____
1940	*Wrong Murder, The*	Craig Rice	_____
1908	*Circular Staircase, The*	Mary Roberts Rinehart	_____
1997	*Blood at the Root (Dead Right)*	Peter Robinson	_____
1984	*Strike Three You're Dead*	R.D. Rosen	_____
1994	*Broken Vessel, A*	Kate Ross	_____
1995	*Concourse*	S.J. Rozan	_____
1933	*Murder Must Advertise*	Dorothy L. Sayers	_____
1970	*Laughing Policeman, The*	Maj Sjowall & Per Wahloo	_____
1938	*Some Buried Caesar (The Red Bull)*	Rex Stout	_____
1949	*Brat Farrar (Come and Kill Me)*	Josephine Tey	_____
1978	*Chinaman's Chance*	Ross Thomas	_____
1996	*Test of Wills, A*	Charles Todd	_____
1987	*Presumed Innocent*	Scott Turow	_____
1931	*Sands of Windee, The*	Arthur W. Upfield	_____
1992	*Ice House, The*	Minette Walters	_____
1990	*Sanibel Flats*	Randy Wayne White	_____
1948	*I Married a Dead Man*	Cornell Woolrich (William Irish)	_____

www.topmystery.com/books1.htm
www.mysterybooksellers.com/favorites.html

100 Favorite Mysteries of the Century
Additional Books Selected by the
Independent Mystery Booksellers Association (IMBA)
Edited by Jim Huang

The title suggestions are from Part II of *100 Favorite Mysteries of the Century*, selected by the *Independent Mystery Booksellers Association*, edited by Jim Huang, 2000. These are titles suggested by contributors who could submit up to five titles each that did not make the above list. There are 120 titles dating from 1905 to 2000.

IMBA Additional Books

1996	*Night Dogs*	Kent Anderson	___
1954	*Caves of Steel, The*	Isaac Asimov	___
1991	*Scandal in Belgravia, A*	Robert Barnard	___
1930	*Hidden Staircase, The* (Nancy Drew, #2)	Mildred Wirt Benson	___
1929	*Poisoned Chocolates Case, The*	Anthony Berkeley	___
1926	*Chinese Parrot, The*	Earl Derr Biggers	___
1998	*Everybody Dies*	Lawrence Block	___
1998	*Hit Man*	Lawrence Block	___
1987	*Neon Rain, The*	James Lee Burke	___
1993	*Goodnight, Irene*	Jan Burke	___
1998	*Hocus*	Jan Burke	___
1940	*Death at the Dog*	Joanna Cannan	___
1985	*Audition for Murder*	P.M. Carlson	___
1969	*Whispering Wall, The*	Patricia Carlon	___
1997	*Killing Floor*	Lee Child	___
1999	*Final Detail, The*	Harlan Coben	___
1992	*Bucket Nut*	Liza Cody	___
1980	*Dupe*	Liza Cody	___
1941	*Toast to Tomorrow, A (Pray Silence)*	Manning Coles	___
1998	*Flying Blind*	Max Allan Collins	___
1983	*True Detective*	Max Allan Collins	___
1995	*Breakheart Hill*	Thomas H. Cook	___
1999	*L.A. Requiem*	Robert Crais	___
1964	*In the Last Analysis*	Amanda Cross	___
1989	*Silver Pigs*	Lindsey Davis	___
1996	*Strange Files of Fremont Jones, The*	Dianne Day	___
1995	*Maiden's Grave, A*	Jeffery Deaver	___
1984	*First Hit of the Season*	Jane Dentinger	___
1977	*Silent World of Nicholas Quinn, The*	Colin Dexter	___
1996	*Cosi Fan Tutti*	Michael Dibdin	___
1927	*House on the Cliff, The* (Hardy Boys, #2)	Franklin W. Dixon	___
1983	*Name of the Rose, The*	Umberto Eco	___
1987	*Black Dahlia, The*	James Ellroy	___

1994	*Portland Laughter, The*	Earl Emerson	___
1999	*Hours of the Virgin, The*	Loren D. Estleman	___
1959	*Goldfinger*	Ian Fleming	___
1966	*King of the Rainy Country, The*	Nicolas Freeling	___
1988	*Question of Guilt, A*	Frances Fyfield	___
1999	*Anonymous Rex*	Eric Garcia	___
1980	*Paladin, The*	Brian Garfield	___
1977	*Judas Pair, The*	Jonathan Gash	___
1975	*Clairvoyant Countess*	Dorothy Gilman	___
1979	*Tightrope Walker, The*	Dorothy Gilman	___
1998	*Dead Cat Bounce, The*	Sarah Graves	___
1938	*Brighton Rock*	Graham Greene	___
1982	*Gravedigger*	Joseph Hansen	___
1942	*Tragedy at Law*	Cyril Hare	___
1989	*Lonely Hearts*	John Harvey	___
1992	*Off Minor*	John Harvey	___
1994	*What's a Girl Gotta Do?*	Sparkle Hayter	___
1987	*Malice in Maggody*	Joan Hess	___
1987	*Double Whammy*	Carl Hiaasen	___
1994	*Pictures of Perfection*	Reginald Hill	___
1996	*Grass Widow, The*	Teri Holbrook	___
1939	*Rogue Male (Man Hunt)*	Geoffrey Household	___
1946	*Ride the Pink Horse*	Dorothy B. Hughes	___
1934	*Murder of My Aunt, The*	Richard Hull	___
1993	*Point of Impact*	Stephen Hunter	___
1931	*Malice Aforethought*	Francis Iles	___
1988	*Grave Designs (The Canaan Legacy)*	Michael A. Kahn	___
1991	*Thousand Yard Stare, The*	Rob Kantner	___
1964	*Friday the Rabbi Slept Late*	Harry Kemelman	___
1996	*With Child*	Laurie R. King	___
1987	*Watchers*	Dean Koontz	___
1964	*Accounting for Murder*	Emma Lathen	___
1979	*Family Vault, The*	Charlotte MacLeod	___
1988	*Bimbos of the Death Sun*	Sharyn McCrumb	___
1996	*Death at Rainy Mountain*	Mardi Oakley Medawar	___
1993	*Houses of Stone*	Barbara Michaels (Elizabeth Peters)	___
1992	*Seneca Falls Inheritance*	Miriam Grace Monfredo	___
1987	*Voyage of the Chianti, The*	B.J. Morison	___
1967	*Murder Fantastical*	Patricia Moyes	___
1998	*Legwork*	Katy Munger	___
1998	*Cursed in the Blood*	Sharan Newman	___
1994	*Death Comes as Epiphany*	Sharan Newman	___
1993	*Pomona Queen*	Kem Nunn	___
1997	*Stone Angel (Flight of the Stone Angel)*	Carol O'Connell	___
1983	*Cop Without a Shield*	Lillian O'Donnell	___

1998	*Blue*	Abigail Padgett	___
1985	*Kill Fee*	Barbara Paul	___
1991	*Raphael Affair, The*	Iain Pears	___
1997	*King Suckerman*	George P. Pelecanos	___
1988	*Cater Street Hangman, The*	Anne Perry	___
1990	*Face of a Stranger, The*	Anne Perry	___
1961	*Death and the Joyful Woman*	Ellis Peters	___
1918	*Complete Uncle Abner, The*	Melville Davisson Post	___
1970	*Labyrinth Makers, The*	Anthony Price	___
1988	*Shackles*	Bill Pronzini	___
1997	*Wasteland of Strangers, A*	Bill Pronzini	___
2000	*Set in Darkness*	Ian Rankin	___
1999	*Remedy for Treason*	Caroline Roe	___
1992	*Long-Legged Fly, The*	James Sallis	___
1996	*Sudden Prey*	John Sandford	___
1989	*Miss Lizzie*	Walter Satterthwait	___
1935	*Gaudy Night*	Dorothy L. Sayers	___
1993	*Catilina's Riddle*	Steven Saylor	___
1970/72	*Maigret and the Madwoman*	Georges Simenon	___
1931/39	*Maigret and the Yellow Dog (A Face for a Clue; Maigret and the Concarneau Murders)*	Georges Simenon	___
1985	*Last Seen Alive*	Dorothy Simpson	___
1990	*New Orleans Mourning*	Julie Smith	___
1981	*Gorky Park*	Martin Cruz Smith	___
1948	*I, the Jury*	Mickey Spillane	___
1992	*Cold Day for Murder, A*	Dana Stabenow	___
1971	*Slayground*	Richard Stark (Donald E. Westlake)	___
1998	*Angels Will Not Care, The*	John Straley	___
1996	*Sex and Salmonella*	Kathleen Taylor	___
1951	*Daughter of Time, The*	Josephine Tey	___
1944	*Dead Ernest*	Alice Tilton (Phoebe Atwood Taylor)	___
1940	*Left Leg, The*	Alice Tilton (Phoebe Atwood Taylor)	___
1994	*Absolution by Murder*	Peter Tremayne	___
1975	*Outsider in Amsterdam*	Janwillem van de Wetering	___
1959	*Chinese Gold Murders, The*	Robert van Gulik	___
1947	*Department of Dead Ends, The*	Roy Vickers	___
1996	*Under the Beetle's Cellar*	Mary Willis Walker	___
1911	*Four Just Men, The*	Edgar Wallace	___
1997	*Ax, The (Axe, The)*	Donald E. Westlake	___
1993	*Don't Ask*	Donald E. Westlake	___
1984	*Miami Blues*	Charles Willeford	___
1991	*Cool Breeze on the Underground, A*	Don Winslow	___
1965	*Though I Know She Lies*	Sara Woods	___

They Died in Vain
Overlooked, Underappreciated and Forgotten Mystery Novels

Edited by Jim Huang (2002)

This list grew out of the Independent Mystery Booksellers Association's list of 100 favorite mysteries of the twentieth century (published in 2000). These titles are seen as omissions and other favorites that they wanted readers to experience in the mystery field. As Jim Huang states in the introduction, "We go beyond the bestsellers, beyond the familiar." In fact they did not include bestsellers! There are 103 titles and essays written by various contributors. Only one book per author was selected. The titles date from 1878 to 2000.

They Died in Vain			
1969	*Stately Home Murder, The (The Complete Steel)*	Catherine Aird	____
1996	*Night Dogs*	Kent Anderson	____
2000	*Death From the Woods*	Brigitte Aubert	____
2000	*Death's Favorite Child*	Frankie Y. Bailey	____
1995	*Complicity*	Iain Banks	____
1991	*Death and Other Lovers*	Jo Bannister	____
1987	*Trouble of Fools, A*	Linda Barnes	____
1995	*Done Wrong*	Eleanor Taylor Bland	____
1989	*Working Murder*	Eleanor Boylan	____
1950	*Hardly a Man is Now Alive (Murder Now and Then)*	Herbert Brean	____
1969	*Whispering Wall, The*	Patricia Carlon	____
1943	*Laura*	Vera Caspary	____
1954	*According to the Evidence*	Henry Cecil	____
1977	*Shadow of a Broken Man*	George C. Chesbro	____
2000	*Running Blind (The Visitor)*	Lee Child	____
1994	*Famine of Horses, A*	P.F. Chisholm	____
1992	*Bucket Nut*	Liza Cody	____
1943	*Without Lawful Authority*	Manning Coles	____
1988	*Man in the Green Chevy, The*	Susan Rogers Cooper	____
1997	*Show of Hands, A*	David A. Crossman	____
1994	*Rough Cut*	Stan Cutler	____
1998	*Good Cop, Bad Cop*	Barbara D'Amato	____
1941	*Murders in Volume 2*	Elizabeth Daly	____
1999	*Victim in Victoria Station, The*	Jeanne M. Dams	____
1994	*Irene's Last Waltz (Another Scandal in Bohemia)*	Carole Nelson Douglas	____
1994	*Matricide at St. Martha's*	Ruth Dudley Edwards	____
1994	*Portland Laughter, The*	Earl Emerson	____
1998	*Jitterbug*	Loren D. Estleman	____

1992	*Death of the Duchess*	Elizabeth Eyre	____
1996	*Kill Me Again*	Terence Faherty	____
1997	*Pest Control*	Bill Fitzhugh	____
1942	*Murder in the O.P.M. (The Priority Murder)*	Leslie Ford	____
1984	*Asia Rip (Tidal Race)*	George Foy	____
1988	*Question of Guilt, A*	Frances Fyfield	____
1979	*Paladin, The*	Brian Garfield	____
1929	*Unpunished*	Charlotte Perkins Gilman	____
1979	*Tightrope Walker, The*	Dorothy Gilman	____
1979	*Zero Trap, The*	Paula Gosling	____
1950	*Beyond a Reasonable Doubt*	C.W. Grafton	____
1878	*Leavenworth Case, The*	Anna Katharine Green	____
1990	*Not a Creature was Stirring*	Jane Haddam	____
1989	*Dog in the Dark*	Gerald Hammond	____
1946	*With a Bare Bodkin*	Cyril Hare	____
1965	*Last Known Address, The*	Joseph Harrington	____
1993	*Christening Day Murder, The*	Lee Harris	____
1995	*Edge of the Crazies, The*	Jamie Harrison	____
1989	*Lonely Hearts*	John Harvey	____
1994	*Comedy of Murders, A*	George Herman	____
1941	*Envious Casca*	Georgette Heyer	____
1978	*Falling Angel*	William Hjortsberg	____
1993	*Midnight Baby*	Wendy Hornsby	____
1984	*Bridge of Birds*	Barry Hughart	____
1932	*Before the Fact*	Francis Iles	____
1997	*Panicking Ralph*	Bill James	____
2000	*Bearing Witness*	Michael A. Kahn	____
1993	*Red, White, and Blues, The*	Rob Kantner	____
1990.	*Park Lane South, Queens*	Mary Anne Kelly	____
1998	*Iron Lake*	William Kent Krueger	____
1991	*Loud Adios, The*	Ken Kuhlken	____
1996	*Debt to Pleasure, The*	John Lanchester	____
1987	*Nightrunners, The*	Joe R. Lansdale	____
1989	*Burn Season*	John Lantigua	____
1991	*Killing Suki Flood*	Robert Leininger	____
1992	*Death at La Fenice*	Donna Leon	____
1908	*Mystery of the Yellow Room, The (Murder in the Bedroom)*	Gaston Leroux	____
1938	*Warrant for X (The Nursemaid Who Disappeared)*	Philip MacDonald	____
1984	*Back Room in Somers Town, A*	John Malcolm	____
1956	*Mecca for Murder*	Stephen Marlowe	____
1995	*Fugitive Colors*	Margaret Maron	____
1990	*Borderlines*	Archer Mayor	____
1991	*Boy's Life*	Robert R. McCammon	____

1991	*Murders of Mrs. Austin and Mrs. Beale, The*	Jill McGown	___
1992	*Dead Letters*	Sean McGrady	___
1986	*Beyond the Grave*	Marcia Muller & Bill Pronzini	___
1998	*Blanche Cleans Up*	Barbara Neely	___
1997	*Dogs of Winter, The*	Kem Nunn	___
1980	*Pew Group, The*	Anthony Oliver	___
1938	*Fast Company*	Marco Page	___
1993	*Apostrophe Thief, The*	Barbara Paul	___
1996	*Big Blowdown, The*	George P. Pelecanos	___
1982	*Butcher's Boy, The*	Thomas Perry	___
1972	*Seventh Sinner, The*	Elizabeth Peters	___
1989	*Down in the Valley*	David M. Pierce	___
1945	*Common or Garden Crime*	Sheila Pim	___
1967.	*Dover and the Unkindest Cut of All*	Joyce Porter	___
1956	*Wailing Frail, The*	Richard S. Prather	___
1988	*Shackles*	Bill Pronzini	___
1990	*I was Dora Suarez*	Derek Raymond	___
1997	*Bird Dog*	Philip Reed	___
1934	*Line-Up, The*	Helen Reilly	___
1985	*Latimer Mercy, The*	Robert Richardson	___
1909	*Man in Lower Ten, The*	Mary Roberts Rinehart	___
1994	*Chicken Little was Right*	Jean Ruryk	___
1994	*Hotel Detective, The*	Alan Russell	___
1991	*Wilde West*	Walter Satterthwait	___
1996	*Concrete River, The*	John Shannon	___
1989	*Never Quite Dead*	Seymour Shubin	___
1959	*Nine Coaches Waiting*	Mary Stewart	___
1940	*Left Leg, The*	Alice Tilton	___
		(Phoebe Atwood Taylor)	
1969	*Just What the Doctor Ordered*	Colin Watson	___
	(The Flaxborough Crab)		
1959	*Sleep Long, My Love (Jigsaw)*	Hillary Waugh	___
1982.	*Kahawa*	Donald E. Westlake	___
1991	*Cool Breeze on the Underground, A*	Don Winslow	___

Mystery Muses:
100 Classics That Inspire Today's Mystery Writers

Edited by Jim Huang and Austin Lugar (2006)

One hundred mystery writers were asked to list a title that inspired them to write. These titles are referred to as classics in that they were seen as important to each of the writer's pasts. Several of the selections are short stories, other are collections of stories, and others are youth or children's stories. Each of these 100 titles has a short essay written by the presenter that helps to illustrate why that work influenced them. The year span was from 1846 to 1998. Fifty were published prior to 1952 and fifty published after 1952.

Four women had three or more titles listed: Agatha Christie with seven titles, Dorothy L. Sayers with six, Josephine Tey with four, and Margery Allingham with three. The 1930s had the most titles at 26. Titles are listed as they appear in the book.

Mystery Muses 100 Classics			
1846	*"Cask of Amontillado, The"*	Edgar Allan Poe	___
1843	*"Tell-Tale Heart, The"*	Edgar Allan Poe	___
1868	*Moonstone, The*	Wilkie Collins	___
1892	*"Speckled Band, The"*	Arthur Conan Doyle	___
1907	*Red Thumb Mark, The*	R. Austin Freeman	___
1911	*Innocence of Father Brown, The*	G.K. Chesterton	___
1920	*Mysterious Affair at Styles, The*	Agatha Christie	___
1924	*Three Hostages, The*	John Buchan	___
1926	*Murder of Roger Ackroyd, The*	Agatha Christie	___
1927	*Tower Treasure, The* (Hardy Boys, #1)	Franklin W. Dixon	___
1929	*Poet and the Lunatics, The*	G.K. Chesterton	___
1929	*Red Harvest*	Dashiell Hammett	___
1930	*Mystery Mile*	Margery Allingham	___
1930	*Murder at the Vicarage, The*	Agatha Christie	___
1927	*Complete Sherlock Holmes, The*	Arthur Conan Doyle	___
1930	*Maltese Falcon, The*	Dashiell Hammett	___
1930	*Strong Poison*	Dorothy L. Sayers	___
1932	*Freddy the Detective* (youth)	Walter R. Brooks	___
1932	*Have His Carcase*	Dorothy L. Sayers	___
1933	*Fear Sign, The (Kingdom of Death; Sweet Danger)*	Margery Allingham	___
1933	*Sign of the Twisted Candles, The* (Nancy Drew, #9)	Carolyn Keene	___
1933	*Murder Must Advertise*	Dorothy L. Sayers	___
1934	*Postman Always Rings Twice, The*	James M. Cain	___
1934	*Murder on the Orient Express (Murder in the Calais Coach)*	Agatha Christie	___

1934	*Chinese Orange Mystery, The*	Ellery Queen	___
1934	*Nine Tailors, The*	Dorothy L. Sayers	___
1934	*Fer-de-Lance (Meet Nero Wolfe)*	Rex Stout	___
1935	*Saint in New York, The*	Leslie Charteris	___
1935	*Case of the Counterfeit Eye, The*	Erle Stanley Gardner	___
1935	*Gaudy Night*	Dorothy L. Sayers	___
1937	*Burning Court, The*	John Dickson Carr	___
1937	*Busman's Honeymoon*	Dorothy L. Sayers	___
1938	*Rebecca*	Daphne du Maurier	___
1938	*Lament for a Maker*	Michael Innes	___
1938	*Dance of Death (Design for Dying)*	Helen McCloy	___
1939	*Mask of Dimitrios, The (A Coffin for Dimitrios)*	Eric Ambler	___
1939	*Big Sleep, The*	Raymond Chandler	___
1939	*And Then There Were None (Ten Little Niggers)*	Agatha Christie	___
1936/43	*Double Indemnity*	James M. Cain	___
1946	*Miss Pym Disposes*	Josephine Tey	___
1948	*Franchise Affair, The*	Josephine Tey	___
1949	*Cat of Many Tails*	Ellery Queen	___
1949	*Brat Farrar (Come and Kill Me)*	Josephine Tey	___
1950	*Trouble is My Business* (collection)	Raymond Chandler	___
1950	*Murder is Announced, A*	Agatha Christie	___
1950	*Strangers on a Train*	Patricia Highsmith	___
1951	*They Came to Baghdad*	Agatha Christie	___
1951	*Big Kill, The*	Mickey Spillane	___
1951	*Daughter of Time, The*	Josephine Tey	___
1952	*Killer Inside Me, The*	Jim Thompson	___
1954	*Caves of Steel, The*	Isaac Asimov	___
1955	*Beckoning Lady, The (The Estate of the Beckoning Lady)*	Margery Allingham	___
1955	*Scales of Justice*	Ngaio Marsh	___
1955	*Strip for Murder*	Richard S. Prather	___
1957	*Door Into Summer, The*	Robert Heinlein	___
1959	*Pink Motel, The* (youth)	Carol Ryrie Brink	___
1960	*Watcher in the Shadows*	Geoffrey Household	___
1961	*Death and the Joyful Woman*	Ellis Peters	___
1961	*Ivy Tree, The*	Mary Stewart	___
1962	*Dead Cert*	Dick Francis	___
1962	*Moon-Spinner, The*	Mary Stewart	___
1963	*Night of the Generals, The*	Hans Hellmut Kirst	___
1964	*Harriet the Spy* (youth)	Louise Fitzhugh	___
1964	*Chill, The*	Ross Macdonald	___
1964	*Pop. 1280*	Jim Thompson	___
1965	*Odds Against*	Dick Francis	___
1966	*Darker Than Amber*	John D. MacDonald	___
1967	*Secret Agents Four* (youth)	Donald J. Sobol	___

1968	*Photogenic Soprano, The (Dolly and the Singing Bird; Rum Affair)*	Dorothy Dunnett (Dorothy Halliday) ___
1968	*Ammie, Come Home*	Barbara Michaels (Elizabeth Peters) ___
1969	*Murder to Go*	Emma Lathen ___
1969	*Goodbye Look, The*	Ross Macdonald ___
1970	*Blessing Way, The*	Tony Hillerman ___
1971	*Day of the Jackal, The*	Frederick Forsyth ___
1971	*Murder in the Walls*	Richard Martin Stern ___
1972.	*Unsuitable Job for a Woman, An*	P.D. James ___
1973	*Godwulf Manuscript, The*	Robert B. Parker ___
1973	*First Deadly Sin, The*	Lawrence Sanders ___
1974	*Tinker, Tailor, Soldier, Spy*	John le Carre ___
1975	*Salem's Lot*	Stephen King ___
1976	*Buyer Beware*	John Lutz ___
1977	*Judgement in Stone, A*	Ruth Rendell ___
1978	*Compromising Positions*	Susan Isaacs ___
1978	*Empty Copper Sea, The*	John D. MacDonald ___
1978	*Judas Goat, The*	Robert B. Parker ___
1979	*Tightrope Walker, The*	Dorothy Gilman ___
1983	*Name of the Rose, The*	Umberto Eco ___
1984	*Briarpatch*	Ross Thomas ___
1986	*"C" is for Corpse*	Sue Grafton ___
1987	*Presumed Innocent*	Scott Turow ___
1988	*Silence of the Lambs, The*	Thomas Harris ___
1988	*Thief of Time, A*	Tony Hillerman ___
1988	*Eight, The*	Katherine Neville ___
1989	*Black Cherry Blues*	James Lee Burke ___
1989	*Time's Witness*	Michael Malone ___
1992	*Bootlegger's Daughter*	Margaret Maron ___
1994	*She Walks These Hills*	Sharyn McCrumb ___
1995	*Breakheart Hill*	Thomas H. Cook ___
1996	*What's the Worst That Could Happen?*	Donald E. Westlake ___
1998	*Gone, Baby, Gone*	Dennis Lehane ___

crumcreekpress.com/titles/muses.htm

International Thriller Writers

The International Thriller Writers, Inc. web site began in 2004 and has compiled a list of 70 novels/stories (as a works in progress) as a place for the public to start reading and collecting in that field. The list is called "Must-Read Thrillers" and a short article by David Morrell accompanies it on the web site.

The thriller novel or story embraces a wide variety of worlds including law, espionage, action-adventure, medicine, police and crime, romance, history, politics, high-tech, and religion. It tells a story that is to provide a sudden rush of emotions, excitement, suspense, apprehension, and exhilaration that drives the narrative with peaks and lulls for the reader to enjoy. Many times an ordinary man or woman is challenged to move ahead from one situation to another and many times it is on a global stage. Numerous disciplines such as science, politics, psychology, crime procedures, intelligence, and history are employed, and the characters who rise to challenges find themselves in the midst of these situations.

Only one book per author was selected and 1995 was the cut-off date for this list. Check out their web site below for additional information. A new revised list of thrillers is being developed and will appear in a book in the near future with articles on each of the selected titles.

Must-Read Thrillers

1838	*Narrative of Arthur Gordon Pym, The*	Edgar Allan Poe	____
1845	*Count of Monte Cristo, The*	Alexandre Dumas	____
1860	*Woman in White, The*	Wilkie Collins	____
1885	*King Solomon's Mines*	H. Rider Haggard	____
1886	*Strange Case of Dr. Jekyll and Mr. Hyde*	Robert Louis Stevenson	____
1891	*Picture of Dorian Gray, The*	Oscar Wilde	____
1897	*Dracula*	Bram Stoker	____
1901	*Kim*	Rudyard Kipling	____
1902	*Heart of Darkness*	Joseph Conrad	____
1902	*Hound of the Baskervilles, The*	Arthur Conan Doyle	____
1903	*Riddle of the Sands, The*	Erskine Childers	____
1912	*Tarzan of the Apes*	Edgar Rice Burroughs	____
1913	*Lodger, The*	Marie Belloc Lowndes	____
1915	*Thirty-Nine Steps, The*	John Buchan	____
1921	*Scaramouche*	Rafael Sabatini	____
1924	*"Most Dangerous Game, The"*	Richard Connell	____
1928	*Ashenden; or, The British Agent*	W. Somerset Maugham	____
1934	*Postman Always Rings Twice, The*	James M. Cain	____
1939	*Coffin for Dimitrios, A (The Mask of Dimitrios)*	Eric Ambler	____
1939	*Rogue Male (Man Hunt)*	Geoffrey Household	____
1941	*Above Suspicion*	Helen MacInnes	____
1945	*Night Has a Thousand Eyes*	Cornell Woolrich (Irish/Hopley)	____
1946	*Big Clock, The (No Way Out)*	Kenneth Fearing	____

1950	Third Man, The (The Third Man and the Fallen Idol)	Graham Greene	___
1950	Strangers on a Train	Patricia Highsmith	___
1952	"Birds, The"	Daphne du Maurier	___
1952	Campbell's Kingdom	Hammond Innes	___
1952	Killer Inside Me, The	Jim Thompson	___
1954	Invasion of the Body Snatchers, The	Jack Finney	___
1957	From Russia, With Love	Ian Fleming	___
1959	Manchurian Candidate, The	Richard Condon	___
1962	Ipcress File, The	Len Deighton	___
1962	Seven Days in May	Fletcher Knebel & Charles W. Bailey	___
1963	Spy Who Came in From the Cold, The	John le Carre	___
1963	Ice Station Zebra	Alistair MacLean	___
1965	Quiller Memorandum, The (The Berlin Memorandum)	Adam Hall	___
1969	Andromeda Strain, The	Michael Crichton	___
1970	Deliverance	James Dickey	___
1971	Day of the Jackal, The	Frederick Forsyth	___
1972	Death Wish	Brian Garfield	___
1972	First Blood	David Morrell	___
1972	Eiger Sanction, The		___
1973	Onion Field, The	Joseph Wambaugh	___
1974	Jaws	Peter Benchley	___
1974	Marathon Man	William Goldman	___
1974	Six Days of the Condor (Three Days of the Condor)	James Grady	___
1974	Dog Soldiers	Robert Stone	___
1975	Eagle Has Landed, The	Jack Higgins	___
1976	Raise the Titanic!	Clive Cussler	___
1976	Boys From Brazil, The	Ira Levin	___
1976	Interview With the Vampire	Anne Rice	___
1977	Coma	Robin Cook	___
1978	Eye of the Needle (Storm Island)	Ken Follett	___
1979	Dead Zone, The	Stephen King	___
1979	Green Ripper, The	John D. MacDonald	___
1980	Bourne Identity, The	Robert Ludlum	___
1980	Ninja, The	Eric Van Lustbader	___
1981	Red Dragon (Manhunter)	Thomas Harris	___
1984	Hunt for Red October, The	Tom Clancy	___
1987	Flight of the Old Dog (Flight of the Wild Dog)	Dale Brown	___
1988	Charm School, The	Nelson DeMille	___
1988	Watchers	Dean Koontz	___
1988	Eight, The	Katherine Neville	___
1991	Firm, The	John Grisham	___

1992	*Along Came a Spider*	James Patterson	____
1993	*Point of Impact*	Stephen Hunter	____
1994	*Alienist, The*	Caleb Carr	____
1994	*Thirteenth Juror, The*	John Lescroart	____
1995	*Absolute Power*	David Baldacci	____
1995	*Night Sins*	Tami Hoag	____

www.thrillerwriters.org/mustread.html

H.R.F. Keating—The 100 Best Books of Crime and Mystery

In his 1987 book *Crime and Mystery: The 100 Best Books,* H.R.F. Keating offers a brief commentary on 100 books that he selected for mystery fans to consider reading. There is one extra offering suggested by the publisher. This list contains books published between 1845 and 1986.

Keating's 100 C & M

1845	*Tales of Mystery and Imagination*	Edgar Allan Poe	____
1868	*Moonstone, The*	Wilkie Collins	____
1870	*Mystery of Edwin Drood, The*	Charles Dickens	____
1892	*Adventures of Sherlock Holmes, The*	Arthur Conan Doyle	____
1899	*Amateur Cracksman, The (Raffles, the Amateur Crasksman; Raffles)*	E.W. Hornung	____
1902	*Hound of the Baskervilles, The*	Arthur Conan Doyle	____
1907	*Thinking Machine, The*	Jacques Futrelle	____
1908	*Circular Staircase, The*	Mary Roberts Rinehart	____
1911	*Innocence of Father Brown, The*	G.K. Chesterton	____
1918	*Uncle Abner, Master of Mysteries*	Melville Davisson Post	____
1925	*Mind of Mr. J.G. Reeder, The (The Murder Book of J.G. Reeder)*	Edgar Wallace	____
1926	*Murder of Roger Ackroyd, The*	Agatha Christie	____
1929	*Red Harvest*	Dashiell Hammett	____
1929	*Death of My Aunt*	C.H.B. Kitchin	____
1930	*Documents in the Case, The*	Dorothy L. Sayers & Robert Eustace	____
1930	*Maltese Falcon, The*	Dashiell Hammett	____
1931	*Sands of Windee, The*	Arthur W. Upfield	____
1932	*Before the Fact*	Francis Iles	____
1933	*Case of the Sulky Girl, The*	Erle Stanley Gardner	____
1934	*Murder on the Orient Express (Murder in the Calais Coach)*	Agatha Christie	____
1934	*Postman Always Rings Twice, The*	James M. Cain	____
1934	*Nine Tailors, The*	Dorothy L. Sayers	____
1935	*Hollow Man, The (The Three Coffins)*	John Dickson Carr	____
1935	*League of Frightened Men, The*	Rex Stout	____
1936	*Wheel Spins, The (The Lady Vanishes)*	Ethel Lina White	____
1938	*Beast Must Die, The*	Nicholas Blake	____
1940	*Bride Wore Black, The (Beware the Lady)*	Cornell Woolrich	____
1940	*Surfeit of Lampreys (Death of a Peer)*	Ngaio Marsh	____
1942	*Calamity Town*	Ellery Queen	____
1942	*Tragedy at Law*	Cyril Hare	____

1942	*High Window, The*	Raymond Chandler	___
1944	*Green for Danger*	Christianna Brand	___
1945	*Appleby's End*	Michael Innes	___
1946	*Murder Among Friends (Cheat the Hangman)*	Elizabeth Ferrars	___
1946	*Horizontal Man, The*	Helen Eustis	___
1946	*Moving Toyshop, The*	Edmund Crispin	___
1947	*Fabulous Clipjoint, The*	Fredric Brown	___
1948	*Franchise Affair, The*	Josephine Tey	___
1948	*Devil Take the Blue-Tail Fly*	John Franklin Bardin	___
1948	*More Work for the Undertaker*	Margery Allingham	___
1949/57	*My Friend Maigret (Methods of Maigret)*	Georges Simenon	___
1949	*Asphalt Jungle, The*	W.R. Burnett	___
1950	*Smallbone Deceased*	Michael Gilbert	___
1948/50	*Stain on the Snow, The (The Snow was Black)*	Georges Simenon	___
1951	*Daughter of Time, The*	Josephine Tey	___
1952	*Last Seen Wearing...*	Hillary Waugh	___
1952	*Tiger in the Smoke, The*	Margery Allingham	___
1953	*Five Roundabouts to Heaven (The Tender Poisoner)*	John Bingham	___
1953	*Long Goodbye, The (The Long Good-bye)*	Raymond Chandler	___
1953	*Post Mortem*	Guy Cullingford	___
1954	*Party at No. 5, The (The Cellar at No. 5)*	Shelley Smith	___
1955	*Talented Mr. Ripley, The*	Patricia Highsmith	___
1955	*Beast in View*	Margaret Millar	___
1956	*Gideon's Week*	John Creasey (as, J.J. Marric)	___
1956	*Mystery Stories (Quiet Horror)*	Stanley Ellin	___
1960/61	*Maigret in Court*	Georges Simenon	___
1960	*New Sonia Wayward, The (The Case of Sonia Wayward)*	Michael Innes	___
1963	*Gun Before Butter (Question of Loyalty)*	Nicolas Freeling	___
1963	*Expendable Man, The*	Dorothy B. Hughes	___
1964	*Pop. 1280*	Jim Thompson	___
1965	*R.S.V.P. Murder*	Mignon G. Eberhart	___
1967	*Man Who Killed Himself, The*	Julian Symons	___
1967	*Murder Against the Grain*	Emma Lathen	___
1967	*Roseanna*	Maj Sjowall & Per Wahloo	___
1967	*Last Best Friend, The*	George Sims	___
1968	*Glass-Sided Ants' Nest, The (Skin Deep)*	Peter Dickinson	___
1968	*Mr. Splitfoot*	Helen McCloy	___
1968	*Private Wound, The*	Nicholas Blake	___
1969	*Tremor of Forgery, The*	Patricia Highsmith	___
1969	*Blind Man With a Pistol (Hot Day, Hot Night)*	Chester Himes	___
1970	*Young Man, I Think You're Dying*	Joan Fleming	___
1970	*Beyond This Point are Monsters*	Margaret Millar	___
1972	*Sadie When She Died*	Ed McBain	___

1972	*Friends of Eddie Coyle, The*	George V. Higgins	____
1972	*Players and the Game, The*	Julian Symons	____
1972	*Mirror, Mirror on the Wall*	Stanley Ellin	____
1973	*Dance Hall of the Dead*	Tony Hillerman	____
1974	*Poison Oracle, The*	Peter Dickinson	____
1974	*Fletch*	Gregory McDonald	____
1975	*Black Tower, The*	P.D. James	____
1975	*Long Shadow, The*	Celia Fremlin	____
1975	*Naked Nuns, The (Six Nuns and a Shotgun)*	Colin Watson	____
1976	*Blue Hammer, The*	Ross Macdonald	____
1976	*Sleeping Murder*	Agatha Christie	____
1976	*Death in the Life, A*	Dorothy Salisbury Davis	____
1976	*Investigation, The*	Dorothy Uhnak	____
1977	*Judgement in Stone, A*	Ruth Rendell	____
1977	*Laidlaw*	William McIlvanney	____
1977	*Nobody's Perfect*	Donald E. Westlake	____
1978	*Pinch of Snuff, A*	Reginald Hill	____
1979	*Skinflick*	Joseph Hansen	____
1979	*Kill Claudio*	P.M. Hubbard	____
1979	*Green Ripper, The*	John D. MacDonald	____
1981	*All on a Summer's Day*	John Wainwright	____
1981	*Death in a Tenured Position (A Death in the Faculty)*	Amanda Cross	____
1981	*Glitter Dome, The*	Joseph Wambaugh	____
1982	*To Make a Killing (Portrait of Lilith)*	June Thomson	____
1982	*False Inspector Dew, The*	Peter Lovesey	____
1984	*Artful Egg, The*	James McClure	____
1986	*Taste for Death, A*	P.D. James	____
1986	*Under a Monsoon Cloud*	H.R.F. Keating	____

www.topmystery.com/books5.htm
www.classiccrimefiction.com/keating100.htm
home.comcast.net/~dwtaylor1/keating.html

Marvin Lachman—150 Favorite Novels

Marvin Lachman originally published in *Deadly Pleasures* (Summer 1997) a list of his favorite mystery novels. He has offered that list here with updates and additional selections. Now there are 150 titles from 1913 to 2001.

Lachman's 150			
1970	*Late Phoenix, A*	Catherine Aird	___
1967	*Most Contagious Game, A*	Catherine Aird	___
1966	*Religious Body, The*	Catherine Aird	___
1934	*Death of a Ghost*	Margery Allingham	___
1938	*Fashion in Shrouds, The*	Margery Allingham	___
1952	*Tiger in the Smoke, The*	Margery Allingham	___
1927	*Trail of Fear, The (Jimmie Rezaire)*	Anthony Armstrong	___
1956	*Dram of Poison, A*	Charlotte Armstrong	___
1962	*Burden of Proof, The*	Jeffrey Ashford	___
1976	*Enemy, The*	Desmond Bagley	___
1974	*Death of an Old Goat*	Robert Barnard	___
1997	*Embarrassment of Corpses, An*	Alan Beechey	___
1931	*Death Walks in Eastrepps*	Francis Beeding	___
1959	*End of Violence, The*	Ben Benson	___
1953	*Target in Taffeta*	Ben Benson	___
1913	*Trent's Last Case (The Woman in Black)*	E.C. Bentley	___
1954	*Evil of Time, The*	Evelyn Berckman	___
1929	*Poisoned Chocolates Case, The*	Anthony Berkeley	___
1937	*Trial and Error*	Anthony Berkeley	___
1938	*Beast Must Die, The*	Nicholas Blake	___
1939	*Smiler With the Knife, The*	Nicholas Blake	___
1949	*Dead Lion*	John & Emery Bonett	___
1937	*Case of the Seven of Cavalry, The*	Anthony Boucher	___
1944	*Green for Danger*	Christianna Brand	___
1948.	*Wilders Walk Away*	Herbert Brean	___
1951	*Far Cry, The*	Fredric Brown	___
1956	*Lenient Beast, The*	Fredric Brown	___
1955	*Wench is Dead, The*	Fredric Brown	___
1941	*Case of the Constant Suicides, The*	John Dickson Carr	___
1938	*Crooked Hinge, The*	John Dickson Carr	___
1956	*Patrick Butler for the Defense*	John Dickson Carr	___
1940	*Farewell, My Lovely*	Raymond Chandler	___
1936	*ABC Murders, The (The Alphabet Murders)*	Agatha Christie	___
1939	*And Then There Were None (Ten Little Niggers)*	Agatha Christie	___
1975	*Curtain*	Agatha Christie	___
1926	*Murder of Roger Ackroyd, The*	Agatha Christie	___
1992	*Black Echo, The*	Michael Connelly	___

1994	*Concrete Blonde, The*	Michael Connelly	___
1995	*Last Coyote, The*	Michael Connelly	___
1920	*Cask, The*	Freeman Wills Crofts	___
1922	*Pit-Prop Syndicate, The*	Freeman Wills Crofts	___
1951	*Gentle Murderer, A*	Dorothy Salisbury Davis	___
1955	*Dark Place, The*	Mildred Davis	___
1953	*They Buried a Man*	Mildred Davis	___
1963	*Sad Song Singing, A*	Thomas B. Dewey	___
1944	*He Wouldn't Kill Patience*	Carter Dickson	___
1939	*Reader is Warned, The*	Carter Dickson	___
1943	*She Died a Lady*	Carter Dickson	___
1957	*Method in Madness (Quiet Violence; Too Innocent to Kill)*	Doris Miles Disney	___
1959	*No Next of Kin*	Doris Miles Disney	___
1946	*Who Rides a Tiger (Sow the Wind)*	Doris Miles Disney	___
1946	*Horizontal Man, The*	Helen Eustis	___
1948	*Halo for Satan*	John Evans (as, Howard Browne)	___
1949	*Halo in Brass*	John Evans (as, Howard Browne)	___
1926	*Payment Deferred*	C.S. Forester	___
1967	*Blood Sport*	Dick Francis	___
1965	*For Kicks*	Dick Francis	___
1964	*Nerve*	Dick Francis	___
1965	*Odds Against*	Dick Francis	___
1969.	*Ascent of D-13, The*	Andrew Garve	___
1953	*Cuckoo Line Affair, The*	Andrew Garve	___
1961	*House of Soldiers, The*	Andrew Garve	___
1957	*Convertible Hearse, The*	William Campbell Gault	___
1951	*Death Has Deep Roots*	Michael Gilbert	___
1980	*Killing of Katie Steelstock, The (Death of a Favourite Girl)*	Michael Gilbert	___
1950	*Smallbone Deceased*	Michael Gilbert	___
1961	*Operation Terror (Experiment in Terror)*	The Gordons	___
1987	*Killings at Badger's Drift, The*	Caroline Graham	___
1937	*Tenant for Death*	Cyril Hare	___
1942	*Tragedy at Law*	Cyril Hare	___
1955	*Enormous Shadow, The*	Robert Harling	___
1927	*Bellamy Trial, The*	Frances Noyes Hart	___
2001	*Dialogues of the Dead*	Reginald Hill	___
1973	*Dance Hall of the Dead*	Tony Hillerman	___
1971	*Fly on the Wall, The*	Tony Hillerman	___
1989	*Talking God*	Tony Hillerman	___
1959	*Man Who Followed Women, The*	Bert & Dolores Hitchens	___
1942	*Rocket to the Morgue*	H.H. Holmes (Anthony Boucher)	___
1932	*Before the Fact*	Francis Iles	___
1937	*Hamlet, Revenge!*	Michael Innes	___

1942	*Phantom Lady*	William Irish (Cornell Woolrich)	___
1964	*Friday the Rabbi Slept Late*	Harry Kemelman	___
1957	*Room to Swing*	Ed Lacy	___
1967	*Murder Against the Grain*	Emma Lathen	___
1966	*Murder Makes the Wheels Go 'Round*	Emma Lathen	___
1944	*Blood Upon the Snow*	Hilda Lawrence	___
1985	*Dunn's Conundrum*	Stan Lee	___
1953	*Kiss Before Dying, A*	Ira Levin	___
1941	*Murder Out of Turn*	Frances & Richard Lockridge	___
1995	*Summons, The*	Peter Lovesey	___
1970	*Wobble to Death*	Peter Lovesey	___
1947	*One More Unfortunate (A Case to Answer)*	Edgar Lustgarten	___
1957	*Executioners, The (Cape Fear)*	John D. MacDonald	___
1938	*Warrant for X (The Nursemaid Who Disappeared)*	Philip MacDonald	___
1950	*Drowning Pool, The*	Ross Macdonald (as, John Ross Macdonald)	___
1953	*Meet Me at the Morgue (Experience With Evil)*	Ross Macdonald (as, John Ross Macdonald)	___
1964	*Chill, The*	Ross Macdonald	___
1962	*Name of the Game is Death, The (Operation Overkill)*	Dan J. Marlowe	___
1961	*Gideon's Fire*	J.J. Marric (John Creasey)	___
1962	*Gideon's March*	J.J. Marric (John Creasey)	___
1938	*Death in a White Tie*	Ngaio Marsh	___
1982	*Light Thickens*	Ngaio Marsh	___
1939	*Overture to Death*	Ngaio Marsh	___
1960	*Heckler, The*	Ed McBain	___
1946	*Pick Your Victim*	Patricia McGerr	___
1952	*Big Heat, The*	William P. McGivern	___
1957	*Odds Against Tomorrow*	William P. McGivern	___
1955	*Beast in View*	Margaret Millar	___
1960	*Stranger in My Grave, A*	Margaret Millar	___
1952	*Vanish in an Instant*	Margaret Millar	___
1981	*Death in the Past*	Richard A. Moore	___
1959	*Dead Men Don't Ski*	Patricia Moyes	___
1974	*God Save the Child*	Robert B. Parker	___
1957	*Bunny Lake is Missing*	Evelyn Piper	___
1957	*Midnight Plumber, The*	Maurice Procter	___
1956	*Pub Crawler, The*	Maurice Procter	___
1973	*Undercurrent*	Bill Pronzini	___
1942	*Calamity Town*	Ellery Queen	___
1949	*Cat of Many Tails*	Ellery Queen	___
1934	*Chinese Orange Mystery, The*	Ellery Queen	___
1932	*Egyptian Cross Mystery, The*	Ellery Queen	___

1929	*Roman Hat Mystery, The*	Ellery Queen	___
1932.	*Tragedy of X, The*	Ellery Queen (as, Barnaby Ross)	___
1932	*Tragedy of Y, The*	Ellery Queen (as, Barnaby Ross)	___
1944	*Puzzle for Puppets*	Patrick Quentin	___
1964	*From Doon With Death*	Ruth Rendell	___
1985	*Latimer Mercy, The*	Robert Richardson	___
1945	*Green December Fills the Graveyard (Murder at Shots Hall)*	Maureen Sarsfield	___
1935	*Gaudy Night*	Dorothy L. Sayers	___
1933	*Murder Must Advertise*	Dorothy L. Sayers	___
1931	*Prime Minister is Dead, The (Vantage Striker)*	Helen Simpson	___
1965	*Fidelio Score, The*	Gerald Sinstadt	___
1951	*House Without a Door, The*	Thomas Sterling	___
1934	*Fer-de-Lance (Meet Nero Wolfe)*	Rex Stout	___
1936	*Rubber Band, The (To Kill Again)*	Rex Stout	___
1938	*Too Many Cooks*	Rex Stout	___
1950	*31st of February, The*	Julian Symons	___
1951	*Daughter of Time, The*	Josephine Tey	___
1946	*Miss Pym Disposes*	Josephine Tey	___
1953	*Death of an Intruder*	Nedra Tyre	___
1955	*Dying Fall, A*	Henry Wade	___
1952	*Last Seen Wearing...*	Hillary Waugh	___
1997	*Ax, The (Axe, The)*	Donald E. Westlake	___
1932	*Fear Stalks the Village*	Ethel Lina White	___
1960	*Sailcloth Shroud, The*	Charles Williams	___
1955	*Scorpion Reef (Gulf Coast Girl)*	Charles Williams	___
1984	*Murder on Ice (The Killing Cold)*	Ted Wood	___
1943	*Black Angel, The*	Cornell Woolrich	___
1948	*Rendezvous in Black*	Cornell Woolrich	___
1962	*Fifth Passenger, The*	Edward Young	___

Marvin Lachman—Favorite 1st Mystery Novels

Mystery reviewer and writer of nonfiction books, Marvin Lachman, offers his list of 102 favorite first mysteries. The titles date from 1887 to 2002.

Lachman 102 1st Mysteries

1887	*Study in Scarlet, A*	Arthur Conan Doyle	___
1913	*Trent's Last Case (The Woman in Black)*	E.C. Bentley	___
1920	*Cask, The*	Freeman Wills Crofts	___
1920	*Mysterious Affair at Styles, The*	Agatha Christie	___
1923	*Whose Body?*	Dorothy L. Sayers	___
1925	*Layton Court Mystery, The*	Anthony Berkeley	___
1926	*Verdict of You All, The*	Henry Wade	___
1927	*Bellamy Trial, The*	Frances Noyes Hart	___
1929	*Red Harvest*	Dashiell Hammett	___
1929	*Roman Hat Mystery, The*	Ellery Queen	___
1929	*Man in the Queue, The (Killer in the Crowd)*	Josephine Tey (Gordon Daviot)	___
1931	*Put Out the Light (Sinister Light)*	Ethel Lina White	___
1934	*Man Lay Dead, A*	Ngaio Marsh	___
1934	*Murder of My Aunt, The*	Richard Hull	___
1936	*Death at the President's Lodging (Seven Suspects)*	Michael Innes	___
1937	*Case of the Seven of Calvary, The*	Anthony Boucher	___
1937	*Tenant for Death*	Cyril Hare	___
1939	*Big Sleep, The*	Raymond Chandler	___
1940	*Verdict of Twelve*	Raymond Postgate	___
1940	*Norths Meet Murder, The (Mr. & Mrs. North Meet Murder; A Taste for Murder)*	Frances & Richard Lockridge	___
1943	*Smell of Money, The*	Matthew Head	___
1944	*Blood Upon the Snow*	Hilda Lawrence	___
1944	*Case of the Gilded Fly, The (Obsequies at Oxford)*	Edmund Crispin	___
1945	*Green December Fills the Graveyard (Murder at Shots Hall)*	Maureen Sarsfield	___
1946	*Horizontal Man, The*	Helen Eustis	___
1946	*Pick Your Victim*	Patricia McGerr	___
1947	*Case to Answer, A (One More Unfortunate)*	Edgar Lustgarten	___
1947	*Fabulous Clipjoint, The*	Fredric Brown	___
1947	*Close Quarters*	Michael Gilbert	___
1948	*Wilders Walk Away*	Herbert Brean	___
1949	*Dead Lion*	John & Emery Bonett	___
1949	*Walk the Dark Streets*	William Krasner	___
1949	*What a Body!*	Alan Green	___
1950	*House Without a Door, The*	Thomas Sterling	___
1950	*Nightmare in Manhattan*	Thomas Walsh	___

1951	*Wooden Overcoat, The*	Pamela Branch	___
1952	*Don't Cry for Me*	William Campbell Gault	___
1952	*Mouse in Eternity (Death is a Lover)*	Nedra Tyre	___
1953	*Kiss Before Dying, A*	Ira Levin	___
1953	*Whistle Up the Devil*	Derek Smith	___
1954	*Alibi Innings*	Barbara Worsley-Gough	___
1954	*Go, Lovely Rose*	Jean Potts	___
1954	*Evil of Time, The*	Evelyn Berckman	___
1955	*In His Blood*	Harold R. Daniels	___
1956	*Landscape with Dead Dons*	Robert Robinson	___
1958	*Revenge*	Jack Ehrlich	___
1959	*Gray Flannel Shroud, The*	Henry Slesar	___
1959	*Dead Men Don't Ski*	Patricia Moyes	___
1961	*Banking on Death*	Emma Lathen	___
1962	*Cover Her Face*	P.D. James	___
1962	*Dead Cert*	Dick Francis	___
1963	*Fifth Passenger, The*	Edward Young	___
1964	*From Doon with Death*	Ruth Rendell	___
1964	*Friday the Rabbi Slept Late*	Harry Kemelman	___
1964	*Dover One*	Joyce Porter	___
1965	*In the Heat of the Night*	John Ball	___
1965	*Last Known Address, The*	Joseph Harrington	___
1965	*Fidelio Score, The*	Gerald Sinstadt	___
1966	*Religious Body, The*	Catherine Aird	___
1967	*Death of an Old Girl*	Elizabeth Lemarchand	___
1969	*You'll Like My Mother (The House with the Watching Eye)*	Naomi Hintze	___
1970	*Clubbable Woman, A*	Reginald Hill	___
1970	*Wobble to Death*	Peter Lovesey	___
1970	*Blessing Way, The*	Tony Hillerman	___
1971	*Ask the Right Question*	Michael Z. Lewin	___
1974	*Death of an Old Goat*	Robert Barnard	___
1975	*Paperback Thriller*	Lynn Meyer	___
1975	*Cast, in Order of Disappearance*	Simon Brett	___
1977	*Fan, The*	Bob Randall	___
1977	*Capitol Crime, A*	Lawrence Meyer	___
1978	*Death and the Maiden (Death in the Morning)*	Sheila Radley	___
1980	*Zero Factor, The*	William Oscar Johnson	___
1980	*Hands of Healing Murder, The*	Barbara D'Amato	___
1980	*Death and the Pregnant Virgin (Death of a Pregnant Virgin)*	S.T. Haymon	___
1981	*Man with a Load of Mischief, The*	Martha Grimes	___
1981	*Old Dick, The*	L.A. Morse	___
1981	*Death in the Past*	Richard A. Moore	___
1981	*One Coffee With*	Margaret Maron	___

1982	*Case of the Hook-Billed Kites, The*	J.S. Borthwick	____
1982	*Butcher's Boy, The*	Thomas Perry	____
1983	*Dead in the Water*	Ted Wood	____
1984	*Generous Death*	Nancy Pickard	____
1984	*Blunt Darts*	Jeremiah Healy	____
1985	*Dunn's Conundrum*	Stan Lee	____
1985	*Latimer Mercy, The*	Robert Richardson	____
1985	*Sleeping Dog*	Dick Lochte	____
1985.	*Double Exposure*	Jim Stinson	____
1986	*Murder for Lunch*	Haughton Murphy	____
1987	*Monkey's Raincoat, The*	Robert Crais	____
1988	*Carolina Skeletons*	David Stout	____
1988	*Murder Once Done*	Mary Lou Bennett	____
1989	*Unorthodox Practices*	Marissa Piesman	____
1989	*Cold Front, The*	Sean Hanlon	____
1989	*Cheerio Killings, The*	Doug Allyn	____
1990	*Body in the Belfry, The*	Katherine Hall Page	____
1992	*Black Echo, The*	Michael Connelly	____
1992	*Cold Day for Murder, A*	Dana Stabenow	____
1993	*Killing of Ellis Martin, The*	Lucretia Grindle	____
1996	*Lie Down with Dogs*	Jan Gleiter	____
1997	*Embarrassment of Corpses, An*	Alan Beechey	____
1998	*Contrary Blues, The*	John Billheimer	____
2002	*In the Bleak Midwinter*	Julia Spencer-Fleming	____

Lori L. Lake—Lesbian and Gay Sleuths

Lesbian author and crime fiction aficionado Lori L. Lake offers a selection of her favorite mystery novels with lesbian and gay sleuths. The twelve titles in each category, dating from 1970 to 2005, are in alphabetical order. The gay and lesbian authors below are some of the most honored and talented in the mystery field.

Lori L. Lake Lesbian Sleuths			
2005	*Grave Silence*	Rose Beecham	___
1994	*Calendar Girl*	Stella Duffy	___
2004	*Hancock Park*	Katherine V. Forrest	___
1998	*Blue Place, The*	Nicola Griffith	___
2005	*Iron Girl, The*	Ellen Hart	___
2005	*Son of a Gun*	Randye Lordon	___
1992	*Dead Beat*	Val McDermid	___
1991	*I Left My Heart*	Jaye Maiman	___
1990	*Death by the Riverside*	J.M. Redmann	___
1996	*Let's Face the Music and Die*	Sandra Scoppettone	___
2001	*Moving Targets*	Pat Welch	___
1984	*Murder in the Collective*	Barbara Wilson	___

Lori L. Lake Gay Sleuths			
1980	*Vermilion*	Nathan Aldyne	___
2001	*Boy Toy*	Michael Craft	___
1998	*FreeForm*	Jack Dickson	___
1970	*Fadeout*	Joseph Hansen	___
2004	*Fingering the Family Jewels*	Greg Lilly	___
1988	*Goldenboy*	Michael Nava	___
1979	*Lure, The*	Felice Picano	___
1996	*Chain of Fools*	Richard Stevenson	___
2001	*Someone Killed His Boyfriend: A Summer of Sex, Sun and Murder in Provincetown*	David Stukas	___
1999	*Justice at Risk*	John Morgan Wilson	___
1997	*Hostage*	R.D. Zimmerman	___
1990	*Why Isn't Becky Twitchell Dead?*	Mark Richard Zubro	___

David Lehman Further Reading

In his book, *The Perfect Murder: A Study in Detection* (1989/2000), David Lehman provides a list of recommended titles. They "were chosen for their importance in the evolution of the mystery genre or simply for the pleasure they reliably give; in many cases, both reasons apply." He lists them by categories, and then he adds more titles in a second edition (2000). All of them are listed here. He also uses other forms including critical documents, resource books, nonfiction, films, poems, plays, etc. The novels total 159 titles between Greek literature (Sophocles, 425 B.E.) and 1998.

I. Detective Novels and Stories

A. Origins

1845	*Tales*	Edgar Allan Poe	____
1868	*Moonstone, The*	Wilkie Collins	____
1887	*Study in Scarlet, A*	Arthur Conan Doyle	____
1892	*Adventures of Sherlock Holmes, The*	Arthur Conan Doyle	____
1894	*Memoirs of Sherlock Holmes, The*	Arthur Conan Doyle	____
1902	*Hound of the Baskervilles, The*	Arthur Conan Doyle	____
1907	*Red Thumb Mark, The*	R. Austin Freeman	____
1905	*Club of Queer Trades, The*	G.K. Chesterton	____
1908	*Man Who was Thursday, The*	G.K. Chesterton	____
1911	*Innocence of Father Brown, The*	G.K. Chesterton	____
1914	*Wisdom of Father Brown, The*	G.K. Chesterton	____

B. The Classic Whodunit, 1912-41

1913	*Trent's Last Case (The Woman in Black)*	E.C. Bentley	____
1926	*Murder of Roger Ackroyd, The*	Agatha Christie	____
1934	*Murder on the Orient Express (Murder in the Calais Coach)*	Agatha Christie	____
1936	*ABC Murders, The (The Alphabet Murders)*	Agatha Christie	____
1939	*And Then There Were None (Ten Little Niggers)*	Agatha Christie	____
1929	*Poisoned Chocolates Case, The*	Anthony Berkeley	____
1930	*Strong Poison*	Dorothy L. Sayers	____
1933	*Murder Must Advertise*	Dorothy L. Sayers	____
1934	*Chinese Orange Mystery, The*	Ellery Queen	____
1935	*Heir Presumptive*	Henry Wade	____
1935	*Three Coffins, The (The Hollow Man)*	John Dickson Carr	____
1937	*Burning Court, The*	John Dickson Carr	____
1938	*Crooked Hinge, The*	John Dickson Carr	____
1938	*Judas Window, The (The Crossbow Murder)*	Carter Dickson	____
1939	*Reader is Warned, The*	Carter Dickson	____
1936	*Thou Shell of Death (Shell of Death)*	Nicholas Blake	____
1938	*Beast Must Die, The*	Nicholas Blake	____
1941	*Corpse in the Snowman, The (The Case of the Abominable Snowman)*	Nicholas Blake	____

1939	*Overture to Death*	Ngaio Marsh	___
1937	*Hamlet, Revenge!*	Michael Innes	___
1938	*Fashion in Shrouds, The*	Margery Allingham	___
1940	*Verdict of Twelve*	Raymond Postgate	___

C. The Hard-boiled Romance, 1929-

1929	*Red Harvest*	Dashiell Hammett	___
1930	*Maltese Falcon, The*	Dashiell Hammett	___
1931	*Glass Key, The*	Dashiell Hammett	___
1936/43	*Double Indemnity*	James M. Cain	___
1939	*Big Sleep, The*	Raymond Chandler	___
1940	*Farewell, My Lovely*	Raymond Chandler	___
1942	*High Window, The*	Raymond Chandler	___
1953	*Long Goodbye, The (The Long Good-bye)*	Raymond Chandler	___
1952	*Killer Inside Me, The*	Jim Thompson	___
1959	*Getaway, The*	Jim Thompson	___
1964	*Chill, The*	Ross Macdonald	___
1969	*Goodbye Look, The*	Ross Macdonald	___
1971	*Underground Man, The*	Ross Macdonald	___
1974	*Death of the Detective, The*	Mark Smith	___
1974	*Big Fix, The*	Roger L. Simon	___
1974	*Big Kiss-Off of 1944, The*	Andrew Bergman	___
1977	*Falling Angel*	William Hjortsberg	___
1981	*Hard Trade*	Arthur Lyons	___
1984	*Strike Three You're Dead*	R.D. Rosen	___
1985	*Dancing Bear*	James Crumley	___
1986	*Kiss Me Once*	Thomas Maxwell	___
1986	*Singing Detective, The*	Dennis Potter	___
1986	*"C" is for Corpse*	Sue Grafton	___
1987	*Bitter Medicine*	Sara Paretsky	___

D. The Postwar Era, 1945-

1946	*Big Clock, The (No Way Out)*	Kenneth Fearing	___
1946	*Moving Toyshop, The*	Edmund Crispin	___
1947	*Too Many Women*	Rex Stout	___
1948	*And Be a Villain (More Deaths Than One)*	Rex Stout	___
1949	*Second Confession, The*	Rex Stout	___
1947	*Minute for Murder*	Nicholas Blake	___
1959	*Widow's Cruise, The*	Nicholas Blake	___
1950	*Strangers on a Train*	Patricia Highsmith	___
1955	*Talented Mr. Ripley, The*	Patricia Highsmith	___
1950	*Daughter of Time, The*	Josephine Tey	___
1950	*31st of February, The*	Julian Symons	___
1953	*Kiss Before Dying, A*	Ira Levin	___
1956	*Mystery Stories (Horror Stories)*	Stanley Ellin	___

1958	*Eighth Circle, The*	Stanley Ellin	____
1963	*Death Over Deep Water*	Simon Nash	____
1963	*Ten Plus One*	Ed McBain	____
1977	*Long Time No See*	Ed McBain	____
1983	*Ice*	Ed McBain	____
1964	*Friday the Rabbi Slept Late*	Harry Kemelman	____
1971	*Words for Murder Perhaps*	Edward Candy	____
1975	*Curtain*	Agatha Christie	____
1977	*Means of Evil*	Ruth Rendell	____
1985	*Killing Doll, The*	Ruth Rendell	____
1977	*Death of an Expert Witness*	P.D. James	____
1986	*Taste for Death, A*	P.D. James	____
1983	*Name of the Rose, The*	Umberto Eco	____
1985	*Glitz*	Elmore Leonard	____
1985-6	*New York Trilogy, The*	Paul Auster	____
1987	*Fatal Inversion, A*	Barbara Vine	____

www.topmystery.com/books3.htm
home.comcast.net/~dwtaylor1/lehman.html

II. Related Genres

A. Spies and Such

1903	*Riddle of the Sands, The*	Erskine Childers	____
1906	*Secret Agent, The*	Joseph Conrad	____
1915	*Thirty-Nine Steps, The*	John Buchan	____
1920	*Great Impersonation, The*	E. Phillips Oppenheim	____
1928	*Ashenden; or, The British Agent*	W. Somerset Maugham	____
1939	*Coffin for Dimitrios, A (The Mask of Dimitrios)*	Eric Ambler	____
1940	*Journey into Fear*	Eric Ambler	____
1969	*Intercom Conspiracy, The (Quiet Conspiracy)*	Eric Ambler	____
1939	*Confidential Agent, The*	Graham Greene	____
1943	*Ministry of Fear, The*	Graham Greene	____
1978	*Human Factor, The*	Graham Greene	____
1963	*Spy Who Came in From the Cold, The*	John le Carre	____
1974	*Tinker, Tailor, Soldier, Spy*	John le Carre	____
1978	*Chinaman's Chance*	Ross Thomas	____

B. The Gothic Tradition

1765	*Castle of Otranto, The*	Horace Walpole	____
1794	*Mysteries of Udolpho, The*	Ann Radcliffe	____
1794	*Adventures of Caleb Williams, The (Things as They Are; or, The Adventures of Caleb Williams; Caleb Williams)*	William Godwin	____
1818	*Frankenstein (The Modern Prometheus)*	Mary Shelley	____
1820	*Melmoth: The Wanderer*	C.K. Maturin	____

1824	*Private Memoirs and Confessions of a Justified Sinner, The*	James Hogg	____
1840	*Tales of the Grotesque and Arabesque*	Edgar Allan Poe	____
1886	*Strange Case of Dr. Jekyll and Mr. Hyde*	Robert Louis Stevenson	____
1890	*Picture of Dorian Gray, The*	Oscar Wilde	____
1897	*Dracula*	Bram Stoker	____
1898	*Turn of the Screw, The*	Henry James	____

C. Comparative Fictions

425 B.C.	*Oedipus Rex*	Sophocles	____
1748	*Zadig; or, The Book of Fate*	Voltaire	____
1925	*Trial, The*	Franz Kafka	____
1941	*Real Life of Sebastian Knight, The*	Vladimir Nabokov	____
1959	*Pledge, The*	Friedrich Dürrenmatt	____
1962	*Ficciones*	Jorge Luis Borges	____
1968	*Real Inspector Hound, The*	Tom Stoppard	____
1977	*Enough!* (contains: *A Travesty* and *"Ordo"*)	Donald E. Westlake	____
1984	*Mysteries of Winterthurn*	Joyce Carol Oates	____
1985	*Suspects*	David Thomson	____

III. Critical Documents

1827-39-54			
	"On Murder Considered as One of the Fine Arts"	Thomas De Quincey	____
1880	"On the Method of Zadig"	T.H. Huxley	____
1901	"Defense of Detective Stories, A"	G.K. Chesteron	____
1936	"What are Master-pieces and Why are There So Few of Them"	Gertrude Stein	____
1941	"Detective Novel as Game, The"	Roger Caillois	____
1944	"Who Cares Who Killed Roger Ackroyd?"	Edmund Wilson	____
1944	"Simple Art of Murder, The"	Raymond Chandler	____
1948	"Guilty Vicarage, The"	W.H. Auden	____
1949	"Detective Stories and the Primal Scene"	Geraldine Pederson-Krag	____
1959	"House of Poe, The"	Richard Wilbur	____
1973	"Writer as Detective Hero, The"	Ross Macdonald	____
1984	*Postscript to The Name of the Rose*	Umberto Eco	____
1988	*Gumshoe: Reflections in a Private Eye*	Josiah Thompson	____

IV. Resource Books

1933	*Private Life of Sherlock Holmes, The*	Vincent Starrett	___
1941	*Murder for Pleasure: The Life and Times of the Detective Story*	Howard Haycraft	___
1946	*Art of the Mystery Story, The: A Collection of Critical Essays*	Howard Haycraft, ed.	___
1970	*Mystery Writer's Art, The*	Francis M. Nevins, Jr., ed.	___
1989	*Catalogue of Crime, A: Being a Reader's Guide to the Literature of Mystery, Detection, and Related Genres*	Jacques Barzun & Wendell Hertig Taylor	___
1975	*Crime on Her Mind: Fifteen Stories of Female Sleuths From the Victorian Era to the Forties*	Michele Slung, ed.	___
1976	*Adventure, Mystery, and Romance: Formula Stories as Art and Popular Culture*	John G. Cawelti	___
1976	*Life of Raymond Chandler, The*	Frank MacShane	___
1976	*Dimensions of Detective Fiction*	Larry N. Landrum, Pat & Ray Browne, eds.	___
1976	*Mystery Story, The: Introduction to Detective-Mystery Fiction*	John Ball, ed.	___
1976	*Encyclopedia of Mystery and Detection*	Chris Steinbrunner & Otto Penzler, eds., Marvin Lachman & Charles Shibuk, senior eds.	___
1978	*World of Mystery Fiction, The: A Guide*	Elliott L. Gilbert, ed.	___
1979	*Mystery and Its Fictions: From Oedipus to Agatha Christie*	David I. Grossvogel	___
1982	*Modus Operandi: An Excursion into Detective Fiction*	Robin W. Winks	___
1983	*Poetics of Murder, The: Detective Fiction and Literary Theory*	Glenn W. Most & William W. Stowe, eds.	___
1984	*Murder Ink: Revived, Revised, Still Unrepentant Prepetrated by Dilys Winn*	Dilys Winn, ed.	___
1985	*Bloody Murder: From the Detective Story to the Crime Novel - A History*	Julian Symons	___
1985	*In the Circles of Fear and Desire: A Study of Gothic Fantasy*	William Patrick Day	___
1987	*Talent to Deceive, A: An Appreciation of Agatha Christie*	Robert Barnard	___
1988	*Silk Stalkings: When Women Write of Murder*	Victoria Nichols & Susan Thompson	___

V. Addendum to the New Edition (2000)

A. Novels and Plays

1933	*Oxford Tragedy, An*	J.C. Masterman	____
1952	*Deep End, The*	Fredric Brown	____
1953	*Hot Spot, The (Hell Hath No Fury)*	Charles Williams	____
1954	*Street of No Return*	David Goodis	____
1955	*After Dark, My Sweet*	Jim Thompson	____
1971	*Burnt Orange Heresy, The*	Charles Willeford	____
1975	*Outsider in Amsterdam*	Janwillem van de Wetering	____
1982	*Dark Wind, The*	Tony Hillerman	____
1984	*Miami Blues*	Charles Willeford	____
1986	*Perfume: The Story of a Murderer*	Patrick Suskind	____
1990	*Nemesis*	Rosamond Smith	____
1990	*New Orleans Mourning*	Julie Smith	____
1990	*Kindred Crimes*	Janet Dawson	____
1990	*Maximum Bob*	Elmore Leonard	____
1990	*"G" is for Gumshoe*	Sue Grafton	____
1994	*Hapgood*	Tom Stoppard	____
1994	*Red Scream, The*	Mary Willis Walker	____
1995	*American Tabloid*	James Ellroy	____
1995	*Bet Against the House*	Catherine Dain	____
1995	*Justice*	Faye Kellerman	____
1995	*Wild and Lonely Place, A*	Marcia Muller	____
1996	*Poet, The*	Michael Connelly	____
1996	*Name Withheld*	J.A. Jance	____
1993/97	*Luneberg Variation, The*	Paolo Maurensig	____
1998	*Instance of the Fingerpost, An*	Iain Pears	____
1997	*Crime Novels: American Noir of the 1930s and 1940s* (6 below)	Robert Polito, ed.	____
1934	*Postman Always Rings Twice, The*	James M. Cain	____
1935	*They Shoot Horses, Don't They?*	Horace McCoy	____
1937	*Thieves Like Us*	Edward Anderson	____
1946	*Big Clock, The (No Way Out)*	Kenneth Fearing	____
1946	*Nightmare Alley*	William Lindsay Greshman	____
1948	*I Married a Dead Man*	Cornell Woolrich	____
1997	*Crime Novels: American Noir of the 1950s* (includes the five novels below)	Robert Polito, ed.	____
1952	*Killer Inside Me, The*	Jim Thompson	____
1955	*Talented Mr. Ripley, The*	Patricia Highsmith	____
1955	*Pick-up*	Charles Willeford	____
1956	*Down There (Shoot the Piano Player)*	David Goodis	____
1959	*Real Cool Killers, The*	Chester Himes	____
1998	*Times Square Story, The*	Geoffrey O'Brien	____
1999	*Billy Straight*	Jonathan Kellerman	____

B. Nonfiction

1990	*Journalist and the Murder, The*	Janet Malcolm	____
1990	*Detective Fiction and Literature: The Figure on the Carpet*	Martin Priestman	____
1991	*Agatha Christie: The Woman and Her Mysteries*	Gillian Gill	____
1995	*Savage Art: A Biography of Jim Thompson*	Robert Polito	____
1996	*Secret Marriage of Sherlock Holmes and Other Eccentric Readings, The*	Michael Atkinson	____
1996	*My Dark Places: An L.A. Crime Memoir*	James Ellroy	____
1997	*Somewhere in the Night: Film Noir and the American City*	Nicholas Christoper	____
1997	*Napoleon of Crime, The: The Life and Times of Adam Worth, Master Thief*	Ben Macintyre	____
1998	*More Than Night: Film Noir in Its Context*	James Naremore	____
1999	*Detective Agency: Women Rewriting the Hard-Boiled Tradition*	Priscilla L. Walton & Manina Jones	____

David Lehman Personal Favorites

The second appendix in *The Perfect Murder: A study in Detection*, David Lehman offers a list of 15 titles as his personal favorites. All of these titles are listed in his "Further Reading" above.

1902	*Hound of the Baskervilles, The*	Arthur Conan Doyle	____
1911	*Innocence of Father Brown, The*	G.K. Chesterton	____
1930	*Maltese Falcon, The*	Dashiell Hammett	____
1936	*Three Coffins, The (The Hollow Man)*	John Dickson Carr	____
1936	*ABC Murders, The (The Alphabet Murders)*	Agatha Christie	____
1936	*Thou Shell of Death (Shell of Death)*	Nicholas Blake	____
1939	*Big Sleep, The*	Raymond Chandler	____
1939	*Coffin for Dimitrios, A (The Mask of Dimitrios)*	Eric Ambler	____
1946	*Big Clock, The (No Way Out)*	Kenneth Fearing	____
1947	*Too Many Women*	Rex Stout	____
1958	*Eighth Circle, The*	Stanley Ellin	____
1964	*Chill, The*	Ross Macdonald	____
1978	*Long Time No See*	Ed McBain	____
1983	*Name of the Rose, The*	Umberto Eco	____
1986	*Singing Detective, The*	Dennis Potter	____

Mystery Writers of America

These titles were selected by the Mystery Writers of America from a questionnaire sent to their active members. The results were tabulated by the compiler Mickey Friedman and published in 1995 in *The Crown Crime Companion: The Top 100 Mystery Novels of All Time*. Each title was annotated by Otto Penzler with a short comment. The 107 titles were published between 1841 and 1991.

Top 100 Mystery Novels of All Time

1927	Top 100 MWA 1	*Complete Sherlock Holmes, The*	Arthur Conan Doyle	____
1902	Top 100 MWA 1 - a	*Hound of the Baskervilles, The*	Arthur Conan Doyle	____
1887	Top 100 MWA 1 - b	*Study in Scarlet, A*	Arthur Conan Doyle	____
1892	Top 100 MWA 1 - c	*Adventures of Sherlock Holmes, The*	Arthur Conan Doyle	____
1890	Top 100 MWA 1 - d	*Sign of the Four, The*	Arthur Conan Doyle	____
1930	Top 100 MWA 2	*Maltese Falcon, The*	Dashiell Hammett	____
1845	Top 100 MWA 3	*Tales of Mystery and Imagination*	Edgar Allan Poe	____
1843	Top 100 MWA 3 - a	*Gold Bug, The*	Edgar Allan Poe	____
1841	Top 100 MWA 3 - b	*Murders in Rue Morgue, The*	Edgar Allan Poe	____
1951	Top 100 MWA 4	*Daughter of Time, The*	Josephine Tey	____
1987	Top 100 MWA 5	*Presumed Innocent*	Scott Turow	____
1963	Top 100 MWA 6	*Spy Who Came in From the Cold, The*	John le Carre	____
1868	Top 100 MWA 7	*Moonstone, The*	Wilkie Collins	____
1939	Top 100 MWA 8	*Big Sleep, The*	Raymond Chandler	____
1938	Top 100 MWA 9	*Rebecca*	Daphne du Maurier	____
1939.	Top 100 MWA 10	*And Then There Were None (Ten Little Niggers)*	Agatha Christie	____
1958	Top 100 MWA 11	*Anatomy of a Murder*	Robert Traver	____
1926	Top 100 MWA 12	*Murder of Roger Ackroyd, The*	Agatha Christie	____
1953	Top 100 MWA 13	*Long Goodbye, The (The Long Good-bye)*	Raymond Chandler	____
1934	Top 100 MWA 14	*Postman Always Rings Twice, The*	James M. Cain	____
1969	Top 100 MWA 15	*Godfather, The*	Mario Puzo	____
1988	Top 100 MWA 16	*Silence of the Lambs, The*	Thomas Harris	____
1939	Top 100 MWA 17	*Coffin for Dimitrios, A (The Mask of Dimitrios)*	Eric Ambler	____
1935	Top 100 MWA 18	*Gaudy Night*	Dorothy L. Sayers	____
1948	Top 100 MWA 19	*Witness for the Prosecution*	Agatha Christie	____
1971	Top 100 MWA 20	*Day of the Jackal, The*	Frederick Forsyth	____
1940	Top 100 MWA 21	*Farewell, My Lovely*	Raymond Chandler	____
1915	Top 100 MWA 22	*Thirty-Nine Steps, The*	John Buchan	____
1983	Top 100 MWA 23	*Name of the Rose, The*	Umberto Eco	____

1866	**Top 100 MWA 24**	*Crime and Punishment*	Fyodor Dostoevsky	____
1978	**Top 100 MWA 25**	*Eye of the Needle (Storm Island)*	Ken Follett	____
1978	**Top 100 MWA 26**	*Rumpole of the Bailey*	John Mortimer	____
1981	**Top 100 MWA 27**	*Red Dragon (Manhunter)*	Thomas Harris	____
1934	**Top 100 MWA 28**	*Nine Tailors, The*	Dorothy L. Sayers	____
1974	**Top 100 MWA 29**	*Fletch*	Gregory McDonald	____
1974	**Top 100 MWA 30**	*Tinker, Tailor, Soldier, Spy*	John le Carre	____
1934	**Top 100 MWA 31**	*Thin Man, The*	Dashiell Hammett	____
1860	**Top 100 MWA 32**	*Woman in White, The*	Wilkie Collins	____
1913	**Top 100 MWA 33**	*Trent's Last Case (The Woman in Black)*	E.C. Bentley	____
1936/43	**Top 100 MWA 34**	*Double Indemnity*	James M. Cain	____
1981	**Top 100 MWA 35**	*Gorky Park*	Martin Cruz Smith	____
1930	**Top 100 MWA 36**	*Strong Poison*	Dorothy L. Sayers	____
1973	**Top 100 MWA 37**	*Dance Hall of the Dead*	Tony Hillerman	____
1970	**Top 100 MWA 38**	*Hot Rock, The*	Donald E. Westlake	____
1929	**Top 100 MWA 39**	*Red Harvest*	Dashiell Hammett	____
1908	**Top 100 MWA 40**	*Circular Staircase, The*	Mary Roberts Rinehart	____
1934	**Top 100 MWA 41**	*Murder on the Orient Express (Murder in the Calais Coach)*	Agatha Christie	____
1991	**Top 100 MWA 42**	*Firm, The*	John Grisham	____
1962	**Top 100 MWA 43**	*Ipcress File, The*	Len Deighton	____
1942	**Top 100 MWA 44**	*Laura*	Vera Caspary	____
1947	**Top 100 MWA 45**	*I, the Jury*	Mickey Spillane	____
1970	**Top 100 MWA 46**	*Laughing Policeman, The*	Maj Sjowall & Per Wahloo	____
1972	**Top 100 MWA 47**	*Bank Shot*	Donald E. Westlake	____
1950	**Top 100 MWA 48**	*Third Man, The (The Third Man and the Fallen Idol)*	Graham Greene	____
1952	**Top 100 MWA 49**	*Killer Inside Me, The*	Jim Thompson	____
1975	**Top 100 MWA 50**	*Where are the Children?*	Mary Higgins Clark	____
1982	**Top 100 MWA 51**	*"A" is for Alibi*	Sue Grafton	____
1973	**Top 100 MWA 52**	*First Deadly Sin, The*	Lawrence Sanders	____
1988	**Top 100 MWA 53**	*Thief of Time, A*	Tony Hillerman	____
1966	**Top 100 MWA 54**	*In Cold Blood: A True Account of a Multiple Murder and Its Consequences*	Truman Capote	____
1939	**Top 100 MWA 55**	*Rogue Male (Man Hunt)*	Geoffrey Household	____
1933	**Top 100 MWA 56**	*Murder Must Advertise*	Dorothy L. Sayers	____
1911	**Top 100 MWA 57**	*Innocence of Father Brown, The*	G.K. Chesterton	____
1979	**Top 100 MWA 58**	*Smiley's People*	John le Carre	____
1943	**Top 100 MWA 59**	*Lady in the Lake, The*	Raymond Chandler	____
1960	**Top 100 MWA 60**	*To Kill a Mockingbird*	Harper Lee	____
1958	**Top 100 MWA 61**	*Our Man in Havana*	Graham Greene	____
1870	**Top 100 MWA 62**	*Mystery of Edwin Drood, The*	Charles Dickens	____

1970	**Top 100 MWA 63**	*Wobble to Death*	Peter Lovesey	___
1928	**Top 100 MWA 64**	*Ashenden; or, The British Agent*	W. Somerset Maugham	___
1974	**Top 100 MWA 65**	*Seven-Per-Cent Solution, The*	Nicholas Meyer	___
1965	**Top 100 MWA 66**	*Doorbell Rang, The*	Rex Stout	___
1983	**Top 100 MWA 67**	*Stick*	Elmore Leonard	___
1983	**Top 100 MWA 68**	*Little Drummer Girl, The*	John le Carre	___
1938	**Top 100 MWA 69**	*Brighton Rock*	Graham Greene	___
1897	**Top 100 MWA 70**	*Dracula*	Bram Stoker	___
1955	**Top 100 MWA 71**	*Talented Mr. Ripley, The*	Patricia Highsmith	___
1946	**Top 100 MWA 72**	*Moving Toyshop, The*	Edmund Crispin	___
1989	**Top 100 MWA 73**	*Time to Kill, A*	John Grisham	___
1952	**Top 100 MWA 74**	*Last Seen Wearing…*	Hillary Waugh	___
1929	**Top 100 MWA 75**	*Little Caesar*	W.R. Burnett	___
1972	**Top 100 MWA 76**	*Friends of Eddie Coyle, The*	George V. Higgins	___
1927	**Top 100 MWA 77**	*Clouds of Witness*	Dorothy L. Sayers	___
1957	**Top 100 MWA 78**	*From Russia, With Love*	Ian Fleming	___
1955	**Top 100 MWA 79**	*Beast in View*	Margaret Millar	___
1950	**Top 100 MWA 80**	*Smallbone Deceased*	Michael Gilbert	___
1948	**Top 100 MWA 81**	*Franchise Affair, The*	Josephine Tey	___
1975	**Top 100 MWA 82**	*Crocodile on the Sandbank*	Elizabeth Peters	___
1971	**Top 100 MWA 83**	*Shroud for a Nightingale*	P.D. James	___
1984	**Top 100 MWA 84**	*Hunt for Red October, The*	Tom Clancy	___
1978	**Top 100 MWA 85**	*Chinaman's Chance*	Ross Thomas	___
1907	**Top 100 MWA 86**	*Secret Agent, The*	Joseph Conrad	___
1975	**Top 100 MWA 87**	*Dreadful Lemon Sky, The*	John D. MacDonald	___
1931	**Top 100 MWA 88**	*Glass Key, The*	Dashiell Hammett	___
1977	**Top 100 MWA 89**	*Judgement in Stone, A*	Ruth Rendell	___
1950	**Top 100 MWA 90**	*Brat Farrar (Come and Kill Me)*	Josephine Tey	___
1964	**Top 100 MWA 91**	*Chill, The*	Ross Macdonald	___
1990	**Top 100 MWA 92**	*Devil in a Blue Dress*	Walter Mosley	___
1975	**Top 100 MWA 93**	*Choirboys, The*	Joseph Wambaugh	___
1967	**Top 100 MWA 94**	*God Save the Mark*	Donald E. Westlake	___
1944	**Top 100 MWA 95**	*Home Sweet Homicide*	Craig Rice	___
1935	**Top 100 MWA 96**	*Three Coffins, The (The Hollow Man)*	John Dickson Carr	___
1982	**Top 100 MWA 97**	*Prizzi's Honor*	Richard Condon	___
1974	**Top 100 MWA 98**	*Steam Pig, The*	James McClure	___
1970	**Top 100 MWA 99**	*Time and Again*	Jack Finney	___
1977	**Top 100 MWA 100 - T**	*Morbid Taste for Bones, A*	Ellis Peters	___
1967	**Top 100 MWA 100 - T**	*Rosemary's Baby*	Ira Levin	___

Top 100 Mystery Novels of All Time — Additional Selections

The following titles are additional works selected by the Mystery Writers of America that did not make the Top 100 (above) but did receive a significant number of votes and are listed in "The Top Ten Books by Category." These titles cover suspense, hard-boiled/private eye, police procedural, cozy/traditional, historical, legal/courtroom, and humorous categories. There are 28 titles dating from 1920 to 1991.

1952	*Tiger in the Smoke, The*	Margery Allingham	____
1965	*In the Heat of the Night*	John Ball	____
1982	*Eight Million Ways to Die*	Lawrence Block	____
1986	*When the Sacred Ginmill Closes*	Lawrence Block	____
1944	*Green for Danger*	Christianna Brand	____
1989	*Black Cherry Blues*	James Lee Burke	____
1951	*Devil in Velvet, The*	John Dickson Carr	____
1949	*Little Sister, The (Marlow)*	Raymond Chandler	____
1936	*ABC Murders, The (The Alphabet Murders)*	Agatha Christie	____
1942	*Body in the Library, The*	Agatha Christie	____
1937	*Death on the Nile*	Agatha Christie	____
1963	*Mirror Crack'd, The (The Mirror Crack'd from Side to Side)*	Agatha Christie	____
1920	*Mysterious Affair at Styles, The*	Agatha Christie	____
1978	*Last Good Kiss, The*	James Crumley	____
1946	*Big Clock, The (No Way Out)*	Kenneth Fearing	____
1933	*Case of the Velvet Claws, The*	Erle Stanley Gardner	____
1989	*Skin Tight*	Carl Hiaasen	____
1979	*Green Ripper, The*	John D. MacDonald	____
1971	*Underground Man, The*	Ross Macdonald	____
1978	*Rest You Merry*	Charlotte MacLeod	____
1983	*Ice*	Ed McBain	____
1987	*Bimbos of the Death Sun*	Sharyn McCrumb	____
1991	*I.O.U.*	Nancy Pickard	____
1942	*Calamity Town*	Ellery Queen	____
1990	*Burden of Proof, The*	Scott Turow	____
1961	*Chinese Nail Murders, The*	Robert van Gulik	____
1976	*Dancing Aztecs (A New York Dance)*	Donald E. Westlake	____
1951	*Caine Mutiny, The*	Herman Wouk	____

Francis M. Nevins—Top Ten Authors

Francis M. Nevins, professor of law, is also well-known as a mystery writer, critic, editor, and speaker. He has twice received the Edgar® Allan Poe Award for criticism in the mystery field. *Grand Connections,* a publication of Saint Louis University, listed his "Top 10" mystery authors who were American, male, and dead. The authors are listed in no particular order. These were offered at a panel discussion during the Bouchercon Conference in Chicago in 2005. See remarks on page 11.

Dashiell Hammett	1894-1961
Raymond Chandler	1888-1959
Erle Stanley Gardner	1889-1970
Cornell Woolrich	1903-1968
David Goodis	1917-1967
John Dickson Carr	1906-1977
Ellery Queen	Frederic Dannay 1905-1982 and Manfred B. Lee 1905-1971
Rex Stout	1886-1975
Anthony Boucher	1911-1968
Harry Stephen Keeler	1890-1967

Queen's Quorum

Ellery Queen (in the person of Frederic Dannay) compiled "Queen's Quorum: A History of the Detective-Crime Short Story as Revealed by the 125 Most Important Books Published in this Field," 1845-1967, a list of the 106 (later expanded to 125; there is one extra title #73a, therefore there are really 126 titles) greatest collections of short stories in the history of mystery fiction. These stories are found in many places since they were first printed. Check the web for locations in various mystery and short story anthologies and also some of the titles can be found with the complete text on the web.

Queen's Quorum

1845	Queen's Quorum 1	*Tales*	Edgar Allan Poe	___
1856	Queen's Quorum 2	*Recollections of a Detective Police-Officer*	Waters(Wiliam Russelll)	___
1859	Queen's Quorum 3	*Queen of Hearts, The*	Wilkie Collins	___
1860	Queen's Quorum 4	*Hunted Down*	Charles Dickens	___
1861-4	Queen's Quorum 5	*Revelations of a Lady Detective, The (The Lady Detective; The Experiences of a Lady Detective)*		___
1862	Queen's Quorum 6	*Out of His Head*	Thomas Bailey Aldrich	___
1867	Queen's Quorum 7	*Celebrated Jumping Frog of Calaveras County, The*	Mark Twain	___
1876	Queen's Quorum 8	*Little Old Man of Batignolles, The*	Émile Gaboriau	___
1878.	Queen's Quorum 9	*Brought to Bay; or, Experiences of a City Detective*	James M'Govan	___
1881	Queen's Quorum 10	*Detective Sketches*	By a New York Detective	___
1882	Queen's Quorum 11	*New Arabian Nights*	Robert Louis Stevenson	___
1884	Queen's Quorum 12	*Lady, or the Tiger, The?*	Frank R. Stockton	___
1888	Queen's Quorum 13	*My Adventure in the Flying Scotsman"*	Eden Phillpotts	___
1888	Queen's Quorum 14	*Man-Hunter, The*	Dick Donovan	___
1892	Queen's Quorum 15	*Big Bow Mystery, The*	Israel Zangwill	___
1892	Queen's Quorum 16	*Adventures of Sherlock Holmes, The*	Arthur Conan Doyle	___
1894	Queen's Quorum 17	*Stories From the Diary of a Doctor*	L.T. Mead & Dr. Clifford Halifax	___
1894	Queen's Quorum 18	*Martin Hewitt, Investigator*	Arthur Morrison	___
1895	Queen's Quorum 19	*Prince Zaleski*	M.P. Shiel	___
1896	Queen's Quorum 20	*Strange Schemes of Randolph Mason, The (Randolph Mason: The Strange Schemes)*	Melville Davisson Post	___
1897	Queen's Quorum 21	*African Millionaire, An*	Grant Allen	___

1897	Queen's Quorum 22	*Dorcas Dene, Detective*	George R. Sims	____
1898	Queen's Quorum 23	*Paul Beck, the Rule of Thumb Detective*	M. McDonnell Bodkin	____
1898	Queen's Quorum 24	*Final Proof (Final Proof: or, The Value of Evidence)*	Rodrigues Ottolengui	____
1899	Queen's Quorum 25	*Detective's Pretty Neighbor, The*	Nicholas Carter	____
1899	Queen's Quorum 26	*Amateur Cracksman, The (Raffles, the Amateur Crasksman; Raffles)*	E.W. Hornung	____
1899	Queen's Quorum 27	*Brotherhood of the Seven Kings, The*	L.T. Eustace & Robert Meade	____
1900	Queen's Quorum 28	*Adventures of a Journalist, The*	Herbert Cadett	____
1901	Queen's Quorum 29	*In the Fog*	Richard Harding Davis	____
1902	Queen's Quorum 30	*Adventures of Romney Pringle, The*	Clifford Ashdown (R. Austin Freeman & John James Pitcairn)	____
1902	Queen's Quorum 31	*Condensed Novels* (second series)	Bret Harte	____
1903	Queen's Quorum 32	*Lingo Dan*	Percival Pollard	____
1905	Queen's Quorum 33	*Chronicles of Addington Peace, The*	B. Fletcher Robinson	____
1905	Queen's Quorum 34	*Loot of Cities, The*	Arnold Bennett	____
1906	Queen's Quorum 35	*Triumphs of Eugene Valmont, The*	Robert Barr	____
1906	Queen's Quorum 36	*Confessions of a Detective*	Alfred Henry Lewis	____
1907	Queen's Quorum 37	*Arsene Lupin, Gentleman-Cambrioleur (The Exploits of Arsene Lupin; "The Seven of Hearts)*	Maurice Leblanc	____
1907	Queen's Quorum 38	*Thinking Machine, The*	Jacques Futrelle	____
1908	Queen's Quorum 39	*Get-Rich-Quick Wallingford*	George Randolph Chester	____
1908	Queen's Quorum 40	*Gentle Grafter, The*	O. Henry	____
1909	Queen's Quorum 41	*Old Man in the Corner, The (The Man in the Corner)*	Baroness Orczy	____
1909	Queen's Quorum 42	*John Thorndyke's Cases (Dr. Thorndyke's Cases)*	R. Austin Freeman	____
1909	Queen's Quorum 43	*Adventures of Archer Dawe, Sleuth-hound (Contents of the Coffin)*	J.S. Fletcher	____
1910	Queen's Quorum 44	*Detective Dagobert's Deeds and Adventures*	Balduin Groller	____
1910	Queen's Quorum 45	*Man of the Forty Faces, The (Cleek, the Master Detective)*	T.W. Hanshew	____
1910	Queen's Quorum 46	*Achievements of Luther Trant, The*	Edwin Balmer & William MacHarg	____
1911	Queen's Quorum 47	*Innocence of Father Brown, The*	G.K. Chesterton	____

1911	**Queen's Quorum 48**	*Average Jones*	Samuel Hopkins Adams	____
1912	**Queen's Quorum 49**	*Silent Bullet, The (The Black Hand)*	Arthur B. Reeve	____
1912	**Queen's Quorum 50**	*Master of Mysteries, The*	Gelett Burgess	____
1912	**Queen's Quorum 51**	*Thrilling Stories of the Railway (Stories of the Railway)*	Victor L. Whitechurch	____
1912	**Queen's Quorum 52**	*Singing Bone, The (The Adventures of Dr. Thorndyke)*	R. Austin Freeman	____
1913	**Queen's Quorum 53**	*Carnacki, the Ghost Finder*	William Hope Hodgson	____
1913	**Queen's Quorum 54**	*Masterpieces of Mystery*	Anna Katharine Green	____
1913	**Queen's Quorum 55**	*November Joe (November Joe, the Detective of the Woods)*	Hesketh Prichard	____
1914	**Queen's Quorum 56**	*Max Carrados*	Ernest Bramah	____
1914	**Queen's Quorum 57**	*Diane and Her Friends*	Arthur Sherburne Hardy	____
1916	**Queen's Quorum 58**	*Limehouse Nights*	Thomas Burke	____
1917	**Queen's Quorum 59**	*Four Corners of the World, The*	A.E.W. Mason	____
1918	**Queen's Quorum 60**	*Uncle Abner, Master of Mysteries*	Melville Davisson Post	____
1918	**Queen's Quorum 61**	*Philo Gubb*	Ellis Parker Butler	____
1919	**Queen's Quorum 62**	*Red Mark, The (Where the Pavement Ends)*	John Russell	____
1920	**Queen's Quorum 63**	*Mysteries of a Great City*	William Le Queux	____
1920	**Queen's Quorum 64**	*Dream-Detective, The*	Sax Rohmer	____
1920	**Queen's Quorum 65**	*Carrington's Cases*	J. Storer Clouston	____
1920	**Queen's Quorum 66**	*Unique Hamlet, The*	Vincent Starrett	____
1920	**Queen's Quorum 67**	*Tutt and Mr. Tutt*	Arthur Train	____
1920	**Queen's Quorum 68**	*Call Mr. Fortune*	H.C. Bailey	____
1922	**Queen's Quorum 69**	*Eight Strokes of the Clock, The*	Maurice Leblanc	____
1923	**Queen's Quorum 70**	*Jim Hanvey, Detective*	Octavus Roy Cohen	____
1924	**Queen's Quorum 71**	*Poirot Investigates*	Agatha Christie	____
1925	**Queen's Quorum 72**	*Mind of Mr. J.G. Reeder, The (Murder Book of J.G. Reeder)*	Edgar Wallace	____
1926	**Queen's Quorum 73**	*Luigi of Catanzaro*	Louis Golding	____
1936	**Queen's Quorum 73a**	*Pale Blue Nightgown*	Louis Golding	____
1927	**Queen's Quorum 74**	*Sinners Go Secretly*	Anthony Wynne	____
1927	**Queen's Quorum 75**	*Jury of Her Peers, A*	Susan Glaspell	____
1928	**Queen's Quorum 76**	*Lord Peter Views the Body*	Dorothy L. Sayers	____
1928	**Queen's Quorum 77**	*Superintendent Wilson's Holiday*	G.D.H. & Margaret Cole	____
1928	**Queen's Quorum 78**	*Ashenden; or, The British Agent*	W. Somerset Maugham	____
1929	**Queen's Quorum 79**	*Rogues in Clover*	Percival Wilde	____
1929	**Queen's Quorum 80**	*Clues of the Caribbees (Clues of the Caribees)*	T.S. Stribling	____
1929	**Queen's Quorum 81**	*Detective Duff Unravels It*	Harvey J. O'Higgins	____

1930	**Queen's Quorum 82**	*Book of Murder, The*	Frederick Irving Anderson	___
1931	**Queen's Quorum 83**	*Solange Stories, The*	F. Tennyson Jesse	___
1931	**Queen's Quorum 84**	*Guys and Dolls*	Damon Runyon	___
1932	**Queen's Quorum 85**	*Thirteen Culprits, The*	Georges Simenon	___
1933	**Queen's Quorum 86**	*Brighter Buccaneer, The*	Leslie Charteris	___
1933	**Queen's Quorum 87**	*Policeman's Lot*	Henry Wade	___
1934	**Queen's Quorum 88**	*Cases of Susan Dare, The*	Mignon G. Eberhart	___
1934	**Queen's Quorum 89**	*Faith, Hope and Charity*	Irvin S. Cobb	___
1934	**Queen's Quorum 90**	*Adventures of Ellery Queen, The*	Ellery Queen	___
1935	**Queen's Quorum 91**	*Curious Mr. Tarrant, The*	C. Daly King	___
1939	**Queen's Quorum 92**	*Mr. Campion and Others*	Margery Allingham	___
1938	**Queen's Quorum 93**	*Trent Intervenes*	E.C. Bentley	___
1940	**Queen's Quorum 94**	*Department of Queer Complaints, The*	Carter Dickson	___
1940	**Queen's Quorum 95**	*Affairs of O'Malley, The (Smart Guy)*	William MacHarg	___
1942	**Queen's Quorum 96**	*Six Problems for Don Isidro Parodi"*	H. Bustos Domecq	___
1944	**Queen's Quorum 97**	*After-Dinner Story (Six Times Death)*	William Irish (Cornell Woolrich)	___
1944	**Queen's Quorum 98**	*Adventures of Sam Spade, The (They Can Only Hang You Once)*	Dashiell Hammett	___
1944	**Queen's Quorum 99**	*Five Murderers*	Raymond Chandler	___
1946	**Queen's Quorum 100**	*Dr. Sam: Johnson, Detector*	Lillian de la Torre	___
1946	**Queen's Quorum 101**	*Turbulent Tales*	Rafael Sabatini	___
1946	**Queen's Quorum 102**	*Compulsion to Murder, The*	Antonio Helu	___
1947	**Queen's Quorum 103**	*Riddles of Hildegarde Withers, The*	Stuart Palmer	___
1947	**Queen's Quorum 104**	*Department of Dead Ends, The*	Roy Vickers	___
1949	**Queen's Quorum 105**	*Knight's Gambit*	William Faulkner	___
1950	**Queen's Quorum 106**	*Diagnosis: Homicide*	Lawrence G. Blochman	___
1951	**Queen's Quorum 107**	*Fancies and Goodnights*	John Collier	___
1952	**Queen's Quorum 108**	*Something to Hide (Fingers of Fear)*	Philip MacDonald	___
1952	**Queen's Quorum 109**	*Little Tales of Smethers, The*	Lord Dunsany	___
1953	**Queen's Quorum 110**	*Beware of the Trains*	Edmund Crispin	___
1953	**Queen's Quorum 111**	*Someone Like You*	Roald Dahl	___
1954	**Queen's Quorum 112**	*Appleby Talking (Dead Man's Shoes)*	Michael Innes	___
1956	**Queen's Quorum 113**	*Mystery Stories (Quiet Horror)*	Stanley Ellin	___
1956	**Queen's Quorum 114**	*Jungle Kids, The*	Evan Hunter	___
1957	**Queen's Quorum 115**	*Albatross, The*	Charlotte Armstrong	___
1958	**Queen's Quorum 116**	*Name is Malone, The*	Craig Rice	___

1958	Queen's Quorum 117	*Malice in Wonderland*	Rufus King	____
1959	Queen's Quorum 118	*Short Cases of Inspector Maigret, The*	Georges Simenon	____
1961	Queen's Quorum 119	*Ordeal of Mrs. Snow, The*	Patrick Quentin	____
1963	Queen's Quorum 120	*People vs. Withers and Malone*	Stuart Palmer & Craig Rice	____
1965	Queen's Quorum 121	*Surprise, Surprise!* (The Singing Diamonds)	Helen McCloy	____
1966	Queen's Quorum 122	*Incredible Schlock Homes, The*	Robert L. Fish	____
1967	Queen's Quorum 123	*Theme is Murder, The*	Miriam Allen deFord	____
1967	Queen's Quorum 124	*Game Without Rules*	Michael Gilbert	____
1967	Queen's Quorum 125	*Nine Mile Walk, The*	Harry Kemelman	____

www.classiccrimefiction.com/queensquorum.htm

Ellery Queen's Twelve Best Detective Stories

In 1950, *Ellery Queen's Mystery Magazine* took a vote of 11 experts, among them Vincent Starrett, Charles Honce, and Lew D. Feldman asking for the experts' pick of the best detective stories ever written. There were 83 detective stories nominated and the final selection of the best is listed below. The results were published in the July 1950 issue of the magazine. Titles date from 1845 to 1938. Copies may be found in many locations.

1935	"Yellow Slugs, The"	H.C. Bailey	Windsor Mag, Mar 35; Mr. Fortune Objects; Meet Mr. Fortune; Churchyard Shadows, Carolan, ed.	____
1905	"Absent-Minded Coterie, The"	Robert Barr	*Sat Evening Post, May 13, 05;* EQMM, May 50; 50 Greatest Mysteries of All Time, Penzler, ed.	____
1938	"Genuine Tabard, The"	E.C. Bentley	*Trent Intervenes; The Strand, Jan 38;* AHMM Feb 94; Churchyard Shadows, Carolan, ed.	____
	"Avenging Chance,The"	Anthony Berkeley	Pearson's Mag, Sept 29; Avenging Chance & Other Mysteries, 04	
1929	"Hands of Mr. Ottermole, The"	Thomas Burke	The Story-Teller, Feb 29; 50 Greatest Mysteries of All Time, Penzler, ed.	____
1911	"Invisible Man,The"	G.K. Chesterton	chapter 5: Innocence of Father Brown; Murder British Style, Greenberg, ed.; 50 Greatest Mysteries of All Time, Penzler, ed.	____
1891	"Red-Headed League, The"	Arthur Conan Doyle	read on-line	____
1907	"Thinking Machine, The"	Jacques Futrelle	read on-line	____

1921	"Gioconda Smile,The"	Aldous Huxley	*English Review, Aug 21; EQMM* Sept 50; 50 Greatest Mysteries of all Time, Penzler, ed.	___
1845	"Purloined Letter, The"	Edgar Allan Poe	Tales	___
1912	"Naboth's Nineyard"	Melville D. Post	*Uncle Abner, 18 Metropolitian Mag, Dec 12; AHMM,* May 00; Best American Mystery Stories of the Century, Hillerman, ed.; Classic Mysteries Stories, Greene, ed.	___
1933	*"Suspicion"*	Dorothy L. Sayers	Mystery League Mag, Oct 33; 101 Years' Entertainment, Queen, ed.; In the Teeth of Evidence	___

www.topmystery.com/books14.htm
home.comcast.net/~netaylor1/elleryqueenstwelve.html

Reader's Guides to Mystery Novels
Susan Oleksiw, series editor

Mary J. Jarvis—Notable Suspense Novels

In her book, *A Reader's Guide to the Suspense Novel,* Mary J. Jarvis presents a list of 32 novels in the suspense field. These novels date from 1934-1994.

1934	*Postman Always Rings Twice, The*	James M. Cain	___
1992	*All Around the Town*	Mary Higgins Clark	___
1980	*Cradle Will Fall, The*	Mary Higgins Clark	___
1982	*Cry in the Night, A*	Mary Higgins Clark	___
1993	*I'll Be Seeing You*	Mary Higgins Clark	___
1991	*Loves Music, Loves to Dance*	Mary Higgins Clark	___
1994	*Remember Me*	Mary Higgins Clark	___
1984	*Stillwatch*	Mary Higgins Clark	___
1977	*Stranger is Watching, A*	Mary Higgins Clark	___
1987	*Weep No More, My Lady*	Mary Higgins Clark	___
1975	*Where Are the Children?*	Mary Higgins Clark	___
1989	*While My Pretty One Sleeps*	Mary Higgins Clark	___
1860	*Woman in White, The*	Wilkie Collins	___
1938	*Rebecca*	Daphne du Maurier	___
1965	*Jealous One, The*	Celia Fremlin	___
1950	*Strangers on a Train*	Patricia Highsmith	___
1944	*Deadline at Dawn*	William Irish (Cornell Woolrich)	___
1970	*Walter Syndrome, The*	Richard Neely	___
1955	*Madam, Will You Talk?*	Mary Stewart	___
1959	*Getaway, The*	Jim Thompson	___
1963	*Grifters, The*	Jim Thompson	___
1954	*Hell of a Woman, A*	Jim Thompson	___
1952	*Killer Inside Me, The*	Jim Thompson	___
1957	*Kill-Off, The*	Jim Thompson	___
1964	*Pop. 1280*	Jim Thompson	___
1972	*Listen for the Whisperer*	Phyllis A. Whitney	___
1962	*Window on the Square*	Phyllis A. Whitney	___
1942	*Black Alibi*	Cornell Woolrich	___
1943	*Black Angel, The*	Cornell Woolrich	___
1941	*Black Curtain, The*	Cornell Woolrich	___
1944	*Black Path of Fear, The*	Cornell Woolrich	___
1948	*Rendezvous in Black*	Cornell Woolrich	___

Marvin Lachman—100 Notable American Novels of Detection

In his *A Reader's Guide to the American Novel of Detection* (1993), Marvin Lachman includes a list of "One Hundred Notable Novels of Detection." He writes: "Though I did consider historical importance, my primary criterion was quality....The detective plot and the ingenuity and fairness of the solution are also basic to the detective story, so certain writers of the Golden Age of Detection (Queen, Carr, and Stout) appear frequently. Yet also included are many more recent writers, people who have substituted regional insights, humor, and exploration of social problems for sheer brilliance of puzzle. Though this list is, of course, subjective, it is based on 50 years of reading mysteries and 25 years of reviewing them." The titles date from 1878 to 1991.

1943	*Shudders, The (Deadly Secret)*	Anthony Abbot	___
1930	*Charlie Chan Carries On*	Earl Derr Biggers	___
1948	*Wilders Walk Away*	Herbert Brean	___
1950	*Hardly a Man is Now Alive (Murder Now and Then)*	Herbert Brean	___
1985	*Triple Crown*	Jon L. Breen	___
1987	*Junkyard Dog, The*	Robert Campbell	___
1937	*Burning Court, The*	John Dickson Carr	___
1941	*Case of the Constant Suicides, The*	John Dickson Carr	___
1938	*Crooked Hinge, The*	John Dickson Carr	___
1933	*Hag's Nook*	John Dickson Carr	___
1956	*Patrick Butler for the Defense*	John Dickson Carr	___
1935	*Three Coffins, The (The Hollow Man)*	John Dickson Carr	___
1984	*Kill Your Darlings*	Max Allan Collins	___
1981	*Death in a Tenured Position (A Death in the Faculty)*	Amanda Cross	___
1967	*James Joyce Murder, The*	Amanda Cross	___
1980	*Hands of Healing Murder, The*	Barbara D'Amato	___
1951	*Gentle Murderer, A*	Dorothy Salisbury Davis	___
1956.	*Fear is the Same*	Carter Dickson	___
1942	*Gilded Man, The (Death and the Gilded Man)*	Carter Dickson	___
1944	*He Wouldn't Kill Patience*	Carter Dickson	___
1938	*Judas Window, The (The Crossbow Murder)*	Carter Dickson	___
1939	*Reader is Warned, The*	Carter Dickson	___
1943	*She Died a Lady*	Carter Dickson	___
1957	*Method in Madness (Quiet Violence; Too Innocent to Kill)*	Doris Miles Disney	___
1946	*Who Rides a Tiger (Sow the Wind)*	Doris Miles Disney	___
1988	*Old Bones*	Aaron Elkins	___
1946	*Horizontal Man, The*	Helen Eustis	___
1944	*Case of the Black-Eyed Blonde, The*	Erle Stanley Gardner	___
1935	*Case of the Counterfeit Eye, The*	Erle Stanley Gardner	___
1944	*Case of the Crooked Candle, The*	Erle Stanley Gardner	___
1934	*Case of the Howling Dog, The*	Erle Stanley Gardner	___
1937	*Case of the Lame Canary, The*	Erle Stanley Gardner	___

1939	*Case of the Perjured Parrot, The*	Erle Stanley Gardner	____
1949	*What a Body!*	Alan Green	____
1878	*Leavenworth Case, The*	Anna Katharine Green	____
1927	*Bellamy Trial, The*	Frances Noyes Hart	____
1945	*Devil in the Bush, The*	Matthew Head	____
1971	*Fly on the Wall, The*	Tony Hillerman	____
1940	*Nine Times Nine*	H.H. Holmes (Anthony Boucher)	____
1942	*Rocket to the Morgue*	H.H. Holmes (Anthony Boucher)	____
1969	*Case of Need, A*	Jeffery Hudson (Michael Crichton)	____
1964	*Friday the Rabbi Slept Late*	Harry Kemelman	____
1966	*Saturday the Rabbi Went Hungry*	Harry Kemelman	____
1935	*Obelists Fly High*	C. Daly King	____
1984	*Emily Dickinson is Dead*	Jane Langton	____
1964	*Accounting for Murder*	Emma Lathen	____
1961	*Banking on Death*	Emma Lathen	____
1967	*Murder Against the Grain*	Emma Lathen	____
1966	*Murder Makes the Wheels Go 'Round*	Emma Lathen	____
1970	*When in Greece*	Emma Lathen	____
1949	*Dishonest Murderer, The*	Frances & Richard Lockridge	____
1941	*Murder Out of Turn*	Frances & Richard Lockridge	____
1940	*Norths Meet Murder, The (Mr. & Mrs. North Meet Murder; A Taste for Murder)*	Frances & Richard Lockridge	____
1978	*Rest You Merry*	Charlotte MacLeod	____
1950	*Through a Glass, Darkly*	Helen McCloy	____
1946	*Pick Your Victim*	Patricia McGerr	____
1975	*Paperback Thriller*	Lynn Meyer	____
1976.	*Ask for Me Tomorrow*	Margaret Millar	____
1955	*Beast in View*	Margaret Millar	____
1945	*Iron Gates, The (Taste of Fears)*	Margaret Millar	____
1952	*Vanish in an Instant*	Margaret Millar	____
1981	*Death in the Past*	Richard A. Moore	____
1986	*Murder for Lunch*	Haughton Murphy	____
1986	*120-Hour Clock, The*	Francis M. Nevins, Jr.	____
1991	*Body in the Belfry, The*	Katherine Hall Page	____
1937	*Puzzle of the Blue Banderilla, The*	Stuart Palmer	____
1984	*Remember to Kill Me*	Hugh Pentecost	____
1984	*Generous Death*	Nancy Pickard	____
1986	*No Body*	Nancy Pickard	____
1989	*Unorthodox Practices*	Marissa Piesman	____
1942	*Calamity Town*	Ellery Queen	____
1949	*Cat of Many Tails*	Ellery Queen	____
1934	*Chinese Orange Mystery, The*	Ellery Queen	____

1932	*Egyptian Cross Mystery, The*	Ellery Queen	___
1930	*French Powder Mystery, The*	Ellery Queen	___
1932	*Greek Coffin Mystery, The*	Ellery Queen	___
1929	*Roman Hat Mystery, The*	Ellery Queen	___
1944	*Puzzle for Puppets*	Patrick Quentin	___
1938	*Death From a Top Hat*	Clayton Rawson	___
1984	*Gold Gamble, The*	Herbert Resnicow	___
1939	*8 Faces at 3 (Death at Three; Murder Stops the Clock)*	Craig Rice	___
1984	*Strike Three You're Dead*	R.D. Rosen	___
1932	*Tragedy of X, The*	Barnaby Ross (Ellery Queen)	___
1932	*Tragedy of Y, The*	Barnaby Ross (Ellery Queen)	___
1960	*Gray Flannel Shroud, The*	Henry Slesar	___
1974	*Reverend Randollph and the Wages of Sin*	Charles Merrill Smith	___
1985	*Double Exposure*	Jim Stinson	___
1989	*Carolina Skeletons*	David Stout	___
1954	*Black Mountain, The*	Rex Stout	___
1965	*Doorbell Rang, The*	Rex Stout	___
1975	*Family Affair, A*	Rex Stout	___
1934	*Fer-de-Lance (Meet Nero Wolfe)*	Rex Stout	___
1950	*In the Best Families (Even in the Best Families)*	Rex Stout	___
1936	*Rubber Band, The (To Kill Again)*	Rex Stout	___
1946	*Silent Speaker, The*	Rex Stout	___
1938	*Some Buried Caesar (The Red Bull)*	Rex Stout	___
1938	*Too Many Cooks*	Rex Stout	___
1944	*Rim of the Pit*	Hake Talbot	___
1938	*Cut Direct, The*	Alice Tilton (Phoebe Atwood Taylor)	___
1928	*Greene Murder Case, The*	S.S. Van Dine	___

home.comcast.net/~dwtaylor1/lachman.html
www.topmystery.com/books17.htm

Gary Warren Niebuhr—The Private Eye Novel: 100 Classics & Highly Recommended Titles

In his *A Reader's Guide to the Private Eye Novel,* Gary Warren Niebuhr list "One Hundred Classics and Highly Recommended Titles" to consider. He intends this to be a "reader's guide" for the P.I. subgenre to provide "many hours of entertainment." The titles date from 1926 to 1990.

The Classics

1959	*As Bad as I Am (Wanted: Danny Fontaine)*	William Ard	____
1947	*Fabulous Clipjoint, The*	Fredric Brown	____
1939	*Big Sleep, The*	Raymond Chandler	____
1940	*Farewell, My Lovely*	Raymond Chandler	____
1943	*Lady in the Lake, The*	Raymond Chandler	____
1953	*Long Goodbye, The (The Long Good-bye)*	Raymond Chandler	____
1939	*Urgent Hangman, The*	Peter Cheyney	____
1984	*True Crime*	Max Allan Collins	____
1983	*True Detective*	Max Allan Collins	____
1958	*Eighth Circle, The*	Stanley Ellin	____
1939	*Bigger They Come, The (Lam to the Slaughter)*	A.A. Fair (Erle Stanley Gardner)	____
1930	*Maltese Falcon, The*	Dashiell Hammett	____
1929	*Red Harvest*	Dashiell Hammett	____
1927/43	*$106,000 Blood Money (Blood Money; The Big Knockover)*	Dashiell Hammett	____
1939	*Red Gardenias (Some Dames are Deadly)*	Jonathan Latimer	____
1950	*Drowning Pool, The*	Ross Macdonald (as, John Ross Macdonald)	____
1946	*Deadly Weapon*	Wade Miller	____
1948	*Uneasy Street*	Wade Miller	____
1987	*Bitter Medicine*	Sara Paretsky	____
1973	*Death of the Detective, The*	Mark Smith	____
1948	*I, the Jury*	Mickey Spillane	____

Highly Recommended Titles

1940	*Sabotage (Death at the Dam; Death Before Breakfast)*	Cleve F. Adams	____
1955	*Shady Lady*	Cleve F. Adams	____
1987	*Get Off at Babylon*	Marvin H. Albert	____
1955	*Hell is a City (The Naked and the Innocent)*	William Ard	____
1954	*Mr. Trouble*	William Ard	____
1968	*Dark Power, A*	William Arden (Dennis Lynds)	____
1983	*Bitter Finish*	Linda Barnes	____
1990	*Coyote*	Linda Barnes	____
1984	*Dead Heat*	Linda Barnes	____
1989	*Snake Tattoo, The*	Linda Barnes	____

1960	*Cain's Woman* (revised: *Cain's Wife*)	O.G. Benson	___
1982	*Eight Million Ways to Die*	Lawrence Block	___
1949	*Bloody Moonlight, The (Murder in the Moonlight)*	Fredric Brown	___
1949	*Little Sister, The (Marlow)*	Raymond Chandler	___
1977	*Shadow of a Broken Man*	George C. Chesbro	___
1939	*Dangerous Curves (Callaghan)*	Peter Cheyney	___
1941	*It Couldn't Matter Less (The Unscrupulous Mr. Callaghan; Set-Up for Murder)*	Peter Cheyney	___
1944	*They Never Say When*	Peter Cheyney	___
1946	*Uneasy Terms*	Peter Cheyney	___
1949	*You Can Call It a Day (The Man Nobody Saw)*	Peter Cheyney	___
1980	*Dupe*	Liza Cody	___
1988	*Neon Mirage*	Max Allan Collins	___
1967	*Act of Fear*	Michael Collins (Dennis Lynds)	___
1975	*Blue Death*	Michael Collins (Dennis Lynds)	___
1927	*Snarl of the Beast, The*	Carroll John Daly	___
1943	*Mouse in the Mountain, The (Rendezvous with Fear; Dead Little Rich Girl)*	Norbert Davis	___
1973	*Woman in Marble*	Carl Dekker (Dennis Lynds)	___
1966	*Deadline*	Thomas B. Dewey	___
1947	*Draw the Curtain Close (Dame in Danger)*	Thomas B. Dewey	___
1964	*Only on Tuesdays*	Thomas B. Dewey	___
1983	*Dark Fantastic, The*	Stanley Ellin	___
1979	*Star Light, Star Bright*	Stanley Ellin	___
1984	*Sugartown*	Loren D. Estleman	___
1948	*Halo for Satan*	John Evans (as, Howard Browne)	___
1957	*Taste of Ashes, The*	John Evans (as, Howard Browne)	___
1942	*Owls Don't Blink*	A.A. Fair (Erle Stanley Gardner)	___
1961	*Hundred-Dollar Girl, The*	William Campbell Gault	___
1972	*Dead Skip*	Joe Gores	___
1985	*"B" is for Burglar*	Sue Grafton	___
1986	*"C" is for Corpse*	Sue Grafton	___
1990	*"G" is for Gumshoe*	Sue Grafton	___
1980	*Death Bed*	Stephen Greenleaf	___
1944	*Michael Shayne's Long Chance*	Brett Halliday	___
1949	*Taste for Violence, A*	Brett Halliday	___
1984	*Blunt Darts*	Jeremiah Healy	___
1987	*Bad August*	Daniel Hearn	___
1990	*Black Light*	Daniel Hearn	___
1946	*Double Take, The*	Roy Huggins	___
1978	*Murder on the Yellow Brick Road*	Stuart M. Kaminsky	___
1989	*March Violets*	Philip Kerr	___

1990	*Pale Criminal, The*	Philip Kerr	___
1957	*Room to Swing*	Ed Lacy	___
1952	*Sin in Their Blood (Death in Passing)*	Ed Lacy	___
1938	*Dead Don't Care, The*	Jonathan Latimer	___
1935	*Headed for a Hearse (The Westland Case)*	Jonathan Latimer	___
1936	*Lady in the Morgue, The*	Jonathan Latimer	___
1941	*Solomon's Vineyard (The Fifth Grave)*	Jonathan Latimer	___
1988	*And Baby Will Fall (Childproof)*	Michael Z. Lewin	___
1984	*Out of Season (Out of Time)*	Michael Z. Lewin	___
1990	*Flame*	John Lutz	___
1988	*Kiss*	John Lutz	___
1986	*Tropical Heat*	John Lutz	___
1984	*San Quentin*	Jack Lynch	___
1985	*Seattle*	Jack Lynch	___
1980	*Castles Burning*	Arthur Lyons	___
1987	*Fast Fade*	Arthur Lyons	___
1948	*Fatal Step*	Wade Miller	___
1947	*Guilty Bystander*	Wade Miller	___
1984	*Leave a Message for Willie*	Marcia Muller	___
1990	*Burn Marks*	Sara Paretsky	___
1989	*Poodle Springs*	Raymond Chandler & Robert B. Parker	___
1976	*Promised Land*	Robert B. Parker	___
1960	*Girl's Number Doesn't Answer, The*	Talmage Powell	___
1984	*Quicksilver*	Bill Pronzini	___
1973	*Undercurrent*	Bill Pronzini	___
1958	*Hoods Come Calling, The*	Nick Quarry (Marvin H. Albert)	___
1970	*Falling Man, The*	Mark Sadler (Dennis Lynds)	___
1953	*Shakedown*	Roney Scott (William Campbell Gault)	___
1986	*Life's Work*	Jonathan Valin	___

Susan Oleksiw—Classic British Mystery 100 Classics of the Genre

In *A Reader's Guide to the Classic British Mystery* (1988), Susan Oleksiw listed "one hundred novels that are outstanding for various reasons: some are historically important as well as being well written; some are fascinating stories; and others are ingenious tales that capture and hold the reader until the surprise ending." She discusses each title in her book; dates range from 1886 to 1984.

1969	Complete Steel, The (The Stately Home Murder)	Catherine Aird	____
1940	Black Plumes	Margery Allingham	____
1950	Corpse Diplomatique	Delano Ames	____
1975	Affair of the Blood-Stained Egg-Cosy, The	James Anderson	____
1980	Assault and Matrimony	James Anderson	____
1978	Sprig of Sea Lavender, A	J.R.L. Anderson	____
1979	So Soon Done For	Marian Babson	____
1940	Bishop's Crime, The	H.C. Bailey	____
1974	Death of an Old Goat	Robert Barnard	____
1931	Death Walks in Eastrepps	Francis Beeding	____
1928	Six Proud Walkers, The	Francis Beeding	____
1944	Death at the Medical Board	Josephine Bell	____
1974	Pigeon Among the Cats, A	Josephine Bell	____
1913	Trent's Last Case (The Woman in Black)	E.C. Bentley	____
1929	Poisoned Chocolates Case, The	Anthony Berkeley	____
1938	Beast Must Die, The	Nicholas Blake	____
1941	Case of the Abominable Snowman, The (The Corpse in the Snowman)	Nicholas Blake	____
1954	Whisper in the Gloom, The (Catch and Kill)	Nicholas Blake	____
1944	Green for Danger	Christianna Brand	____
1954	Bones of Contention	Edward Candy	____
1908	Man Who was Thursday, The	G.K. Chesterton	____
1964	Caribbean Mystery, A	Agatha Christie	____
1937	Death on the Nile	Agatha Christie	____
1930	Murder at the Vicarage, The	Agatha Christie	____
1926	Murder of Roger Ackroyd, The	Agatha Christie	____
1934	Murder on the Orient Express (Murder in the Calais Coach)	Agatha Christie	____
1984	Dead Letter	Douglas Clark	____
1977	Gimmel Flask, The	Douglas Clark	____
1948	Buried for Pleasure	Edmund Crispin	____
1946.	Moving Toyshop, The	Edmund Crispin	____
1920	Cask, The	Freeman Wills Crofts	____
1946	Death of a Train	Freeman Wills Crofts	____
1922	Pit-Prop Syndicate, The	Freeman Wills Crofts	____
1977	Silent World of Nicholas Quinn, The	Colin Dexter	____
1968	Skin Deep (The Glass-Sided Ants' Nest)	Peter Dickinson	____
1956	Death in the Quadrangle	Eilis Dillon	____

411

1975	*Harriet Farewell*	Margaret Erskine	___
1929	*Mysterious Partner, The*	A. Fielding	___
1953	*Midsummer Malice*	Nigel Fitzgerald	___
1959	*This Won't Hurt You*	Nigel Fitzgerald	___
1919	*Middle Temple Murder, The*	J.S. Fletcher	___
1962	*Dead Cert*	Dick Francis	___
1907	*Red Thumb Mark, The*	R. Austin Freeman	___
1950	*Smallbone Deceased*	Michael Gilbert	___
1981	*Man With a Load of Mischief, The*	Martha Grimes	___
1951	*English Murder, An (The Christmas Murder)*	Cyril Hare	___
1949	*When the Wind Blows (The Wind Blows Death)*	Cyril Hare	___
1938	*Blunt Instrument, A*	Georgette Heyer	___
1983	*Deadheads*	Reginald Hill	___
1886	*Mystery of a Hansom Cab, The*	Fergus Hume	___
1931	*Malice Aforethought*	Francis Iles	___
1936	*Death at the President's Lodging (Seven Suspects)*	Michael Innes	___
1938	*Lament for a Maker*	Michael Innes	___
1960	*New Sonia Wayward, The (The Case of Sonia Wayward)*	Michael Innes	___
1975	*Black Tower, The*	P.D. James	___
1977	*Death of an Expert Witness*	P.D. James	___
1970	*Inspector Ghote Breaks an Egg*	H.R.F. Keating	___
1980	*Murder of the Maharajah, The*	H.R.F. Keating	___
1929	*Death of My Aunt*	C.H.B. Kitchin	___
1928	*Footsteps at the Lock, The*	Ronald A. Knox	___
1925	*Viaduct Murder, The*	Ronald A. Knox	___
1972	*Cyanide With Compliments*	Elizabeth Lemarchand	___
1976	*Step in the Dark*	Elizabeth Lemarchand	___
1946	*Fire in the Thatch*	E.C.R. Lorac	___
1976	*Swing, Swing Together*	Peter Lovesey	___
1938	*Nursemaid Who Disappeared, The (Warrant for X)*	Philip MacDonald	___
1933	*R.I.P. (Menace)*	Philip MacDonald	___
1924	*Rasp, The*	Philip MacDonald	___
1945	*Died in the Wool*	Ngaio Marsh	___
1951	*Opening Night (Night at the Vulcan)*	Ngaio Marsh	___
1940	*Surfeit of Lampreys (Death of a Peer)*	Ngaio Marsh	___
1933	*Oxford Tragedy, An*	J.C. Masterman	___
1922	*Red House Mystery, The*	A.A. Milne	___
1932	*Saltmarsh Murders, The*	Gladys Mitchell	___
1976	*Over the Sea to Death*	Gwen Moffat	___
1967	*Murder Fantastical*	Patricia Moyes	___
1961	*Sunken Sailor, The (Down Among the Dead Men)*	Patricia Moyes	___
1961	*Death and the Joyful Woman*	Ellis Peters	___
1972	*Death to the Landlords!*	Ellis Peters	___

1976	*Never Pick Up Hitch-Hikers!*	Ellis Peters	___
1968	*Hidden Wrath, The*	Stella Phillips	___
1977	*Judgement in Stone, A*	Ruth Rendell	___
1980	*Lake of Darkness, The*	Ruth Rendell	___
1946	*Death in Harley Street*	John Rhode	___
1956	*Landscape With Dead Dons*	Robert Robinson	___
1933	*Murder Must Advertise*	Dorothy L. Sayers	___
1934	*Nine Tailors, The*	Dorothy L. Sayers	___
1928	*Unpleasantness at the Bellona Club, The*	Dorothy L. Sayers	___
1978	*Blackheath Poisonings, The*	Julian Symons	___
1964	*End of Solomon Grundy, The*	Julian Symons	___
1970	*Man Who Lost His Wife, The*	Julian Symons	___
1952	*Singing Sands, The*	Josephine Tey	___
1973	*Death Cap*	June Thomson	___
1931	*Murder at School (Was It Murder?)*	Glen Trevor (James Hilton)	___
1974	*Pinch of Snuff, A*	Michael Underwood	___
1951	*Sole Survivor and The Kynsard Affair, The*	Roy Vickers	___
1929	*Duke of York's Steps, The*	Henry Wade	___
1935	*Heir Presumptive*	Henry Wade	___
1967	*Lonelyheart 4122*	Colin Watson	___
1978	*Treasure Up in Smoke*	David Williams	___

www.topmystery.com/books20.htm
home.comcast.net/~dwtaylor1/oleksiw.html

Nancy-Stephanie Stone—100 Spy and Thriller Novels

In *A Reader's Guide to the Spy and Thriller Novel* (1997), Nancy-Stephanie Stone lists 99 novels in the spy and thriller genre. These novels date from 1915-1993.

1955	*Assignment to Disaster*	Edward S. Aarons	____
1981	*Other Side of Silence, The*	Ted Allbeury	____
1938	*Cause for Alarm*	Eric Ambler	____
1939	*Mask of Dimitrios, The (A Coffin for Dimitrios)*	Eric Ambler	____
1963	*Green Wound, The (The Green Wound Contract)*	Philip Atlee	____
1976	*Last Domino Contract, The*	Philip Atlee	____
1973	*Tightrope Men, The*	Desmond Bagley	____
1966	*Thief Who Couldn't Sleep, The*	Lawrence Block	____
1990	*Kaddish in Dublin*	John Brady	____
1980	*Blood Group O*	David Brierley	____
1979	*Cold War*	David Brierley	____
1915	*Thirty-Nine Steps, The*	John Buchan	____
1976	*Saving the Queen*	William F. Buckley, Jr.	____
1984	*Story of Henri Tod, The*	William F. Buckley, Jr.	____
1966	*Naked Runner, The*	Francis Clifford	____
1970	*Defector, The*	Charles Collingwood	____
1985	*Disorderly Elements*	Bob Cook	____
1987	*Questions of Identity*	Bob Cook	____
1983	*When Fish Begin to Smell*	Matthew Heald Cooper	____
1969	*Embassy*	Stephen Coulter	____
1977	*Soyuz Affair, The*	Stephen Coulter	____
1968	*Stranger Called the Blues, A (Players in a Dark Game; Death in the Sun)*	Stephen Coulter	____
1966	*Hong Kong Incident, The (Assignment Hong Kong)*	James Dark	____
1991	*Russian Singer, The*	Leif Davidsen	____
1983	*Berlin Game*	Len Deighton	____
1964	*Funeral in Berlin*	Len Deighton	____
1962	*Ipcress File, The*	Len Deighton	____
1988	*Spy in Chancery*	P.C. Doherty	____
1973	*Wilby Conspiracy, The*	Peter Driscoll	____
1984	*Last Assassin, The*	Daniel Easterman	____
1980	*Murder of Lawrence of Arabia, The*	Matthew Eden	____
1972	*Judas Mandate, The*	Clive Egleton	____
1971	*Last Post for a Partisan*	Clive Egleton	____
1970	*Piece of Resistance, A*	Clive Egleton	____
1981	*Winter Touch, The (The Eisenhower Deception)*	Clive Egleton	____
1953	*Casino Royale (You Asked for It)*	Ian Fleming	____
1958	*Doctor No*	Ian Fleming	____
1957	*From Russia, With Love*	Ian Fleming	____
1983	*Leader and the Damned, The*	Colin Forbes	____

1971	*Day of the Jackal, The*	Frederick Forsyth	___
1974	*Dogs of War, The*	Frederick Forsyth	___
1977	*Charlie Muffin (Charlie M)*	Brian Freemantle	___
1973	*Goodbye to an Old Friend*	Brian Freemantle	___
1991	*Dark Star*	Alan Furst	___
1988	*Night Soldiers*	Alan Furst	___
1980	*Garden of Weapons, The*	John Gardner	___
1979	*Nostradamus Traitor, The*	John Gardner	___
1982	*Quiet Dogs, The*	John Gardner	___
1987	*Death's Head Berlin*	Jack Gerson	___
1979	*November Man, The*	Bill Granger	___
1958	*Our Man in Havana*	Graham Greene	___
1955	*Quiet American, The*	Graham Greene	___
1950	*Third Man, The (The Third Man and the Fallen Idol)*	Graham Greene	___
1972	*Sahara Road*	Simon Harvester	___
1991	*Eagle Has Flown, The*	Jack Higgins	___
1975	*Eagle Has Landed, The*	Jack Higgins	___
1980	*Oxford Gambit, The (The Flowers of the Forest)*	Joseph Hone	___
1988	*Friends, Russians and Countrymen*	Hampton Howard	___
1985	*Red Fox, The*	Anthony Hyde	___
1983	*Beaver to Fox*	Derek Kartun	___
1984	*Flittermouse*	Derek Kartun	___
1991	*German Reguiem, A*	Philip Kerr	___
1989	*March Violets*	Philip Kerr	___
1990	*Pale Criminal, The*	Philip Kerr	___
1989	*Burn Season*	John Lantigua	___
1977	*Orchids for Mother*	Aaron Latham	___
1961	*Call for the Dead (The Deadly Affair)*	John le Carre	___
1977	*Honourable Schoolboy, The*	John le Carre	___
1980	*Smiley's People*	John le Carre	___
1963	*Spy Who Came in From the Cold, The*	John le Carre	___
1974	*Tinker, Tailor, Soldier, Spy*	John le Carre	___
1975	*Robespierre Serial, The*	Nicholas Luard	___
1975	*Travelling Horseman*	Nicholas Luard	___
1975	*Road to Gandolpho, The*	Robert Ludlum (as, Michael Shepherd)	___
1966	*Shooting Script*	Gavin Lyall	___
1976	*Man From Yesterday, The*	George Markstein	___
1964	*Drum Beat—Berlin*	Stephen Marlowe	___
1966	*Gold of Malabar, The*	Berkely Mather	___
1983	*Last Supper, The*	Charles McCarry	___
1975	*Tears of Autumn, The*	Charles McCarry	___
1980	*In the Secret State*	Robert McCrum	___
1989	*Mamur Zapt and the Night of the Dog, The*	Michael Pearce	___

1988	*Mamur Zapt and the Return of the Carpet, The*	Michael Pearce	——
1970	*Labyrinth Makers, The*	Anthony Price	——
1975	*Our Man in Camelot*	Anthony Price	——
1988	*Spy in Question, The*	Tim Sebastian	——
1975	*Harry's Game*	Gerald Seymour	——
1986	*Song in the Morning, A (Shadow on the Sun)*	Gerald Seymour	——
1953	*China Coaster*	Don Smith	——
1981	*Gorky Park*	Martin Cruz Smith	——
1993	*Playing With Cobras*	Craig Thomas	——
1978	*Chinaman's Chance*	Ross Thomas	——
1966	*Cold War Swap, The (Spy in the Vodka)*	Ross Thomas	——
1971	*Fools in Town Are on Our Side, The*	Ross Thomas	——
1954	*Death Hits the Jackpot*	John Tiger (Walter Wager)	——
1983	*Man Called Kyril, A (Kyril)*	John Trenhaile	——
1980	*Man Who Lost the War, The*	W.T. Tyler	——
1973	*Beria Papers, The*	Alan Williams	——
1974	*Gentleman Traitor, The*	Alan Williams	——

Jo Ann Vicarel—100 Police Procedural Novels

A Reader's Guide to the Police Procedural, Jo Ann Vicarel offers the following 98 titles in the Police Procedural detection. The titles date from 1957 to 1992.

1977	*Police Chief*	John Ball	___
1976	*Yesterday is Dead*	Dallas Barnes	___
1984	*Switch*	William Bayer	___
1977	*Moment of Truth, The*	K. Arne Blom	___
1988	*Bad Guys*	Anthony Bruno	___
1992	*Stained White Radiance, A*	James Lee Burke	___
1984	*Strip Search*	Rex Burns	___
1978	*Jacobs Park Killings, The*	William Camp	___
1986	*Suspects*	William J. Caunitz	___
1988	*Butcher's Dozen*	Max Allan Collins	___
1992	*Black Echo, The*	Michael Connelly	___
1974	*Blank Page, The*	K.C. Constantine	___
1989	*Streets of Fire*	Thomas H. Cook	___
1991	*Body of Evidence*	Patricia Cornwell	___
1990	*Hundred Percent Squad, The*	E.W. Count	___
1983	*Dangerous Edge, The*	Robert Daley	___
1973	*Oktoberfest*	Frank De Felitta	___
1987	*Limbo*	Joseph P. De Sario	___
1987	*Dinner to Die For, A*	Susan Dunlap	___
1990	*Choke Hold*	Lew Dykes	___
1990	*Help Wanted: Orphans Preferred*	Earl Emerson	___
1985	*Alchemist*	Kenneth Goddard	___
1983	*Balefire*	Kenneth Goddard	___
1978.	*Running Duck, A (Fair Game)*	Paula Gosling	___
1988	*Silent Knives (Death on a No. 8 Hook)*	Laurence Gough	___
1987	*Just a Shot Away*	James Grady	___
1980	*Public Murders*	Bill Granger	___
1990	*Night Walker*	Jean Hager	___
1966	*Blind Spot*	Joseph Harrington	___
1989	*Tincture of Death*	Ray Harrison	___
1991	*Cutting Edge*	John Harvey	___
1992	*Off Minor*	John Harvey	___
1970	*Blessing Way, The*	Tony Hillerman	___
1978	*Listening Woman*	Tony Hillerman	___
1980	*People of Darkness*	Tony Hillerman	___
1988	*Thief of Time, A*	Tony Hillerman	___
1990	*Grootka*	Jon A. Jackson	___
1970	*God Keepers, The*	F. Richard Johnson	___
1977	*Death Squad (Hit Squad)*	Herbert Kastle	___
1989	*Death Spiral*	Bill Kelly & Dolph Le Moult	___
1983	*Hanging Tree, The*	Bill Knox	___

1987	*Heat Lightning*	John Lantigua	____
1989	*Captain Butterfly*	Bob Leuci	____
1986	*Late Payments*	Michael Z. Lewin	____
1989	*Shadow Dancers*	Herbert Lieberman	____
1984	*Heat From Another Sun*	David L. Lindsey	____
1990	*Point Blank*	Jayson Livingston	____
1957	*Con Man, The*	Ed McBain	____
1980	*Ghosts*	Ed McBain	____
1960	*Heckler, The*	Ed McBain	____
1970	*Jigsaw*	Ed McBain	____
1988	*Redemption (Murder at the Old Vicarage)*	Jill McGown	____
1977	*Laidlaw*	William McIlvanney	____
1987	*Fatal Command*	Joseph D. McNamara	____
1991	*Target Blue*	Terry Marlow	____
1961	*Gideon's Fire*	J.J. Marric (John Creasey)	____
1959	*Gideon's Staff*	J.J. Marric (John Creasey)	____
1981	*Perfect End*	William Marshall	____
1988	*Whisper*	William Marshall	____
1961/89	*Inspector Immanishi Investigates*	Seicho Matsumoto	____
1990	*Echo of Justice, An*	Hugh Miller	____
1988	*Crosskiller, The*	Marcel Montecino	____
1991	*Midtown North*	Christopher Newman	____
1992	*Nineteenth Precinct*	Christopher Newman	____
1987	*Body in Sokolniki Park, The (The Fair at Sokolniki)*	Fridrikh Neznansky	____
1991	*Private Crime, A*	Lillian O'Donnell	____
1975	*Scapegoat (The Whipping Boy)*	Poul Orum	____
1987	*Nowhere Man*	Jerry Oster	____
1989	*Midnight Club, The*	James Patterson	____
1961	*Nose on My Face, The (The First Body)*	Laurence Payne	____
1992	*Hard Fall*	Ridley Pearson	____
1989	*Earth Angels*	Gerald Petievich	____
1990	*Face of a Stranger, The*	Anne Perry	____
1986	*Cop Killer*	Tom Philbin	____
1970	*Reardon*	Robert L. Pike (Robert L. Fish)	____
1962	*Body to Spare, A*	Maurice Procter	____
1985	*Devil's Home on Leave, The*	Derek Raymond	____
1990	*And Leave Her Lay Dying*	John Lawrence Reynolds	____
1989	*Necessary End, A*	Peter Robinson	____
1988	*1199*	Charles G. Rogers	____
1991	*Crimes of the City*	Robert Rosenberg	____
1990	*Shadow Prey*	John Sandford	____
1988	*Undercover*	Soledad Santiago	____
1986	*Vendetta*	Steve Shagan	____
1971	*Murder at the Savoy*	Maj Sjowall & Per Wahloo	____

1989	*Force of Nature*	Stephen Solomita	___
1986	*Rainbow Drive*	Roderick Thorp	___
1984	*Big Money*	Peter Turnbull	___
1989	*Condition Purple*	Peter Turnbull	___
1978	*Blond Baboon, The*	Janwillem van de Wetering	___
1985	*Rattle-Rat, The*	Janwillem van de Wetering	___
1981	*All on a Summer's Day*	John Wainwright	___
1987	*Forgotten Murders The*	John Wainwright	___
1975	*Landscape With Violence*	John Wainwright	___
1989	*Man Who Wasn't There, The*	John Wainwright	___
1972	*Blue Knight, The*	Joseph Wambaugh	___
1992	*Sweet Deal*	John Westermann	___
1985	*New Hope for the Dead*	Charles Willeford	___

James Sandoe—Honor Roll of Crime Fiction

James Sandoe was a major mystery critic in the middle part of the last century. He worked for the *Chicago Sun-Times,* the *New York Herald Tribune,* and *Library Journal.* He was also at the *University of Colorado* as professor in English and Humanities. Sandoe was awarded two Edgars® for reviewing mysteries by the MWA.

This list was published in a chapter entitled, "Readers' Guide to Crime," in *The Art of the Mystery Story*, edited by Howard Haycraft, 1976. The list is offered with the suggestions of others and has 217 novels plus two nonfiction titles; covering 1841 to 1945. In addition, there are 20 titles plus the suggestion of *Ellery Queen Mystery Magazine* under the section entitled "Anthologies." Several times Sandoe gives a title of an "omnibus" to cover many works by an author. I have added some of those individual titles after listing the omnibus title for the clarification.

This began a conversation that saw Howard Haycraft offer suggestions to this list of books and that follows in the next list.

Sandoe Honor Roll

1934	*Death of a Ghost*	Margery Allingham	____
1936	*Flowers for the Judge (Legacy in Blood)*	Margery Allingham	____
1943	*Intrigue (Omnibus; 4 below)*	Eric Ambler	____
1937	*Background to Danger (Uncommon Danger)*	Eric Ambler	____
1938	*Cause for Alarm*	Eric Ambler	____
1939	*Coffin for Dimitrios, A (The Mask of Dimitrios)*	Eric Ambler	____
1940	*Journey into Fear*	Eric Ambler	____
1933	*He Arrived at Dusk*	R.C. Ashby	____
1942	*Meet Mr. Fortune (The Bishop's Crime & 12 stories)*	H.C. Bailey	____
1941	*Orphan Ann (The Little Captain)*	H.C. Bailey	____
1910	*Achievements of Luther Trant, The*	Edwin Balmer & William MacHarg	____
1931	*Death Walks in Eastrepps*	Francis Beeding	____
1939	*From Natural Causes*	Josephine Bell	____
1937	*Murder in Hospital*	Josephine Bell	____
1942	*Death of a Busybody*	George Bellairs	____
1902	*Grand Babylon Hotel, The (T. Racksole and Daughter)*	Arnold Bennett	____
1913	*Trent's Last Case (The Woman in Black)*	E.C. Bentley	____
1938	*Trent Intervenes (stories)*	E.C. Bentley	____
1929	*Poisoned Chocolates Case, The*	Anthony Berkeley	____
1937	*Trial and Error*	Anthony Berkeley	____
1926	*Chinese Parrot, The*	Earl Derr Biggers	____
1938	*Beast Must Die, The*	Nicholas Blake	____

1940	*Case of the Baker Street Irregulars, The (Blood on Baker Street)*	Anthony Boucher	____
1937	*Case of the Seven of Calvary, The*	Anthony Boucher	____
1939	*Death Has a Past*	Anita Boutell	____
1942.	*Fear and Miss Betony (Fear for Miss Betony)*	Dorothy Bowers	____
1924	*Eyes of Max Carrados, The*	Ernest Bramah	____
1914	*Max Carrados*	Ernest Bramah	____
1938	*Bullet in the Ballet, A*	Caryl Brahms & S.J. Simon	____
1944	*Case of the Giant Killer*	H.C. Branson	____
1943	*Pricking Thumb, The*	H.C. Branson	____
1927	*Kink, The (Colonel Gore's Third Case)*	Lynn Brock	____
1940	*Stoat, The*	Lynn Brock	____
1915	*Thirty-Nine Steps, The*	John Buchan	____
1941.	*Death at the Dog*	Joanna Cannan	____
1943	*Experiment Perilous*	Margaret Carpenter	____
1937	*Burning Court, The*	John Dickson Carr	____
1936	*Murder of Sir Edmund Godfrey, The*	John Dickson Carr	____
1935	*Three Coffins, The (The Hollow Man)*	John Dickson Carr	____
1939	*Big Sleep, The*	Raymond Chandler	____
1942	*High Window, The*	Raymond Chandler	____
1939	*No Orchids for Miss Blandish (Villain and the Virgin)*	James Hadley Chase	____
1945	*Father Brown Omnibus, The* (all Father Brown stories below and one story not in earlier volumes*)*	G.K. Chesterton	____
1911	*Innocence of Father Brown, The* (stories)	G.K. Chesterton	____
1914	*Wisdom of Father Brown, The* (stories)	G.K. Chesterton	____
1926	*Incredulity of Father Brown, The* (stories)	G.K. Chesterton	____
1927	*Secret of Father Brown, The* (stories)	G.K. Chesterton	____
1936	*Scandal of Father Brown, The* (stories)	G.K. Chesterton	____
1943	*Dark Duet (The Counter Spy Murders) (3 novelettes: It Doesn't Hurt Much; Sweet Conga; You Can Always Duck)*	Peter Cheyney	____
1936	*ABC Murders, The (The Alphabet Murders)*	Agatha Christie	____
1942	*Murder in Retrospect*	Agatha Christie	____
1926	*Murder of Roger Ackroyd, The*	Agatha Christie	____
1938	*Man From Tibet, The*	Clyde B. Clason	____
1942	*Perhaps a Little Danger*	E.H. Clements	____
1934	*Death in the Quarry*	G.D.H. & Margaret Cole	____
1941	*Drink to Yesterday*	Manning Coles	____
1940	*Toast to Tomorrow, A (Pray Silence)*	Manning Coles	____
1868	*Moonstone, The*	Wilkie Collins	____
1932	*Sweepstake Murders, The*	J.J. Connington	____
1943	*Painted for the Kill*	Lucy Cores	____
1920	*Cask, The*	Freeman Wills Crofts	____

1934	*Wilful and Premeditated (The 12:30 From Croydon)*	Freeman Wills Crofts	___
1941	*Strange Death of Manny Square, The*	A.B. Cunningham	___
1944	*Arrow Pointing Nowhere (Murder Listens In)*	Elizabeth Daly	___
1941	*Murders in Volume 2*	Elizabeth Daly	___
1945	*Elizabeth is Missing*	Lillian de la Torre	___
1870	*Mystery of Edwin Drood, The (Starrett, ed)*	Charles Dickens	___
1938	*Judas Window, The (The Crossbow Murder)*	Carter Dickson	___
1935	*Red Widow Murders, The*	Carter Dickson	___
1927	*Complete Sherlock Holmes, The*	Arthur Conan Doyle	___
1935	*Skin for Skin*	Winifred Duke	___
1936	*Fair Warning*	Mignon G. Eberhart	___
1929	*Patient in Room 18, The*	Mignon G. Eberhart	___
1939	*Bigger They Come, The (Lam to the Slaughter)*	A.A. Fair (Erle Stanley Gardner)	___
1903	*Nebuly Coat, The*	John Meade Falkner	___
1918	*Middle Temple Murder, The*	J.S. Fletcher	___
1937	*Simple Way of Poison, The*	Leslie Ford	___
1932	*Thorndyke's Omnibus (5 below)*	R. Austin Freeman	___
1912	*Singing Bone, The (The Adventures of Dr. Thorndyke)*	R. Austin Freeman	___
1941	*Dr. Thorndyke's Crime File*	R. Austin Freeman	___
1911	*Eye of Osiris, The (The Vanishing Man)*	R. Austin Freeman	___
1924	*Mystery of Angelina Frood, The*	R. Austin Freeman	___
1930	*Mr. Pottermack's Oversight*	R. Austin Freeman	___
1932	*Man From Scotland Yard, The (Mr. Simpson Finds a Body)*	David Frome	___
1926	*Payment Deferred*	C.S. Forester	___
1941	*Reunion With Murder*	Timothy Fuller	___
1907	*Problem of Cell 13, The*	Jacques Futrelle	___
1868/79	*Monsieur Lecoq (Lecoq the Detective)*	Emile Gaboriau	___
1866/73	*Widow Lerouge, The (Lerouge Case)*	Emile Gaboriau	___
1935	*Case of the Counterfeit Eye, The*	Erle Stanley Gardner	___
1942	*Mystery in the Woodshed (Something Nasty in the Woodshed)*	Anthony Gilbert	___
1878	*Leavenworth Case, The*	Anna Katharine Green	___
1939	*Confidential Agent, The*	Graham Greene	___
1936	*Death in the Deep South*	Ward Greene	___
1942	*Momentary Stoppage*	A.F. Grey	___
1939	*French Key, The (The French Key Mystery; Once Over Deadly)*	Frank Gruber	___
1941	*Last Doorbell (Kiss the Boss Goodbye)*	Frank Gruber (as, John K. Vedder)	___
1944	*Adventures of Sam Spade and Other Stories, The (They Can Only Hang You Once)*	Dashiell Hammett	___
1945	*Continental Op, The* (stories)	Dashiell Hammett	___
1945	*Return of the Continental Op, The* (stories)	Dashiell Hammett	___

1942	*Complete Dashiell Hammett, The (5 below)*	Dashiell Hammett	___
1929	*Red Harvest*	Dashiell Hammett	___
1929	*Dain Curse, The*	Dashiell Hammett	___
1930	*Maltese Falcon, The*	Dashiell Hammett	___
1931	*Glass Key, The*	Dashiell Hammett	___
1934	*Thin Man, The*	Dashiell Hammett	___
1927/43	*$106,000 Blood Money (Blood Money; The Big Knockover)*	Dashiell Hammett	___
1942	*Tragedy at Law*	Cyril Hare	___
1927	*Bellamy Trial, The*	Frances Noyes Hart	___
1943	*Smell of Money, The*	Matthew Head	___
1941	*Taste for Honey, A (A Taste for Murder)*	H.F. Heard	___
1941	*Envious Casca*	Georgette Heyer	___
1933	*Was It Murder? (Murder at School)*	James Hilton (as, Glen Trevor)	___
1942	*Lady Killer*	Elisabeth Sanxay Holding	___
1938	*Obstinate Murderer, The (No Harm Intended)*	Elisabeth Sanxay Holding	___
1942	*Rocket to the Morgue*	H.H. Holmes (Anthony Boucher)	___
1936	*Doctor Died at Dusk, The*	Geoffrey Homes	___
1905	*Thief in the Night, A*	E.W. Hornung	___
1939	*Rogue Male (Man Hunt)*	Geoffrey Household	___
1944	*Delicate Ape, The*	Dorothy B. Hughes	___
1942	*Fallen Sparrow, The*	Dorothy B. Hughes	___
1934	*Murder of My Aunt, The*	Richard Hull	___
1937	*Murder at Government House*	Elspeth Huxley	___
1938	*Murder on Safari*	Elspeth Huxley	___
1932	*Before the Fact*	Francis Iles	___
1931	*Malice Aforethought*	Francis Iles	___
1937	*Hamlet, Revenge!*	Michael Innes	___
1938	*Lament for a Maker*	Michael Innes	___
1942	*Phantom Lady*	William Irish (Cornell Woolrich)	___
1933	*Night Over Fitch's Pond*	Cora Jarrett	___
1940	*Keep Murder Quiet*	Selwyn Jepson	___
1941	*Singing Widow, The*	Veronica Parker Johns	___
1942	*Widening Stain, The*	W. Bolingbroke Johnson	___
1934	*Pattern in Black and Red*	Faraday Keene	___
1935	*Profile of a Murder*	Rufus King	___
1932	*Valcour Meets Murder*	Rufus King	___
1926	*Viaduct Murder, The*	Ronald A. Knox	___
1936	*Lady in the Morgue, The*	Jonathan Latimer	___
1945	*Time to Die, A*	Hilda Lawrence	___
1912	*Crystal Stopper, The*	Maurice Leblanc	___
1922	*Eight Strokes of the Clock, The* (stories)	Maurice Leblanc	___
1914	*Teeth of the Tiger, The*	Maurice Leblanc	___
1910	*813*	Maurice Leblanc	___

1941	*G-String Murders, The (Strip-Tease Murders; Lady of Burlesque)*	Gypsy Rose Lee (ghost written by Georgiana Ann Randolph Craig, aka, Craig Rice)	___
1943	*Death in the Doll's House*	Hannah Lees & Lawrence Bachmann	___
1908	*Mystery of the Yellow Room, The (Murder in the Bedroom)*	Gaston Leroux	___
1941	*Murder Out of Turn*	Frances & Richard Lockridge	___
1937	*Death of an Author*	E.C.R. Lorac	___
1913	*Lodger, The*	Marie Belloc Lowndes	___
1942	*Cue for Murder*	Helen McCloy	___
1943	*Goblin Market, The*	Helen McCloy	___
1924	*Rasp, The*	Philip MacDonald	___
1938	*Warrant for X (The Nursemaid Who Disappeared)*	Philip MacDonald	___
1940	*Enter Three Witches (The Spanish Steps)*	Paul McGuire	___
1938	*Funeral in Eden, A (Burial Service)*	Paul McGuire	___
1943	*Colour Scheme*	Ngaio Marsh	___
1938	*Death in a White Tie*	Ngaio Marsh	___
1939	*Overture to Death*	Ngaio Marsh	___
1910	*At the Villa Rose*	A.E.W. Mason	___
1924	*House of the Arrow, The*	A.E.W. Mason	___
1924	*Ashenden; or, The British Agent*	W. Somerset Maugham	___
1934	*East and West* (omnibus; collected short stories)	W. Somerset Maugham	___
1922	*Red House Mystery, The*	A.A. Milne	___
1942	*Laurels are Poison*	Gladys Mitchell	___
1945	*Rising of the Moon, The*	Gladys Mitchell	___
1943	*Sunset Over Soho*	Gladys Mitchell	___
1942	*When Last I Died*	Gladys Mitchell	___
1894	*Martin Hewitt: Investigator*	Arthur Morrison	___
1944	*Glass Mask*	Lenore Glen Offord	___
1943	*Skeleton Key*	Lenore Glen Offord	___
1920	*Great Impersonation, The*	E. Phillips Oppenheim	___
1938	*Fast Company*	Marco Page	___
1937	*Puzzle of the Blue Banderilla, The*	Stuart Palmer	___
1935	*Grindle Nightmare, The (Darker Grows the Valley)*	Q. Patrick	___
1933	*S.S. Murder*	Q. Patrick	___
1843	"Gold Bug, The"	Edgar Allan Poe	___
1841	"Murders in the Rue Morgue, The"	Edgar Allan Poe	___
1842	"Mystery of Marie Roget, The"	Edgar Allan Poe	___
1844	"Purloined Letter, The"	Edgar Allan Poe	___
1844	"Thou Art the Man"	Edgar Allan Poe	___
1896	*Strange Schemes of Randolph Mason, The (Randolph Mason: The Strange Schemes)*	Melville Davisson Post	___

1918	*Uncle Abner, Master of Mysteries*	Melville Davisson Post	____
1943	*Somebody at the Door*	Raymond Postgate	____
1940	*Verdict of Twelve*	Raymond Postgate	____
1942	*Calamity Town*	Ellery Queen	____
1934	*Chinese Orange Mystery, The*	Ellery Queen	____
1938	*Death From a Top Hat*	Clayton Rawson	____
1928	*Murders in Praed Street, The*	John Rhode	____
1944	*Home Sweet Homicide*	Craig Rice	____
1941	*Trial by Fury*	Craig Rice	____
1908	*Circular Staircase, The*	Mary Roberts Rinehart	____
1930	*Door, The*	Mary Roberts Rinehart	____
1932	*Tragedy of X, The*	Barnaby Ross (Ellery Queen)	____
1942.	*Lazarus #7*	Richard Sale	____
1937	*Busman's Honeymoon*	Dorothy L. Sayers	____
1930	*Documents in the Case, The*	Dorothy L. Sayers & Robert Eustace	____
1935	*Gaudy Night*	Dorothy L. Sayers	____
1932	*Have His Carcase*	Dorothy L. Sayers	____
1934	*Nine Tailors, The*	Dorothy L. Sayers	____
1930	*Strong Poison*	Dorothy L. Sayers	____
1938	*Listening House, The*	Mabel Seeley	____
1939	*Blanche Fury: or, Fury's Ape*	Joseph Shearing	____
1941	*Crime of Laura Sarelle, The (Laura Sarella)*	Joseph Shearing	____
1940	*Maigret Keeps a Rendezvous* (2 below)	Georges Simenon	____
1940	*Sailors' Rendezvous, The*	Georges Simenon	____
1932/40	*Saint-Fiacre Affair, The (Maigret Goes Home)*	Georges Simenon	____
1940	*Maigret to the Rescue* (2 below)	Georges Simenon	____
1940	*Flemish Shop, The*	Georges Simenon	____
1940	*Guinguette by the Seine, The*	Georges Simenon	____
1936	*Midnight and Percy Jones*	Vincent Starrett	____
1939	*Judas, Incorporated*	Kurt Steel	____
1941	*Good Night, Sheriff*	Harrison R. Steeves	____
1891	*Wrecker, The*	Robert Louis Stevenson & Lloyd Osbourne	____
1937	*Red Box, The (Case of the Red Box)*	Rex Stout	____
1938	*Too Many Cooks*	Rex Stout	____
1943	*Look Your Last*	John Stephen Strange	____
1929	*Clues of the Caribbees (Clues of the Caribees)*	T.S. Stribling	____
1944	*Rim of the Pit*	Hake Talbot	____
1927	*Slype, The*	Russell Thorndike	____
1943	*Murder Down Under (Mr. Jelly's Business)*	Arthur W. Upfield	____
1933	*Murder in Trinidad*	John Vandercook	____
1929	*Bishop Murder Case, The*	S.S. Van Dine	____
1936	*Wheel Spins, The (The Lady Vanishes)*	Ethel Lina White	____
1931	*Death in a Bowl*	Raoul Whitfield	____

1940	*Inquest*	Percival Wilde	____
1941.	*Footsteps Behind Her*	Mitchell Wilson	____
1940	*Bride Wore Black, The (Beware the Lady)*	Cornell Woolrich	____

Critical works

| 1945 | *Baker Street Inventory: A Sherlockian Bibliography* | Edgar W. Smith (compiler) | ____ |
| 1933 | *Private Life of Sherlock Holmes, The* | Vincent Starrett | ____ |

Anthologies

These are, of course, older suggestions, but there are many wonderful stories and articles for the mystery reader. Again, check online for used copies.

1945	*Great American Detective Stories*	Anthony Boucher, ed.	____
1927	*Before Scotland Yard: Classic Tales of Roguery and Detection, Ranging From the Apochrypha to Charles Dickens*	Peter Haworth, ed.	____
1927	*Great Detective Stories*	Willard Huntington, ed. (S.S. Van Dine)	____
1931	*Sleuths*	Kenneth MacGowan, ed.	____
1941	*101 Years' Entertainment: The Great Detective Stories, 1941-1941*	Ellery Queen, ed.	____
1938	*Challenge to the Reader*	Ellery Queen, ed.	____
1943	*Female of the Species, The: The Great Women Detectives and Criminals*	Ellery Queen, ed.	____
1944	*Misadventures of Sherlock Holmes, The*	Ellery Queen, ed.	____
1945	*Rogues' Gallery: The Great Criminals of Modern Fiction*	Ellery Queen, ed.	____

(Note: *Ellery Queen's Mystery Magazine* — since its first issue in 1941, has distinguished itself for the unusual diversity and quality of its stories.)

1942	*Sporting Blood: The Great Sports Detective Stories*	Ellery Queen, ed.	____
1939	*Detection Medley*	John Rhode, ed.	____
1940	*Line-Up* (a selection from *Detection Medley*)	John Rhode, ed.	____
1929	*Omnibus of Crime, The*	Dorothy L. Sayers, ed.	____
1932	*Second Omnibus of Crime, The: The World's Great Crime Stories*	Dorothy L. Sayers, ed.	____
1935	*Third Omnibus of Crime, The*	Dorothy L. Sayers, ed.	____
1936	*Tales of Detection*	Dorothy L. Sayers, ed.	____
1928	*Fourteen Great Detective Stories*	Vincent Starrett, ed.	____
1944	*World's Great Spy Stories*	Vincent Starrett, ed.	____
1929	*World's Best Detective Stories*	Eugene Thwing, ed.	____
1926	*Crime and Detection*	E.M. Wrong, ed.	____

Howard Haycraft's Additions to James Sandoe's Honor Roll of Crime Fiction

Howard Haycraft, in his editor's notes to James Sandoe's chapter "Readers' Guide to Crime" in *The Art of the Mystery Story* (1946) offered the importance of Sandoe's list: 1) up-to-date and refreshing, 2) the input of several informed minds, and 3) a place for conversation on the list.

At that point, he offers conversation in several areas. In the area of titles, it was not the authors he questioned, but the titles from some authors. He gave an example and then offered a different title by that author. At one point, he amended his own list of several years earlier (*Murder for Pleasure*, 1941) by offering two different titles by John Dickson Carr (earlier he had listed: *The Arabian Nights Murder* and *The Plague Court Murder*) and amended that with *The Crooked Hinge* and *The Judas Window*). Thus, Haycraft knew the continuing conversation that must take place in considering a "best" or "cornerstone" list of titles.

He then discussed "borderline" novels that opened the gate for further considerations. If one (borderline) title could be suggested, why not another? He went on to offer numerous "borderline" suggestions.

He also pointed out that Sandoe's list had a shortcoming in the "medium-to-hard-boiled school of crime writing," and he suggested additional titles. He mentioned the following authors who should be considered (without offering titles) that Sandoe's list omitted: Whitman Chambers, George Harmon Coxe, John Spain, H.C. Grafton, H.W. Roden, Brett Halliday, and Dana Chambers.

Finally, Haycraft turned to the "non-tough or general category" titles and gave authors and volumes that he thought should be added to Sandoe's list.

I have taken those titles from Haycraft's notes and list them below as possible additions for the collector. The titles have dates between 1898 to 1945; there are 67 titles in all.

In 1951, Fred Dannay (half of the famous writing team known as Ellery Queen) would have conversation with Haycraft's original list of 1941 and add a great many titles causing that list to become the *Haycraft-Queen* list (1952). The conversation continues.

Haycraft's Additions to Sandoe

1940	*Sabotage (Death at the Dam; Death Before Breakfast)*	Cleve F. Adams	___
1940	*Journey into Fear*	Eric Ambler	___
1914	*Adventures of the Infallible Godahl*	Frederick Irving Anderson	___
1930	*Book of Murder, The*	Frederick Irving Anderson	___
1932	*Red Castle, The (The Red Castle Mystery)*	H.C. Bailey	___
1906	*Tracks in the Snow*	Godfrey R. Benson (Lord Charnwood)	___
1936	*Trent's Own Case*	E.C. Bentley & H. Warner Allen	___

1942	*Full Crash Dive (The Submarine Signaled...*	Allan R. Bosworth	___
	Murder!; Murder Goes to Sea;		
	Hang and Rattle)		
1936/43	*Double Indemnity*	James M. Cain	___
1934	*Postman Always Rings Twice, The*	James M. Cain	___
1919	*Skeleton Key, The (The Mystery of the*	Bernard Capes	___
	Skeleton Key)		
1943	*Laura*	Vera Caspary	___
1940	*Farewell, My Lovely*	Raymond Chandler	___
1939	*Let Him Die*	E.H. Clements	___
1932	*Re-Enter Sir John*	Clemence Dane &	___
		Helen Simpson	
1939	*Murder is a Collector's Item*	Elizabeth Dean	___
1940	*Murder by Marriage, A*	Robert George Dean	___
1943	*Compound for Death*	Doris Miles Disney	___
1940	*Balcony, The*	Dorothy Cameron Disney	___
1941	*Death and Taxes*	David Dodge	___
1938	*Death Wears a White Coat*	Theodora Du Bois	___
1938	*Rebecca*	Daphne du Maurier	___
1936	*Harvard Has a Homicide (J for Jupiter)*	Timothy Fuller	___
1927	*Astounding Crime on Torrington Road, The*	William Gillette	___
1935	*Merely Murder (Death in the Stocks)*	Georgette Heyer	___
1941	*Justice Be Damned*	A.R. Hilliard	___
1940	*Deadly is the Evil Tongue (Old Mrs. Fitzgerald)*	Anne Hocking	___
1940	*So Blue Marble, The*	Dorothy B. Hughes	___
1898	*Turn of the Screw, The*	Henry James	___
1940	*Matter of Iodine, A*	David Keith	___
1941	*Odor of Violets, The (Eyes in the Night)*	Baynard Kendrick	___
1930	*Man in the Red Hat, The*	Richard Keverne	___
1930	*Death of My Aunt*	C.H.B. Kitchin	___
1944	*Darkness of Slumber*	Rosemary Kutak	___
1944	*Blood Upon the Snow*	Hilda Lawrence	___
1940	*Norths Meet Murder, The (Mr. & Mrs. North*	Frances & Richard Lockridge	___
	Meet Murder; A Taste for Murder)		
1941	*Longbow Murder, The*	Victor Luhrs	___
1942	*Uninvited, The (Uneasy Freehold)*	Dorothy Macardle	___
1932	*Escape (Mystery in Kensington Gore)*	Philip MacDonald	___
1941	*Above Suspicion*	Helen MacInnes	___
1928	*Death in the Dusk*	Virgil Markham	___
1915	*Beetle, The (The Mystery of the Beetle;*	Richard Marsh	___
	The House With the Open Window)		
1945	*Iron Gates, The (Taste of Fears)*	Margaret Millar	___
1942	*Murder, Chop Chop*	James Norman	___
1939	*Mysterious Mickey Finn, The; or, Murder*	Elliot Paul	___
	at the Café du Dome		

1939	*Cancelled in Red*	Hugh Pentecost	____
1944	*Alarum and Excursion*	Virginia Perdue	____
1943	*He Fell Down Dead*	Virginia Perdue	____
1921	*Grey Room, The*	Eden Phillpotts	____
1936	*Puzzle for Fools, A*	Patrick Quentin	____
1944	*Don't Look Behind You!*	Samuel Rogers	____
1932	*Clerical Error (The Vicar's Experiments)*	Anthony Rolls	____
1939	*Stars Spell Death, The (Murder in the Stars)*	Jonathan Stagge	____
1934	*Fer-de-Lance (Meet Nero Wolfe)*	Rex Stout	____
1931	*Cape Cod Mystery, The*	Phoebe Atwood Taylor	____
1938	*Cut Direct, The*	Alice Tilton	____
		(Phoebe Atwood Taylor)	
1939	*Escape*	Ethel Vance	____
1929	*Duke of York's Steps, The*	Henry Wade	____
1925	*Murder Book of J.G. Reeder, The*	Edgar Wallace	____
	(The Mind of Mr. J.G. Reeder)		
1934	*Portcullis Room, The*	Valentine Williams	____
1932	*Fatal Five Minutes, The*	R.A.J. Walling	____
1942	*Once Off Guard (The Woman in the Window)*	J.H. Wallis	____
1944	*Bride's Castle*	P.W. Wilson	____
1934	*Murder in a Walled Town*	Katherine Woods	____
1940	*Rope for a Convict*	R.C. Woodthrope	____
1933	*Ask a Policeman* (anthology)	Detection Club	____
1932	*Floating Admiral, The* (anthology)	Detection Club	____

James Sandoe—The Private Eye: A Personal Checklist

James Sandoe originally offered a list of *Hardboiled Dicks* in 1952 when Arthur Lovell, a Chicago bookseller, gave a gift to friends and clients. It was then updated and published in the January 1968 issue of *The Armchair Detective* and then updated in an article "The Private Eye" in *The Mystery Story* that was edited by John Ball in 1976. There are 83 titles dating from 1929 to 1962.

Sandoe Private Eye

1940	*Sabotage (Death at the Dam; Death Before Breakfast)*	Cleve F. Adams	____
1952	*Diary, The*	William Ard	____
1942	*Anything for a Quiet Life*	A.A. Avery	____
1948	*Dealing Out Death*	W.T. Ballard	____
1936	*"Policeman Only Taps Once, The"* (in, Six Against Scotland Yard)	Anthony Berkeley	____
1946	*3-13 Murders, The*	Thomas B. Black	____
1944	*No Good From a Corpse*	Leigh Brackett	____
1934	*Postman Always Rings Twice, The*	James M. Cain	____
1933	*Fast One*	Paul Cain	____
1946	*Seven Slayers* (stories)	Paul Cain	____
1939	*Big Sleep, The*	Raymond Chandler	____
1940	*Farewell, My Lovely*	Raymond Chandler	____
1947	*Finger Man, and Other Stories* (stories)	Raymond Chandler	____
1944	*Five Murderers (stories)*	Raymond Chandler	____
1945	*Five Sinister Characters* (stories)	Raymond Chandler	____
1942	*High Window, The*	Raymond Chandler	____
1943	*Lady in the Lake, The*	Raymond Chandler	____
1949	*Little Sister, The (Marlow)*	Raymond Chandler	____
1950	*Simple Art of Murder, The* (stories)	Raymond Chandler	____
1943	*Dark Duet (The Counter Spy Murders)* (3 novelettes: It Doesn't Hurt Much; Sweet Conga; You Can Always Duck)	Peter Cheyney	____
1936	*"Angelfish"* (in, *Black Mask*, Dec 1936)	Lester Dent (Joseph T. Shaw)	____
1941	*Death and Taxes*	David Dodge	____
1946	*It Ain't Hay (A Drug on the Market)*	David Dodge	____
1942	*Shear the Black Sheep*	David Dodge	____
1947	*Bandaged Nude, The*	Robert Finnegan	____
1948	*Many a Monster*	Robert Finnegan	____
1942	*Deadlier Than the Male*	James Gunn	____
1944	*Adventures of Sam Spade and Other Stories, The (They Can Only Hang You Once)*	Dashiell Hammett	____
1948	*Big Knockover, The (Blood Money; $106,000 Blood Money)*	Dashiell Hammett	____
1945	*Continental Op, The* (stories)	Dashiell Hammett	____

1950	*Creeping Siamese, The* (stories)	Dashiell Hammett	____
1929	*Dain Curse, The*	Dashiell Hammett	____
1947	*Dead Yellow Women* (stories)	Dashiell Hammett	____
1931	*Glass Key, The*	Dashiell Hammett	____
1946	*Hammett Homicides* (stories)	Dashiell Hammett	____
1930	*Maltese Falcon, The*	Dashiell Hammett	____
1962	*Man Named Thin, A* (stories)	Dashiell Hammett	____
1948	*Nightmare Town* (stories)	Dashiell Hammett	____
1929	*Red Harvest*	Dashiell Hammett	____
1934	*Thin Man, The*	Dashiell Hammett	____
1945	*Return of the Continental Op, The* (stories)	Dashiell Hammett	____
1952	*Woman in the Dark* (stories)	Dashiell Hammett	____
1927/43	*$106,000 Blood Money (Blood Money; The Big Knockover)*	Dashiell Hammett	____
1944	*Murder of a Stuffed Shirt*	M.V. Heberden	____
1940	*Subscription to Murder*	M.V. Heberden	____
1951	*Carry My Coffin Slowly*	Lee Herrington	____
1946	*Build My Gallows High*	Geoffrey Homes	____
1947.	*Halo for Nobody, A (Martinis and Murder)*	Henry Kane	____
1938	*If I Die Before I Wake (The Lady from Shanghai; Price for Murder)*	Sherwood King	____
1947	*Search for a Scientist*	Charles L. Leonard (M.V. Heberden)	____
1949	*Sinister Shelter*	Charles L. Leonard (M.V. Heberden)	____
1942	*Stolen Squadron, The*	Charles L. Leonard (M.V. Heberden)	____
1950	*Drowning Pool, The*	Ross Macdonald (as, John Ross Macdonald)	____
1952	*Ivory Grin, The (Marked for Murder)*	Ross Macdonald (as, John Ross Macdonald)	____
1949	*Moving Target, The (Harper)*	Ross Macdonald (as, John Ross Macdonald)	____
1948	*Three Roads, The*	Ross Macdonald (as, Kenneth Millar)	____
1951	*Way Some People Die, The*	Ross Macdonald (as, John Ross Macdonald)	____
1947	*Bury Me Deep*	Harold Q. Masur	____
1948	*Fatal Step*	Wade Miller	____
1945	*Guilty Bystander*	Wade Miller	____
1950	*Murder Charge*	Wade Miller	____
1951	*Shoot to Kill*	Wade Miller	____
1949	*Viewless Winds, The*	Murray C. Morgan	____
1952	*Obit Delayed*	Helen Nielsen	____

1946	"Farewell, My Lovely Appetizer" (in, *Keep It Crisp*)	S.J. Perelman	____
1945	"Somewhere a Roscoe" (in, *Crazy Like a Fox*)	S.J. Perelman	____
1951	*Pagoda*	James Atlee Phillips	____
1949	*Suitable for Framing*	James Atlee Phillips	____
1940	*No Mourners Present*	Frank G. Presnell	____
1936	*One Man's Muddle*	E(leanor) Baker Quinn	____
1939	*Dead and Done For*	Robert Reeves	____
1946	*Hard-Boiled Omnibus, The: Early Stories from Black Mask*	Joseph T. Shaw, ed.	____
1944	*Death is Like That*	John Spain (Cleve F. Adams)	____
1942	*Dig Me a Grave*	John Spain (Cleve F. Adams)	____
1950	*Blues for the Prince*	Bart Spicer	____
1949	*Dark Light, The*	Bart Spicer	____
1951	*Golden Door, The*	Bart Spicer	____
1952	*Long Green, The (Shadow of Fear)*	Bart Spicer	____
1945	*Dead Lie Still, The (Dead Ahead)*	William L. Stuart	____
1948	*Night Cry*	William L. Stuart	____
1952	*Night Watch, The*	Thomas Walsh	____
1950	*Nightmare in Manhattan*	Thomas Walsh	____
1931	*Death in a Bowl*	Raoul Whitfield	____

Charles Shibuk—105 Best Mystery Novels of All Time: A Preliminary List

(Subject to Change Without Notice)

In the #51 issue of *CADS*, the editor, Geoff Bradley, invited Charles Shibuk, mystery reviewer and writer of nonfiction books, to offer his list of 100 best mysteries of all time. He did so with the following comment:

> The following list was composed some ten years ago and with much haste and little thought. I think a substantial number of the titles could probably be eliminated in favour of other volumes of equal or greater merit. However, this is what was set down, for better or for worse, and I hope the readers will find it of some value.

He also listed five additional titles in 2007 to make the total of 105 novels, dating from 1906 to 1999.

Shibuk 105 Best Mysteries

1943	*Shudders, The (Deadly Secret)*	Anthony Abbot	___
1940	*Journey into Fear*	Eric Ambler	___
1939	*Mask of Dimitrios, The (A Coffin for Dimitrios)*	Eric Ambler	___
1933	*He Arrived at Dusk*	R.C. Ashby	___
1906	*Rock in the Baltic, A*	Robert Barr	___
1913	*Trent's Last Case (The Woman in Black)*	E.C. Bentley	___
1932	*Murder in the Basement*	Anthony Berkeley	___
1937.	*Trial and Error*	Anthony Berkeley	___
1925	*House Without a Key, The*	Earl Derr Biggers	___
1938	*Beast Must Die, The*	Nicholas Blake	___
1951	*Banner for Pegasus, A (Not in the Script)*	John & Emery Bonett	___
1944	*Green for Danger*	Christianna Brand	___
1955	*Tour de Force*	Christianna Brand	___
1948	*Wilders Walk Away*	Herbert Brean	___
1955	*Wench is Dead, The*	Fredric Brown	___
1957	*Taste of Ashes, The*	Howard Browne (John Evans)	___
1952	*Cold Blood*	Leo Bruce	___
1919	*Mr. Standfast*	John Buchan	___
1943	*Nobody Lives Forever*	W.R. Burnett	___
1937	*Case of the Missing Minutes, The (Eight O'Clock Alibi)*	Christopher Bush	___
1954	*Case of the Three Lost Letters, The*	Christopher Bush	___
1934	*Case of the 100% Alibis, The (The Kitchen Cake Mruder)*	Christopher Bush	___
1938/44	*Embezzler, The (in, Three of a Kind; The Baby in the Icebox; also as, "Money and the Woman")*	James M. Cain	___

433

1952	*Corpse in the Crevasse, The*	Glyn Carr	____
1937	*Burning Court, The*	John Dickson Carr	____
1936	*Three Coffins, The (The Hollow Man)*	John Dickson Carr	____
1953	*Long Goodbye, The (The Long Good-bye)*	Raymond Chandler	____
1936	*ABC Murders, The (The Alphabet Murders)*	Agatha Christie	____
1939	*And Then There Were None (Ten Little Niggers)*	Agatha Christie	____
1920	*Mysterious Affair at Styles, The*	Agatha Christie	____
1938	*Man From Tibet, The*	Clyde B. Clason	____
1944	*Case of the Gilded Fly, The (Obsequies at Oxford)*	Edmund Crispin	____
1920	*Cask, The*	Freeman Wills Crofts	____
1946	*Death of a Train*	Freeman Wills Crofts	____
1924	*Inspector French's Greatest Case*	Freeman Wills Crofts	____
1934	*12.30 from Croydon, The (Wilful and Premeditated)*	Freeman Wills Crofts	____
1975	*Wrong Case, The*	James Crumley	____
1927	*Snarl of the Beast, The*	Carroll John Daly	____
1983	*Riddle of the Third Mile, The*	Colin Dexter	____
1938	*Judas Window, The (The Crossbow Murder)*	Carter Dickson	____
1915	*Valley of Fear, The*	Arthur Conan Doyle	____
1939	*Bigger They Come, The (Lam to the Slaughter)*	A.A. Fair (Erle Stanley Gardner)	____
1946	*Big Clock, The (No Way Out)*	Kenneth Fearing	____
1985	*Break In*	Dick Francis	____
1965	*Odds Against*	Dick Francis	____
1930	*Mr. Pottermack's Oversight*	R. Austin Freeman	____
1974	*Return of Moriarty, The (Moriarty)*	John Gardner	____
1969	*Ascent of D-13, The*	Andrew Garve	____
1952	*Death in Captivity (The Danger Within)*	Michael Gilbert	____
1950	*Smallbone Deceased*	Michael Gilbert	____
1927	*Astounding Crime on Torrington Road, The*	William Gillette	____
1964	*Antagonists, The*	William Haggard	____
1936	*Dead Reckoning (Middle Class Murder)*	Bruce Hamilton	____
1963	*Ambushers, The*	Donald Hamilton	____
1964	*Shadowers, The*	Donald Hamilton	____
1964	*Ravagers, The*	Donald Hamilton	____
1931	*Glass Key, The*	Dashiell Hammett	____
1930	*Maltese Falcon, The*	Dashiell Hammett	____
1951	*English Murder, An (The Christmas Murder)*	Cyril Hare	____
1942	*Tragedy at Law*	Cyril Hare	____
1949	*Wind Blows Death, The (When the Wind Blows)*	Cyril Hare	____
1946	*With a Bare Bodkin*	Cyril Hare	____
1940	*Nine Times Nine*	H.H. Holmes (Anthony Boucher)	____
1939	*Rogue Male (Man Hunt)*	Geoffrey Household	____
1963	*Expendable Man, The*	Dorothy B. Hughes	____
1934	*Murder of My Aunt, The*	Richard Hull	____
1932	*Before the Fact*	Francis Iles	____

1942	*Phantom Lady*	William Irish (Cornell Woolrich)	___
1948	*Outrun the Constable (Killer By Proxy; Man Running)*	Selwyn Jepson	___
1936	*Iron Spiders, The (The Iron Spiders Murders)*	Baynard Kendrick	___
1941	*Odor of Violets, The (Eyes in the Night)*	Baynard Kendrick	___
1938	*Arrogant Alibi*	C. Daly King	___
1937	*Careless Corpse*	C. Daly King	___
1935	*Obelists Fly High*	C. Daly King	___
1994	*Beekeeper's Apprentice, The*	Laurie R. King	___
1986	*Rough Cider*	Peter Lovesey	___
1938	*Funeral in Eden, A (Burial Service)*	Paul McGuire	___
1942	*Calamity Town*	Ellery Queen	___
1932	*Greek Coffin Mystery, The*	Ellery Queen	___
1948	*Ten Days' Wonder*	Ellery Queen	___
1932	*Tragedy of X, The*	Ellery Queen (as, Barnaby Ross)	___
1946	*Death in Harley Street*	John Rhode	___
1932	*Fire At Greycombe Farm, The (Mystery at Greycombe Farm)*	John Rhode	___
1954	*Lucinda*	Howard Rigsby	___
1933	*Murder Must Advertise*	Dorothy L. Sayers	___
1930	*Strong Poison*	Dorothy L. Sayers	___
1952	*Kiss Me, Deadly*	Mickey Spillane	___
1980	*Man Who Killed His Brother, The*	Reed Stephens	___
1950	*In the Best Families (Even in the Best Families)*	Rex Stout	___
1931	*Death Flies High*	Darwin L. Teilhet	___
1929	*Barrakee Mystery, The (The Lure of the Bush)*	Arthur W. Upfield	___
1954	*Death of a Lake*	Arthur W. Upfield	___
1928	*Greene Murder Case, The*	S.S. Van Dine	___
1955	*Dying Fall, A*	Henry Wade	___
1935	*Heir Presumptive*	Henry Wade	___
1933	*Mist on the Saltings*	Henry Wade	___
1953	*Too Soon to Die*	Henry Wade	___
1944	*Bride's Castle*	P.W. Wilson	___
1941	*Measure for Murder*	Clifford Witting	___
1929	*Blood Royal*	Dornford Yates	___
1945	*House that Berry Built, The*	Dornford Yates	___

Addenda:

1927	*White Yawl, The*	J.B. Harris-Burland	___
1999	*Place of Execution, A*	Val McDermid	___
1945	*Red Right Hand, The*	Joel Townsley Rogers	___
1940	*Bride Wore Black, The (Beware the Lady)*	Cornell Woolrich	___

Grobius Shortling Mystery Lists

Grobius Shortling was a mystery fan and critic whose real name was Wyatt Edgar Frederic James; he died on January 12, 2006. Shortling created a tremendous web site listing his selections in depth with comment, it is listed at the end of his entries.

He has a list of 50 best mystery novels, but looking over the list one sees that he really has about 50 authors with 120 titles. He originally began his list in the 1980s and updated and made changes from time to time. I have kept the older titles and the new ones on the list. Dates range from 1853 though 1998. Several other lists follow below.

Grobius Shortling—50 Best Mystery Novels

1939	*Coffin for Dimitrios, A (The Mask of Dimitrios)*	Eric Ambler	___
1981	*Death of a Literary Widow (Posthumous Papers)*	Robert Barnard	___
1980	*Death of a Mystery Writer (Unruly Son)*	Robert Barnard	___
1981	*Death of a Perfect Mother (Mother's Boys)*	Robert Barnard	___
1974	*Death of an Old Goat*	Robert Barnard	___
1985	*Out of the Blackout*	Robert Barnard	___
1931	*Death Walks in Eastrepps*	Francis Beeding	___
1929	*Poisoned Chocolates Case, The*	Anthony Berkeley	___
1937	*Trial and Error*	Anthony Berkeley	___
1987	*When the Sacred Ginmill Closes*	Lawrence Block	___
1985	*Death is a Lonely Business*	Ray Bradbury	___
1979	*Comedian Dies, A*	Simon Brett	___
1984	*Not Dead, Only Resting*	Simon Brett	___
1981	*Situation Tragedy*	Simon Brett	___
1950	*Night of the Jabberwock*	Fredric Brown	___
1937	*Burning Court, The*	John Dickson Carr	___
1941	*Case of the Constant Suicides, The*	John Dickson Carr	___
1951	*Devil in Velvet, The*	John Dickson Carr	___
1957	*Fire, Burn!*	John Dickson Carr	___
1946	*He Who Whispers*	John Dickson Carr	___
1933	*Mad Hatter Mystery, The*	John Dickson Carr	___
1935	*Three Coffins, The (The Hollow Man)*	John Dickson Carr	___
1943	*Lady in the Lake, The*	Raymond Chandler	___
1939	*And Then There Were None (Ten Little Niggers)*	Agatha Christie	___
1965	*At Bertram's Hotel*	Agatha Christie	___
1942	*Body in the Library, The*	Agatha Christie	___
1961	*Pale Horse, The*	Agatha Christie	___
1957	*What Mrs. McGillicuddy Saw! (4:50 from Paddington)*	Agatha Christie	___
1868	*Moonstone, The*	Wilkie Collins	___
1860	*Woman in White, The*	Wilkie Collins	___

1944	*Case of the Gilded Fly, The (Obsequies at Oxford)*	Edmund Crispin	___
1950	*Frequent Hearses (Sudden Vengeance)*	Edmund Crispin	___
1951	*Long Divorce, The (Noose for Her, A)*	Edmund Crispin	___
1975	*Last Bus to Woodstock*	Colin Dexter	___
1983	*Riddle of the Third Mile, The*	Colin Dexter	___
1979	*Service of All the Dead*	Colin Dexter	___
1853	*Bleak House*	Charles Dickens	___
1870	*Mystery of Edwin Drood, The*	Charles Dickens	___
1969	*Glass-Sided Ants' Nest, The (Skin Deep)*	Peter Dickinson	___
1971	*Sleep and His Brother*	Peter Dickinson	___
1974.	*Poison Oracle, The*	Peter Dickinson	___
1940	*And So to Murder*	Carter Dickson	___
1945	*Curse of the Bronze Lamp, The (Lord of the Sorcerers)*	Carter Dickson	___
1938	*Judas Window, The (The Crossbow Murder)*	Carter Dickson	___
1946	*My Late Wives*	Carter Dickson	___
1943	*She Died a Lady*	Carter Dickson	___
1902	*Hound of the Baskervilles, The*	Arthur Conan Doyle	___
1946	*Big Clock, The (No Way Out)*	Kenneth Fearing	___
1957	*From Russia, With Love*	Ian Fleming	___
1954	*Live and Let Die*	Ian Fleming	___
1963	*On Her Majesty's Secret Service*	Ian Fleming	___
1964	*You Only Live Twice*	Ian Fleming	___
1926	*D'Arblay Mystery, The*	R. Austin Freeman	___
1930	*Mr. Pottermack's Oversight*	R. Austin Freeman	___
1936	*Penrose Mystery, The*	R. Austin Freeman	___
1967	*Too Many Magicians*	Randall Garrett	___
1979	*Gold by Gemini (Gold from Gemini)*	Jonathan Gash	___
1977	*Judas Pair, The*	Jonathan Gash	___
1950	*Smallbone Deceased*	Michael Gilbert	___
1951	*Death Has Deep Roots*	Michael Gilbert	___
1980	*Killing of Katie Steelstock, The (Death of a Favourite Girl)*	Michael Gilbert	___
1991	*Queen Against Karl Mullen, The*	Michael Gilbert	___
1985	*Twelfth Juror, The*	B.M. Gill	___
1930	*Maltese Falcon, The*	Dashiell Hammett	___
1942	*Tragedy at Law*	Cyril Hare	___
1958	*Untimely Death (He Should Have Died Hereafter)*	Cyril Hare	___
1975	*April Shroud, An*	Reginald Hill	___
1980	*Killing Kindness, A*	Reginald Hill	___
1973	*Ruling Passion*	Reginald Hill	___
1988	*Underworld*	Reginald Hill	___
1986	*Skinwalkers*	Tony Hillerman	___
1970	*Hot Day, Hot Night (Blind Man With a Pistol)*	Chester Himes	___

1965	*Hive of Glass, A*	P.M. Hubbard	____
1965	*Holm Oaks, The*	P.M. Hubbard	____
1934	*Murder of My Aunt, The*	Richard Hull	____
1932	*Before the Fact*	Francis Iles	____
1931	*Malice Aforethought*	Francis Iles	____
1962	*Atlantic Fury*	Hammond Innes	____
1956	*Wreck of the Mary Deare, The (The Mary Deare)*	Hammond Innes	____
1949	*Case of the Journeying Boy, The (The Journeying Boy)*	Michael Innes	____
1937	*Hamlet, Revenge!*	Michael Innes	____
1938	*Lament for a Maker*	Michael Innes	____
1977	*Honourable Schoolboy, The*	John le Carre	____
1965	*Spy Who Came in From the Cold, The*	John le Carre	____
1980	*Smiley's People*	John le Carre	____
1974	*Tinker, Tailor, Soldier, Spy*	John le Carre	____
1967	*Last One Left, The*	John D. MacDonald	____
1998	*Ballad of Frankie Silver, The*	Sharyn McCrumb	____
1993	*Hangman's Beautiful Daughter, The*	Sharyn McCrumb	____
1991	*If Ever I Return, Pretty Peggy-O (If Ever I Return)*	Sharyn McCrumb	____
1996	*Rosewood Casket, The*	Sharyn McCrumb	____
1995	*She Walks These Hills*	Sharyn McCrumb	____
1967	*Crimson Madness of Little Doom, The*	Mark McShane	____
1961	*Seance (Seance on a Wet Afternoon)*	Mark McShane	____
1989	*King of the Nightcap, The*	William Murray	____
1972	*Colonel Butler's Wolf*	Anthony Price	____
1983	*Gunner Kelly*	Anthony Price	____
1979	*Tomorrow's Ghost*	Anthony Price	____
1949	*Cat of Many Tails*	Ellery Queen	____
1932	*Egyptian Cross Mystery, The*	Ellery Queen	____
1932	*Greek Coffin Mystery, The*	Ellery Queen	____
1997	*Innocent Graves*	Peter Robinson	____
1975	*Family Affair, A*	Rex Stout	____
1961	*Final Deduction, The*	Rex Stout	____
1938	*Some Buried Caesar (The Red Bull)*	Rex Stout	____
1938	*Too Many Cooks*	Rex Stout	____
1978	*Chinaman's Chance*	Ross Thomas	____
1979	*Eighth Dwarf, The*	Ross Thomas	____
1990	*Twilight at Mac's Place*	Ross Thomas	____
1952	*Killer Inside Me, The*	Jim Thompson	____
1964	*Pop. 1280*	Jim Thompson	____
1954	*Death of a Lake*	Arthur W. Upfield	____
1951	*New Shoe, The (The Clue of the New Shoe)*	Arthur W. Upfield	____
1926	*Benson Murder Case, The*	S.S. Van Dine	____
1929	*Bishop Murder Case, The*	S.S. Van Dine	____
1993	*Anna's Book (Asta's Book)*	Barbara Vine	____

1995	*Brimstone Wedding, The*	Barbara Vine	____
1987	*Dark-Adapted Eye, A*	Barbara Vine	____
1962	*Hopjoy was Here*	Colin Watson	____
1967	*Lonelyheart 4122*	Colin Watson	____

Grobius Shortling—50 Mysteries to Take to a Desert Island

He referred to this list as the 50 mysteries to take to your desert island, but he rounds that total to 59 by adding some sets and reference works. Titles date from 1853 though 1995.

1939	*Coffin for Dimitrios, A (The Mask of Dimitrios)*	Eric Ambler	____
1980	*Death of a Mystery Writer (Unruly Son)*	Robert Barnard	____
1931	*Death Walks in Eastrepps*	Francis Beeding	____
1937	*Trial and Error*	Anthony Berkeley	____
1987	*When the Sacred Ginmill Closes*	Lawrence Block	____
1985	*Death is a Lonely Business*	Ray Bradbury	____
1985	*Dead Giveaway*	Simon Brett	____
1950	*Night of the Jabberwock*	Fredric Brown	____
1946	*He Who Whispers*	John Dickson Carr	____
1943	*Lady in the Lake, The*	Raymond Chandler	____
1942	*Body in the Library, The*	Agatha Christie	____
1868	*Moonstone, The*	Wilkie Collins	____
1944	*Case of the Gilded Fly, The (Obsequies at Oxford)*	Edmund Crispin	____
1975	*Last Bus to Woodstock*	Colin Dexter	____
1853	*Bleak House*	Charles Dickens	____
1969	*Glass-Sided Ants' Nest, The (Skin Deep)*	Peter Dickinson	____
1938	*Judas Window, The (The Crossbow Murder)*	Carter Dickson	____
1902	*Hound of the Baskervilles, The*	Arthur Conan Doyle	____
1946	*Big Clock, The (No Way Out)*	Kenneth Fearing	____
1954	*Live and Let Die*	Ian Fleming	____
1936	*Penrose Mystery, The*	R. Austin Freeman	____
1967	*Too Many Magicians*	Randall Garrett	____
1977	*Judas Pair, The*	Jonathan Gash	____
1950	*Smallbone Deceased*	Michael Gilbert	____
1985	*Twelfth Juror, The*	B.M. Gill	____
1930	*Maltese Falcon, The*	Dashiell Hammett	____
1942	*Tragedy at Law*	Cyril Hare	____
1980	*Killing Kindness, A*	Reginald Hill	____
1986	*Skinwalkers*	Tony Hillerman	____
1970	*Hot Day, Hot Night (Blind Man With a Pistol)*	Chester Himes	____
1965	*Holm Oaks, The*	P.M. Hubbard	____
1934	*Murder of My Aunt, The*	Richard Hull	____
1931	*Malice Aforethought*	Francis Iles	____
1956	*Wreck of the Mary Deare, The (The Mary Deare)*	Hammond Innes	____
1938	*Lament for a Maker*	Michael Innes	____
1965	*Spy Who Came in From the Cold, The*	John le Carre	____

1967	*Last One Left, The*	John D. MacDonald	____
1967.	*Crimson Madness of Little Doom, The*	Mark McShane	____
1989	*King of the Nightcap, The*	William Murray	____
1983	*Gunner Kelly*	Anthony Price	____
1932	*Greek Coffin Mystery, The*	Ellery Queen	____
1975	*Urn Burial (Beyond the Bone)*	Patrick Ruell (Reginald Hill)	____
1938	*Too Many Cooks*	Rex Stout	____
1978	*Chinaman's Chance*	Ross Thomas	____
1952	*Killer Inside Me, The*	Jim Thompson	____
1964	*Pop. 1280*	Jim Thompson	____
1954	*Death of a Lake*	Arthur W. Upfield	____
1929	*Bishop Murder Case, The*	S.S. Van Dine	____
1995	*Brimstone Wedding, The*	Barbara Vine	____
1962	*Hopjoy was Here*	Colin Watson	____

Shortling Desert Island Collection

1928	*World's Great Detective Stories*	Walter J. Black, ed.	____
1951	*Father Brown Anthology, The*	G.K. Chesterton	____
1853	*Bleak House (he repeats it here, see above)*	Charles Dickens	____
1927	*Complete Sherlock Holmes, The*	Arthur Conan Doyle	____
1864	*Uncle Silas*	J. Sheridan Le Fanu	____
1845	*Tales of Mystery and Imagination*	Edgar Allan Poe	____

Reference Books

1989	*Catalogue of Crime, A: Being a Reader's Guide to the Literature of Mystery, Detection, and Related Genres*	Jacques Barzun & Wendell Hertig Taylor	____
1941	*Murder for Pleasure: The Life and Times of the Detective Story*	Howard Haycraft	____
1982	*Gun in Cheek: A Study of "Alternative" Crime Fiction*	Bill Pronzini	____
1987	*Son of Gun in Cheek*	Bill Pronzini	____
1972	*Mortal Consequences*	Julian Symons	____

Grobius Shortling—One of a Kind

He offers books he referred to as "one-of-a-kind" that have extraordinary plotting, supernatural elements, or something else for the reader. The 24 titles date from 1824 to 2001.

1987	*Chatterton*	Peter Ackroyd	____
1915	*Thirty-Nine Steps, The*	John Buchan	____
1979	*Musclebound*	Liza Cody	____
1866	*Armadale*	Wilkie Collins	____
1979	*Leaven of Malice, A*	Clare Curzon	____
1991	*Drity Tricks*	Michael Dibdin	____
1989	*Tryst, The*	Michael Dibdin	____
1853	*Bleak House*	Charles Dickens	____

1938	*Rebecca*	Daphne du Maurier	___
1992	*Rune*	Christopher Fowler	___
2001	*Dangerous D@ta*	Lury Gibson (Adam Lury & Simon Gibson)	___
1794	*Adventures of Caleb Williams, The (Things as They Are; or, The Adventures of Caleb Williams; Caleb Williams)*	William Godwin	___
1968	*It Happened in Boston?*	Russell H. Greenan	___
1991	*Perfect Murder, The*	Jack Hitt (with other writers)	___
1978	*Falling Angel*	William Hjortsberg	___
1824	*Private Memoirs and Confessions of a Justified Sinner, The*	James Hogg	___
1934	*Cadaver of Gideon Wyck, The*	Alexander Laing	___
1864	*Uncle Silas*	J. Sheridan Le Fanu	___
1953	*Kiss Before Dying, A*	Ira Levin	___
1937	*Face on the Cutting Room Floor, The*	Cameron McCabe (Ernest Borneman)	___
1989	*Felidae*	Akif Pirincci	___
1945	*Red Right Hand, The*	Joel Townsley Rogers	___
1956	*Ka of Gifford Hillary, The*	Dennis Wheatly	___
1933	*Shadows of Ecstasy*	Charles Williams	___

members.aol.com/grobius/top50.htm

Rex Stout's 10 Favorite Detective Novels

Rex Stout (1886-1975), the detective storywriter and creator of Nero Wolfe, offered his ten favorite detective novels that were published in Vincent Starrett's *Books and Bipeds* in 1947. The titles date from 1868 to 1938.

Rex Stout List			
1920	*Call Mr. Fortune*	H.C. Bailey	___
1911	*Innocence of Father Brown, The*	G.K. Chesterton	___
1926	*Murder of Roger Ackroyd, The*	Agatha Christie	___
1868	*Moonstone, The*	Wilkie Collins	___
1920	*Cask, The*	Freeman Wills Crofts	___
1930	*Maltese Falcon, The*	Dashiell Hammett	___
1927	*Bellamy Trial, The*	Frances Noyes Hart	___
1938	*Lament for a Maker*	Michael Innes	___
1930	*Documents in the Case, The*	Dorothy L. Sayers & Robert Eustace	___
1926	*Benson Murder Case, The*	S.S. Van Dine	___

www.topmystery.com/books21.htm
home.comcast.net/~dwtaylor1/rexstoutsten.html

Julian Symons 100 Best Crime Stories

In 1957-58, Julian Symons selected the 100 Best Crime Stories for the London Sunday Times. His selection spanned 1794 through 1957. He was awarded the British Crime Writer's Association Cartier Diamond Dagger for lifetime achievement, named a Grand Master by the Mystery Writers of America, served as President of the Detection Club in London, and was a distinguished critic of the mystery genre. Mr. Symons (1912-94) was a British writer best known for his crime fiction, but he also wrote social and military history, biography, and on crime and literature, and was a poet.

Symons 100 Crime

1794	*Adventures of Caleb Williams, The (Things as They Are; or, The Adventures of Caleb Williams; Caleb Williams)*	William Godwin	___
1845	*Tales of Mystery and Imagination*	Edgar Allan Poe	___
1860	*Woman in White, The*	Wilkie Collins	___
1864	*Uncle Silas*	J. Sheridan Le Fanu	___
1866	*Crime and Punishment*	Fyodor Dostoevsky	___
1868	*Moonstone, The*	Wilkie Collins	___
1870	*Mystery of Edwin Drood, The*	Charles Dickens	___
1882	*New Arabian Nights*	Robert Louis Stevenson	___
1867/71	*Mystery of Orcival, The (Crime at Orcival)*	Emile Gaboriau	___
1887	*Mystery of a Hansom Cab, The*	Fergus Hume	___
1894	*Memoirs of Sherlock Holmes, The*	Arthur Conan Doyle	___
1895	*Three Impostors, The*	Arthur Machen	___
1899	*Raffles (The Amateur Cracksman; Raffles, the Amateur Crasksman)*	E.W. Hornung	___
1902	*Hound of the Baskervilles, The*	Arthur Conan Doyle	___
1907	*Thinking Machine, The*	Jacques Futrelle	___
1907	*Seven of Hearts, The (Arsene Lupin, Gentleman-Cambrioleur; The Exploits of Arsene Lupin)*	Maurice Leblanc	___
1908	*Mystery of the Yellow Room, The (Murder in the Bedroom)*	Gaston Leroux	___
1909	*Old Man in the Corner, The (The Man in the Corner)*	Baroness Orczy	___
1910	*At the Villa Rose*	A.E.W. Mason	___
1911	*Innocence of Father Brown, The*	G.K. Chesterton	___
1912	*Singing Bone, The (The Adventures of Dr. Thorndyke)*	R. Austin Freeman	___
1913	*Trent's Last Case (The Woman in Black)*	E.C. Bentley	___
1914	*Max Carrados*	Ernest Bramah	___
1915	*Thirty-Nine Steps, The*	John Buchan	___
1920	*Bulldog Drummond (Bull-Dog Drummond)*	"Sapper" (H.C. McNeile)	___
1922	*Crimson Circle, The*	Edgar Wallace	___

1922	*Red House Mystery, The*	A.A. Milne	____
1922	*Pit-Prop Syndicate, The*	Freeman Wills Crofts	____
1924	*House of the Arrow, The*	A.E.W. Mason	____
1926	*Murder of Roger Ackroyd, The*	Agatha Christie	____
1926	*Payment Deferred*	C.S. Forester	____
1928	*Greene Murder Case, The*	S.S. Van Dine	____
1927	*Bellamy Trial, The*	Frances Noyes Hart	____
1928	*Ashenden; or, The British Agent*	W. Somerset Maugham	____
1929	*Poisoned Chocolates Case, The*	Anthony Berkeley	____
1929	*Mr. Fortune Speaking*	H.C. Bailey	____
1931	*Pleasantries of Old Quong, The* (*A Tea-Shop in Limehouse*)	Thomas Burke	____
1931	*Glass Key, The*	Dashiell Hammett	____
1931	*Sanctuary*	William Faulkner	____
1931	*Malice Aforethought*	Francis Iles	____
1931	*Above the Dark Circus (Above the Dark Tumult)*	Hugh Walpole	____
1932	*Greek Coffin Mystery, The*	Ellery Queen	____
1933	*Murder Must Advertise*	Dorothy L. Sayers	____
1936	*Wheel Spins, The (The Lady Vanishes)*	Ethel Lina White	____
1934	*Death of a Ghost*	Margery Allingham	____
1934	*Postman Always Rings Twice, The*	James M. Cain	____
1934	*Pin to See the Peep-Show, A*	F. Tennyson Jesse	____
1934	*Adventures of Ellery Queen, The*	Ellery Queen	____
1934	*Fer-de-Lance (Meet Nero Wolfe)*	Rex Stout	____
1935	*Hollow Man, The (The Three Coffins)*	John Dickson Carr	____
1935	*We, the Accused*	Ernest Raymond	____
1935	*Gaudy Night*	Dorothy L. Sayers	____
1936	*Case of the Sleepwalker's Niece, The*	Erle Stanley Gardner	____
1936	*Gun For Sale, A (This Gun for Hire)*	Graham Greene	____
1937	*Hamlet, Revenge!*	Michael Innes	____
1937	*Lady in the Morgue, The*	Jonathan Latimer	____
1938	*Rebecca*	Daphne du Maurier	____
1938	*Nursemaid Who Disappeared, The (Warrant for X)*	Philip MacDonald	____
1939	*Mask of Dimitrios, The (A Coffin for Dimitrios)*	Eric Ambler	____
1939	*Rogue Male (Man Hunt)*	Geoffrey Household	____
1939	*Overture to Death*	Ngaio Marsh	____
1940	*Verdict of Twelve*	Raymond Postgate	____
1941	*Hangover Square*	Patrick Hamilton	____
1941	*Never Come Back*	John Mair	____
1942	*Tragedy at Law*	Cyril Hare	____
1942	*Phantom Lady*	William Irish (Cornell Woolrich)	____
1943	*High Window, The*	Raymond Chandler	____
1943	*Lodger, The* (in, *Escape in Vain;* with, *One Way Out*)	Georges Simenon	____
1944	*Laura*	Vera Caspary	____

1945	*Death Comes as the End*	Agatha Christie	___
1946	*Moving Toyshop, The*	Edmund Crispin	___
1946	*Horizontal Man, The*	Helen Eustis	___
1946	*Big Clock, The (No Way Out)*	Kenneth Fearing	___
1947	*Case to Answer, A (One More Unfortunate)*	Edgar Lustgarten	___
1948	*Devil Take the Blue-Tail Fly*	John Franklin Bardin	___
1948	*With My Little Eye*	Roy Fuller	___
1949	*Asphalt Jungle, The*	W.R. Burnett	___
1949	*Department of Dead Ends, The*	Roy Vickers	___
1950	*Mischief*	Charlotte Armstrong	___
1950	*Cat and Mouse*	Christianna Brand	___
1950	*Smallbone Deceased*	Michael Gilbert	___
1951	*Venetian Bird (Bird of Prey)*	Victor Canning	___
1951/54	*Maigret in Montmartre (Inspector Maigret and the Strangled Stripper)*	Georges Simenon	___
1951	*Daughter of Time, The*	Josephine Tey	___
1952	*My Name is Michael Sibley*	John Bingham	___
1952	*Reputation for a Song*	Edward Grierson	___
1952	*Last Seen Wearing…*	Hillary Waugh	___
1953	*Long Goodbye, The (The Long Good-bye)*	Raymond Chandler	___
1953	*Kiss Before Dying, A*	Ira Levin	___
1953	*Ivory Grin, The (Marked for Murder)*	Ross Macdonald (as, John Ross Macdonald)	___
1955	*Man Who Didn't Fly, The*	Margot Bennett	___
1955	*Man From the Sea, The (Death by Moonlight)*	Michael Innes	___
1955	*Beast in View*	Margaret Millar	___
1955	*Man With Two Wives, The*	Patrick Quentin	___
1956	*Tangled Web, A (Death and Daisy Bland)*	Nicholas Blake	___
1956	*Blunderer, The (Lament for a Lover)*	Patricia Highsmith	___
1956	*Lord Have Mercy, The (The Shrew Is Dead)*	Shelley Smith	___
1957	*Mystery Stories (Quiet Horror)*	Stanley Ellin	___
1957	*From Russia, With Love*	Ian Fleming	___
1957	*Compulsion*	Meyer Levin	___

www.topmystery.com/books23.htm
home.comcast.net/~dwtaylor1/symonsbest.html
www.classiccrimefiction.com/symons100.htm

Robin Winks—A Personal List of Favorites

In the Appendix to *Detective Fiction, A Collection of Critical Essays*, Robin W. Winks (editor) includes "A Personal List of Favorites." He writes that some people would like a list or entry point to read in the mystery field, and he offers this list as a guide. Authors are limited to no more than three titles and many books from the early classic period (pre-1930) are omitted; coverage is between 1903-1987. There are 304 titles.

Winks Mystery List

1982	*Cobalt*	Nathan Aldyne	____
1973	*Choice of Enemies, A*	Ted Allbeury	____
1929	*Crime at Black Dudley, The (The Black Dudley Murder)*	Margery Allingham	____
1937	*Dancers in Mourning (Who Killed Chloe?)*	Margery Allingham	____
1952	*Tiger in the Smoke, The*	Margery Allingham	____
1975	*Goodey's Last Stand*	Charles Alverson	____
1937	*Background to Danger (Uncommon Danger)*	Eric Ambler	____
1939	*Coffin for Dimitrios, A (The Mask of Dimitrios)*	Eric Ambler	____
1940	*Journey into Fear*	Eric Ambler	____
1975	*Affair of the Blood-Stained Egg Cosy, The*	James Anderson	____
1969	*Death of a Hittite*	Sylvia Angus	____
1976	*Murder at the ABA (Authorized Murder)*	Isaac Asimov	____
1976	*Enemy, The*	Desmond Bagley	____
1965	*High Citadel*	Desmond Bagley	____
1970	*Running Blind*	Desmond Bagley	____
1965	*In the Heat of the Night*	John Ball	____
1980	*Rembrandt Panel, The (The Rembrandt File)*	Oliver Banks	____
1979	*Death of a Literary Widow (Posthumous Papers)*	Robert Barnard	____
1974	*Death of an Old Goat*	Robert Barnard	____
1966	*Kremlin Letter, The*	Noel Behn	____
1957	*Running Man, The*	Ben Benson	____
1913	*Trent's Last Case (The Woman in Black)*	E.C. Bentley	____
1974	*Big Kiss-Off of 1944, The*	Andrew Bergman	____
1937	*Trial and Error*	Anthony Berkeley	____
1967	*Repeat the Instructions*	R. Vernon Beste	____
1940	*Corpse in the Snowman, The (The Case of the Abominable Snowman)*	Nicholas Blake	____
1947	*Minute for Murder*	Nicholas Blake	____
1976	*Sins of the Fathers, The*	Lawrence Block	____
1962	*Ficciones*	Jorge Luis Borges	____
1937	*Case of the Seven of Calvary, The*	Anthony Boucher	____
1952	*Death in the Fifth Position*	Edgar Box (Gore Vidal)	____
1944	*Green for Danger*	Christianna Brand	____
1948	*Wilders Walk Away*	Herbert Brean	____

1947	*Fabulous Clipjoint, The*	Fredric Brown	___
1956	*Lenient Beast, The*	Fredric Brown	___
1925	*John Macnab*	John Buchan	___
1941	*Mountain Meadow (Sick Heart River)*	John Buchan	___
1915	*Thirty-Nine Steps, The*	John Buchan	___
1987	*Mongoose R.I.P*	William F. Buckley, Jr.	___
1976	*Saving the Queen*	William F. Buckley, Jr.	___
1959	*Pyx, The (The Chosen Girl)*	John Buell	___
1966	*Tremor of Intent*	Anthony Burgess	___
1979	*Angle of Attack*	Rex Burns	___
1986	*Ground Money*	Rex Burns	___
1958	*Or Be He Dead*	James Byrom	___
1936/43	*Double Indemnity*	James M. Cain	___
1934	*Postman Always Rings Twice, The*	James M. Cain	___
1971	*Finding Maubee (The Calypso Murders)*	A.H.Z. Carr	___
1941	*Case of the Constant Suicides, The*	John Dickson Carr	___
1935	*Three Coffins, The (The Hollow Man)*	John Dickson Carr	___
1981	*Thus was Adonis Murdered*	Sarah Caudwell	___
1939	*Big Sleep, The*	Raymond Chandler	___
1940	*Farewell, My Lovely*	Raymond Chandler	___
1943	*Lady in the Lake, The*	Raymond Chandler	___
1911	*Innocence of Father Brown, The*	G.K. Chesterton	___
1903	*Riddle of the Sands, The*	Erskine Childers	___
1926	*Murder of Roger Ackroyd, The*	Agatha Christie	___
1940	*Patriotic Murders, The (One, Two, Buckle My Shoe; An Overdose of Death)*	Agatha Christie	___
1939	*Ten Little Niggers (And Then There Were None)*	Agatha Christie	
1985	*Hunt for Red October, The*	Tom Clancy	___
1967	*All Men are Lonely Now*	Francis Clifford	___
1965	*Third Side of the Coin, The*	Francis Clifford	___
1948	*Wisteria Cottage (The Night Before Dying)*	Robert M. Coates	___
1982	*Bad Company*	Liza Cody	___
1940	*Drink to Yesterday*	Manning Coles	___
1941	*Toast to Tomorrow, A (Pray Silence)*	Manning Coles	___
1974	*Blank Page, The*	K.C. Constantine	___
1982	*Man Who Liked Slow Tomatoes, The*	K.C. Constantine	___
1967	*Murder's Burning*	S.H. Courtier	___
1968	*Gideon's River*	John Creasey (as, J.J. Marric)	___
1956	*Gideon's Week*	John Creasey (as, J.J. Marric)	___
1971	*Trial of Lobo Icheka, The*	David Creed	___
1946	*Moving Toyshop, The*	Edmund Crispin	___
1926	*Cheyne Mystery, The (Inspector French and the Cheyne Mystery)*	Freeman Wills Crofts	___
1946	*Death of a Train*	Freeman Wills Crofts	___

1981	*Death in a Tenured Position*	Amanda Cross	____
	(A Death in the Faculty)		
1970	*Poetic Justice*	Amanda Cross	____
1978	*Last Good Kiss, The*	James Crumley	____
1960	*Sylvia*	E.V. Cunningham	____
1964	*Out of the Dark (Child's Play)*	Ursula Curtiss	____
1960	*Night of Wenceslas*	Lionel Davidson	____
1962	*Rose of Tibet, The*	Lionel Davidson	____
1978	*Killed in the Ratings*	William L. DeAndrea	____
1962	*Ipcress File, The*	Len Deighton	____
1978	*SS-GB*	Len Deighton	____
1955	*Sunlit Ambush, The*	Mark Derby	____
1977	*Silent World of Nicholas Quinn, The*	Colin Dexter	____
1968	*Glass-Sided Ants' Nest, The (Skin Deep)*	Peter Dickinson	____
1983	*Hindsight*	Peter Dickinson	____
1980	*One Foot in the Grave*	Peter Dickinson	____
1950	*Long Escape, The*	David Dodge	____
1957	*Rebecca's Pride*	Donald McNutt Douglass	____
1964	*Q Document, The*	Robert Duncan	____
		(as, James Hall Roberts)	
1983	*Name of the Rose, The*	Umberto Eco	____
1958	*Eighth Circle, The*	Stanley Ellin	____
1985	*Very Old Money*	Stanley Ellin	____
1983	*Glass Highway, The*	Loren D. Estleman	____
1946	*Horizontal Man, The*	Helen Eustis	____
1946	*Big Clock, The (No Way Out)*	Kenneth Fearing	____
1979	*Pursuit*	Robert L. Fish	____
1941	*I Wake Up Screaming*	Steve Fisher	____
1957	*From Russia, With Love*	Ian Fleming	____
1978	*Eye of the Needle (Storm Island)*	Ken Follett	____
1926	*Payment Deferred*	C.S. Forester	____
1971	*Day of the Jackal, The*	Frederick Forsyth	____
1967	*Blood Sport*	Dick Francis	____
1962	*Dead Cert*	Dick Francis	____
1969	*Forfeit*	Dick Francis	____
1972	*Aupres de ma blonde (A Long Silence)*	Nicolas Freeling	____
1962	*Love in Amsterdam (Death in Amsterdam)*	Nicolas Freeling	____
1935	*Case of the Caretaker's Cat, The*	Erle Stanley Gardner	____
1944	*Case of the Crooked Candle, The*	Erle Stanley Gardner	____
1939	*D.A. Draws a Circle, The*	Erle Stanley Gardner	____
1964	*Liquidator, The*	John Gardner	____
1969	*Ascent of D-13, The*	Andrew Garve	____
1953	*Cuckoo Line Affair, The*	Andrew Garve	____
1958	*Galloway Case, The*	Andrew Garve	____
1977	*Judas Pair, The*	Jonathan Gash	____

1956	*Day of the Ram, The*	William Campbell Gault	____
1975	*Wind Chill Factor, The*	Thomas Gifford	____
1951	*Death Has Deep Roots*	Michael Gilbert	____
1952	*Death in Captivity (The Danger Within)*	Michael Gilbert	____
1979	*Death Drop*	B.M. Gill	____
1974	*Marathon Man*	William Goldman	____
1974	*River Gets Wider, The*	R.L. Gordon	____
1938	*Brighton Rock*	Graham Greene	____
1943	*Ministry of Fear, The*	Graham Greene	____
1932	*Stamboul Train (Orient Express)*	Graham Greene	____
1983	*Fatal Obsession*	Stephen Greenleaf	____
1984	*Dirty Duck, The*	Martha Grimes	____
1953	*Night of the Hunter, The*	Davis Grubb	____
1973	*Wild Pitch*	A.B., Jr. Guthrie	____
1975	*Scorpion's Tail, The*	William Haggard	____
1958	*Teleman Touch, The*	William Haggard	____
1959	*Venetian Blind*	William Haggard	____
1975	*Mandarin Cypher, The*	Adam Hall	____
1965	*Quiller Memorandum, The (The Berlin Memorandum)*	Adam Hall	____
1973	*Tango Briefing, The*	Adam Hall	____
1977	*Exit Sherlock Holmes*	Robert Lee Hall	____
1975	*Search for Joseph Tully, The*	William H. Hallahan	____
1960	*Death of a Citizen*	Donald Hamilton	____
1964	*Ravagers, The*	Donald Hamilton	____
1930	*Maltese Falcon, The*	Dashiell Hammett	____
1929	*Red Harvest*	Dashiell Hammett	____
1987	*Early Graves*	Joseph Hansen	____
1951	*English Murder, An (The Christmas Murder)*	Cyril Hare	____
1927	*Bellamy Trial, The*	Frances Noyes Hart	____
1982	*Ritual Murder*	S.T. Haymon	____
1986	*Staked Goat, The (The Tethered Goat)*	Jeremiah Healy	____
1941	*Taste for Honey, A (A Taste for Murder)*	H.F. Heard	____
1973	*Through the Dark and Hairy Wood*	Shaun Herron	____
1938	*Blunt Instrument, A*	Georgette Heyer	____
1972	*Friends of Eddie Coyle, The*	George V. Higgins	____
1984	*Deadheads*	Reginald Hill	____
1973	*Ruling Passion*	Reginald Hill	____
1970	*Blessing Way, The*	Tony Hillerman	____
1984	*Ghostway, The*	Tony Hillerman	____
1964	*Cotton Comes to Harlem*	Chester Himes	____
1963	*Florentine Finish*	Cornelius Hirschberg	____
1968	*Dance of the Dwarfs (The Adversary)*	Geoffrey Household	____
1939	*Rogue Male (Man Hunt)*	Geoffrey Household	____
1951	*Rough Shoot, A*	Geoffrey Household	____

1959	*Ossian's Ride*	Fred Hoyle	___
1982	*Trotsky's Run*	Richard Hoyt	___
1946	*Ride the Pink Horse*	Dorothy B. Hughes	___
1964	*From Cuba, With Love (Ring Around Rosy)*	E. Howard Hunt (Gordon Davis)	___
1938	*Murder on Safari*	Elspeth Huxley	___
1932	*Before the Fact*	Francis Iles	___
1956	*Wreck of the Mary Deare, The (The Mary Deare)*	Hammond Innes	___
1937	*Hamlet, Revenge!*	Michael Innes	___
1962	*Cover Her Face*	P.D. James	___
1971	*Shroud for a Nightingale*	P.D. James	___
1972	*Unsuitable Job for a Woman, An*	P.D. James	___
1954	*Beat Not the Bones*	Charlotte Jay	___
1955	*Yellow Turban, The*	Charlotte Jay	___
1964	*Perfect Murder, The*	H.R.F. Keating	___
1961	*Rush on the Ultimate, A*	H.R.F. Keating	___
1961	*Spoilt Kill, The*	Mary Kelly	___
1964	*Friday the Rabbi Slept Late*	Harry Kemelman	___
1961	*Court of Crows*	Robert A. Knowlton	___
1986	*Floater*	Joseph Koenig	___
1984	*Emily Dickinson is Dead*	Jane Langton	___
1966	*Death Shall Overcome*	Emma Lathen	___
1967	*Murder Against the Grain*	Emma Lathen	___
1965	*Passport to Oblivion (Where the Spies Are)*	James Leasor	___
1963	*Spy Who Came in From the Cold, The*	John le Carre	___
1974	*Tinker, Tailor, Soldier, Spy*	John le Carre	___
1976	*Swag*	Elmore Leonard	___
1983	*LaBrava*	Elmore Leonard	___
1976	*Night Cover*	Michael Z. Lewin	___
1984	*Man in the Middle, The (A Suitable Case for Corruption)*	Norman Lewis	___
1981	*Amateur, The*	Robert Littell	___
1979	*Debriefing, The*	Robert Littell	___
1973	*Defection of A.J. Lewinter, The*	Robert Littell	___
1982	*False Inspector Dew, The*	Peter Lovesey	___
1970	*Wobble to Death*	Peter Lovesey	___
1947	*One More Unfortunate (A Case to Answer)*	Edgar Lustgarten	___
1965	*Midnight Plus One*	Gavin Lyall	___
1964	*Most Dangerous Game, The*	Gavin Lyall	___
1980	*Castles Burning*	Arthur Lyons	___
1973	*Hail to the Chief*	Ed McBain	___
1983	*Ice*	Ed McBain	___
1973	*Miernik Dossier, The*	Charles McCarry	___
1985	*Artful Egg, The*	James McClure	___
1971	*Steam Pig, The*	James McClure	___

1978	*Fletch's Fortune*	Gregory McDonald	___
1953	*Dead Low Tide*	John D. MacDonald	___
1963	*Drowner, The*	John D. MacDonald	___
1964	*Quick Red Fox, The*	John D. MacDonald	___
1959	*List of Adrian Messenger, The*	Philip MacDonald	___
1964	*Far Side of the Dollar, The*	Ross Macdonald	___
1959	*Galton Case, The*	Ross Macdonald	___
		(as, John Ross Macdonald)	
1969	*Goodbye Look, The*	Ross Macdonald	___
1981	*Bogmail*	Patrick McGinley	___
1977	*Laidlaw*	William McIlvanney	___
1941	*Above Suspicion*	Helen MacInnes	___
1963	*Venetian Affair, The*	Helen MacInnes	___
1962	*Satan Bug, The*	Alistair MacLean (as, Ian Stuart)	___
1958	*South by Java Head*	Alistair MacLean	___
1935	*Enter a Murderer*	Ngaio Marsh	___
1977	*Thin Air*	William Marshall	___
1933	*Oxford Tragedy, An*	J.C. Masterman	___
1960	*Pass Beyond Kashmir, The*	Berkely Mather	___
1928	*Ashenden; or, The British Agent*	W. Somerset Maugham	___
1974	*Seven-Per-Cent Solution, The*	Nicholas Meyer	___
1955	*Beast in View*	Margaret Millar	___
1957	*Soft Talkers, The (Air that Kills, An)*	Margaret Millar	___
1922	*Red House Mystery, The*	A.A. Milne	___
1967	*Third Policeman, The*	Flann O'Brien	___
1920	*Great Impersonation, The*	E. Phillips Oppenheim	___
1982	*Indemnity Only*	Sara Paretsky	___
1974	*God Save the Child*	Robert B. Parker	___
1980	*Looking for Rachel Wallace*	Robert B. Parker	___
1975	*Mortal Stakes*	Robert B. Parker	___
1981	*Outside Man, The*	Richard North Patterson	___
1973	*Dreamland Lake*	Richard Peck	___
1982	*Butcher's Boy, The*	Thomas Perry	___
1980	*One Corpse too Many*	Ellis Peters	___
1940	*Verdict of Twelve*	Raymond Postgate	___
1975	*Other Paths to Glory*	Anthony Price	___
1956	*Pub Crawler, The*	Maurice Procter	___
1971	*Stalker, The*	Bill Pronzini	___
1942	*Calamity Town*	Ellery Queen	___
1929	*Roman Hat Mystery, The*	Ellery Queen	___
1932	*Tragedy of X, The*	Ellery Queen (as, Barnaby Ross)	___
1978	*Death in the Morning (Death and the Maiden)*	Sheila Radley	___
1980	*Euro-Killers, The*	Julian Rathbone	___
1976	*Demon in My View, A*	Ruth Rendell	___
1926	*Bat, The*	Mary Roberts Rinehart	___

1945	*Red Right Hand, The*	Joel Townsley Rogers	____
1970/73	*Sacrificial Pawn*	Francis Ryck	____
1973	*First Deadly Sin, The*	Lawrence Sanders	____
1935	*Gaudy Night*	Dorothy L. Sayers	____
1934	*Nine Tailors, The*	Dorothy L. Sayers	____
1930	*Strong Poison*	Dorothy L. Sayers	____
1938	*Listening House, The*	Mabel Seeley	____
1938/42	*Man Who Watched the Trains Go By, The*	Georges Simenon	____
1973	*Big Fix, The*	Roger L. Simon	____
1970	*Fire Engine that Disappeared, The*	Maj Sjowall & Per Wahloo	____
1967	*Roseanna*	Maj Sjowall & Per Wahloo	____
1961	*Ballad of the Running Man, The*	Shelley Smith	____
1955	*Day of the Dead, The*	Bart Spicer	____
1948	*And Be a Villain (More Deaths Than One)*	Rex Stout	____
1959	*Plot It Yourself (Murder in Style)*	Rex Stout	____
1938	*Too Many Cooks*	Rex Stout	____
1967	*Man Who Killed Himself, The*	Julian Symons	____
1950	*31st of February, The*	Julian Symons	____
1986	*Criminal Comedy, A (The Criminal Comedy of the Contented Couple)*	Julian Symons	
1985	*Dutch Blue Error, The*	William G. Tapply	____
1986	*Marine Corpse, The (A Rodent of Doubt)*	William G. Tapply	____
1951	*Daughter of Time, The*	Josephine Tey	____
1936	*Shilling for Candles, A*	Josephine Tey	____
1976	*Family Arsenal, The*	Paul Theroux	____
1969	*Brass Go-Between, The*	Ross Thomas (as, Oliver Bleeck)	____
1966	*Cold War Swap, The (Spy in the Vodka)*	Ross Thomas	____
1967	*Seersucker Whipsaw, The*	Ross Thomas	____
1952	*Killer Inside Me, The*	Jim Thompson	____
1977	*Death Cap*	June Thomson	____
1972	*Eiger Sanction, The*	Trevanian	____
1981	*Deep and Crisp and Even*	Peter Turnbull	____
1958	*Bachelors of Broken Hill, The*	Arthur W. Upfield	____
1951	*New Shoe, The (The Clue of the New Shoe)*	Arthur W. Upfield	____
1987	*Fire Lake*	Jonathan Valin	____
1986	*Life's Work*	Jonathan Valin	____
1981	*Mind-Murders, The*	Janwillem van de Wetering	____
1976	*Stateline*	John Van der Zee	____
1926	*Benson Murder Case, The*	S.S. Van Dine	____
1958	*Chinese Bell Murders, The*	Robert van Gulik	____
1961	*Chinese Nail Murders, The*	Robert van Gulik	____
1949	*Department of Dead Ends, The*	Roy Vickers	____
1911	*Four Just Men, The*	Edgar Wallace	____
1963	*Death and Circumstance*	Hillary Waugh	____
1952	*Last Seen Wearing…*	Hillary Waugh	____

1970	*Hot Rock, The*	Donald E. Westlake	___
1984	*Victims*	Collin Wilcox	___
1963	*Catfish Tangle, The (River Girl)*	Charles Williams	___
1985	*New Hope for the Dead*	Charles Willeford	___
1940	*Bride Wore Black, The (Beware the Lady)*	Cornell Woolrich	___
1966	*Tree Frog*	Martin Woodhouse	___
1985	*Death in the Old Country*	Eric Wright	___
1984	*Smoke Detector*	Eric Wright	___
1985	*Suspect, The*	L.R. Wright	___
1963	*Fifth Passenger, The*	Edward Young	___
1974	*Hazell Plays Solomon*	P.B. Yuill	___

www.topmystery.com/books6.htm
home.comcast.net/~netaylor1/winks.html
www.classiccrimefiction.com/winks-recommended-detective-fiction.htm

Name Index

459

Name Index

O

O'Brien, Bob 74
O'Brien, Charles 22, 218
O'Brien, Darcy 161, 163, 294
O'Brien, Flann 451
O'Brien, Geoffrey 391
O'Brien, Kevin 277
O'Brien, Robert C. 183
O'Callaghan, Maxine 261
O'Callaghan, Sean 107
O'Callahan, Maxine 46
O'Connell, Carol 38, 59, 128, 138, 361, 364
O'Connor, Ed 62
O'Connor, Flannery 288
O'Dea, Brian 198
O'Donnell, Lawrence Jr. 165
O'Donnell, Lillian 364, 418
O'Donnell, Michael 98
O'Donnell, Peter 313, 350
O'Donovan, Gerard 101
O'Faolain, Nuala 105
O'Farrell, William 158, 285, 304, 318
O'Finn, Thaddeus 144
O'Flaherty, Liam 356
O'Hara, John 288
O'Hara, Kenneth 88
O'Higgins, Harvey J. 356, 400
O'Malley, Martin 201
O'Malley, Suzanne 159
O'Neil, Vincent H. 258
O'Neill, Judith 153
O'Rourke, Rebecca 97
O'Toole, G.J.A. 346
Oates, Joyce Carol 151, 156, 389
O'Brien, Charles 22
Obstfeld, Ray 148
OConnell, Carol 331
Oddie, James L. 125
Odell, Lilias 103
Odell, Robin 107, 159
O'Donnell, Peter 313
O'Donovan, Gerard 101
Oellrichs, Inez 305
O'Farrell, William 304
Offord, Lenore Glen 320, 424
Ogan, George 267
Olcott, Anthony 83, 98, 140
Old Sleuth (Harlan Page Halsey) 354
Olde, Nicholas 349
Olden, Marc 149
Olesker, Harry 143, 309
Oliphant, B.J. 42, 147
Oliver, Anthony 82, 329, 368
Oliver, Steve 127
Olsen, D.B. 317, 318

Olsen, Jack 52, 162, 163, 165
Olson, Donald 44, 66, 155, 156
Olson, Karen E. 213
One More Unfortunate (A Case to Answer) 358
Oney, Steve 160
Onions, Oliver 296
Oppenheim, E. Phillips 301, 311, 332, 348, 356, 388, 424, 451
Opyr, Joan 223
Orczy, Baroness 295, 323, 329, 332, 347, 355, 399, 443
Orgill, Douglas 86
Orlev, Uri 181
Orum, Poul 418
Osborne, Mary Pope 180
Oster, Jerry 418
Oswald, James 101
Ottolengui, Rodrigues 399
Ouimet, Gilles & Anne- Marie Pons 206
Ousby, Ian 26, 250
Overture to Death 357
Owen, James 105
Owens, Barbara 155

P

Paciocco, David M. 199
Packard, Frank L. 348
Packer, Vin 309
Padgett, Abigail 23, 38, 243, 247, 361, 365
Padgett, Lewis 303
Page, Katherine Hall 18, 19, 23, 27, 28, 180, 187, 252, 384, 406
Page, Marco 368, 424
Page, Marco (Harry Kurnitz) 297
Pain, Barry 348
Palmer, Alex 71
Palmer, Linda 236
Palmer, Liz 207
Palmer, Stuart 356, 401, 406, 424
Palmer, Stuart & Craig Rice 402
Palmtag, Dinah 149
Panek, Leroy Lad 170, 173, 175
Papazoglou, Orania (Jane Haddam) 140
Paradis, Peter 198
Paretsky, Sara 36, 77, 80, 81, 98, 244, 245, 263, 286, 291, 331, 362, 387, 408, 410, 451
Paretsky, Sara, ed. 48
Park, Jacqueline 149
Park, Tony 71
Parker, Ann 232
Parker, Barbara 138
Parker, Daniel 176
Parker, I.J. 272
Parker, Richard 308
Parker, Robert B. 57, 133, 263, 264, 294, 326, 331, 362, 371, 380, 410, 451

W

Title Index

Short Stories

Book Titles

L

N

S

557

Z

Roger M. Sobin is a mystery fan, reader, collector, and has written several short stories. He spent twenty years as an Air Force chaplain, served as a Presbyterian minister, and has published a number of articles in religious education journals. Rev. Dr. Sobin is a member of the Society of Biblical Literature, the American Academy of Religion, and the International Bonhoeffer Society. Among his varied interests is the study of the Dead Sea Scrolls. He lives near San Antonio in Helotes, Texas and is currently working on a novel.

CPSIA information can be obtained at www.ICGtesting.com
Printed in the USA
BVOW08s0617190116

433451BV00001B/34/P